D0906531

ARBA Guide to Biographical Dictionaries

ARBA Guide to
Biographical Dictionaries

BOHDAN S. WYNAR

Editor

WITHDRAWN
IOWA STATE UNIVERSITY
LIBRARY

LIBRARIES UNLIMITED, INC.
Littleton, Colorado
1986

Copyright © 1986 Libraries Unlimited, Inc.
All Rights Reserved
Printed in the United States of America

No part of this publication may be reproduced, stored in a retrieval system, or transmitted, in any form or by any means, electronic, mechanical, photocopying, recording, or otherwise, without the prior written permission of the publisher.

LIBRARIES UNLIMITED, INC.
P.O. Box 263
Littleton, Colorado 80160-0263

Library of Congress Cataloging-in-Publication Data

ARBA guide to biographical dictionaries.

Includes indexes.
1. Biography--Dictionaries--Bibliography. I. Wynar,
Bohdan S. II. American reference books annual.
Z5301.A82 1986   016.92   86-2851
[CT103]
ISBN 0-87287-492-3

Libraries Unlimited books are bound with Type II nonwoven material that meets and exceeds National Association of State Textbook Administrators' Type II nonwoven material specifications Class A through E.

Contents

Part II
Biographies in Professional Fields

Journals Cited

FORM OF CITATION	JOURNAL TITLE
BL	Booklist
Choice	Choice
C&RL	College & Research Libraries
JAL	Journal of Academic Librarianship
LJ	Library Journal
RBB	Reference Books Bulletin
RQ	RQ
SBF	Science Books & Films
SLJ	School Library Journal
SLMQ	School Library Media Quarterly
WLB	Wilson Library Bulletin

Introduction

The purpose of this book is to offer a representative selection of biographical dictionaries and directories that would be useful in the reference and information process in libraries of all types. We expect that this bibliographic guide will also assist in the acquisition process, providing not only complete bibliographic description, including price information, but also a critical evaluation of each work. *ARBA Guide to Biographical Dictionaries* covers significant biographical sources, serial and non-serial, published chiefly during the last twenty years. Most of the material was carefully selected from *American Reference Books Annual* (*ARBA*), which in the last seventeen years has reviewed over 28,500 titles, including about 2,500 biographical sources. Reviews selected from *ARBA* were carefully re-edited, and occasionally completely rewritten to bring them up-to-date. In such cases, the name of the editor was added to the name of the original reviewer. In addition, all bibliographic information was updated—prices of books were checked against information from recent publishers' catalogs and *Books in Print*. New exclusive distributors and new publishers were added for most recent editions, as well as additional citations to published reviews. This was accomplished with the assistance of *Book Review Digest* and *Book Review Index*. About two hundred new reviews were written by the editor for this compilation, primarily in the first part, "Universal and National Biographies," but also in the second part "Biographies in Professional Fields." In such chapters as "Education," "Political Science," and "Science and Technology" the arrangement of material—reflected in the table of contents—is quite different from that in *ARBA*.

Part 1, "Universal and National Biographies," begins by covering general sources or biographical dictionaries not limited in their coverage to a particular nationality, topic, description, or territory. This is followed by the national or territorial coverage, starting with the United States. The second part, "Biographies in Professional Fields," incorporates twenty-one subject-oriented chapters or areas starting with "Applied Arts," "Communications and

Mass Media," "Economics and Business," down to "Science and Technology," "Social Sciences," and "Sports." Obviously, chapter subdivisions reflect both publishing practices and individual disciplines or areas. In addition, chapter length varies; for example, there are over 110 main entries in the literature section versus only 5 in geography.

In terms of criteria, the editor attempted to select only the most useful biographical sources that were published primarily in the last twenty years. All reviews adequately describe a given work and then provide well-documented comments, positive or negative. Usually they discuss such things as usefulness of a given work, organization or contents, and similarity to other works and/or previous editions. Many related titles are mentioned in the reviews as is a practice in *ARBA*, and in this book such comparative notes are significantly expanded by the editor. Citations to additional reviews in major periodicals follow most annotations. Sometimes page numbers are absent from these, following an older *ARBA* style.

Occasionally it will be noted that Libraries Unlimited staff have written descriptive notes on Libraries Unlimited publications. This reflects an *ARBA* convention 1970-1984.

Generally speaking, only books still in print are included in the *ARBA Guide to Biographical Dictionaries*. However, there are some exceptions for significiant out-of-print titles, primarily in such areas as religion, music, and fine arts. Most reprints are not included, neither are biographies of individuals and membership directories that offer minimum biographical information. On several occasions, as a service to the profession, we have included some substandard titles with negative reviews.

All chapters in part 2 are preceded by brief introductions that discuss the arrangement, the most significant or interesting titles, as well as additional sources of biographical information, some of them in languages other than English. These brief introductions usually include information on indexes and abstracting services and conclude with references to existing bibliographical guides to a given discipline that should assist the reader in finding additional information.

We would like to thank all of the *ARBA* reviewers who have contributed to this volume; without their help this book could not have been completed. They are listed on the pages following this introduction. In addition, we would like to thank the members of our staff who contributed to this book: G. Kim Dority, who assisted in the initial preparations; Hannah L. Kelminson, whose general assistance lent cohesion and consistency to the volume; Carolyn Kallemeyn, who copyedited the material; Kay Minnis, who did the composition work; Ellen Thompson and Gloria Powell, who assisted in checking bibliographic information; Sharon Kincaide, who compiled the author/title index and proofread the manuscript; and Ruth Blackmore, who prepared the subject index.

Bohdan S. Wynar

Contributors

Patricia M. Aldrich, Reference Reader's Service Librarian, Washington Univ. Law Library, St. Louis, Mo.

Brian Alley, Univ. Librarian and Assoc. Dean, Sangamon State Univ., Springfield, Ill.

Donald Altschiller, Asst. Librarian, American Jewish Historical Society, Waltham, Mass.

Rao Aluri, Asst. Professor, Division of Librarianship, Emory Univ., Atlanta, Ga.

Emily J. Alward, Consumer and Family Sciences Librarian, Purdue Univ. Libraries, West Lafayette, Ind.

Frank J. Anderson, Librarian Emeritus, Sandor Teszler Library, Wofford College, Spartanburg, S.C.

James D. Anderson, Assoc. Professor, Graduate School of Library and Information Studies, Rutgers Univ., New Brunswick, N.J.

Margaret Anderson, Assoc. Professor, Faculty of Library Science, Univ. of Toronto, Ont.

Charles R. Andrews, Dean of Library Services, Hofstra Univ., Hempstead, N.Y.

Karen L. Andrews, Head, Engineering and Mathematical Sciences Library, Univ. of California, Los Angeles.

Theodora Andrews, Pharmacy Librarian and Professor of Library Science, Purdue Univ., West Lafayette, Ind.

Susan B. Ardis, Head Librarian, Engineering Library, Univ. of Texas, Austin.

Judith Armstrong, Director of the Library, Drury College, Springfield, Mo.

Theodore M. Avery, Jr., formerly of Brooklyn Public Library, N.Y.

Robert Balay, Head, Reference Dept., Yale Univ. Library, New Haven, Conn.

Doris H. Banks, Public Services Librarian, Whitworth College, Spokane, Wash.

Charla Banner, Researcher, Features Unlimited, Kokoma, Ind.

Gary D. Barber, Coordinator of Reference Services, Daniel A. Reed Library, State Univ. of New York, Fredonia.

Ruth E. Bauner, Morris Library, Southern Illinois Univ., Carbondale.

Irene Wood Bell, Media Specialist, Denver Public Schools, Colo.

Jane A. Benson, Reference Librarian, Kent State Univ. Libraries, Kent, Ohio.

Bernice Bergup, Reference Librarian, Humanities Reference Dept., Univ. of North Carolina Library, Chapel Hill.

Robert C. Berring, Law Librarian and Professor, Univ. of California, Berkeley,

Alexander S. Birkos, General Manager, Mercury Book Co., Mount Shasta, Calif.

Ron Blazek, Professor, School of Library Science, Florida State Univ., Tallahassee.

Marty Bloomberg, Head of Library Operations, California State College, San Bernardino.

Nancy G. Boles, Curator of Manuscripts, Maryland Historical Society, Baltimore.

Peggy Clossey Boone, Librarian, Joseph A. Leonard Jr. High School, Old Town, Maine.

William Brockman, Reference/Documents Librarian, Drew Univ. Library, Madison, N.J.

Barbara E. Brown, Head, General Cataloging Section, Library of Parliament, Ottawa.

David W. Brunton, Acting Assoc. Director, Arapahoe Regional Library, Englewood, Colo.

Richard M. Buck, Asst. to the Chief, Performing Arts Research Center, New York Public Library at Lincoln Center, New York.

Brower R. Burchill, Professor, Physiology and Cell Biology, Univ. of Kansas, Lawrence.

Dwight F. Burlingame, Director of Univ. Libraries, Bowling Green State Univ., Bowling Green, Ohio.

G. Joan Burns, Principal Art Librarian, Art and Music Dept., Public Library of Newark, N.J.

Hans E. Bynagle, Director, Cowles Memorial Library, Whitworth College, Spokane, Wash.

Jerry Cao, Asst. Library Director, Woodbury Univ., Los Angeles, Calif.

Jennifer Cargill, Acquisitions Librarian, Miami Univ. Libraries, Oxford, Ohio.

Susan Dedmond Casbon, Teacher-Librarian, Ananda Schools, Nevada City, Calif.

Jefferson D. Caskey, Professor of Library Science and Instructional Media, Western Kentucky Univ., Bowling Green.

Joseph H. Cataio, Chicago, Ill.

Dianne B. Catlett, Lecturer, Dept. of Library Science, East Carolina Univ., Greenville, S.C.

Frances Neel Cheney, Professor Emeritus, School of Library Science, George Peabody College for Teachers, Nashville, Tenn.

Boyd Childress, Social Sciences Reference Librarian, Auburn Univ., Ala.

Diane J. Cimbala, Asst. Librarian for Circulation, Reese Library, Augusta College, Ga.

Cecil F. Clotfelter, Asst. Director, Eastern New Mexico Univ. Library, Portales.

Paul B. Cors, Collection Development Librarian, Univ. of Wyoming Library, Laramie.

Brian E. Coutts, History/Social Sciences Bibliographer, Fondren Library, Rice Univ., Houston, Tex.

Milton H. Crouch, Asst. Director for Reader Services, Bailey/Howe Library, Univ. of Vermont, Burlington.

Doris Cruger Dale, Professor, Dept. of Curriculum, Instruction, and Media, Southern Illinois Univ., Carbondale.

William J. Dane, Supervising Art and Music Librarian, Public Library of Newark, N.J.

Donald G. Davis, Jr., Assoc. Professor, Graduate School of Library Science, Univ. of Texas, Austin.

Lorelei D. Davis, Fashion and Styling Consultant, Chicago, Ill.

Eleanor DeLashmitt, Lawyer-Librarian, Tarlton Law Library, Univ. of Texas, Austin.

Dominique-René De Lerma, Professor of Music, Morgan State Univ., Baltimore.

Mary Alice Deveny, Youth Librarian, Venice Area Public Library, Venice, Fla.

Donald C. Dickinson, Professor, Graduate Library School, Univ. of Arizona, Tucson.

Dennis Dillon, Map Librarian, General Libraries, Univ. of Texas, Austin.

Carol A. Doll, Asst. Professor, Davis College, Univ. of South Carolina, Columbia.

Lamia Doumato, Head of Reference, National Gallery of Art, Library and Study Center, Washington, D.C.

John E. Druesedow, Jr., Director of the Conservatory Library, Oberlin College, Ohio.

Ronald W. Dunbar, Asst. Professor, Dept. of Foreign Languages, West Virginia Univ., Morgantown.

Ralph M. Edwards, Asst. Professor, School of Librarianship, Western Michigan University, Kalamazoo.

David Eggenberger, Director, Publications, U.S. National Archives and Records Service, Washington, D.C.

Donald L. Ehresmann, Assoc. Professor, History of Architecture and Art, Univ. of Illinois, Chicago.

Julia M. Ehresmann, Instructor, William Rainey Harper College, Palatine, Ill.

Marie Ellis, English and American Literature Bibliographer, Univ. of Georgia Libraries, Athens.

Donald Empson, Reference Librarian, Minnesota Historical Society, St. Paul.

Claire England, Assoc. Professor of Library Science, Univ. of Toronto, Ont.

Jonathon Erlen, Curator, History of Medicine, Univ. of Pittsburgh, Pa.

Judith Ann Erlen, School of Nursing, Univ. of Pittsburgh, Pa.

G. Edward Evans, Assoc. Dean, Graduate School of Librarianship and Information Management, Univ. of Denver, Colo.

Gwynneth Evans, Executive Secretary, National Library of Canada, Ottawa.

Joyce Duncan Falk, Data Services Coordinator and Reference Librarian, Univ. of California, Irvine.

Joseph Riss Fang, Professor of Library Science, Simmons College, Boston.

Ralph J. Folcarelli, Professor of Library Science, Palmer Graduate Library School, C. W. Post Center, Long Island Univ., Greenvale, N.Y.

Donald D. Foos, formerly staff, Libraries Unlimited, Inc.

Carole Franklin. *See* Carole Franklin Vidali.

Susan J. Freiband, Vice-President for Research, Hispanic Foundation, Washington, D.C.

Lewis Fried, Assoc. Professor, Dept. of English, Kent State Univ., Ohio.

Ronald H. Fritze, Asst. Professor, Dept. of History, Lamar Univ., Beaumont, Tex.

Stephen M. Fry, Head, Music Library, Schoenberg Hall, Univ. of California, Los Angeles.

Sherrilynne Fuller, Director, Bio-Medical Library, Univ. of Minnesota, Minneapolis.

Andrew Garoogian, Librarian, Brooklyn College Library, N.Y.

Betty Gay, Central Library Director, Los Angeles Public Library, Calif.

Charlotte Georgi, Librarian for Management Bibliography, Univ. of California Graduate School of Management Library, Los Angeles.

Ray Gerke, Librarian, Education/Reference, Wessell Library, Tufts Univ., Medford, Mass.

Edwin S. Gleaves, Chair, Dept. of Library Science, George Peabody College, Vanderbilt Univ., Nashville, Tenn.

Allie Wise Goudy, Music Librarian, Western Illinois Univ. Macomb.

Frank Wm. Goudy, Assoc. Professor, Univ. Libraries, Western Illinois Univ., Macomb.

Eric Gould, Assoc. Professor of English, Univ. of Denver, Colo.

Richard A. Gray, Littleton, Colo.

Suzanne K. Gray, formerly Coordinator of Science, Boston Public Library, Sharon Mass.

Richard W. Grefrath, Instructional Services Librarian, Univ. of Nevada Library, Reno.

Helen Gregory, Toledo-Lucas County Public Library, Reynolds Corners Branch, Toledo, Ohio.

Lawrence Grieco, former Consultant/Librarian, Colorado State Library, Denver.

James J. Groark, Bibliographer, Univ. Libraries, State Univ. of New York, Albany.

Laurel Grotzinger, Dean, Graduate College, and Chief Research Officer, Western Michigan Univ., Kalamazoo.

Deborah Hammer, Asst. Div. Head, History, Travel and Biography, Div., Queens Borough Public Library, Jamaica, N.Y.

Beverley Hanson, Cincinnati, Ohio.

Constance Hardesty, staff, Libraries Unlimited, Inc.

Thomas S. Harding, Librarian Emeritus, Washburn Univ. of Topeka, Kans.

Roberto P. Haro, Academic Asst. to the Vice-Chancellor, and Lecturer, Ethnic Stuides Dept., Univ. of California, Berkeley.

Chauncy D. Harris, Samuel N. Harper Distinguished Service Professor of Geography, Univ. of Chicago, Ill.

Ann Hartman, formerly staff, Libraries Unlimited, Inc.

Ann J. Harwell, formerly staff, Libraries Unlimited, Inc.

Robert J. Havlik, Univ. Engineering Librarian, Univ. of Notre Dame, Ind.

James P. Heitzer, Asst. Manager, Industrial Data Base, Standard & Poor's Compustat Services, Inc., Englewood, Colo.

Peter Hernon, Ph.D. candidate, Graduate Library School, Indiana Univ., Bloomington.

Jean Herold, Reference Librarian, General Libraries, Univ. of Texas, Austin.

George R. Hill. Asst. Professor and Music Bibliographer, Baruch College, City Univ. of New York, N.Y.

Charles L. Hinkle, Professor of Business and Admin., Univ. of Colorado, Colorado Springs.

Linda Keir Hinrichs, Reference Librarian, Univ. of Dayton, Ohio.

Marjorie K. Ho, Head, Bibliographic Services, Western Michigan Univ. Libraries, Kalamazoo.

George V. Hodowanec, Director, William Allen White Library, Emporia State Univ., Kans.

Susan C. Holte, formerly staff, Libraries Unlimited, Inc.

Norman Horrocks, Director, School of Library Service, Dalhousie Univ., Halifax, Nova Scotia.

Don D. Insko, Asst. Acquisitions Librarian, Univ. of Wyoming, Laramie.

David Isaacson, Asst. Head of Reference and Humanities Librarian, Western Michigan Univ., Kalamazoo.

Janet R. Ivey, Head of Support Services, Boynton Beach City Library, Fla.

Miles M. Jackson, Professor, Graduate School of Library Studies, Univ. of Hawaii, Honolulu.

Maggie Johnson, Kansas City, Mo.

Beatrice J. Kalisch, Professor and Chair of Parent-Child Health, Univ. of Michigan, Ann Arbor.

Thomas A. Karel, Asst. Director for Public Services, Snadek-Fackenthal Library, Franklin and Marshall College, Lancaster, Pa.

Sharad Karkhanis, Professor, Kingsborough Community College Library, Brooklyn N.Y.

Dean H. Keller, Curator, Special Collections, Kent State Univ. Libraries, Ohio.

Richard J. Kelly, Asst. Professor and Reference/Bibliographer, Univ. of Minnesota Libraries, Minneapolis.

Barbara E. Kemp, Head, Humanities/Social Sciences Public Services, Washington State Univ., Pullman.

Michael Keresztesi, Assoc. Professor of Library Science, Wayne State Univ., Detroit.

Sharon Kincaide, staff, Libraries Unlimited, Inc.

Philip H. Kitchens, Reference Librarian, U.S. Army Missile Command, Redstone Scientific Information Center, Huntsville, Ala.

Susan Beverly Kuklin, Law Librarian, Santa Clara County Law Library, San Jose, Calif.

Colby H. Kullman, Dept. of English, Univ. of Mississippi, University.

Jovian P. Lang, Asst. Professor, Dept. of Library and Information Science, St. John's Univ., Jamaica, N.Y.

Mary Larsgaard, Map Librarian, Arthur Lakes Library, Colorado School of Mines, Golden.

Norman Lederer, Lower Columbia College, Longview, Wash.

Hwa-Wei Lee, Director of Libraries, Ohio Univ., Athens.

Donald J. Lehnus, Assoc. Professor, Graduate School of Library and Information Sciences, Univ. of Mississippi, University.

Dorothy E. Litt, Flushing, N.Y.

Janet H. Littlefield, Mayer, Brown & Platt, Denver, Colo.

Catherine R. Loeb, Asst. to the Women's Studies Librarian-at-Large, Univ. of Wisconsin, Madison.

Koert C. Loomis, Jr., Denver, Colo.

Irving Lowens, Music Critic, *Washington Star-News,* Washington, D.C.

Anna Mary Lowrey, Asst. Professor, School of Library and Information Science, State Univ. of New York, Buffalo.

Amy Gische Lyons, Senior Asst. Librarian, Health Sciences Library, State Univ. of New York, Buffalo.

H. Robert Malinowsky, President, Special Libraries Association.

Betty Malkus, Dept. of Music, Morgan State Univ., Baltimore, Md.

Guy A. Marco, Washington, D.C.

Lorranie Mathies, formerly Head, Education and Psychology Library, Univ. of California, Los Angeles.

Steven J. Mayover, Head, Films Dept., Northeast Regional Library, Free Library of Philadelphia, Pa.

James P. McCabe, Librarian, Allentown College of St. Frances de Sales, Center Valley, Pa.

Kathryn McChesney, Asst. Professor, School of Library Science, Kent State Univ., Ohio.

Kathleen McCullough, Bibliographer, School of Humanities, Social Science and Education, and Assoc. Professor of Library Science, Purdue Univ., West Lafayette, Ind.

Joseph McDonald, Doctoral candidate, Drexel Univ., Philadelphia, Pa.

Laura H. McGuire, Documens Librarian, Eastern New Mexico Univ. Library, Portales.

Robert W. Melton, Asst. Special Collections Librarian, Kenneth Spencer Research Library, Univ. of Kansas, Lawrence.

Shirley Miller, Reference Librarian, Kalamazoo Public Library, Mich.

Necia A. Musser, Head, Acquisitions and Collection Development, D. B. Waldo Library, Western Michigan Univ., Kalamazoo.

Elma M. Natt, Asst. Science and Technology Librarian and Assoc. Professor, Eastern Michigan Univ., Ypsilanti.

Marjorie N. Nelson, Librarian I, Science and Technology Dept., Los Angeles Public Library, Calif.

Eldo Neufeld, Music Librarian, Univ. of British Columbia, Vancouver.

Walter L. Newsome, Documents Librarian, Univ. of Virginia Library, Charlottesville.

Eric R. Nitschke, Reference Librarian, Robert W. Woodruff Library, Emory Univ., Atlanta, Ga.

Cleon Robert Nixon, III, Freelance writer, Platteville, Wis.

Margaret Norden, Reference Librarian, Falk Library, Univ. of Pittsburgh, Pa.

Dennis North, Head Librarian, Dayton Memorial Library, Regis College, Denver.

Marshall E. Nunn, Reference Librarian, Glendale Community College, Calif.

L. Terry Oggel, Assoc. Professor of English, Northern Illinois Univ., DeKalb.

Jeanne Osborn, formerly Professor, School of Library Science, Univ. of Iowa, Iowa City.

Henry S. Otterson, Jr., Senior Librarian, Attica Correctional Facility, N.Y.

Elliot Palais, Reference and Collection Development Librarian, Arizona State Univ. Library, Tempe.

Roberta R. Palen, Political Science, Public Admin. and Social Work Librarian, Syracuse Univ., N.Y.

Joseph W. Palmer, Asst. Professor, School of Information Studies, State Univ. of New York, Buffalo.

Robert Palmieri, Professor and Coordinator, Div. of Keyboard Instruments, School of Music, Kent State Univ., Ohio.

Maureen Pastine, Director, San Jose State Univ. Library, Calif.

Anna Grace Patterson, staff, Libraries Unlimited, Inc.

Charles D. Patterson, Professor, Graduate School of Library Science, Louisiana State Univ., Baton Rouge.

Gari-Anne Patzwald, Consultant, Sordoni-Burich Library, National College of Chiropractic, Lombard, Ill.

Sharon L. Paugh, Music Librarian, University of Wisconsin, Milwaukee.

Susan V. Peck, Business Reference Specialist, Cuyahoga County Library System, Maple Heights, Ohio.

Daniel F. Phelan, Head, Audio Visual Dept., North Bay Public Library, Ont.

Jack E. Pontius, Head, Microforms Section, Pattee Library, Pennsylvania State Univ., University Park.

Edwin D. Posey, Engineering Librarian, Engineering Library, Purdue Univ., Libraries, West Lafayette, Ind.

Gloria Palmeri Powell, staff, Libraries Unlimited, Inc.

Randall Rafferty, Asst. Professor and Humanities Reference Librarian, Mississippi State Univ. Library, Mississippi State.

F. W. Ramey, Denver, Colo.

Ronald Rayman, Assoc. Professor and Reference Librarian, Western Illinois Univ., Macomb.

Bernard D. Reams, Jr., Assoc. Professor of Law and Law Librarian, Washington Univ. School of Law, St. Louis, Mo.

Mary Reichel, Head, Reference Dept., William R. Pullen Library, Georgia State Univ., Atlanta.

James Rettig, Head Reference Librarian, Univ. of Illinois, Chicago.

Margaret Rich, Librarian, Drake Memorial Library, State Univ. College, Brockport, N.Y.

John V. Richardson, Jr., Assoc. Professor, Graduate School of Library and Information Science, Univ. of California, Los Angeles.

Edward A. Richter, Reference Librarian, Eastern New Mexico Univ., Portales.

Philip R. Rider, Instructor of English, Northern Illinois Univ., DeKalb.

Ilene F. Rockman, Reference Librarian, California Polytechnic State Univ., San Luis Obispo.

A. Robert Rogers, formerly Dean, School of Library Science, Kent State Univ., Ohio.

David Rosenbaum, Reference Librarian, Education Library, Wayne State Univ., Detroit.

Judith Campbell Rosenberg, Children's Librarian, Chamberlain Branch, Akron-Summit County Public Library, Akron, Ohio.

Kenyon C. Rosenberg, Assoc. Director for Bibliographic and Document Services, National Technical Information Service, Springfield, Va.

Julia Sabine, formerly Special Asst. to the Director, Munson-Williams-Proctor Institute, Utica, N.Y.

Edmund F. SantaVicca, Humanities Bibliographer/Reference Librarian, Cleveland State Univ. Library, Ohio.

William Z. Schenck, Head, Acquisitions Dept., Wilson Library, Univ. of North Carolina, Chapel Hill.

John P. Schmitt, Reference Librarian, Purdue Univ., West Lafayette, Ind.

Frederic Schoettler, Asst. Professor of Music, Kent State Univ., Ohio.

Alan Edward Schorr, Univ. Librarian, California State Univ., Fullerton.

Helen Q. Schroyer, Documents and Special Collections Librarian, Purdue Univ. Libraries, West Lafayette, Ind.

Eleanor Elving Schwartz, Assoc. Professor and Coordinator, Library/Media Program, Dept. of Communication Sciences, Kean College of New Jersey, Union.

LeRoy C. Schwarzkopf, formerly Govt. Documents Librarian, Univ. of Maryland, College Park.

Robert A. Seal, Director of Library Public Services, Bizzell Library, Univ. of Oklahoma, Norman.

Nat Shapiro, New York, N.Y.

Ravindra Nath Sharma, Head Librarian, Pennsylvania State Univ., Beaver Campus, Monaca.

Avery T. Sharp, Music Librarian, Baylor Univ., Waco, Tex.

Patricia Tipton Sharp, Asst. Professor of Library Science, Baylor Univ., Waco, Tex.

Jesse H. Shera, formerly Dean Emeritus, School of Library Science, Case Western Reserve Univ., Cleveland, Ohio.

Joan Sargent Sherwood, Vice President of Student Affairs/Dean of Students, Western Washington Univ., Bellingham.

Gerald R. Shields, Asst. Dean, School of Information and Library Studies, State Univ. of New York, Buffalo.

Bruce A. Shuman, Alpha Systems Resource, Shelbyville, Ind.

Jacqueline Sisson, Head, Fine Arts Library, and Assoc. Professor, Ohio State Univ., Columbus.

Sally S. Small, Head Librarian, Berks Campus, Pennsylvania State Univ., Reading.

Phillip Smith, Reference Librarian, Univ. of California, San Diego.

Miluse Soudek, Professor and Subject Specialist for Psychology/Philosophy/Religion. Northern Illinois Univ. Libraries, DeKalb.

Lawrence E. Spellman, Curator of Maps, Princeton Univ. Library, N.J.

Paul H. Spence, Univ. College Librarian, Mervyn H. Sterne Library, Univ. of Alabama, Birmingham.

Bill Sperry, Englewood, Colo.

Lee Steinberg, Programmer, City Univ. of New York, New York.

Clara Steuermann, Librarian, Cleveland Institute of Music, Ohio.

Norman D. Stevens, Univ. Librarian, Univ. of Connecticut, Storrs.

Esther F. Stineman, formerly Librarian-at-Large for Women's Studies, Memorial Library, Univ. of Wisconsin, Madison.

Leon J. Stout, Head, Pennsylvania State Room, Pennsylvania State Univ. Libraries, University Park.

James H. Sweetland, Head Librarian, State Historical Society of Wisconsin, Madison.

D. Bernard Theall, Assoc. Professor of Library Science, Catholic Univ. of America, Washington, D.C.

Ellen C. Thompson, formerly staff, Libraries Unlimited, Inc.

Lawrence S. Thompson, Professor of Classics, Classics Dept., Univ. of Kentucky, Lexington.

Bruce H. Tiffney, Dept. of Biology, Yale Univ., New Haven, Conn.

Andrew G. Torok, Asst. Professor, Dept. of Library Science, Northern Illinois Univ., DeKalb.

Peggy M. Tozer, Director, Library, Eastern New Mexico Univ., Portales.

Joanne Troutner, Media Specialist, Klondike Jr. High School, West Lafayette, Ind.

Dean Tudor, Professor, School of Journalism, Ryerson Polytechnical Institute, Toronto.

Robert L. Turner, Jr., Asst. Library Director for Public Services, Radford Univ., Va.

Daniel Uchitelle, Reference Librarian, Sterling Memorial Library, Yale Univ., New Haven, Conn.

Robert F. Van Benthuysen, Library Director, Monmouth College, West Long Branch, N.J.

Barbara Van Deventer, Director, Cubberley Library, Stanford Univ. Libraries, Calif.

Carole Franklin Vidali, Syracuse, N.Y.

George M. Vogler, C.P.A., Denver, Colo.

Kathleen J. Voight, Head, Reference Dept., Carlson Library, Univ. of Toledo, Ohio.

Mary Jo Walker, University Archivist and Special Collections Librarian, Eastern New Mexico Univ., Portales.

Lillian Biermann Wehmeyer, Superintendent for Instruction, San Mateo City School District, Calif.

Darlene E. Weingand, Asst. Professor, Library School, Univ. of Wisconsin, Madison.

Ina J. Weis, Asst. to the Director for Special Projects, Univ. of Toledo Libraries, Ohio.

Robert L. Welker, Professor and Chairman of the English Dept., Univ. of Alabama, Huntsville.

Erwin K. Welsch, Social Studies Bibliographer, Memorial Library, Univ. of Wisconsin, Madison.

Lucille Whalen, Professor, School of Library and Information Science, State Univ. of New York, Albany.

Helen Wheeler, Assoc. Professor, School of Library Science, Louisiana State Univ., Baton Rouge.

Wayne A. Wiegand, Asst. Professor, College of Library Science, Univ. of Kentucky, Lexington.

Constance D. Williams, formerly staff, Libraries Unlimited, Inc.

Wiley J. Williams, Professor, School of Library Science, Kent State Univ., Ohio.

John G. Williamson, Humanities Bibliographer, Yale Univ. Library, New Haven, Conn.

Patty Wood, Denver, Colo.

Raymund R. Wood, Editor, *The Westerners,* Encino, Calif.

Ross Wood, Music Librarian, Wellesley College, Mass.

Anna Wynar, Certified Rehabilitation Counselor, Ravenna, Ohio.

Christine Gehrt Wynar, President, Corona Press, Littleton, Colo.

Lubomyr R. Wynar, Professor, School of Library Science, and Director, Program for the Study of Ethnic Publications in the U.S., Kent State Univ., Ohio.

Sally Wynkoop, formerly Asst. Editor, *American Reference Books Annual.*

Mark R. Yerburgh, Library Director, Trinity College, Burlington, Vt.

A. Neil Yerkey, Asst. Professor, School of Information and Library Studies, State Univ. of New York, Buffalo.

Victoria L. Young, Reference/Instruction Librarian, Bowling Green State Univ. Libraries, Ohio.

William Curtis Young, author, Lawrence, Kans.

Part I
Universal and National Biographies

INTRODUCTION

Part I, "Universal and National Biographies," constitutes the smaller portion of this book. The material is divided into several chapters. "Universal Sources" covers general biographical dictionaries not limited to a particular territory or nation. It is subdivided into two sections: "Current Biographies" and "Retrospective Biographies" with a total of thirty-five entries. It includes such well-known works as Wilson's *Current Biography Yearbook* (see entry 3) or Marquis's *Who's Who in the World* (see entry 10), or such monumental works (in the retrospective section) as *The McGraw-Hill Encyclopedia of World Biography* (see entry 23). Most annotations provide references to related works and offer a number of critical comments.

"Universal Sources" is followed by a chapter on national and regional sources. The "United States" (fifty-one entries) is treated first in this chapter. Here the material is subdivided into three sections: "Current Biographies," "Retrospective Biographies," and "States and Regions." The section on "Current Biographies" contains such well-known works as *Who's Who in America* (see entry 37) and *Who's Who of American Women* (see entry 39). "Retrospective Biographies" includes such outstanding scholarly works as *Dictionary of American Biography* (see entry 43), *Notable American Women, 1607-1950* (see entry 63), and *Notable American Women, the Modern Period* (see entry 64). There is also a comprehensive review of *Who Was Who in America* (see entry 70) with references to companion volumes.

The section on "States and Regions" is not as complete as the preceding two sections because many biographical sources are published locally and are not included in such standard sources as *Books in Print* and *American Reference Books Annual*. Several sources offer comprehensive listings of such biographies; thus, for example, Robert B. Slocum's *Biographical Dictionaries and Related Works* (Gale, 1967 and *Supplement*, 1972) lists under "National or Area Biography—Local" many biographical sources. Unfortunately, bibliographic citations are not always accurate and over 50 percent of the material deals with history rather than biography. The new edition, now in preparation, may correct such inaccuracies. Two other sources might also be of some importance: *Dictionary Catalog of the Local History and Genealogy Division* (18v. G. K. Hall, 1974), which shows the New York Public Library holdings in this subject area, and *United States Local Histories in the Library of Congress: A Bibliography*, edited by M. Kaminkow (4v. Magna Carta Book Co., 1975). The quality of the material in this area is rather uneven. There are some outstanding works, e.g., *Dictionary of Georgia Biography* (see entry 77). There are other works, such as

Colorado Who's Who (see entry 78) that remind us of a typical vanity press publication. As a matter of fact, Gormezano Reference Publications is a vanity press (see entry 82), and they have issued a number of biographical dictionaries covering all states. We felt that our readers should know about it. The section on the United States is followed by eight subject-oriented sections: "Africa," "Asia," "Australia and New Zealand," "Canada," "Europe," "Great Britain and Commonwealth," "Latin America," and "Middle East." The biographical sources pertaining to Great Britain constitute the greatest number and include such well-known works as *Who's Who: 1985-86* (see entry 128) or such outstanding works as *The Dictionary of National Biography* (see entry 137) or *Dictionary of Labour Biography* (see entry 132).

In addition to the 161 sources listed here and several hundred related titles mentioned in the annotations, there are a number of older biographical directories that still may be useful for retrospective searching. In international sources there is, of course, Joseph Thomas's *Universal Pronouncing Dictionary of Biography and Mythology* (5th ed. Lippincott, 1930. 2250p.) best known as *Lippincott's Biographical Dictionary* with the first edition published in 1870. Equally well known is *New Century Cyclopedia of Names*, edited by C. L. Barnhart (3v. Appleton, 1954), that contains about one hundred thousand entries ranging from two or three lines in length to more than half a page. It is a revision of the *Century Cyclopedia of Names*, originally published as volume 2 of the *Century Dictionary and Cyclopedia* (12v. Century, 1911) that was first published in six volumes in 1889-1891.

There are also a number of older biographical sources published in other languages. One of the best known in French is *Biographie universelle . . .* , known as "Michaud" (45v. Paris, Mme. C. Desplaces, 1843-1865), with the first edition published in 1811-1857 and continued by *Nouvelle biographie générale . . .* (46v. Paris, Firmin Didot, 1853-1866), usually cited as "Hoefer." C. G. Jöcher's *Allgemeines Gelehrten—Lexikon . . .* (4v. Leipzig, Gleditsch, 1750-1751) plus supplements is an example of one of the best German biographies. The same is true of E. M. Oettinger's *Moniteur des Dates. Biographisch-genealogisch-historisches Welt-Register . . .* (9v. Leipzig, Denicke, 1869-1873; Hermann, 1873-1882) containing over one hundred thousand entries.

Most countries have a number of retrospective biographical dictionaries. Thus, for the United States, still useful is *Appleton's Cyclopaedia of American Biography*, edited by J. G. Wilson and J. Fiske (7v. Appleton, 1894-1900; repr. Gale, 1968). For Australia we have *Australian Dictionary of Biography* (Melbourne, University Press, 1966- . In progress), and for Austria, *Biographisches Lexikon des Kaiserthums Oesterreich . . .* (60v. Vienna, Zamarski, 1856-1891). For France there is *Dictionnaire de bibliographie française* (Paris, Letouzey, 1933- . In progress), and for Germany, *Allgemeine deutsche Biographie* (56v. Leipzig, Duncker, 1875-1912).

A fairly complete listing (except for developing countries) of biographical works (current and retrospective) can be found in Eugene P. Sheehy's *Guide to Reference Books* (9th ed. American Library Association, 1976. 1015p.) and the two supplements published in 1980 and 1982. All entries are annotated briefly and provide a very good publishing history of a given work. Sheehy can be supplemented by A. J. Walford's *Guide to Reference Material* (3rd ed. London, Library Association, 1975-1980) that provides a good coverage of smaller European countries and is more comprehensive in discussing biographical sources of the British Commonwealth.

In addition to biographical sources, a number of general and subject encyclopedias contain a large amount of biographical data. The most famous encyclopedia in English,

Encyclopaedia Britannica, was first published in 1768-1771 in three volumes, and, starting with the fifteenth edition (1974), consists of three parts (*Micropaedia, Macropaedia,* and *Propaedia*). Most important personalities are included in *Britannica* and length of biographical sketches ranges from several lines to several pages, depending on the relative historical importance of a given individual. Biographies are included in most other American and English encyclopedias, e.g., *Encyclopedia Americana* (16v. 1st ed. 1903-1904), *Chambers' Encyclopaedia* (1st ed. 1850-1868), *Collier's Encyclopedia* (20v. 1st ed. 1949-1951), *Academic American Encyclopedia* (21v. 1980), as well as in several juvenile encyclopedias, e.g., *Compton's Pictured Encyclopedia* (1st ed. 1922), *World Book Encyclopedia* (8v. 1st ed. 1917), and many others. The reader will find a good evaluation of general encyclopedias in K. F. Kister's *Encyclopedia Buying Guide: A Consumer Guide to General Encyclopedias in Print* (3rd ed. R. R. Bowker, 1981. 530p.) as well as in Sheehy, Walford, *American Reference Books Annual,* and *Reference and Subscription Books Reviews* (in 1983 the title changed to *Reference Books Bulletin*).

A number of subject encyclopedias or dictionaries also offer biographical information. Thus, for the Middle Ages, one can consult *Dictionary of the Middle Ages* to be published in twelve volumes (Scribner's, 1982-), or A. Grabois's *The Illustrated Encyclopedia of Medieval Civilization* (Octopus Books, 1980. 751p.), or especially I. Rachum's *The Renaissance: An Illustrated Encyclopedia* (Mayflower Books, 1980. 611p.) that offers some two thousand articles, most of them biographical in nature. For the modern period there is A. Palmer's *The Facts on File Dictionary of 20th Century History* (Facts on File, 1979. 402p.) or Palmer's other two works, *The Penguin Dictionary of Modern History 1789-1945* (2nd ed. Penguin Books, 1983. 315p.) and *The Penguin Dictionary of Twentieth-Century History* (2nd ed. Penguin Books, 1983. 411p.).

Several works specifically cover World Wars I and II, and biographical information is offered in *The Marshall Cavendish Illustrated Encyclopedia of World War I,* edited by P. Young (12v. Marshall Cavendish, 1984) and *The Historical Encyclopedia of World War II,* edited by M. Baudot (Facts on File, 1980. 548p.).

E. N. Williams's *The Facts on File Dictionary of European History, 1485-1789* (Facts on File, 1980. 509p.) offers biographical information on figures in European history and there are, of course, many other sources.

Several hundred encyclopedias and dictionaries deal with individual countries, for example, *Historical Dictionary of the French Revolution, 1789-1799,* edited by S. F. Scott and B. Rothaus (2v. Greenwood Press, 1985) and L. Snyder's *Encyclopedia of the Third Reich* (McGraw-Hill, 1976. 410p.). Again, the reader will find most important reference sources in Sheehy, Walford, and *American Reference Books Annual.*

Biographical information published in periodicals (occasionally also in books) can be located through indexes and abstracting services. The most popular is a quarterly publication, *Biography Index: A Cumulative Index to Biographical Material in Books and Magazines* (Wilson, 1947-) covering over fifteen hundred periodicals. That publication can be supplemented in retrospective searching by M. Arnim's *Internationale Personalbibliographie, 1800-1943* (2v. 2nd ed. Leipzig. Hiersemann, 1944-1952). It indexes books, periodicals and biographical dictionaries published during that period. Another Wilson publication, *Essay and General Literature Index* (Wilson, 1934-) also provides a substantial amount of biographical information. The basic volume of this work, covering 1900-1933, was published in 1934 and is now kept up-to-date by several cumulations. All major indexing services are adequately described by Sheehy, Walford, and *American Reference Books Annual*.

1 Universal Sources

CURRENT BIOGRAPHIES

1. Andersen, Christopher P. **The Book of People: Photographs, Capsule Biographies and Vital Statistics of Over 500 Celebrities.** New York, Putnam, 1981. 425p. illus. (A Perigee Book). $9.95pa. LC 81-82857. ISBN 0-399-50530-X.

The Book of People is filled with information about celebrities, for the most part the superstar variety that "people watchers" like to know about. The "now generation" representing wealth, power, and talent, as well as the notorious, get special recognition. Among the wealthy are Daniel Ludwig, billionaire tanker owner; Christina Onassis, heiress of a shipping fortune; George Lucas, the force behind *Star Wars*; and Peter Frampton, a rock star who struck it rich. Among the talented and accomplished are Mikhail Baryshnikov, the greatest living classical dancer; the Bee Gees, rock singers who at least rank with the Beatles; and Mark Hamil of *Star Wars* fame. For the notorious, samples are Idi Amin and Charles Manson.

But the older generation is not ignored here. A casual browsing will reveal biographical information and usually photographs of such personalities as Ingrid Bergman, Bob Hope, Katharine Hepburn, Cary Grant, Greta Garbo, and a goodly number of others. Nor are the notables in other areas disregarded. For instance, there are Pope John Paul, II, David Brinkley, Jimmy Carter, Billy Graham, Betty Ford, and Richard Nixon.

Perhaps the most appealing part of *The Book of People* will be the vital statistics given at the end of each biographical sketch. These include birth dates, height, weight, color of eyes, and interesting measurements (Dolly Parton's are 39-25-39); the sign of the Zodiac under which each was born (a disproportionate number have their fates sealed with Taurus); education (many finished high school, a few went to college, and more than a few are high school dropouts); religion; marriages (usually at least two are listed); and income (astronomically high).

Photographs are often missing. None seemed to be available for Robert Woodward, Natalie Wood, Abigail Van Buren, Gloria Steinem, Jean Stapleton, and numerous others; the income figures tend to be vague (one must assume that those stated are for a twelve-month period); and the professions are not readily in view for quick reference.

The Book of People will make a hit on the newsstand alongside *People Magazine* because people will find these small things fascinating; and reference librarians — academic, high school, junior high school, and public — will find it of some value to supplement *Current Biography*. [R: LJ, 15 Oct 81, p. 2013; SLJ, Nov 81, p. 118]

Jefferson D. Caskey

2. **Biography News: A Compilation of News Stories and Feature Articles from American Newspapers Covering Personalities of National Interest in All Fields**. Frank Bair and Barbara Nykoruk, eds. Detroit, Gale, 1974-1975. Frequency varies. illus. o.p.

This publication, published monthly in 1974 and bimonthly in 1975, reproduces biographical information that originally appeared in approximately fifty newspapers that represent the geographical areas of the United States. About fifteen hundred pages of illustrated material are included in a single year, with a monthly cumulative index for all previously published articles for that year. The individuals included are people of general interest making news; the comments about them can be considered as updatings of traditional biographical sources, so that this publication supplements rather than replaces these sources.

Approximately one-third of the names listed in the cumulated index we checked were associated with the entertainment world and the performing arts. Sports figures, authors, and some national political figures were represented, with only minimal coverage of regionally or locally important people. In contrast, the *New York Times Biographical Edition*, which has essentially the same format, includes, in addition to the general coverage of newsworthy people, more international personages and obituaries of lesser-known individuals.

The coverage of newsworthy people offered by *Biography News* was not sufficiently different from that of the *New York Times Biographical Edition* and by the end of 1975 *BN* ceased publication. [R: WLB, Oct 74, p. 180]   Jean Herold

3. **Current Biography Yearbook 1984**. Charles Moritz, ed. New York, H. W. Wilson, 1984. 488p. illus. index. $35.00. LC 40-27432. ISSN 0084-9499.

One of the most durable of all reference works is *Current Biography*. And deservedly so. Widely used by libraries of all types as a monthly magazine, *Current Biography* is also available as a cloth-bound *Yearbook*, published annually in December. Like its forty-four annual predecessors, the 1984 yearbook presents a timely biography of some 140 leaders in all fields of endeavor — government, entertainment, business, science, religion, the arts. Each biography runs from two thousand to three thousand words and carries a portrait, an address, and a list of references consulted.

The coverage is thoroughly international and includes all races, colors, and creeds. Women are well represented; the "D" section alone has Mary Decker, Judianne Densen-Gerber, Diana of Wales, Anne Dillard, and Elizabeth Dole. The *CB* also does well in contemporaneity. Many "scholarly" reference works disdain biographies of the living but this publication thrives on the here and now. For example, a list of the 1984 subjects shows the following, all born after 1950 — Michael Jackson, Jennifer Holliday, Steven Jobs, Joe Montana, Sally Ride, and Curtis Sliwa.

The editorial procedures may be summarized as follows. Constant research and writing help produce eleven monthly issues with each article checked, whenever possible, for accuracy and timeliness with the appropriate biographer. The *Yearbook* is then compiled to include revised sketches on previous subjects that have had a major career change, obituaries of previous subjects who have died in the past year, appropriate cross-references, a classification by profession, and a cumulative index (for 1984 it covers the 1980, 1981, 1982, 1983, and 1984 yearbooks). Earlier cumulative yearbooks are available from the publisher.

David Eggenberger and Bohdan S. Wynar

4. **The International Who's Who, 1985-86**. 49th ed. London, Europa Publications; distr., Detroit, Gale, 1985. 1530p. $130.00. LC 35-10257. ISBN 0-946653-07-0; ISSN 0074-9613.

For many years *The International Who's Who* has been considered a reliable reference source throughout the world. Now in its 49th edition, it has been updated and apparently offers the same quality of usefulness.

This new edition contains approximately fifteen thousand biographies, with over fifteen hundred of them new additions. The individual entries have been revised and updated; and for those entrants who have retired or whose biographies underwent no changes, users are referred to earlier editions in which their biographies may be located. At the beginning of the volume there is an obituary list of those personalities whose deaths occurred after the copy for this edition went to press. The list of abbreviations, which appears in the front matter, will be needed in reading the biographies in this work, as virtually all of the entries have some abbreviations in them.

The section entitled "Reigning Royal Families," also in the front matter, lists these persons alphabetically by country, beginning with Bahrain and continuing through the United Kingdom. Most of these names can also be found in more detail in their expected alphabetical place in the text, sometimes requiring *see* references for complicated names.

The International Who's Who encompasses biographical material for countries whose who's whos are inadequate. It also includes a wide range of prominent men and women in international affairs, government, administration, diplomacy, science, medicine, law, finance, business, education, religion, literature, music, art, entertainment, and sports. Addresses are given, and frequently, telephone numbers.

Although the biographies in *The International Who's Who* are the formula type, and contain many abbreviations, they are remarkably detailed and accurate. The print is clear and most readable. *The International Who's Who* offers a reference service that would make it essential in university, college, and public libraries; and international business and government organizations would certainly want to have access to it.

Jefferson D. Caskey

5. Kay, Ernest, ed. **Dictionary of International Biography: A Biographical Record of Contemporary Achievement. Volume 18**. Cambridge, England, International Biographical Centre; distr., Totowa, N.J., International Biographical Centre, 1984. 893p. illus. $117.50. ISBN 0-900332-75-1.

Although the present edition does incorporate some changes from the earlier formats, it is difficult to conceive of previous reviewers giving the eighteenth volume more favorable reviews than they gave the others. This volume does include the third edition of *Men and Women of Distinction* appended at the end, and there is a new section at the beginning as well. This edition features "the full life stories and photographs" of a select few men and women (twenty-five) to whom the book is dedicated. They represent every continent, but six come from the United States and three each from Australia and Canada. Photographs are also supplied for many of the entries in "Men and Women of Distinction."

The same poor quality of informational content which was described in the previous reviews continues — entries are uneven in the type and quantity of information supplied, even with respect to birthdates and places. Sometimes a country is given but no place or date, or some variation of this theme. While most of the people listed, regardless of which section of the work one is considering, appear to be worthy citizens of their country and of the world, the particular posts to which they have risen are not, in most cases, sufficiently eminent to look for them in a work of this type. Most would be sought in national biographical directories or in a Who's Who devoted to particular subject specializations where more relevant information might be expected. It is indeed difficult to determine what use this book is likely to be, and to whom.

Margaret Anderson

6. Kay, Ernest, ed. **The World Who's Who of Women**. 7th ed. Cambridge, England, International Biographical Centre; distr., Totowa, N.J., International Biographical Centre, 1984. 800p. illus. $125.00. ISBN 0-900332-68-9.

A key problem with this Who's Who, endemic to this type of reference book, lies in the selection process itself. "Inclusion is entirely by invitation and achievement," the editor tells us. So many notable American names, luminaries from academe, business, entertainment, government, and sports, are absent from this publication (that frankly draws most of its biographees from the United States) that one begins to wonder whether selection was solely the result of returning the response form. It is, however, good to see praise accorded in the form of short chronicles of "ordinary women" — women who struggle along in the mainstream of ordinary lives, achieving rather ordinary honors.

The work is set up rather like a yearbook; the editor has gathered many photographs of those "selected," and it is not surprising that most of the women are white, though some effort has been made to include women from developing nations.

Reviewing this book clarified my awareness of a personal bias I have toward biographical references identifying "extraordinary" and famous women, women who are already identified in many other sources, of course. Hence, biographical sources on women being what they are — methods of identification probably depending on self-selection — I would not favor Kay's book in a reference area. However, for sociological purposes alone, this volume may well prove useful in contemporary and future international analysis of women's interests and achievements.

Esther Stineman

7. **Men of Achievement. Volume 10**. Cambridge, England. International Biographical Centre; distr., Totowa, N.J., Biblio Distribution Centre, 1984. 650p. illus. $75.00. ISBN 0-900332-66-2.

Selection of biographees included in *Men of Achievement* "is entirely dependent upon achievement, whether this be on an international, national, regional or local level." These vague statements are not made clearer by the provision of any details on how individuals are discovered. My guess — and it is only that — is that the publisher relies heavily on mailing lists of various professional organizations. Biographical information, at any rate, is supplied in most cases by those selected.

By not limiting the scope of this volume, the publisher or editor hopes to escape the responsibility of providing systematic coverage in any given field of endeavor. The volume includes Senator Inouye (though it fails to give his party affiliation) but not Senators Dole, Kennedy, or Helms, or Speaker O'Neill; Vice President Bush but not President Reagan; conductor Claudio Abbado but not van Karajan; the presidents of Duke and Kansas State universities but not those of Harvard or Yale; and so forth. With such uneven coverage among people of international stature, surely the coverage at the lesser levels of achievement is even more arbitrary.

It is undoubtedly true, as the editor states in the preface, that the book contains "many biographies which cannot be found elsewhere." And it is entirely possible that some of the people included will be the object of some library users' search for information. Of particular value may be the information on those university professors, consultants, medical specialists, and corporate executives and managers who were included. But a very large percentage of persons included fall into one of two categories: people for whom adequate information is available elsewhere, and people who are not likely to be the subject of anyone else's information need. Thus, the volume does not belong on the ready-reference shelf, and only those libraries for which providing exhaustive biographical information is a high priority should consider spending the exorbitant sum for this volume. Robert W. Melton

8. **New York Times Biographical Service: A Compilation of Current Biographical Information of General Interest**. Ann Arbor, Mich., University Microfilms International, 1970- . Monthly. $110.00/yr. LC 70-20206.

This monthly service supplies, in hard copy, more than two thousand biographical profiles a year. They are reproduced exactly as they appear in the *New York Times* and the *New York Times Magazine* and range from short news stories to lengthy "think" pieces. The majority of the articles are on sports figures, entertainers, and politicians, although all walks of life are represented. The December 1984 edition included such people as rock singer Sting, quarterback Archie Manning, actor Peter Lawford, the Polish General Wojciech Jaruzelski, and Herbert A. Blaize, Prime Minister of Grenada. The service is most useful for its obituaries; since it is published monthly one can learn here about important deaths much more quickly than is possible through most other sources. An index of names is included in each issue and semiannual and annual cumulative indexes are printed with the biographical material. Intelligent use of this service will save countless hours of research on the part of the library user. Bohdan S. Wynar

9. Weis, Frank W. **Lifelines: Famous Contemporaries from 600 B.C. to 1975**. New York, Facts on File, 1982. 437p. illus. index. $19.95. LC 80-23132. ISBN 0-87196-466-X.

Lifelines lists, groups, and comments on over two thousand famous people who lived during the time span of 600 B.C. to 1975. Organized into twenty-five-year periods, each section gives a brief (several paragraphs) synopsis of those years. These narrative parts, highlighted in shaded boxes, are capsule history written in a lively, readable style. Then follow biographies of people then living who made contributions to world history. By necessity in a volume of this scope, the biographies are brief, limited to several sentences each. The names of the people are also listed in the previous and the following groupings of twenty-five years, in separate columns, with birth and death dates. Initially, this reviewer found the format somewhat confusing.

The summary biographies are less complete than those found in a multivolume encyclopedia. For example, Hirohito, emperor of Japan, is listed in the 1925-1950 grouping. His life is described in three sentences. Next to his name is his age, twenty-four years, in 1925. (Hirohito was born in 1901. This information is found in the 1950-1975 grouping.) However, neither the date listings nor the biographical entries are in alphabetical order. The names are arranged by birth date and an alphabetical name index at the end of the book provides access to the biographical entries.

A somewhat related title is *Regents of Nations: Systematic Chronology of States and Their Political Representatives in Past and Present. A Biographical Reference Book*, edited by Peter Truhart (3v. New York, K. G. Saur, 1985. $200.00). It enumerates heads of state around the world, from ancient Assyrian kings and dynasts to African tribal leaders and modern American cabinet officers. Some thirty thousand individuals are covered in this set. [R: Choice, July-Aug 82, p. 1544; WLB, June 82, p. 784]   Mary Alice Deveny and Bohdan S. Wynar

10.   **Who's Who in the World, 1984-1985**. 7th ed. Chicago, Marquis Who's Who, 1984. 1178p. $130.00. LC 79-139215. ISBN 0-8379-1107-9.

The current edition contains brief biographical sketches of some twenty-five thousand persons. Criteria for admission are stated and methods of spelling and alphabetizing names from non-Roman alphabet languages are described in the prefatory matter. Cross-references are provided when they are considered necessary. The standard Marquis format is followed, and abbreviations are explained. Biographical information was secured from, and then verified by, biographees whenever possible. When this was not possible, biographical sketches of internationally prominent people (e.g., the Ayatollah Ruhollah Khomeini) were prepared from other sources. Entries prepared in this fashion are indicated by asterisks. A spot check of a small sample of prominent persons in the news failed to reveal any omissions. A quick scan of addresses on selected pages suggested wide international coverage. A check for prominent librarians revealed some unevenness. It was gratifying to find Elizabeth Stone—but why not Robert Wedgeworth? For reference departments with a sufficient volume of questions about personages of international consequence.

For a number of years St. Martin's Press published a competitive volume to *Who's Who in the World*, namely *The Blue Book: Leaders of the English Speaking World*. The last volume we examined was for 1975. We compared *The Blue Book* with *Who's Who* and *Who's Who in America*, clearly the two most pertinent sources for "leaders of the English speaking world." Using a rough sample of entries appearing in *WW* and *WWA* in the "B-Bac" segment of the alphabet, we found that about one-half of them were not duplicated in *The Blue Book*. Conversely, about the same percentage of *The Blue Book* entries did not appear in the other two sources.

Obviously since *The Blue Book* is no longer published, this exercise is purely academic. But *The Blue Book* is listed in a number of standard sources (e.g., Walford), and most libraries probably will retain those volumes.

A. Robert Rogers and Bohdan S. Wynar

RETROSPECTIVE BIOGRAPHIES

11.   **The Annual Obituary, 1983**. Chicago, St. James Press, 1983. 900p. index. $74.50. ISBN 0-312-03877-4.

This annual volume must rank as one of the major reference books. It is a standard purchase since all editions published since 1981 carry on the initial high level of selection, writing, and completeness.

Basically an international biographical work, it describes and evaluates the lives of three hundred notable people who died during the year. Selection of entries was based on major historical importance, international renown, and national prominence. Each entry opens with a brief identification of the person, plus birth and death information. The heart of the presentation is a signed essay followed by full biographical data in a compressed format, a bibliography (if applicable), and sometimes (but unfortunately not always) photographs of the subject. Essays range in length from three hundred to five thousand words.

Entries are arranged chronologically, balanced out by an alphabetical index and an index by professions. In all volumes, both the alphabetical and professions indexes are cumulative.

This annual can be supplemented by *Atlantic Brief Lives: A Biographical Companion to the Arts*, edited by L. Kronenberger (Little, Brown, 1971. 898p. o.p.). *Brief Lives* contains 1,081 brief biographies covering 1,103 personages important in the literature, art, and music of the Western world. Living figures are excluded. Besides these succinct, factual accounts of the biographees, 211 persons were selected for extended essays following the regular biographical entry which explicate those individuals' works.

Among the contributors who have written these essays are Jacques Barzun, Stanley Kunitz, Lewis Mumford, Mark Schorer, and John Updike. Useful inclusions, in the brief biographies, are the subject's major works with dates and a selective bibliography of critical and biographical studies.   David Eggenberger and Bohdan S. Wynar

12.   Bietenholz, Peter G., and Thomas B. Deutscher, eds. **Contemporaries of Erasmus: A Biographical Register of the Renaissance and Reformation. Volume 1: A-E.** Buffalo, N.Y., University of Toronto Press, 1985. 462p. illus. $72.50. ISBN 0-8020-2507-2.

This handsome volume is an offshoot of the project to publish the collected works of Erasmus. To avoid the necessity of the editors having to fully and repetitiously identify the many persons who appear in the works and the correspondence, the decision was made to publish a separate biographical register. *Contemporaries of Erasmus* will be complete in three volumes. The present part, A-E, covers Henry Abingdon through Hendrik van den Eynde.

As with the collected works themselves, this book is a joint project. Over one hundred scholars from fifteen nations contributed biographies of persons great and small. The size of each biography is generally proportional to the person's importance and the availability of information. Thus, figures such as Pope Adrian VI, Martin Bucer, and John Colet have entries of approximately three double-column pages each, while others have only a line or two to indicate that they are mentioned by Erasmus but cannot be otherwise identified. For each entry, there is reference to where the person is named by Erasmus, and wherever possible there is a bibliography directing the reader to further information.

This is very much a work for specialists. Its narrow scope and high price will keep it out of most undergraduate and public libraries. Specialists in the Reformation and early Renaissance will find it helpful, and for Erasmus scholars it will be indispensable.

Philip R. Rider

13.   Biography Almanac: A Comprehensive Reference Guide to More Than 23,000 Famous and Infamous Newsmakers from Biblical Times to the Present as Found in Over 300 Readily Available Biographical Sources. 2nd ed. Susan L. Stetler, ed. Detroit, Gale, 1983. 2v. index. $85.00/set; $48.00/vol. ISBN 0-8103-1634-X (set); 0-8103-1632-3 (vol. 1); 0-8103-1633-1 (vol. 2); ISSN 0738-0097.

The more than twenty-three thousand persons who appear on these pages are those who have " 'made it' in television, or in the theatre, or in science, sports, business, government, religion, or industry," or are noteworthy historical figures. The first volume, containing the biographical summaries, is a self-contained directory of entries, each of which includes, where possible, the full name, nationality, occupation, cause of the individual's fame, birth and death dates and places, and references to additional listings in one or more of the three hundred readily available reference sources that appear, with their abbreviations, on the endpapers of the volume.

The second volume consists of three indexes: (1) a chronological index by year and then date, with each person listed by birth and death date, the most recent being Tennessee Williams, 24 February 1983; (2) a chronological index by calendar month and day, in which birth and death dates appear for each person; and (3) a geographic index, which begins with the United States, subdivided by state and then city, and then continues with Canada and other countries. If a town is not known, the listing appears under the state or country. Fore-edge markings help to distinguish the indexes.

Like the smaller first edition, this moderately priced work differs from the publisher's comprehensive *Biography and Genealogy Master Index*. *Biography Almanac* selects "famous" people from the pool of biographical reference works searched; it allows for cross-referencing by variant name forms, including nicknames; and it serves (through the first volume) as a direct source for biographical information. The index volume is new with this edition and is available separately. The two volumes together present a great deal of difficult-to-locate information in an easy-to-use format and will be useful in all types of libraries.

A supplement that will cover over twenty-five hundred individuals, including new names and some revisions from the first edition published in 1981, is in preparation (ca. 200p., $42.00). [R: WLB, Oct 83, p. 144]

Donald G. Davis, Jr., and Bohdan S. Wynar

14.   Chambers' Biographical Dictionary. rev. ed. Edited by T. C. Collocott, Edinburgh and London, Chambers, Ltd.; New York, Littlefield, 1974. 2v. index. $7.95pa./set. LC 76-85529. ISBN 0-8226-0498-1.

First published in 1897, this is one of the standard British biographical dictionaries. The major revision was undertaken in 1961 and at that time the editors reviewed most of the entries. The entries vary in length, depending on the relative importance of a given person, and most of them, in addition to the usual biographical data, include published works of the biographees, important critical works about them, with an editorial policy "of clothing the bare facts with human interest and critical observation, listing in its archives the infamous along with the worthy." The 1974 edition includes some fifteen thousand biographies as against some eleven thousand in the previous edition. There are two major criticisms of this otherwise satisfactory work. Some bibliographic references are rather sketchy and titles lack complete bibliographical description. Secondly, there is some tendency to elaborate on contemporary political personalities out of proportion to their relative historical importance. For example, a Soviet politician Shepilov received nine lines in comparison to Shevchenko (seven lines), the most prominent

Ukrainian poet of the nineteenth century. Many American modern poets and writers are also omitted. But, all in all, this is one of the best one-volume biographical dictionaries, showing a constant improvement with every new edition published. [R: LJ, 1 Jan 1970]
Bohdan S. Wynar

15. **The Dictionary of Biography**. rev. and enlarged ed. By Herbert Spencer Robinson and a staff of editors. Totowa, N.J., Rowman and Littlefield, 1975. 530p. index. $10.00; $4.95pa. (from Littlefield, Adams). LC 75-12775; 74-32346pa. ISBN 0-87471-647-0; 0-8226-0281-4pa.

A handy quick reference to more than thirty-five hundred individuals including the famous and infamous, the living and the dead, and personalities as diverse as the Biblical Moses and Grandma Moses. Length of entries varies considerably, ranging from a two-liner for Boris Spassky to twenty-four lines for William Shakespeare. In addition to a short biographical account, each alphabetically arranged entry gives occupation, pronunciation, and date of birth (and death, when appropriate). There are adequate cross-references.

Also included is a useful category index of important personalities; however, one might wonder why Billy Graham, Martin Luther King, Jr., and Norman Vincent Peale are listed under three separate categories. One might wonder also why Frank Sinatra is found under "Stage and Screen Personalities" rather than "Popular Singers." Nevertheless, this concise dictionary will serve as a useful companion volume to *Webster's Biographical Dictionary* (forty thousand entries) and *Chambers' Biographical Dictionary* (fifteen thousand entries), which serve the same general purpose, but with surprisingly little overlapping of names.

Somewhat related is *Celebrity Register* (Simon and Schuster, 1973. 562p. o.p.) that provides a listing of movie stars, politicians, film and television personalities, religious leaders, businessmen and women, astronauts, etc. It is written in a journalistic style with anecdotes and photographs of each celebrity. The biographical data (birth date, spouse's name, education, etc.) are usually there but are buried in the narrative of interesting events in the celebrity's life.   Ralph J. Folcarelli and Bohdan S. Wynar

16.   Fines, John. **Who's Who in the Middle Ages**. First Scarborough Books ed. New York, Stein and Day Publishers, 1980 (c1970). 217p. index. (A Scarborough Book). $8.95pa. LC 72-127225. ISBN 0-8128-6074-8.

John Fines is a British historian who has long been committed to improvement of the teaching of history. This book, originally published in 1970, is a companion to Betty Radice's *Who's Who in the Ancient World*. The author contends that history as it is presently approached, without attention to the interesting people, is complicated and obscure. To compensate for neglect of the biographical approach, he presents here brief portraits of his personal choice of the hundred people who show particularly well a facet of the society in which they lived, between the fall of the Roman Empire and the Renaissance. He gives the savour of medieval Christendom, to be sure tasted with English tongue. Fines tells their stories briefly from the best biographical material and available original sources in translation. He is alert to the sin of anecdotalism, and he writes well and tells many good stories. His intent is to tempt the reader into more detailed reading. He wants to arouse the interest of the bored generation, who have been recognized as "half our future," in what is by some measures half our past. This work is designed to be a beginning, an aid for the reader who wants to start general reading on the Middle Ages, a handbook beside such a reader during that reading, and a guide for further reading.

Companion volumes are *Who's Who in the Ancient World* by Betty Radice (New York, Penguin, 1971. 225p. $6.95pa.) and *Who's Who in Modern History, 1860-1980* (Holt, Rinehart and Winston, 1980. 332p. o.p.) containing six hundred biographies, each about two hundred words in length.   Doris H. Banks and Bohdan S. Wynar

17.   Hart, Michael H. **The 100: A Ranking of the Most Influential Persons in History**. New York, Hart Publishing, 1978. 572p. illus. index. o.p. LC 77-77090. ISBN 0-8055-1256-X.

To list the one hundred most influential persons in history is an arresting and challenging idea. Then to take the selections and rank them from one to one hundred is really intriguing. The author's guidelines are simple: not greatness (Stalin is here, Mother Cabrini is not); not fame (Gregory Pincus is here, Pelé is not); not charisma (Homer is here, Leonardo Da Vinci is not); but individual personal influence, affecting generations past, present, or both. And it is this yardstick that ranks Muhammed first, Isaac Newton second, and Jesus Christ third.

The biographical information is generally limited to facts related to the person's career, contribution to society, and extent of personal influence. It reads well and is nicely illustrated with a variety of maps, photographs, and art reproductions. The design by Stefan Salter is appropriate.

And now to the fun part. Why this one and not that one? Why does a philosopher outrank a world conqueror? Why? Why? Why? The author has anticipated many of the questions by listing, unranked, a second one hundred, replete with such figures as Bismarck, Churchill, Gandhi, and the Virgin Mary. In addition he invites the reader to compose similar lists with the same or different criteria.

What can be said about the list given here? Very little in a short review but there are some sightings that may help describe the book. Hart is strong on scientific figures, from Ts'ai Sun (no. 7) to Heisenberg (no. 43). The first pope to make the team is Urban II (no. 50) — so much for launching the Crusades. There are two women — queens Isabella I of Castile (no. 68) and Elizabeth I of England (no. 95) (which says less about the author than mankind in general) — and three U.S. presidents — Washington (no. 27), Jefferson (no. 70), and, surprisingly, Kennedy (No. 80). All in all it is an entertaining and instructive book from start to finish.

Related, but less successful, is Donald Robinson's *The 100 Most Important People in the World Today* (Putnam, 1970. 384p. o.p.) that serves as a collection of dehydrated biographies of influential international figures selected by commentator/newsman Robinson, with the aid of such varied agencies as the Atomic Energy Commission, the UN, U.S. State Department and World Council of Churches. Each essay averages twelve hundred words and concentrates on the more recent aspects of that person's life. The biographies are categorized into ten types of professional activities with public affairs having the most (twenty-two) and religion the least (five); other classes include fine arts, economy, letters and science. Written in a sprightly style, each prose portrait is broad brush but compactly informative. The sixteen-page index is well arranged and complete. Inclusion of a bibliography or list of references for those seeking more definite biographical information would enhance the value of this work.

David Eggenberger and Lawrence E. Spellman

18. Herwig, Holger H., and Neil M. Heyman. **Biographical Dictionary of World War I**. Westport, Conn., Greenwood Press, 1982. 424p. bibliog. index. $49.95. LC 81-4242. ISBN 0-313-21356-9.

The 265 individuals featured in this dictionary are all statesmen, diplomats, heads of state, or military leaders from Great Britain, Western, Eastern, or Central Europe, Russia, Turkey, Japan, or the United States. The biographies vary in length from about 350 words (Otto Bauer) to a high of 3,000 words (Wilhelm II), but the majority seem to run about 900 words. As befits a dictionary of the First World War, two-thirds of each entry is devoted to the subject's wartime experiences, the remainder dealing with his life before and after the war. Pétain, for example, is given five columns, of which three-and-one-quarter cover the years 1914-1918. Each entry is followed by a list of from three to six references to standard histories, biographies, or biographical dictionaries (such as the *DNB* or *Neue Deutsche Biographie*).

In addition to the dictionary proper, the work includes a sixty-page summary history of the war (with four pages of notes), an eight-page chronology of the war, and an appendix which lists each biographee by country and gives the pre-war, wartime, and post-war occupation or title of each. A twelve-page bibliography gives full citations to all references used in the biographical entries. Finally, there is an outstanding index to the entire work, which permits access to places, persons, battles, and other topics covered in one or more places in the book.

Obviously, information on many of these famous people will be easily found elsewhere. It is in the bringing together in one volume of biographies of both the famous and the unfamiliar that this work has its merit. It is a scholarly work, based on standard, authoritative works, and is a good example of what a biographical dictionary should be. [R: LJ, 15 Dec 82, p. 2330; WLB, Dec 82, p. 347]   Eric R. Nitschke

19. Keegan, John E. **Who Was Who in World War II**. New York, Thomas Y. Crowell, 1978. 224p. (A Bison Book). o.p. LC 77-95149. ISBN 0-690-01753-7.

This is a well-illustrated biographical dictionary of military, diplomatic, and political personalities of World War II from belligerent as well as neutral nations. The biographical sketches generally cover only the war years, although in some cases brief mention is made of events prior to 1939; we are not told of the careers or fates of any biographees subsequent to the war except those convicted of war crimes. Excellent color photographs open the work, while the clear black-and-white pictures which accompany the text are placed near the entry for the subject. There is no bibliography or index.

The short, choppy sentences might suggest that this work was intended for young readers were it not for the fact that a substantial amount of background knowledge is required to make use of the entries. The writing style is exemplified by such constructions as "France's rule in Indo-China led to a very costly war which the country could ill afford after the war," and "He damaged the Forces's flagship and sank two destroyers so the Japanese lost 700 men and withdrew in confusion." Errors of fact occur: *SS* stands for *Schutzstaffel*, not *Sicherheitsdienst*; the picture on page 162 is not of General Patch, but of General Patton; General H. M. Smith's famous row with the army occurred at Saipan, not Iwo Jima.

Professor Keegan also edited the *Rand McNally Encyclopedia of World War II*, which does not exhibit the tortured style of the *Who Was Who*, but has fewer biographical entries. A far better resource than either of these is the *Simon & Schuster Encyclopedia of World War II* which, while not as fully illustrated, has twice as many biographies as the *Who Was Who*, is superior in content and style, and is well indexed.

A related work is *A Biographical Dictionary of World War II*, by Christopher Tunney (St. Martin's Press, 1972. 216p. o.p.), that covers over four hundred individuals who in some way "made noteworthy contributions . . . to the prosecution of war." The entries include military leaders, actors, authors, poets, journalists, scientists, secret agents, conscientious objectors, politicians, and other assorted heroes and villains. The entries range in length from a short paragraph to several pages, depending upon both the individual's importance and the amount of information available. The biographical sketch includes information only about the individual's wartime contributions. The entry for George Marshall, for example, does not mention his pre-war career or his distinguished post-war achievements. [R: Choice, Feb 79, p. 1644]

Eric R. Nitschke and Marty Bloomberg

20.   Lane, Hana Umlauf, ed. **The World Almanac Book of Who**. New York, World Almanac Publications; distr., New York, Ballantine Books, a division of Random House, 1980. 360p. index. $5.95pa. LC 79-67561. ISBN 0-345-29177-8. (Hardbound ed. available from Prentice Hall, Englewood Cliffs, N.J. $15.95. ISBN 0-13-967844-1).

First in a new (1980) line of World Almanac Publications reference books is *The Book of Who*, a biographical dictionary containing nearly seven thousand names spanning time from B.C. (Isaiah) to the present (Billy Joel). Entries are brief, well balanced, apparently well researched, and concise, including: name (and pseudonym), birth date and place, death date if applicable, and major works, accomplishments, or claim to fame or infamy (Tokyo Rose). Names are alphabetically listed and well organized, divided by fifteen professional categories, including: business leaders (Samuel Waters Allerton), explorers (Edwin Eugene Aldrin), statesmen and political leaders (Bella Abzug), artists (Berenice Abbott), educators (Cyrus Adler), inventors and scientists (Cleveland Abbe), entertainers (Don Adams), and other noted or notorious personalities (Abigail Adams). Professional groupings are further divided by nationality. Twenty-three appendix pages list world rulers by country, date, affiliation, and pertinent data, and Nobel, Pulitzer, Oscar, and Miss America winners. Both a name and a subject index make this volume a useful and welcome reference tool.

Mary Alice Deveny

21.   Levy, Felice, comp. **Obituaries on File**. New York, Facts on File, 1980. 2v. $75.00/set. LC 79-12907. ISBN 0-87196-385-5/set.

Since its first appearance in 1940, *Facts on File* has provided a valuable running reference summary of the more important events that have taken place in the nation and the world. Among the more interesting sections in each edition is that devoted to a necrology of noteworthy persons dying during the time period covered. The names included in these lists are not only the leading lights of politics, economics, business and industry, and entertainment, but also individuals whose fame may have been transitory, notorious, or downright obscure. Author T. S. Eliot (died 4 January 1965) finds a place, as does Adolf Hitler (a suicide in Berlin, 30 April 1945); but so does Clarence (Ginger) Beaumont, the first man to bat in a World Series game (died 10 April 1956), and J. Frank Honeywell, author of boys' adventure books (died 6 August 1951).

The almost twenty-five thousand names included in the two volumes of this set cover the period 1940 through 1978, with each entry containing the name of the person deceased, age at the time of death, significant aspects of his or her life, date of death, and place of death. At the end of the second volume are a list of dates on which persons died and a comprehensive subject index, providing means of tracing persons through their major areas of renown and their geographical location. The set will be a useful acquisition for larger public and most academic libraries. [R: BL, 15 Oct 80, p. 348; Choice, Apr 80, p. 204; WLB, May 80, pp. 590-91]   Norman Lederer

22.   Macksey, Joan, and Kenneth Macksey. **The Book of Women's Achievements**. New York, Stein and Day, 1976 (c1975). 288p. illus. index. (A Scarborough Book). $6.95pa. LC 75-38771. ISBN 0-8128-2238-2.

Consistent with the introductory statement ("our wish is as much to entertain as to inform though it is hoped that a useful reference work results"), *The Book of Women's Achievements* proves to be a compendium of unusual if entertaining information and a moderately useful reference book. The cover, which mentions Guinness Superlatives Ltd. as an author along with Joan and Kenneth Macksey, provides a clue to the type of information to be mined from this volume—a wealth of names of women "who were either first in their field of endeavor or at least first among the ladies." Categories under which these "firsts" have been arranged include, among others, "Homemakers," "As Explorers," "As Sportswomen," and "In Literature, Journalism and Publishing."

The approximately fifteen hundred biographies are short, though they vary in length; the writing style in most cases is snappy rather than scholarly. Groupings of individuals can yield odd results. In the somewhat sensational category "Mistresses, Courtesans and Salonnières," for example, we find an incredible mixture of women from Lucrezia Borgia to Jacqueline Kennedy. The ordering and arrangement of the information in all categories is arbitrary, though dates of specific achievements appear in most cases. The authors do provide an index.

The "Sources and Bibliography" section, although identified as a very select list, misses many of the most important titles that should have been consulted for doing a work of this scope; this may be responsible for a few of the authors' grosser editorial comments. A sample commentary is their assessment of the Brontë sisters: "Emily Brontë's *Wuthering Heights* is probably the family's supreme contribution, yet it is hard to claim that they advanced literature since their style was mainly a copy of an earlier period" (p. 185).

Though the authors cite selection as a "major problem" and excuse their exclusions on the grounds that "no work such as this can be fully comprehensive," the rationale for excluding such pioneers of scientific achievement as Margaret Mead is incomprehensible.

Still, *The Book of Women's Achievements*, with its attractive format and illustrations, its international scope, and its snippets of fascinating information about women in broad fields of human endeavor should mark this title for inclusion in almost every type of reference collection. The user should be aware, however, that this is neither a definitive nor a scholarly chronicle of women's achievements, but rather a novel approach to an enormous subject.   Esther F. Stineman

23.   **The McGraw-Hill Encyclopedia of World Biography**. David I. Eggenberger, ed.-in-chief. New York, McGraw-Hill, 1973. 12v. illus. (part col.). index. $550.00. LC 70-37402. ISBN 0-07-079633-5.

According to the introduction, this encyclopedia "has been designed to meet a growing need in school and college libraries as well as in public libraries. Written entirely by academic authorities and other specialists, and enriched with illustrations, bibliographies, Study Guides, and Index, this work, we believe, combines more useful features for the student than any other multivolume biographical encyclopedia" (Vol. 1,

p. v). In other words, *EWB* was conceived primarily for the use of students. The editors have provided five thousand biographies, averaging about eight hundred words in length, with a curriculum orientation. Each article concludes with a "further reading" section, consisting of references to Study Guides in Volume 12 and to related articles in other volumes. An annotated bibliography of English language books is appended to each article. Access to the material is enhanced by the one hundred thousand-entry index located in the last volume; the last volume also contains a list of contributors, showing their institutional affiliation.

It is almost impossible to provide a formula for selection of five thousand biographees who might be "universally appealing" to students. Inclusions (or exclusions) can be debated. With respect to politicians, Beria, head of the Soviet secret police until his execution, is included (although with an inadequate bibliography), as is Trotsky (who is provided much better coverage). Benesh, however, the president of Czechoslovakia from 1935 to 1938 and 1940 to 1948, is treated in less detail. A comparison of the *EWB* with *Dictionary of Scientific Biography* shows that the coverage of famous scientists who have a popular appeal is quite adequate.

This set will be very useful in public schools; college students, however, will often need more detailed information and will have to rely on more specialized biographical directories, such as *Dictionary of Scientific Biography*.   Bohdan S. Wynar

24. **Obituaries from The Times 1951-1960**; including an index to all obituaries and tributes appearing in *The Times* during the years 1951-1960. Reading, England, Newspaper Archive Developments Ltd.; Westport, Conn., Meckler Books, 1979. 896p. index. $85.00.

25. **Obituaries from The Times 1961-1970**; including an index to all obituaries and tributes appearing in *The Times* during the years 1961-1970. Reading, England, Newspaper Archive Developments Ltd., 1975. 952p. index. $60.00.

26. **Obituaries from The Times 1971-1975**; including an index to all obituaries and tributes appearing in *The Times* during the years 1971-1975. Reading, England, Newspaper Archive Developments Ltd.; Westport, Conn., Meckler Books, 1978. 647p. index. $60.00.

The first volume provides a full text of selected obituaries from *The Times* of London plus an index to all obituaries covered during 1951-1960. According to the preface, "In this volume, there are 1,450 entries. There is of course some overlap with the relevant volume of the *Dictionary of National Biography* . . . , but twenty-eight per cent of the notices refer to British subjects who do not appear in the *Dictionary of National Biography* and twenty-nine per cent are foreign subjects."

The second volume (1961-1970) reprints a selection of fifteen hundred obituaries. And the third, according to the preface, contains an index of all entries appearing in the obituary columns of *The Times* from 1971-1975. The first part of this volume reprints in full an alphabetically arranged selection of about one thousand obituary notices of the period.

The selection for these volumes has been made with regard to the public importance of the subject of the obituary, the intrinsic interest of what was written about him/her, and the need to reflect the wide range of nationalities and walks of life which *The Times* obituary columns encompass. After 1978 this series ceased publication.

                Bohdan S. Wynar

27. Opfell, Olga S. **The Lady Laureates: Women Who Have Won the Nobel Prize.** Metuchen, N.J., Scarecrow, 1978. 267p. bibliog. index. o.p. LC 78-15995. ISBN 0-8108-1161-8.

The lives and achievements of the seventeen women Nobel Prize winners are described in *The Lady Laureates.* Introductory chapters provide background information on Alfred Nobel and the Nobel prizes and a third chapter attempts to explain why so few women have been presented the award ("in 77 years, 17 women and 437 men [three of whom declined] have won Nobel Prizes in peace, literature, and science"). The greater portion of the information presented in the short biographies is taken from anecdotes, observations of families and friends, and quotations from letters, diaries, and literary works, which accounts for the informal and rather melodramatic tone of the book. Speculation is freely intermixed with fact, resulting in interesting (but hardly serious) reading. Thus, Gabriela Mistral, in Stockholm to receive the award, is said to have "captivated the onlookers with her charming smile that belied her tragic eyes," and readers will be relieved to know that "Alfred Nobel certainly was not prejudiced against women achievers. A lifelong bachelor, he was particularly devoted to his mother, Caroline." Obviously, *Lady Laureates* would be useful only to young readers. As with many books now being published on women's topics, this work is of note, not because of its execution, but simply because it is the first to bring the information together in one volume. A twelve-page bibliography, a time-line (1833-1977), and a general index are included.   Susan C. Holte

28. Raven, Susan, and Alison Weir. **Women of Achievement: Thirty-five Centuries of History**. New York, Harmony Books/Crown, 1981. 288p. illus. index. $19.95. LC 80-24239. ISBN 0-517-53982-9.

No one will quibble with the divisions of achievement selected by the authors: "Politics and Power," "Education and Social Reform," "The Written Word," "Travel and Exploration," "The Performing Artist," and several more predictable areas. Nor will readers be stunned by the names that surface in these short, interesting biographical pieces: Mother Jones, Rosa Luxemburg, Jane Addams, Helen Keller, St. Joan, Jane Austen, The Brontë sisters, Sappho, Dorothea Lange, Madam Curie, Marilyn Monroe, and hundreds more, including some lesser-known sports and explorer types. There are many striking photographs and prints to enliven the text. The emphasis is clearly on nineteenth- and twentieth-century North American and European women, "not only because their lives are normally far better documented, but also because modern women in the Western world have had more opportunities for achievement than all but a handful of women in the ancient world or in today's developing world" (introduction).

Less entertaining and non-bookish than *Womanlist*, less scholarly and more global than Harvard's *Notable American Women*, *Women of Achievement*, nevertheless, has its place. It provides handy biographical reference to almost five hundred prominent women (some still living), and could be a fascinating one-stop source for those who haven't yet considered the authors' premise that "women must be reckoned with in any history of human achievement." The authors have compiled a proper name index. No bibliography or further references appear, which seems appropriate for a glossy, quick-fix, biographical collection. [R: SLJ, Dec 81, p. 90; WLB, Sept 81, p. 63]
                    Esther F. Stineman

29. Rogers, J. A. **World's Great Men of Color**. Edited, with an introduction, commentary and new bibliographical notes, by John Henrik Clarke. 1946-1947; repr., New York, Macmillan, 1972. 2v. illus. index. $9.95/vol. LC 73-186437. ISBN 0-02-081300-7.

Rogers's two-volume biographical work was completed in 1947 and published in a small private edition, years before black history and black studies were popularized. The long introduction by the author, an anthropologist who died in 1966, sets down his reasons for preparing the book and reflects the level of racism at the time. The purpose, as he points out, "was not to write highly critical and psychoanalytical, or even literary essays, but rather principally success stories, chiefly for Negro youth" (p. 24). Rogers maintained that knowledge of the contributions of black people had consistently been ignored and denied; his work in black history aimed to bring to light the significant accomplishments of nonwhite people and put aside the myth of black inferiority. Criteria for inclusion were based on evidence he obtained that an individual was at least one-eighth Negro.

The two hundred biographical articles, arranged geographically, include Imhotep, Hatshepsut, Hannibal, Terence, Al-Jahiz, Eugene Chen, Abu Hassanali, Chaka, Alfred A. Dodds, Aleksander Pushkin, Alexandre Dumas, Samuel Coleridge-Taylor, Vicente Guerrero, Nat Turner, and Arthur A. Schomburg. Portraits of some biographees are included. A separate section gives brief mention of a selected number of great men of color who are not recognized as blacks. John H. Clarke has added introductory matter to both volumes, surveying recent research in support of some of Rogers's findings. References at the ends of articles are updated in this new edition to include recent research on those subjects. Unfortunately, no index was added to the new edition. [R: BL, 15 June 73, p. 957; Choice, 15 June 73, p. 602; LJ, 1 Mar 73, p. 735; WLB, Apr 73, p. 701]   Bohdan S. Wynar

30. Uglow, Jennifer S., comp. and ed. **The International Dictionary of Women's Biography**. New York, Continuum; distr., New York, Crossroad/Continuum, 1982. 534p. bibliog. index. $29.50. LC 82-7417. ISBN 0-8264-0192-9.

Included here are fifteen hundred women whose contribution to society is remarkable "regardless of their sex." Entrants are mostly from North America, Europe, and the British Commonwealth and flourished during the last two centuries. Biographical coverage is necessarily brief; entries average three for each double-columned page. Social contributions are emphasized. The selection is excellent and the writing style lively. The format and typeface contribute to the book, but the binding is not sturdy.

An "Additional Reference Sources" section, containing a good listing of recommended biographical dictionaries and national biographies, is included, and a suggested biography or autobiography follows many entries. All these bibliographical references are much abbreviated: surname with initial, publisher not named, no edition statement. Suggested sources following entries are not always the most scholarly works available. The index is divided into four sections ("Public Life," "Cultural Life," "Physical Achievements," and "Colourful Characters") and further divided into primary fields such as "Politics," "Arts and Entertainment," "Exploration and Travel," and "National Heroines." Some personalities (actresses, dancers, lawyers) stand out, but subdivisions such as "Mathematics, Pure and Applied, Medicine," "Humanities and Social Sciences," "Communications: Journalism, Publishing, Broadcasting" are too broad; many users will need to check all entries to locate doctors, nurses, classicists, editors, etc. Cross-referencing is well done. [R: BL, 15 Dec 83, p. 618; Choice, May 83, p. 1266; WLB, Mar 83, p. 608]   Milton H. Crouch

31. **Webster's Biographical Dictionary**. Springfield, Mass., G. & C. Merriam, 1980. 1697p. (A Merriam-Webster). $15.00. LC 79-23607. ISBN 0-87779-443-X.

The aim of *Webster's Biographical Dictionary* "is to provide in a single handy volume a work of biographical reference not restricted in its selection of names by considerations of historical period, nationality, race, religion, or occupation." In this effort the work is successful, and it has become a standard on the ready reference shelf. Some forty thousand names have been amassed in the volume, approximately the same number as in the original 1943 edition. It is interesting that this volume carries a 1980 copyright, but it is not a numbered edition, nor are previous copyright years listed. In fact, remarkably little is revealed about the selection processes used to update the volume. "Only in certain classes of contemporaries may some consultants feel an inadequacy. The names of persons prominent (sometimes only briefly) in sports, in motion pictures, in the contemporary theater, and in radio are so numerous that the editors were compelled, however reluctantly, to curtail their representation to the minimum" (preface). In reality, the omissions are a little more widespread than in the areas stated. Jimmy Carter and Walter Mondale are included; Ronald Reagan and George Bush are not. Also missing are Golda Meir, Ian Smith, and Suharto.

Because the process of updating is not explained, and the editors do not claim comprehensive coverage of current notables, a library might carefully consider ordering each new edition. Nonetheless, *Webster's Biographical Dictionary* is an excellent single source reference, and every library should own a recent edition.

An abridged version advertised as *Webster's New Biographical Dictionary* covering thirty thousand biographies (1148p.) sells for $18.95. [R: BL, 15 July 70, p. 1353; RQ, Summer 73, p. 411; WLB, Jan 70, p. 563]   Janet H. Littlefield

32. Whitman, Alden. **The Obituary Book**. New York, Stein and Day, 1971. 284p. o.p. LC 70-127026. ISBN 8128-1354-5.

This volume is a compilation of thirty-seven obituary articles about contemporary international personalities. The articles appeared from 1964, when the *New York Times* obituary policy was expanded, to 1970. In an essay which precedes the anthology, chief obituary writer Whitman describes "The Art of the Obituary" and the developments at the *New York Times* which produced the book. The articles cover such diverse figures as Martin Buber, Sherman Billingsly, Elizabeth Arden, J. Robert Oppenheimer, Dorothy Parker, John Nance Garner, Helen Keller, Norman Thomas, Boris Karloff, Theodor Reik, Albert Schweitzer, Mies van der Rohe. If one considers a reference book in the conventional sense (designed by arrangement and treatment to be consulted for definite items of information rather than to be read consecutively), *The Obituary Book* does not qualify; moreover, articles in *Current Biography*, for example, are generally more readable. It does, of course, provide primary source material (presumably accessible via *Biography Index* as well as the *New York Times Index* itself). The value of some of the articles is enhanced by Whitman's having been able to interview the subject, which provides unique insights. [R: LJ, 15 Jan 71, p. 184; RQ, Summer 71, p. 366]
                                                                            Helen Wheeler

33. **Who Did What: The Lives and Achievements of the 5000 Men and Women— Leaders of Nations, Saints and Sinners, Artists and Scientists—Who Shaped Our World**. Gerald Howat, general ed. New York, Crown, 1974. 383p. illus. (part col.). o.p. LC 73-81194. ISBN 0-517-505673.

Although there is no preface in this biographical directory to provide us with the editorial criteria used in compiling it, the publisher states on the book jacket that "achievement is the simple yardstick that has been used to decide the inclusion of each entry." The blurb also indicates that "*Who Did What* gives an informed digest of the actions, ideas or circumstances that have given immortality to five thousand well-known names." Generally speaking, the biographical sketches are brief; occasionally they are too brief to be useful (see, for example, the forty-word entry for Jules Verne, the thirty-eight-word entry for Herbert Spencer, or the thirty-nine-word entry for Oswald Spengler). The appendix, "A Time Chart of Human Achievement," contains six chronological divisions with capsule descriptions under the headings of principal events, religion, philosophy, literature, art, architecture, music, and technology. There is also a listing (by nationality) of dynasties, popes, and heads of state. We examined the listing of Russian heads of state (House of Rurik) and found it most incomplete. Instead of starting this list with Rurik (as the name of the dynasty would seem to dictate), this list starts with Ivan III, The Great, in the fifteenth century. The whole period of Kievan Rus' is thus omitted.

The review in *Booklist* indicated that this work "will be useful in homes and libraries serving readers with no special knowledge who need essential information on notables of all times and places." This recommendation might be apt, since books of this type always have a rather broad appeal. Nevertheless, it seems to us that libraries would be better served by more comprehensive, standard biographical directories that have better-defined editorial criteria. We are referring here to the well-known *Webster's Biographical Dictionary* (forty thousand names) or even *Chambers' Biographical Dictionary* (fifteen thousand names).

A related work, somewhat smaller in scope, is *Famous Kings and Emperors* by Theodore Rowland-Entwistle and Jean Cooke (David & Charles, 1977. 124p. o.p.) that serves as a quick guide to ninety-six male and seven female rulers of some note; about sixty of these are European, though monarchs are included for Japan, Egypt, Mexico, and other places. Those listed are alphabetically arranged from Akbar the Great to William II of Germany.

Entries include birth and death dates (if known), and easy-to-read, concise, biographical material ranging in length from a single paragraph to over three pages. Anglicized forms of names are used. [R: BL, 15 Nov 74, p. 352]   Bohdan S. Wynar

34. Wintle, Justin, ed. **Dictionary of Modern Culture**. Boston, Ark Paperbacks/ Routledge & Kegan Paul, 1984. 469p. index. $9.95pa. ISBN 0-7448-0007-2.

This work is an abridgement of the author's *Makers of Modern Culture* (Facts on File, 1981). It contains 320 of the 537 biographical entries in the parent volume. Wintle, along with his over two hundred contributors, purports to have included all those twentieth-century figures who "initiated cultural change . . . , whose names occur most frequently in the critical press, and whose achievements seem most significant" (preface).

Beginning with Alfred Adler and ending with Yeats, Yevtushenko, and Zamyatin, each entry attempts to interpret the importance of a particular personality, taking between half a page and three pages to do so. The articles are well written, each one signed by its expert contributor, and each including a short bibliography; unfortunately, most entries are concise to a fault, being almost always too short to give these important historical figures their due.

It is difficult to use this work as a reference tool; criteria for inclusion are so vague that one can never be certain of finding any particular personage within its pages. The subject indexing is very poor, the print size is almost microscopic. Yet the entries are quite readable, making this a book that encourages browsing. Perhaps that is its best quality.   Daniel Uchitelle

35. Wintle, Justin, ed. **Makers of Nineteenth Century Culture: 1800-1914**. Boston, Routledge & Kegan Paul, 1982. 709p. index. $37.50. ISBN 0-7100-9295-4.

This volume, the second of a projected five-volume biographical series, could well serve, as its book jacket states, as a "comprehensive guide to the ideas of the 19th century." The 493 prominent figures of the period, from Lord Acton to Emile Zola, who were included were selected for their cultural importance; their ideas and achievements are considered to be significant today. Included are artists, composers, novelists, poets, dramatists, philosophers, scientists, social thinkers, and theologians; performing artists are excluded, and the politicians who are here presumably qualified by virtue of their philosophies. Men and women from English-speaking and European nations predominate, but other parts of the world are represented only meagerly. As is the case for any volume of this kind, one can always question inclusions or omissions. The editorial policies followed are explained fully in the first volume of the series, *Makers of Modern Culture* (Facts on File, 1981. 624p. $34.95), which covers 1914 to date and includes some 537 names.

The biographies appear in alphabetical order by the name by which the personage is commonly known—e.g., George Sand, Mark Twain, George Eliot—with the real name in parentheses. Written by some two hundred contributors, mostly British, who are well qualified by education or experience to make judgments, the articles are factually accurate but do not attempt a historical construction of a life; rather, they are interpretative accounts that assess the significance of the subject's life and work as a whole. Lengths of the essays vary from one column to several pages, depending on the complexity of the subject as well as the style of the biographer. The quality of the writing varies also, but a sampling found articles that are directed to the general reader and interesting enough to lead to exploring other entries. Cross-references are liberally sprinkled throughout, and a short bibliography follows each essay.

The thorough index refers to themes (communism, impressionism, social Darwinism) as well as to persons. It includes persons not separately treated as well as some treated in other volumes of the series. Index numbers refer to entries, not pages, a system that works well enough for the subject of an entry but that can be annoying when one is looking for individuals and themes given only passing reference within a lengthy article. The binding of the review copy is not as sturdy as it should be, and the cover is already pulling off.

On the whole, this biographical dictionary will be very useful in libraries and in homes, as a supplement to the national biographies, for quick reference, to provide an overview of the period, and—perhaps most of all—for pleasant browsing. [R: BL, 1 Nov 83, p. 414; Choice, June 83, p. 1434; LJ, 15 Mar 83, pp. 576-77]

                                                                      Laura H. McGuire

2 National and Regional Sources

UNITED STATES

Current Biographies

36. **Community Leaders of America: Outstanding, Distinguished**. Raleigh, N.C., American Biographical Institute, 1973. 580p. o.p. LC 70-127176.

According to the preface, "those selected for *Community Leaders of America* have gained special recognition through political leadership, educational research and guidance, business management, artistic excellence . . . ," etc. There are four more lines of these "criteria." In fact, of course, there are no criteria at all, since the remittance of a certain sum guarantees one's inclusion. (For additional sums one can receive "a personally inscribed plaque" or "a beautiful wall certificate laminated on wood," either of which will amply testify to one's importance.) There are many biographical reference tools of this type, and they vary only in the price one has to pay and the amount of "window-dressing" — that is, the number of biographical sketches poorly edited or taken at random from more reliable sources. Occasionally one finds biographees of genuine prominence listed here, usually submitted by innocents who do not know what this is all about — namely, money. Librarians should certainly know better; but one finds quite a few librarians listed here. Bohdan S. Wynar

37. **Who's Who in America 1984-1985**. 43rd ed. Chicago, Marquis Who's Who, 1984. 2v. index. $140.00/set. LC 4-16934. ISBN 0-8379-0-143-X.

38. **Who's Who in America Index 1984-1985**. 43rd ed. Chicago, Marquis Who's Who, 1984. 578p. $65.00. LC 4-16934. ISBN 0-8379-1503-1.

The goal of the editors of the forty-third edition of *Who's Who in America* is the same as that of its founder, A. N. Marquis, in 1898: to provide information on the lives of individuals "whose achievements and contributions to society made them subjects of widespread reference interest." Requiring two years of preparation, this edition of

Who's Who contains seventy-five thousand biographies of people in the United States, Canada, and Mexico. Subjects were chosen on the basis of their reference value (i.e., position of responsibility held or level of achievement attained). Position categories covered include high-ranking federal, state, and local officials; military officers on active duty; ranking officials of major universities; principal officers of major businesses; heads of major cultural, educational, and scientific organizations; chief ecclesiastics; and recipients of major awards. Included in the "level of achievement" category are writers, artists, etc.

Information provided on these individuals includes name, occupation, vital statistics, parents, marriage, children, education, professional certifications, career, writings, civic and political activities, awards, professional memberships, political affiliation, religion, clubs, and home and business addresses. In some cases, the biographee has submitted a statement of principles or goals, which appears at the end of the entry. In this edition, for the first time, computer technology has been applied to the entries to improve consistency in definition and arrangement of information.

Who's Who Index 1984-1985 is arranged by geographic and professional area. Subjects are listed in alphabetical order with occupation given; no references to page numbers in the main volumes are provided.

Marquis also produces an annual master index. The current edition, *Index to Who's Who Books 1985* (Chicago, Marquis Who's Who, 1985. 481p. $49.95. LC 74-17540. ISBN 0-8379-1419-1), contains an alphabetical listing of approximately 220,000 individuals whose personal and career data are listed in *Who's Who in America* (43rd ed.), *Who Was Who in America* (vol. 7), *Who's Who in the East* (20th ed.), *Who's Who in the Midwest* (19th ed.), *Who's Who in the West* (19th ed.), *Who's Who in the South and Southwest* (19th ed.), *Who's Who in the World* (7th ed.), *Who's Who of American Women* (14th ed.), *Who's Who in Finance and Industry* (23rd ed.), *Who's Who in American Law* (3rd ed.), and *Who's Who in Frontier Science and Technology* (1st ed.).   Sharon Kincaide

39. **Who's Who of American Women, 1985-1986**. 14th ed. Chicago, Marquis Who's Who, 1984. 898p. $94.00. LC 58-13264. ISBN 0-8379-0414-5.

The fourteenth edition of this standard reference work includes brief biographical sketches for over twenty-one thousand women. Entries continue to follow a uniform format giving useful biographical information: occupation, vital statistics, education, writings and creative works, civic and political activities. Previous reviewers criticized the work for being incomplete, for failing to adhere to stated "Standards of Admission," and for not defining these standards. Another concern was that not all women found in the same publisher's *Who's Who in America* were included. None of these important concerns have been resolved in this new edition; it is still relatively easy to identify important women not included.

However, biographical information for thousands of women is included. A review of the most recent edition of *Bio-Base* (Gale, 1984), an index to biographical information included in five hundred current and historical biographical dictionaries, indicates that biographical information for thousands of women is found only in *WWOAW*. The reference value of this and other Marquis publications would be much improved if a topical subject or professional listing were maintained, serving to group biographees by birthplace (state, foreign country), colleges attended, and occupation.

                                                                        Milton H. Crouch

Retrospective Biographies

40. **The Biographical Cyclopaedia of American Women**. Compiled under the supervision of Mabel Ward Cameron. New York, The Halvord Publishing Company, Inc., 1924; repr., Detroit, Gale, 1974. 2v. illus. index. $110.00/set. LC 24-7615. ISBN 0-8103-3999-0.

This title has never appeared in any edition of Mudge/Winchell. A random sampling of the entries quickly reveals why it was omitted from the standard compendia of reference books. The women included in these volumes were not those whose achievements will endear them to the feminists of the mid-1970s. There is a pronounced aristocratic slant to the inclusion policy of Ms. Cameron's cyclopaedia, according to which she tended to view with favor women who either were born to, or achieved through marriage, a position of wealth and privilege. Such women often did perform important services in a volunteer capacity. A typical Cameron biographical entrant is first, rich; second, active in numerous board memberships; third, a world traveller; fourth, a member in good standing of the social register; and fifth, probably a member of "the 400."

Comparing this work with *Notable American Women, 1607-1950: A Biographical Dictionary* (3v. Cambridge, The Belknap Press of Harvard University Press, 1971), one makes some remarkable discoveries. *Notable American Women* means exactly what the title implies. Comparing even at random one finds that most of Harvard's notable women are not in Cameron, and vice versa. The evidence favors the Harvard compilation. Without exception, the women memorialized in its three volumes deserve the tribute. Considering that we now have the Harvard volumes, it is clear that Cameron is an appropriate purchase only for those libraries that collect comprehensively in American social history. This book could have research value for a scholar seeking to assess the quality of feminism in the early 1920s.

Somewhat related is *Twelve American Women* by Elizabeth Anticaglia (Chicago, Nelson-Hall, 1974. 272p. $23.95; $11.95pa.) that describes such persons as Anne Hutchinson, Mercy Otis Warren, Margaret Fuller, Dorothea Dix, and Margaret Mead.

Richard A. Gray and Bohdan S. Wynar

41. **Concise Dictionary of American Biography**. 3rd ed., complete to 1960. New York, Scribner's, 1980. 1333p. $75.00. LC 80-13892. ISBN 0-684-16631-3.

The second edition of this standard reference work was published in 1977; it updated the first edition to 1950. The current edition is complete to 1960, but the decade 1951-1960 is contained in a separate section. Approximately one thousand biographies have been added in the new section, bringing the total to over seventeen thousand. In keeping with the original philosophy of the parent work, the *Dictionary of American Biography* (*DAB*), no living persons are included. At least ten years elapse after the death of a potential subject before the person is considered for inclusion. All entries included in the *DAB* appear in the *Concise Dictionary*, but their contents are summarized. Three types of entries are employed: minimal (birth, death, and a short statement of the person's achievements), median (slightly more extended, with critical comments on achievements and influence), and extended (which preserve the original entry as fully as possible). The *Concise Dictionary*, at $75, is handy to have for quick reference, even in libraries owning the complete *DAB*. [R: WLB, Oct 80, pp. 140-41]

Janet H. Littlefield

42.   Dickerson, Robert B., Jr. **Final Placement: A Guide to the Deaths, Funerals, and Burials of Notable Americans**. Algonac, Mich., Reference Publications, 1982. 250p. illus. index. $19.95. LC 81-52598. ISBN 0-917256-18-2.

At first glance, *Final Placement* might not seem to offer anything more than a purely morbid interest. On closer examination, however, it is strangely pleasing and fascinating, and readers may find themselves picking it up time and again.

Presenting a unique contribution to Americana, it encompasses 312 names of notable people from the United States' historic past up to the present decade. Included are presidents, statesmen, actresses and actors, writers, founding fathers, musicians, inventors, industrialists, sports figures, adventurers, and others. In comparing practices from different eras, the author shows the changing fabric of the United States' social history and culture.

Vital statistics as well as a summary of each person's life are given. The author has presented meaningful insights via details on a more personal level: last words (when recorded) and particulars of the personalities' deaths, funerals, and burials (giving exact addresses when known).

The terse writing style is appropriate. With rare exception, though, the first sentence of each entry follows the same pattern (name of person is reiterated, reason is given for the person's fame, date and place of birth are supplied), thus rendering a certain monotony to the presentation. Also, a more careful job of editing and proofreading would have eliminated a number of minor errors.

The book, well researched, is a good biographical source with a unique slant. Very entertaining and meaningful, it is apt to end up not only in public libraries but also in private homes. [R: BL, 1 Mar 83, p. 858]   Beverley Hanson

43.   **Dictionary of American Biography**. Edited under the auspices of The American Council of Learned Societies. New York, Scribner's, 1928-1937. 20v. and index; repr., Scribner's, 1943, 21v.; 1946, 10v. on thin paper. Supplements 1-7. $1,100.00/base set [of 10 vols.] and supplements. LC 44-41895.

44.   **Dictionary of American Biography Complete Index Guide, Volumes I-X, Supplements 1-7**. New York, Scribner's, 1981. 214p. $12.95pa. LC 81-9216. ISBN 0-684-17152-X.

Until the publication of *Dictionary of American Biography*, the first volume of which appeared in 1928, America did not have a really authoritative national biography. The *DAB* is an American counterpart of the *British Dictionary of National Biography*. Adolph S. Ochs, owner of the *New York Times*, financed the *DAB* and appointed two men to a Committee of Management which was to determine policy and direct the work. Four more men, appointed by the American Council of Learned Societies, completed the group. The committee's first action was to elect Allen Johnson as editor, a position he held for five years. Upon Johnson's death in 1931, Dumas Malone assumed responsibility.

In defining an "American," the committee determined that residents of the original thirteen colonies, inhabitants of territories which later became part of the United States, and citizens by birth or naturalization were eligible for inclusion. However, British officers who served in America after the colonies declared their independence were not considered "Americans." Because of this, Robert De LaSalle, the French explorer, is found in the *DAB*, but Charles Cornwallis, British officer who inadvertently helped the American colonists conclude the war of independence, is not. A further qualification for inclusion states that candidates must have distinguished themselves in some fashion, even if that distinction was of a negative nature. Thus are included both Abraham Lincoln and John Wilkes Booth.

Primary sources were used whenever possible for information which included ancestry, parentage, childhood, education, and marital status, along with a short account of the biographee's achievements, and a bibliography.

Each biography is signed by the initials of its author, and an author key is provided in each volume. No biography is shorter than 500 words, and the longest, that of George Washington, is 16,500 words. There were 2,243 contributors, including such distinguished ones as Carl Van Doren, Mark Van Doren, Allan Nevins, Crane Brinton, Bernard DeVoto, and Carl Sandburg.

The twenty volumes of the *DAB* were published during ten-and-a-half years. In 1937 an index to the work was published. The index's divisions are alphabetical by name, birthplace, occupation, schools attended, topics of importance, and contributors. Two supplements have appeared, the first in 1944 and the second in 1958. They are both concerned only with biographies of those who died not later than 1940.

The third supplement covers 1941-1945 (1973), the fourth 1946-1950 (1974), the fifth 1951-1955 (1977), the sixth 1956-1960 (1980), and the seventh 1961-1965 (1981). The main set covers 17,500 people and each supplement contains about 500 biographies.

Complete Index Guide serves as a combined alphabetical listing of all entries in volumes 1-10 and supplements 1-7. Smaller libraries that cannot afford this source may rely on *Concise Dictionary of American Biography*.   Bohdan S. Wynar

45. **Dictionary of American Biography, Including Men of the Time**. By Francis S. Drake. Boston, James R. Osgood, 1872; repr., Detroit, Gale, 1974. 1019p. $95.00. LC 73-11061. ISBN 0-8103-3731-2.

According to Burke and Howe in *American Authors and Books*, the late Francis Samuel Drake (1828-1885) was a historian with three books to his credit — the title listed above, *Tea Leaves* (1884), and *Indian History for Young Folks* (1885). The *Harvard Guide to American History* does not cite this work nor has any edition of Kroeger/ Mudge/Winchell/Sheehy. However, according to the publisher (not verified), Sonnenschein does cite Drake in *Best Books*, as does Gert A. Zischka in his *Index Lexicorium* (Vienna, Brüder Hollinek, 1959. 290p.).

In view of this relative neglect, it is something of a mystery why Gale has chosen to reprint the title. With very little to go on, it becomes a reviewer's responsibility to arrive at a judgment on the possible utility of Drake's 1872 title in American reference departments today.

In his introduction Drake states that his intention was to correct an imbalance that existed in biographical directories of his day. According to him, most such works grossly over-represented public figures — politicians and military men — to the neglect of men who really make civilization advance: engineers, scientists, physicians, clergymen, newspaper editors, teachers, etc. Glancing through his pages, one finds that a high percentage of his entries are of professional people in the above categories. It is possible that this reprint will occasionally provide information on obscure eighteenth- and nineteenth-century figures who are not treated in the standard sources.

Suitable for consideration by libraries needing additional retrospective sources of American biographical reference.   Richard A. Gray

46.　Downs, Robert B., John T. Flanagan, and Harold W. Scott. **Memorable Americans 1750-1950**. Littleton, Colo., Libraries Unlimited, 1983. 400p. index. $23.50. LC 82-22871. ISBN 0-87287-360-9.

This book focuses on 150 men and women whose achievements and actions made a permanent impression on the nation's culture and history. Literature, science and invention, business and industry, social reform, the arts, and politics are but a few of the fields represented by the biographees in this work, who include Ernest Hemingway, Cyrus McCormick, Margaret Sanger, Frederic Remington, and Horace Greeley. Names nominated for inclusion by specialists in various fields were carefully screened by the authors to determine those persons whose impact was permanent and whose contributions indicated something of the richness and variety of U.S. history and culture. The authors have excluded individuals who died after 1950, whose great work was accomplished prior to coming to the United States, or whose work had little impact on their successors. The sketches are arranged alphabetically and include basic dates related to the person, the individual's major writings, and selected references. Lists of the individuals, arranged both by birth date and field of endeavor, are offered in the appendix. This one-volume source of biographical information on selected notable Americans can be used for ready reference and by U.S. history teachers to supplement the curriculum. It can also be enjoyed by anyone interested in obtaining an overview of U.S. history through the accomplishments of some of the nation's most prominent personalities. [R: WLB, June 83, p. 883]　　　　　　　　　　　　　　Ann Hartman

47.　Downs, Robert B., John T. Flanagan, and Harold W. Scott. **More Memorable Americans 1750-1950**. Littleton, Colo., Libraries Unlimited, 1985. 383p. index. $30.00. LC 84-27780. ISBN 0-87287-421-4.

More Memorable Americans is a supplement to *Memorable Americans 1750-1950*. The general content and format have not changed, concentrating on individuals making contributions in politics, the arts and entertainment, science, education, the military, business, and other fields of endeavor. The first volume included 150 entries, and this supplement numbers 151 names. Of these, only 11 (7 percent) are not in the *Dictionary of American Biography* and its supplements. Pearl Buck, Walt Disney, Upton Sinclair, and Helen Keller are representative of this handful of *DAB* exclusions. Each name carries a brief biographical sketch centering on the major achievements of the individual as well as selected references. The entries are necessarily concise but contain sufficient biographical information for a work of this type. It is, as is *Memorable Americans*, a useful ready-reference which is well written and makes interesting reading. Included are two appendixes arranged by date of birth and principal careers of the biographees.

A volume of this type is obviously a worthwhile collection, but this one is marred by the inconsistent quality of the selected references for each entry. For example, the entry for Anthony Wayne includes no references published since 1929 and excludes Charles J. Stille's book on Wayne in the American Revolution (1968). On the other hand, the sketch of John Steinbeck lists three references, one as late as 1984. The entry for John Adams omits Peter Shaw's *The Character of John Adams* (1976). Dated references are a definite drawback of this title, but it is, nevertheless, a handy one-volume biographical collection.　　　　　　　　　　　　　　　　　　　Boyd Childress

48.　Dupuy, Trevor N., and Gay M. Hammerman, eds. **People and Events of the American Revolution**. New York, R. R. Bowker, 1974. 473p. index. o.p. LC 74-7896. ISBN 0-8352-0777-3.

The first of the two main sections of this book is a day-by-day chronology of some twelve hundred events related to the American Revolution. In 278 pages it covers the legislation, battles, troop movements, executions, appointments, foreign affairs, etc., from the 1733 Molasses Act to the 1784 ratification of the Treaty of Paris. In the second main section (153 pages), some fourteen hundred individuals receive a biographical sketch that may contain as few as fourteen or fifteen words. These biographies cover loyalists, patriots, Europeans, Indians, local heroes, and military people of general and flag rank. Among the three appendixes is a breakdown of Revolutionary people into more than sixty categories (e.g., traders, women, spies, and college presidents). A seven-page bibliography is included.

Colonel Dupuy is an experienced and respected writer on military affairs, and Ms. Hammerman has also published in this field. Their book aims at a worthy objective, but it covers so much ground that the treatment will satisfy few readers other than trivia fans. And the publisher will receive no compliments for the design.

David Eggenberger

49.   Felton, Bruce, and Mark Fowler. **Felton and Fowler's Famous Americans You Never Knew Existed**. New York, Stein and Day, 1979. 293p. illus. index. o.p. LC 78-56944. ISBN 0-8128-2511-X.

This is a humorous collection of sketches about Americans nobody knows existed. The compilation contains biographical essays on four hundred unknown Americans who lived from colonial times to the present day. The essays are divided into fifteen topical chapters with captions like "Inventors and Innovators," "Overdoers," "Prophets," and "Sexy People." The subject index is useful for finding the name of the inventor of the safety pin, the oldest living man, and the first person elected to federal office while serving a jail term. No separate alphabetical listing for these non-famous individuals is included, nor are they listed in the subject index. The individuals selected for inclusion may be home-town or college pranksters, quacks, eccentrics, blunderers, or other outcasts who never achieved notice for their deeds. The book is humorous, relaxing, and fun to read, but it is not intended for serious reference work. [R: LJ, 1 May 79, p. 1042]

Sally S. Small

50.   Garraty, John A., ed. **Encyclopedia of American Biography**. New York, Harper & Row, 1974. 1241p. o.p. LC 74-1807. ISBN 0-06-011438-4.

A handy, one-volume biographical directory containing one thousand entries for notable Americans from the earliest period to the present day. Each biographical sketch consists of two parts: a factual chronological summary (about 350 words) of the biographee's personal data, and an interpretive essay of his achievements. All the essays are signed.

Although this volume overlaps somewhat in coverage with *Webster's American Biographies*, their different approaches keep them from being competitive; they can be used together. The average user might find Garraty's compilation more interesting, primarily because of the evaluative interpretations following the biographical sketch. As was pointed out in the *New York Times* review, Garraty's comments occasionally go haywire. For example, in the 1950s, Frank Sinatra was "straight, alcoholic, compensatory, lithe, neurotic, masculine, childlike, petulant and romantic." He was "the kind of man who had been through hell, who tells his story to you, and transforms you into the ever patient waitress who gives him another cup of coffee on the house."

The selection criteria for the two works were practically the same; both include Americans in all professions, living and dead, aiming at more popular figures that will be of interest to the general reader. [R: WLB, Dec 74, p. 313]   Bohdan S. Wynar

51.   Howes, Durwood, ed. **American Women, 1935-1940: A Composite Biographical Dictionary: A Consolidation of All Material Appearing in the 1939-1940 Edition of** *American Women*, **with a Supplement of Unduplicated Biographical Entries from the 1935-1937 and 1937-1938 Editions**. Detroit, Gale, 1981. 2v. index. (Gale Composite Biographical Dictionary Series, No. 6; A Firenze Book). $160.00. LC 80-17368. ISBN 0-8103-0403-1.

Designed as a biographical directory of eminent American women of the time, *American Women: The Official Who's Who among the Women of the Nation* was issued biennially from 1935/36 to 1939/40. New biographies were published in each successive volume along with updated versions of earlier biographical entries, resulting in a total of over ten thousand biographies in the third and final edition. The two-volume set published by Gale Research Company is a reprint of the third edition (1939/40), along with a supplement of biographical entries which appeared in only the 1935/36 or 1937/38 editions. About twelve thousand women (born 1842-1929) are listed, representing a broad spectrum of occupations and involvements. Entries include the following information (solicited by means of a questionnaire): date and place of birth, parents' names, education, marriage, children, hobbies and recreations, occupation, politics, religion, memberships, achievements, honors, and home and business addresses. In addition, the biographical data are broken down into a statistical summary (comparing volumes 1 through 3), and geographical and occupational indexes. An index of national women's organizations is also included.

Catherine R. Loeb

52.   Hughes, Langston, Milton Meltzer, and C. Eric Lincoln. **A Pictorial History of Black Americans**. 5th ed. of *A Pictorial History of the Negro in America*. New York, Crown, 1983. 400p. $19.95. illus. LC 83-7742. ISBN 0-517-55072-5.

This is the fifth revised edition of a work that first appeared over twenty years ago and that was prepared under the direction of the late Langston Hughes. In this updated edition, Meltzer and Lincoln give only limited and superficial discussion to the important developments in the lives of black Americans during more recent years. The revisions attempt to cover the new styles of protest, black political progress, problems and progress in public and higher education, and significant developments in black religion and in the arts. Coverage in these areas is through 1982. Much of the material, however, is unchanged from the previous edition. As an example, biographical information on living persons has not been updated. Basically, coverage is complete through the 1970s and the historical information is solid and accurate. The positive features of this work are: (1) it is a relatively inexpensive edition; (2) it is superbly illustrated with over one thousand photographs, paintings, broadsides, drawings, woodcuts, cartoons, and reproductions of letters, posters, and handbills; (3) the historical information is well written and suitable for most age levels. Except for its failure to provide a thorough updating, this is a recommended source for public and academic libraries. [R: LJ, 1 June 84, p. 1128]   Miles M. Jackson

53.   Leavitt, Judith A. **American Women Managers and Administrators: A Selective Biographical Dictionary of Twentieth-Century Leaders in Business, Education, and Government**. Westport, Conn., Greenwood Press, 1985. 317p. bibliog. index. $45.00. LC 84-12814. ISBN 0-313-23748-4.

This volume arose from the need to identify twentieth-century women leaders in business, education, and government. In doing so, Leavitt compiled the biographies of 226 outstanding women managers, administrators, and leaders who have held or now hold positions of prominence. The criteria for inclusion were as follows: women who were "firsts" or who had achieved some significant accomplishment in a particular field or occupation; women who were founders of business or educational institutions; and women who have held some position of national prominence. Women who were "firsts" make up nearly half the entries in this collection.

The biographies, which vary in length, are arranged in alphabetical order. In most cases, a bibliography citing works by and about the subject follows each entry. The appendix includes an alphabetical listing by category of the women cited in the directory. The volume also includes a general bibliography and an index.

Because of its subject content, this book will be a useful reference tool in public, school, and college libraries. It will be useful for guidance and career counselors and in programs of women's studies.   Lorraine Mathies

54.   **Liberty's Women**. Robert McHenry, ed. Springfield, Mass., G. & C. Merriam, 1980. 482p. index. o.p. LC 79-23772. ISBN 0-87779-064-7.

In an attempt to give recognition to American women's contributions throughout history, Robert McHenry presents sketches of over one thousand women, deceased and living, who "compiled striking records of accomplishment" in various fields of endeavor. The alphabetically arranged biographies, averaging about four hundred words in length, cover such figures as Erma Bombeck, Grace Kelly, and even Lizzie Borden (a striking record of accomplishment?), while Gloria Steinem apparently did not merit inclusion. The women excluded and included suggest a random selection, and as might be expected, no selection criteria are provided. Included for each biographee are date and place of birth and date and place of death, if applicable. The sketches themselves are well written, and facts appear to be accurate, although neither the biographers nor their sources are indicated. An interesting volume, but certainly not a necessary addition to women's studies collections.   Susan C. Holte

55.   Logan, Rayford W., and Michael R. Winston. **Dictionary of American Negro Biography**. New York, W. W. Norton, 1982. 680p. $50.00. LC 81-9629. ISBN 0-393-01513-0.

Some 250 specialists have been instrumental in this compilation of more than seven hundred biographical descriptions of U.S. blacks who were important to their community and/or region. The purpose of the book is to illustrate the participation and impact of blacks in the growth and development of the United States. Inclusion is dependent not on fame, but on the individual's contribution to history. Each of the entries ends with a briefly annotated bibliography of primary and secondary sources. Some notable persons are omitted from the book, but the omissions do not detract from the value of this contribution to U.S. black biography. [R: BL, 15 Sept 83, p. 149; Choice, June 83, pp. 1433-34; WLB, June 83, p. 881]   Bohdan S. Wynar

56. McLachlan, James. **Princetonians 1748-1768: A Biographical Dictionary**. Princeton, N.J., Princeton University Press, 1976. 706p. illus. index. $60.00. LC 76-4063. ISBN 0-691-04639-5.

57. Harrison, Richard A. **Princetonians, 1769-1775: A Biographical Dictionary**. Princeton, N.J., Princeton University Press, 1980. 585p. illus. index. $55.00. LC 80-7526. ISBN 0-691-04675-1.

58. Harrison, Richard A. **Princetonians, 1776-1783: A Biographical Dictionary**. Princeton, N.J., Princeton University Press, 1981. 498p. illus. index. $45.00. LC 81-47074. ISBN 0-691-05336-7.

The Princetonians of the title are men who attended the College of New Jersey, now Princeton University. The lives of these men are described in sketches that average two pages in length, with some as long as thirteen pages. The biographies are arranged alphabetically by year of graduation, and each sketch is followed by a list of sources, such as local histories, journal articles, and documents; the repository of the subject's own manuscripts is indicated. Portraits accompany many of the biographies. At the end of the volumes are indexes of birthplaces, occupations, and Revolutionary War service.

These biographical sketches provide valuable insight into the history of the era. Reflecting exhaustive research, the work will be useful to historians and genealogists.

Robert F. Van Benthuysen

59. **National Cyclopedia of American Biography**. Edited by John Dickson. New York, J. T. White, 1892- . In progress. 44 permanent volumes. Price varies. LC 21-2156. ISBN 0-88371-029-3.

60. **National Cyclopedia of American Biography**. New York, J. T. White, 1892- . In progress. 14v. (current series). Price varies. LC 21-2156. ISBN 0-88371-030-7.

61. **National Cyclopedia of American Biography: Index Volume**. New York, J. T. White, 1984. 1v. $85.00. ISBN 0-88371-040-4.

62. **White's Conspectus of American Biography**. Clifton, N.J., J. T. White, 1973. 725p. $44.95. LC 73-6885. ISBN 0-88371-002-1.

The *National Cyclopedia of American Biography* is called the most comprehensive American work of its type and as such is less limited and less selective than the *Dictionary of American Biography*. Articles on deceased persons are collected in the permanent series which numbered forty-four volumes in 1985. The current series is composed of biographies of living persons. It is marked by letters of the alphabet and consists of fourteen volumes.

The aim of the *National Cyclopedia* is to include biographies of people who have been prominent in some way in shaping the history of the United States. More space is devoted to men and women of importance after 1850; however, some space is given to outstanding people before that time. According to the inclusion policy stated in the preface, the work includes "all persons who held or are holding high positions in international and state government as well as those occupying positions of leadership and distinction in professional, scientific, financial, industrial and religious spheres."

The names of persons who have recently died are deleted from the current series and placed in the latest volume of the permanent series. Revisions are also made in the current series to add significant facts to the lives of prominent living persons. Thus both series are quite up-to-date.

The articles, which are unsigned, are usually written by the editorial staff from questionnaires and other information supplied by families of the biographees. When possible, the information is checked by the editorial staff. Because of this procedure the treatment in the articles is uneven. Bibliographies are generally not included.

A dictionary arrangement is not used. Instead, individuals are grouped with reference to their work and also by important events and prominent movements. There are individual indexes to each volume and a combined looseleaf index which is divided into three parts, each covering a specific group of volumes. There are both personal and topical indexes, and *White's Conspectus* also provides indexing by various subjects to biographies included in the main sets.

Published originally in 1906 in combination with the indexes to the *National Cyclopedia of American Biography*, *White's Conspectus* was revised and modernized in 1970. The *Conspectus* is a tabulated chronological record of Americans who have achieved distinction in some field of endeavor. It consists largely of lists of leaders in state and national government, religion, education, the arts and sciences, and the professions. The time span ranges from colonial times up to publishing date.

As with any work of this type, the *Conspectus* must be selective. Therefore, criticism of inclusions and omissions is to be expected and can be found in various reviews. In some cases the material was not brought up-to-date as of 1 December 1970, the closing date for revision. The *Conspectus* is now becoming out of date as a guide to the current series of the *National Cyclopedia* but is still useful for older historical reference. While it can be used as an independent reference work, it is more useful if the library has a copy of the *National Cyclopedia*. [R: BL, 1 June 74, pp. 1066-67; Choice, Apr 74, p. 238; WLB, Feb 74, p. 507]   Bohdan S. Wynar

63. **Notable American Women 1607-1950. A Biographical Dictionary**. Edward T. James, ed. Cambridge, Mass., Harvard University Press, 1971. 3v. $60.00. $32.50pa. LC 76-152274. ISBN 0-674-62731-8; 0-674-62734-2pa.

This biographical dictionary, the first large-scale scholarly work in its field, was prepared under the auspices of Radcliffe College. A total of 1,359 biographical sketches is included and the entries are patterned after the well-known *Dictionary of American Biography*, which includes some seven hundred biographies of women out of a total of nearly fifteen thousand entries. According to the preface, "for each biography the editors endeavored to find an author with special knowledge of the subject or of her field. Seven hundred and thirty-eight contributors were enlisted, the scholarly community making a generous response in time and effort for which the modest honorarium was a purely token recompense. The few unsigned articles are the product of editorial collaboration. The length of the article varies according to the importance of the individual, the complexity of her career, and the availability of the material: the two longest (more than seven thousand words) are the biographies of Mary Baker Eddy, founder of the Church of Christ, Scientist, and the author Harriet Beecher Stowe; the shortest is the four hundred-word sketch of the Colonial printer Ann Timothy." It should also be pointed out that "only one group of women, the wives of the presidents of the United States, were admitted to *Notable American Women* on their husbands' credentials. For the others the criterion was distinction in their own right of more than local significance." It is worth noting that of the 706 women who appear in the

Dictionary of American Biography, 179 were omitted in this biographical dictionary —
"mostly individuals who seemed to have lost significance with the passage of time or . . .
marginal figures about whom so little material was available that there seemed no point
in attempting a fresh sketch." A classified list of selected biographies is appended,
including names of seventeen librarians. Highly recommended as an authoritative
scholarly work for women's history.   Bohdan S. Wynar

64. **Notable American Women, the Modern Period: A Biographical Dictionary**.
Barbara Sicherman and Carol Hurd Green, eds. Cambridge, Mass., Belknap Press/
Harvard University Press, 1980. 773p. $45.00; $12.95pa. LC 80-18402. ISBN
0-674-62732-6; 0-674-62733-4pa.

The first three volumes of this biographical dictionary, *Notable American Women
1607-1950*, appeared in 1971. This one-volume supplement, which now extends
coverage to women who died between 1951 and 1975, continues in a tradition of
scholarly, fascinating, and well-written articles.

An advisory board of eight leading scholars from various disciplines and the editors
worked with more than seven hundred experts to select the 442 women who were
eventually included in this directory. The criteria used for selection, as stated in the
preface, were similar to those used in the first three volumes: "the individual's influence
on her time or field; important or significant achievements; pioneering or innovative
quality of her work; and the relevance of her career on the history of women." In
addition, they considered a wide variety of fields which illustrated "the diverse ways in
which women have defined themselves and made an impact on their culture. . . ." The
result of this selection and outstanding research based on primary sources is a collection
of 1½- to 2-page signed biographies of women who have achieved recognition in both
traditional and nontraditional fields. Individuals were chosen from business, science,
arts, humanities, and government, as well as the more traditional disciplines of education, home economics, librarianship, and social work. Subjects such as Elizabeth Arden
(business), Margaret Morse Nice (science), Maria Cadilla de Martínez (writer), Marilyn
Monroe (actress), Mary McLeod Bethune (politics), and Janis Joplin (musician) are
found here.

Each biographical article includes crucial dates, ancestry, birth order, education,
marital status, children, and cause of death (when known). The focus of each sketch is
on the woman's life and personality, and an evaluation of her career, placed in its
historical framework. At the end of each article is a bibliography of primary and
secondary sources. A classified list of the biographies located at the end of the work
provides further access to the alphabetically arranged directory.

Although the user may find some overlap in other sources which deal with women
in specific fields, or those which cover notable Americans in general, such as *Dictionary
of American Biography*, this source brings together biographies of significant women
from various disciplines, and treats them in a manner which is scholarly, yet engaging.
[R: Choice, Jan 81, p. 640]   Ann Hartman

65. Shipton, Clifford K. **Sibley's Harvard Graduates: Biographical Sketches of
Those Who Attended Harvard College in the Classes 1768-1771, Volume XVII,
1768-1771**. Boston, Massachusetts Historical Society, 1975. 724p. illus. index. $35.00.

The biographical sketches of which the present volume is the seventeenth is known
to scholars as the *Sibley-Shipton Harvard Graduates*. Begun in 1859 by John Langdon
Sibley, by the time of his death in 1880 it had proceeded through three volumes,

covering Harvard classes of 1642 through 1689. The project then lapsed for many years. It did not revive until 1933, when Shipton brought out volume 4, *Classes of 1690-1700*. Volume 16, covering 1764-1767 was published in 1972. Volumes 4-17, published during 1933-1975, are available from the Massachusetts Historical Society at a cost of $35.00 each.

Each volume is arranged first by graduating class and then alphabetically by name. Each sketch is an authentic piece of historical research; the bountiful footnotes indicate that all possible primary and secondary sources were used as authorities.

It is appropriate that this particular volume appeared during the Bicentennial year, for most of the men treated had some involvement in the Revolutionary War.

The Sibley-Shipton volumes are a major resource for seventeenth- and eighteenth-century American biography, an important supplement to the *DAB* and the *National Cyclopedia of American Biography*. This is not to imply that the Harvard graduates were all distinguished men. The majority of them were quite mediocre and hence were not eligible for the *DAB*; but enough of them were of sufficient importance to make the set a worthwhile supplemental source. In addition, the entire set is indispensable for New England genealogy, since the sketches contain full particulars on birth and death dates, parents and children.   Richard A. Gray

66.   Stern, Madeleine B., comp. **A Phrenological Dictionary of Nineteenth-Century Americans**. Westport, Conn., Greenwood Press, 1982. 430p. illus. bibliog. index. $49.95. LC 82-991. ISBN 0-313-23286-5.

Assessing the character and mental capacity of individuals from the contours of a skull is the basis of the "pseudoscience" of phrenology. In this "pseudo-dictionary" (actually, largely a series of reprints from *The Phrenological Journal* and other phrenological publications of the last century), compiler Stern has assembled a group of biographical sketches of the famous and near famous, ranging from Edgar Allan Poe and Mark Twain to P. T. Barnum and Lizzie Borden. Curiously, even Moby Dick is scrutinized (it is one of the only non-Americans examined).

Arranged by categories such as writers, artists, performers, feminists, and criminals and introduced by an essay on phrenology, this volume attempts to combine the curious and the outré with a touch of social and cultural history. Each sketch is accompanied by a drawing or photograph of its subject and reveals as much about the opinions, prejudices, and mores of the time as does the phrenological explanation. An especially interesting entry on the black educator Booker T. Washington treads a fine line between adulation and racism. The section on Edgar Allan Poe, featuring three separate reprints, displays more interest in his personal life and dipsomania than in his skull.

Despite the marginality of this book as a reference, one cannot help being fascinated by it, and a bibliographical essay at the end along with a substantial index gives it enough scholarly credentials to make its high price at least partially justified. It remains a highly specialized work suitable only for the collections on Americana, sociology, and psychology that must be exhaustive.   Daniel F. Phelan

67.   Wakelyn, Jon L. **Biographical Dictionary of the Confederacy**. Westport, Conn., Greenwood Press, 1977. 601p. bibliog. index. $45.00. LC 72-13870. ISBN 0-8371-6124-X.

This is actually two books—a biography of Confederate leaders plus a quantitative study of them. Although the two sections are connected, each stands alone and deserves separate evaluation.

The biographical section contains 651 short (about five hundred to six hundred words) biographies of Confederate leaders—military, political, economic, and social. The criterion for inclusion is a broadly defined: "Contribution to the War Effort." The biographies are listed alphabetically, and the main source for each biography is cited. There is a bibliography, plus five appendixes, which break down the names into lists based on geographical mobility before and after the Civil War, principal occupations, religious affiliation, education, and pre- and postwar political affiliation.

The other section of the book analyzes the biographical information. Wakelyn has quantified up to seventy-two variables in each biography, and in four chapters at the beginning of the book he presents an excellent examination of these Confederate elites, emphasizing their background and preparation (including education), their leadership, and postwar activity. The analysis is based on the computerized comparisons of the individual biographies.

The main value of the book is its compilation of biographies, although historians will find the quantitative study of collective biography very interesting. Although the biographies are taken mostly from secondary sources, this volume makes them readily available. Unfortunately, the information is only as good as the original sources, and the author did not indicate when or where he has gone for further elaboration or verification. Also, while standard biographies are usually cited in the biography, several have been excluded. Thus, a reader may still need to check other sources, such as Ezra Warner's *Generals in Gray* (Louisiana State University Press, 1959). This compilation by Wakelyn serves as not only a valuable quantitative study but also an excellent one-volume reference work. [R: Choice, Sept 77, p. 836; WLB, Sept 77, p. 85]

William Z. Schenck

68. **Webster's American Biographies**. Charles Van Doren, ed. Robert McHenry, associate ed. Springfield, Mass., G. & C. Merriam, 1979. 1233p. (A Merriam-Webster). $15.00. LC 78-13719. ISBN 0-87779-253-4.

The first edition of *Webster's American Biographies* appeared in 1974. It was recommended as an excellent source for concise biographies of over three thousand significant Americans. The new edition gives no clues about the amount of revising performed, but revisions seem to be minimal. In comparing the 1974 and 1979 editions, the total paging was discovered to be identical, and randomly selected pages matched in most cases. The article for Vladimir Nabokov was updated to include his death, as was Elvis Presley's. Jimmy Carter, Walter Mondale, and John Paul Stevens were added. Ronald Reagan is not included. A "Careers and Professions Index" concludes the volume. Carter, Mondale, and Stevens were not added to the appropriate index listings, suggesting that no index changes were made. *Webster's American Biographies* is a handy ready-reference tool, but it is strongest for historical figures. The minimal revisions in the 1979 edition do not seem to justify purchase if a library already owns an earlier volume.

Janet H. Littlefield

69. **Who Was Who during the American Revolution**. Compiled by the editors of Who's Who in America with Jerry Kail. Indianapolis, Bobbs-Merrill, 1976. 515p. illus. o.p. LC 75-34514. ISBN 0-672-52216-0.

According to the introduction, this lists nearly fifteen hundred people who made contributions to the American Revolution. The entries average one hundred words, offering the barest fragments of information (and sometimes nothing) about the subjects' actual contributions to the Revolution. Some of the individuals had nothing whatsoever to do with the American Revolution (e.g., a poet who came to the United States after the War is listed because he wrote verses praising George Washington after his death). The information that is given is so little that virtually all users will have to consult other works of American history and biography for any substantive information.

Readers wanting more historical detail will turn to the *Dictionary of American Biography*, and readers in need of only brief statements of the subjects' involvement will do better with the clear and pertinent entries found in a general encyclopedia. This work cannot be recommended as source material for the American Revolution. [R: LJ, 1 Jan 77, p. 92]   Lee Steinberg

70. **Who Was Who in America: Historical Volume, 1607-1896, a Component Volume of Who's Who in American History**. Chicago, Marquis Who's Who, 1963. 670p. $67.50. ISBN 0-8379-0200-2.

71. **Who Was Who in America: A Companion Biographical Reference Work to Who's Who in America**. Chicago, Marquis Who's Who, 1942- . In progress. $67.50/vol. (ISBN assigned separately to each volume.)

72. **Who Was Who in America with World Notables Index, 1607-1981: Volumes I-VII and Historical Volume**. Chicago, Marquis Who's Who, 1981. 256p. $29.50. LC 81-84493. ISBN 0-8379-0212-6.

The historical volume published in 1963 precedes the three-volume set of *Who Was Who in America* for 1897-1942, 1943-1950, 1951-1962. It incorporates biographies of 13,300 individuals who have made contributions to, or whose activity was in some way related to, the history of the United States. It should be noted that this historical volume includes biographies of some individuals who died before 1607 and quite a few people not listed in *Who Was Who in America*. There are several appendixes listing first governors, members of federal government, etc. The revised edition published in 1967 (689p.) adds some two hundred individuals.

The seven volumes of *Who Was Who in America* cover the following years: volume 1 (1897-1942) ISBN 0-8379-0201-0; volume 2 (1943-1950) ISBN 0-8379-0206-1; volume 3 (1951-1960) ISBN 0-8379-0203-7; volume 4 (1961-1968) ISBN 0-8379-0204-5; volume 5 (1969-1973) ISBN 0-8379-0205-3; volume 6 (1974-1976) ISBN 0-8379-0207-X; volume 7 (1977-1981) ISBN 0-8379-0210-X; index volume (1607-1981) ISBN 0-8379-0212-6.

It includes biographical sketches removed from *Who's Who in America* because of death of the biographee. On the average, there are about six thousand to eight thousand entries in each volume, and the total number of entries in all seven volumes amounts to over 105,000. Essentially all entries are reproduced from *Who's Who in America*, with death date and place of interment added. No attempt has been made to assess the life or accomplishments of any biographee in a historical perspective, as this is done in the more scholarly and selective *DAB*. Nevertheless, this is an important set, and these retrospective volumes are heavily used in most libraries as supplements to current volumes of *Who's Who*. It should also be noted that starting with volume 6 (1974-1976), the editors have included deceased Marquis biographees "whose careers had been of an essentially regional significance and whose listings were in publications other than *Who's Who in America*" (p. vi). This is a significant departure from the previous practice, and we are not sure it is for the better. The index volume of *Who's Who in America* also lists biographees from regional volumes. Why not include such biographees in a separate "regional volume of deceased biographees"? Or at least indicate by using symbols that a particular biography was taken from a regional volume (and identify the volume) so that the user of this standard source may go back to the source for additional information, if need be. As it is known, biographical sketches in *Who's Who in America* are slightly edited by the editorial staff, with information supplied by the legal representatives of the deceased biographee. Two other changes should be noted. This new volume includes sketches of some Marquis biographees known to be ninety-five years of age or older. "Lacking current information regarding these individuals, however, we made such inclusions in the hope that our apologies will be accepted should errors occur" (p. vi). Secondly, included in this volume is a comprehensive index to the now more than ninety-five thousand sketches in the *Who Was Who* series. This is an excellent addition that will make the set more usable.

Through volume 6 of *Who Was Who in America with World Notables*, a cumulative index was found at the end of each edition. Having reached an unwieldy 256-page index with volume 7, Marquis has ceased this practice and issued a separate publication indexing the historical volume (1607-1896) and volumes 1 through 7 (1897-1981) of *Who Was Who in America*.

This index contains over 105,000 deceased biographees who previously appeared in either *Who's Who in America* or one of the regional Who's Who publications. With entries alphabetically arranged by surname, numbers following each name indicate the volume in which the biographical sketch containing personal and career information can be found. An "H" after a name designates the historical volume. Entries are in tediously small typeface with a five-column-per-page format. The binding and construction are sturdy and color-coordinated to the *Who Was Who* set. "Index" is clearly marked on the spine.

At this point it is necessary to search only the cumulative index in volume 6 and the entries in volume 7 to determine if an individual is listed. Considering the price of the separate cumulative index, this is a minor inconvenience for those who use the set infrequently. Yet, as this trend of a separate index is likely to continue, future cumulations should prove to be obvious time-savers. In conclusion, an essential set for all large and medium-sized libraries. Bohdan S. Wynar

73. **Who Was Who in American History: Arts and Letters**. Chicago, Marquis Who's Who, 1975. 604p. $57.50. LC 75-29617. ISBN 0-8379-3301-3.

A biographical reference work containing brief sketches of ten thousand great and near-great American artists, performers, and writers now deceased. Coverage extends from 1607 through mid-1973. Entries for post-1899 decedents are largely autobiographical; Marquis editors compiled the remainder. Approximately 10 percent of all entries are officially unverified. Some are inexplicable: why include Camus? Quiller-Couch? Chester Morris? but not Clara Bow? A number of birth and/or death dates are omitted, and more than one entry ends in mid-sentence. Hard-to-pronounce names are spelled phonetically, but no pseudonymic cross-references are provided. Abbreviations abound in each entry and are defined in a separate table. The small print will plague more than a few readers. Summation: a hasty culling of Marquis's original *Who Was Who in America*, with some updating.

There are two companion volumes: *Science and Technology* ($57.50) and *The Military* ($57.50). [R: BL, 1 Nov 76, p. 422; Choice, Oct 76, p. 964]

Lawrence E. Spellman

States and Regions

74. **Biographical Cyclopedia of the Commonwealth of Kentucky: Embracing Biographies of Many of the Prominent Men and Families of the State**. Chicago, John M. Gresham, 1896; repr., Easley, S.C., Southern Historical Press, 1980. 631p. illus. index. $40.00. ISBN 0-89308-193-0.

Most any biographical dictionary can be useful if the reader knows the limitations and caveats in its use. Many of the southern and midwestern works of the last century are execrable as reference works, but they often contain information not readily available elsewhere. They were frequently based on interviews with a publisher's representative, who collected a fee for inclusion.

The special value of this reprint is not only the fact that it lists 1,104 biographical sketches, but also that it includes an index of names, both of biographees and others. The text of the original edition is in miscellaneous alphabetical order, indexed by biographee only. The present reprint provides an index of other names, prepared by Eileene Sandlin, on thirty-five unnumbered pages at the end. The information is generally, but not invariably, accurate, and, by the standards of inclusion, the work could be expanded several times. It would be a genuine service to historians and genealogists if dozens of other similar works could have a new index similar to Sandlin's.   Lawrence S. Thompson

75. **The Biographical Encyclopaedia of Kentucky of the Dead and Living Men of the Nineteenth Century**. Cincinnati, Ohio, J. M. Armstrong, 1878; repr., Easley, S.C., Southern Historical Press, 1980. 792p. illus. index. $42.50. ISBN 0-89308-192-2.

This old mug book contains 1,408 biographical sketches that are generally, but not invariably, accurate, and portraits that are often not readily available elsewhere. It could have been greatly expanded if uniform policies of selection had been applied. The entries in the original work were printed in random order, but there was an alphabetical index. Much more important is the index of all names following the original index (twenty-seven unnumbered pages) by Mary Elizabeth Phillips. It is invaluable for genealogists and local historians. If Phillips can continue the arduous task of supplementary indexing for dozens of other similar regional biographical works, it would be a priceless source for biographical information about the United States in general.

Lawrence S. Thompson

76. Carrington, Evelyn M., ed. **Women in Early Texas**. Sponsored by American Association of University Women, Austin Branch. Austin, Tex., Jenkins Publishing Co., The Pemberton Press, 1975. 308p. illus. o.p. LC 75-27032.

This engaging book, sponsored by the Austin (Texas) Branch of the American Association of University Women as a contribution to the American Revolution Bicentennial Celebration, contains short biographical sketches of forty-two pioneer women of Texas, most of which are affectionately written by descendants from family records and oral traditions. The trials, tribulations, and successes of these sturdy pioneer women make wonderful reading, but the book is of limited reference value.

Paul H. Spence

77. Coleman, Kenneth, and Charles Stephen Gurr, eds. **Dictionary of Georgia Biography**. Athens, Ga., University of Georgia Press, 1983. 2v. $60.00/set. LC 82-17341. ISBN 0-8203-0662-2.

The new *Dictionary of Georgia Biography* fills a reference gap of seventy-one years' standing. Its predecessors, Allen Daniel Candler and Clement A. Evans's *Georgia: Comprising Sketches of Counties, Towns, Events, Institutions, and Persons* (1906) and William J. Northen's *Men of Mark in Georgia* (1907-1912), are still useful, but the perception of historical significance has changed over the ensuing eight decades, and researchers needed an up-to-date biographical work on luminaries from the Peach State.

In their preface, editors Coleman and Gurr explain their criteria for the selection of subjects for the dictionary. Those included are no longer living, and they "must have done something of statewide significance while a resident of Georgia." Strictly local dignitaries do not appear here. Omissions may be attributed to the subject's having left Georgia before gaining prominence, there being insufficient research material with which to compose a sketch, or the editors' inability to secure an author for the entry. Historians wrote most sketches, but librarians, family members, and independent researchers submitted others. The alphabetically-arranged entries range in length from a short paragraph to several pages.

The editors deserve commendation for their careful inclusion of prominent blacks and women in the dictionary. Among those Georgians profiled here are artists, writers, slaves, Reconstruction officers, suffragists, civil rights and labor leaders, librarians, and even viticulturalists. A short bibliography concludes each entry, greatly increasing the reference value of the work.   Diane J. Cimbala

78. **Colorado Who's Who 1984**. Littleton, Colo., TY Publishing, 1984. 337p. No price indicated. LC 84-51399. ISBN 0-930613-00-7.

According to the preface, *Colorado Who's Who 1984* "provides up-to-date biographical information on men and women of distinction who are residents of the State of Colorado." It is further indicated that nominees for this work are people whose accomplishments have distinguished them from the ordinary, "and inclusion in *Colorado Who's Who* is reserved only for these achievers. Wealth, social status, or desire are not justification for inclusion." So much for that. What do we find here? Many important and not-so-prominent people: business executives, physicians, some teachers and faculty members, artists, and many politicians. Former governor John Love is not included, nor is Carl Akers, a well-known personality on local TV. The author of this review also received a questionnaire from the publisher with a post office box number for return. All attempts to contact the publisher were unsuccessful, so this questionnaire was not answered. The value of this publication for a local library will be marginal. Important people (many are omitted) receive, quite frequently, less coverage than people of lesser importance. Some that are included are not even important in local affairs. In short, it reminds us of a typical vanity-press publication.

Bohdan S. Wynar

79. Marks, Henry S., comp. **Who Was Who in Alabama**. Huntsville, Ala., Strode Publishers, 1972. 200p. o.p. LC 74-188627. ISBN 0-87397-017-9.

According to the preface, this work "is designed to be a permanent one-volume biographical record of outstanding residents of Alabama who have passed away." Unfortunately, the criteria for inclusion—beyond the requirement to have "passed away"—are not explained, and it is rather difficult to determine from the listings whether indeed any scholarly judgment was brought to bear during the selection process. The biographical sketches are informal, as two examples might illustrate. The entry for Samuel Wootten Averett is, in its entirety: "He is chiefly known in Alabama history as the president of Judson College from 1887 to 1896"; the entire entry for Alfred Baker notes that "Chilton County was originally named Baker, in honor of this early citizen of Autauga County." In justice to this rather interesting work, we must admit that most entries are more complete; in particular, they usually do provide date of birth and death and some career information. Nevertheless, a work of this type should reflect closer editorial attention; Alabama history certainly merits a better biographical record.   Bohdan S. Wynar

80. Marks, Henry S., comp. **Who Was Who in Florida**. Huntsville, Ala., Strode Publishers, 1973. 276p. $12.95. LC 73-83503. ISBN 0-87397-039-X.

The author of *Who Was Who in Alabama* (1972) has performed a similar service for Florida. The thirteen hundred entries (for deceased "outstanding residents or developers" of Florida) vary in length from a dozen to four hundred words. The work purports to list persons from "the period of initial discovery and exploration to November 30, 1972" about whom questions may be asked by librarians and historians. Paucity of information provided has resulted from an attempt to include "as many people as possible . . . in a single volume"; inquirers seeking more data are directed to an appendix of local source materials. Despite the cooperation of many librarians, an unusually large number of entries lack vital dates—e.g., Lue Gim Gong, "the Luther Burbank of Florida." There are many entries for persons who wintered in or retired to Florida. Since this is a first venture in retrospective Florida biography, concerned persons will want to answer the author's request to "correct either flagrant omissions or incorrect or misleading biographies." [R: BL, 1 July 74, p. 1166]

Donald G. Davis, Jr.

81. O'Neal, Bill. **Encyclopedia of Western Gunfighters**. 1st ed. Norman, Okla., University of Oklahoma Press, 1979. 386p. illus. bibliog. index. $29.95. LC 78-21380. ISBN 0-8061-1508-4.

This encyclopedia contains a wealth of information, listing a total of 255 western gunfighters and 587 gunfights under an alphabetical arrangement by name of gunfighter. Each entry provides the gunfighter's name, any known alias(es) and/or nickname(s), a short biographical sketch with birth and death dates if known, and descriptions of all verified gunfights, including the date and location of each if known. An abbreviated list of sources used to write and verify each entry follows, referring the reader to a bibliography at the end of the book. Introductory material is brief but useful, and very interesting. O'Neal provides a definition of gunfighter as a yardstick to determine whether an individual is truly a gunfighter and merits inclusion in the book. Also provided is comprehensive information on the listed gunfighters' vital statistics, causes of death, occupations pursued, number of gunfights, etc.

O'Neal's writing style is interesting, smooth, and well suited to his subject matter. Well-placed photographs (some of which are extraordinary and unforgettable) help to relieve the repetitive format of the entries, although extended reading of this encyclopedia is not difficult. This is a first-rate effort and fascinating reading. [R: BL, 1 June 80; p. 1437; WLB Jan 80, p. 332]   Ronald Rayman

82. **Who's Who in Arizona, 1982: Four Thousand Brief Biographies**. Edited by Gormezano Reference Publications Staff. Seattle, Wash., Gormezano Reference Publications, 1981. 200p. (Who's Who Reference Series, No. 9). $59.95. LC 81-70636. ISBN 0-935954-19-8.

Gormezano Reference Publications published in 1981 a number of biographical dictionaries covering practically all states, from Arizona to Wyoming. The number of biographical sketches varies from state to state. Larger states like Pennsylvania or New York contain four thousand or five thousand entries, while smaller states such as Vermont or Alabama contain two thousand or three thousand entries. There are a few exceptions; for example, Nevada contains forty-two hundred entries and Colorado includes four thousand entries. Occasionally it is indicated on the title page that a particular work was edited by Beacon Presse. Gormezano Reference Publications is a subsidiary of Beacon. This is a typical vanity-press publication, and it is hoped that librarians realize that. There are no criteria or standards. We have examined a few volumes in libraries. Worthless publications.   Bohdan S. Wynar

83. **Who's Who in the East, 1985-1986**. 20th ed. Chicago, Marquis Who's Who, 1984. 819p. $99.50. LC 43-18522. ISBN 0-8379-0620-2.

The twentieth edition is not radically different from the twelfth (1970-1971) and seventeenth (1979-1980) editions. "The East" is now defined as Connecticut, Delaware, the District of Columbia, Maine, Maryland, Massachusetts, New Hampshire, New Jersey, New York, Pennsylvania, Rhode Island, Vermont, New Brunswick, Newfoundland, Nova Scotia, Prince Edward Island, Quebec, and the eastern half of Ontario. (West Virginia, included in this region through the fifteenth [1975-1976] edition, is now included in the publisher's companion regional volume, *Who's Who in the South and Southwest*). The present work contains about eighteen thousand names—some three thousand fewer than in the nineteenth edition. The difference is nowhere explained unless it is that the list of Eastern biographees to be found in *Who's Who in America* (which appeared in the nineteenth edition and some, but not all, of the earlier editions) has been deleted.

Assessment of the current edition should weigh carefully certain editorial statements in the preface: (1) in most cases biographees furnished their own data, "thus assuring a high degree of accuracy"—but in some cases, Marquis staff members compiled the data and (2) "in the editorial evaluation that resulted in the ultimate selection of names in this directory, an individual's desire to be listed was not sufficient reason for inclusion; rather it was the person's achievement that ruled. Similarly, wealth or social position was not a criterion—only occupational stature or achievement in a field within the eastern region of North America influenced selection." These editorial remarks notwithstanding, academic, public, and many special libraries in the area covered and elsewhere will acquire this volume for their patrons and/or the comprehensiveness of their biographical collections.   Wiley J. Williams

84. **Who's Who in the Midwest 1984-1985**. 19th ed. Chicago, Marquis Who's Who, 1984. 915p. $99.50. LC 50-289. ISBN 0-8379-0719-5.

The nineteenth edition of *Who's Who in the Midwest* contains biographies of 21,400 leading figures in twelve American states—Illinois, Indiana, Iowa, Kansas, Michigan, Minnesota, Missouri, Nebraska, North Dakota, Ohio, South Dakota, and Wisconsin, as well as the contiguous areas of Canada—Manitoba and western Ontario. Although the publishers claim minimal duplication of names between this volume and *Who's Who in America*, nearly fourteen thousand of the biographees are also listed in *Who's Who in America*, a 60 percent duplication. However, since it is the aim of the publishers to include both persons of localized reference interest and persons of national reference interest in the regional volume, duplication would seem to be inevitable.

Commendably, the publishers strive to keep information current and accurate by asking biographees to update their entries on an average of three times per biennium. Any library maintaining a reference department will need this title for its coverage of interdisciplinary subjects in a geographical area.

As previous reviews concluded, this member of the Marquis family of Who's Whos is a valuable reference tool for all types and sizes of libraries.   Necia A. Musser

85. **Who's Who in the South and Southwest, 1984-1985**. 19th ed. Chicago, Marquis Who's Who, 1984. 847p. $99.50. LC 50-58231. ISBN 0-8379-0819-1.

This latest edition contains some nineteen thousand entries from fourteen Southern states (excluding Maryland and Missouri, but including West Virginia and Oklahoma), Puerto Rico, the U.S. Virgin Islands, and Mexico (apparently very selective). Entries contain the familiar stock of information expected from Marquis publications, and some sample checks of names familiar to the reviewer reflect the usual meticulous accuracy. Individuals in *Who's Who in America* are not included except for a few major personalities (e.g., university presidents) who are as significant regionally as nationally. This means that the bulk of the biographees are individuals of secondary importance. Some reference librarians, even in the region, say they rarely use it. Would it not be worthwhile to study the possibility of miniaturizing this and some dozens of other biographical reference works that are expensive and of marginal utility (and most of them much less adequately edited than Marquis publications) and putting them in a consolidated and cumulating work? On the other hand, this present edition, with three gilt edges and in imitation leather, is likely to have a home on the desk of thousands of its biographees with the marker ribbon in the appropriate place.

Lawrence S. Thompson

86. **Who's Who in the West, 1984-1985**. 19th ed. Chicago, Marquis Who's Who, 1983. 832p. $99.50. LC 49-48186. ISBN 0-8379-0919-8.

This is one of four regional biographical directories published by Marquis Who's Who as a companion to *Who's Who in America*. *Who's Who in the West* includes biographical information on people in the states of Alaska, Arizona, California, Colorado, Hawaii, Idaho, Montana, Nevada, New Mexico, Oregon, Utah, Washington, Wyoming, and the contiguous western provinces of Canada. Although the print is small, it is very readable. Reflecting the diversity of western life, this nineteenth edition contains twenty thousand entries, two thousand more than the seventeenth edition. Included are such people as Erskine Caldwell, novelist; Bob Packwood, senator; Peterson Zah, chairman, Navajo Tribal Council; Pat Schroeder, congresswoman; Dianne Feinstein, mayor; Cesar Chavez, president of United Farm Workers of America; and Jennifer McDowell, composer of music for Paramount Pictures. It contains a list of biographees of the Western region not listed in this volume but who may be found in the 42nd edition of *Who's Who in America*. This title, along with its companions, is necessary for comprehensive biographical collections.

Anna Grace Patterson

AFRICA

87.   **Africa Year Book and Who's Who 1977**. London, Africa Journal, 1977; distr., New York, Unipub, 1977. 1364p. illus. (part col.). maps. $44.00. ISBN 0-903274-05-1.

The major parts of this work are a seven-hundred-page description of all African countries and a "Who's Who in Africa" as of 1977. Other contents include a short diary of events for 1975 and 1976; a general section on the continent's geography, people, economy, and communication; two sections on organizations, regional and international; and a ten-page section on sports.

The first reaction to this source must be to question what it adds to the reference material on Africa. The preface emphasizes the importance of treating the continent as a whole and of presenting the information from the African point of view. Despite the validity of these sentiments, the source manages to make only limited additions to available works.

The diary can only serve to supplement the information in *Deadline Data on World Affairs* (Deadline Data Inc., 1955-) and Colin Legum's *Africa Contemporary Record, 1974-75* (Holmes and Meier, Vol. 7, 1975). Regional and international organizations are adequately covered in other sources, notably the Europa publications. The country material is presented well and the visitors' guide for each country is not duplicated elsewhere in this type of source. However, the other information is not notably different from that in *Africa South of the Sahara* and *The Middle East and North Africa*. The latter sources have the advantage of including short bibliographies for each country.

The biographical section does make a substantial contribution. Out of fifteen names checked (starting arbitrarily with "M" and taking the first fifteen), only seven appeared in *International Who's Who, 1976-77* (40th ed., Europa, 1976) and only three in John Dickie and Alan Rake's *Who's Who in Africa* (African Development, 1973).

The book should be in large reference collections or those specializing in Africa. [R: BL, 15 Oct 77, pp. 399-400; Choice, Sept 77, p. 825; WLB, Sept 77, pp. 85-86]

Mary Reichel

88.   Deane, Dee Shirley. **Black South Africans: A Who's Who, 57 Profiles of Natal's Leading Blacks**. New York, Oxford University Press, 1978. 210p. illus. o.p. ISBN 0-19-570148-8.

This biographical dictionary of black South Africans includes forty-seven men and ten women from the province of Natal who were chosen by a Natal selection committee consisting of five black trustees. The selection criteria agreed upon included, in order of priority, willingness to sacrifice self in the interests of others; dedication to the black community and contributions made; leadership qualities; and personal, vocational, avocational, and educational achievements (p. ix). This is the first of three planned volumes, the other two to cover black leaders in the Transvaal and in the Cape province and the Orange Free State.

Prefatory material includes a cross index by fields of activity, the names of eleven persons from Natal living abroad who met the criteria for selection but whose biographies could not be gathered for use in the book, a map of Natal, explanatory notes, a preface by Mangosuthu G. Buthelezi, and an introduction by the author, who, in obtaining the material for this book, had to contend with various impediments and barriers but who visited all the biographees and spoke with them at length (with some of them, a number of times). Each sketch includes a full-page photograph (by themselves, worth the price of the book); brief facts such as personal information, education, career, published works, foreign travel, memberships and offices, and addresses; and a narrative essay. Although many of the people included in this volume are unknown in the United States, it is a very important book and should be useful in all libraries from the secondary school to the university. It is hoped that the author can obtain the financial support needed to complete this project.

A much more substantial work is *Dictionary of South African Biography* (Pretoria, National Council for Social Research, 1968- . In progress) that is also published in Afrikaans. Patterned after *DNB*, it is a scholarly work covering "all those who have, since the earliest European contact with the southern extremity of Africa, made a contribution of importance to the course of South African history" (introduction). An older work is *Southern African Dictionary of National Biography* edited by Eric Rosenthal (London, Warne, 1966. 430p.) that includes over two thousand brief biographies of deceased persons. For current information one should consult *Who's Who of Southern Africa* (Philadelphia, International Publications Service, 1982. 845p. $70.00. LC 15-10690. ISBN 0-8002-2989-4) that started in 1915 and is now in its 67th edition. [R: BL, 1 Oct 79, p. 304; LJ, 15 Jan 79, p. 179]

Doris Cruger Dale and Bohdan S. Wynar

89.   Dickie, John, and Alan Rake. **Who's Who in Africa: The Political, Military and Business Leaders of Africa**. London, African Development; distr., New York, International Publications Service, 1973. 602p. illus. map. o.p. ISBN 0-9502755-0-6.

Contains biographical sketches ranging in length from three hundred to twelve hundred words. There are entries for some 650 prominent Africans living in forty-seven countries, with an emphasis on governmental officials. Biographies are arranged alphabetically by country, but there is no general index of names, thus making it rather difficult to use this directory. There is also a brief (one-page) introduction for each country, providing data on population, geography, economy, etc. Unfortunately, the information provided here is rather superficial, and the reader interested in more substantial information would be well advised to use Europa publications. There are also, of course, other biographical directories that cover Africa—e.g., *The Encyclopaedia Africana Dictionary of African Biography*. Nevertheless, this one-volume compilation will be of some use in larger libraries that have strong collections of materials on Africa. [R: WLB, May 74, p. 764; Choice, Apr 74, p. 233]

Bohdan S. Wynar

90.   **The Encyclopaedia Africana Dictionary of African Biography (in 20 Volumes)**. New York, Reference Publications, 1977- . In progress. illus. maps. index. $59.95/vol. LC 76-17954.

The appearance in 1977 of the first volume (Ethiopa-Ghana) under the aegis of the *Encyclopaedia Africana* is a major publishing event. It is the first tangible outcome of W. E. B. Du Bois's dream (conceived in 1909) of a monumental synoptic work devoted to the contributions of Africa and Africans to civilization. The idea has been kept alive for more than one-half century, but not until 1961 was it possible to translate it into concrete work plans. That year, Du Bois moved to Ghana to organize and direct the project with Nkrumah's financial and moral support. Following Du Bois's death in 1963, the editorial board of the *Encyclopaedia* decided to implement the plan by initially publishing volumes of biographical articles on a country-by-country basis covering the entire sweep of African history. Subsequent financial support came from some African governments and from American and West German foundations.

The first volume brings together 146 Ethiopian and 138 Ghanian biographies spanning many centuries. They include rulers, statesmen, politicians, religious leaders, intellectuals, and people from all walks of life who have influenced the course of events in these countries in one way or another. Many of the people highlighted had been previously overlooked by Western literature. All biographies are treated in a broad historical framework in the context of events contemporary with the biographee. Consequently, the whole historical epoch comes alive through the vivid individual portraiture.

The articles resulted from meticulous research carried out by leading Africanists in the world, half of whom are African nationals associated with leading universities on the continent. Uniformly, the tone of discourse is elevated. Attempts to assess objectively a person's significance and efforts to present historical events in a balanced manner are in evidence throughout the whole work. The articles dealing with Graziani in Ethiopia and Padmore in Ghana could be cited as examples. Collectively, these biographies accomplish the project's objective, which Kenneth Kaunda, president of the Republic of Zambia, defined in the *Dictionary*'s prefatory note: "to reveal the genius of her [Africa's] people, their history, culture and institutions, their achievements as well as their shortcomings."

The articles are cross-referenced and followed by substantial bibliographies both of materials in various Western languages and of citations to local source materials when available. A detailed index at the end of the volume provides excellent topical penetration into the contents of the articles, making the *Dictionary* a superb tool for researching many aspects of Ethiopia and Ghana. A large number of the biographies are accompanied by portraits and illustrations. Each section of the work is preceded by a twenty-page overview of the history of these two countries. Other features include a glossary of unfamiliar terms and maps of provinces, principal rivers, towns, and ethnic distribution of the population.

In 1979 the second volume was published (*Sierra Leone-Zaire*), and again the articles were based on materials ranging from archival resources to standard treatises listed in the source bibliographies that follow each biography. The third volume (*South Africa, Botswana—Lesotho Swaziland*) was published in 1985.

The *Dictionary of African Biography* should be hailed as a landmark achievement in every respect. When completed, it will close a vast gap in our knowledge. In restoring the dignity of Africa's contribution to the civilization of mankind, it will become an effective instrument for the promotion of cultural understanding between Africa and the West. [R: BL, 1 Mar 78, p. 1127; Choice, Dec 78, p. 1346]   Michael Keresztesi

91.   Lipschutz, Mark R., and R. Kent Rasmussen. **Dictionary of African Historical Biography**. 1st U.S. ed. Chicago, Aldine Publishing, 1978. 292p. illus. maps. bibliog. index. o.p. LC 76-54337. ISBN 0-202-24144-0.

There are approximately eight hundred biographical sketches included in this *Dictionary*, arranged in alphabetical order and averaging a paragraph in length. Brief citations following each entry indicate the work from which the information was extracted. The entries cover all of the African continent, but only personalities from pre-colonial times and from the most "popular" areas of the continent. The appendixes include a subject guide to the names, arranged by broad occupational and chronological headings. An index of variant spellings is also included, which helps explain the lack of cross-references in the main body of the work. This *Dictionary* is by no means a "definitive" work on African personalities—nor did its authors intend it to be one. It is, rather, a handbook that may be of some value to the general student. I see little necessity in including it in a collection for the serious scholar of Africa and its peoples.

Margaret Rich

92. Who's Who of Southern Africa, Including Mauritius and Incorporating South African Who's Who and the Central African Who's Who. 67th ed. Johannesburg, The Argus Printing and Publishing Co.; distr., Philadelphia, International Publications Service, 1985. 900p. $85.00. ISBN 0-8002-3158-9.

This annual, first published in 1907, changed its title from *South African Who's Who* in 1959 (43rd ed.). The volume consists of several sections: a South African section; a South West African section; a section on Zimbabwe, Malawi, and Botswana; and a section on Mauritius, Lesotho, Swaziland, etc. and includes several thousand biographical sketches of prominent personalities in all walks of life. In addition to biographies, there are official guides and several directories, covering such things as the president's council, universities, governmental agencies, and representatives of the Republic of South Africa abroad. Biographies too late to classify and obituaries are also listed.

Bohdan S. Wynar

ASIA

93. Association for Asian Studies. Ming Biographical History Project Committee. **Dictionary of Ming Biography, 1368-1644.** L. Carrington Goodrich, ed. New York, Columbia University Press, 1976. 2v. illus. index. $140.00/set. LC 75-26938. ISBN 0-685-62034-4/set.

This excellent, scholarly biographical dictionary complements two other compilations (*Eminent Chinese of the Ch'ing Period (1644-1912)*, edited by Arthur W. Hummel, and *Biographical Dictionary of Republican China*, edited by Howard L. Boorman and Richard C. Howard) and extends their coverage back to the fourteenth century. Together they constitute the most authoritative source for Chinese biographical information in the English language, and perhaps in any language. The *Dictionary of Ming Biography* includes some 650 biographies ranging from one page to thirteen pages in length. Although rulers and officials predominate, persons of many other occupations are included—especially artists, writers, and scholars. Most of the subjects are of Chinese nationality, but Europeans, as well as persons of other East Asian nationalities who were important in Chinese history, are included. Very few women are included, probably because historical records for women, other than those related to rulers, are very rare for this period. The biographies are written in a clear, unpretentious style. The important aspects of each subject's life are described and an effort is made to evaluate the contribution to Chinese society. The biographies are signed by their authors, all eminently suited for this task, and conclude with extensive but highly abbreviated bibliographies of basic sources, most of which are in East Asian languages.

Among the most valuable contributions of this work are its extensive indexes. An index of names includes not only the names of the biographees, but some six thousand other persons described in the biographies. The value of this work for bibliographical research is greatly enhanced by a title index to some thirty-five hundred books mentioned in the biographical articles. The subject index locates discussions of some twenty-five hundred specific events and topics.

This fundamental tool is an indispensable addition to any library that has an interest in China and its history. [R: BL, 1 Nov 76, p. 424; Choice, Sept 76, p. 794; LJ, 1 June 76, p. 1275]   James D. Anderson

94.   Bartke, Wolfgang. **Who's Who in the People's Republic of China**. Armonk, N.Y., M. E. Sharpe; distr., Chicago, Marquis Who's Who, 1981. 729p. illus. (A Publication of the Institute of Asian Affairs in Hamburg). $125.00. LC 80-27599. ISBN 0-87332-183-9.

Research for this reference work was supported by the Deutsche Forschungs-gemeinschaft (German Research Society) in Bonn. Franciscus Verellen made the English translation. The biographies are based on files primarily from the daily Chinese press and unofficial sources recorded by the compiler since 1958. The book is intended as a reference guide to the "current active leadership" of China.

"Standards for Inclusion" (p. xi) try to define the groups of cadres listed, who are mostly the heads and deputies of political, military, and cultural organizations and institutions. A small number of deceased or purged leaders considered of political significance are listed in a special section (pp. 571-93). The reliance on the Chinese press created unavoidable inaccuracies, and the compiler decided to include mainly those persons mentioned in the press since August 1978. Since 1975, 1,030 biographies had to be deleted from the compiler's records as a result of extensive purges, and by and large replaced by re-activated cadres who had held high ranks before the cultural revolution.

Some two thousand persons are listed, and, as can be expected, they are mostly men. The biographies are alphabetically arranged according to the Pinyin spelling. The Wade-Giles transcription is given in parentheses, as well as the Chinese character. There are many photographs for the entries, mostly taken from the Chinese press, and although some are of poor quality, they are still useful. A conversion table of names from Wade-Giles to Pinyin is added as an appendix and facilitates use. Each biography is preceded by a list of posts held as of March 1980, when work on biographies in this volume was completed. These posts are arranged in the following order: party, government, National People's Congress, military, provincial administration, mass organizations, and others. Thus, the present status of a cadre can be sized up at a glance. Pre-1949 information is given as continuous text after that, followed by the official post-1949 data, which are arranged chronologically by year and month. This arrangement makes the information on each person very quickly and easily available. The biographies are printed in two columns and cover 570 pages. An informative appendix on "The Organization of the People's Republic of China" (pp. 595-713) provides extensive tables and statistics on military, political, and other organizations, with names of people in charge.

Handsomely bound in red buckram, the volume lies flat when opened and will stand frequent use. Typography and legibility are very good. An impressive, highly informative, and scholarly reference source, recommended for libraries with interest in current Chinese affairs and studies.

This work can be supplemented by *Who's Who in Communist China*, 2nd ed. (2v. Hong Kong, Union Research Institute, 1969-1970) that includes sixteen hundred biographies of major personalities in contemporary life, emphasizing political leaders, scientists and diplomatic personnel. Biographies of some deceased persons are retained, primarily members of the Communist party. [R: LJ, July 81, p. 1403]

Josephine Riss Fang and Bohdan S. Wynar

95. **Biographical Dictionary of Republican China**. Howard L. Boorman, ed. New York, Columbia University Press, 1967-1971. 4v. $50.00/vol. LC 67-12006.

96. Krompart, Janet. **Biographical Dictionary of Republican China, Volume 5: A Personal Name Index**. Howard L. Boorman and Richard C. Howard, eds. New York, Columbia University Press, 1979. 75p. $50.00. LC 67-12006. ISBN 0-231-08958-9.

Intended as a supplement to A. W. Hummel's *Eminent Chinese of the Ch'ing Period (1644-1912)* (2v. Washington, Library of Congress, 1943-1944) that covered eight hundred prominent personalities in this period, *Biographical Dictionary* concentrates on the period 1911-1949 and includes six hundred biographies. The articles are arranged by the Wade-Giles romanization of the subject's surname, with the exception of the biographies of Chiang Kai-shek, Eugene Ch'en, H. H. K'ung and a few others that appear under the name most familiar to Western readers. Chinese characters are also supplied for most Chinese names. This work, indeed, is the most scholarly biographical dictionary on China, including a comprehensive bibliography listing all known works on all the subjects of the biographies and the sources used in writing the articles on them.

Krompart's personal name index lists and provides page references for all persons mentioned in the biographical sketches, including Western authors and Japanese figures cited. Cross-referencing is thorough, and death dates are supplied for biographees who died since the completion of the main volumes in 1971.

Biographical Dictionary of Republican China will remain for years as the standard source on this subject. [R: Choice, Sept 70; Choice, Apr 72, p. 195; Choice, Nov 79, p. 1148; WLB, Mar 69, p. 673; WLB, Mar 70; WLB, Apr 72, p. 741; WLB, Oct 79, p. 134]
Bohdan S. Wynar

97. Buckland, C. E. **Dictionary of Indian Biography**. London, Sonnenschein, 1906; repr., New York, Greenwood Press, 1969. 494p. bibliog. $21.00. LC 69-13848. SBN 8371-0331-2.

Contains twenty-six hundred biographical sketches of Who's Who type for Indian, English and foreign persons "who have been conspicuous in the history of India, or distinguished in the administration of the country," covering the period 1750-1905. In addition to biographical listings this volume includes a brief bibliography of reference works consulted and a bibliography of biographical works on some prominent personalities arranged under the name of the biographee or subject. This biographical dictionary is a valuable reference work for historical research; it is supplemented by other biographical dictionaries, e.g., *Who's Who in India* (Lucknow, Newul Kishore Press, 1911-1914) and *The Times of India Directory and Year Book* (Bombay, The Times of India, 1915- . Annual). [R: RQ, Summer 69, p. 288; WLB, June 69, p. 1019]
Bohdan S. Wynar

98. **Dictionary of National Biography**. Edited by Siba Pada Sen. Calcutta, Institute of Historical Studies; distr., Columbia, Mo., South Asia Books, 1974. 4v. $90.00.

According to the preface, this four-volume dictionary is "the first attempt of its kind in India, on the lines of similar works in other countries." Its purpose is to cover "people from all walks of life—politics, religious and social reform, education, journalism, literature, science, law, business and industry, etc.—who made some tangible contribution to national life from the beginning of the nineteenth century to the achievement of independence" (1800-1947). In fact, this dictionary includes among its fourteen hundred entries quite a few personalities of only regional importance, omitting, however, many artists and sports figures who achieved national importance. Promised supplementary volumes that may rectify some of these omissions have not yet been published. [R: Choice, June 73, p. 596]   Bohdan S. Wynar

99. Heussler, Robert. **British Malaya: A Bibliographical and Biographical Compendium**. New York, Garland, 1981. 193p. index. (Themes in European Expansion: Exploration, Colonization, and the Impact of Empire, Vol. 1; Garland Reference Library of Social Science, Vol. 79). $33.00. LC 80-8968. ISBN 0-8240-9369-0.

Compiled by a well-known historian of British colonial administration in Africa and Asia, this research aid is apparently a by-product of the author's *British Rule in Malaya: The Malayan Civil Service and Its Predecessors, 1867-1942*, also published in 1981. There are several themes that appear in Heussler's published works that are reflected here: the importance of understanding the accomplishments of colonial administrations, the continuity of certain of their attitudes and practices after independence, and the propensity of these civil servants to record their experiences and observations. In fact, Heussler's earlier work has been criticized on occasion for these emphases, although such criticism may only reflect disapproval of a positive treatment of colonial civil servants.

The work at hand gives 499 bibliographic citations and almost six hundred biographical notes on civil officials who served in Malaya during this period. The bibliography is divided into eight general topical sections and includes books, articles, and manuscript collections. Almost every entry is annotated with one or two sentences summarizing the quality and scope of the work. Authors who are represented in the biographical section are marked with an asterisk. Biographical notes, drawn from civil lists and including Malays as well as Englishmen, provide vital dates, father's occupation, education, and posts. There is a brief subject and author index to the bibliography.

This is a workmanlike tool, although little enhanced by the Garland style of production.

A related title is *Who's Who in Malaysia, Singapore and Brunei*. Edited by J. Victor Morais (16th ed. Kuala Lumpur, Malaysia, Who's Who Publications SDN.; BHD.; distr., Philadelphia, International Publications Service, 1985. 650p. $85.00. ISBN 0-8002-3686-6) that started as a biennial in 1956 and originally was published in Kuala Lumpur by Economy Printers. Since that time it has been published under several titles, e.g., *Leaders of Malaya and Who's Who* or *Who's Who in Malaysia*. In addition to brief biographical sketches on Malaysians, it contains separate sections on Singapore and Brunei, as well as a supplement containing biographies received after the volume's compilation deadline. The section "Who's Who in Business" contains profiles of several major companies as well as biographies of business people.

Leon J. Stout and Bohdan S. Wynar

100. **India Who's Who, 1969-** . New Delhi, INFA Publications, 1969- . Annual. 1985 ed. distr., Philadelphia, International Publications Service. 450p. $35.00. LC 73-906738. ISBN 0-8002-3846-X.

One of several contemporary biographical dictionaries on India, this work covers prominent personalities arranged by professional occupations. It contains some four thousand biographics of people prominent in all walks of life, including government officials, civil servants, business executives; it also covers such areas as sports, law, education, and art. Each entry is revised periodically by means of a questionnaire sent every year to each biographee. Entries not confirmed for three consecutive years are dropped as a matter of editorial policy.

The biographical entries are divided into seven main sections: "Public Affairs," "Business," "Humanities," "Sciences," "Sciences Applied," "Social Sciences and Law," and "Miscellaneous." Under each section individual disciplines are listed, e.g., under social sciences and law: anthropology and sociology, economics, history, philosophy, psychology, and law. Some four hundred new entries are added in this edition out of eight hundred recommended to the editorial board. The volume concludes with a general index, a list of abbreviations, and an index of advertisers.

India Who's Who can be supplemented by *The Times of India Directory and Year Book Including Who's Who* (Bombay and London, Bennet, Coleman and Co., 1915- . Annual) or *Who's Who in India, 1967-* (New Delhi, Guide Pub., 1967-) published on an irregular basis.   Bohdan S. Wynar

101. Sharma, Jagdish Saran. **The National Biographical Dictionary of India**. New Delhi, Sterling Publishers (P) Ltd.; distr., Columbia, Mo., South Asia Books, 1972. 302p. index. o.p.

Although there appears to be a need for a good comprehensive Indian biographical dictionary covering men and women, past and present, who have made significant contributions to India's culture, art, literature and independence, *The National Biographical Dictionary of India* is not the kind of work which will fulfill that need. This dictionary, in its 265 pages, attempts to list in alphabetical order men, women, and even some Indian gods who have supposedly "played vital roles in the history of India."

One is compelled to point out the serious shortcomings and gross misrepresentations in this work. First, the preface claims "nearly five thousand entries." On actual count, however, there are only 1,247. About 343 entries are nothing but listings of some well-known, and many never-heard-of, freedom fighters who were killed during demonstrations against the British Raj or died in jails for India's freedom struggle. About two hundred additional entries list people who fought for India's independence and later served the Government of India in some capacity or other. This means that in fewer than seven hundred entries, the compiler covers a period of five thousand years and deals with areas as important and broad as literature, art, culture, kings, emperors, sportsmen, gods, and the rest.

Secondly, the entries are uneven in terms of both text and factual material. The entry length ranges anywhere from one line to several paragraphs. Some entries do not have any dates at all; others do not tell us when the person was born or died. A generous spread of names of freedom fighters is evident throughout the text, with one-line descriptions of how they died. Phrases such as "shot dead by army patrol," "killed during firing by police," "died by indiscriminate machine-gun fire," "died by bullet wound," "fired upon and killed by police," "tortured by police," "sentenced to death," "executed," "knocked down and killed by military truck," and so on abound on every single page of this work.

Numerous vague and unnecessary sentences consume a great deal of space in the biographical entries, as the following examples illustrate: "she was all positive, there was nothing negative in her," "wrote several books," "wrote eight books," "visited Europe many a time and died in London," "editor of *Navajivan Weekly* for some time," "he was very handsome."

One fails to understand why the compiler felt the need to include the Indian gods in this national biography. Selection of some gods and the exclusion of others is still another mystery which cannot be explained. For example, Ekvira, a relatively unknown goddess, is included, but Sarasvati, wife of Brahma and goddess of eloquence, learning, and wisdom, is omitted.

Although the print is clear and legible, spelling errors, misspelled names and awkward sentences are noticeable in the text as well as in the index.

Sharad Karkhanis

102. **Who's Who in China 1918-1950**. Hong Kong, Chinese Materials Center; distr., San Francisco, Calif., Chinese Materials Center, 1982. 3v. illus. index. $130.00/set. ISBN 0-89644-626-3.

Probably the first modern English-language publication of the Who's Who genre for China, this work was originally published in nine volumes (consisting of six editions and three supplements) issued between 1919 and 1950. It was begun by *Millard's Review of the Far East*, better known by its later name, the *China Weekly Review*, a leading English-language newspaper published in China from June 1907 until it went out of existence in July 1953. This current work, published in 1982 by the Chinese Materials Center in Hong Kong, is a reprint in three volumes of the entire original with a cumulative index prepared by Jerome Cavanaugh. This index contains 2,908 names of some of the best-known personalities in China. For many, biographical sketches were updated in subsequent editions. The cumulative index also incorporates the names, in alphabetical order, of about 580 alumni of Tsing-Hua College who studied in the United States on funds from the American remission of the Boxer Indemnity. These names were included in "Directory of American Returned Scholars" which was appended to the third edition published in 1925.

When begun, *Who's Who in China* was intended to be an annual, but successive wars and chaotic conditions within China frequently delayed publishing schedules, resulting in the nine volumes over a thirty-one-year span. In the early editions, the biographies were taken from a regular column in the weekly newspapers and were published in the order in which they appeared. With the third edition, all entries were arranged in alphabetical order by surname and the scope of the coverage was greatly expanded. For example, the first edition included only fifty-nine biographies while the third contained over one thousand and the fifth over fifteen hundred. To permit this expanded scope, biographies were sought from sources such as newspaper stories, official records, and individually submitted autobiographies.

Although other biographical works have appeared in recent years, such as Howard L. Boorman's *Biographical Dictionary of Republican China* in four volumes for which a separate index was published and the two-volume *Biographic Dictionary of Chinese Communism, 1921-1965*, this *Who's Who in China 1918-1950* remains the original and contemporary biographical publication on leading Chinese personalities in the first half of the twentieth century. The cumulative index greatly enhances the utility of this reprint.

Hwa-Wei Lee

103. **Who's Who in Japan 1984-85**. New York, International Culture Institute; distr., Chicago, Marquis Who's Who, 1984. 1083p. $185.00.

The first edition of *Who's Who in Japan* includes short biographical entries for individuals in government, commerce, medicine, journalism, and the arts. Governmental listings cover ministers, Diet members, and ranking members of governmental units and the civil service. Business biographies include the major executives in large industrial, commercial, and service firms.

Entries typically contain vital statistics, educational background, career history, honors, and a current address. Ephemeral information such as hobby interests is also listed.

The binding is insubstantial and no doubt constructed to warrant the purchase of the next edition in those libraries finding this directory useful.

No criteria for admission of entries are given. The expertise of the selectors is not indicated. Each entry is brief; and, in contrast to *Who's Who in America*, the more important individuals do not have longer, more extensive biographies. For example, the entry for the prime minister is the same length as the entry for the vice president of a national bakery. The size of corporations or the depth of management level in the corporation whose executives are included is not explained. As the parameters for selection are not indicated, it is impossible to check comprehensiveness. The major members of the current cabinet and the editors of major newspapers are included, however. Entry arrangement is alphabetical. There is neither a glossary of the types of businesses included nor an index. Because of its limitations, this directory is recommended only for libraries with extensive Japanese collections or a need for this type of specific information.

A more reliable work is *Japan Biographical Encyclopedia and Who's Who* (Tokyo, Japan Biographical Research Dept., Rengo Press, 1958-) that provides, in English, coverage of all prominent personalities, in all fields, of all periods, living and dead.

Eleanor DeLashmitt and Bohdan S. Wynar

AUSTRALIA AND NEW ZEALAND

104. **Australian Dictionary of Biography**. Carlton, Victoria, Melbourne University Press; distr., Portland, Oreg., International Scholarly Book Services, 1966- . In progress. (To be published in 12v.) $41.00/vol.

The *Australian Dictionary of Biography* is a projected twelve-volume compilation of biographical sketches, of which nine volumes have already been published. The first two volumes cover 1788-1850; volumes 3 and 4, 1851-1890; volumes 5 and 6, 1851-1890; volumes 7, 8, and 9, 1891-1939. Sketches range in length from under a page to seven pages, and when completed, the project will include some seven thousand biographies. All articles are signed and include a short list of reference sources, personal data, and information on careers and other contributions. According to the preface, this scholarly work is based on consultation and cooperation, and the "burden of writing has been shared by university historians and by members of historical and genealogical societies and other specialists." Some two thousand contributors are involved in this project, and "the placing of each individual's name in the appropriate section has been generally determined by when he did his most important work. For articles that overlap the chronological division, preference has usually been given to the earlier period, although all the important Federationists will appear in the third section, 1891-1939." A complete index of names will be published in the last volume.

A related title is *Who's Who in Australia* (23rd ed. Philadelphia, International Publications Service, 1980. 925p. $67.50. ISBN 0-8002-2541-4) that started in 1922 and was published by Herald and Weekly Times in Melbourne. The title and frequency of this current biography vary. The twentieth edition incorporated John's *Notable*

Australians, first published in 1906. Occasionally this work carries a subtitle, *An Australian Biographical Dictionary and Register of Titled Persons*.

Most larger libraries may also have *Debrett's Handbook of Australia and New Zealand* (2nd ed. distr., Chicago, Marquis Who's Who, 1984. $85.00. ISBN 0-949-137-006) that contains eight hundred brief biographies of prominent people in Australia and New Zealand. In addition to biographical sketches this handbook provides gazetteer-type information on both countries.   Bohdan S. Wynar

105. **Who's Who in New Zealand**. Edited by J. E. Traue. 11th ed. Wellington, New Zealand, A. H. and A. W. Reed; distr., Rutland, Vt., Charles E. Tuttle, 1978. 300p. $24.75. ISBN 0-589-01113-8.

Continuing a series begun in 1908, with the tenth edition having been published in 1971, this is the usual Who's Who type of publication, containing over three thousand entries covering living New Zealanders, including natives now resident elsewhere in the world and non-natives now resident in New Zealand. The entries are abbreviated, as is customary, and tend to be extremely brief, with many of ten lines or less in a double column format. In addition to the entries, there is a considerable amount of prefatory material, although somewhat less than in the tenth edition, providing listings not only of the current governmental structure and incumbents but the usual British-type listings of those people holding various awards, decorations, and honors. Among the more useful sections is an obituary listing giving the names, and place and date of death of those listed in the tenth edition who died between 1971-1977.

In a country as small as New Zealand, it is possible to include a wide range of people in this kind of directory, so one will find here not only figures considered prominent by American standards but many more from all walks of life with an emphasis on the intellectual, political, economic, and social side of New Zealand society. One will find included here, for example, the librarians of all of the larger New Zealand cities and of all the academic institutions. Virtually everyone from New Zealand that those using reference collections in American libraries are likely to be interested in will be found here, but since the number of such inquiries is likely to be somewhat limited, this volume is of value only to large libraries and those with a special interest in New Zealand.

For retrospective coverage, one should consult *A Dictionary of New Zealand Biography*, edited by G. H. Scholefield (2v. Wellington, Dept. of Internal Affairs, 1940). It is a national biography modeled after *DAB* and includes most notables for this territory since European migration.   Norman D. Stevens and Bohdan S. Wynar

CANADA

106. **Canadian Who's Who 1979, Volume XX**. Keiran Simpson, ed. Toronto and Buffalo, University of Toronto Press, 1985. 1362p. $85.00. ISBN 0-8020-4626-6. ISSN 0068-9963.

The first edition of *Canadian Who's Who* was published in 1910 by the Times Publishing Company (London); the second edition appeared in 1936, published by A. L. Tunnell, who had acquired the rights. It has been published triennially ever since. In 1978, Tunnell sold it to the University of Toronto Press, which will presumably maintain the publishing schedule. Unfortunately, recent volumes were not available for inspection.

Beyond updating, adding (eleven hundred new names), and deleting through demise, differences between the thirteenth (1975) edition and the fourteenth (1979) edition are slight. It is the same bulky book in red cover, presenting data on seven thousand or so Canadians who are living at home or abroad. Thus it is very similar to *Who's Who in America*, using the questionnaire technique to verify data on vital facts, education, awards, writings, current occupations, addresses, and so forth. And, of course, there is no charge for this service (fees are paid for *Who's Who in Canada*). Checking through the book for names of friends and others (there is no point in questioning selection principles), I have uncovered several errors and omissions—one librarian has apparently dropped out of sight after 1964; one writer's entry has no mention of her academic occupation; one address has the street but not the number; several hundred addresses are not even given. It is hoped that some of these errors will be corrected through the supplements (available as four semiannual issues). Other spinoffs include a *Who's What* occupation index and a *Who's Where* geographic index, both separately published.

Canadian Who's Who can be supplemented by *Who's Who in Canada: An Illustrated Biographical Record of Canada's Leading Men and Women in Business, Government and Academia*, seventy-fifth anniversary edition (Ernest W. Whelpton, ed. Agincourt, Ont., Global Press; distr., Philadelphia, International Publications Service, 1985. 1600p. $150.00. ISBN 0-771-539-57-6). First published in 1910 by International Press Ltd., it was acquired in 1983 by Global Press, a division of Gage Publishing Ltd. It contains over three thousand brief biographies of the Who's Who type, plus portraits. Biographical sketches are preceded by sections on the governor general, the prime minister, the leader of the opposition, and premiers. A corporate index concludes the volume.   Dean Tudor and Bohdan S. Wynar

107. Creative Canada. A Biographical Dictionary of Twentieth-Century Creative and Performing Artists. 1971-1972. Compiled by Reference Division, McPherson Library, University of Victoria. Toronto, Buffalo, N.Y., published in association with McPherson Library, University of Victoria, by University of Toronto Press. 1971-1972. 2v. $35.00/vol. LC 71-1513837. ISBN 0-8020-3262-1 (vol. 1); 0-8020-3285-0 (vol. 2).

The purpose of this set is to cover those "creative and performing artists who have contributed as individuals to the culture of Canada in the twentieth century, and who have had this individual contribution recognized in print. The amount of critical acclaim in print has been a guide to the compilers, since it is inconceivable in this era of the media and the message that any artist will be of significance if he has not received critical acclaim in books, journal articles, or newspapers" (p. v). According to the stated objectives, the first volume includes authors of "works of the imagination," such as "artists and sculptors, musicians, and performing artists in the fields of ballet, modern dance, radio, theatre, television, and motion pictures; directors, designers, and producers in theatre, cinema, radio and television, and the dance." Excluded are architects, commercial artists, creators of handicraft and patrons of the arts, as well as journalists, historians, etc., "unless they have an established reputation as individual artists in one of the categories listed above." The first volume contains about five hundred entries in one alphabet and the length of the biographical sketches varies from a few lines to several pages. Many entries offer a great deal of detail that will not be found elsewhere (e.g., for the film producer Tom Daly we have over six pages, including even some minor awards, although for many writers (e.g., Mary E. Q. Innis) there is about half a column. Using the reasoning employed for film producers, one can justify the inclusion of critical works about writers.

Like the first volume, the second volume also contains about five hundred entries, with an approximate breakdown of 27 percent authors, 28 percent artists (painters, sculptors), 19 percent musicians, and 26 percent performing artists.

Our critical comments about the first volume apply for the second volume as well. The preface to the second volume justifies this imbalance with a statement that "because this dictionary is limited to an objective presentation of the facts of a given artist's life and career, the entry for each will depend on those facts. An artist of some stature producing very little actual material will not have as lengthy an entry as another of equal or lesser importance who has produced a great deal" (p. vi). Well, it seems to us that this is not a sound criterion; it is not enough simply to provide inventory-type information. One has to evaluate the information and put it in a proper perspective. Indeed, this is an interesting work, but in terms of editorial attention, it is still out of balance.

Bohdan S. Wynar

108. **Dictionary of Canadian Biography**. Frances G. Halpenny, ed. Toronto and Buffalo, N.Y., University of Toronto Press, 1966- . In progress. $45.00/vol.

Also published in French under the title *Dictionnaire biographique du Canada*, by Les Presses de l'Université Laval, Quebec. This is the most important Canadian retrospective biography patterned after *DNB* and *DAB*. It should be noted that the *Dictionary of Canadian Biography* is not being published in sequence. Volume 1, covering subjects who died before 1701, was published in 1966; volume 2, for the period 1701-1740, appeared in 1969; volume 10, for the decade 1871-1880, was published in 1972. The other volumes published at this writing are: volume 3, 1741-1770 in 1974; volume 4, 1771-1800 in 1979; volume 9, 1861-1870 in 1976; volume 11, 1881-1890 in 1982. A limited deluxe edition, Laurentian Edition, is also available at $100/vol., bound in morocco and buckram.

There is a major difference between *DCB* and the *DNB* and *DAB*. The Canadian work is being produced on the premise that coverage of a segment of time creates the most coherent frame for the consideration of a nation's major figures. In contrast, *DNB* and *DAB* were, in their main volumes, issued in straight alphabetical order. Their supplementary volumes, however, are appearing on a time-segment basis.

Editorial policy as stated in the preface includes the "Directives" supplied to contributors: "Each biography should be an informative and stimulating treatment of its subject, presented in readable form. All factual information should be precise and accurate, and be based upon reliable (preferably primary) sources. Biographies should not, however, be mere catalogues of dates and events, or compilations of previous studies of the same subject. The biographer should try to give the reader an orderly account of the personality and achievements of the subject against the background of the period in which the person lived and the events in which he or she participated."

Thus, for example, to reinforce the background of 1741-1770, the editor has included two clearly written historical review essays on the French forces and the British forces in the Seven Years War, written by W. J. Eccles and C. P. Stacey, respectively. These essays are particularly apposite because most of the 550 figures who died between 1741 and 1770 and are therefore treated in this volume were in one way or another involved in that eighteenth century struggle between Britain and France for commercial dominance of the North American continent.

Persons qualified for inclusion are those who took an active part or exerted major influences in that part of North America which later became Canada. Thus, we find many prominent French officers (e.g., the Marquis de Montcalm), British officers (e.g., General James Wolfe), and Indian chiefs (e.g., Pontiac).

An examination of sample biographies shows that the editors have accomplished their main goal: the sketches do indeed "give the reader an orderly account of the personality and achievements of the subject against the background of the period."

On the average, each volume contains some five hundred biographies ranging from four hundred to twelve hundred words in length. There are copious bibliographies, a full name index, and cross-references to other people and other volumes. A new feature in the eleventh volume is a regional index, subdivided by primary area of occupation. In short, *DCB* is an irreplaceable source of documentation on Canada and should find its place in any respectable library.   Bohdan S. Wynar

109.   Wallace, W. Stewart, ed. **The Macmillan Dictionary of Canadian Biography**. 4th ed. Revised, enlarged, and updated by W. A. McKay. Toronto, Macmillan of Canada, 1978. 914p. $49.95. ISBN 0-7705-1462-6.

The fourth edition of the *Macmillan Dictionary of Canadian Biography* contains over five thousand biographies of prominent Canadians and others with significant places in Canadian history who died before 1976. As in the past editions, there is a preponderance of political and military figures among the biographees; however, the editor has made an effort to include more artists, writers, scientists, and businessmen. All entries from the previous edition have been reviewed and changes made to insure accuracy. Particular attention has been paid to bibliographies that have been updated to include new sources. A few entries have been deleted in the interest of saving space.

Entries are concise, including full name, birth and death dates (including day and year), a brief account of the subject's life and contributions, and a bibliography of books and entries from standard biographical sources. Cross-references are provided, as are references to pseudonyms and other names or titles by which biographees may have been known. The *Dictionary*, an essential work that is all too infrequently revised (first edition, 1926; revisions: 1945, 1963, and 1978), should be in the collections of all academic libraries and all but the smallest public libraries.

To some extent, it can be supplemented by *Standard Dictionary of Canadian Biography: The Canadian Who Was Who*, edited by Charles G. D. Roberts and Arthur L. Tunnell (2v. Toronto, Trans-Canada Press, 1934-1938) that contains fairly long biographical sketches of Canadians who died during 1875-1937.

Gari-Anne Patzwald and Bohdan S. Wynar

EUROPE

110.   **International Biographical Dictionary of Central European Emigrés 1933-1945**. Herbert A. Strauss and Werner Röder, eds. Munich, New York, K. G. Saur, 1980-1983. 3v. $375.00. ISBN 3-598-10089-2.

Publication of these three volumes completes an important project concerning the emigrés that fled Nazi Germany between the years 1933 and 1945. It is a representative sampling of eighty-seven hundred individuals who achieved prominence in the arts, science, and literature among the more than five hundred thousand who fled. Each entry provides a brief paragraph of vital statistics (including religion, emigration information, and destination), a more descriptive paragraph describing activities, and a bibliography. Volume 3 is a complete index to volumes 1 and 2.

As far as could be determined, the information is accurate and complete and is marred only by occasional typographical errors that closer proofreading might have found but that do not interfere with the works' usefulness. Since a number of the individuals are listed in other sources, this may not be an essential source for all libraries. But for those interested in the period, in Central European history, or in American intellectual history, this is a vital publication. [R: Choice, Sept 84, p. 64]

Erwin K. Welsch

111.   Kay, Ernest, ed. **Dictionary of Scandinavian Biography**. London, Melrose Press; distr., Totowa, N.J., Biblio Distribution Centre, 1972-1976. 2v. $55.00/set. LC 73-189270. ISBN 0-900332-204 (vol. 1); 0-900332-352 (vol. 2).

Contains some thirty-six hundred biographical sketches of the Who's Who type, covering prominent personalities of Denmark, Finland, Iceland, Norway, and Sweden. It has more listings than the *International Who's Who*, but not as many as biographical dictionaries published in several of the above-mentioned countries. There are some notable omissions on the same order as those apparent in another work by the same editor and publisher—*Dictionary of Latin American and Caribbean Biography*. [R: Choice, Mar 73, p. 60; WLB, Sept 72, p. 95]

Bohdan S. Wynar

112.   Kay, Ernest, ed. **Who's Who in Western Europe**. 2nd ed. Cambridge, England, International Biographical Centre; distr., Totowa, N.J., International Biographical Centre, 1984 (c1983). 670p. illus. $135.00. ISBN 0-900332-67-0.

When the first edition of this work was reviewed in publications, including *ARBA*, it was "not recommended" for purchase. Unfortunately, seemingly very little (if anything) has been done to improve the work in the interim.

A potpourri of sources (in addition to questionnaires) has been used to compile the biographical information included. This hodgepodge of sources is clearly evident in the hodgepodge of entries—they represent an uneven catchall of individuals, a number of whom would be of dubious value to any biographical reference work.

Another curious inclusion is a group of eight individuals highlighted in detail, including photographs, at the beginning of the work. There is no rationale offered for their inclusion other than the statement that they are "distinguished people from European countries." One can only speculate as to why they were included and not others.

Because of its poor quality (and accompanying high price tag), this second edition is still not recommended.

Apparently the third edition will be published in 1985 and will be distributed in Philadelphia by International Publications Service ($150.00. ISBN 0-90033-261-1).

Ronald Rayman

113.   Lewytzkyj, Borys, and Juliusz Stroynowski, eds. **Who's Who in the Socialist Countries: A Biographical Encyclopedia of 10,000 Leading Personalities in 16 Communist Countries**. 1st ed. New York, K. G. Saur; Munich, Verlag Dokumentation, 1978. 736p. $95.00. LC 78-4068. ISBN 0-89664-011-6.

As most specialists know, communist countries do not publish biographical directories of the Who's Who type. One can find only a minimum of biographical information in numerous Soviet or Eastern European general or subject encyclopedias, and the few directories that do exist provide information only on full and associate members of the Soviet Academy of Sciences and on the most prominent Soviet scholars. It is extremely difficult to find biographical information on Soviet or Eastern European officials, and one must search hundreds of "official sources" (usually newspapers and journals) to get bits and pieces of biographical data. As a result, biographical directories published in the West are incomplete and provide only fragmentary information. This is the case with *Who's Who in Communist China* (published already in several editions by Union Research Institute, Hong Kong); *Party and Government Officials of the Soviet Union, 1917-1967* (Scarecrow, 1969); *The Soviet Diplomatic Corps, 1917-1967* (Scarecrow, 1970); and especially *Who Was Who in the USSR: A Biographic Directory Containing Five Thousand and Fifteen Biographies of Prominent Soviet Historical Personalities* (compiled by the Institute for the Study of the USSR and published by Scarecrow in 1972).

The present volume is no exception; there are obvious gaps in its coverage. Out of twenty thousand biographical sketches, at least half are of Soviet personalities, primarily government officials, party functionaries, and some prominent scholars. The information for these biographies comes primarily from Lewytzkyj's archives — clippings and notes from all available Soviet reference books, hundreds of daily and weekly Soviet newspapers, and other sources. (Lewytzkyj is the author of many books on the Soviet Union in several languages and, with the possible exception of Professor Armstrong from Wisconsin University, has the most extensive private archives on this subject.)

Somewhat weaker is the representation of biographies of people from fifteen other communist countries prepared by Professor Stroynowski who left his native Poland in 1969. The emphasis is again on government and party officials, but there are also rather lengthy biographies on scholars, writers, and other personalities, not all of national importance. Obviously, it is much easier to obtain biographical data on Polish or Yugoslav officials than on Soviet personalities. Thus, coverage is uneven, and biographical sketches vary in length, depending on the relative importance of the biographee. Nevertheless, considering the magnitude of this work, both editors should be congratulated on preparing a unique reference work that will be of great interest to all students of Eastern European studies. [R: Choice, Dec 78, p. 1350; LJ, 1 Sept 78, p. 1626; WLB, Nov 78, p. 275]   Bohdan S. Wynar

114.   Partington, Paul G. **Who's Who on the Postage Stamps of Eastern Europe**. Metuchen, N.J., Scarecrow, 1979. 498p. illus. bibliog. index. $34.00. LC 79-22183. ISBN 0-8108-1266-5.

This is a comprehensive biographical dictionary in English of individuals who have appeared on the postage stamps of Albania, Bulgaria, Czechoslovakia, East Germany, Hungary, Poland, Rumania, and Yugoslavia. It required an enormous effort to go through the *Scott Standard Postage Stamp Catalogue*, identifying personalities, locating biographical sketches in dictionaries and encyclopedias, and then having them translated; and Editor Partington, a philatelic writer and stamp collector, has engaged the services of an impressive array of talent, which includes librarians, academics, and philatelists. What results is a fine contribution to the study of Eastern European personalities based on the major biographical sources of those countries. In the case of minor personalities and others not covered by biographical tools (Albania is extremely weak in biographical coverage), the biographies are written by area specialists.

The book is divided into three sections, the major one being "Native Personalities," which provides alphabetical access to thousands of East Europeans who have been honored on postage stamps. Included here are detailed biographical sketches; Scott Catalog numbers of stamps issued, together with dates and country of issue; and in some cases illustrations of the stamps. Of importance is the inclusion of abbreviations of the biographical tools used. Section 2 is an alphabetical listing of foreign personalities honored, giving dates of birth and death, nationality, and occupation, followed by Scott Catalog number and dates and place of issue. Section 3 is a topical index, listing by occupation or activity the various people covered. The topic "Communists" seems to be an anomaly of logic here, since, as a general category, it embraces people who properly might have been placed under an occupation. For example, Marx and Engels are found here but not in the "Philosophers" category. The book concludes with a listing of the one hundred biographical sources employed, together with their abbreviation symbols. Owing to the paucity of English-language tools of this nature, the work should prove to be an important source of reference and research information for librarians, scholars, and philatelists. Ron Blazek

115. Who Was Who in the Greek World: 776 BC-30 BC. Edited by Diana Bowder. Ithaca, N.Y., Phaidon Book/Cornell University Press, 1982. 227p. illus. maps. bibliog. index. $29.95; $8.50pa. LC 82-71594. ISBN 0-8014-1538-1; 0-671-50159-3pa.

This title is the companion volume to *Who Was Who in the Roman World, 753 B.C.—A.D. 476*. Alphabetically arranged, the entries contain biographical information about important Greeks and non-Greeks who were important in Greek history. With each biographical sketch, the length of which varies from very brief to extensive, there is at least one bibliographic citation. Well illustrated with pertinent maps, the book also contains a helpful glossary and bibliography. [R: BL, 1 Feb 83, p. 712; Choice, Apr 83, p. 1116; LJ, Jan 83, p. 122] Bohdan S. Wynar

116. Who Was Who in the Roman World, 753 B.C.—A.D. 476. Edited by Diana Bowder. Ithaca, N.Y., Cornell University Press, 1980. 256p. illus. maps. bibliog. index. (A Phaidon Book). $32.50. LC 80-67821. ISBN 0-8014-1358-3.

An entertaining, highly readable, and comprehensive biographical dictionary covering the twelve hundred years from the founding of the city of Rome to the collapse of the Western Empire. It is comprised of entries about one thousand persons, "statesmen and philosophers, saints and scoundrels," but not limited to Roman citizens. The scope includes individuals who influenced the Roman world regardless of nationality, including the principals involved in the establishing of Christianity; the Ptolemys of Egypt; and Attila, king of the Huns.

The biographic entries are extensively supported through the use of maps, stemmata of the important houses, a chronology table to place rulers and major events in time, and over 250 photographs of statuary, commemorative coins, wood cuts, monuments, and sites, giving life and personality to ancient names. The entries are nicely cross-referenced and are even supplemented by an index of persons considered too minor to list in the body. A brief glossary is included along with a modest bibliography.

This book is an asset to the student of Roman history and is highly recommended for any library concerned with ancient history. [R: Choice, Apr 81, p. 1078; LJ, 15 Feb 81, p. 439; WLB, Feb 81, p. 461] George Vogler

117. **Who Was Who in the USSR: A Biographic Directory Containing 5,015 Biographies of Prominent Soviet Historical Personalities**. Compiled by the Institute for the Study of the USSR. Metuchen, N.J., Scarecrow, 1972. 687p. index. o.p. LC 70-161563. ISBN 0-8108-0441-7.

This biographical directory covers important Soviet persons no longer living. According to the preface, "it includes a certain number of biographies of people who actively campaigned against the Soviet regime or were later exiled or put to death by the Soviet authorities." Criteria for selection are stated in the preface: "contains 5,015 biographies of prominent individuals who made major contributions to the political, intellectual, scientific, social and economic life of the country." Thus, this is a sequel to other of the Institute's publications, such as *Biographic Directory of the USSR* (Scarecrow, 1958), two volumes of *Who's Who in the USSR* for 1961-1962 and 1965-1966 (published by International Book and Publishing Co. in 1962 and 1966), *Prominent Personalities in the USSR* (Scarecrow, 1968), and *Party or Government Officials of the Soviet Union 1917-1967* (Scarecrow, 1969).

Biographical sketches vary in length, depending on the relative importance of the biographee and, of course, on the availability of sources. Thus, we find a fairly lengthy article on M. S. Grushevskiy (which should actually be Hrushevskyi—to use the Ukrainian transliteration found in all standard sources, including Horecky's bibliographical guides), but rather inadequate treatment of Mykola Khvylovyi (real name Fitilov and not Fitilyova), a Ukrainian writer who committed suicide in 1933. The coverage is meager, also, for S. V. Petlura, ranking in importance with Hrushevskyi with respect to Ukrainian affairs in the Soviet Union. Thus, the coverage of Ukrainians is rather uneven, a fact which applies, to some extent, to other prominent non-Russians as well. In addition, citations of the original works of non-Russian authors are inaccurate. They are given in Russian translation, rather than in the original language—and often in poor Russian translation. We find much better coverage of Russian personalities, including some of only minor importance—e.g., F. K. Mironov, military commander; diplomat A. I. Plakhin; or the Russian critic Adrian I. Piotrovskiy, to name only a few. Occasionally the editors have problems with English terminology (e.g., M. M. Pistrak is called an "educationist," rather than an "educator"). The treatment provided for L. G. Kornilov, one of the co-founders of the Russian Volunteer Army, is rather inadequate, in spite of the fact that there are many biographical studies about him. And occasionally the editors take official Soviet material at face value—see the biography of I. P. Kripyakevich or, an even better example, the noted literary historian V. N. Peretts.

Summing up, the coverage is uneven. However, considering the magnitude of the undertaking, this biographical directory is among the best works compiled by the Institute. [R: Choice, Sept 72, p. 795; LJ, 15 May 72, p. 1799]

Bohdan S. Wynar

118. **Who's Who in Austria: A Biographical Dictionary of Prominent Personalities from and in Austria**. 10th ed. Zurich, Who's Who AG; distr., Chicago, Marquis Who's Who, 1983. 1225p. (International Red Series). $100.00. ISBN 3-921220-44-0.

This tenth edition contains approximately fifty-five hundred biographies of typical Who's Who type information. Each volume has two parts: (1) who's who section and (2) directory of organizations, institutions, associations, and societies. Emphasis is on contemporary political personalities, scholars, artists, writers, business executives, and other categories of prominent personalities in contemporary Austria. More strict criteria for selection were evident in the German work *Österreicher der Gegenwart* (Vienna, Österreichische Staatsdruckerrei, 1951) edited by Österreich Institut that contained biobibliographical data on some twenty-five hundred Austrians plus vocational index. This volume is also available from International Publications Service in Philadelphia at $174.00 (ISBN 0-8002-3836-2).   Bohdan S. Wynar

119. **Who's Who in France. Qui est qui en France**. 16th ed. Paris, Lafitte; distr., Philadelphia, International Publications Service, 1983. 1436p. $150.00. ISBN 2-85784-016-0.

The first edition was published in 1953, covering 1953-1954 and providing some five thousand biographical sketches of Who's Who type. Subsequently it became a biennial and the present edition contains some twenty thousand biographies covering a wide range of prominent personalities in France, including not only those in the metropolitan area of Paris as it did in the 1950s. It is an excellent work, superior in graphics to *Who's Who in America* or *Who's Who*.   Bohdan S. Wynar

120. **Who's Who in Germany**. 8th ed. Zurich, Who's Who AG, 1983; distr., Chicago, Marquis Who's Who, 1983. 1388p. (International Red Series). $100.00. ISBN 3-921220-46-7.

The eighth edition contains approximately 17,500 biographies of prominent Germans including politicians, scholars, writers, community leaders, artists, and business people. Information is typical of Who's Who. There is an extensive appendix listing German associations, societies, and institutions. A more comprehensive coverage is provided in the German language *Wer ist Wer? Das deutsche Who's Who* (Berlin, Arani, 1905- . Title and frequency vary) that starting with the fourteenth edition (1962-1965), is published in two volumes, covering Federal Republic and West Berlin in the first and German Democratic Republic in the second. The most important retrospective biography is *Neue Deutsche Biographie* 1953- (supercedes the 56-volume *Allgemeine deutsche Biographie*, 1875-1912) that is still in progress, with more than fifteen volumes published.   Bohdan S. Wynar

121. **Who's Who in Italy**. 4th ed. Zurich, Who's Who AG; distr., Chicago, Marquis Who's Who, 1983. 700p. (International Red Series). $100.00. ISBN 3-921220-38-6.

Started in 1958, this biography of contemporaries is now published by Who's Who AG, Zurich, an international publishing house that has branches in several countries. It includes some seven thousand personalities from Italy and the Vatican. Appendixes provide listings of important organizations and associations. *Chi è? Dizionario degli Italiani d'oggi* (Rome, Scarano, 1928-) provides a more comprehensive coverage of some seven thousand prominent Italians but, unfortunately, is not issued on a regular basis.   Bohdan S. Wynar

122. **Who's Who in Poland**. 1st ed. Zurich, Who's Who AG; distr., Chicago, Marquis Who's Who, 1983. 1107p. (International Red Series). $100.00. ISBN 3-921229-56-4.

This is the only biographical dictionary of Polish contemporaries in English including some seventy-five hundred biographical sketches of prominent people from all walks of life: government officials, members of the Party, military personnel, writers, artists, faculty members, etc. The appendix lists important organizations, institutions, and societies. For retrospective coverage, one should consult *Polski*

Stownik biograficzny (Krakow, Akademja Umiejetnósci, 1935- . In progress), a multi-volume set of scholarly biographies (three thousand to five thousand words per entry) patterned after *DNB*. Over twenty volumes have been published so far.

Bohdan S. Wynar

123. **Who's Who in Switzerland, Including the Principality of Liechtenstein, 1950/51-** . Geneva, Nagel, 1985; distr., Philadelphia, International Publications Service. 1985. 620p. $135.00. ISBN 2-8263-0790-8.

The first volume was published in 1950 and included over thirty-nine hundred brief biographies. The present edition, the thirteenth, includes over four thousand biographical sketches of Who's Who type, plus a glossary and list of abbreviations. It can be supplemented by the *Swiss Who's Who*, 1st ed. (distr., Chicago, Marquis Who's Who, 1983. 600p. $100.00. ISBN 3-921220-74-2) that is somewhat more comprehensive, covering both Switzerland and Liechtenstein, and includes fifty-five hundred personalities.   Bohdan S. Wynar

124. **Who's Who in the Soviet Union: A Biographical Encyclopedia of 5,000 Leading Personalities in the Soviet Union.** Edited by Borys Lewytzkyj. New York, K. G. Saur, 1984. 428p. $125.00. ISBN 3-598-10467-7.

Complements *Who's Who in Socialist Countries* also edited by Lewytzkyj, who unfortunately died not very long ago, though this fact is not noted by the publisher. The emphasis in this volume is on government officials and prominent members of the Communist party, Komsomol, trade union and other bodies, with more selective coverage of scholars, artists, writers, and teaching faculty. The period covered is approximately 1976-1982. The late Dr. Lewytzkyj relied on his extensive archives plus clippings and notes from all available Soviet reference sources, newspapers, journals, etc. Selected major figures who have died, retired, or been dismissed are also listed. Concluding this volume is a listing of several appendixes, e.g., listing of several official Soviet bodies (Politbureau of the Central Committee of the Soviet Union, as well as all republics, members of the Central Committee, first secretaries, oblast committees, etc.). There is also a separate listing of the members of government, including ministries of foreign affairs, and defense. This type of information is repeated for all the republics, and the volume concludes with separate name indexes for scientists, authors, artists, military leaders, jurists, journalists, cosmonauts, architects, athletes, etc. Dissidents (with the exception of Sakharov and a few others) are not listed. All in all, this is an essential biographical work, with better execution than *Who's Who in the Socialist Countries.*   Bohdan S. Wynar

125. Wistrich, Robert. **Who's Who in Nazi Germany**. New York, Macmillan, 1982. 359p. bibliog. $17.75. LC 82-4704. ISBN 0-02-630600-X.

Essentially a biographical dictionary of almost 350 figures who exerted significant influence during the rise, zenith, and demise of Nazi power in Germany, this work should be titled *Who Was Who*. Narrative style entries average three hundred words, and the treatment in each is chronological. Personalities include both friends and foes of Nazism. Many represent the military, but more than a few were notable in contemporary art, science, academia, industry, and entertainment. Career highlights are delineated succinctly, footnotes are eschewed, and q.v. cross-referencing is frequent. The author attempts, with mixed success, to link each biographee to the Third Reich and the enormously intricate machine that was Hitlerian Germany. His admittedly subjective opinion of de-Nazification court actions is not complimentary. In all other aspects, however, his approach is relatively unbiased. Much background data has been drawn from German publications which form the bulk of an appended bibliography. In addition, there are a glossary of terms plus a comparative list of ranks vis-à-vis U.S. and British counterparts.

Targeted for the lay reader or tyro researcher, this work is both readable and informative. It constitutes a valuable basic insight into the Nazi phenomenon. [R: BL, 1 Oct 82, p. 187; LJ, 15 Sept 82, p. 1745; WLB, Dec 82, p. 352]

Lawrence E. Spellman

GREAT BRITAIN AND COMMONWEALTH

Current Biographies

126. **Debrett's Handbook, 1982: Distinguished People in British Life**. Charles Mosley, ed. London, Debrett's Peerage; distr., Chicago, Marquis Who's Who, 1981. 1648p. $80.00. ISBN 0-905649-38-9.

As the title page says, this "comprises short biographies of The Royal Family, the peerage, baronetage, bearers of courtesy titles, businessmen, industrialists, and prominent people with correct forms of epistolary address." There are excellent articles on the social recognition of titles of honor and precedence of peerages. Also included are an introduction, preface, lists of abbreviations and symbols, alphabetization guide, and a section of advertisements.

This thick (1,648 pages, mostly double-column) volume is complete as of late 1981. It is not only a Who's Who of England, Scotland, Wales, and Northern Ireland, but also of the Irish peerage plus residents of past and present Commonwealth nations who hold British titles and/or orders. The short biographies are only of the living, but are connected to the past by quotations, anecdotes, and comments. In certain cases, there are tidbits of fascinating information about the biographee or his/her forebears. Listings include all subsidiary titles for the Royal Family and the peerage. Addresses are given for almost all those included, and phone numbers are noted for many.

A new edition of this standard work is most welcome and will be especially useful for students of Great Britain, the nobility, and genealogy. It should be noted, however, that there is another biographical source of long tradition, namely *Kelly's Handbook of the Titled, Landed and Official Classes* (London, Kelly Directories, 1880-) published annually. Biographies are brief and factual and the coverage includes members of Parliament, government officials, prominent writers, artists, and business people. The emphasis is on landed proprietors. In addition, Debrett's has also published *Debrett's Peerage and Baronetage: Comprises Information concerning the Royal Family, the Peerage and Baronetage*, edited by Charles Kidd and David Williamson (1v. London, Macmillan; distr., Chicago, Marquis Who's Who, 1985. (various paging). $125.00), which gives information on individuals in the aristocracy exclusively.

Eleanor Elving Schwartz and Bohdan S. Wynar

127. **Who's Who in the Commonwealth**. Edited by Ernest Kay. Totowa, N.J., International Biographical Centre, 1982. 672p. $75.00. ISBN 0-900332-63-8.

As the title of this work indicates, it is concerned with providing biographical information about significant people in Commonwealth nations, including the United

Kingdom. Entries are based on questionnaires that the publisher sent to the individuals selected for inclusion. It claims to be the first biographical reference book to concentrate on the Commonwealth, a group of nations it compares in significance to the United States and the USSR. A random sample of entries from ten pages indicates that men predominate (seventy-seven of eighty-three entries examined). Residents of Australia and the United Kingdom comprised twenty-three and twenty of these entries, respectively. Nigerians form the next most common group, with fourteen. In contrast, India and Canada seem somewhat underrepresented, with one and four entries each.

The method used to select biographees is never stated, although the editor points out that there is no charge for an entry and no obligation for biographees to buy the book. Educators, politicans, civil servants, lawyers, doctors, and more are included. Still, the absence of people like Canadian writer Robertson Davies, Australian film director Peter Weir, former Indian prime minister Morarji Desai, Tanzanian president Julius Nyerere, and Australian actor Mel Gibson casts doubt on this work's comprehensiveness. The well-known people appearing in this work also appear in *Who's Who* or *International Who's Who*, often with identical entries. Therefore, if a library already possesses those works, it should only consider the book under review if there is a need for information about less well-known residents of the Commonwealth.

Ronald H. Fritze

128. **Who's Who, 1985-1986: An Annual Biographical Dictionary**. 137th ed. New York, St. Martin's Press, 1985. 2143p. $115.00. LC 4-16933. ISBN 0-312-87474-X.

This 1985-1986 edition of *Who's Who* announces the continuation of work that has a proud tradition. With its beginning in 1849 and continuing through 1896, it was limited to lists of names, without biographies, of British nobility. Beginning with the year 1897, it became a biographical dictionary, including the nobility as well as prominent people regardless of class.

The typical biography in *Who's Who* is detailed and factual: facts such as date of birth, spouse's and children's names, education, positions held, address, recreation, and, if the entrant is an author, a list of his or her work. *Who's Who* remains primarily British, and this is announced early in the volume with "*Who's Who* 1985: The Royal Family." Also included throughout are some notables of other countries in the arts, politics, and entertainment.

For the most part, *Who's Who* is easy to use. The biographies are arranged alphabetically beginning with "page 1." It is rather confusing, however, to find that there are thirty-five prefatory pages, also with Arabic numbers beginning with "page 1." Also included in this section are abbreviations used in the volume, an obituary list of persons whose biographies will be included later in *Who Was Who*, and a supplement which includes alterations received too late for inclusion in this edition.

Who's Who is the pioneer work of this type of biographical dictionary, and over the years has been regarded as a dependable, accurate reference. All of the larger libraries will want to have it in their reference collections. For the smaller libraries, it will be well to compare *Who's Who* with *International Who's Who*, as both are expensive publications and there is some duplication.   Jefferson D. Caskey

Retrospective Biographies

129.   Aubrey, John. **Brief Lives**. Edited by Richard Barber. Totowa, N.J., Barnes & Noble Books, 1982. 332p. $22.50. LC 82-24416. ISBN 0-386-20366-1.

Most of the material in Aubrey's *Brief Lives* was written between 1679 and 1680. The present volume is an attempt to reproduce the lives of some two hundred figures of sixteenth- and seventeenth-century England as described by Aubrey, but in modern spelling and with the Latin words and phrases omitted or translated. Since Aubrey died leaving his work incomplete and mostly in confused notebooks, Barber, the editor, had a considerable task. He points out in the introduction that for each biographical sketch, the material found in the manuscripts of the *Lives* is given first, followed by material from other sections of Aubrey's works or his letters. A symbol is used in the text to indicate a change in the source or that the material was written at a different time. Barber includes brief introductory notes before each of the biographical sketches, which are arranged alphabetically by the name of the biographee, except for the sketch of Aubrey, written by himself, which comes first. The sketches are of little-known and well-known Englishmen (almost all are men) and range in length from three lines for the daughter of a wealthy merchant who married her footman to fifteen pages for Thomas Hobbes. There is no table of contents or index, so one must page through sections of the work to find a specific person.

Information about most of the people included in the volume can be found in standard biographical dictionaries, but probably none of those has the human interest and sometimes gossipy accounts found in Aubrey. As a reference work, this might be included as supplementary to standard works, but it must be used with some caution in seeking factual information. It should, however, be included in a general collection for the pleasure it provides readers interested in the period.   Lucille Whalen

130.   Banks, Olive. **The Biographical Dictionary of British Feminists. Volume One: 1800-1930**. New York, New York University Press; distr., New York, Columbia University Press, 1985. 239p. index. $55.00. LC 85-3110. ISBN 0-8147-1078-6.

This biographical dictionary is designed for persons interested in the development of the British feminist movement between 1800 and 1930. It is made up of sketches of both women and men who contributed their time, effort, and money to advancing the progress of the women's movement in Great Britain. The time limit of 1930 represents the closing of an era when women's suffrage was a primary issue. It is anticipated that descriptions of later generations of feminists who faced different problems will be included in the next volume. The subjects presented here were chosen to convey both the variety and complexity of the issues, recognizing the fact that individuals frequently changed their positions over time.

Entries in the *Dictionary* are alphabetical under the name by which the individual is most likely to be recognized, with cross-references to others in the index of names. Insofar as possible, each sketch includes a full account of the subject's life, with an emphasis upon facts and situations that affected her/his involvement in the feminist movement. A summary of additional biographical sources of information and cross-references to other listings in the book are found with each essay.

A concise history of the feminist movement is included in the introduction. An index of topics completes this well-written work.   Lorraine Mathies

131.   Baylen, Joseph O., and Norbert J. Gossman, eds. **Biographical Dictionary of Modern British Radicals**. Brighton, England, Harvester Press; distr., Salem, N.H., Salem House, 1979-1980. 3v. $75.00/vol.

According to the intentions of its editors (two American professors of history), this new biographical dictionary is intended to "supplement and in some cases correct the biographical sketches in the *Dictionary of National Biography*." A six-page introduction sets forth the aims and limitations of the dictionary and provides a brief historical background. The term "radical" receives a fairly broad interpretation and is meant to include anyone who advocated a substantial change in Britain's political, economic, and social institutions.

Each entry begins with a short paragraph that identifies the individual, placing him (only five women were selected in the first volume) within the political, social, or cultural movements of the time. The biographical sketch itself ranges in length from one-half page to seven pages, and concludes with a short bibliography (in narrative form, rather than merely a listing of sources). Some of the lengthier sketches are for Robert Owen, Thomas Paine, David Ricardo, William Blake, Charles James Fox (a leader of parliamentary opposition), and William Roscoe (a reformer and leader in the abolition movement). Some other well-known names merit lesser consideration: Percy Bysshe Shelley, John Witherspoon, William Hazlitt, Jeremy Bentham, and, surprisingly, Josiah Wedgwood.

Since most of the important figures are adequately treated in the *DNB*, the chief value of this set for libraries lies in the information provided about the less-widely-known radicals. Ralph Eddowes is an appropriate example. He was a reformer in the city of Chester before emigrating to the United States, where he became an important Unitarian leader. He is not mentioned at all in the *DNB*, but rates six pages in *Modern British Radicals*. Likewise, William Duckett (an Irish supporter of the French Revolution) and John McCreery (a printer and organizer) received only short entries in the *DNB*, but have five and six pages, respectively, in *MBR*. However, a few of the radicals fared much better in the *DNB*: Fox received seventeen pages, compared to five in *MBR*; and there are eighteen pages for O'Connell and ten pages for Paine.

The entries in *Modern British Radicals* are signed, and a list of contributors (with academic affiliations) is included. There is an index, which is nothing more than a table of contents for the volumes. For libraries with extensive research holdings in British history, there are cross-references to entries in the *Dictionary of Labour Biography*. This set should be an important acquisition for most academic libraries. Unfortunately, the inordinately high price tag will probably restrict availability to only the largest research libraries. [R: Choice, Dec 79, p. 1283]   Thomas A. Karel

132.   Bellamy, Joyce M., and John Saville, eds. **Dictionary of Labour Biography**. Fairfield, N.J., Augustus M. Kelley, 1972- . vol. 1- . In progress. $37.50/vol. LC 78-185417.

The dictionary has been planned as a multivolume project, each volume of which will be a self-contained unit with a comprehensive subject index and a cumulative index of entries. The time span of the dictionary covers the period of modern industrialism — from the last decades of the eighteenth century to the present. Living persons are excluded. Its aim is to include anyone who was active, at any level, in the organizations and institutions of the British labour movement as well as those who influenced the development of radical and socialist ideas.

So far seven volumes have been published. Each volume contains between seventy and one hundred entries, from six hundred to eight thousand words each, with twenty-five hundred to three thousand being a typical length. Entries are based on primary sources, with heavy drafts, where possible, on personal information from colleagues, friends, and relatives (among whom the authors of the sketches, when not subject specialists, are frequently found). The unique opportunity presented here to give full treatment to hitherto neglected or local figures is not lost. Also admirable are the bibliographies, a treasure trove of manuscript and archival sources, newspaper references, pamphlets, documents, and lists of personal informants. The biographee's own writings are listed in full and secondary sources are also well represented.

The editors foresee no end to this project either by number of volumes or by closing date. The project will continue until all potential biographees have been written up. The volumes follow no alphabetic or chronologic sequence, the entries in each volume clustering loosely around a variety of movements or periods. The present volume, for instance, contains (to quote the dust jacket) "entries concerned with the Chartist, Secularist, and Clarion movements, with New Unionism, and with a cross-section of MPs, trade unionists and others active in the labour movement in the late nineteenth and twentieth centuries."   David Rosenbaum and Bohdan S. Wynar

133. **Biographical Dictionary of British Radicals in the Seventeenth Century**. Richard L. Greaves and Robert Zaller, eds. Brighton, England, Harvester Press; distr., Atlantic Highlands, N.J., Humanities Press, 1982-1984. 3v. $200.00/set; $75.00/vol. ISBN 0-85527-133-7 (vol. 1); 0-7108-0430-X (vol. 2); 0-7108-0486-5 (vol. 3).

This new dictionary is similar in purpose, style, and format to the three-volume *Biographical Dictionary of Modern British Radicals*. The 1600s in England were more than a time of exploration and colonization (Jamestown, Plymouth, William Penn, etc.). It was, first, the period of Stuart rule—James I and Charles I; the Great Protestation; the Petition of Right; the Long Parliament; Civil War; Cromwell's Commonwealth; the Restoration; the Declaration of Rights; and the acceptance of the Crown by William and Mary. It was a turbulent time; many of those included in this dictionary were imprisoned, and some were executed. The term *radical* is somewhat ambiguous during this period, though the editors provide a lengthly introduction in which their concept is explained. Thus, a diverse group wears the label radical— politicians, poets, Puritans, Quakers, and soldiers. Most of these radicals were seeking reforms in the existing political system and were opposed to the excesses of arbitrary government. Ultimately, they helped establish "the principle that England would be governed not by men but by law."

The first volume (A-F) contains over 350 entries written by contributors who are affiliated, mostly, with British and American universities. These biographical sketches tend to be fairly brief, averaging about half a page in length. There are, however, many substantial entries for the major figures: Oliver Cromwell, George Fox, Sir John Eliot, Sir Anthony Ashley Cooper (First Earl of Shaftesbury), Sir Edward Coke, John Bunyan, Daniel Defoe, Robert Cotton, William Fiennes, and Margaret Fell. A brief bibliography accompanies each entry, though the works cited are usually abbreviated. The reader must then consult a list of bibliography abbreviations in the front of the volume, where the citations are still incomplete.

In the second volume (G-O), the editors have compiled biographical sketches of 303 British "radicals." As in the first volume, quite a diverse group was selected— religious and literary radicals as well as political. Most of these names will not be familiar to the average reader, though the intended audience for this work is specialists in British history or politics. Still, by browsing through the biographies, a reader will gain a general flavor of the period and will encounter such familiar people as John Locke, Thomas Hobbes, John Milton (the focus is on his political writings), Anne Hutchinson, and the poet Andrew Marvell (who was also well known as a political pamphleteer and satirist). Among the other radicals who receive longer-than-average entries are the Quaker theologian George Keith; James Harrington, a republican theorist best known for *The Republic of Oceana* (1656); George Griffith, one of the independent ministers who signed *A Renuntiation and Declaration of the Ministers* in 1661; Henry Ireton, author of the important manifesto *A Remonstrance of the Army*, which was central to the High Court's charge against Charles I; and John Hampden, one of the most influential opponents of Charles I in Parliament.

The third volume (P-Z) is similar to the first two, covering British radicals in the seventeenth century. It also contains a supplementary bibliography, corrigenda to volumes 1 and 2, and an index to all three volumes.

Even though many of the seventeenth-century radicals are included in the *Dictionary of National Biography* and other compilations, this set provides a much-needed scope to radical activities and will be useful in graduate history collections. [R: Choice, Nov 82, p. 406]   Thomas A. Karel

134.   **A Biographical Dictionary of Irish Writers**. Edited by Anne Brady and Brian Cleeve. New York, St. Martin's Press, 1985. 480p. $35.00. LC 85-40074. ISBN 0-312-07871-4.

This book encompasses Ireland's tradition of the written word from the days of St. Patrick to the present. Over fifteen hundred biographical entries describe authors of Irish birth and cultural influence along with details of their work. The writers included here have been selected for their contribution to literature or for their social and historical interest.

Part one of the resource features writers in English of fiction, non-fiction, poetry, and drama, philosophers, scientists, pamphleteers, and propagandists. Writers range from the internationally recognized such as Beckett, Berkeley, and Swift, to those of more local significance—Drennan, Kickham, and Zozimus. Part two focuses on writers in Irish and Latin. Also described are anonymous literature, scribal compilations and annals.   Bohdan S. Wynar

135.   Boylan, Henry. **A Dictionary of Irish Biography**. New York, Barnes & Noble/Harper & Row, 1978. 385p. bibliog. $28.50. LC 79-102572. ISBN 0-06-490620-5.

The first comprehensive biographical dictionary of Ireland to appear in fifty years, the *Dictionary of Irish Biography* will be a valuable addition to collections of Irish reference materials. John S. Crone produced the *Concise Dictionary of Irish Biography* (New York, Longman) in 1928, and Alfred Webb wrote the standard *Compendium of Irish Biography* in 1878 (repr., Humanities Press, 1970). Both earlier biographical dictionaries could be considered more comprehensive than Boylan, up to the dates of publication. Boylan, however, had to sacrifice minor figures in Irish history to allow inclusion of important twentieth-century personalities. The introduction carefully explains how selections were made, and discusses the difficulties in determining the selection criteria. The comprehensiveness of individual entries varies, of course, depending not only on the importance of the person, but on the source materials available.

It can be supplemented by *Who's Who, What's What and Where in Ireland* (London, G. Chapman, 1973-) that contains separate sections for the Republic of Ireland and Northern Ireland. In addition to biographical sketches, it also includes directory-type information of government agencies, professional organizations, etc. [R: Choice, June 79, p. 5061]   Janet H. Littlefield and Bohdan S. Wynar

136.   The Compact Edition of the Dictionary of National Biography. Complete text reproduced micrographically. New York, Oxford University Press, 1975. 2v. index. $149.00 (in slipcase with magnifying glass). ISBN 0-19-865102-3.

The compact edition of the *DNB* includes the complete and unaltered texts of the twenty-two volumes reissued by Oxford University Press in 1938 and the six volumes of supplements which make up the twentieth-century *DNB*. For description see *Dictionary of National Biography*, (entry 137). [R: BL, 15 July 76, p. 1627]

Bohdan S. Wynar

137.   Dictionary of National Biography, From the Earliest Times to 1900. Edited by Sir Leslie Stephen and Sir Sidney Lee. London, Smith, Elder; repr., New York, Oxford University Press, 1938. 22v. $998.00. ISBN 0-19-865101-5.

138.   Dictionary of National Biography. Supplements (The Twentieth Century D.N.B.): The D.N.B. 1901-1911. Edited by Sir Sidney Lee. 1912. 2084p. $89.00. ISBN 0-19-865201-1; **The D.N.B. 1912-1921.** Edited by W. H. C. Davis and J. R. H. Weaver. With a cumulative index covering 1901-1921. 1927. 650p. $89.00. ISBN 0-19-865202-X; **The D.N.B. 1922-1930.** Edited by J. R. Weaver. With a cumulative index covering 1901-1930. 1937. 976p. $65.00. ISBN 0-19-856203-8; **The D.N.B. 1931-1940.** Edited by L. G. Wickham Legg. With a cumulative index covering 1901-1940. 1949. 984p. $89.00. ISBN 0-19-865204-6; **The D.N.B. 1941-1950.** Edited by L. G. Wickham Legg and E. T. Williams. With a cumulative index covering 1901-1950. 1959. 1054p. $89.00. ISBN 0-19-865205-4; **The D.N.B. 1951-1960.** Edited by E. T. Williams and Helen M. Palmer. With a cumulative index covering 1901-1960. 1971. 1171p. $89.00. ISBN 0-19-865206-2; **The D.N.B. 1961-1970.** Edited by E. T. Williams and C. S. Nichols. 1981. 1178p. $74.00. ISBN 0-19-865207-0.

Founded in 1882 by George Smith, the *Dictionary of National Biography* (*DNB*) is the first major biographical tool of the English-speaking world. There were other British biographies, but none whose scope or completeness could match the *DNB*. At first the plan was to make a universal biography, but it was decided that such an undertaking would be too impractical. The project was begun by Mr. George Smith, the publisher who took on the financial responsibility, and Sir Leslie Stephen, the editor. In 1889 Stephen resigned because of poor health and was succeeded by Sir Sidney Lee. After his retirement Stephen continued to be a major contributor; in all he wrote 820 biographies consisting of over 1,370 pages.

The editors intended to include all noteworthy inhabitants of Great Britain, Ireland, and the Colonies, exclusive of living persons, from the earliest historical period to the time of publication. Included are Britons who lived abroad and foreigners who became British subjects during their lifetime. Names of important legendary figures, such as Robin Hood, are also listed. Among the names included are the very famous, the famous, and the infamous.

The *DNB* staff gathered names from a wide range of sources in historical and scientific literature and from an endless amount of miscellaneous records and reports. A preliminary list was compiled and sent to specialists of literary experience competent to write articles for the proposed dictionary. Subsequent lists were published in the *Athenaeum* and readers' comments were invited.

Included in the basic set are 29,120 articles. The contributors were urged to get their information from original sources whenever possible, especially from unpublished papers. The articles had to be accompanied by bibliographies. The average length of a biography is a little less than one page, although some run much longer (Shakespeare, forty-nine pages) and others are less than one column. The articles are signed with the initials of the contributor, and a key to their names is included in every volume.

The original work was completed in 1900 and decennial supplements have covered the lives of those who died during the decade, making it possible to have the lives written by persons many of whom knew their subjects intimately. So, for example, in the most recent supplement covering 1961-1970, we find records of lives of 745 British men and women who died between 1961 and 1970. Like the previous supplements and the *DNB* itself, this volume is an outstanding model for all biographical dictionaries. It shows careful scholarship, providing lengthy, well-researched biographies of prominent individuals from the vast field of human endeavor. Bibliographical notes listing important secondary and primary sources follow each signed biography. The biographies have been written by people, often as eminent as their subjects, who knew their subjects personally and who could often add private knowledge to the biographical facts. Thus, the sketches of Winston Churchill, T. S. Eliot, Vivian Leigh, Bernard Russell, Dame Edith Sitwell, Charles Onions, Mervyn Peake, Clement Attlee, Nancy Astor, and the others come alive, making this a reference work of great interest to the general reader as well as the historian. [R: LJ, 1 Sept 82, p. 1648]

Bohdan S. Wynar

139.   **The Dictionary of National Biography: The Concise Dictionary. Part I, From the Beginning to 1900. Part II, 1901-1970.** New York, Oxford University Press, 1906-1982. $55.00/vol. ISBN 0-19-865301-8 (part 1); 0-19-865303-4 (part 2).

This epitome of the twentieth-century portion of the celebrated *Dictionary of National Biography* offers short notices for over six thousand outstanding British personalities who died between the end of 1900 and the beginning of 1971. Its complementary part 1, last published in 1953, summarizes selected main work entries "from the beginnings to 1900." This edition replaces *The Concise DNB 1901-1950 and 1951-1960*. The entries are extracts of the lives in the twentieth-century *DNB* supplements, and in each case, give the essential biographical information, i.e., name, title, profession, dates of birth and death, and main features of the career.

The first one hundred entries in this latest edition include eight women, seventeen individuals who died in the 1960s, and seven entries cumulated into the 1901-1950 alphabet from its 1951-1960 supplement. The pre-1961 biographies show no alterations, although certain criticisms of their choice and balance were heard at the time of first publication. Men of action are still favored over artists, writers, thinkers, and the like, reflecting an original bias in the full *Dictionary*. [R: LJ, 1 Sept 82, p. 1648]

Jeanne Osborn and Bohdan S. Wynar

140.   Emden, A. B. **A Biographical Register of the University of Oxford A.D. 1501 to 1540.** New York, Oxford University Press, 1974. 742p. o.p. ISBN 0-19-951008-3.

This is a supplementary volume to the author's three-volume set, *A Biographical Register of the University of Oxford to A.D. 1500.* Published by Oxford University

Press from 1957 to 1959, this work contains some fifteen thousand biographical entries. The present volume uses an identical structure for the biographical entries, and also provides a brief historical introduction for the period covered. There are two older compilations on the same subject, by Joseph Foster: *Alumni Oxonienses: The Members of the University of Oxford, 1500-1714* (4v. Oxford, Parker, 1891-1892); and its continuation, *Alumni Oxonienses, 1715-1886* (4v. 1888). Mr. Emden is also the author of *A Biographical Register of the University of Cambridge to 1500* (Cambridge University Press, 1963).

The present register is an essential biographical history for the period; it will be indispensable to all scholars interested in the history of this great university and the political influence of its alumni.   Bohdan S. Wynar

141.   Hoffmann, Ann. **Lives of the Tudor Age 1485-1603**. New York, Barnes and Noble, 1977. 500p. illus. index. (Lives of the . . . Age Series). $25.00. LC 76-15685. ISBN 0-06-494331-3.

Third in a proposed series of biographical dictionaries covering important periods of English history, this work should find its way into many collections. The entries, while concise, contain all the basics and then some, presented in an unbiased, readable form.

The entries are arranged alphabetically by last name, or title with "see" references to the main entries. Dates and profession are followed by the biography itself, with bibliographic references to the major biography of the entrant plus several other sources of special note. Reproductions of paintings or engravings of many subjects are included, along with their original location.

The chief of the two indexes lists not only the main entrants but also subsidiary persons mentioned within the text. Paginations of the main entries are indicated here in boldface. The second index contains main entrants only, with no pagination, and is arranged according to profession or status.

The 308 entries include some for important foreign figures. Subjects whose lives overlap two periods are listed in the volume relating to the peak of their careers.

This excellent source presents easily accessible information on many important personages and should prove essential in university and public libraries. [R: Choice, June 77, p. 513; LJ, 1 May 77, pp. 1003-4]   Judith K. Rosenberg

142.   Laurence Urdang Associates, comp. **Lives of the Stuart Age, 1603-1714**. Edwin Riddell, ed. New York, Barnes and Noble, 1976. 500p. illus. index. $25.00. LC 75-39126. ISBN 0-06-494330-5.

The first of five "Lives" books that Barnes and Noble hopes to publish on prominent Englishmen. *Lives of the Stuart Age* consists of 322 biographies of individuals with significant impact on English society from 1603 to 1714, including several new World founders and foreigners who exerted influence on the Stuart period. Biographees whose lives cross the "Ages" are referred to the Tudor Georgian volumes.

Entries are arranged alphabetically by surname (in boldface), though the reader will find numerous cross-references from titles. Each entry includes the biographee's birth and death dates, followed by a listing of titles, positions, or vocations. Length of these highly readable sketches is determined by importance to the Age: James I merits six pages; musician John Wilbye, one column. Also included are selective bibliographies consisting of the standard biography, the definitive editions of collected works (if available), and iconographies (where possible).

Two indexes facilitate use. The first is alphabetical and refers the reader to each place the surname occurs in the text. For those appearing more than once, the main entry is in bold type. The second index is classified by vocation or historical significance (Charles II's mistresses can be found under "Ladies of Society"), but includes no references to page numbers. Some individuals, like John Churchill, First Duke of Marlborough, appear under more than one classification.

The series will update but not replace the *Dictionary of National Biography*, which remains substantially more complete: Guy Fawkes is awarded three pages in *DNB*—in *Lives*, one; in *DNB* John Milton merits seventeen pages—in *Lives*, five. Typography is even and clear, the paper heavy, and the binding attractive and strong. [R: Choice, Dec 76, p. 1274]   Wayne A. Wiegand

143.   Newman, P. R. **Royalist Officers in England and Wales, 1642-1660: A Biographical Dictionary**. New York, Garland, 1981. 429p. (Garland Reference Library of Social Science, Vol. 72). $99.00. LC 80-8594. ISBN 0-8240-9503-0.

One of the problems faced by a historian interested in the English Civil War is that many of the contemporary documents have been destroyed and many of those still extant are available only in major research institutions. Even when the records are available, however, there is another equally common and equally frustrating problem—the welter of individuals' names. Newman's work goes far in resolving both problems, at least for the Royalist side.

This book provides biographical information for 1,629 Royalist field officers commanding fighting men between May 1642 and the restoration of Charles II in 1660. For each, Newman attempts to give "his family origin, his social status, his educational record, his involvement in local and national government, his religious persuasion, and his career subsequent to the . . . war." For some individuals, of course, much of this information is simply not obtainable. Most officers, however, receive at least a short paragraph, and a few of the more well-known figures such as Edward Somerset, Henry Hastings, and Marmaduke Langdale are each allotted a full page or more. All entries are alphabetical by surname, including peers of the realm who are cross-referenced from their titles. Following each entry is a citation of sources in primary documents. There is a helpful introductory essay, "Some Notes on the Royalist Command Structure 1642-46 and the King's Two Nephews."

Historians will find this both a welcome compendium and a convenient guidepost to further research in the primary materials.   Philip R. Rider

144.   Ormond, Richard, and Malcolm Rogers, eds. **Dictionary of British Portraiture, Four Volumes**. New York, Oxford University Press, 1979. 4v. $42.50/vol. 1; $49.50/vol. 2; $62.50/vol. 3; $62.50/vol. 4. LC 79-22598. ISBN 0-19-520180-9 (vol. 1); 0-19-520181-7 (vol. 2); 0-19-520182-5 (vol. 3); 0-19-520183-3 (vol. 4).

Catalogs of the National Portrait Gallery, the British Museum, and other sources have been used in compiling this dictionary of famous figures from the Middle Ages to 1900. Chosen from the *Dictionary of National Biography*, with omission of minor names and a few additions, are men and women whose portraits are in galleries, institutions, or other collections open to the public. A few are found outside Britain, e.g., the Ellesmere Chaucer at the Huntington Library. The first two volumes, covering the Middle Ages to 1700 and 1700 to 1800, are alphabetically arranged, giving the following information for each entry: name of sitter, birth and death dates, profession or occupation, genre (painting, drawing, sculpture, photograph, etc.), name of artist, date of portrait, size (i.e., half length, full length), other distinguishing features, medium, and location. Illustrations would have enlivened the volumes but would have made them prohibitively large and expensive. The concise information found in these volumes will be very useful for identification, especially since this is the first comprehensive handbook of its kind.   Frances Neel Cheney

145.   Palmer, Alan, and Veronica Palmer. **Who's Who in Shakespeare's England**. New York, St. Martin's Press, 1981. 280p. illus. $32.50. ISBN 0-312-87096-5.

This is a guide to some seven hundred persons who were important in England or to Shakespeare during the years 1590 to 1623. Entries are brief, with, in some cases, one to three bibliographical citations or a portrait of the subject. Women are given generous inclusion as subjects. There are maps of London and Stratford-on-Avon, an index of names by occupation and relation to Shakespeare: for family, legends, London and Stratford connections, and a brief glossary of terms.

The book reveals good planning for usefulness and ease in locating information. A sample check of biographies found them to be accurate, albeit somewhat telescoped, as is, of course, to be expected in this type of guide. *Who's Who in Shakespeare's England* should make an excellent introductory work of reference. [R: BL, 1 Sept 82, p. 69; Choice, Feb 82, p. 746]   Dorothy E. Litt

146.   Pickrill, D. A. **Ministers of the Crown**. Boston, Routledge & Kegan Paul, 1981. 135p. bibliog. $18.95. ISBN 0-7100-0916-X.

"This book lists, in chronological order, holders of ministerial posts, senior and junior, in most cases from the earliest known date" (p. vii). While its title, *Ministers of the Crown*, could imply holders of similar posts in those parts of the Commonwealth acknowledging the Crown as their head of state, the compiler has limited his list to the United Kingdom.

For the seventeenth century and later, the date of the person's appointment to a position is the one given, but for earlier years the date listed may simply be one at which time the person was *known* to hold the office. Verification was obtained from one of the sources listed in the bibliography. Certain of the offices have the lists of their incumbents compiled from the date at which the office took on political character. Examples of these are—the Lord High Admiral, where the political association dates from the 1540 appointment of Lord Russell, and the Lord President of the Council, which first appeared in some semblance of its present form in 1679.

Except for listing the name of the person holding the office, and the date he held it, very little other information is supplied. For individuals, we are given information concerning changes of name or title, or another office also held during part of the same time span. For the various offices themselves, we are given the various titles as they changed over time, with some indication of the scope of each position in the respective periods. There is a separate listing for the various wartime offices, a section for Ministers without Portfolio (an office dating from 1830), and one for the various offices in Scotland, Ireland, and Wales. A list of Speakers of the House of Commons concludes the work.

Since the previous listing of such officeholders, *Haydn's Book of Dignitaries*, appeared nearly a century before and was less comprehensive in scope, this work (although its compiler acknowledges there may be a few errors or omissions due mainly to the possible inaccuracies of his sources) will be a useful tool for identifying individuals holding particular positions at certain times. [R: Choice, July-Aug 82, p. 1542]   Margaret Anderson

147.   Routh, C. R. N., ed. **Who's Who in History.** Oxford, England, Basil Blackwell, 1964-1974; distr., New York, Barnes & Noble, 1975. o.p. Vol. I. **British Isles 55 BC-1485.** By W. O. Hassall. Vol. II. **England 1485-1603.** By C. R. N. Routh. Vol. III. **England 1603-1714.** By C. P. Hill. Vol. IV. **England 1714-1789.** By Geoffrey Treasure. Vol. V. **England 1789-1837.** By G. R. R. Treasure.

This set of five volumes (with one more volume forthcoming) is a series of historical biographies covering the history of the British Isles from the earliest times to the nineteenth century. Within each volume, the arrangement is chronological (and sometimes by profession) rather than alphabetical. This is a nuisance, requiring in most cases that one look in the index first. Approximately half the biographical sketches have a suggestion or two for further reading, usually a recent biography; however these bibliographies are extremely superficial, for the most part just window dressing. The books cited are usually those published in Britain. There are some major omissions; for example, there is no bibliography after the biography of William Hogarth.

Those selected for inclusion are the usual famous, e.g., Samuel Johnson, John Newbery, Horace Walpole, James Watt. A brief check indicated that everyone included here could be found, in considerably more detail, in the *Dictionary of National Biography*. The text, while accurate, is fairly simple, and certainly understandable to those from high school on up.   Donald Empson

148.   Valentine, Alan. **The British Establishment, 1760-1784: An Eighteenth-Century Biographical Dictionary.** Norman, Okla., University of Oklahoma Press, 1976. 2v. $35.00; $17.50pa. LC 69-16734. ISBN 0-8061-0877-0; 0-8061-1378-2pa.

The pyramid of British society in the eighteenth century was headed by a small, select "establishment," here defined as "the influential levels of court, government, army, navy, church, law, trade, finance and society." Its members shared many ties—birth, marriage, education, profession, business or club membership. Alan Valentine has spent many years studying and writing of this period. Now he provides this useful finding list, containing some three thousand entries, bringing out many of these interrelated facets of British society. It will be helpful as a checklist for names appearing in writings of this key period in British and American history, especially as nearly half of them are not represented in the current *Dictionary of National Biography*. No bibliographical citations are attached to the entries; this fact reduces its effectiveness for further research purposes. [R: LJ, Aug 70; RQ, Fall 70]

Norman Horrocks

149.   Wallace, Martin. **100 Irish Lives.** Totowa, N.J., Barnes & Noble Books, 1983. 184p. illus. map. index. $18.50. LC 82-24289. ISBN 0-389-20364-5.

Wallace, an Irish writer and editor, has presented in this volume brief biographies of what he terms "a disparate lot" of Irish men and women from the time of St. Patrick (390?-461?) to Patrick Kavanagh, an Irish literary figure who died in 1967. Most of the biographees were born and lived in Ireland; however, some who were not Irish but spent most of their lives in Ireland and made a distinctive contribution to its history are also included. Likewise, a few who were Irish but lived most of their lives elsewhere—George Bernard Shaw, for example—were also included. No rigid criteria account for the selection of biographees: Some are well known and others are rather obscure; many contributed substantially to Irish culture, though some were "rogues and vagabonds."

The material is arranged chronologically by date of birth. A list in this order is given in the table of contents, but access is also possible through the index of names in the appendix. Appended to most of the biographical accounts are references to further readings and also to places and things related to the person. The author intended the book to be used as a guidebook and therefore included five pages of maps with many of the places of interest numbered to correspond to the number of the biography. Thus a person interested in Frank O'Connor can go from the footnote to his biography, which gives the address of O'Connor's final home, to the map of Dublin and find the exact location for visiting. Other features of the work are the photographs of people and places interspersed throughout the text and a list of important dates in Irish history. Although the book makes delightful reading, as a reference book it should be considered only as an added source of information to such standard works as *A Dictionary of Irish Biography* by Henry Boylan (Gill and Macmillan, 1978. 385p.). Boylan itself succeeds J. S. Crane's *Concise Dictionary of Irish Biography* (Longmans, 1937. 290p.) "giving the important facts and events of the subject's career in chronological order and including, where possible, a sentence or quotation to give the flavour of the man" (introduction).   Lucille Whalen and Bohdan S. Wynar

150. Watt, D. E. R. **A Biographical Dictionary of Scottish Graduates to A.D. 1410**. New York, Oxford University Press, 1977. 607p. index. $89.00. ISBN 0-19-822447-8.

A major biographical source for Scottish history, this specialized work lists all Scots trained at a university for a 250-year period (roughly A.D. 1150 to 1410). A Scot is defined as a person born or reared within the boundaries of modern Scotland. The arrangement is alphabetical, using the standardized form of surname. Entries are well-documented with primary sources. A comprehensive introduction defines the procedures followed for each entry, with valuable background information on the schools and the church during this period. An index of Christian names follows the body of this most carefully researched work, which is intended for scholarly use. [R: BL, 15 June 78, p. 1634; C&RL, July 78, p. 303]   Bernice Bergup

151. **Who Was Who**. London, Block; New York, St. Martin's Press, 1897- . Vol. I. 1897-1915. $69.50. ISBN 0-312-87570-3. Vol. II. 1916-1928. $69.50. ISBN 1-312-87605-X. Vol. III. 1929-1940. $69.50. ISBN 0-312-87640-8. Vol. IV. 1941-1950. $69.50. ISBN 0-312-87675-0. Vol. V. 1951-1960. $69.50. ISBN 0-312-87710-2. Vol. VI. 1961-1970. $69.50. ISBN 0-312-87745-5. Vol. VII. 1971-1980. $74.50. ISBN 0-312-87746-3.

Who Was Who consists mainly of original sketches as they appeared in *Who's Who*. They have been reprinted with the date of death added. In some instances additional information is added.

Who Was Who was first published in 1920 and covered the period from 1897 through 1916. A new edition was published in 1929. The following three volumes cover the years 1915-1928, 1929-1940, 1941-1950, 1951-1960, 1961-1970 and 1971-1980 respectively. The editors plan to publish a new volume at the close of each decade.

          Bohdan S. Wynar

LATIN AMERICA

152. Camp, Roderic A. **Mexican Political Biographies, 1935-1981**. 2nd ed., rev. and expanded. Tucson, Ariz., University of Arizona Press, 1982. 447p. bibliog. $35.00. LC 82-2768. ISBN 0-8165-0743-0.

The second edition of Camp's work (first published in 1977) will be a welcome addition to major libraries and others with users interested in Mexico. The revised work covers the period 1935 to 1981 and includes new information. Additional biographies of public figures in the Mexican political arena, living and deceased, are available.

This expanded version incorporates updated information. Approximately 400 of the original biographies have been redone. Moreover, 450 new biographies were added. Information about family ties was added, along with the names of important party persons and ambassadors.

The work is highly useful as a quick source of information. This is important because there are very few reliable reference books that provide the library client with numerous entries and accurate data about Mexican political persons.

The format is a straightforward, alphabetical listing by biographee surname. Unfortunately, there are no cross-references (particularly useful where double surnames are involved). Articles are interfiled. This practice may seem odd to some librarians and scholars, but it will be acceptable to others. I am surprised by the absence of a list (in chronological order) of Mexico's presidents and ambassadors to the United Nations. Aside from the above criticisms and format concerns, this is a good revision. [R: Choice, May 83, p. 1261]   Roberto P. Haro

153. Henderson, James, and Linda Roddy Henderson. **Ten Notable Women of Latin America**. Chicago, Nelson-Hall Publishers, 1973. 320p. $23.95; $11.95pa. LC 73-88510. ISBN 0-88229-426-1; 0-88229-596-9pa.

Extensive treatment of such personalities as Malinche, Ines de Saurez, Sor Juana Ines de la Cruz, Gabriela Mistral, and Eva Peron. The volume is well illustrated and indexed.   Bohdan S. Wynar

154. Kay, Ernest, ed. **Dictionary of Latin American and Caribbean Biography**. 2nd ed. London, Melrose Press; distr., Totowa, N.J., Rowman and Littlefield, 1971. 458p. $25.00.

This work contains thirty-five hundred biographical sketches of the Who's Who type. This new edition seems to be a considerable improvement over the first edition, but the lack of entries for many important personalities (say, some presidents and prime ministers) soon rouses one's suspicions. In addition, there are three separate alphabets to consult! The concept is sound—such a biographical directory is badly needed—but this one has to be much improved in order to fill the gap successfully. [R: Choice, Jan 72, p. 1438]   Bohdan S. Wynar

155. **Who's Who in Latin America. A Biographical Dictionary of Notable Living Men and Women of Latin America**. 3rd ed. Ronald Hilton, ed. Stanford, Calif., Stanford University Press, 1951; repr., Detroit, Blaine Ethridge Books, 1971. 2v. $47.50/set. LC 76-165656. ISBN 0-87917-021-2.

Originally this edition was published in seven parts: Mexico (1946); Central America and Panama (1945); Colombia, Ecuador, and Venezuela (1951); Bolivia, Chile, and Peru (1947); Argentina, Paraguay, and Uruguay (1950); Brazil (1948); and

Cuba, the Dominican Republic, and Haiti (1951). The first two editions in one volume (1935, 1940) were edited by P. A. Martin. This is a reprint of the third edition, substantially enlarged, which includes over eight thousand biographical sketches of Latin Americans prominent in the post-World War II period, compared with fifteen hundred entries in the second edition. This is a standard work on this subject, providing the usual information of the Who's Who type. It should be noted that a number of alphabets must be consulted in using this dictionary, since the listings are under country (e.g., in the first volume, Mexico, Central America and Panama), and occasionally the user may not know the country of origin for the biographee. Bohdan S. Wynar

MIDDLE EAST

156. Comay, Joan. **Who's Who in Jewish History after the Period of the Old Testament**. New York, McKay, 1974. 448p. illus. (part col.). index. o.p. LC 73-93915. ISBN 0-679-50455-9.

Karpman's *Who's Who in World Jewry: A Biographical Dictionary of Outstanding Jews* (Pitman, 1972. 999p.) includes some ten thousand biographies written in a standard Who's Who format. The present work, actually a sequel to Comay's *Who's Who in the Old Testament*, is quite different in format as well as in execution. As a general rule, persons alive at the time of writing have been omitted, except for some Israeli leaders and persons who have gained international reputations in scholarship, the arts, or politics. Entries vary in length from fifty words to more than a page, depending on the relative importance of the subject. One of the longest entries is for Dr. Theodor Herzl, founder of the modern Zionist movement.

A questionable editorial policy is the inclusion of non-Jewish leaders—Hitler is listed, as is Winston Churchill, who "early in his political career . . . took a sympathetic interest in Jewish matters" (p. 114). One finds here also entries for King Hussein, Boris Pasternak (whose mother, Rosa Kaufmann, was of Jewish origin), and Joseph Pulitzer, whose father was a Jew. Marcel Proust, a Catholic, was "clearly influenced by his half-Jewish background" (p. 326). Instead of concentrating on such entries, this dictionary might better serve its purpose by including entries for such persons as Kantor, founder of the first Hebrew daily newspaper, of Kaplansky, the Zionist labor leader, to suggest only two examples.

We think that this dictionary is trying to do too much. Most scholars will prefer to consult the biographical material in the prestigious *Encyclopaedia Judaica*; nevertheless, this compilation can be a handy ready reference tool for smaller institutions, if it is used with caution. Bohdan S. Wynar

157. **The International Who's Who of the Arab World**. 2nd ed. London, International Who's Who of the Arab World, 1984. 600p. $155.00. ISBN 0-9506122-1-9.

Its purpose is to present current information on "leading personalities of the Arab World in all walks of life" (preface) including "prominent Arabs living outside their countries of birth." This second edition contains some three thousand biographical sketches plus directory-type information listing biographees by country, and then by occupation or field of activity. Bohdan S. Wynar

158.   **Who's Who in Israel and Jewish Personalities from All Over the World**. 20th ed. Tel-Aviv, Bronfman Publishers; distr., Philadelphia, International Publications Service, 1985. 496p. $140.00. LC 46-6380. ISBN 0-8002-3946-6.

The first edition of this work was published in 1945 in Tel-Aviv by Who's Who in the State of Israel Publishing House. The title of this publication varies. For example, the 1947 edition was titled *Palestine and Transjordan Who's Who* and the 1949 edition was called *Who's Who in the State of Israel*. The present volume is in several parts. The first part, "Personalia," provides three thousand brief biographical sketches of prominent statesmen, scholars, politicians, artists, journalists, etc. in the State of Israel and several hundred individuals abroad, primarily in the United States. The second part, "Public and Private Bodies," is a directory of national institutions, political parties, universities, cultural centers, banks, industry and other institutions. In addition, there are small sections on the presidency of the State of Israel, members of the Eleventh Knesset and members of government.   Bohdan S. Wynar

159.   **Who's Who in Lebanon, 1982-1983**. 8th ed. Beirut, Publitec Publications; distr., New York, Unipub, 1983. 782p. $85.00. LC 65-2366. ISBN 2-90-3188-01-7.

Edited by Gabriel M. Bustros, the newest edition of this biennial publication that started in 1964 consists of three parts. Part 1, an almanac, features a readable account of war in Lebanon, a concise overview of Lebanon's history, geography, population, government, etc. Part 2 is a biographical listing of some three thousand prominent personalities, including political figures, government officials, scholars, and artists. The biographies are brief, but in most cases provide the basics: date of birth, lineage, marriage, educational background, current career, and address. Part 3 provides biographical sketches of noted Lebanese living abroad.   Bohdan S. Wynar

160.   **Who's Who in Saudi Arabia, 1983-1984**. 3rd ed. Jeddah, Saudi Arabia, Tihama; distr., Detroit, Gale, 1983. 375p. index. $65.00.

The stated purpose of this particular work is to permit "the international community to acquire a true knowledge of the country, its heritage, vast possibilities and people" (p. vii). The Kingdom of Saudi Arabia is steadily increasing in importance within the community of nations while retaining its vital position in the world of Islam. Such importance makes it essential that greater access to pertinent biographical data on its most prominent public figures be widely available. Not only does the country possess the largest oil reserves in the Middle East, it also stands as guardian for the two holiest Islamic shrines, the cities of Mecca and Medina.

In addition to supplying biographical data on some twelve hundred prominent Saudis, representing every possible public field—from administration to communications, medicine, education, entertainment, and culture—the work also includes a "Survey of Saudi Arabia," a fact-filled essay dealing with social and economic matters, including material on Saudi Arabia's role in the world economic structure and on long-term marketing prospects for oil and petrochemicals. This section is illustrated with diagrams and bar graphs.

While the book is both useful and important, supplying information not often so readily available in English, the biographical entries are somewhat uneven in quality. This is caused not so much by the fact that they vary in length, but by the fact that they often do not supply the same amount of information. In some cases we are told about the individual's education, including the degrees held and where they were obtained, something useful in professional contacts; in other cases we are told simply that the person has a particular degree; and sometimes we are not told in what area the degree was earned. Information concerning publications is also spotty and this is especially unfortunate when we are told that the person has published research articles and/or monographs. Although such materials may be only in Arabic, and, therefore, not easily handled by Western readers, the business and professional world, for whom this work is intended, ought to be informed more fully of the productivity and backgrounds of people with whom they will have contact. Such details will likely be corrected as future editions of this useful tool appear. This volume is also available from International Publications Service at $60.00 (ISBN 0-9466-53-X).   Margaret Anderson

161. **Who's Who in the Arab World 1984-1985**. 7th ed. rev. Gabriel M. Bustros, ed. Beirut, Lebanon, Publitec Publications; distr., New York, Unipub [1984]. 1207p. $135.00. LC NE 677-1244. ISBN 2-903-188-02-5.

The fifth edition of this work was published in 1980, first in 1965. The work is divided into three parts: part 1, "Outline of the Arab World," part 2, "Survey of the 20 Arab Countries," and part 3, the biographical section. In the first part we find data on such topics as the League of Arab States, OPEC, petroleum development and marketing, the Palestinians, the Maghreb Consultative Committee, and the Gulf Cooperation Council. Part 2 provides information on twenty Arab countries, excluding Lebanon which is served with a volume of its own, *Who's Who in Lebanon*. The "Survey," partly statistical and partly descriptive, is useful, but much less detailed than the information provided in *The Middle East and North Africa*. Since *The Middle East and North Africa* covers a greater number of countries but provides no biographical information, the two works complement each other quite well.

This volume's greatest claim to usefulness is found in the third section where biographical information is provided for over seven thousand names. Along with most of the major figures among the Arab population (and this edition does include a biographical reference to Muammar al-Kadhafi, missing from the fifth), there are references to several non-Arabs living and working in the area—teachers, bankers, archeologists, from various parts of Europe. The information for each entry is not as precise as one might wish; one does not always find birth dates, nor even birthplaces, but the country of birth is usually given. (For some persons the year of birth is listed; for others one is left to speculate.) The length of the biography does not necessarily reflect the importance of the individual; the biography of the prime minister of Tunisia is longer by a good deal than that of the president of the Republic of Tunisia, and much longer than that of the president of Egypt. There is still, as was remarked before, some inconsistency with the Romanization of Arabic spellings, particularly with first names, but occasionally with family names, making some individuals more difficult to find. The information provided, however, is generally useful, and the work is a valuable reference tool.   Margaret Anderson

Part II
Biographies in Professional Fields

3 Applied Arts

Introduction

Because of their position between art and technology, and between the fine arts and crafts, there is no clear and universally accepted definition of what constitutes the applied arts. In this chapter we follow the more narrow definition as found in *American Reference Books Annual* and in Sheehy's *Guide to Reference Books*. Included are "Decorative Arts," "Fashion," and "Photography," with a total of eight entries. Collecting and crafts are not included in this chapter.

Some standard works in applied arts include Jervis Simon's *The Facts on File Dictionary of Design and Designers* (see entry 162) and *Contemporary Photographers* (see entry 167). There are also some subject dictionaries that contain a fair amount of biographical information. As first choice one should mention *The Oxford Companion to the Decorative Arts* (Oxford University Press, 1975. 865p.) that contains biographies of major artists and craftsmen. More in-depth coverage of furniture designers is found in Hugh Honour's *Cabinet Makers and Furniture Designers* (Putnam, 1969. 320p.) that contains fifty-two biographies of the world's greatest. *Fairchild's Dictionary of Fashion* (Fairchild, 1975. 693p.) is probably the best subject dictionary in this area and includes some five hundred biographical sketches of fashion designers. Not as adequate is Martin Pegler's *The Dictionary of Interior Design* (Crown, 1966. 500p.) providing somewhat brief biographical sketches of famous designers and architects. In the area of photography, the International Center of Photography produced the *Encyclopedia of Photography* (Crown, 1984. 607p.) that covers 250 noted photographers and pioneers in photography active between 1840 and 1940. In addition, H. W. Wilson's *Art Index* covers not only fine arts, but also periodical articles in interior design, fashion, and photography. For general orientation the best bibliographic guide is Donald Ehresmann's *Applied and Decorative Arts: A Bibliographic Guide to Reference Works, Histories, and Handbooks* (Libraries Unlimited, 1977. 232p.) and older guides the reader will find in Walford and Sheehy.

DECORATIVE ARTS

162.   Jervis, Simon. **The Facts on File Dictionary of Design and Designers**. New York, Facts on File, 1984. 533p. $24.95. LC 83-25350. ISBN 0-87196-891-6.

The emphasis of this dictionary is on historical design and designers, providing brief biographies of designers from 1450 to the present, including minor as well as major figures. The scope is broad, listing noted patrons and historians as well as designers; important exhibitions, especially those of the nineteenth century; schools and institutions; and major serial and periodical publications. Design types subject to extensive coverage encompass ceramics, furniture, glass, interior decoration, metal-work, ornament, and textiles, while graphic design and typography are only occasionally touched upon. Heavy industrial design, theatre design, and dress design are essentially excluded. Geographically, the concentration is upon Europe and North America.

In his six-page introduction, the author notes that recent design history has focused on practical design and the influence of craftsmanship while neglecting the historic design role of the goldsmith, the engraver, the painter, the sculptor, and the architect from the fifteenth through the eighteenth centuries.

The dictionary proper consists of 516 double-column pages in strict alphabetical arrangement. Biographies usually include birth and death dates, place of birth, training of and influences upon the person, as well as the person's contributions to and relative importance in the design discipline. Most entries include many cross-references to other dictionary topics which are indicated in boldface type, making for ease in pursuing related subjects.

Excellently organized and very inclusive, this is not only a most useful reference tool to the broad subject of design but opens up many new areas for future design history study. [R: Choice, Dec 84, p. 538; LJ, Aug 84, p. 1438]   G. Joan Burns

163.   Prather-Moses, Alice Irma, comp. **The International Dictionary of Women Workers in the Decorative Arts: A Historical Survey from the Distant Past to the Early Decades of the Twentieth Century**. Metuchen, N.J., Scarecrow, 1981. 200p. bibliog. index. $15.00. LC 81-8947. ISBN 0-8108-1450-1.

This is an alphabetical dictionary of women throughout the ages who were known for their work in the decorative arts. It includes textile workers, metal and ceramic workers, architects, jewelers, and assorted other craftspeople. In most cases, the biographies are quite brief, short paragraphs which give an account of the woman's career, her major works and/or exhibitions, and limited material on her personal life. The introduction traces women's involvement in the decorative arts scene from prehistoric times to the present, and Prather-Moses also provides a large bibliography and subject index. While undeniably presenting the reader with a wealth of previously inaccessible information, this rather specialized work will be an essential purchase only for major art and all-inclusive university collections.   Deborah Hammer

164.   Pyke, E. J. **A Biographical Dictionary of Wax Modellers**. New York, Oxford University Press, 1973. 528p. illus. bibliog. index. o.p. ISBN 0-19-817194-3.

Although the demand for information on wax modellers is light, answering any questions pertaining to this subject has in the past been difficult if not impossible. Far more complete than the title implies, the text also includes descriptions of methods of wax analysis and wax conservation, lists of private and public collections, a sizeable bibliography, and an excellent index. Arranged alphabetically and spanning seven centuries of wax modelling, the biographical entries vary in length from three lines to several pages. Major entries include techniques, catalogs of extant works, bibliographies, and quotations from principal and primary sources. Only artists employing wax as an art form are included; those using wax as a preliminary step to bronze casting are, of course, omitted. Specialized libraries serving collectors will find that the convenience of owning this title will justify the expense of obtaining it. The author of this well-illustrated and carefully researched book is to be commended for undertaking such a monumental task.

In 1981 Mr. Pyke produced a supplement, *Biographical Dictionary of Wax Modellers: Supplement* (London, Pyke, 1981. 528p. £16.50. ISBN 0-9507518-0-4) in a limited edition of eight hundred copies. [R: LJ, 15 Sept 73, p. 2538]

Jacqueline Sisson

FASHION

165. Stegemeyer, Anne. **Who's Who in Fashion**. New York, Fairchild, 1980. 179p. bibliog. index. $15.50. LC 79-89755. ISBN 0-87005-257-8.

Who's Who in Fashion is a collection of illustrated biographical entries of influential couturiers, designers, and fashion editors divided into three categories. The purpose of the volume, as noted in the preface, is to provide a needed source from which a student might gain "an awareness of the contribution of individuals to the field of fashion."

The preface also includes a disclaimer explaining that "the fashion business is a constantly changing cast of characters. Talents appear, star for a while and drop out of sight. . . . Recording this scene is a continuing process, never finished, always incomplete." The author is correct in describing the difficulty of her task. Deciding who's who in a business which "comes-out" five times a year in the United States and twice yearly in Europe is nearly impossible. Several award-winning manufacturing house designers have been overlooked (Nicole Miller, P. J. Walsh) as well as several influential fashion "personalities," such as Levi Strauss. Still, the book has some valuable material, and the inclusion of relatively new and avant garde designers such as Perry Ellis and Montana Claude is a welcome surprise. The print is easily read, and many of the "Horatio Alger" stories are inspirational. However, the entries are inconsistent in length and detail. The sketches and photographs are wonderful but are not provided for each designer or personality. An index and bibliography are included.

This volume is sure to be obsolete soon. A yearly alphabetical directory of the New York, Paris, and Milan markets, including designer biographies and a short historical section of famous designers of the past, might fill the need for a source book in this field better than this volume. Meanwhile, the traditional and practical method of "shopping Bloomingdale's" or your local better department store, in which students and buyers can see who's designing, who's selling, and who's new, may still be the preferred method. [R: BL, 15 Apr 80, p. 1169; Choice, May 80, p. 367; LJ, 1 Mar 80, p. 601]

Lorelei D. Davis

166.   Strute, Karl, and Theodor Doelken, eds. **Who's Who in Fashion: A Biographical Encyclopedia of the International Red Series Containing Some 6,000 Biographies of Living Prominent Personalities in the Fields of Fashion, Beauty and Jewellery**. Zurich, Who's Who AG; distr., New York, Unipub, 1983. 3v. in 2. (International Red Series). $160.00/set. ISBN 3-921220-32-7 (vol. 1); 3-921220-33-5 (vol. 2).

In this first edition, important personalities and international institutions in the fields of fashion, cosmetics, and jewelry from most Western European countries are covered. Biographies of over five thousand people who operate in the economic, artistic, and scientific sectors of these fields are given. The entries include such information as birth date, parents, spouse, children, home and/or work address, education, career information, current position, publications, memberships, awards, specialty, qualifications, and hobbies. Occasionally, home or business telephone or telex numbers are given. The lengths of the biographies vary according to how the information was obtained. The name indexes (one for each volume) include a few photographs, mostly black and white.

There are occasional errors, but they are minor when one considers all other aspects of this voluminous work. The extremely detailed appendixes give the names and addresses of about three thousand national and international organizations, schools and training institutes, museums, fairs, associations and societies, professional journals and publishers, prizes and awards, etc.

The information in this title could be extremely useful for anyone interested in establishing contact with individuals in the areas of fashion design, manufacturing, or marketing. The publisher intends to update this title every three years.

Additional information on designers can be found in *Contemporary Designers* (St. Martin's Press, 1985. $65.00) that covers 650 figures of international reputation.

Elma M. Natt

PHOTOGRAPHY

167.   **Contemporary Photographers**. George Walsh, Colin Naylor, and Michael Held, eds. New York, St. Martin's Press, 1982. 1124p. illus. (part col.). $70.00. LC 82-3337. ISBN 0-312-16791-1.

With this volume, St. Martin's Press has contributed another important work to their series on contemporary arts. Although there are other scattered reference sources which offer biographical information on photographers, nothing quite compares to this volume in its coverage, scope, and research value.

Each person selected for coverage was recommended by an advisory board of distinctive individuals, e.g., Cornell Capa, Helmut Gernsheim, and Sir Tom Hopkinson. International in scope with photographers from the Eastern bloc being well represented, this work covers 650 prominent contemporary photographers, both those who are living and those who have died in recent years. The entries include the standard biographical data found in other works in the series, e.g., *Contemporary Artists*. In addition, the following information is given: a listing of individual exhibitions (two- and three-man shows are included here); a selection of up to ten group expositions; galleries and museums that have the work of an entrant in their collection (up to ten); and a bibliography of books and articles by and about the person. Two features which make this reference work so delightful and informative are the statements made by many of the living photographers about their own work or about contemporary photography in general, as well as the signed critical essays provided by the 155 contributors. The essays range from scholarly and critical, reflecting a great deal of original research, to personal and provocative, such as the essay by Judy Dater on Ansel Adams. More than six hundred black-and-white and thirty color photographs, chosen as being representative of the artists' work, are also presented.

Since the publisher plans a revised edition every five years, this valuable tool will continue to provide a wealth of information for users of library collections which support art and photography programs. Ann L. Hartman

168. **Macmillan Biographical Encyclopedia of Photographic Artists & Innovators**. New York, Macmillan, 1983. 722p. illus. (part col.). $45.00. LC 82-4664. ISBN 0-02-517500-9.

This is a collection of more than two thousand biographies of photographers and photographic artists who may be noted initiators and innovators, but may not necessarily be well-known. Nevertheless, if they have made significant contributions and if their works are widely recognized, they have been included. The intent of the authors is to "inform the readers about the world of photography as well as the photographers in it." The selection of candidates for inclusion is international in scope. Dedication to photography, and visibility through publication, showings, and awards formed the basis for selection criteria.

In this first Who's Who in photography, approximately a quarter of the biographees come from the nineteenth and the early part of the twentieth centuries. The giants are all represented along with those lesser-known photographers who have passed the dedication and visibility test.

The volume includes a collection of representative photographs reproduced in black and white and color, 144 plates in all. In the appendix there are separate listings of museums and galleries, with addresses.

This is a major reference work and is recommended for medium and large public and academic libraries. [R: Choice, May 84, p. 1272; RBB, 1 Oct 84, pp. 202-4]

Brian Alley

169. Willis-Thomas, Deborah. **Black Photographers, 1840-1940: An Illustrated Bio-Bibliography**. New York, Garland, 1985. 141p. illus. index. (Garland Reference Library of the Humanities, Vol. 401). $40.00. LC 82-49145. ISBN 0-8240-9147-7.

Americans have always loved the camera. Professional and amateur alike have recorded the nation's daily life and historic events since the daguerreotype was introduced in the late 1830s. Many historic photographs have been collected in the numerous volumes of pictorial histories published over the past few decades, but one group that has been largely ignored in these collections has been the black photographers who chronicled Afro-American life.

Willis-Thomas seeks to right this wrong with her bio-bibliography of American-born black photographers who practiced their craft during its first one hundred years. The biographical sketches are divided into four chronological groups: "Daguerreans, 1840-1859"; "Daguerreans and Photographers, 1860-1899"; "Photographers, 1900-1919"; and "Photographers, 1920-1940." Biographical information is scarce for many of the artists profiled, but Willis-Thomas has at least located where and when the photographer was active in the trade. She also lists where each artist's works are collected, along with bibliographic listings of published work by and about these men.

The best feature of the book is the selection of photographs reproduced from collections of these artists' works. The photos range from portraits of brides to black political leaders, from Harlem street scenes to scenes of the rural south. They are wonderful images, recording pieces of Americana too often omitted in photographic histories of this country.

Willis-Thomas's book is a valuable reference tool for students of photography or Afro-Americana. But because of the photographs included in the volume, I recommend its acquisition to all libraries.   Diane J. Cimbala

4 Communications and Mass Media

Introduction

In this chapter we include "Authorship," "Films," "Journalism," and "Television and Cable," with a total of forty entries. Related titles are mentioned in the annotations. Twenty-three entries pertain to films, and are subdivided into three categories: "General Works," "Actors and Actresses," and "Directors, Cinematographers, and Designers." Some standard works in this area include *American Writers: A Collection of Literary Biographies (see entry 171), Who Was Who on Screen* (see entry 196), and *Who's Who in Television and Cable* (see entry 208).

In addition to biographical sources, some subject dictionaries, primarily dealing with films, contain a fair amount of biographical information. *The Oxford Companion to Film* (Oxford University Press, 1976. 767p.) is probably one of the best sources, with international coverage. Less useful in this respect will be *Filmgoer's Companion* (6th ed. Avon, 1978. 825p.) with very brief biographical information pertaining primarily to the United States. International coverage is provided by the *International Dictionary of Films and Filmmakers* (4v. St. James Press, 1984-1985). Two foreign encyclopedias should also be mentioned: Roger Boussinot's *L'encyclopédie du Cinéma* (2v. Paris, Bordas, 1967-1970), international in coverage, with many biographies of film personalities; and a Russian work, *Kinoslovar'* (2v. Moscow, Sovetskaia Entsiklopediia, 1966-1970) that concentrates on the Soviet Union and Eastern Europe. For television, one of the best subject encyclopedias is *The New York Times Encyclopedia of Television* (Times Books, 1977. 492p.) that covers TV personalities in brief biographical sketches of one hundred to two hundred words.

Several indexes and abstracting services, including Wilson indexes, cover communications and mass media. One specialized source, *Communication Abstracts* (Sage, 1978-) covers some one hundred journals and a certain number of books. There are only a few bibliographic guides in the area of mass media. One of the best is Eleanor Blum's *Basic Books in the Mass Media: An Annotated, Selected Booklist Covering General Communications, Book Publishing, Broadcasting, Editorial Journalism, Film,*

Magazines and Advertising (2nd ed. University of Illinois Press, 1980. 426p.). For films one can recommend Alan Dyment's *The Literature of the Film: A Bibliographical Guide to the Film as Art and Entertainment, 1936-1970* (Gale, 1975).

AUTHORSHIP

170.   **American Society of Journalists and Authors Directory 1982-83: A Listing of Professional Free-Lance Writers**. New York, American Society of Journalists and Authors, 1982. 84p. index. $40.00pa.

This work lists for 1982-1983 the more than 650 members of this organization, a national group of professional freelance writers. The directory is arranged alphabetically by name and contains geographical and subject specialty indexes. The membership listings contain useful information, including address, phone number, publications, awards, and professional experience. The directory seems aimed primarily at editors and publishers seeking writers, but it is also a useful companion volume to *Contemporary Authors*, providing supplementary information and, perhaps, additional names. Although the price is steep for such a slim work, it is nevertheless a worthwhile collection. [R: BL, 15 Dec 83, p. 612]   Donald Altschiller

171.   **American Writers: A Collection of Literary Biographies**. Leonard Unger, ed.-in-chief. New York, Scribner's, 1974. 4v. $160.00. LC 73-1759. ISBN 0-684-13662-7.

172.   **American Writers, Supplement I: A Collection of Literary Biographies**. A. Walton Litz, ed.-in-chief. New York, Scribner's, 1979. 2v. $110.00. LC 73-1759. ISBN 0-684-15797-7.

173.   **American Writers, Supplement II, Parts 1 and 2: A Collection of Literary Biographies**. A. Walton Litz, ed.-in-chief. New York, Scribner's, 1981. 2v. index. $100.00/set; $55.00/vol. LC 73-1759. ISBN 0-684-16482-5.

The biographical essays that comprise *American Writers* were originally published as the University of Minnesota's *Pamphlets on American Writers* from 1959 to 1972. For this collection, most of the essays have been revised and updated, and an index to the whole set has been added. There are about one hundred essays in all, starting with Henry Adams and ending with Richard Wright. All the essays are well documented with a selected bibliography of works about and by the given author. A brief biographical sketch is provided in each essay, but the emphasis is on the critical evaluation and analysis of the writer's literary achievements. Recommended only for those libraries that do not have the original University of Minnesota series.

The first supplement was published in 1979, and the second in 1981, each reviewing twenty-nine authors. They have the same objectives and audience in mind. (An important difference between these essays and those in the initial volumes is that these are all original essays, published here for the first time. The problem of superfluity which plagued the first volumes is no longer.)

If one accepts the objectives—a sort of once-over-lightly approach—one must judge these essays to be well executed. Despite their brevity, they include a good deal of information and are often well written (particularly Kent Bales's essay on O. Henry and Paul Doyle's on Pearl Buck). Some of them are produced by well-known authorities who have published on their author or on closely allied subjects. The volumes are supplied with a thorough subject index. Both supplements seek to include more women and minority writers, writers who have been neglected in past volumes, and literary critics, as well as writers who have but recently gained wide recognition, which means that the essays cover a very wide spectrum of American writing, from Cotton Mather to Imamu Amiri Baraka and Joyce Carol Oates.

We have no quarrel with the objectives of these essays nor with the rigorously uniform and light treatment which those objectives necessarily produce, but it does seem that these characteristics militate against higher institutions' acquiring the volumes. The essays are entirely undocumented and frequently tend to be more appreciative than analytical. Even "college students" would be expected to do much more in the way of reading or research than these essays and their *highly* selected bibliographies offer. And it is stretching the point a good deal to claim, as the editor does, that essays like the one on W. E. B. DuBois are the "Fullest account to date of the writer's life and works." For college and university libraries, the Twayne books on American writers are better as introductions. These volumes are very appropriate for public libraries, however. L. Terry Oggel and Bohdan S. Wynar

174. **ASCAP Biographical Dictionary**. 4th ed. Compiled for the American Society of Composers, Authors and Publishers by Jaques Cattell Press. New York, R. R. Bowker, 1980. 589p. o.p. LC 80-65351. ISBN 0-8352-1283-1.

The American Society of Composers, Authors and Publishers was founded in 1914 as a voluntary, unincorporated, nonprofit association set up to collect royalties for the use of copyright music and to distribute the revenue among the persons entitled to it. In its first appearance, in 1948, the dictionary contained close to two thousand biographies; the present updated fourth edition has over eight thousand member entries, this reportedly being only a portion of the society's membership. Also, with this edition, the *Biographical Dictionary* is being offered commercially to the public, this being the result of many requests from the nonmusic industry to do so.

The biographical entries are organized alphabetically and as to: name (and professional name if that is the case) — pseudonyms are cross-referenced; year joined ASCAP; professional category; birthplace and date; study and training; outline of career; chief collaborators; and major published works. Questionnaire forms sent to qualified ASCAP members, their heirs, or representatives were the prime means of information collection. The main biographical section is followed by a listing of over seven thousand publisher members. The dictionary is unique in one sense: it contains biographies of select musicians and authors side by side. Nevertheless, don't expect to find every composer or every author listed, only those who are or have been members of ASCAP. Yet there will be names listed that cannot be found in other sources. [R: Choice, May 81, p. 1229] Frederic Schoettler

175. **The Author's and Writer's Who's Who**. 6th ed. New York, Hafner, 1971. 887p. o.p.

This is a well-known work that needs little introduction. The last edition was published seven years ago and many new names (four thousand, in fact) in the literary world have been introduced in this volume. Others were deleted. The biographical information remains essentially the same: date of birth, place, education, career, address, and, obviously, a list of published works. For major works new editions (and publisher) are indicated, which is certainly helpful. This work was produced in cooperation with the British Society of Authors; obviously, for international coverage the reader has to look elsewhere. The list of pseudonyms printed in a very small typeface may irritate many users, as well as the similarly printed list of abbreviations.

Unfortunately, there is no new edition of this work, and the 1971 imprint makes combined information and personal data rather obsolete.   Bohdan S. Wynar

176.   **Authors in the News: A Compilation of News Stories and Feature Articles from American Newspapers and Magazines Covering Writers and Other Members of the Communications Media**. By the staff of *Biography News*. Barbara Nykoruk, ed. Detroit, Gale, 1975-1976. 2v. illus. index. (Biography News Library). $70.00/vol. LC 75-13541. ISBN 0-8103-0043-5 (vol. 1); 0-8103-0045-1 (vol. 2).

Authors in the News is an extension of the work of the staff of *Biography News*, which seeks to present in depth five hundred articles concerning persons of prominence. The articles are taken from newspapers and magazines. *Authors in the News* focuses on authors, both new and established, and covers the entire world of communications. This is a gargantuan undertaking.

The main criticism concerns the sources used. Scanning the newspapers consulted for articles, the reader is rather astounded to learn that such newspapers as the *Boston Globe*, the *Chicago Tribune*, the *Los Angeles Times*, *Newsday*, the *New York Times*, the *St. Louis Post-Dispatch* and the *Washington Post* were completely neglected, and such a magazine as the *Saturday Review* was not consulted. There seems to have been a very heavy reliance on the *Miami Herald*, which, although an excellent newspaper, is only one of many sources.

A second criticism is the subject selection. For every major writer, such as Joseph Heller and Tennessee Williams, there are three or four unknown or very minor authors.

The book is well printed with excellent photographs. The index is accurate and complete. The series will be a good buy for any library. [R: LJ, July 76, p. 1512; WLB, Sept 76, pp. 85-86]   William C. Young

177.   **The International Authors and Writers Who's Who**. 9th ed. Adrian Gaster, ed. Cambridge, England, Melrose Press; distr., Detroit, Gale, 1982. 1093p. $120.00. ISBN 0-8103-0428-7.

This work incorporates both *The Authors and Writers Who's Who*, published by Burke's Peerage Ltd. since 1934, and Melrose Press's ill-conceived *County Authors Today* series, abandoned after nine volumes were published. In addition, some twenty-five hundred poets that would have been listed in the sixth edition of *International Who's Who in Poetry* are represented in this work.

The format and the information included in the twelve thousand or so biographical entries are essentially the same as those in Burke's last edition: date and place of birth, career, education, published works, honors and memberships, and address. Type is smaller and the entries are generally briefer, with references to spouses and children eliminated and bibliographies often more selective. While the number of biographies has not substantially changed, the scope has been expanded from primarily English-language authors to those throughout the world. Thus, fewer English-language authors are found here than in the past. Still, there are biographees here who are not covered in *Contemporary Authors*. Therein lies the chief value this work might have. However, the majority of authors that are likely to need finding are more thoroughly covered in other sources. Also provided is a list of pseudonyms of included authors and a list of literary agents. Recommended only for those who found Burke's editions useful and/or for those who want everything in this area. [R: BL, 1 Nov 76, pp. 417-18; LJ, 15 Apr 76, p. 1001]   Richard J. Kelly

178.   **The Writers Directory 1984-86**. 6th ed. New York, St. Martin's Press, 1983. 1250p. index. $85.00. LC 77-166289. ISBN 0-912289-02-3.

This is an "all purpose" directory listing professional and part-time authors, journalists, and editors writing in the English language. The biographical information is of the usual type, e.g., name; pen-names, if any; area of writing; publishers of given works (but not titles of written books); major current and past appointments; and address. All names are arranged in one alphabet, with an index to writing categories and a list of publishers. In glancing at the index we can see that most professions are represented—e.g., literature (subdivided by novels, poetry, etc.), nonfiction (again subdivided by subject area, such as agriculture, anthropology), journalists, columnists and correspondents, and book editors. The directory provides information on more than fifteen thousand contemporary writers from America and the British Commonwealth. In comparison to Gale's *Contemporary Authors* (to mention just one well-known directory) the entries are very brief—frankly, too brief.

In most cases biographical sketches tell us very little. In general, for prominent authors there are many better directories. Secondly, the criteria for selection are not clear. Apparently, authors simply nominate each other. Consequently, we will not recommend this book.   Bohdan S. Wynar

FILMS

General Works

179.   Dolmatovskaya, Galina, and Irina Shilova. **Who's Who in the Soviet Cinema**. Vladislav Kostin, ed. Translated by L. Shkanov. Moscow, Progress Publishers, 1979; distr., Chicago, Imported Publications. 685p. $12.50. ISBN 0-8285-1553-0.

This book presents seventy portraits of Soviet directors, actors, and actresses active in the contemporary cinema. Each entry includes a photograph of the biographee and stills from his or her films. Birth dates, relevant educational background, work experience, and awards precede each entry; a list of movies which the biographee directed or acted in follows the text.

The articles average three pages in length and contain descriptions of selected films of each biographee. Incidental personal information in the text usually consists only of a brief mention of where the person grew up. The authors emphasize the techniques and themes of the director, or the screen persona of the actor or actress; specific movies or characters are discussed in some detail. The authors do not state their selection criteria in any detail, saying that they have chosen subjects "whose work is the fullest and most vivid reflection of all that is original in our cinema today" (p. 684). They state that they included men who have been making films since the twenties but yet they have omitted some of the best known names, such as Parazhanov.

Usage is sometimes a little sloppy and, since this was published in 1979, the work is now somewhat outdated. Interesting to browse through, the book might be more helpful to the general student of Soviet film than to someone needing a detailed biographical source.   Gloria Palmeri Powell

180.   Halliwell, Leslie. **Halliwell's Filmgoer's Companion**. 8th ed. New York, Scribner's, 1984. 704p. illus. bibliog. $42.50. LC 84-51624. ISBN 0-684-18183-5.

This eighth edition has added or revised some seven thousand entries with the information current through early 1984. Besides film people there are entries on specific films—although no criteria are given for selection—and on film topics such as air balloons, leprechauns, etc. Over one hundred photographs replace the movie posters of the seventh edition. In addition, nearly the entire contents of two other books, *Halliwell's Movie Quiz* (Penguin, 1978) and the *Filmgoer's Book of Quotes* have been added to this edition making it both informative and fun to read. Included in the entries are personal dates (birth and death), film dates and titles (with those Halliwell thinks are most significant in italics), an indicator of which films have won the Academy Award or the British Film Academy Award, a rosette for people entered into Halliwell's Hall of Fame, and often, quotations about and/or by the person discussed. Quizzes are included throughout the book with answers provided. The print has been reduced in size from the previous edition in order to accommodate more information in fewer pages. The entries here are shorter than in Ephraim Katz's *The Film Encyclopedia* (Crowell, 1979), but are more current.

As always it is relatively easy to find errors in a work of this magnitude. For example, the entries for Dean Martin and Jerry Lewis give conflicting dates on the releases of several of their films as well as the breakup of their partnership.

This book is a standard reference that is improving gradually with each edition.

Robert L. Turner, Jr.

181.   Kaplan, Mike, ed. **Variety Who's Who in Show Business**. New York, Garland, 1983. 330p. $15.95pa. LC 83-11654. ISBN 0-8240-9096-9.

Variety Who's Who offers extremely wide, if not deep, coverage of people currently in show business. In addition to actors, actresses, producers, writers, and directors, it includes dancers, executives, singers, composers, and TV journalists, among others. Entries include date and place of birth, occupation(s), place where educated or trained, career changes, credits, and awards won. Variations in name and relationship to other famous people are noted. Dates for films, TV shows, and stage plays are not given, nor are addresses for the personalities. The more than six thousand current biographies included here, plus the authority lent by the name *Variety*, make this a useful and dependable book for reference work.

In connection with this work one should also mention *Who's Who in Show Business: The International Directory of the Entertainment World*, published in New York by Who's Who in Show Business, Inc., in 1968 and 1971. It lists choreographers, composers, lyricists, music arrangers, producers and directors and even some writers. This work is now out-of-print.   Randall Rafferty and Bohdan S. Wynar

182.   Lloyd, Ann, and Graham Fuller, eds. **The Illustrated Who's Who of the Cinema**. New York, Macmillan, 1983. 480p. illus. (part col.). $65.00. LC 83-790. ISBN 0-02-923450-6.

An encyclopedia of mainstream cinema, *The Illustrated Who's Who of the Cinema* celebrates films and their producers and directors, actors and actresses, screenwriters, cinematographers, inventors, scene designers, costume designers, art directors, composers, conductors, arrangers, animators, critics, and censors.

A total of twenty-five hundred biographies is included, with brief biographical data plus more than fifteen hundred photographs, most in color.

As editors Lloyd and Fuller explain, the "fullest treatment" has been given the great decades of the 1920s and the 1930s, with the 1940s not far behind. Since the films of the 1950s and the 1960s are probably better known, the presentation of these is "more straightforward." The selections from recent cinema are based on intelligent guesses as to what names will be known in twenty or thirty years. Since the films of the avant-garde and underground cinema have to a large extent entered the mainstream, masters such as Louis Delluc, Germanie Dulac, Jean Vigo, and Viking Eggeling are included.

In the filmographies, complete lists were not possible, so the editors marked the beginning and end (if there is one) of a career, citing the films that seem characteristic of the artist's best work.

Thanks to repertory cinemas, films on television, and video players, a wide variety of films is now available for the film enthusiast, who will find *The Illustrated Who's Who of the Cinema* a reliable armchair companion. This work may be supplemented by *Who's Who in the Motion Picture Industry*, 4th edition by Rodman W. Gregg (Packard, 1981. 250p. $17.95pa.), and by *Who's Who in American Film Now*, revised edition by James Monaco (New York, Zoetrope, 1981. $19.95; $9.95pa.). [R: Choice, Oct 83, p. 252; LJ, Aug 83, p. 1471; WLB, Sept 83, p. 66]

Colby H. Kullman and Bohdan S. Wynar

183.   Sadoul, Georges. **Dictionary of Films**. Translated, edited, and updated by Peter Morris. Berkeley, University of California Press, 1972. 432p. $36.50; $8.95pa. LC 74-136027. ISBN 0-520-01864-8; 0-520-02152-5pa.

184.   Sadoul, Georges. **Dictionary of Film Makers**. Translated, edited, and updated by Peter Morris. Berkeley, University of California Press, 1972. 288p. $27.50; $5.95pa. LC 78-136028. ISBN 0-520-01864-8; 0-520-02151-7pa.

These complementary volumes were originally published in France in 1965; this is their first appearance in English. *Films* includes about twelve hundred entries (in the original languages with cross-references from English) that attempt to give a historical view of film throughout the world. Each entry includes credit list, running time, short plot summary, and a critical note.

Film Makers includes over "a thousand entries devoted to directors, scriptwriters, cinematographers, art directors, composers, producers, inventors," but "no technicians, . . . exhibitors, distributors or exporters" (preface). The directors' filmographies are the key—each director's entry includes his own filmography (not always complete, although Morris has expanded the originals) and a critical appraisal. The works included in *Films* are not evaluated here, but their inclusion in *Films* is noted by an asterisk. For this reason—and also because neither work has a separate index and each must act as an index to the other—both should be available to gain full value from either.

The one great lack for English-speaking monolinguists is that titles in *Film Makers* are in French. German and Italian titles have not been translated when the English release title is a simple translation. For example, if using the Jean Renoir entry in *Film Makers* to find the listing for a specific Renoir film in the other volume, one must know it by its French title. In *Films*, although the English release titles are cross-referenced to the original language entry, this presupposes that one knows the release title, which is not always the case.

A sampling of the entries in both dictionaries indicates critical comments in most cases, usually the expected ones, to only a few of which one could take exception. Some landmark films such as *Greed* (three columns) and *Intolerance* (two columns) are covered very thoroughly; other entries seem arbitrary: Disney's *Snow White* gets two columns to one for *Wild Strawberries*; *2001* gets one and one-half to one for *The Silence.*

Despite any shortcomings, omissions, errors, or critical misjudgments, these dictionaries are valuable reference tools, are less specialized than either *The American Movies Reference Book* or *The New York Times Film Reviews* (abridged), and supplement any other bibliographies available in English, including the in-progress multi-volume catalog produced under the aegis of the American Film Institute. [R: LJ, 1 Oct 72, p. 3138]   Richard M. Buck

185.   Stewart, William T., Arthur F. McClure, and Ken D. Jones. **International Film Necrology**. New York, Garland, 1981. 328p. (Garland Reference Library of the Humanities, Vol. 215). $42.00. LC 80-17636. ISBN 0-8240-9552-9.

The authors have compiled a necrology of significant personalities connected with the film (motion picture) industry from 1900 to the publication date of February 1980. Actors, actresses, composers, writers, directors, and cinematographers as well as producers are included. Listed alphabetically, the information appears under the person's professional name followed by the real name (if applicable). Dates of birth and death, age at death, and occupation are included. In addition to many published biographies and reports, statistics from the California Department of Public Health (which keeps records regarding births and deaths back to 1905) were used. This is a very good quick reference item and is recommended for large libraries dealing in many quick reference questions for which this can provide adequate information. [R: Choice, May 81, p. 1244; LJ, 15 Feb 81, p. 441]   .   Steven J. Mayover

186.   Thomson, David. **A Biographical Dictionary of Film**. 2nd ed. New York, William Morrow, 1981. 682p. $15.95; $10.95pa. LC 80-20499. ISBN 0-688-00131-9; 0-688-00132-7pa.

As Jonathan Rosenbaum has asserted in *American Film*, film book publishers have only two markets to chase—the scholarly and the mass market—and anything falling between these two will encounter difficulty in being placed. This *Biographical Dictionary of Film* asserts itself as the indispensable reference work, yet the entries strike a strangely approachable and paradoxically unstarstruck tone. Thomson hides no prejudice, and his biases have caused a few slipups—where are Alan Rudolph, Jill Clayburgh, Richard Gere? Didn't Steve McQueen die in 1980? Randy Quaid was an Academy Award nominee; doesn't he deserve an entry? How can John Carpenter's filmography end with *Halloween*, even in a work with a 1981 imprint? But one must review affectionately a collection of biographical sketches which asserts that, "directed by Warhol, Buñuel, or von Sternberg, Connery could have been a marvellous cruel stud James Bond."

The volume is a pleasure. It is compassionate and cynical by turns. It is a surprise. Any film buff would enjoy turning to it repeatedly. But as a reference work it is a bit idiosyncratic and should be considered only after the more authoritative titles have been purchased.

Probably a better balanced work is *Who Was Who on Screen* (3rd ed. New York, R. R. Bowker, 1983. 571p. $65.00) that is also available in an abridged edition (1984. 438p. $23.95pa.). The unabridged version contains thirteen thousand brief biographies of stars, actors, stunt people, dancers, musicians, and animals. The abridged edition provides thirty-three hundred entries. [R: LJ 1 Apr 81, p. 784]

F. W. Ramey and Bohdan S. Wynar

Actors and Actresses

187.   Palmer, Scott. **A Who's Who of British Film Actors**. Metuchen, N.J., Scare-crow, 1981. 561p. $27.50. LC 80-26016. ISBN 0-8108-1388-2.

"This book includes some 1,400 actors and actresses," the majority of them English but including Scottish, Irish, Welsh, Australian, Canadian, South African, and those from former or present British Commonwealth members (p. v). Actors born in other countries but working in the United Kingdom are included. Listings are comprehensive but are not claimed to be complete, omissions including bit parts by later stars and players who appeared only in bit parts. Entries include birth and death dates, brief characterization of players, and generally complete, chronological listings of films. Silent films are included, except that those players who appeared only in silents are omitted.

It is interesting to compare names from this work with their listings in Halliwell's *Filmgoer's Companion* (6th ed. Avon Books, 1978), which includes some supposedly complete filmographies. Sampling of three players (Sara Allgood, Lionel Atwill, and Peter Ustinov) revealed larger film totals for Allgood and Ustinov in Palmer by significant numbers of films, and the same totals for Atwill. Incidentally, some of Palmer's brief characterizations of actors are strikingly close to those found in Halliwell for the same players. Reference uses for this work would seem to be limited to determining whether certain players appeared in certain films and, of course, browsing. Paper, type, and binding are first class.

A related title is Denis Gifford's *British Cinema: An Illustrated Guide* (London, A. Zwemmer; distr., Cranbury, N.J., A. S. Barnes, 1969. 176p. $2.25pa.) which provides brief biographical sketches of about 546 British actors and directors. [R: BL 15 June 82, p. 1388]

Jerry Cao

188.   Parish, James Robert. **Hollywood Character Actors**. With Earl Anderson and others. New Rochelle, N.Y., Arlington House, 1978. 542p. illus. o.p. LC 78-17553. ISBN 0-87000-384-4.

This is a very simple reference source with very simple contents. The volume consists of an alphabetical arrangement of entries under the names of several hundred character actors (male and female), each with an illustrative still, a skimpy paragraph of biographical information, a dialog quotation from one of the actor's films, and surely the most complete list extant of films (with company and release dates) in which the actor appeared. The quotations were surely unnecessary—some are amusing, but most are inane. The filmographies would have been enhanced by naming the character played. There is no foreword or preface, except the author's note that the film listing includes all known features over four reels in length and serials. No short subjects or made-for-TV films are included. There is no index. [R: LJ, 1 Dec 78, p. 2443; WLB, Dec 78, p. 344]

Richard M. Buck

189.   Parish, James Robert, and Lennard DeCarl. **Hollywood Players: The Forties**. New Rochelle, N.Y., Arlington House, 1976. 544p. illus. index. o.p. LC 75-33146. ISBN 0-87000-322-4.

This is a movie buff's delight. Where else would one hope to find fairly detailed career/personal sketches of such diverse performers as Evelyn Ankers, Billy De Wolfe, Mona Freeman, Lon McCallister, Dennis O'Keefe, and Martha Vickers? These players, and seventy-seven others, are each represented by a three- to four-page sketch, several well-chosen stills, and a filmography. Dolled up in coffee-table format, *Hollywood Players* will provide many pleasurable hours for the older filmgoer with a memory or for any devotee of old movies on TV.

Despite these virtues, there are some flaws. A basic repetitiveness is probably unavoidable in such a compilation. Still, following each sketch from the performer's birth and rearing to establishment in Hollywood to career decline becomes monotonous. The writing style is genial but tends toward overly sympathetic treatment (as when a minor contribution to a grade-C film is viewed with near-reverence). Factual inaccuracies seem minimal, but typographical errors pop up on an average of one per page.

A more important quibble concerns the authors' (unstated) criteria for inclusion. When examined alongside the full shelf of related books by Parish and various collaborators, *Hollywood Players* takes on something of a "leftover" quality. For example, two earlier Parish products, *The Paramount Pretties* (Arlington House, 1972) and *The Fox Girls* (Arlington House, 1971), detailed the careers of these studios' leading women contract players. Missing from these volumes were, respectively, Paramount's extremely pretty Gail Russell and Fox's eminently foxy Vivian Blaine, both of whom have found a place in the present work. Parish's *The MGM Stock Company* (Arlington House, 1973) covered that studio's contract players quite well; consequently, only one (Ann Blyth) is included here. The large number of sketches on actresses from the stables of Warner Brothers, Columbia, and Universal, and on actors associated with studios other than MGM, seems attributable to the fact that previous Parish books have not covered these categories of performers.

All of this leads to a curious mix. Talented, established players such as Teresa Wright and Robert Preston share the spotlight with the less vivid Susanna Foster and Robert Hutton. Although most of the performers received star billing at the time, others (e.g., Sydney Greenstreet, Barry Fitzgerald, Arthur Kennedy) were distinguished supporting players. An attempt at more cohesive selection would have given the book greater unity.

Still, rather than complain, one is inclined to respect the authors' decision not to recycle previous material. And one must decidedly applaud the effort to document the careers of the many lesser but still-remembered performers who have received no attention elsewhere.   Phillip Smith

190.   Parish, James Robert, and William T. Leonard. **The Funsters**. With Gregory W. Mank and others. New Rochelle, N.Y., Arlington House, 1979. 752p. illus. index. o.p. LC 78-32095. ISBN 0-87000-418-2.

The sixty-two profiles in this collection, averaging ten pages in length and including several photographs each, continue the sequence of Hollywood biography titles turned out by Parish and his staff. An attempt seems to have been made to select relatively few subjects and to provide intense coverage of those chosen. This time, the focus is on "Funsters," a reasonably accurate but perhaps ill-chosen name for comedians, especially as they are found in the movies. Both those of bygone days (Chaplin, Arbuckle, Normand) and those of more recent times (Woody Allen, Dick Van Dyke, Jack

Lemmon) are included, with ample information concerning the person, his or her films, and specific or summarized critical reception, with an overall attempt at an evaluation.

Following the Parish mold, this book wastes no space on preface or introduction (unless one reads the blurb), but dives right into the alphabetically arranged sketches, which constitute the major section. The general tenor of the sketches is casual and conversational, with no obligation to a strict chronological arrangement. This provides a wealth of fascinating detail, but makes searching for specific nuggets of information, such as birth date or other salient facts, rather slow going. The tone is affectionate; clearly, Parish has chosen those comics he feels warrant the most interest, and details appear not as highlighted items of gossip but as part of the narrative. Quotes from the subjects and their costars, producers, and directors abound, and these entries may be read for pleasure as well as for specific information.

While this book will provide such interesting details as what Laurel really thought of Hardy, and vice versa, it is not a quick reference source of vital statistics on the stars; it should be employed as a supplement to more highly structured film-bio books. Recommended for its knack of making accessible the personalities behind the personae of the cinema.   Bruce A. Shuman

191.   Parish, James Robert, and William T. Leonard. **Hollywood Players: The Thirties**. New Rochelle, N.Y., Arlington House, 1976, 1978pa. 576p. illus. index. $19.95; $7.95pa. LC 76-17647. ISBN 0-87000-365-8; 0-89508-003-6pa.

The authors have compiled a list of seventy-one actors and actresses who were among those forming the backbone of the movie industry in the thirties. Although they occasionally rose to starring roles in major productions, they spent most of their film careers in second leads and character parts or starring in the Bs. Each performer is profiled in a brief biographical essay, written in a breezy style reminiscent of gossip columns and fan magazines. The essays trace both personal and professional activities, including all aspects of show business: stage, film, radio, and television. Concluding each essay is the performer's filmography. The index consists of film titles, with no entries for titles of stage, radio, or television productions although these are mentioned in the text. The only personal names listed are those of the persons profiled.

The work has limited reference value. Lack of in-depth indexing severely limits its usefulness. The essays themselves will appeal to nostalgia buffs rather than to serious students and researchers. As a guide to film credits, it must be compared to John T. Weaver's *Forty Years of Screen Credits*. Although Weaver's book only covers 1929 to 1969, and Parish and Leonard include work before 1929 and up to the present, there is much duplication of coverage. In actual fact, many of the performers profiled began their film careers after 1930 and either died or retired before 1970. Spot comparisons of the two works show that Weaver often lists more credits for the time period covered by both works. [R: LJ, 15 Oct 76, p. 2192]   Barbara E. Kemp

192.   Pickard, Roy. **Who Played Who in the Movies: An A-Z**. London, F. Muller, 1979; repr., New York, Schocken Books, 1981. 248p. illus. index. $14.95; 5.95pa. LC 80-26546. ISBN 0-8052-3766-6; 0-8052-0676-0pa.

Who Played Who in the Movies is a moderately useful volume identifying actors and actresses who have played well-known historical and fictional characters and the films in which they have appeared. The scope is international, with primary emphasis given to the sound era. Entries include an introductory paragraph about each character, followed by a listing of the actor or actress, title, director, country of origin, and year of release for each film in which the character appeared. Arrangement is by name of the character, and there is an index of players. Although this is the first work devoted to this topic, much of the information it supplies can be found in such film encyclopedias as Leslie Halliwell's *Filmgoer's Companion*. Also, the selection of characters included seems, at times, arbitrary: Nick Adams, but not Robert Jordan; William Cody, but not Kit Carson; the Lone Wolf, but not the Lone Ranger. Still, most of the characters likely to be sought after will be found here—and in more plentiful numbers than in any other available source. [R: BL, 15 June 81, p. 1328; RQ, Fall 81, pp. 90-91]

Richard J. Kelly

193. Pitts, Michael R. **Horror Film Stars**. Jefferson, N.C., McFarland, 1981. 324p. illus. bibliog. index. $16.95; $12.95pa. LC 80-11241. ISBN 0-89950-003-X; 0-89950-004-8pa.

This selective presentation of performers who have depended on the horror film genre for at least a part of their careers provides reasonable accounts of those careers. There are fifteen performers given "star" status, and to them go the more detailed entries. Many of the names here, such as Boris Karloff, Lon Chaney, Sr., and Bela Lugosi, have more extensive biographies available, and some of the other names appear in other previously published collections. However, there is a sense of reference orientation in this work. The "stars" get a listing of all of their films; the group called "players," which includes John Agar, Henry Daniell, Rondo Hatton, and Glenn Strange, have lists of their genre films. The index covers all personal names and the titles of films mentioned. The text is devoted solely to the performers, with no mention of other artists connected with the production or the releasing company. There are sufficient stills and portraits to cover all of the performers mentioned. *Horror Film Stars* would be handy as a reference work or for general reader interest. This is a far superior work to the usual "fanzine" type previously published in this subject field. [R: LJ, 1 Mar 81, p. 574; RQ, Fall 81, pp. 90-91; WLB, Oct 81, p. 142]

Gerald R. Shields

194. Ragan, David. **Who's Who in Hollywood 1900-1976**. New Rochelle, N.Y., Arlington House, 1976. 864p. o.p. LC 76-25542. ISBN 0-87000-349-6.

Touted on the jacket blurb as "Finally—the definitive biographical reference of the film," this oddly compiled reference work proves to be a massive hodge-podge of strange biographical "facts" about screen personalities. Directors are included only if they have appeared in films as actors. The author divides the more than twenty thousand entries into five sections: "Living Players," "Late Players (1900-1974)," "Players Who Died in 1975 and 1976," " 'Lost' Players," and " 'Lost' Child Players,"— an unfortunate arrangement, particularly if one forgets who is living, who is dead, and who is lost. There is no index.

The treatment of living Hollywood actors is anecdotal and inconsistent in length and type of information. As a rule, obscure stars often have the longest entries, consisting mainly of fulsome, subjective descriptions of the individual's personal appearance. The typical format for entries of well-known screen personalities is a listing of screen credits, unaccompanied by dates, with little or no biographical information. Similarly, dates are missing for Oscar nominations and awards. The author chooses to omit a birth date in most cases, even when this vital statistic is readily available. The John Wayne entry, for example, gives little more than a listing of his films, despite the fact that biographical and film dates can be located easily in such common sources as

Who's Who in America and Leslie Halliwell's *The Filmgoer's Companion* (4th ed. 1974). Though the author does provide the subject's current place of residence, users might find mention of the individual's nationality a more helpful feature.

Generally omitted is information about a player's education and training. Even the longer entries seldom assess the dramatic contributions of the actor or list the studios for which he/she worked.

Still, this is a source of information, albeit peripheral, about obscure screen personalities impossible to locate elsewhere. [R: Choice, Sept 77, p. 834; WLB, Apr 77, p. 682]

Esther F. Stineman

195.   Rainey, Buck. **Saddle Aces of the Cinema**. 1st ed. San Diego, Calif., A. S. Barnes; London, Tantivy Press, 1980. 307p. illus. index. $19.95. LC 78-75328. ISBN 0-498-02341-9.

For the nostalgia buff who still fondly remembers the Saturday matinee shoot-em-up westerns, this book provides an enjoyable trip through the past; for the serious student of American film history and criticism, Buck Rainey has made a welcome addition to the literature of the western genre. The author, who is an authority on the cowboy film, surveys the lives and assesses the screen careers of fifteen cowboy stars, including Tom Mix, Hoot Gibson, Harry Carey, Buck Jones, Gene Autry, and Jack Holt. The personalities selected are primarily those whose careers spanned the silent and sound eras of motion pictures, i.e., pre-1920s through the 1940s.

Although not every afficionado of the western will be pleased by Rainey's choices, there is no doubt that the author has full mastery over his subject. Each profile is written with a graceful ease in a breezy, captivating manner, and is followed by a meticulous filmography. The reader, whether a film buff or serious student, will come to appreciate that the American cowboy film was multifaceted, due in large part to the styles and preferences of the saddle aces. The book contains many rare photos and posters (all from the author's private collection), and is very well bound and excellent in its graphic qualities. In all aspects, this is a work that is worthy of attention by students of American film, and Rainey is to be commended for producing a book that satisfies both research needs and nostalgic reading interests.

A related title is *The Hall of Fame of Western Movie Stars* by Ernest N. Corneau (North Quincy, Mass., Christopher Publishing House, 1969. 307p.), covering some 150 actors and actresses, with many illustrations. A somewhat different book is *The Great Cowboy Stars of Movies and Television* (New Rochelle, N.Y., Arlington House, 1979. 384p.). The text consists of three main parts divided among fifteen "living legends" such as Bob Steele and Randolph Scott, eleven "new breed of cowboy TV-movie star" like James Arness and Richard Boone, seventeen "ghost riders in the sky," among them William S. Hart, Hoot Gibson, Buck Jones, and thirty-six more straight-shooting Saturday afternoon heroes. Each tribute, varying in length from three to twelve pages, fondly profiles the actor's life, career, and films. In a few cases the author talked to the stars themselves, and with some, like Johnny Mack Brown, Tim McCoy, and Ken Maynard, he was the last to interview them before their death.

Great for trivia players is the listing for each cowboy of birth date; place of birth; year married, divorced, remarried; and names of wives and children. Every western film credit is also listed with the date and name of studio or network. There is an alphabetical index by name of performer and title of film. Probably the most appealing feature for nostalgia fans is the 152 photographs, many full page.

Andrew Garoogian and Alexander S. Birkos

196. Truitt, Evelyn Mack. **Who Was Who on Screen**. 3rd ed. New York, R. R. Bowker, 1983. 571p. $65.00. LC 77-22651.

The first edition of this basic reference tool appeared in 1974 and contained over six thousand entries covering mainly United States, British, and French screen personalities who had died between 1920 and 1971. The second edition contained over nine thousand entries covering 1905 to 1975. The present edition contains thirteen thousand entries of persons who died between 1905 and 1981. In addition, many sketches from the second edition have been revised.

Entries are arranged alphabetically with complete film credits following the basic biographical information. Only people who have actually appeared on screen are listed, although this is not limited to professional actors. Picasso, G. B. Shaw, and Somerset Maugham, for example, are listed for their brief appearances in dramatic films. As was the case in the first edition, U.S. release dates are taken from information in *Film Daily*, and the definitions of short (one to four reels) and feature (five reels or more) remain the same. The purpose of the first edition was to provide the researcher, the buff, or the audience member with facts "completely and accurately." Although not stated in the same way, the purpose obviously remains the same in this revision.

This is indeed a *basic* tool. The film credit listings give no information except title and release date. The biographical information is absolutely skeletal. For any fleshing-out of professional or personal background, one would have to turn to other sources. Presumably to save space, there are no breaks between letters of the alphabet. I do not believe I have ever seen continuous listing like this without even a space between the letters, except in the Marquis biographical series, in which it is also somewhat jarring. In any case, this is an important tool for large libraries with collections of film material, but a luxury for most smaller libraries, which would not have the necessary supplementary material in any case.

An abridgment of this work was published in paperback in 1984 (438p. $23.95).

Richard M. Buck

197. Wlaschin, Ken. **The Illustrated Encyclopedia of the World's Great Movie Stars and Their Films**. New York, Harmony Books/Crown, 1979. 256p. illus. (part col.). index. (A Salamander Book). $24.95; $9.95pa. LC 78-26866. ISBN 0-517-53714-1; 0-517-53715-Xpa.

The distinction has often been made between actors and movie stars. Many are both (Katharine Hepburn, Michel Simon); some move from one category to the other (Marcello Mastroianni, Monica Vitti); others from one to the other and back again (Jane Fonda). But most every personality whose face or figure is recognizable to the moviegoer, late show addict, or HBO subscriber appears in this heavily illustrated "encyclopedia."

Wlaschin's faith in the transcendent effectiveness of the star leads to some interesting if at times petulant 1-1½-column evaluations. But he often provides only lists of roles and adjectives—"She made a terrific impact as the very beautiful but slightly pregnant hostess in *Airport*; she was excellent as the object of the affections of a disturbed French boy in *The Secret World* and she superficially explored the women's liberation movement in *Stand Up and Be Counted*." Wlaschin's faith also denies Sean Connery and Roger Moore star status; rather, both are discussed in the entry for the personality/image they shared—James Bond.

The first line of the introduction proclaims, "This is a book of opinions"; and so it is. N. B. Max von Sydow, Bibi Andersson, Liv Ullmann, Victor Sjöström (director of and actor in many films, both in Sweden and the United States, but star of *Wild Strawberries*), et al., share an entry under "Ingmar Bergman's 'Stars,' " the "greatest group star in the history of cinema." Interestingly, Wlaschin designates ten best films for each entry, and this "group star" also has but ten.

Few will agree with all of the author's opinions, and this work has little reference value in spite of five hundred sketchy biographies. But the stills in this "encyclopedia" are often rare and usually interesting, and, frankly, the opinions are more provocative than anything in most star books. [R: BL, 15 Sept 79, p. 81; LJ, 1 Oct 79, p. 2085; WLB, Nov 79, p. 192]   F. W. Ramey

Directors, Cinematographers, and Designers

198. Coursodon, Jean-Pierre, with Pierre Sauvage. **American Directors**. New York, McGraw-Hill, 1983. 2v. index. $21.95; $11.95pa. LC 82-15199. ISBN 0-07-013263-1 (vol. 1); 0-07-013261-5pa. (vol. 1); 0-07-013264-X (vol. 2); 0-07-013262-3pa. (vol. 2).

Extremely up-to-date is this two-volume work featuring 118 readable essays on U.S. directors and giving background, influences, evaluation, and complete filmography for each subject. Coursodon, author of *Trente ans de cinema americain*, and Sauvage, a director himself, write very effectively in English and provide penetrating insights into the psychology of film and the psychology of the directors portrayed in their essays. Thus, this book can be used for pleasure reading by any amateur film buff, as well as for nuggets of useful information in the reference context.

One could pick, however. Nowhere are we told how the work is divided into its two volumes. Only from the promotional material did this reviewer glean that the birth year 1907 divides those directors included in volume 1 from those in its companion. The indexes, while helpful, do not provide cross listings between the volumes, which would have helped, and there is definitional ambiguity as to what constitutes an "American" director. Then, some are omitted who should be there. George Lucas is probably neglected because he is young, but what accounts for Mel Brooks's not being present, when so many little-known and mostly forgotten names are in evidence? Despite these criticisms, this book definitely belongs in every collection concerned with the performing arts, and the attractive price makes it even more desirable. [R: Choice, Oct 83, p. 249; LJ, 15 Apr 83, p. 836]   Bruce A. Shuman

199. **The International Dictionary of Films and Filmmakers: Volume II: Directors/ Filmmakers**. Christopher Lyon and Susan Doll, eds. Chicago, St. James Press, 1984. 611p. $50.00. LC 83-24616. ISBN 0-912289-05-8.

This is the second volume of a four-volume set which, when completed, will be the most substantial English-language film encyclopedia available. Volume 1, *Films*, provides detailed information on some six hundred of the world's "most widely-studied films." Volume 3, *Actors and Actresses* and volume 4, *Writers and Production Artists* are yet to come.

Volume 2, *Directors/Filmmakers*, covers more than 450 internationally-known directors. Entries consist of a brief biography, a filmography, a selective bibliography of books and articles (including interviews) by and about the director, and a signed, critical essay on the director's work.

The volume deals with roughly half the number of directors found in Georges Sadoul's *Dictionary of Film Makers*. The selections have been judiciously made, however, and the information provided here is much more extensive than in Sadoul and, of course, much more up-to-date. The quality of the essays and the completeness of the data supplied vary considerably—and a few of the entries (Jan Kadar, Billy Wilder) lack essays altogether. Despite these occasional first-edition lapses, though, the set promises to become a standard source for film studies.

A related title is Wheeler W. Dixon's *The "B" Directors: A Biographical Directory* (Scarecrow, 1985. 594p. $47.50), which provides filmographies and brief evaluative career biographies for over 350 directors who have made low-budget features. This work is opinionated and fun to read although its reference value is vastly reduced by an inadequate index.   Richard J. Kelly and Joseph W. Palmer

200.   **International Directory of Cinematographers, Set- and Costume Designers in Film**. Alfred Krautz, ed. Munich, New York, K. G. Saur, 1981-1983. 3v. index. $98.00. ISBN 3-598-21433-2.

Three volumes cover the following: volume 1, German Democratic Republic (1946-1978) and Poland (from the beginning to 1978); volume 2, France to 1980; and volume 3, Albania, Bulgaria, Greece, Rumania, and Yugoslavia to 1980.

A unique but highly specialized reference tool for research libraries, these first three volumes in a projected series provides very brief information about cinematographers and set and costume designers and lists films made by them in those countries. (Films they made elsewhere will appear in the appropriate volumes.) According to the preface, these film workers, unlike actors and directors, "have never been properly documented except in a few rare cases."

Information has been culled from materials in the International Federation of Film Archives (FIAF). No claim for completeness of filmographies is made, and only very basic information is provided. Jerzy Goscik, for instance, is described as "Cinematographer. Born 1934. Trained at the Moscow Film Institute. Also director and cameraman for documentaries." There follows a year-by-year list of films for which he was cinematographer, with the film's director named in parentheses (e.g., 1976 *Ocalic Miastro* [Jan Lomnicki]). While there are indexes to directors and film titles, the title is given only in the original language. Therefore, anyone wanting to identify the cinematographer of *Ashes and Diamonds* would first have to research the Polish title. No bibliographic references of any kind are provided.

In 1984 the fourth volume of this series was published under the title *International Directory of Cinematographers, Set- and Costume Designers in Film: Germany, From the Beginning to 1945* (New York, K. G. Saur, 1984. 605p. $62.00. ISBN 3-598-21434-0). The information is similar to the previous volumes providing brief biographical information and filmographies for the period covered. Although important for large cinema collections, the book is too esoteric for most libraries. Subsequent volumes that deal with countries such as the United States, England, and France could be of more widespread interest.

Joseph W. Palmer and Bohdan S. Wynar

201.   Singer, Michael, comp. and ed. **Film Directors: A Complete Guide**. Beverly Hills, Calif., Lone Eagle, 1985. 436p. illus. index. $34.95. ISBN 0-943728-15-0; ISSN 0740-2872.

The third edition of this annual guide has expanded to cover some fourteen hundred living film directors from around the world. Arranged alphabetically by director, each entry provides a chronological list of full-length feature-film and telefeature titles—with release year, country of origin, and distributor. Also furnished for most directors are birthplace and birth date as well as agent's name, address and phone number (especially useful for those wishing to contact lesser-known directors not found in other sources). Singer's international coverage and concentration on living filmmakers (including many new ones) further distinguish his guide from otherwise similar sources such as Larry Langman's *A Guide to American Film Directors: The Sound Era: 1929-1979* and James Robert Parish's *Film Director's Guide: Western Europe*. Indexed by directors, film titles, and agents.

　　Those who still want some biographical prose on many of the directors should consult David Thomson's highly opinionated *Biographical Dictionary of Film* and Georges Sadoul's *Dictionary of Film Makers*. Sharon Smith's *Women Who Make Movies* (New York, Hopkinson and Blake, 1975. 307p.) provides a general historical survey of women filmmakers, brief biographical sketches of porminent personalities, and a directory of contemporary women filmmakers. Unfortunately this work is now out-of-print.　　　　　　　　　　　　　　　　Richard J. Kelly and Bohdan S. Wynar

JOURNALISM

202.　Ashley, Perry J., ed. **American Newspaper Journalists, 1873-1900**. Detroit, Gale, 1983. 392p. illus. bibliog. index. (Dictionary of Literary Biography, Vol. 23). $78.00. LC 83-20582. ISBN 0-8103-1145-3.

　　This twenty-third volume of the *Dictionary of Literary Biography*, covering the last three decades of the nineteenth century, focuses on the time in American history when the newspaper was going through the final stages of its evolution from a vehicle of opinion into a medium which emphasized news, human interest, and entertainment. It was a period of great growth; the number of daily newspapers and their circulation increased at a far greater pace than did the population during this era of rapid industrialization.

　　Against this background, this work presents heavily illustrated biographical and critical essays on forty-two individuals who figured prominently. Many persons covered in the volume have long been recognized as literary figures, political leaders, and social and political observers. The essays presented here, however, focus on their journalistic activities, placing those in perspective with their other accomplishments. Among the journalists covered who achieved fame in other areas are Samuel Clemens, Ambrose Bierce, Jane Cunningham Croly, Richard Harding Davis, and Joel Chandler Harris.

　　Each essay has been written by a scholar or expert chosen for his or her knowledge of the subject. The volume follows the format and style of the previous highly regarded *DLB* volumes, the first of which was published in 1978 and most of which have been reviewed in past *American Reference Books Annuals*. The essays present a discussion of the subjects' professional and, where appropriate, personal lives. Each varies in length from two to sixteen pages, depending on the prolificacy of the individual.

　　Preceding each essay is a listing of the major position(s) held by the individual, and if he or she authored books, these are listed as well. Inconsistently, other headings are included—birth, marriage, and death information; awards and honors; and education. It would have been helpful had such headings been given for each subject, though even when not given in this form at the beginning of the piece, the information can usually be found in the body of the essay. Following each essay are such listings as biographies, letters, references, periodical publications, and papers. A checklist for further reading and a cumulative index are found at the end of the book.

Depicting the forerunners of the fourth estate as we know it today, the work is certainly of interest and value. Its price, though, may be prohibitive for smaller libraries. [R: Choice, June 84, p. 1435]   Beverley Hanson

203.   Ashley, Perry J., ed. **American Newspaper Journalists, 1901-1925**. Detroit, Gale, 1984. 385p. illus. bibliog. index. (Dictionary of Literary Biography, Vol. 25). $80.00. LC 83-25395. ISBN 0-8103-1704-4.

This new volume (the twenty-fifth) of the *Dictionary of Literary Biography* expands the coverage that began in volume 23, *American Newspaper Journalists, 1873-1900*.

Volume 25, in focusing on the 1901-1925 period, covers a transition from the personalized journalism of the nineteenth century to today's corporate-style journalism. It is one of the more interesting historical periods, as journalistic personalities were highly individualistic and colorful, some noteworthy newspapers such as *The New York Times* and the *Christian Science Monitor* began operations, and a publishing peak of about twenty-six hundred daily newspapers occurred around 1915.

Biographical and critical essays spotlight the career achievements of forty-seven journalists, including William Randolph Hearst, Ring Lardner, and Elizabeth Cochrane (Nellie Bly). Essays are structured chronologically; additional information in each entry includes birth and death dates, major position(s) held, a list of major books, a bibliography of secondary sources, and the location of the subject's collected papers. Numerous illustrations add much to the historical documentation. Additional features include a checklist for further reading and a cumulative index (*DLB*, vols. 1-25; *DLB Yearbook*, 1980-82; and *DLB Documentary Series*, vols. 1-4).

An excellent addition to any reference collection, the *Dictionary of Literary Biography* is an informative and readable examination of the preeminent literary personalities from 1600 to the present. Since volume 10 in 1982, the scope of *DLB* has been enlarged beyond the literature of the United States and now includes British, Commonwealth, and modern European literature. As a chronicle of the "intellectual commerce of a nation," the *DLB* is an invaluable library reference tool.

                                                                Darlene E. Weingand

204.   **Who Was Who in Journalism 1925-1928**. Detroit, Gale, 1978. 664p. index. (Gale Composite Biographical Dictionary Series, No. 4; A Firenze Book). $42.00. LC 78-13580. ISBN 0-8103-0401-5.

Journalism is sparsely covered by biographical dictionaries; this one contributes to historical interests. It is a complete reissue, including advertisements, of two publications (*Who's Who in Journalism*, 1925 and 1928) edited by Mihran Nicholas Ask and Sinai Gershanek. The reissue is justified, according to the Gale editors, by the fact that the late twenties were "the era of Mencken, Lippmann, Swope and tabloid journalism." However, those and other illustrious names from the originals are updated and treated more fully in later general sources, although sometimes their earlier journalistic work is not so specifically cited or is omitted altogether. The book is useful also for lesser-known names specific to the field and outstanding in local journalism, but not sufficiently widely known to be included in general biographical sources. An accurate sense of timing is needed to start a search with this book; it is, however, indexed in *Journalists Biographical Master Index* (Gale, 1978). Omissions in the originals (inclusion depended on returning questionnaires) are, of course, carried over into the present volume: Claudia Cassidy, Red Smith, Paul Gallico, Robert Casey, Don Marquis, A. B. Guthrie, Jr., among others working in the 1920s.

The book is in type. Newspapers are predominant, but trade journals and magazines are included. Entries — in abbreviated, truncated form — include place and date of birth, education, position in 1928, previous posts, professional affiliations, and addresses. Supplementary material includes an index to entries by a directory of job classifications; a geographical directory of newspapers, with officers and department heads named; a bibliography on journalism; schools of journalism; clubs and associations; syndicates; and foreign agencies.   Kathleen McCullough

205. **Who's Who in Journalism 1970.** 2nd ed. London, Haymarket Press; distr., Philadelphia, International Publications Service, 1970. 424p. o.p.

Includes British press organizations, newspaper and magazine groups, national daily newspapers, regional newspapers, magazines, news agencies, photo agencies, radio and TV services, foreign newspapers, list of specialized writers and editors, information services, news sources, personnel lists and government information services.   Bohdan S. Wynar

TELEVISION AND CABLE

206. Jakubowski, Maxim, and others, eds. **MTV, Music Television, Who's Who in Rock Video**. New York, Quill/William Morrow, 1984. 190p. illus. (part col.). index. $13.95pa. LC 84-60325. ISBN 0-688-04042-X.

The major portion of this book is devoted to a brief description of one hundred bands and individual performers who "have played an important role" in the development of video music and Music Television (MTV). The lavish use of illustrations tends to lengthen each entry, but actual text usually amounts to less than one full page so the information is necessarily brief. Typically an entry gives the background of the group or individual, lists relevant personnel changes, and briefly discusses major releases. Surprisingly, there is usually little information about the related videos or their impact. For most entries there is also a list of albums and videos released as of October 1983. Introductory material includes a discussion of MTV and the development of music video and brief biographies of the five MTV VJs (video jockeys). There are also lists of video directors with reference to the performers and videos for which they are responsible and an index to these directors by artist.

Given the rapidly changing nature of rock music and its performers and this book's 1983 compilation date, there are some glaring omissions of creative rock-video artists. No mention is made of Madonna, Cyndi Lauper, Elton John, Phil Collins, the Eurhythmics and others. Although brief, the information given will be helpful, but an updated, expanded version is needed.   Barbara E. Kemp

207. Morsberger, Robert E., Stephen O. Lesser, and Randall Clark, eds. **American Screenwriters**. Detroit, Gale, 1984. 382p. illus. index. (Dictionary of Literary Biography, Vol. 26). $80.00. LC 83-25414. ISBN 0-8103-0917-3.

Purists may quibble about the inclusion of a volume on screenwriters in the Dictionary of Literary Biography series, yet this is a genre that deserves serious critical examination. A screenwriter is essentially a dramatist, once-removed from the legitimate theatre. Thus, it is not surprising to find a number of important American playwrights included in this volume (e.g., Clifford Odets, Robert E. Sherwood, Sidney Howard, Ben Hecht). The editors, however, attach new significance to screenwriters. They feel that "the screenplay has emerged as a new form of literature" in the past decade, justifying a close examination of the careers of the important screenwriters, present and past.

In this volume, sixty-five such "major" writers are discussed in separate, signed essays, which average between five and six pages in length. This group is composed of those "who wrote primarily for the screen or who had noteworthy film achievements while writing in other media." Many of the writers found here will be familiar to anyone with a moderate knowledge of the American cinema: Charles Brackett, I. A. L. Diamond, Philip Dunne, Jules Furthman, Nunnally Johnson, Ring Lardner, Jr., Anita Loos, Herman Mankiewicz, Stirling Silliphant, Donald Ogden Stewart, Dalton Trumbo. A few of the major screenwriters were also prominent directors: John Huston, Preston Sturges, Billy Wilder (Wilder "never directed a film he did not write"). In addition to the playwrights mentioned above, several important television writers are represented (Rod Serling, Reginald Rose, Horton Foote), as are a few novelists (James Agee, Budd Schulberg, Daniel Fuchs). The essays here on these writers are good supplements to the fuller accounts found in previous volumes. Excluded are those novelists, like Faulkner and Fitzgerald, who wrote part-time for films, and playwrights who have primarily adapted their own work for the screen (Neil Simon).

The biographical essays contain a photo of the writer and, usually, several film stills (most are half a page in size). There is a short list of references at the end of most essays, plus an extensive list entitled "Books for Further Reading" which fills nine pages in the back of the volume. This particular volume also contains a cumulative index to the entire DLB series to date.

There is no comparable reference work available on American screenwriters; Richard Corliss's *Talking Pictures: Screenwriters in the American Cinema, 1927-1973* (Overlook Press, 1974) provides similar coverage, but only thirty-eight writers are discussed. Even though this DLB volume is more comprehensive, there are many important omissions (e.g., Ernest Lehman, S. J. Perelman, Walter Bernstein, William Goldman, Woody Allen), though that may be rectified in a projected second volume on screenwriters. Despite the inclusion of Stanley Kubrick and Buck Henry, most of the new generation of screenwriters (Robert Towne, Robert Benton, Elaine May, Nancy Dowd, et al.) are not covered. Nonetheless, this will be a popular volume in the DLB series—informative, readable, and great for browsing. [R: Choice, Nov 84, p. 397]

Thomas A. Karel

208.   Scheuer, Steven H., ed. **Who's Who in Television and Cable**. New York, Facts on File, 1983. 579p. illus. index. $49.95. LC 82-12045. ISBN 0-87196-747-2.

This is a serviceable biographical guide to more than two thousand individuals in TV, video, and cable. A majority of those included are top executives of the three major commercial networks, public TV, the large cable services, and local TV stations in New York, Washington, and Los Angeles. Covered, too, are a substantial number of writers, directors, designers, actors and actresses, on-air journalists, critics, and agents. Most entries provide job title, address, birth date, education, career highlights, achievements and awards, and "personal information." Scheuer, a well-known TV critic, acknowledges that "due to constraints of both space and time, various deserving candidates have been omitted" from this volume—a deficiency one hopes will be remedied in future editions. The present effort also writes off too many facts as not available (e.g., Dan Rather's educational background and Alistaire Cooke's birthplace, both of which are readily available in many other biographical directories). Still, for the industries it covers, this volume is the most comprehensive source of biographical information to date. Adding to its usefulness are some four hundred photographs as well as corporation and job title indexes. [R: Choice, Sept 84, p. 72; LJ, July 84, p. 1316; RBB, 1 Dec 84, p. 513; WLB, June 84, p. 757]   Richard J. Kelly

209. **Who's Who on Television: A Fully Illustrated Guide to a Thousand of the Best Known Faces on British Television**. Compiled and produced by ITV Books. London, Independent Television Books Ltd.; distr., Salem, N.H., Merrimack Pub. Cir., 1983. 272p. $6.95pa. ISBN 0-900727-95-0.

This guide features the most popular British stars and many American celebrities whose shows have been successful in Britain, such as Alan Alda, Linda Evans, Johnny Carson and Robert Wagner, to name just a few. Many biographical sketches are accompanied by photographs. There are a number of other biographical sources available on this subject, e.g., *Who's Who in Television*, edited by Rodman W. Gregg (Packard, 1984. $17.95pa. LC 81-64574. ISBN 0-941710-11-4) or *Who's Who on British Television* (ITV Books, 1981. distr., Zoetrope. 255p. $5.95pa. ISBN 0-900727-72-1).

Bohdan S. Wynar

5 Economics and Business

Introduction

The material in this chapter is arranged under seven headings. The first two sections, "Economics" and "Business," cover general works that pertain to all aspects of economic and business activities. They are followed by specific subject-oriented sections, e.g., "Banking and Finance," "Consulting," "Labor," "Public Relations," and "Real Estate." Twenty-one reference books are discussed in this chapter, with many related titles mentioned in the annotations. This chapter contains a number of outstanding biographical sources, e.g., *Biographical Dictionary of American Business Leaders* (entry 214), *Dictionary of Business Biography* (entry 215), *Biographical Dictionary of American Labor* (entry 224), and *Who's Who in Finance and Industry* (entry 220). It is hoped that all of these titles will be found in most libraries.

Obviously biographical information on prominent people in economics and business can also be found in other sources. Many dictionaries and encyclopedias contain some biographical information. For example, Ammer's *Dictionary of Business and Economics* (Free Press/Macmillan, 1984. 507p.) contains three thousand entries, including biographies of leading economists and business executives, past and present, and is international in scope. Auld's *The American Dictionary of Economics* (Facts on File, 1983. 342p.) is more selective. It contains sixteen hundred entries, but coverage is limited to such persons as Myrdal or Galbraith, and in this respect it is similar to Bannock's *The Penguin Dictionary of Economics* (2nd ed. Penguin Books, 1979). Pearce's *The Dictionary of Modern Economics* (MIT Press, 1983. 481p.) contains twenty-five hundred entries, but again the coverage is limited primarily to Nobel prize winners in economics.

For retrospective coverage there are three outstanding works. Palgrave's *Dictionary of Political Economy* (Macmillan, 1910; 3v. repr., Gale, 1976) offers excellent coverage of leading figures from the nineteenth century to 1908. Comprehensive coverage is also provided by two non-English works, namely L. Elster's *Wörterbuch der Volkswirtschaft* (3v. 4th ed. Jena, Fischer, 1931-1933) and *Dictionnaire des Sciences Économiques* (2v. Paris, Presses Universitaires de France, 1956-1958) that excludes living persons.

Additional biographical information can be located in periodicals and magazines, and in this respect, several indexing and abstracting services will be of primary importance. One should at least mention ABI/INFORM database (INF), *Business Index, Business Periodicals Index, Business Publications Index and Abstracts* (BPIA), MANAGEMENT CONTENTS database, *Public Affairs Information Service Bulletin, Social Sciences Index, Social Sciences Citation Index* and several other indexing services described in some detail in Lorna Daniells's *Business Information Sources* (University of California Press, 1985. pp. 20-25). Daniells also provides a selective listing of published bibliographies of business literature. In this connection one should also mention P. Melnyk's *Economics. Bibliographic Guide to Reference Books and Infortion Sources* (Libraries Unlimited, 1971. 263p.) that will be useful in locating basic sources of biographical information published internationally.

ECONOMICS

210. Blaug, Mark. **Great Economists since Keynes: An Introduction to the Lives & Works of One Hundred Modern Economists.** Totowa, N.J., Barnes & Noble Books, 1985. 267p. illus. index. $32.50. LC 85-12443. ISBN 0-389-20517-6.

This listing of one hundred modern economists would be a useful addition to both public and academic libraries since it covers a number of notable economists who are not included in standard reference sources. One hundred is an arbitrary listing but major figures and schools of thought are covered. Each entry is self-contained and covers major contributions of the economist as well as biographical and academic information. The essays are fair and well written. A basic knowledge of economics is helpful. While this is primarily a reference volume, it may be read through as an overview of post-Keynesian economic thought.   Maggie Johnson

211. Mai, Ludwig H. **Men and Ideas in Economics: A Dictionary of World Economists Past and Present.** Totowa, N.J., Littlefield, Adams, 1977. 270p. bibliog. (A Littlefield, Adams Quality Paperback No. 284). $11.50; $2.95pa. LC 77-9556. ISBN 0-87471-867-8; 0-8226-0284-9pa.

This volume contains brief (from a paragraph to a page) biographies of some seven hundred persons – mainly economists, with a few others thrown in who are important in matters of doctrine or policy (such as Lenin). One of the appendixes lists, by country, currently active economists and their principal works, and another outlines (in seven pages) a history of economic doctrine, covering the more important schools and movements and those associated with them. Although coverage is everywhere extremely summary, even economists are likely to find the work useful. They will in some cases doubtless be irritated by the shortcomings in the technical treatment of those economists whose work they know well, but they will need the work for the majority of those with whose work they have only slight acquaintance. Librarians and other laymen with an interest in matters economic will find the work very helpful for ready reference. For the money, hard to equal.

A related title is *Who's Who in Economics: A Biographical Dictionary of Major Economists, 1700-1981*, edited by Mark Blaug and Paul Sturges (MIT Press, 1983. 416p. $70.00) that covers more individuals, emphasizing primarily biographical data. [R: WLB, Dec 77, p. 345]   John G. Williamson and Bohdan S. Wynar

BUSINESS

212. **Business People in the News: A Compilation of News Stories and Feature Articles from American Newspapers and Magazines Covering People in Industry, Finance, and Labor**. Barbara Nykoruk, ed. Detroit, Gale, 1976. 402p. illus. index. (Biography News Library). $62.00. LC 76-4617. ISBN 0-8103-0044-3.

This new series by Gale follows the same format and pattern as their *Biography News*. The biographical articles on prominent business leaders are reproduced from various U.S. magazines and newspapers. Volume one includes approximately three hundred biographical sketches.

Because of the price and nature of this new reference series, it is most appropriate for larger libraries that need additional biographical information on business leaders — information that they have not been able to find in the standard sources. Many of the entries are included in the *Who's Who* series. [R: Choice, Nov 76, p. 115; LJ, 1 Nov 76, p. 2266; WLB, Nov 76, p. 262]   Dwight F. Burlingame

213. Fucini, Joseph J., and Suzy Fucini. **Entrepreneurs: The Men and Women behind Famous Brand Names and How They Made It**. Boston, G. K. Hall, 1985. 297p. illus. bibliog. index. $19.95; $7.95pa. LC 84-15846. ISBN 0-8161-8708-8; 0-8161-8736-3pa.

This little book is all about the most American of heroes — the entrepreneur who named his product after him(or her)self. "Any commercial good or item widely known and used in the United States today, and named after an actual person or persons, was fair game for this book," state the authors in their introduction. Not exactly precise selection criteria, but we get the idea. As long as readers are not disappointed that their favorite was excluded — mine was, Frank Perdue — this book is a delight. The authors do cheat a little; Wendy was a real little girl, and she had pig tails and freckles, but it was her father who invented the hamburger.

The book itself is divided into two parts. The first consists of extensive (two- to four-page) biographies, and the second of cameos. The bibliography is well annotated and extensive. The text is very readable, and the authors have found really interesting things about the persons described. (How many people know that the inventor of electric trains started by illuminating the inside of flower pots?) One suspects that this book will be a favorite of trivia buffs.

The book will be used two ways in most libraries: one, as a biographical source for elusive persons such as Alfred Fuller, Famous Amos, and Mary Kay Ash; and two, it is fun to read. Is it a reference book? It is well indexed, and the facts are correct. For harried reference librarians who need biographical sources to satisfy students writing papers, it will be a godsend.   Constance D. Williams

214. Ingham, John N. **Biographical Dictionary of American Business Leaders**. Westport, Conn., Greenwood Press, 1983. 4v. index. $195.00/set. LC 82-6113. ISBN 0-313-21362-3.

This set contains 835 entries covering eleven hundred "significant figures in American industry and commerce." All are written by the same author and reviewed by a panel of historians. Biographies range in length from a paragraph to several pages for someone like Henry Ford. This set certainly represents a massive undertaking for one person.

The lengthy index covers company, industry, person, place, and, less extensively, general topic and catch phrase, such as "most hated woman in America." Appendixes group the biographies by industry, company, birthplace, place of business, religion, ethnicity, year of birth, and sex. These appendixes add to the book's usefulness for those doing studies of business leaders. Each entry also includes a bibliography. Many of the older biographies cite reference works that are widely available, such as the *Dictionary of American Biography* or the *National Cyclopedia of American Biography*, but people are included who were not covered in either work, such as William Webster Browne, founder of the "first all-Negro bank in America." In fact, the author has made an effort to include blacks and women who have been ignored in earlier reference works. Coverage extends to people who are still active, such as Lee Iacocca and Diane von Furstenburg, but most entries are for deceased people.

Despite the fact that the author, as he states in the preface, did not have time or resources to do primary research, the secondary research, as judged by looking at the bibliographies, seems extensive. Ingham's work fills a void, as there are a number of biographical works on contemporary business executives, but none that the reviewer is aware of to cover historically significiant figures. [R: LJ, 15 June 83, pp. 1249-50]

Susan V. Peck

215.   Jeremy, David J., ed. **Dictionary of Business Biography: Biographical Dictionary of Business Leaders Active in Britain in the Period 1860-1980. Volume I: A-C.** Woburn, Mass., Butterworth Publishers, 1984. 878p. illus. $185.00. ISBN 0-406-27341-3.

The *Dictionary of Business Biography* is a substantial and authoritative contribution to British biography. Over one thousand biographies of British businessmen from 1860 to 1980 will be contained in five volumes; there is a separately bound index volume. The first volume, covering the letters A to C, has now appeared. The others will follow at intervals of six months to a year.

Each of the biographies includes the name; a brief identification; a biographical sketch, sometimes as long as five pages; and a bibliography of works by and about the biographee. Many biographies are accompanied by portraits, and some have other illustrations as well. Entries are under family name, with cross-references, when necessary, to titles of nobility. For example, Lord Beaverbrook is entered under Aitken, William Maxwell.

The physical presentation is excellent: good layout, clear typeface, sharp reproduction of the portraits and illustrations, use of a heavy line to separate each biography. The binding and cover are sturdy, a necessary feature since the volume is large.

While the price is substantial (over $900 for the set), it is definitely worth the cost for those who can make use of such a valuable reference tool: large university and public libraries, historical research centers, and certain business libraries. It is highly recommended.

Barbara E. Brown

216.   Leavitt, Judith A. **American Women Managers and Administrators: A Selective Biographical Dictionary of Twentieth-Century Leaders in Business, Education, and Government.** Westport, Conn., Greenwood Press, 1985. 317p. bibliog. index. $45.00. LC 84-12814. ISBN 0-313-23748-4.

This volume arose from the need to identify twentieth-century women leaders in business, education, and government. In doing so, Leavitt compiled the biographies of 226 outstanding women managers, administrators, and leaders who have held or now hold positions of prominence. The criteria for inclusion were as follows: women who were "firsts" or who had achieved some significant accomplishment in a particular field or occupation; women who were founders of business or educational institutions; and women who have held some position of national prominence. Women who were "firsts" make up nearly half the entries in this collection.

The biographies, which vary in length, are arranged in alphabetical order. In most cases, a bibliography citing references by and about the subject follows each entry. The appendix includes an alphabetical listing by category of the various women cited in the directory. The volume also includes a general bibliography and an index.

Because of its subject content, this book will be a useful reference tool in public, school and college libraries. It will be useful for guidance and career counselors and in programs of women's studies.   Lorraine Mathies

217. **Who's Who in Black Corporate America**. Edna Doggett, ed. Washington, D.C., Who's Who in Black Corporate America, 1982. 256p. index. $65.00. ISBN 0-686-43317-3; ISSN 0277-5336.

The main body of this listing consists of half-page biographies of approximately three hundred figures. These entries, offered in clear typescript, trace the individual's business affiliations, education, honors, and fraternal memberships. Also cited are family members (with children's ages sometimes provided) and the city of residence. Addresses are absent, and there are few dates. Some who have been included were yet engaged in undergraduate study (although a separate section cares for "most promising students").

Users living in large cities who know the business community can expect to spot lacunae immediately and may wonder if the entries were written by the subjects themselves. There is a listing of "blacks on boards of some major U.S. corporations" (addresses are provided here), but no biographies for these figures. Reference to the business schools of black colleges is incomplete. The "Business Executive Guide" lists names by states in which the figures reside or work, all of which requires a final index. The book cover is elegant, but the pages are held together by internal plastic spikes that break after one or two uses, disbinding the sheets. This publication is of restricted reference application. [R: BL, Aug 83, 1491; Choice, Apr 83, p. 1116]

Dominique-René de Lerma

BANKING AND FINANCE

218. **American Banker Directory of U.S. Banking Executives**. 1st ed. New York, American Banker; distr., Salem, N.H., Ayer Co. 1981. 824p. o.p.

This directory is a bargain for those who need to know names, backgrounds, and affiliations of bank executives. The gold-stamped, library-bound volume was compiled by publishers of the nation's only daily newspaper devoted exclusively to banking. *Polk's World Bank Directory* and Rand McNally International's *Bankers Directory* publish names of top managers along with data on their banks, but contain nothing like the biographical sketches provided in this first-edition *American Banker* volume. *Who's Who in Banking: The Directory of the Banking Profession* (Business Press, New York), which last appeared in 1972, contained some eight thousand biographical profiles of officers in a variety of financial institutions and regulatory agencies.

The *American Banker Directory* profiles about fifteen thousand bank executives, all prominent in their own milieus and many whose reputations are national and international. Biographies are alphabetically arranged, with such vital information as birth date and place; spouses and children; home address; educational background;

military service; previous bank affiliations; special awards; and career, civic, political, and club affiliations. Also, banks are indexed by state, accompanied by listings of bank officers and their positions. A table of abbreviations explains shorthand such as acronyms and military rank. As in any similar work, some names are missing, presumably those who did not submit the requested data.

This volume will occupy a useful niche in the business, financial, and banking sections of reference libraries, and could benefit sales and marketing organizations dealing with upper-level executives in the commercial banking field.

A related title is *Who's Who in Banking in Europe* (4v. International Publications Service, 1983. $550.00. ISBN 0-905589-02-5) that provides brief biographical data on some thirty thousand European bank executives. [R: Choice, July-Aug 81, p. 1525]

Charles L. Hinkle and Bohdan S. Wynar

219. **Who's Who in British Finance**. London, Gower Press; distr., New York, R. R. Bowker, 1972. 615p. index. o.p.

This biographical directory contains information about three thousand individuals holding influential positions in the public and private sectors of British finance. Included are the finance directors in the top one thousand companies in the United Kingdom; investment managers in insurance, pension funds, unit trusts; department heads in major banks; leading stock brokers and jobbers; and many others. Entries are alphabetically arranged, with name, home and business addresses, profession, current position and company, other concurrent positions, previous positions held, education, birthplace, marital status, children, honors received, club and organization memberships, publications, public service commitments. Biographees are indexed by employment and by company categories. A list of all professional organizations and groups is included. This work is now obsolete and hopefully will be revised soon. [R: LJ, Aug 72, p. 563; WLB, Oct 72, p. 201]   Bohdan S. Wynar

220. **Who's Who in Finance and Industry, 1983-84**. 23rd ed. Chicago, Marquis Who's Who, 1983. 945p. $84.50. LC 70-616550. ISBN 0-8379-0323-8.

This twenty-third edition of *Who's Who in Finance and Industry* includes biographical data on approximately twenty-one thousand business executives. The biographies include name, position held, vital statistics, education, family information, professional activities, publications, and addresses. Candidates for inclusion are invited to submit biographical data about their business careers. In the event that a reference-worthy individual fails to submit biographical data, the publisher's research staff prepares a sketch after researching the subject. A random sample of the entries revealed that the coverage is somewhat uneven for some geographical areas. Although not comprehensive, this directory is a useful reference work for libraries with extensive business collections.   James J. Groark

CONSULTING

221. Johnson, Richard R., ed. **Directory of Evaluation Consultants**. New York, Foundation Center, 1981. 191p. index. o.p. LC 80-67499. ISBN 0-87954-035-4.

Full descriptions, including addresses, telephone numbers, background, and experience, for 491 qualified evaluation consultants and 159 organizations are given. Three indexes to the names of these individuals and organizations, and lists by geographical area and by subject specialty are helpful in locating the exact information needed. A preface and introduction give practical information on agreements and contracts between clients and consultants, with useful advice on assessing and selecting consultants before working with them. Relevant bibliographical materials are cited.

The editor, Richard R. Johnson of Exxon Education Foundation, is to be congratulated on producing an impressive reference tool, no mean job for a directory of this scope.   Charlotte Georgi

222. **Who's Who in Consulting: A Reference Guide to Professional Personnel Engaged in Consultation for Business, Industry and Government**. 2nd ed. Paul Wasserman, managing ed.; Janice McLean, associate ed. Detroit, Gale, 1973. 1011p. index. $150.00. LC 73-16373. ISBN 0-8103-0360-4.

223. **Supplement**. Detroit, Gale, 1982-1983. 3 issues. $160.00/set. ISBN 0-8103-0361-2.

A list of individuals from many different fields who offer consulting services. The work is intended to supplement and serve as a companion to Gale's *Consultants and Consulting Organizations* by providing factual information about more than seventy-five hundred individual consultants. The arrangement is alphabetical by last name, and information contained in each entry was provided by the persons listed. The preface points out that the sole criterion for inclusion was active service in either full-time or part-time consulting and that all who could be identified, through either their companies, their associations, or their professional efforts, were invited to complete questionnaires and that those who did so were listed. The editors caution the user that a listing does not, therefore, constitute an endorsement of the consultant or his qualifications. Nor do the editors claim comprehensiveness in their listing of consultants. A useful feature is the list of individuals arranged by city and state under their subject fields of expertise.

The supplements, also edited by Wasserman and McLean, provide more current information. In three issues, they provide biographical and career information on more than three thousand active consultants in all fields.

Ralph M. Edwards and Bohdan S. Wynar

LABOR

224. Fink, Gary M., ed. **Biographical Dictionary of American Labor**. Westport, Conn., Greenwood Press, 1984. 767p. index. $49.95. LC 84-4687. ISBN 0-313-22865-5.

This basic resource in the field of labor history first made its appearance in 1974 under the title *Biographical Dictionary of American Labor Leaders*. The 1984 edition promises to be even more useful. Two hundred thirty-four new sketches have been added to the five hundred which appeared in the earlier edition. A special effort has been made to incorporate the biographies of women who were prominent in the labor movement. Also emphasized in the new edition are the labor leaders of the last quarter of the nineteenth century. In addition, many sketches from the first edition have been updated to include more recent biographical data or additional bibliographical references.

The entries in the *Dictionary* focus upon the role which each individual played in the story of American labor, whether as a trade union leader, a political radical, a labor publicist, or an academician. The sketches also touch on relevant personal information. Each entry provides a list of sources for further research.

As in the earlier edition, there are appendixes which list labor leaders by union affiliations, religious preference, place of birth, formal education, political preference, and major appointive and elective public offices.

Appearing for the first time in the 1984 edition is a seventy-seven-page introduction which offers a quantitative and qualitative examination of American labor leadership in the twentieth century. Using four sample years—1900, 1925, 1946, and 1976—the study traces the evolving characteristics of this leadership. In addition to reporting and analyzing statistical data, the introduction employs fictionalized biographies to dramatize the nature of the transitions.

The *Biographical Dictionary of American Labor* will be an important acquisition for academic libraries, labor libraries, and larger public libraries.   Shirley Miller

225. Gifford, Courtney D., and William P. Hopgood. **Directory of U.S. Labor Arbitrators: A Guide for Finding and Using Arbitrators**. Washington, D.C., Bureau of National Affairs, 1985. 445p. $40.00pa. LC 85-18562. ISBN 0-87179-494-2.

This directory, used in conjunction with the Bureau of National Affairs's LABORLAW database, "is designed to accelerate the process of selecting an arbitrator or establishing a permanent panel of arbitrators to be used on a rotating basis" (p. v). The BNA is a respected private publishing service.

The book begins with a brief introductory survey of the history of arbitration. Its main section contains capsule biographies of arbitrators as prepared by themselves, as of February 1985. Each entry has this valuable information: the arbitrator's business and home addresses and telephone numbers; occupation (many arbitrators not surprisingly work as professors and attorneys); membership in professional associations, rosters, and panels; a summary of the arbitrator's experience; lists of industries and issues arbitrated; year of birth; education; and amount of per diem and other fees.

There is also a state-by-state list of arbitrators. Finally, the directory contains the Code of Professional Responsibility for Arbitrators; procedures and rules of the American Arbitration Association and the Federal Mediation and Conciliation Service; and sample agreements for the selection of panel arbitrators and the mediation of grievances.

This reference work provides reasonably recent and accurate information in a thoroughly professional manner and is the only such directory in print.

Marshall E. Nunn

226. **Who's Who in Labor**. Salem, N.H., Ayer Co., 1976. 807p. bibliog. index. (Arno Press Who's Who Series). $71.50. LC 75-7962. ISBN 0-405-06651-1.

This book provides biographical information concerning over thirty-eight hundred people active in the labor movement itself, in neutral capacities (arbitration, etc.), or as government officials. Data were gathered and entries were chosen with the cooperation of the AFL-CIO, the United Mine Workers, the United Auto Workers, the American Arbitration Association, and the Federal Mediation and Conciliation Service. Also included are a list of AFL-CIO and other labor federations, national unions and employee associations, government offices serving labor, and labor studies centers. A glossary of basic labor terms is included, as is a bibliography of labor periodicals, and an index to people included, this arranged according to organization. The only other work on labor leaders is Gary Fink's *Biographical Dictionary of American Labor*, and both works complement and supplement each other. [R: BL, 1 Feb 77, p. 407; C&RL July 77, p. 324; Choice, Nov 76, p. 1121]   Bohdan S. Wynar

PUBLIC RELATIONS

227.   Barbour, Robert L., ed.-in-chief. **Who's Who in Public Relations (International)**. 5th ed. Meriden, N.H., PR Publishing; distr., Canaan, N.H., Phoenix, 1976. 731p. $35.00. LC 62-4348. ISBN 0-914016-25-3.

The fifth edition of *Who's Who in Public Relations* represents a much-needed reference book in this subject field. The words "Who's Who" in the title were used with the permission of Marquis Who's Who, Inc., but the two publishers have nothing else in common. Individual biographical entries vary from two to twenty-one lines. The average entry includes essential personal information, educational background, professional experience, awards received, and business address. Information included was provided by the biographees themselves. Arranged alphabetically, entries list some five thousand public relations executives from sixty countries.

The editors make an effort to define the field of public relations as well as to express their opinion on its past and present. A brief discussion of PR methods and procedures is included. People in the public relations field experience an extraordinarily high rate of transfers, promotions, and other employment changes. Therefore, the editors feel that a reference source such as *Who's Who in Public Relations* will have inevitable omissions and will quickly become out of date.

In the back of the volume, biographees are listed alphabetically by country, state, province, and city. The problem here is that only major cities are listed; entries for people in smaller cities are listed within a given state under an "elsewhere" rubric. Therefore, there is no way to locate a person from a smaller city unless one happens to know that person's name. However, the geographical listing is a special feature worth noting. No doubt *Who's Who in Public Relations*, being the only reference source of its kind, represents a very useful compilation of valuable information. [R: BL, 1 Sept 76, p. 59; Choice, July/Aug 76, p. 648]   George V. Hodowanec

228.   **Directory of Personal Image Consultants, 1984-85**. Edited by Editorial Services Co. New York, Fairchild, 1984. 130p. $22.50pa. ISBN 0-686-83189-6.

Provides comprehensive listings of "image consultants"—describing who these people are and the services they have to offer. Those consultants listed specialize in one or more of the following areas: speech/public appearance; speech/script writers; wardrobe analysis; personal public relations; motivation, goal-setting, career development. Each listing provides a description of services offered including specialties, teaching techniques, and fee schedules. Useful for individuals and corporations who want to polish their public image. Also includes bibliography containing names of self-help books and cassettes.   Bohdan S. Wynar

229.   O'Dwyer, Jack, ed. **O'Dwyer's Directory of Public Relations Executives, 1983**. New York, J.R. O'Dwyer, 1983. 305p. index. $70.00. ISBN 0-941424-02-2; ISSN 0191-0051.

This is the third edition of this title from the publisher of several directories, including *O'Dwyer's Directory of Public Relations Firms*. The volume contains short biographies of business-related public relations executives in corporations, associations, and public relations firms. The preface states that the names of the four thousand executives who responded to a request for information were supplemented with names from the files that the publisher had built over the years. General criteria for inclusion are: at least five years of experience in the business world, the title of manager or above at a corporation or association, or the title of account supervisor or above at an agency. Each name in the alphabetically-arranged directory is followed by the name of the company for which the person works and a short professional biography that includes education, psoitions held, and business address. Following the main part of the work is an index that identifies the companies represented. Libraries and public relations firms should find this work easy to use and helpful. [R: BL, 1 Sept 84, p. 52]

Peggy M. Tozer

REAL ESTATE

230. **Who's Who in Real Estate: The Directory of Real Estate Professions**. Sharon, Conn., Gray House, 1983. 903p. $85.00. ISBN 0-9393-00-14-1.

A comprehensive biographical source to some fifteen thousand real estate people including top executives from the Fortune 1000 firms, leading developers and syndicators, officials from state and federal government agencies, attorneys and bankers specializing in real estate, and mortage and real estate brokers and consultants. Entries are of the usual Who's Who type covering current position, firm, business address and telephone, primary real estate activity, relevant previous employment, professional affiliations and honors, services offered, representative clients, education, home address, date of birth, nonprofessional affiliations, honors, and military service.

A complementary volume is *The Directory of Real Estate Investors* (Gray House, 1984. 497p. $103.00) covering major buyers and sellers of income-producing properties.

Bohdan S. Wynar

6 Education

Introduction

The material in this chapter is arranged under three headings. The first section, "General Works," covers general biographical sources. It is followed by two sections, "Higher Education" and "Elementary and Secondary Education." Ten entries are included, with a number of other titles mentioned in the annotations. The number of biographical sources in education is rather limited, and with the exception of a few retrospective works, e.g., *Biographical Dictionary of American Educators* (see entry 231), and serials, *Directory of American Scholars* (see entry 234) or *Who's Who among American High School Students* (see entry 238), many sources in the field are substandard, e.g., *International Who's Who in Education* (see entry 235).

Biographical entries are located in most encyclopedias and dictionaries covering several aspects of education. The most comprehensive work is *The Encyclopedia of Education* (10v. Macmillan and Free Press, 1971). According to the preface, the more than one thousand articles offer "a view of institutions and people, of the processes and products, found in educational procedure." This encyclopedia contains a number of biographical entries; some of them are rather substantial, containing several pages with proper documentation (e.g., "St. Augustine," vol. 1. pp. 421-27). Macmillan's work actually updates an old classic, Monroe's *A Cyclopedia of Education* (Macmillan, 1911-1913; 5v. repr., Gale, 1968) that should be consulted for the nineteenth century and earlier periods. There are also a number of one-volume dictionaries, e.g., Blishen's *Encyclopedia of Education* (Philosophical Library, 1970. 882p.) or the more recent *American Educators' Encyclopedia*, edited by E. Dejnozka and D. Kapel (Greenwood Press, 1982. 634p.) that contain a fair number of biographical entries.

Additional biographical information can be located in periodical literature, and in this respect, several indexing services should be consulted. The most important is still Wilson's *Education Index* (1929-), followed by *Current Index to Journals in Education* (Oryx Press, 1969-) and its supplement *Resources in Education* (Educational Resources Information Center, 1966-). These and other indexing services are described in some detail by D. Brewer in *ARBA Guide to Education* (Libraries Unlimited, 1985) that also offers a good coverage of important bibliographies in this field. Similar information is also provided in M. Woodbury's *A Guide to Sources of Educational Information* (2nd ed. Information Resources Press, 1982. 430p.).

GENERAL WORKS

231. Ohles, John F., ed. **Biographical Dictionary of American Educators**. Westport, Conn., Greenwood Press, 1978. 3v. index. $150.00/set. LC 77-84750. ISBN 0-8371-9893-3.

The *Biographical Dictionary of American Educators* recognizes 1,665 teachers, reformers, theorists, and administrators, from colonial times to 1976. Many state and regional educators are included along with the more widely known national figures. Women and minority educators have been included also. Biographical format includes a brief description of the person's education, professional accomplishments, contribution to the educational movement, and personal data. In many instances, references for further study are given. Readers are referred to such reliable sources as the *Dictionary of American Biography*, the *National Cyclopedia of American Biography*, and *Notable American Women*.

Five appendixes include groupings according to place of birth, state of major service, and field of work; a chronology of birth years; and important dates in American education. A general index provides further access to the information contained in the 1,665 entries. Unfortunately, the alphabetical contents of each of the three volumes are not indicated on the spines. Also, this information is not provided in the table of contents. This three-volume set would be useful in academic libraries. Since inclusion required that a person had reached the age of sixty, had retired, or had died by 1 January 1975, it serves as a good complement to *Who's Who in Education* and the *Directory of American Scholars*. [R: Choice, Dec 78, p. 1343; LJ, 1 June 78, p. 1161; WLB, Nov 78, p. 277]   Peggy Clossey Boone

HIGHER EDUCATION

232. **The Academic Who's Who, 1975-1976: University Teachers in the British Isles in the Arts, Education and Social Sciences**. 2nd ed. Detroit, Gale, 1975. 784p. $45.00. ISBN 0-8103-2020-7.

The second edition of an excellent British reference work, first published in 1973, has been enlarged to contain accurate biographical information about approximately seven thousand university teachers in non-scientific disciplines throughout the British Isles. Included are faculty members holding the rank of senior lecturer or above, or who have taught for five years as lecturer or assistant lecturer, as well as those holding senior non-teaching university appointments. The publishers state that inclusion is not based on payment or on an obligation to purchase the directory.

Format is like that of *Who's Who*, with personal and career data, education, memberships, publications, and journals contributed to. The twenty-three preliminary pages of abbreviations could be very helpful, especially to those who are unfamiliar with British terminology and titles. [R: LJ, 1 Nov 76, p. 2268]   Laura H. McGuire

233. Carrubba, Robert W., and George A. Borden, eds. **Directory of College and University Classicists in the United States and Canada**. University Park, Pa., Pennsylvania State University Press, 1973. 221p. $18.50. LC 73-6882. ISBN 0-271-01123-8.

Published in cooperation with the Classical Association of the Middle Atlantic States, this work supersedes Edward A. Robinson's survey for *The Classical World* entitled "College Classical Departments 1967-68: I Faculty Rosters." Like many directories of this type, it was compiled from questionnaires distributed to classics departments in accredited institutions and from replies to an article in *The Classical World*. Over eighteen hundred names are included. Completeness is difficult to judge, but the fact that Kent State University is missing from the "list of College and University Departments" would suggest that there may be other omissions as well.

The main part of the *Directory* consists of an "Alphabetic List of Classicists." Information given includes faculty rank, institution, institutional address and telephone number, degrees and institutions, home address and telephone number, and areas of specialization (of which each respondent was asked to select not more than three). This is supplemented by a "Geographic List of Classicists" by state (U.S.) or province (Canada) and by a list of "Areas of Interest or Specialization." Other sections include "List of College and University Departments," "List of Classical Associations," and "List of Classical Journals and Newsletters."

The book is well bound and the paper is pleasantly off-white with only minimal show-through. The typography, though small, is legible. This book should be a useful addition to the reference shelves of college, university, and large public libraries.

A. Robert Rogers

234. **Directory of American Scholars**. 8th ed. Edited by Jaques Cattell Press. New York, R. R. Bowker, 1982. 4v. index. $295.00. LC 57-9125. ISBN 0-8352-1476-1.

Like the fourth through seventh editions (seventh edition published in 1978), this current edition to mostly U.S. and Canadian scholars in the universities appears in four subject volumes: history; English, speech, and drama; foreign languages, linguistics, and philology; and philosophy, religion, and law. Readability has been enhanced noticeably in this edition with larger type and italicized subject headings.

The preface specifies inclusion of thirty-nine thousand entries, with some thirty-eight hundred new entries "obtained from former entrants, academic deans, or citations in professional journals" and selected on the basis of achievement in scholarly work or in attainment of a position of scholarly endeavor. New information appears for over 70 percent of the listings. Excluding those scholars, emeritus or retired, who have not published within the past decade, the sixth, seventh, and current editions closely correspond in total number of entries.

Biographical details again appear, as in the seventh edition, and include such information as citizenship, education, chief fields of research interest, and principal publications. Scholars demonstrating major involvement in other fields are again cross-referenced to other volumes. As before, volume 4 contains an alphabetical index of entries in all four volumes, and each volume offers a geographic index by state and city.

Ray Gerke

235. **International Who's Who in Education**. 2nd ed. Ernest Kay, ed. director. Cambridge, England, International Biographical Centre; distr., Totowa, N.J., Biblio Distribution Center, 1981. 490p. $54.50. ISBN 0-900332-56-5.

More than seven thousand persons from all parts of the world are listed in this biographical dictionary. The persons included are university and college teachers in all fields of knowledge. Entries range in length from ten to fifteen lines and give full name, degrees, date and place of birth, experience, publications, current position, and address. The publisher's foreword states that this second edition has been extended "to include leading teachers, academics, and administrators world-wide, notably throughout the United States and Canada." However, a comparison of the Americans listed therein indicates that very few listed in such publications as *Biographical Dictionary of American Educators* and *Leaders in Education* are found in this work. No criteria are given for the selection of the individuals, but the foreword says that the information for each entry "has been freely provided by each contributor." An index by field, e.g., chemistry, physics, history, sociology, etc., would have greatly enhanced this work. Even though the volume may be considered universal in coverage because it lists persons from Asia, Africa, the Near East, Europe, and North America, South Americans are not represented at all. With no stated criteria for selection, one does wonder about the importance of the individuals or relevance of this publication.

Donald J. Lehnus

236. **Leaders in Education. A Biographical Directory.** 4th ed. Edited by the Jaques Cattell Press. New York, R. R. Bowker, 1971. 1097p. index. o.p. LC 32-10194. ISBN 0-8352-0434-0.

Leaders in Education serves as a companion volume to *American Men of Science*, listing some fifteen thousand biographical sketches of the Who's Who type. The first edition, published in 1932, was recognized as a standard work on the subject. There are other directories of this type, especially in the area of education, e.g., *Directory of American Scholars*. Usually they are based on a questionnaire sent to all known addresses with an "encouragement" to buy this particular "standard" tool at a discount price. *Leaders in Education* is obviously based on the same procedure – that is, the information is gathered with the assistance of a questionnaire – but, unlike *Outstanding Educators of America* (1970. now o.p.) or similar works, it is a reliable reference book with good editing and well-defined criteria for inclusion.

If one can offer a critical comment, it would probably be in the area of comparison with the Who's Who series. *Who's Who in America* lists a number of educators not found in this directory, primarily in the area of "attainment of a position of substantial responsibility." In addition, entries we found in both *Who's Who in America* and this directory have a somewhat different emphasis in categories such as publications. In our sampling we found that *Leaders in Education* provides less emphasis on publications and research activities and probably more details on memberships and positions held. In general, however, *Leaders in Education* is a carefully edited and well-balanced work. It is now superceded by *Directory of American Scholars* and *American Men and Women of Science*. Another well-known publication that ceased to exist is *Who's Who in American Education: An Illustrated Biographical Dictionary of Eminent Living Educators of the United States and Canada* (Nashville, Tenn., Who's Who in American Education, 1928-1968. Biennial) that contained biographies of faculty and administrative officers, plus selective listings in the area of secondary education. [R: RQ, Winter 71, p. 167]

Bohdan S. Wynar

237.   U.S. Library of Congress. **National Directory of Latin Americanists**. 2nd ed. Compiled by the Hispanic Foundation Reference Department. Washington, D.C., GPO, 1971. 683p. (Hispanic Foundation Bibliographical Series, No. 12). o.p. LC 75-37737.

The first edition of this biographical directory, published in 1966, contained 1,884 biographies. This edition contains biographies of 2,695 Latin American specialists in the social sciences and humanities. Each entry contains the biographee's name, birthplace, birth date, major discipline, degrees (including honoraries), professional career, fellowships, honors, awards, etc., membership in professional and honorary associations, research specialities and interests, publications (limited to three), language knowledge (on a scale of one to five for each of the following: reading, understanding the spoken language, speaking, and writing), linguistic studies, home and office addresses. Includes indexes of subject specialties and area specialties with biographees' names under each heading.   Bohdan S. Wynar

ELEMENTARY AND SECONDARY EDUCATION

238.   **Who's Who among American High School Students**. 18th ed. Lake Forest, Ill., Educational Communications, 1984. Annual. 9v. Free copies to schools and libraries. LC 68-43796.

Since 1967 this publication has been committed to celebrating outstanding students for their positive achievements in academics, athletics, and school and community service. The first edition recognized thirteen thousand students; the present edition, published in nine regional volumes, honors 390,000 students representing eighteen thousand public, private, and parochial high schools nationwide. The standard sequence of information for each entry is name of student, name of school, city and state, "nomination source," class year (not always given), rank in class, accomplishments, and "future plans." Photographs are appended at the end of the volume, with the sequence matching that of the entries. Each year the edition is available on a complimentary basis to all participating schools, youth organizations, colleges, and universities.   Bohdan S. Wynar

239.   **Who's Who Biographical Record—Child Development Professionals**. Compiled by the editors of Who's Who in America. Chicago, Marquis Who's Who, 1976. 515p. $55.00. LC 76-27258. ISBN 0-8379-3701-9.

The editors of the Marquis Who's Who famous line of biographical directories introduce what is described as a new series of "Biographical Records," representing a new concept in selection of entrants. The criterion for inclusion in the new series is professional employment in the particular field. In the case of this volume, professional employment in the child development field is the prerequisite. Definition of the term is broad, including child psychologists; guidance and reading counselors; special education teachers; directors of Head Start, day care, and other special programs; and college and university professors of education and psychology. The aim is to compile a reference source that provides concise information directly related to the professional achievements of the persons listed. Entries are structured to include background information on the academic and career experience, professional membership, certification and area of specialization, vital statistics, family, and name and/or office address. Data for the nine thousand individual records were compiled by the Marquis staff and verified by the biographees, a standard practice by Marquis primarily used to guarantee accuracy.

A number of entries were examined to determine whether known specialist writers were included (for example, Samuel A. Kirk, Hans G. Furth, and Herbert Ginsburg were located). The listings provided not only the data that were promised by the editors but, in two cases, listed books authored, a heading now shown in the sample entry. Nearly all the entries that were examined listed people with advanced degrees, specialized certification, a variety of professional positions or active participation in professional organizations related to their specialities. An exception is the occasional entry that appears to lack any reason for being listed—for example, a media specialist with a master's degree in English who plays violin in a local symphony. The range of specialties of biographees is impressive. One can find reading specialists, remedial reading teachers, optometrists specializing in treatment of learning disabilities, resource room teachers, bilingual specialists, speech pathologists, educational researchers, student personnel directors, librarians, school superintendents, migrant teachers, and social workers.

The directory is a very useful reference, but a few critical comments are in order. The editors have not made it entirely clear how the names were selected for inclusion, and in some cases, entries beg for explanation of why they exist. Employment as an elementary school teacher, media specialist, or librarian does not appear to satisfy the primary criterion for inclusion. A few words of explanation by the editors on selection of biographees and on updating are in order. Likewise, the directory would be improved by the deletion of unqualified biographees or by the addition of data to support their inclusion. All in all, the volume successfully brings together information on specialists which was formerly scattered among scores of directories and lists. [R: BL, 1 Mar 78, p. 1138; Choice, Sept 77, p. 838; RQ, Winter 77, p. 190; WLB, Mar 77, p. 602]

Christine L. Wynar

240. **Who's Who Biographical Record—School District Officials.** Compiled by the editors of Who's Who in America. Chicago, Marquis Who's Who, 1976. 666p. $55.00. LC 76-27259. ISBN 0-8379-3801-5.

This is the first publication in a new series of biographical dictionaries by Marquis Who's Who, meant to provide a broad overview of people within a specific professional field. The first volume of the series is devoted to school district officials.

The publisher states that the principal criterion for inclusion is professional employment in school district management. The entries, however, go beyond the generally accepted scope of school district management to include, in addition to superintendents, principals, and district business and planning managers, officials more closely allied to the field of curriculum, such as curriculum coordinators, librarians, guidance counselors, and department heads. Because of this overly ambitious scope, many officials who should have been included have been overlooked. Although unwarranted omissions are inevitable in any first edition, broad coverage attempted here has resulted in an unacceptable number of omissions.

In typical Who's Who format, the volume includes more than twelve thousand entries, is arranged alphabetically, contains a key to information in the directory, and is based on biographical data solicited from the biographee. [R: Choice, Sept 77, p. 838; WLB, Mar 77, p. 602]

Anna Mary Lowrey

7 Ethnic Studies

Introduction

The material in this chapter is arranged under eight section headings. The first section is "General Works," followed by "American Indians," "Blacks," "Chicanos," "Croatians," "Jews," "Poles," and "Ukrainians." In other words, only seven ethnic groups are represented here out of some ninety-plus ethnic communities in the United States. There are seventeen entries in this chapter and a number of additional titles are mentioned in the annotations. Many biographical dictionaries are produced for ethnic communities. Usually they are prepared by religious, social, or fraternal groups for local consumption and will not be reported in such standard sources as *Books in Print* or *American Reference Books Annual*. Several other sources may be consulted for additional information. *Harvard Encyclopedia of American Ethnic Groups* edited by Stephan Thernstrom (Harvard University Press, 1980. 1076p.) is probably the most scholarly publication in this area and a typical ethnic-group entry includes information on historical background, migration, settlement, culture and language, organizations, group maintenance and a brief, rather limited, selective bibliography.

Concerning individual groups and their reference sources, probably the best title is *Encyclopedia of Indians of the Americas* (Scholarly Press, 1974-) to be published in twenty volumes. *Public Affairs Information Service Foreign Language Index* (PAIS, 1972-), the foreign-language counterpart to *Public Affairs Information Service Bulletin*, will be useful in locating periodical articles published in major foreign languages. Paul Wasserman's *Ethnic Information Sources of the United States* (2v. 2nd ed. Gale, 1983) includes the usual directory-type information plus a selective bibliography on books, pamphlets and audiovisual material. Wasserman contains very little information on published reference sources, including biographical dictionaries. More information will be found in *Building Ethnic Collections. An Annotated Guide for School Media Centers and Public Libraries* by L. Buttlar and L. R. Wynar (Libraries Unlimited, 1977. 434p.), but, unfortunately, the information may be dated in some respects. The same is true of *Encyclopedic Directory of Ethnic Organizations in the United States* by L. R. Wynar (Libraries Unlimited, 1975. 414p.) that contains most ethnic organizations active at that time with their publications profile.

GENERAL WORKS

241. **Who's Who of American Immigrants**. Edited by Martin S. Sumers. New York, Stein and Day, 1985. 400p. $39.95. LC 82-40014. ISBN 0-8128-2979-4.

This work includes some eight thousand biographical sketches of "noteworthy immigrants" providing birth and death dates, country of origin, field of endeavor, and succinct synopses of achievements and contributions to American society. Most ethnic groups are covered, with probably more emphasis on Spanish-Americans as compared to Slavic groups.   Bohdan S. Wynar

AMERICAN INDIANS

242. **Dictionary of Indians of North America**. St. Clair Shores, Mich., Scholarly Press, 1978. 3v. illus. $145.00/set. LC 78-65222. ISBN 0-403-01799-8.

Biographical reference works about American Indians are biased in several ways. First, the content and structure of biographies are based upon a European value system. Second, the criteria for selection are culturally biased: Indians who "made it" on white terms—yes; Indians who "made it" on Indian terms—no. What the criteria of selection were for this three-volume set only the publisher knows. The only front matter is a brief essay by Marion Gridley, which outlines the problems of preparing an Indian biographical source book. Unfortunately, the publisher seems not to have taken her warnings to heart.

In a period of tight acquisition funds, this set is a questionable purchase. The *Dictionary* contains more than one thousand biographies, and those that do go beyond two or three sentences tend to be good. However, the lack of editorial control ruins what could have been an outstanding collection. One problem lies with the title. Does North America mean the United States? the United States and Canada? Mexico? We do not really know, since a detailed examination of one of the three volumes indicates that there are probably no more than twenty-five Alaskan Indian and Eskimo biographies. The only Canadian Indian in one volume is Buffy Sainte-Marie, and she grew up in the United States and is now a U.S. citizen. The rest of the New World fared better, with numerous entries for Mexico, some for Panama, Nicaragua, Costa Rica, the Caribbean Islands, and one from Peru (Sumac Yma—also an American citizen). In any event, the limits of the set are unknown. As noted earlier, we have no information on selection criteria for biographies. Why are there so many one-line "biographies" (such as "Guy, Annie [Chickasaw] was a mixed blood"), and individuals such as Daniel Bomberry, Calvin Boy, L. L. Broadfast, and Charles Asa Brown, just to cite some persons missing from the *B* section, are omitted? Another unusual feature is the portraits included in each letter of the alphabet. A number of individuals whose portraits are included have no biographies. One example from the letter *P*: it contains biographies of Arthur Parker, Caroline Parker, and Ely Parker, but in the illustration section, there are portraits of Caroline Parker, Ely Parker, and Quanah Parker. This pattern was repeated over and over again.   G. Edward Evans

243. Dockstader, Frederick J. **Great North American Indians: Profiles in Life and Leadership**. New York, Van Nostrand Reinhold, 1977. 386p. illus. bibliog. index. (A Norback Book). $22.50. LC 77-23733. ISBN 0-442-02148-8.

The lives of three hundred deceased native Americans who significantly influenced the history of their peoples are presented in this volume, which combines both scholarship and readability. Dockstader has taken the view that the American Indians' view of their own history would guide his selection. Thus, even in the discussions themselves, events that non-Indians might see as important are subordinated to those with lasting impact on native Americans themselves, as seen by them.

The primary section is, of course, the biographical sketches. Birth and death dates are given as closely as possible, variants in names are noted, family information is given, and the major events of the biographee's life are then recorded. Coverage is not uniformly even, but sketches note the availability (or lack) of sources when facts are questionable. A significant number of women are included; among them are Kateri Tekakwitha, Degonwadonti (Molly Brant), Roberta Campbell Lawson, and Mountain Wolf Woman. Grounds for inclusion occasionally appear to be a bit shaky, as when people of 1/8 Indian blood are represented (e.g., Gilcrease and Tinker). Coverage is not exclusively historical, and the fairly contemporary LaFlesche family is represented as is the modern artist Jerome Tiger. In general, the coverage is at once broad and representative, including even the semi-mythical Dekanawida.

Appended material includes a bibliography of approximately five hundred items, a tribal-listing index of over seventy divisions, and a chronological listing of the biographees arranged by year of birth. A thorough name index includes variants of names (of which there are many), and these are cross-referenced to the form used in the main entry.

All in all, the book should prove valuable for both pleasure reading and information, although the lack of a subject index does hinder access to a degree. Illustrative material (most often portraits) accompanies each sketch and is interesting if sometimes of only marginal relevance to the sketch itself. The clarity of presentation and the information yielded combine, though, to make this a most attractive candidate for purchase, especially in collections where material on native Americans is limited.

Koert C. Loomis, Jr.

BLACKS

244.   Adams, Russell L., ed. **Great Negroes, Past and Present**. 3rd ed. Chicago, Afro-Am Publishing Co., 1976. 212p. illus. $14.95; $9.95pa. LC 72-87924. ISBN 0-910030-07-3; 0-910030-08-1pa.

This is a revised edition of what has turned out to be, since its inception in 1963, an excellent biographical reference source for young people. The lives of over 175 personalities are discussed in a straight, easy-to-read narrative style. It should be noted that whereas many of the subjects have had their biographies treated in other sources, there are several who are seldom written about, such as John Jasper, Dean Dixon, Ulysses Kay, and Gordon Parks. The work is divided into occupational categories in the main: (1) African heroes, (2) early American, (3) science and industry, (4) business pioneers, (5) religion, (6) education, (7) literature, (8) the theatre, (9) music, and (10) art. Two outstanding features of this work, in addition to the biographical studies, are the bibliographies for each section containing books written specifically for young readers and the handsomely drawn portraits of each subject. A teachers' guide will prove to be helpful in correlating the role of each of the personalities in United States history. Highly recommended as an improvement over the second edition.

Miles M. Jackson

245.   Franklin, John Hope, and August Meier, eds. **Black Leaders of the Twentieth Century**. Urbana, Ill., University of Illinois Press, 1982. 372p. illus. index. (Blacks in the New World). $19.95; $7.95pa. LC 81-11454. ISBN 0-252-00870-7; 0-252-00939-8pa.

This timely book presents biographical essays with portraits of fifteen black leaders: Booker T. Washington, T. Thomas Fortune, Ida B. Wells-Barnett, W. E. B. DuBois, James Weldon Johnson, Marcus Garvey, A. Philip Randolph, Charles Clinton Spaulding, Mary McLeod Bethune, Charles Hamilton Houston, Mabel K. Staupers, Adam Clayton Powell, Jr., Martin Luther King, Jr., Malcolm X, and Whitney M. Young, Jr. Each well-researched essay is interestingly written by a different contributor and outlines the contributions that the leader has made in the history of the United States. The book should appeal to general readers as well as scholars.

H. Robert Malinowsky

246.   Johnson, Frank J. **Who's Who of Black Millionaires**. Fresno, Calif., Who's Who of Black Millionaires, 1984. 182p. illus. index. $9.95pa. LC 83-082591. ISBN 0-915021-00-5.

This paperback offers brief biographies on thirty-seven selected "entertainers" (perhaps Emmanuel Lewis fits that category, but not Leontyne Price), thirty-four "professionals and entrepreneurs" (gospel-singer Shirley Caesar is among these, while Andrae Crouch is classed with the entertainers), and twenty-two athletes. The sketches are designed for the very casual reader, but not the scholar (Stevie Wonder's sound system in his Rolls-Royce cost twelve thousand dollars, Barry White's home has twenty-eight rooms, Michael Jackson's animals include a llama and four swans, Johnny Mathis lives in the home Howard Hughes built for Jean Harlow, Chester Washington has given a lecture tour in Sweden). The introduction provides a four-page history of black-Americans' finances, and the back matter (five pages) includes a breakdown by state of the nation's 574,342 millionaires, an index to the book's main entries, photo credits, and a biography of the author.

Dominique-René de Lerma

247.   Logan, Rayford W., and Michael R. Winston, eds. **Dictionary of American Negro Biography**. New York, W. W. Norton, 1983. 680p. $50.00. LC 81-9629. ISBN 0-393-01513-0.

This is probably one of the best retrospective biographical dictionaries on this subject. It includes prominent blacks who died before 1 January 1970. The execution is quite scholarly and all biographies are signed. Entries vary in length from a column to several pages and cite not only additional biographical listings for biographees, but also primary source material. Indeed, an outstanding and reliable biographical source.

Bohdan S. Wynar

248.   Richardson, Ben Albert, and William A. Fahey. **Great Black Americans**. 2nd rev. ed. New York, Thomas Y. Crowell, 1976. 344p. illus. $14.38. LC 75-12841.

The first edition of this book was published under the title *Great American Negroes* in 1956. This revised edition, which retains the same format, includes figures such as Muhammad Ali and Malcolm X. Many other biographical sketches have been revised, and for the first time, black-and-white photographs accompany the text. [R: BL, 15 Apr 76, p. 1189; SLJ, May 76, p. 72]

Bohdan S. Wynar

249. **Who's Who among Black Americans, 1980-81**. 3rd ed. Publisher, Ann Wolk Krouse; eds., William C. Matney and G. James Fleming. Northbrook, Ill., Who's Who Among Black Americans, 1981. 1006p. index. $59.95. LC 76-643293. ISBN 0-915130-33-5.

Of exceptional value and importance in many ways, this directory of contemporary figures is overpowering to the extent that it offers data not available in any other source, including subject areas which have already been treated in the literature. This is not a vanity Who's Who; the editorial board and their distinguished advisors were determined that the criteria for inclusion would serve the interests of the users. (Among the advisors, who appear not to have served in an "honorary" capacity, are Nikki Giovanni, Eileen Southern, Arthur Ashe, Bayard Rustin, Jesse Jackson, and Clara Jones.) With an increase of three thousand new entries over the 1976 edition (bringing the total to around sixteen thousand), the coverage includes figures from the arts, sports, government, education, law, religion, business, and other areas, ending up as a celebration-in-print of major contributions by Afro-Americans. Yet it is far more than that, even if some information on figures from the second edition should have been revised. This is a publication meriting acquisition consideration by all libraries.

It is much superior to *Contemporary Black Leaders* by Elton Fax (New York, Dodd, Mead, 1970. 243p. o.p.). For retrospective coverage one can recommend *Who's Who of the Colored Race: A General Biographical Dictionary of Men and Women of African Descent* (Chicago, Half-Century Anniversary of Negro Freedom in the U.S., 1915; repr., Detroit, Gale, 1976. 296p.) that contains approximately fifteen hundred profiles of men and women of African descent who achieved prominence in the United States in the arts and sciences and the professions. The profile for each individual includes such information as occupation, place of birth, date of birth, names of parents, education, membership in organizations, and career achievements. The value of this historical source is mostly in the names of blacks who lived in the nineteenth century. In addition to the alphabetical arrangement of the profiles, there are miscellaneous factual data on such matters as the text of the Emancipation Proclamation and the Thirteenth Amendment, statistical data from the United States Census in 1910, and a list of national organizations supported by blacks in the early part of this century.   Dominique René de Lerma and Bohdan S. Wynar

CHICANOS

250. Martinez, Julio A., ed. and comp. **Chicano Scholars and Writers: A Bio-Bibliographical Directory**. Metuchen, N.J., Scarecrow, 1979. 579p. index. $31.50. LC 78-32076. ISBN 0-8108-1205-3.

With an increase of interest in the scholarly contributions of American ethnic scholars to academic disciplines, this bio-bibliographic directory is a valuable reference guide. It is the first reference work to present biographical, professional, educational, and bibliographical information on the achievements of over five hundred Chicanos who have made important contributions in the fields of the humanities, the social sciences, and education both within and outside academic circles. Also included are Anglo-American and Latin-American scholars who have researched the Chicano experience. The purpose of this reference work is to legitimize and provide visibility to Chicano scholarship and academic accomplishments, especially since individual contributions by Chicanos have often been ignored in traditional directories.

The entries are arranged in alphabetical order. Information on the biographees includes personal data, education, professional and community affiliation, distinctions and honors, publications, papers and speeches, lectures and nonprint works, and criticism of works. In order to facilitate reference, a subject index with cross-references to the biographees is also included. This guide is recommended for large public and academic libraries. It is a worthwhile addition for those institutions that emphasize Chicano studies. [R: BL, 15 Sept 80, p. 142; Choice, Mar 80, p. 49; LJ, 1 Dec 79, p. 2557; RQ, Spring 80, p. 297; WLB, Mar 80, p. 463]   Anna T. Wynar

CROATIANS

251. Eterovich, Francis H., comp. **Biographical Directory of Scholars, Artists, and Professionals of Croatian Descent in the United States and Canada**. 3rd enl. ed. Cleveland, Ohio, Institute for Soviet and East European Studies, John Carroll University, 1970. 203p. $10.00. LC 70-13452.

The first edition of this biographical directory, published in 1965, contained biographical information on some 150 individuals plus 220 names without biographical data. The third edition is significantly enlarged. It is based on a questionnaire administered by the compiler and contains three hundred biographies in alphabetical order, lists of names according to field of specialization and by geographical area (United States and Canada), and list of names according to field of specialization of eligible persons not included in this directory (questionnaires were not returned). Biographical information includes the following data: professional position, personalia, collection, major field, languages, membership, publications, and address. There are obviously more professionals of Croatian descent eligible for inclusion in this type of directory; nevertheless, even of such limited scope, this directory provides a good starting point.   Bohdan S. Wynar

JEWS

252. **American Jewish Biographies**. By Lakeville Press. New York, Facts on File, 1982. 493p. bibliog. index. $39.95. LC 80-27105. ISBN 0-87196-462-7.

This is a compilation of biographical information on over four hundred men and women "who have distinguished themselves either in American life or [in] American Jewish life" and who have received public attention because of their achievements. To qualify, individuals must be living U.S. citizens who consider themselves Jewish and have made a "permanent contribution to life in this country" or are identified with a significant event, issue, or movement. The research and writing were done by several journalists and writers. They are not identified, so there is no way to ascertain their qualifications for such an undertaking. This factor places into question the accuracy and reliability of the information presented.

The entries are arranged alphabetically. Some include brief and incomplete bibliographic references. There is a subject index that can be used to identify, for example, Jewish physicists, journalists, educators, or actors. The brief introduction by historian Henry Feingold aims to place the biographies in the context of U.S. Jewish history, but in the discussion of Jewish achievements in U.S. society he overlooks the reality of anti-Semitism in the United States. The book complements rather than duplicates the standard reference work on U.S. Jews, *Who's Who in American Jewry. American Jewish Biographies* presents in essay format information about the life, work, contributions, and impact of each person considered, whereas *Who's Who* is a brief, concise listing with dates of work experience, publications, awards, and memberships. *American Jewish Biographies'* coverage is broad, its format convenient, and its entries written in a popular style. It can strengthen public-library collections of Jewish resources and would also be especially appropriate for secondary-school and community-college libraries. [R: BL, 1 Oct 83, p. 246; LJ, 1 Feb 83, p. 197; RQ, Summer 83, p. 419; WLB, Feb 83, p. 520]   Susan J. Freiband

253.   Greenberg, Martin H. **The Jewish Lists: Physicists and Generals, Actors and Writers, and Hundreds of Other Lists of Accomplished Jews.** New York, Schocken Books, 1979. 327p. index. $12.95. LC 79-14349. ISBN 0-8052-3711-9.

Books of lists depend upon the element of surprise and sheer exhaustiveness. An unearthing of the curious, a seemingly indefatigable, relentless coverage, and some generally unique categories create a new genre of popular encyclopedias. *The Jewish Lists* shares some of these elements with similar works, and it also comes with some caveats as well. This is a partial listing, and one that reflects personal interest and taste, Greenberg points out. Moreover, it is a "celebration of the Jewish presence" and hopes to inspire younger readers in their quest for "roots."

The book is divided into nine general parts that deal with such areas as public life, the professions, business, social sciences, physical sciences, the arts, motion pictures, sports, and prize winners. The annotations are brief, and if not unflavored by personal preference, are made somewhat bland by repetitious phrases. "Important," "world-renowned," "leading," and "influential" appear with regularity, making the "celebration" a high time indeed. Nonetheless, the book should find its niche in the popular market; its instruction may well be a slender enterprise, but its capacity for entertainment and idle pleasure is another matter.[R: BL, 1 Nov 80, pp. 414-15]

Lewis Fried

254.   Postal, Bernard, and Lionel Koppman. **Guess Who's Jewish in American History.** New York, New American Library, 1978. 322p. index. (A Signet Book). o.p. ISBN 0-451-08351-2.

This collection of biographical vignettes about American Jews groups them into broad categories, such as sports, business and banking, arts and journalism. Although much useful information is accumulated in this work, there are several problems: biographees are selected haphazardly (major figures are omitted when minor ones are presented); the unfavorable and controversial are ignored (there are no criminals, spies, or New Left proponents); and the women (who are slighted) are covered in their own category rather than in their fields of endeavor. There is no attempt to relate the subject's Jewishness to his or her claim to fame. The most interesting section of the book, which is not reflected by the title, is a review of the attitudes of America's presidents toward the Jewish community. Like the biographical section, the summary limits itself to the positive, amiable aspects of this interaction. There is no bibliography.

Margaret Norden

255.   **Who's Who in American Jewry: Incorporating** *The Directory of American Jewish Institutions.* 1980 ed. Los Angeles, Standard Who's Who, 1980. 726p. $87.50. ISSN 0196-8009.

A handy, one-volume biographical directory containing over six thousand entries for notable Jewish men and women in the United States and Canada. According to the editor, the principle underlying the selection criteria "has been to choose Jewish men and women who have achieved distinction in a particular field of human endeavor or who hold leadership positions in the Jewish or national community" (preface, p. iv). The volume consists of two major parts: a biographical section and the Directory of American Jewish Institutions. The Directory is arranged by state and covers over nine thousand Jewish institutions. *Who's Who in American Jewry* constitutes a major reference work on American Jewry and is recommended for large academic and public libraries.

It might be supplemented by *Who's Who in World Jewry. A Biographical Dictionary of Outstanding Jews* (Marshfield, Mass., Pitman, 1972. 999p.) that lists some ten thousand biographies written in the standard Who's Who format. The information provided usually includes name, country of residence, occupation, place and date of birth, educational background, publications, etc. Prepared with the aid of a number of well-known advisors, this volume, in general, successfully accomplishes its stated purposes. [R: LJ, 15 Oct 80, p. 2192]   Lubomyr R. Wynar

POLES

256.   Bolek, Francis, ed. **Who's Who in Polish America: A Biographical Directory of Polish-American Leaders and Distinguished Poles Resident in the Americas.** Salem, N.H., Ayer Co., 1970. 581p. $31.50. ISBN 0-405-00545-8.

This is actually a reprint of the 1943 edition published in the American Immigration Collection. It contains a listing of some five thousand brief biographies of prominent personalities in this ethnic group.

Similar works exist for many other ethnic groups, usually published by ethnic organizations and not easily accessible in standard tools of the trade. As an example one can mention *Hungarians in America: A Biographical Directory of Professionals of Hungarian Origin in the Americas*. The second edition of this work was published in 1966 in New York by the Kossuth Foundation (East European Biographies and Studies, vol. 2. 488p.) and was edited by Szy Tibor. The more recent edition was edited by D. K. Bognar and was published in 1981 (New York, Media Forum, 1981. 369p. $25.00. ISBN 0-912460-04-0). Some ethnic biographical sources are published by vanity presses, notably Gormezano, who has released *Who's Who among American Jews* (1985. 996p. $989.85), *Who's Who among Native Americans* (1982. 293p.), *Who's Who among Hispanic or Spanish-Surnamed Americans: Five Thousand Brief Biographies, 1980-81* (1980), *Who's Who among Asian-Americans: Five Thousand Brief Biographies* (1982) and others.   Bohdan S. Wynar

UKRAINIANS

257.   **Ukrainians in North America: A Biographical Directory of Noteworthy Men and Women of Ukrainian Origin in the United States and Canada.** Dmytro M. Shtohryn, ed. Champaign, Ill., Association for the Advancement of Ukrainian Studies, 1975. 424p. $20.00. LC 75-31726. ISBN 0-916332-01-2.

There are approximately two-and-a-half million Americans (including Canadians) of Ukrainian origin who contribute to the scientific and creative fields within these two countries. The present publication constitutes the first comprehensive biographical directory of noted Ukrainians in North America. The biographic data for this directory were obtained from completed questionnaires or secondary biographical sources. Arranged in straight alphabetical order by the surnames of biographees, it contains approximately eighteen hundred biographical sketches. According to the editor, "admission to *Ukrainians in North America* was judged on four main factors: (1) position of responsibility held, (2) scientific-scholarly and/or professional work, (3) cultural, social and/or political activities, and (4) past positions and services" (p. xi). Although this publication omits some notable Ukrainians in the United States and Canada, it constitutes a valuable reference source for historians and researchers involved in ethnic studies as well as for reference librarians. Recommended for university and public libraries.   Lubomyr R. Wynar

8 Fine Arts

Introduction

The material in this chapter is arranged under eleven headings. The first section, "General Works," covers biographical reference sources not limited to a particular country or subject. "General Works" is arranged in two parts: current and retrospective biographical sources. Following the first section are three subject-oriented sections: "Architects," "Graphic Artists," and "Painters," with coverage not limited to a particular country or nationality. The rest of the material is arranged by country: United States; Australia and New Zealand; Canada; France; Germany, Austria, and Switzerland; Great Britain; and Japan. A total of fifty-six main entries is included in this chapter, with many more related titles mentioned in annotations. There are a number of outstanding biographical sources in this area, e.g., *Contemporary Artists* (see entry 258), Wilson's *World Artists* (see entry 271), *Macmillan Encyclopedia of Architects* (see entry 277), *Larousse Dictionary of Painters* (see entry 286), *Dictionary of American Artists* (see entry 294), and many others.

Obviously, biographical information on prominent artists can also be found in other sources, primarily subject dictionaries and encyclopedias. In this respect the most important work is *McGraw-Hill Encyclopedia of World Art* (15v. New York, McGraw-Hill, 1959-1968) that covers some 550 outstanding artists worldwide. *McGraw-Hill Dictionary of Art* edited by Bernard S. Myers (5v. McGraw-Hill, 1969) is not an abridgment of the above-mentioned *Encyclopedia of World Art*, but an independent work. This dictionary contains about fifteen thousand entries with many biographical entries for noted artists. International coverage is also provided by a number of one-volume dictionaries, e.g., Murrays' *A Dictionary of Art and Artists* (3rd ed. Penquin Books, 1972. 457p.) covering some one thousand artists, *Oxford Companion to Art* (Oxford University Press, 1970. 1277p.), and *The Oxford Companion to Twentieth-Century Art* (Oxford University Press, 1981. 656p.). The *Praeger Encyclopedia of Art* (5v. Praeger, 1971), based on the French encyclopedia *Dictionnaire universel de l'art et des artistes* published in 1967, includes some three thousand biographical articles on prominent personalities worldwide. The most comprehensive biographical encyclopedia is the German *Allgemeines Lexikon der bildender Künstler von der Antike bis zur Gegenwart* (37v. Leipzig, Seemann, 1907-1950), a reference source of outstanding scope and scholarship. Artists active chiefly in the twentieth century are not included. American artists are represented in Baigell's *Dictionary of American Art* (Harper & Row, 1979. 390p.) covering some 650 artists, and *The Britannica Encyclopedia of American Art* (Encyclopaedia Britannica, 1973. 669p.).

Additional biographical information can be found in periodical literature with the assistance of existing indexing services. The most popular is *Art Index: A Cumulative Author and Subject Index to a Selected List of Fine Arts Periodicals and Museum Bulletins* (H. W. Wilson, 1933-) that serves as a basic reference tool, especially for material in the English language. Museum bulletins are included only through 1957. The Wilson index can be supplemented by *Index to Art Periodicals* (Boston, G. K. Hall, 1962. 11v. supplement, 1975) that covers some three hundred periodicals not indexed by Wilson. Of some assistance will also be *Art Bibliographies Current Titles* (ABC-Clio Press, 1972-), a monthly index that covers some 250 fine-arts periodicals. In addition to general serial indexes, Patricia Havlice has produced two important indexes. *Index to Artistic Biography* (2v. Scarecrow, 1973) covers seventy-thousand artists from sixty-four art publications. The source books were published between 1902 and 1970 in ten different languages. In a supplement, *Index to Artistic Biography: First Supplement* (Scarecrow, 1981. 953p.), Havlice covers an additional seventy titles which she had combed for artists' biographies and indexed alphabetically by the artist's name. Important bibliographies and other types of reference books are adequately covered by Donald Ehresmann in *Fine Arts. A Bibliographic Guide to Basic Reference Works, Histories, and Handbooks* (2nd ed. Libraries Unlimited, 1979. 349p.).

GENERAL WORKS

Current Biographies

258. **Contemporary Artists**. 2nd ed. Muriel Emanuel and others, eds. New York, St. Martin's Press, 1983. 1041p. illus. $70.00. LC 82-25048. ISBN 0-312-16643-5.

This new edition of a work first published in 1977 includes biographical and critical information about one thousand artists worldwide, 150 of them new to this edition. Four hundred and fifty of the thirteen hundred artists covered in the first edition have been omitted. Despite the use of "contemporary" in the title, dead artists are included if their work still exerts influence in the art world. Matisse, Picasso, Pollock, and Arp are listed, for example. Entries include a short biography, lists of individual and group exhibitions, a list of collections in which the artist is represented, a bibliography of publications by and about the artist, the name of the artist's agent or dealer, and sometimes a short critical essay signed by one of the contributors. In some cases the artists themselves have contributed brief explanations of their work. Entries for artists who appeared in the first edition have been updated. Many entries also have new critical essays, but occasionally the criticism is the same in both editions. Black-and-white photographs of art works decorate the book but are of little value to the librarian seeking biographical information. Bracketing the main body of the work are a list of included artists (at the front) and notes on the contributors (at the back).

This book is valuable more for its entries on lesser-known figures such as Klaus Staeck, the German political poster artist, and Dorothy Iannone, an American feminist artist now working in Berlin. Wider in scope than the *Dictionary of Contemporary American Artists* and offering more information than the *Dictionary of Contemporary Artists*, this volume will be useful to both art librarians and general university reference librarians. Because of the large number of artists omitted from the second edition, libraries which own the first edition should keep it as well. [R: BL, 15 Oct 78, pp. 402-3; Choice, Apr 78, p. 207; LJ, 15 Feb 78, pp. 449-50]   Linda Keir Hinrichs

259. **Guide to Exhibited Artists: Craftsmen**. Santa Barbara, Calif., ABC-Clio, 1985. 211p. index. $19.50pa. ISBN 0-903440-98-4.

260. **Guide to Exhibited Artists: European Painters**. Santa Barbara, Calif., ABC-Clio, 1985. 398p. index. $19.50pa. ISBN 0-903440-94-1.

261. **Guide to Exhibited Artists: North American Painters**. Santa Barbara, Calif., ABC-Clio, 1985. 229p. index. $19.50pa. ISBN 0-903440-96-8.

262. **Guide to Exhibited Artists: Printmakers**. Santa Barbara, Calif., ABC-Clio, 1985. 287p. index. $19.50pa. ISBN 0-903440-93-3.

263. **Guide to Exhibited Artists: Sculptors**. Santa Barbara, Calif., ABC-Clio, 1985. 254p. index. $19.50pa. ISBN 0-903440-97-6.

For several years Clio Press has been gathering and publishing information on living artists, based chiefly on exhibition records. Their computerized files now contain over sixteen thousand artists, and these five volumes are a by-product of this data gathering. For all practical purposes, this is not a typical biographical directory, but rather a fact-finding device to locate exhibiting artists worldwide. The following information is provided in most cases: name, nationality, specialty, personal data (place and year of birth), address, education, and chronological listing of major exhibits. The information has been obtained from two main sources: the exhibition catalogs and from the artists themselves. In confirming listings for *North American Painters*, we found that at least 50 percent of the nationally known artists are not listed here. But, nevertheless, these small volumes might be of some use to the patron when visiting galleries. Reference value is rather limited.   Bohdan S. Wynar

264. Smith, V. Babington. **Dictionary of Contemporary Artists**. Santa Barbara, Calif., ABC-Clio Press, 1981. 451p. index. $47.50. ISBN 0-903450-46-1.

The *Dictionary of Contemporary Artists* is the first of a planned annual series to be published by ABC-Clio Press on beginning and little-known living and working artists whose work is now exhibited in galleries and museums around the world. Unfortunately, no more volumes have been published in this series since 1981. Entries are alphabetical by artist, providing brief bibliographical and biographical information, including exhibition details. All artistic disciplines are covered, including ceramicists, jewelers, painters, printmakers, and video artists. The most useful feature of the work is the inclusion of full addresses for over seven hundred exhibiting galleries and museums which publish catalogs and brochures on artists and their works. This biographical dictionary could well become the easiest and fastest method to trace biographical and exhibition details on contemporary artists. [R: Choice, Nov 81, p. 355; RQ, Fall 81, pp. 92-93]   Maureen Pastine

265.   Smith, Veronica Babington, ed. **International Directory of Exhibiting Artists.** 2nd ed. Santa Barbara, Calif., ABC-Clio, 1983. 2v. index. $65.00/set. ISBN 0-903450-75-5.

According to the editor, there are in excess of fourteen thousand artists listed in this two-volume work, which is international in scope. ABC-Clio received some of the documentary information for the myriad artists listed in this second edition from ARTbibliographies MODERN and some from other sources. Difficulties continue, however, in gathering current biographic data from artists in South America, Australia, and southern European countries. The two principal assets of the directory are the listings of galleries and museum associations for the individual artists, so that contact may be made through these exhibiting institutions in most cases, and the many listings broken down by media. These divisions include not only painters, sculptors, and printmakers but workers in other media prevalent in today's international art world, such as holographers; filmmakers; craftspeople; photographers; and book, glass, mail, paper, textile, and video artists. Listings for the exhibiting institutions, which include commercial galleries, conclude both volumes and should be of real value to collectors, dealers, curators, and appraisers with particular concerns with North American and United Kingdom contacts. This edition is an improvement over the 1982 edition in that it has been expanded by one-third and is therefore more complete. This directory is an important art reference tool and is of particular value to those involved with contemporary artists on a worldwide scale. It is now being updated by *Guide to Exhibited Artists.* (See entries 259-63.) [R: BL, 1 Dec 83, p. 555]

William J. Dane

Retrospective Biographies

266.   Bihalji-Merin, Oto, and Nebojša-Bato Tomašević. **World Encyclopedia of Naive Art.** Belgrade, Yugoslavia, Scala/Philip Wilson; distr., New York, Harper & Row, 1984. 735p. illus. (part col.). bibliog. $60.00. LC 84-051455. ISBN 0-935748-62-8.

In his opening remarks (an excellent and extended essay entitled "A Hundred Years of Naive Art") the senior author of this volume effectively sets the stage for what is to follow. He states the purpose of the work, which, he says, "attempts to explain and summarize our theoretical and practical knowledge of naive art, to offer definitions and, in its main section, to provide biographical entries on the individual artists in alphabetical order." The author describes naive artists "as individuals practising their art world-wide but outside historical and stylistic categories." Without question, this volume represents the finest compilation of these artists and their work on a worldwide basis.

After the opening essay are biographical sketches for 1,560 painters and sculptors. Although no established criteria for inclusion are stated (Clementine Hunter of Louisiana is omitted), the six countries with the greatest number of artists represented, ranked in descending order are: Yugoslavia, 86; USSR, 67; Great Britain, 62; United States, 59; West Germany, 56; and France, 47. The biographical sketches vary in length (the longest is for Rousseau) and most are signed by an authority whose credentials and biography are found near the end of the volume. A typical entry includes the standard factual information, but with the omission of reference to any formal education or training. General characteristics of style and unique quality of a particular artist are also provided. Black-and-white photographs (425 in all) of some of the artists are included, and at least one representative work is illustrated for each artist whose biographical information is given (some are full-page and all are in color).

Following the biographical section, which occupies the major portion of the volume, there are signed essays devoted to historical surveys of naive art in twenty-nine of the countries represented in the volume. An added feature of the book is a chronological listing of important naive art exhibitions, museums, and galleries throughout the world. An extensive bibliography, arranged alphabetically by country, is also provided.

The leaves in this volume are sewn and it is sturdily cased. The pages lie flat when the volume is open.

This volume provides an attractive, extensive, and up-to-date overview of naive art and artists of the world. As such, it should be included in all academic, larger public, and specialized humanities and fine art collections.   Charles D. Patterson

267.   Clement, Clara Erskine and Laurence Hutton. **Artists of the Nineteenth Century and Their Works**. Salem, N.H., Ayer Co., 1969. 2v. in 1. $24.00. LC 70-88820. ISBN 0-405-02222-0.

This book is a reprint of the 1884 edition, containing 1,050 biographical sketches. The author intentionally omitted early and well-known artists, concentrating on later artists of prominence and promise. It is alphabetically arranged by artist. Indexes are provided for authorities quoted and places; a general index concludes the work.

Bohdan S. Wynar

268.   **Female Artists Past and Present**. Berkeley, Calif., Women's History Research Center, 1974. 158p. $7.00.

269.   **Female Artists Past and Present: International Women's Year 1975 Supplement**. Berkeley, Calif., Women's History Research Center, 1975. 66p. index. $4.00pa.

Female Artists is another entry in the current rush to publish women's studies guides and reference aids. As with so many of the works published by dedicated volunteer groups, this one has many good features; but it is so uncritically edited that its use and reliability are severely limited. Its aim is to identify women artists and thereby open up new channels of communication among them. The four main parts are: (1) female artists in art history; (2) individual women artists today, arranged alphabetically under nine media; (3) women working in other areas of the visual arts – art teachers, gallery personnel, critics, researchers; (4) contemporary female artists movement. The typescript pages are so poorly arranged and printed that the resulting jumble requires a dedicated reader in order to make some sense of it. The listings for contemporary artists provide brief citations to published articles and books. Biographical data and address of the individual are given in some cases but not others. The contemporary movement section lists groups, collections and organizations; galleries, museums and slide registries; articles; publications; festivals, etc.

The supplement, issued in 1975, follows the same arrangement but adds additional names. An index covering names listed in the main volume and the supplement is appended. The editor indicates that this supplement is the last publication of the Women's History Research Center (2325 Oak Street, Berkeley, CA 94708).

A much more substantial work is *Dictionary of Woman Artists: An International Dictionary of Women Artists Born before 1900*, by Chris Petteys (Boston, G. K. Hall,

1985. 872p. $49.95) that covers twenty thousand women painters, sculptors, print-makers, and graphic artists world-wide. The following information is provided: name (with maiden and married names cross-referenced); birth and death dates and locations; media in which the artist worked and subjects for which she was best known; artist's place of residence and/or activity; schools in which she enrolled and teachers with whom she studied; summary of her exhibition record, including major solo exhibitions and awards; key to bibliographic sources. Appended to each entry is a bibliography of references to help researchers and librarians locate further information.

Bohdan S. Wynar

270.   Kingston, Jeremy. **Arts and Artists**. New York, Facts on File, 1980. 336p. illus. (part col.). index. $24.95. LC 79-20820. ISBN 0-87196-404-X.

The art critic of *Punch* has produced a kind of *Reader's Digest* of the arts which covers broadly (but not deeply) painting, sculpture, architecture, music, theatre, and film, intended for those who want "to explore and appreciate a wide range of arts." Chapters are augmented by a two-page spread on each of seventy well-selected artists in these fields, illustrated with reproductions of their works, chiefly in color. These vary in clarity, and their sources, chiefly museums, are indicated in an appendix. The simply written text emphasizes biography rather than critical analysis of the works and is calculated to appeal to the general reader. There is no bibliography. The index contains chiefly names of artists and their works. While this British import (originally published by Aldus Books, London) will add little or nothing to libraries with substantial reference collections in these fields, it may serve as a circulating title in high school and small public libraries.   Frances Neel Cheney

271.   Marks, Claude. **World Artists 1950-1980**. New York, H. W. Wilson, 1984. 912p. illus. $70.00. LC 84-13152. ISBN 0-8242-0707-6.

The latest in the H. W. Wilson Company's solid and reliable biographical dictionary series, *World Artists 1950-1980* is a necessary purchase for those libraries which place even limited emphasis upon the fine arts.

Alphabetically arranged, the 312 entries treat artists who lived and were influential in the post-World War II era. As Marks says in his information-packed preface, he was not able to include every significant artist but did attempt to select "outstanding figures from many countries, representing a wide variety of styles and movements and embracing the long-neglected graphic media as well as painting and sculpture." Each entry includes the artist's full name, birth and death dates, a picture in most instances, a two-to-five-page biographical-critical commentary incorporating, where possible, statements by the artist, locations and dates of exhibitions, galleries/museums holding collections, publications about the artist, and proper pronunciation of the artist's name. Additional prefatory material includes a list of the artists and keys to pronunciation and abbreviations.   Charles R. Andrews

272.   Murray, Peter, and Linda Murray. **A Dictionary of Art and Artists**. Baltimore, Md., Penguin Books, 1968; repr., 1984. 384p. (Penguin Reference Books). $6.95pa. ISBN 0-14-051133-4.

This dictionary was first published in 1959, a revised edition was published by Thames and Hudson in 1965, and the final revision by Penguin appeared in 1968. This paperback reprint provides short biographies of some one thousand painters, sculptors and engravers, as well as brief definitions of artistic movements, terminology, and some abbreviations. It will be a useful companion for gallery visitors and provides quick reference data with a number of helpful cross-references.   Bohdan S. Wynar

273. Petteys, Chris, and others. **Dictionary of Woman Artists: An International Dictionary of Women Artists Born before 1900**. Boston, G. K. Hall, 1985. 851p. bibliog. $49.95. LC 84-22511. ISBN 0-8161-8456-9.

This new comprehensive international biographical dictionary of more than twenty-one thousand women painters, sculptors, printmakers, and illustrators born before 1900 is the most important publication on women artists to date. Photographers, architects, craftsworkers, and designers are excluded. Entries include full name, married name, and pseudonyms (all cross-referenced), birth and death dates, the media in which the artist worked, and subject matter for which she is known, place of residence, other artists in the family, formal education and teachers with whom she studied, exhibitions and awards, and further bibliographical references. The references given direct the scholar to collection locations and further materials on the artists included. An extremely valuable asset is the provisions of references consulted for each entry leading the researcher to even more information. Many individuals and publications provided source material, most notably the thirty-six volumes of Thieme-Becker's *Allgemeines Lexicon der bildenden Künstler von der Antike bis zur Gegenwart*.

Used in conjunction with publications by Donna G. Bachmann and Sherry Piland, *Women Artists: An Historical, Contemporary, and Feminist Bibliography* (Scarecrow, 1978), Charlotte Streifer Rubenstein, *American Women Artists: From Early Indian Times to the Present* (G. K. Hall, 1982), Anne Sutherland Harris and Linda Nachlin, *Women Artists: 1550-1950* (Museum/Knopf, 1977), and similar works, this massive volume extends the ability of artists, art historians, art teachers, women's studies scholars, librarians, and others to investigate women's role in our artistic and cultural history. It will also be of inestimable value to art collectors and dealers, art galleries, and museums. The guide to bibliographical references is a superb listing of major references for student and scholar.   Maureen Pastine

274. **Phaidon Encyclopedia of Art and Artists**. London, Phaidon Press; distr., New York, E. P. Dutton, 1978. 704p. illus. (part col.). o.p. LC 77-89312. ISBN 0-7148-1513-6.

The *Phaidon Encyclopedia* is a condensation of the five-volume *Praeger Encyclopedia of Art* (*Pall Mall Encyclopedia of Art* in Great Britain) published in 1971. Although the preface states that the present one-volume work has been "brought up to date and adapted to suit the format of a single volume," in fact updating amounts to little more than adding recent death dates to the biographical entries. No new entries have been added, and no entries have been rewritten to reflect changes in opinion and information in the past eight years. This alone would not be a serious limitation, for the original work is a good general dictionary of Western art history. But the process of condensation has resulted in arbitrarily excised paragraphs from the original entries and has eliminated entirely the very useful bibliographies attached to many of the entries in the original five-volume work. Recommended to those not possessing the Praeger or Pall Mall encyclopedias. [R: BL, 15 Sept 79, p. 144; Choice, Mar 79, p. 58; LJ, 15 Jan 79, p. 180; RQ, Summer 79, p. 409; WLB, Feb 79, p. 469]

                    Donald L. Ehresmann

275.   **The Thames and Hudson Dictionary of Art and Artists**. rev. ed. Herbert Read and Nikos Stangos, eds. London, Thames and Hudson, 1984; distr., New York, W. W. Norton, 1985. 352p. illus. $19.95. LC 84-50342. ISBN 0-500-23402-7.

Attempting to be comprehensive in its coverage of the fine arts, this work is limited in scope to painting, sculpture, drawing, and prints; to various artists; and to a selection of technical and conceptual terms relevant to art and art history. Most of the entries included were originally written for *The Encyclopaedia of the Arts* (Meredith Press, 1966). Some have been revised; others have not. Three hundred and seventy-six black-and-white illustrations (somewhat dark) accompany more than twenty-five hundred entries.

As a quick reference source for high school and small public libraries, this work may prove sufficient. There is however, an evident lack of consistency in entries and cross-references—a quality which will limit usefulness in the academic setting. Non-Western art is given cursory treatment, with the noticeable absence of information on Indian art. Other areas overlooked are American Indian art, folk art, crafts, and photography. Mayan, Aztec and Incan art are included in a general entry for Pre-Columbian art, yet cross-references appear only under "Maya art" and "Aztec art." "Earth art" and "Econological art" have separate entries with similar definitions, yet neither is cross-referenced to the other. Definitions are presented for "Graphic arts" and "Drawing," yet none appear for painting or sculpture.

A work of uneven quality, this dictionary might reasonably be selected when all others are out-of-print, and no encyclopedia can be located.

                                                                Edmund F. SantaVicca

ARCHITECTS

276.   Emanuel, Muriel, ed. **Contemporary Architects**. Dennis Sharp, architectural consultant. New York, St. Martin's Press, 1980. 933p. illus. $70.00. LC 79-67803. ISBN 0-312-16635-4.

Contemporary Architects is a worthy companion to the same publisher's outstanding *Contemporary Artists*. The two bio-bibliographical dictionaries are unquestionably the best current reference tools on contemporary artists and architects. Six hundred signed entries treat major architects, planners, and theorists—either living or recently deceased. A selection of well-known architects of the interwar and immediate postwar periods has been included to round out coverage of twentieth-century architecture. The international board of advisors has assured broad and generally even coverage. Only for Eastern European countries and some areas of the Third World are there lapses; but these are forgivable in view of the great difficulty of obtaining reliable information, and the reader is informed of this in the introduction.

Entries vary in length from a few columns to several pages, with the vast majority having a thorough biography, a very extensive chronological list of major works by the architect, a bibliography of books and articles written by the subject, an essay by the architect that is a brief philosophical statement on architecture, a critical evaluation of the architect's contribution (written by a historian or critic), and a thorough bibliography of literature about the architect. Each entry has one black-and-white illustration of a major building by the architect. *Contemporary Architects* is a must for all reference collections. [R: Choice, Nov 80, p. 372; LJ, 1 Sept 80, p. 1720; RQ, Fall 80, pp. 88-90]   Donald L. Ehresmann

277. **Macmillan Encyclopedia of Architects**. Adolf K. Placzek, ed. New York, Free Press/Macmillan, 1982. 4v. illus. bibliog. index. $275.00/set. LC 82-17256. ISBN 0-02-925000-5.

Any work entitled "Encyclopedia" is immediately and inherently faced with the problem of comprehensiveness: what sound methodology can define its limits for inclusion? The twenty-four hundred biographies of architects herein include those deceased and those born by 31 December 1930 (although such a cutoff date may seem arbitrary, it is nonetheless essential in preventing any biases in contemporary coverage). The biographees, selected by a board of editors and reviewed by international specialist advisers, were chosen for the importance of their work, their creation or expansion of a style, their effect upon a culture (since the list includes architects of all cultures and time periods), or their production of a substantial body of work—all criteria that can be stretched or manipulated by a subjective imagination. Invited authors, most of whom are authorities on their particular biographees, have for the most part produced thoughtful essays accompanied by useful bibliographies, illustrations, and a selective list of works. Supplementing these essays is a glossary of select terms intended to expand on architectural styles and elements that are treated only superficially within the text; a worthwhile enhancement to this glossary would have been phonetic spellings for each term listed. The usual index of names is provided, and a more unusual index of architectural works refers to each building or monument discussed in these four volumes. Also, the chronological list of architects will prove valuable. The value of the bibliography of general biographical sources and handbooks is somewhat negligible due to its general nature.

Slight errors and omissions are bound to be apparent in an undertaking whose scope is so all-encompassing. Errors in dates have been made both for buildings—e.g., Angelo Italia's Chiesa Matrice was rebuilt in Alcamo, Sicily in 1669 rather than 1699, as the encyclopedia says; and for architects, e.g., the years of birth and death for Jean Jacques Marie Huve (1783-1852) are incorrectly cited as 1742-1808 (actually those of his father, Jean Jacques Huve). Another confusion of father with son occurs in the entry for Pierre Lassurance; the text and bibliography confuse Lassurance the younger with Lassurance the elder (who is not included in this work). The most obvious omissions are among women: substantial contributions, like those of Sophia Hayden and Eleanor Raymond, have been ignored. Despite its flaws and lacunae, this encyclopedia represents the most complete source of its kind. [R: BL, 1 Sept 83, pp. 50-52; Choice, Apr 83, pp. 111-12; LJ, 1 Apr 83, pp. 731-32; 1 May 83, p. 964; WLB, Apr 83, pp. 707-8]   Lamia Doumato

278. **Who's Who in Architecture from 1400 to the Present**. Edited by J. M. Richards. New York, Holt, Rinehart and Winston, 1977. 368p. illus. (part col.). o.p. LC 76-44323. ISBN 0-03-017381-7.

The author of this invaluable reference work is an architectural writer, critic, and historian of distinction. For English and American readers interested in architects and their buildings, he provides over six hundred alphabetically arranged entries for architects, engineers, town planners, and landscape architects who have made a significant contribution to the development of architecture. About fifty of the entries constitute fairly substantial, informative, and stimulating essays written by specialists on individuals or periods. The geographical scope is the Western world, plus those other parts of the world whose culture is derived from the West.

Sixteen color pages and 250 black-and-white illustrations are included. Books on individual architects, when they exist in English, are given at the end of each biographical entry. A classified list of other recommended books for further reading is given, along with acknowledgments and a select list of buildings by country.

Kathleen J. Voigt

GRAPHIC ARTISTS

279.   Holt, Tonie, and Valmai Holt. **Picture Postcard Artists: Landscapes, Animals and Characters**. New York, Longman, 1984. 106p. illus. (part col.). bibliog. index. $14.95. LC 82-24949. ISBN 0-582-50318-3.

A subjective selection of artists and postcards, with priority given to artists about whom useful information could be provided and postcards for the most part readily available and reasonably priced to be found in dealers' stocks at most collectors' fairs and in postcard auction catalogs.

The authors are well known in the field of picture postcards, collectors for many years, veterans of TV and radio appearances, and authors of many authoritative articles, catalogs, and books on the subject.

The work is divided into three sections: landscapes and views, the country, mountain, and seaside (six publishers and fifteen artists); animals (nineteen artists); character studies—literary and ethnic types (eleven artists). Most of the forty-five color illustrations and one hundred black-and-white cards selected were published in the Edwardian era, the Golden Age of the picture postcard.

The volume will be useful to the beginning collector, the seasoned collector, and the noncollector. Public libraries and museum libraries should find this title a useful addition to their collection. A bibliography and an index are included.

Kathleen J. Voigt

280.   Kingman, Lee, Grace Allen Hogarth, and Harriet Quimby, comps. **Illustrators of Children's Books, 1967-1976**. Boston, Horn Book, 1978. 290p. illus. bibliog. index. $35.00. LC 78-13759. ISBN 0-87675-018-8.

In 1947 Horn Book launched a book about illustrators of children's books which immediately gained wide recognition. Entitled *Illustrators of Children's Books: 1744-1945*, edited by Bertha E. Mahony and others (Boston, Horn Book, 1947. 527p. $28.00), it contained biographical sketches of 358 illustrators, bibliographies of illustrators and authors of books in which the illustrations appeared, and ten articles on the history and development of illustration. Three sequels have been published so far: *Illustrators of Children's Books: 1946-1956* (Boston, Horn Book, 1958. 229p. $28.00); *Illustrators of Children's Books: 1957-1966* (Boston, Horn Book, 1968. 295p. $28.00); and finally, *Illustrators of Children's Books: 1967-1976*. The last volume retains all the major characteristics of this distinguished series. The book provides biographical sketches of 478 artists chosen as the best or most representative for the period. Again, there are essays that survey the development of children's illustration during this decade; an appendix that includes bibliographical notes to the essays, biographies and bibliographies; and a cumulative index to biographies and bibliographies in all four volumes in the series. [R: BL, 1 Feb 79, p. 871; Choice, June 79, p. 524; WLB, Mar 79, p. 522]

Bohdan S. Wynar

281. Mahony, Bertha E., and Elinor Whitney, comps. **Contemporary Illustrators of Children's Books**. Boston, Bookshop for Boys and Girls, 1930; repr., Detroit, Gale, 1978. 135p. illus. $65.00. LC 79-185381. ISBN 0-8103-4308-8.

One must note immediately that the word "contemporary" in the title means, of course, contemporary to the original publication date of 1930. The compilers obtained information from approximately 150 illustrators, mostly American, each of whom is discussed in a bio-bibliographical sketch approximately one-half page in length. A number of sketches are in the first person, apparently excerpted directly from letters solicited from each biographee. The compilers had asked for birthplace and date, training, address, and a list of books illustrated. The latter are, admittedly, often incomplete, even as of 1930, as are those for an additional twenty-five illustrators listed in the appendix for whom biographical information was unobtainable. Some of the biographees are no longer familiar to us, of course, and others were just at the beginning of a subsequently notable career.

Well over one-third of the volume consists of essays—three on "contemporary," including European, children's book illustration, and five on historical influences. Their authors include Esther Averill and Rachel Field. Although, like some of the biographical sketches, the essays take an adulatory tone that has become suspect in more recent years, they nevertheless offer valuable information about their respective topics as well as insights into the aesthetic sensitivities of their authors. Every page or two presents a black-and-white reproduction, often reduced in size, of a typical illustration by one of the better-known artists. This volume is essential to any collection on the history of children's literature and book illustration that lacks a good copy of the original, but the several more recent, richly illustrated, histories and anthologies of illustrated children's books will better serve most school and small public libraries.

Lillian Biermann Wehmeyer

282. Meyer, Susan E. **A Treasury of the Great Children's Book Illustrators**. New York, Harry N. Abrams, 1983. 272p. illus. (part col.). bibliog. index. $45.00. LC 83-2500. ISBN 0-8109-0782-8.

Susan E. Meyer has again combined an informative text with sumptuous illustrations, well-printed on fine quality paper, to create a useful, handsome volume on illustration. Her first product, *America's Great Illustrators* (Harry N. Abrams, 1978) shares a number of elements with this book; however, the present publication exceeds the former in the quality of paper, print illustrations, and elegant touches (e.g., the refined border design framing each page and the delicate colored diagrams prevalent throughout the text).

The selection includes thirteen children's book illustrators whose work is indicative of the prevalent style and/or trend of a period. The scope encompasses only English-language works and includes such illustrators as Arthur Rackham, *Winnie-the-Pooh*'s E. H. Shepard, Walter Crane, and Kate Greenaway. [R: SLJ, Apr 84, p. 28]

Lamia Doumato

283. Peppin, Brigid, and Lucy Micklethwait. **Book Illustrators of the Twentieth Century**. New York, Arco Publishing, 1984. 336p. illus. bibliog. $39.95. LC 83-3745. ISBN 0-668-05670-3.

Although there are other works of this type, some devoted exclusively to American book illustration (e.g., Bolton's *American Book Illustrators* [1938], Hamilton's *Early American Book Illustrators and Wood Engravers, 1670-1870* [1968], and Pitz's

Treasury of American Book Illustration [1947]), and still others that deal exclusively with illustrators of children's books, the present work fills a void in an important area too long neglected. Its pages represent the first attempt at complete coverage of all British book illustrators working in the twentieth century (to 1975); it includes more than eight hundred individuals whose work, illustrating both fiction and poetry, was first published in Great Britain. Not only are the famous and influential individuals such as Beatrix Potter, Eric Gill, and Mabel Lucie Attwell found here, but also a host of less-celebrated, yet notable figures whose work is liberally represented in leading publications of the period covered.

The work is alphabetically arranged by subject, and a typical entry provides biographical information, which in some cases is all too brief; a discussion of the artist's style; a list of books and periodicals to which the artist contributed (in some instances a selected list as requested by the artist); and a bibliography of references, to which the user can turn for further information. More than 350 of the entries are accompanied by a representative example of the illustrator's work. Although these are extremely useful in providing illustrations of lesser-known artists in particular, all examples are, unfortunately, in black and white. The use of color would have considerably enhanced an already superb reference work.

A very sturdy volume, well-cased, with sections sewn, the book is indispensable in academic and public libraries as well as in specialized fine art, library science, and journalism collections. This book is also published in Great Britain under the title *A Dictionary of British Book Illustrators—The Twentieth Century* (John Murray Publishers). [R: RBB, 1 Dec 84, p. 493]   Charles D. Patterson

PAINTERS

284.   Canaday, John. **The Lives of the Painters**. Vol. 1: **Late Gothic to High Renaissance**. Vol. 2: **Baroque**. Vol. 3: **Neoclassic to Post-Impressionist**. Vol. 4: **Plates and Index**. New York, W. W. Norton, 1969. 4v. illus. index. $24.95/set. LC 67-17666. ISBN 0-393-94231-6.

Mr. Canaday, the art critic of *The New York Times*, provides a highly readable reference history of Western painting and its artists by means of biographic and critical essays on more than 450 individual painters, Giotto through Cezanne. Following an over-all chronological pattern, each of twenty-nine chapters groups the artists around a centralizing theme, be it style, genre, or nationality. Each chapter begins with a unifying historical-critical introduction that is designed to guide the reader through the biographies but is not supported with bibliographic apparatus.

The Lives of the Painters is elegantly produced in four slip-cased volumes. The first three volumes contain the biographies of the painters; the fourth volume contains more than five hundred reproductions of the works of each of the artists Mr. Canaday discusses: 176 full-page, full-color reproductions and 352 monochrome pictures. Certainly, this work lives up to its challenge to Vasari's *Lives of the Great Italian Painters, Sculptors and Architects* and will be of interest to most public libraries. [R: LJ, 15 Sept 69]   Bohdan S. Wynar

285.   Champlin, John Dension and Charles C. Perkins, eds. **Cyclopedia of Painters and Paintings**. New York, Scribner's, 1892; repr., Irvington Publishers, 1969. 4v. illus. $76.00. LC 77-86249. ISBN 0-8046-0535-1.

This standard work was already once reprinted by Empire State Book Company in 1927 and is again available for new libraries. It provides, in one alphabet, biographical articles on painters and descriptive articles on famous paintings. The biographies include: the main facts of the artist's life; a list of his paintings, with references to the museums or collections where they may be found; and some bibliography.

The articles on paintings give brief descriptions, some facts of history, museum locations, statements of whether engraved and by whom, and some bibliographical references. There are over two thousand illustrations consisting of outline drawings of paintings, portraits of painters, and facsimiles of monograms and signatures. [R: WLB, Feb 70, p. 661]   Bohdan S. Wynar

286. **Larousse Dictionary of Painters**. Edited by Michel Laclotte and Alistair Smith. New York, Larousse, 1981. 467p. illus. (part col.). bibliog. $50.00. LC 81-81046. ISBN 0-88332-265-X.

With over 550 entries for selected artists prepared by nearly 140 contributors and illustrated with hundreds of black-and-white and color reproductions, this is a solid concentration on the principal painters of Europe and North America. The entries are packed with facts telling readers of the artist's life and achievements in the world of art and concluding with a summary of locations where the artist's works may be viewed. The writing is crisp, generally free of jargon, and entries for major artists such as Holbein, Picasso, Rembrandt, Rubens, Tintoretto, Cezanne, and Durer, for example, are broken up into segments by the periods of their lives. In addition to the great centers of art, there are entries for artists from Canada, Denmark, Hungary, Norway, and Czechoslovakia, along with an admirable selection from the United States.

The editing gives a nice sense of wholeness to the many parts. The binding is solid, and the pages lie flat, filling two requirements for a good, popular dictionary. Some of the color reproductions are a bit pallid, with the warm red hues frequently toned down. The book is handsome in format and production. Those teaching or studying in a survey approach to the art of the Western World will certainly use the book for reference in addition to individual study. [R: Choice, July-Aug 82, pp. 1538-40; LJ, 1 Feb 82, p. 248; WLB, Feb 82, p. 463]   William J. Dane

287. Norman, Geraldine. **Nineteenth-Century Painters and Painting: A Dictionary**. Berkeley, Calif., University of California Press, 1977. 240p. illus. (part col.). bibliog. index. $70.00. LC 76-24594. ISBN 0-520-03328-0.

Over the years, several fine one-volume English-language dictionaries of modern (i.e., principally twentieth century) art and artists have appeared, but none covering the entire range of nineteenth-century painting. Norman's *Dictionary*, which includes information on "major figures of all the national schools" in Europe and the United States and their interaction with each other, does much to fill this gap in the reference literature. The dictionary proper is prefaced by brief descriptions of major types and styles of nineteenth-century painting, these illustrated by color reproductions. Of the seven hundred or more dictionary entries, most are biographies of individual painters, but also included are entries on artistic movements, techniques, and institutions. The articles are brief, but reliable, and more readable than many drier dictionary accounts. Short bibliographies are appended in most instances; these include primarily monographs and range from studies done in the nineteenth century to very recent scholarly publications. The citations are not duplicated in the bibliography at the end of the book, which provides additional references to dictionaries and studies of nineteenth-century art, academies, individual countries, and movements.

The format is roughly similar to the *Britannica Encyclopedia of American Art.* Small monochrome illustrations run alongside the text. These are identified by painter, title, and date with further information (medium, size, location, and photo source) supplied in a list arranged alphabetically by painter following the bibliography. Norman's book will be useful in all types of libraries. It provides the most up-to-date dictionary coverage of many painters and gives locations for their *oeuvres* in cities and museums throughout Europe and the United States. [R: Choice, Sept 78, p. 843; LJ, 15 May 78, p. 1051]   Carole Franklin

UNITED STATES

Current Biographies

288.   Cummings, Paul. **Dictionary of Contemporary American Artists**. 4th ed. New York, St. Martin's Press, 1982. 653p. illus. bibliog. index. $50.00. LC 82-7337. ISBN 0-312-20097-8.

First published in 1966, and last appearing in 1977, this work has become a "useful and detailed directory of America's leading painters, sculptors and printmakers." Enlarged over the third edition by more than one hundred pages, the present volume is expanded to 923 individuals, seventy-one new artists, but also deleting nineteen. Although criteria for deletion are not provided, death cannot be among them, as at least 201 individuals in this edition are no longer living. However, those included were so because of their representation in both public and private, as well as museum collections; representation in major American and international exhibitions; their influence upon others as teachers; and the acclaim received from critics, dealers, fellow artists, and others having professional interest in the arts.

Divided into several sections, the biographical entries follow the format of previous editions, and information provided includes where the subject attended school or was educated, along with names of prominent teachers; scholarships and/or prizes won; and the subject's teaching experience. Important one-man retrospective and group exhibitions are included in addition to the subject's address and that of his/her dealer(s). Also included is a bibliography of work by and about the subject and, if available, the location in archives of the artist's personal papers and taped conversations. A new selection of nearly 125 black-and-white reproductions of works by as many artists is scattered throughout the volume. Description of each work and location where each resides are given at the front of the volume, with the exception of the works by Ben Shahn, Georgia O'Keeffe, Louise Nevelson, Rockwell Kent, and Andrew Wyeth. Other sections of the volume include an index of artists and a pronunciation guide, and a key to museums and institutions, and galleries representing the artists included in the book. The majority of the latter (eighty-five) are to be found in New York City, with San Francisco, Los Angeles, and Chicago following with fourteen, thirteen, and nine, respectively. The volume closes with a forty-two-page bibliography divided in two parts: the first, books dealing with the artists and their works, and the second, books of general interest. The volume is logically arranged, and various symbols and keys facilitate its use.

Although the *Who's Who in American Art*, which contains more than ten thousand entries, is much broader in scope (including art educators, critics, dealers, museum directors, etc.), its biographical entries do not include the detailed information found in the present work. Consequently, the *Dictionary* is a required purchase for all specialized art collections and is highly recommended for general collections in all public and academic libraries.   Charles D. Patterson

289. **Who's Who in American Art**. 16th ed. Edited by Jaques Cattell Press. New York, R. R. Bowker, 1984. 1186p. index. $85.00. LC 36-27014. ISBN 0-8352-1878-3; ISSN 0000-0191.

Almost eleven thousand active contributors to the visual arts in the United States, Canada, and Mexico are profiled in this sixteenth edition of *Who's Who in American Art*. Some entrants have accomplished more than others, obviously, but even those not quite at midcareer have already made worthwhile contributions to art in America. In addition to successful painters and sculptors, the book also lists important collectors, critics, historians, curators, and dealers. Several distinguished craftspeople, cartoonists, printmakers, and photographers are likewise included.

More than 70 percent of the listings have been updated and over one thousand new entrants have been added to this edition. The names of individuals listed for the first time were obtained from nominations provided by former entrants, art associations, galleries, and museums, or from citations in professional publications.

Arranged alphabetically by surname, each entry runs approximately two hundred words. Besides the expected birth date, education, and training data, information relative to work in public collections, significant commissions, honors and awards, style and techniques, media, dealers, and mailing address are also supplied. Three appended indexes further enhance this valuable reference tool. The first is a geographic index, arranged according to state and city, which allows a user to locate entrants within a given area. The second is a professional classification index which categorizes formal specialties, such as calligrapher, ceramist, conceptual artist, draftsman, designer, glass blower, goldsmith, and restorer. The third is a necrology section which extends from 1953 to 1983.   G. A. Cevasco

Retrospective Biographies

290. Baigell, Matthew. **Dictionary of American Art**. 1st ed. New York, Harper & Row, 1979. 390p. (Icon Editions). $17.95; $8.95pa. LC 78-24824. ISBN 0-06-433254-3; 0-06-430078-1pa.

This outstanding American art history reference book passes all tests with flying colors and includes about 650 articles on our painters, graphic artists, sculptors, and photographers from colonial to contemporary times. Adding greatly to its reference function are sixty-nine highly authoritative articles on themes and movements of primary concern to those interested in a thorough survey in dictionary form of the total history of our national visual arts. These specific topics include: Art-Unions, Bayou School, Federal Art Projects, Gift Books, Luminism, Panoramas, Primary Structures, Taos Artists, and White Marmorean Flock, to list but a few. The biographic entries, which make up the bulk of the book, give a quantity of material on each artist and make for enjoyable reading at the same time. The articles, while concentrating on factual matters, reveal a love of the material and a dedication to the dissemination of information.

Considering its modest price, the book has solid production values, including a firm, attractive binding for heavy use, medium-size type for reading ease, and a few blank pages at the end for personal notes. This is the first edition of this dictionary, which will be of definite value to amateur and specialist alike. [R: BL, 1 July 80, p. 1626; Choice, Mar 80, p. 47]   William J. Dane

291.   Cederholm, Theresa D., comp. and ed. **Afro-American Artists: A Bio-Bibliographical Directory**. Boston, Boston Public Library, 1973. 348p. $10.00pa. LC 73-84951. ISBN 0-89073-007-5.

Includes information on about two thousand black American artists, covering such areas as fine arts, painting, sculpture, graphics, etc. A typical entry provides data on birth date (but not death date), education, specialization, titles of more important works, exhibitions, and awards, plus citation to additional sources of information. All in all, a useful work that fills an important gap in our literature on black American artists. [R: BL, 15 Nov 73, p. 362; WLB, Nov 73, p. 261]   Bohdan S. Wynar

292.   Collins, J. L., and G. Opitz, eds. **Women Artists in America: Eighteenth Century to the Present**. 3rd ed. Poughkeepsie, N.Y., Apollo, 1981. 2v. $60.00. ISBN 0-938290-00-2.

Earlier editions of this work, edited by Collins in 1973 and 1975, are included in this new edition along with an additional 240 pages of biographies.

While some attention has been paid to past women artists, this book tackles the whole problem, as the title indicates. One wishes that there were an introduction by the author that would tell how the information was collected, and whether and what standards for inclusion were set and applied. For example, Jessie Willcox Smith is included but not Frances Tipton Hunter nor Maude Tousey Fangel, whose work was widely reproduced at the same period. Some indication of the sources used might give answers to such questions, since the author may not have had access to regional exhibition catalogs and the holdings of small museums and organizations. If, as Ida Kohlmeyer says in her introduction, "Mr. Collins was too often frustrated by lack of definitive information," the users of this book will find themselves in the same situation with too little or none at all. The author set himself a terrific task and is to be commended for this start. It is too bad that the result leaves the user not much better off than before, since the researcher will probably have to cover the same ground again, just to be sure. The book is well bound, but the typeface is difficult to read, since the pages are set (by varityper?) in small italic. The few illustrations add little to the whole: "White Stone," by Agnes Martin, looks like nothing at all. To end on a positive note, this book will serve as a preliminary index, and it points up the need for a much better dictionary or directory on which research workers and art librarians can rely.

A related title is *American Women Artists: From Early Indian Times to the Present* edited by Charlotte Streifer Rubinstein (Boston, G. K. Hall, 1982. 500p. $42.95). Arranged by historical periods, this volume offers introductory essays surveying women's contributions in each era, followed by in-depth biocritical portraits of the period's leading women painters and sculptors. The lives and careers of several hundred artists are set against the background of American history and the principal artistic movements of their times. *American Women Artists* contains 225 black-and-white and forty-nine full-color illustrations. Many significant works are reproduced for the first time here. An extensive subject index and a wide-ranging bibliography enhance the book's value as a complete information base.   Julia Sabine and Bohdan S. Wynar

293. Dawdy, Doris Ostrander. **Artists of the American West: A Biographical Dictionary**. Athens, Ohio, Swallow Press/Ohio University Press, 1974-1985. 3v. $8.00/vol. 1; $22.95/vol. 2; $35.00/vol. 3. LC 72-91919. ISBN 0-8040-0851-5 (vol. 1); 0-8040-0352-1 (vol. 2); 0-8040-0851-5 (vol. 3).

This comprehensive dictionary covers some forty-one hundred artists born before 1900. Arranged alphabetically, each artist entry lists dates and places of birth, primary area of residence, location of works, and most important, locations of additional sources (books, periodicals, etc.) where additional information can be found. An index (by volume only, not by page) concludes the third volume.

The reference value of the set lies chiefly in its comprehensiveness, but also in the succinct detail of each entry. Little space is given to biographical details except as they relate to artistic studies, art schools attended, famous masters or tutors, and the like. On the other hand, the citations for each painter to *American Art Annual*, *Artists of the American West*, and other standard sources are exhaustive. These are supplemented by monographic works on artists, newspaper obituaries, exhibit catalogs, and the like. A classified bibliography of source materials relating to all three volumes, and covering some nineteen pages, precedes the index. Another reference value to the set lies in the fact that although the birth dates may have been prior to 1900, in practice many of the artists were at the height of their painting careers during the first half of the present century. One woman, who may have been born in 1858, was still painting at age ninety-eight in 1954. Others, born a little later, were still active into the 1960s. So the volumes become a useful reference source for information about many western painters of the present century, as well as of the past. [R: AL, Sept 74, p. 417; LJ, Aug 74, p. 1926; WLB, Dec 74, p. 314]   Raymund F. Wood and Bohdan S. Wynar

294. **Dictionary of American Artists: 19th & 20th Century**. Edited by Alice Coe McGlauflin. Poughkeepsie, N.Y., Apollo, 1982. 372p. illus. (Reprinted from Vol. XXVI *American Art Annual* for the Year 1929). $49.50. ISBN 0-938290-01-0.

Caveat emptor: This "book" is a reprint of the artist directory section of volume 26 of the *American Art Annual* for the year 1929. Entries include brief biographical information on contemporary artists (that is, contemporary to 1929), the material compiled chiefly from membership lists of leading art societies in the United States. A typical entry provides the following data: name of artist, date and place of birth, studies, memberships, awards and prizes, and a list of exhibitions. No revisions or additions have been made to the original edition.   Lamia Doumato

295. Lester, Charles Edwards. **The Artists of America**. New York, Baker & Scribner, 1846; repr., New York, Kennedy Galleries, Inc./DaCapo Press, 1969. 257p. illus. $32.50. LC 68-8689. ISBN 0-306-71169-9.

When first published, this book was a rather modest popularizing biographical work on eight American artists, beginning with Benjamin West. All are treated amply in later collective and individual biographies, except for a rather mysterious James De Veaux, who does not seem to be listed in current reference works. The *Dictionary of American Biography* says of the prolific Mr. Lester and his works: "Though popular rather than erudite, and often compilations designed to meet the demands of the hour, his books are generally clear and vigorous, showing genuine interest in the spread of knowledge and liberal ideas" (*DAB*, XI:189-90). Today, however, this book will be of little interest to anyone but the historiographer of art, or the social historian, as an example of one type of writing of its time. The original edition had no index and the reprint is still innocent of one. Why it should cost so much is indeed a mystery.

Dennis North

296.   Opitz, Glenn B., ed. **Dictionary of American Sculptors: "18th Century to the Present."** Poughkeepsie, N.Y., Apollo, 1984. 656p. illus. $75.00. ISBN 0-938290-03-7.

The documentation of the work of sculptors in general often has been fragmentary, minimal, and elusive. Therefore, this one-volume source of information on over five thousand American sculptors is a welcome addition to the bibliography of our indigenous three-dimensional art history. The editor starts with eighteenth century sculptors but emphasizes those working in the nineteenth and twentieth centuries with many entries for living and recently deceased artists. Some sculptors were solicited directly and their responses are included along with data submitted by individuals from the long run of the *American Art Annual* which was issued from 1898 to 1933.

It is puzzling that many entries for contemporary sculptors omit data on most events after 1970 or so. This is frequently the case as per citations for Joseph Brown, Gwen Lux, James Rosati, David Von Schlegell, and Richard Lippold, for example. With a 1984 copyright, there is a decade or more of unreported data for very active and creative sculptors. The compiler plans a later volume for additions and corrections where these lacunae may be substantially filled. However, with more than two hundred full-page illustrations on glossy stock, a truly solid sewn binding which is so essential for a reference book, and the evident cooperation of the National Sculpture Society, this needed volume for reference amply celebrates and records the diversity and growing importance of America's sculptors.   William J. Dane

297.   Opitz, Glenn B., ed. **Mantle Fielding's Dictionary of American Painters, Sculptors, & Engravers.** New completely rev., enlarged, and updated ed. Poughkeepsie, N.Y., Apollo, 1983. 1041p. $75.00. ISBN 0-938290-02-9.

This new volume, over twice the size of the original 1926 volume, is the first completely revised, enlarged, and updated edition of *Fielding's Dictionary* in almost sixty years. It includes the records and accomplishments of over ten thousand major and minor professional artists. The facts, given in terse, compact statements, do not, however, include complete lists of the artist's achievements.

Some of the entries are unchanged from the original edition because no additional information was found. Some of the original entries have been expanded to include birthplace and birth date, schooling, collections, awards, date of death, etc. More than six thousand new entries have been added, primarily for artists of the nineteenth and early twentieth centuries as well as for over one thousand living artists; these entries include their exhibitions, commissions, awards, memberships, and studies.

This is an indispensable, comprehensive resource for art dealers, collectors, curators, and students of U.S. painting, sculpture, and graphics.

Kathleen J. Voigt

298.   Samuels, Peggy, and Harold Samuels. **The Illustrated Biographical Encyclopedia of Artists of the American West.** Garden City, N.Y., Doubleday, 1976. 496p. illus. bibliog. $30.00. LC 76-2816. ISBN 0-385-01730-8.

Contains seventeen hundred concise biographical sketches of artists associated with the Western region, providing information on the artists' studies and experience, listings of shows, auction prices, etc. It supplements Cummings's *A Dictionary of Contemporary American Artists* (2nd ed. St. Martin's, 1971. 368p.) since the coverage is much more comprehensive for the Western region. Many artists found here are also included in Bowker's *Who's Who in American Art.* [R: LJ, 15 Nov 76, p. 2360]

Bohdan S. Wynar

299. Schwab, Arnold T., in cooperation with the Art Libraries Society of North America. **A Matter of Life and Death: Vital Biographical Facts about Selected American Artists**. New York, Garland, 1977. 64p. (Garland Reference Library of the Humanities, Vol. 90). $17.00. LC 76-52694. ISBN 0-8240-9883-8.

The author, an English professor, provides the reader with an interesting introduction concerning the detective procedures he used in compiling this valuable biographical dictionary of selected American painters, sculptors, and graphic artists. Listed are over five hundred deceased artists, near-contemporaries. Most of the dates listed have come from obituaries in newspapers and magazines or from reference books. The author has attempted to verify dates through the examination of birth records, or, more frequently, death records or through correspondence with the artists' families or friends.

The alphabetical list includes facts previously unrecorded anywhere else — the exact date and place of birth and death and the age at death. The artist's particular field and the *New York Times* obituary are indicated by code. Detailed notes document the sources for entries where discrepancies in information exist. Useful to art librarians, critics and historians, biographers, museums, and dealers.   Kathleen J. Voigt

300. Soria, Regina. **Dictionary of Nineteenth-Century American Artists in Italy, 1760-1914**. East Brunswick, N.J., Fairleigh Dickinson University Press, 1982. 332p. illus. bibliog. $45.00. LC 74-4986. ISBN 0-8386-1310-1.

The main body of this book is devoted to alphabetically arranged biographical sketches of American artists and literary figures who spent a significant portion of their careers in Italy. Many of the artists are relatively unknown today, while others have established reputations both in America and abroad. In every case, author Regina Soria attempts to identify their Italian connection and the influence which Italy has had on so many American artists and their works.

Each entry includes the artist's name, the place and date of birth and death, and dates of visits to Italy. In addition, the author has included information on the artist's relevant works as well as pertinent bibliographic citations.

The book includes a detailed introduction by the author and a short bibliography. There are a helpful list of abbreviations and a brief bibliography of general references which includes many of the artists listed in this work. Also included are a number of illustrations of the works of many of the better-known artists. And although the works represented are excellent examples, the quality of the reproductions is only fair.

Twenty years in the making, this is a significant and thoroughly useful reference work. It is a good choice for any art history collection. It might benefit from an index for use in locating people, places, and works included in the biographical sketches.

Brian Alley

301. Tatman, Sandra L., and Roger W. Moss. **Biographical Dictionary of Philadelphia Architects: 1700-1930**. Boston, G. K. Hall, 1984. 916p. $99.50. ISBN 0-8161-0437-9.

Nationally renowned as an architectural center since the early eighteenth century, Philadelphia has produced numerous building professionals. This biographical dictionary identifies more than twelve hundred architects who worked primarily — but not exclusively — in the Philadelphia area prior to 1930. Each entry contains a narrative biographical sketch, list of documented works, selected bibliography, and a list of repositories where original resources can be viewed.   Bohdan S. Wynar

AUSTRALIA AND NEW ZEALAND

302.   Germaine, Max. **Artists and Galleries of Australia and New Zealand**. Sydney, Australia, Lansdowne Editions; distr., New York, Mereweather Press, 1979. 646p. illus. (col.). $40.00. ISBN 0-868-32-0196.

Although only larger libraries with specialized art collections or an interest in Australia and New Zealand may be interested in this volume, it is well worth their consideration, for it is an outstanding reference tool of its kind and for its subject. *Artists and Galleries* furnishes, in one alphabetical sequence, a comprehensive body of information about contemporary art in Australia and New Zealand, including over two thousand living artists, private and public galleries, journals, museums, prize competitions, institutions, etc. There is also a short addendum providing the same information for about sixty recently deceased artists. For each artist, information is given about date and place of birth, field of work, studies, exhibitions, location of works, and written material relating to the artist. For other items, a concise but detailed descriptive paragraph is provided.

The typography is outstanding, which makes the information both visually appealing and readily available. The text is supplemented by just over sixty color illustrations, which provide a good balance of the kind of work currently being done. The only flaw in the book is that it does not provide enough addresses; addresses are given only for galleries, museums, and competitions, but not for individual artists and often not for other agencies and institutions. The selection of artists for inclusion was based on a reasonable set of criteria relating to their stature, and the information was gathered from questionnaires. The result is indeed a comprehensive listing that should have permanent value for researchers and scholars.   Norman D. Stevens

CANADA

303.   Harper, J. Russell. **Early Painters and Engravers in Canada**. Toronto, Buffalo, University of Toronto Press, 1971; repr., 1981. 376p. bibliog. $45.00. ISBN 0-8020-1630-8.

A comprehensive non-critical dictionary for librarians, collectors, art historians, and dealers compiled from notes collected during fifteen years of research by J. Russell Harper, who has been associated with a number of important Canadian art collections and at present is an associate professor in the department of art at Sir George Williams University. This title includes over four thousand entries listing all known painters and engravers who were born before 1867 (the year of Confederation) and worked in Canada. If their birth date is unknown, artists are included whose works appeared in public exhibitions or whose names were mentioned in pre-1900 directories. Also included are visitors to Canada whose artistic works included Canadian subjects, and nineteenth-century photographers who colored their works. Entries include: date and place of birth and death, important details of life, a listing of public exhibitions where works have appeared, public and semipublic collections in which the artist is represented, and a key to biographical references. A bibliography concludes the volume with directory references appearing in the abbreviation index. This work was originally published in 1971, and the 1981 edition is an actual reprint. [R: Choice, Sept 71, p. 808; LJ, July 71, p. 2294]   Kathleen J. Voigt

FRANCE

304.   Muehsam, Gerd, ed. **French Painters and Paintings from the Fourteenth Century to Post-Impressionism**. New York, Frederick Ungar, 1970. 646p. illus. (A Library of Art Criticism Series). $40.00; $10.95pa. LC 70-98344. ISBN 0-8044-3210-4; 0-8044-6521-5pa.

In contrast to other publications dealing with sources and documents, Gerd Meuhsam's impressive book is solely concerned with art criticism. A concise, lucid introduction provides background on the history of art academies and the development of art criticism in France. The entries, arranged chronologically by artist, consist of brief biographical resumes followed by examples of art criticism pertaining to a specific work of art and in some cases general criticisms of the artist's total *oeuvre*. Frequently the selections include statements by the artist and his contemporaries as well as selections from twentieth-century critics and art historians. For example, the criticism on Poussin's paintings are from works by Bellori, Félibien, Voltaire, Reynolds, Stendhal, Ingres, Delacroix, Ruskin, Cézanne, Magne, Gide, Friedlaender, and De Tolnay. Regrettably, illustrations are not always included. The entries covering the work of anonymous painters, such as the Master of Aix and the Master of Moulins, are especially successful in illustrating the variety of approaches employed by art historians in establishing or attempting to establish attributions. The task of selecting the materials must have been monumental. Although each specialist consulting this valuable reference book will not always agree with all the selections made, there is no doubt that Gerd Meuhsam has a scholarly knowledge of the field and its bibliography. The only serious omissions in our opinion are the small number of negative criticisms, incomplete textual and bibliographic information on Charles Sterling's attribution to Quarton of the School of Avignon *Pièta*, and the omission of K. E. Maison's denial of a Daumier attribution for the final painting of *L'Emeute*. This sizable book will be consulted by scholars and students in all fields of the humanities. The impressive selected bibliography is an excellent check list for libraries. [R: LJ, July 70, p. 2455]

Jacqueline Sisson

GERMANY, AUSTRIA, AND SWITZERLAND

305.   Strute, Karl, and Theodor Doelken, eds. **Who's Who in the Arts and Literature: A Biographical Who's Who by the International Red Series Containing Some 20,000 Prominent Artists and Authors from the Federal Republic of Germany, Austria and Switzerland**. 3rd ed. Zurich, Who's Who AG; distr., New York, Unipub, 1983. 3v. in 4. (The International Red Series). $160.00/set. ISBN 3-921220-50-5; ISSN 0722-916-X.

Although limited in geographic scope, this set provides a wealth of directory-type information regarding the European art and literature communities. With two volumes devoted to fine arts, one to literature, and one to applied arts and music, the editors have assembled a potentially useful reference tool for both comprehensive and specialized library collections.

In addition to basic biographical information such as name, address, education, genealogy, work experience, awards, and publications, photographs of selected individuals are included. In the case of fine arts, selected works are reproduced. A useful name index, arranged by specialty, appears at the end of each volume. This is followed by a variety of appendixes that profile organizations, publications, societies, museums, galleries, festivals, awards, costumers, schools, producers, instrument makers, dealers, and more.

In such a comprehensive work, it seems unusual that the editors fail to identify either the selection criteria or the selection panel. Still, the work functions as a useful guide to current aspects of the arts and literature in Europe and serves as a handy directory of practicing and recently retired professionals.   Edmund F. SantaVicca

GREAT BRITAIN

306.   Colvin, Howard Montagu. **A Biographical Dictionary of British Architects, 1600-1840**. rev. and enlarged ed. New York, Facts on File, 1980. 1080p. index. $75.00. ISBN 0-87196-442-2.

Titled *A Biographical Dictionary of English Architects, 1660-1840* in its first edition (1954), this superior work contains biographical sketches of significant architects who practiced in England, Scotland, and Wales during the seventeenth, eighteenth, and early nineteenth centuries (from Inigo Jones, 1573-1652, to Sir Charles Barry, 1795-1860). This revision expands coverage to include Scotland and Wales and an additional sixty years. Most Victorian architecture is excluded. The lengthy and informative introduction of the first edition has been reprinted in this enlarged edition.

Every building (and some projects that were never executed) considered by the author to be significant and for which the architect can be identified is listed, along with its date of erection and demolition, its style, and references to published descriptions. Each architect's work is given in chronological order, with an evaluation of his contributions to British architectural history. All British architectural publications appearing between 1600 and 1840 are listed by author. Thorough building and name indexes facilitate access to the dictionary's contents. [R: BL, 15 Nov 81, p. 460; Choice, Apr 81, pp. 1069-70]   Bohdan S. Wynar

307.   Foskett, Daphne. **A Dictionary of British Miniature Painters**. New York, Praeger, 1972. 2v. illus. (part col.). o.p. LC 72-112634.

A solid and enduring piece of scholarship, this work is also a luxurious production in terms of illustration. To Basil Long's *British Miniaturists* (1929), Miss Foskett has added over two thousand miniaturists and has extended the period covered by Long to 1910. Volume one lists almost forty-five hundred names or initials of miniaturists who were native to or worked in Great Britain and Ireland. Biographical and stylistic information in the entries is sufficient and succinct. One hundred fine color illustrations are interspersed in the six hundred pages of the first volume, which also contains a brief discussion of miniature materials and techniques as well as a selective but discriminating bibliography. Volume two is devoted to monochrome illustrations — 967 of them. The illustration list for volume two has thoughtfully been included in both volumes. For libraries with the patronage of collectors, dealers, and scholars, this will be a mandatory acquisition. For other large reference departments it should be regarded as a most desirable luxury. [R: LJ, 15 June 72, p. 2172]   Julia M. Ehresmann

308.   Hammelmann, Hanns, and T. S. R. Boase. **Book Illustrators in Eighteenth Century England**. New Haven, Conn., Yale University Press, 1975. 120p. illus. index. o.p. LC 75-2770. ISBN 0-300-01895-9.

At the time of his death in 1969, the distinguished German scholar Hanns Hammelmann was engaged in preparing a book on the subject of eighteenth-century book illustration for the Paul Mellon Foundation, an area of research in which he had earned a considerable reputation as an authority since 1952, when he first wrote on the subject for *The Book Collector*. From the notes and other materials left by Hammelmann, the present annotated and alphabetically arranged listing of illustrators was brought together by T. S. E. Boase, who was an associate of Hammelmann and an authority in the field in his own right.

Following the customary introductory material, the book begins with an informative and well-documented survey of eighteenth-century English book illustration that emphasizes the French influence and the roles of such significant and well-known figures as M. Gravelot, William Hogarth, and Francis Hayman. There is also a brief and interesting section on the copyright law of eighteenth-century England respecting the rights of book illustrators.

The main body of the work is, of course, the alphabetical listing of artists with appropriate annotations. This is followed by an "Index of Authors and Titles" and a general index. The work concludes with a section of selected illustrations.

"Technical works where plates of architecture, archaeology, anatomy, or botany were integral to the scheme of the book" were excluded from the survey, though some of their allegorical frontispieces have been included. What concerned Hammelmann was "the invention of the artist, not his skill as a copyist."

The volume, which is attractively printed by the Yale University Press for the Paul Mellon Centre for Studies in British Art (London) Ltd., is an important contribution to the history of books and printing. It will also be useful to students of English literature and scholarship. [R: LJ, 15 Mar 76, p. 801]   Jesse H. Shera

309.   Parry-Crooke, Charlotte, ed. **Contemporary British Artists**. New York, St. Martin's Press, 1979. (unpaged). illus. $30.00. LC 79-87712. ISBN 0-312-16655-9.

The beauty of this handsome volume lies in its opening section of fine black-and-white photographic portraits (executed by Saranjeet Walia) of each of the 201 artists who, in the opinion of the editor, comprise the contemporary British art world. Norbert C. Lynton, professor of art history at the University of Sussex and advisor to the present work, clearly emphasizes their importance in his introductory remarks and also identifies London as "one of the leading and most productive art worlds of our time." These photographs, one might guess, are presented in order of prominence of the subject, an arrangement not satisfactory from the practical standpoint. Following the photographs is a unique section reproducing facsimiles of signatures of 174 of the artists, useful for identification.

The second major section (reference) of the volume consists of an alphabetical array of biographical information for each subject which includes, in chronological order, important events in the professional life of the person, a black-and-white representative example of work (title, medium, size provided), an artistic/philosophical statement written either by the subject or someone else, and, finally, the dealer for the artist. Although not specifically identified, the page reference to the appropriate photograph is given following the name of the person. A publisher's note states that every effort was made to ensure that information given in this reference section of the book is accurate, but we are not told just how this was accomplished. The volume closes with a directory of selected gallery addresses, emphasizing London and regional galleries primarily used by the artists but including others throughout the world which have shown a particular artist's work.

Although a more utilitarian arrangement would place the biographical reference section before the photographs, the volume is recommended for academic, research, and specialized art collections, particularly those where a geographical emphasis is desired. As such, it includes biographical information and pictures for 109 artists not included in *Contemporary Artists* (St. Martin's Press). [R: JAL, Jan 80, p. 368]

Charles D. Patterson

310.   **Who's Who in Art**. 21st ed. Havant, England, Art Trade Press; distr., Detroit, Gale, 1984. 557p. illus. $90.00. ISBN 0-900083-10-7.

Although the overall format (i.e., sections included) remains unchanged from earlier editions, the present edition opens with "An Appeal to Artists and Agents" not found in the 1982 edition. Basically, this is a call for any artist to submit biographical information for consideration "with no obligation whatsoever to purchase a copy of the book." "Publisher's Notes" remains unchanged and states that the work "is principally concerned with British artists, and so far as overseas artists are concerned we include only a representative selection." Omitted are the names Chagall, Nevelson, O'Keeffe, A. Breker, A. Wyeth, and de Kooning, all of whom, no doubt, are readily available in other works of similar type. However, the overseas representative selection does include Jean Picart LeDoux of France, and Stephen Pace, Azeglio Pancani, Jr., and Helen Phillips, all of the United States. All entries under "Aims and Activities of Academies, Groups, Societies, etc." are unchanged with the exception that the City of London Art Exhibition, Industrial Printers' Group, and the Royal Drawing Society have been omitted. Also, the Royal Ulster Academy of Painting, Sculpture and Architecture has now become the Royal Ulster Academy of Arts. As in previous editions, the present volume also contains appendixes devoted to monograms and signatures, obituaries, and an explanation of abbreviations used throughout the book. Perhaps all of the latter are familiar to the British reader, but F.R.B.S., A.S.T.C., A.R.B.S., and A.S.W.A., used in the entry for Barbara Tribe (one of the longest accounts) are omitted from the list of abbreviations and will thus be unexplained to many who will consult the volume.

This standard art reference (more than doubled in price since the 1980 edition) has endured for more than half a century, and despite the lack of any criteria for selection of those included, it remains, for the larger academic, research, and public library, and for the specialized fine arts collection, the single most important source for biographical information about thousands of British artists, and about the art world in the United Kingdom.

Charles D. Patterson

JAPAN

311. **Biographical Dictionary of Japanese Art**. 1st ed. Yutaka Tazawa, supervising ed. New York, Kodansha International; distr., New York, Harper & Row, 1981. 825p. bibliog. index. (Dictionary of Japan, Vol. 3). $42.00. LC 81-82717. ISBN 0-87011-488-3.

The third volume of a three-volume biographical dictionary of Japan (the first covers history, the second, literature), *Biographical Dictionary of Japanese Art* is a welcome addition to the fine arts reference shelf, which until recently was poor in English-language reference works on Japan. This work stands comfortably with Laurance P. Roberts's *Dictionary of Japanese Artists: Painting, Sculpture, Ceramics, Prints, Lacquer* (New York, Weatherhill, 1976). The new dictionary, produced under the editorship of Yutaka Tazawa, is like Roberts's book in its concentration on figurative artists. But in addition, Tazawa includes architects and artists working in photography, garden design, and metalwork.

The biographical entries are grouped into media, with a brief introductory essay introducing each section. A good index makes this arrangement only slightly inconvenient for quick reference. Within the sections, the artists are arranged alphabetically by transliterated names. The entries are basically factual, but anecdotal material—so familiar in older works on Oriental art—is in evidence and users will have to be more critical than they are accustomed to being when dealing with dictionaries of Western artists. The appendixes are particularly worthwhile. There are useful charts and tables of artistic schools and styles, a brief glossary of Japanese terms, maps, and an extensive bibliography that includes general works and monographic literature. [R: LJ, 15 Mar 82, p. 628]   Donald L. Ehresmann

312. Blakemore, Frances. **Who's Who in Modern Japanese Prints**. New York, Weatherhill, 1975. 263p. illus. index. $13.95. LC 74-28174. ISBN 0-8348-0101-9.

A long-time American resident of Japan, Frances Blakemore presents here a cross-section of 105 Japanese artists, most of whom began their careers in the last decade; they were selected by nominations from artist colleagues and critics.

The author, a collector and director of Franell Gallery, one of Tokyo's leading dealers in modern art, presents a simple reference guide. She neither reports nor acts as a critic; instead, she expresses her views, talking more about the art than the artist. Her interpretations may not be what the artists themselves felt or intended the viewer to see, but the over 270 black-and-white illustrations may help the reader to become his or her own critic.

She includes a brief historical survey of the Japanese print. Information provided for each artist includes: age, principal media, output, and development. A comprehensive appendix index of over four hundred artists, based on a questionnaire, completes the volume. [R: Choice, Nov 75, p. 1152]   Kathleen J. Voigt

313. Roberts, Laurance P. **A Dictionary of Japanese Artists: Painting, Sculpture, Ceramics, Prints, Lacquer**. New York, Weatherhill, 1976. 299p. bibliog. index. $27.50. LC 76-885. ISBN 0-8348-0113-2.

A comprehensive dictionary with about three thousand concise entries for Japanese artists who were born before 1900 or who died before 1972, including painters, sculptors, potters, printmakers, and lacquerers. The dictionary is divided into three sections: the main body alphabetically lists each artist under the name by which he is most commonly known, the index of alternate names gives cross-references to main entries, and the character index lists all names in "kanji."

Each entry gives the artist's various art names, brief biographical information, lists of public collections in which the artist's work can be seen, and a bibliography of books and other publications in which his works are illustrated and/or discussed.

Appendixes include a list of public collections in Japan, the United States, Canada, and Europe in which the work of the artists can be seen; art organizations and institutions mentioned in the dictionary; art periods of Japan, Korea, and China; and Japanese provinces and prefectures. With a glossary of Japanese art terms and a comprehensive bibliography of works on Japanese art in English, French, German, and Japanese, this title, written by a specialist in Oriental art, is an authoritative and informative volume for both the layman and the scholar. [R: BL, 1 Apr 77, p. 1194; Choice, Mar 77, p. 45]   Kathleen J. Voigt

9 Geography

Introduction

This chapter contains five biographical sources in the areas of "General Works," "Cartography," and "Conservation and Ecology." For additional sources, the reader will have to consult other chapters, e.g., part 1, "Universal and National Biographies," and in part 2, the chapters on "Economics and Business," "Ethnic Studies," and "History," which contain some biographies of outstanding geographers. Even subject dictionaries and encyclopedias in this area contain some information on outstanding geographers, e.g., *The Marshall Cavendish Illustrated Encyclopedia: World and Its People* (27v. Marshall Cavendish, 1981) or *Lands and People* (6v. Grolier, 1985). Even *Webster's New Geographical Dictionary* (G. & C. Merriam, 1984. 1376p.), with its listing of fifty thousand entries, serves primarily as a gazetteer similar in its execution to *Columbia Lippincott Gazetteer of the World* (Columbia University Press, 1962. 2148p.) or *Chambers' World Gazetteer and Geographical Dictionary* (Chambers, 1954. 792p.). Biographical data are also to be found in some older subject dictionaries, e.g., *Longmans Dictionary of Geography* (Longmans, 1966. 492p.) that includes entries for individual geographers, or German *Westermann Lexikon der Geographie* (5v. G. Westermann, 1968-1972) that is useful primarily for place names but also includes numerous personal names and obviously, geographical terminology.

For current information one can consult indexes and abstracting services, e.g., *Geo Abstracts* (Geo Abstracts, 1966-) a British publication, published in several parts, or *Social Sciences Citation Index* (Institute for Scientific Information, 1973-). There are several bibliographical guides to the literature of geography. Most of them contain extensive listings about existing bibliographies and incorporate information relating to abstracting and indexing services. James Brewer's *The Literature of Geography: A Guide to Its Organisation and Use* (2nd ed. Linnet Books, 1978. 264p.) is a British publication with good coverage of bibliographical sources published before 1978. A more comprehensive guide, again British, is C. Lock's *Geography and Cartography: A Reference Handbook* (3rd ed. Linnet Books, 1976. 762p.).

GENERAL WORKS

314. Freeman, T. W., ed., **Geographers: Biobibliographical Studies.** London, Mansell; distr., New York, H. W. Wilson, 1977- . Price varies. (Vol. 7. 1983. $34.00pa.). ISSN 0308-6992.

As part of a wider program of studying the history of geography, the Commission on the History of Geographical Thought of the International Geographical Union sponsored the writing of a series of biographical sketches of geographers who have played seminal roles in the development of this field. Each biobibliography includes a brief summary of the subject's education, life, and work; scientific ideas and geographical thought; influence and spread of the person's ideas; sources and bibliography; and a chronological table of the life, career, activities, field work, and publications of the individual, as well as contemporary events. In an average of 6½ pages, the life, contributions, and influence of each person are succinctly summarized.

Volume 1 (published in 1977) contains eighteen biographies. In this initial volume, geographers of the United States (4), United Kingdom (5), and France (4) are well represented, and individuals from Poland, Romania, the Soviet Union, Japan, and Malaya are also included. The authors of the sketches typically come from the same countries as the biographees and are intimately acquainted with their contributions and impact. The biobibliographies are convenient and authoritative summaries in accessible form, more objective and evaluative than some memorials written immediately after the death of an eminent figure and more concise than the full biographies that appear in book form.

The latest volume published is volume 7. It continues the high quality and international coverage of earlier volumes. The twenty-five biobibliographies in this volume are devoted mainly to Europeans, especially geographers of Germany, France, Russia (some of whom continued into the Soviet period), Britain, and Austria, but include three who worked in the United States, two in Australia, and one in Mexico. Most lived in the second half of the nineteenth century and the first half of the twentieth. Most were trained in fields other than geography but engaged in scientific and scholarly work that became increasingly geographic. The three from the United States were active on the margins and frontiers of geography: Robert DeCourcy Ward (1867-1931) in climatology, Clark Wissler (1870-1947) in anthropology, and Jacques M. May (1896-1975) in medical geography. Authors of the biographies are generally from the same country, often the same institution, as the biographees and thus frequently have access to archival material and other special sources. One biographee, Pyotr A. Kropotkin (1842-1921), has two biographies, one by a Soviet historian of science with access to archives in the Soviet Union, the other by a Western scholar with access to archives of the Royal Geographical Society in Britain. Of particular value is the sensitive and balanced appraisal of Walter Christaller (1893-1969), first appreciated more abroad than in his native Germany. A valuable source.   Chauncy D. Harris

315. **Who's Who of Indian Geographers.** New Delhi, Concept Publishing Co.; distr., Atlantic Heights, N.J., Humanities Press, 1982. 139p. $15.25. ISBN 0-391-02808-1.

Who's Who of Indian Geographers serves as a companion volume to the International Geography Series *Perspectives in Agricultural Geography* (five volumes published) and *Perspectives in Urban Geography* (fifty-plus volumes published). This biographical source was provided in cooperation with the Indian National Association of Geographers and is based on a questionnaire administered by the publisher. Over one thousand brief biographical sketches of uneven quality are included.

Bohdan S. Wynar

CARTOGRAPHY

316.   Tooley, Ronald Vere, comp. **Tooley's Dictionary of Mapmakers**. New York, Alan R. Liss; Amsterdam, Meridian Publishing, 1979. 696p. illus. maps. bibliog. $120.00; $40.00pa. LC 79-1936. ISBN 0-8451-1701-7; 0-8451-1702-5pa.

What a beautifully produced, substantial work! It is easy to believe that this work is a reflection of the author's decades of work in the field of cartography. The aim of the publication is to give, in the most compact form, information on persons associated with the production of maps from the earliest times to 1900, and the aim is true. The reader might make minor quibbles with the author concerning the information in some of the cites, but, in the main, this classic reference work is excellent. Approximately one-half of the information first appeared in *Map Collector's Circle* (now discontinued), but even that has been revised and enlarged, thus making this a good purchase even for those libraries that have copies of the *Circle*. There are illustrations to break up the alphabetical entries; sad to say, some of the maps are poorly reproduced and blurry. A good extra touch is the inclusion of signatures of major mapmakers. The only aid this volume lacks is a geographic index, and it is so massive as is, that it seems picky to insist on that point. For all academic libraries that support degrees in geography, this will be a basic reference work in cartography.

Mary Larsgaard

CONSERVATION AND ECOLOGY

317.   Clepper, Henry, ed. **Leaders of American Conservation**. New York, Ronald Press, 1971. 353p. o.p. (Available from Books on Demand, $69.40). LC 75-155206. ISBN 0-8357-9921-2.

It is difficult to assess adequately the real value of this compendium of biographical sketches, alphabetically arranged by name. In one sense, the selection of these three-plus individuals is an attempt to recognize their distinctive contributions to the preservation or wise use of our natural resources; this in itself does not produce a useful reference tool. On the other hand, our contemporary concern for conservation of our national environment has created a need for special information resources within the library collection. From that standpoint, this tool can offer data which are not necessarily available from other biographical sources.

The individuals who are included in this physically attractive volume were chosen by the member organizations of the Natural Resources Council of America. All biographees were considered to have performed "meritorious" activities above and beyond long service within an office relating to conservation. They are, then, significant personages in this field—some living and still active, most dead or in retirement. To this extent, the volume becomes a history of conservation activities in the last century. The perusal of names is fascinating in that the selection achieves some unexpected combinations. In one listing are Ansel Adams, Stephen Forbes, Rachel Carson, John D. Rockefeller, Theodore Roosevelt, Stewart Udall, and Mabel Wright, to name only a few.

The entries average a page in length, are carefully edited, and, in general, are prepared by contributors who knew the "leaders" personally and are themselves active in the field. The editor, Clepper, prepared seventy-two of the entries, thereby providing a significant part of the text. Each entry is signed and usually from one to five sources are cited. Unfortunately, most of the sources are basic biographical dictionaries such as *American Men of Science* or a Who's Who publication. Still, the biographies, presented here in narrative form, add interpretative dimensions to the material. One suspects that this tool will not be used as a reference, but as a browsing source for students interested in the field; only rarely will a question be raised that identifies American conservation leaders specifically. Even then, this compilation admittedly covers only an honored few out of the many individuals who, in one way or another, have made contributions to the conservation movement. [R: Choice, Dec 71, p. 1317; LJ, 15 Dec 71, p. 4082]

Laurel Grotzinger

318.   Cox, Donald W. **Pioneers of Ecology**. Maplewood, N.J., Hammond, 1971. 93p. illus. bibliog. index. o.p. LC 77-158132. ISBN 0-8431-3832-4.

The biographical approach of this book should prove especially valuable in view of the current interest in ecology. Studying the lives of these important men and women, who were dedicated pioneers even in the face of public scorn, teaches us again the sad lesson that a prophet is often without honor in his own country. The fifteen biographees are all American, in the sense of having done most of their work here, and they are from related walks of life—naturalists, biologists, conservationists, and ornithologists. Some of the better-known visionaries are Rachel Carson, George Washington Carver, Theodore Roosevelt, Henry Thoreau, Joseph Krutch, Alexander Wilson, and John James Audubon. The work is arranged chronologically, and emphasis on the inter-relatedness of the biographees allows the reader to see how each one helped in the fight to preserve not just the United States but the world. Reading the stories of these lives provides a different route to an understanding of global ecosystems. The work should appeal to all ages from junior high up.

The graphic presentations are particularly helpful, explaining vividly the difficulties that face the world; in many instances they depict the advances that have been made over the past century in America. The portrait illustrations by Ted Lewin are clear, apt, realistic, and rugged. Also included are a helpful list of environmental organizations and periodicals, a selected bibliography, and an adequate index. Because of the lack of saddle-stitch binding, it is impossible to read the inner columns of this book unless both hands are used to hold it open.   Jovian P. Lang

10 Health Sciences

Introduction

The material in this chapter is arranged under four headings: "Medicine," "Pharmacology," "Psychiatry," and "Public Health and Health Care." Fifteen entries are included in this chapter, with many more related titles mentioned in annotations. There are a number of excellent and comprehensive sources in this area: *Dictionary of American Medical Biography*, probably one of the best in terms of its scholarly execution (see entry 323), and a number of standard biographical directories prepared by Jaques Cattell Press, e.g., *Biographical Directory of the American Academy of Pediatrics* (see entry 319), *Biographical Directory of the American College of Physicians* (see entry 320), and *Marquis Who's Who Directory of Medical Specialists* (see entry 324). There are also a number of older biographical sources. *Dictionary of American Medical Biography*, edited by H. A. Kelly and W. L. Burrage (Appleton, 1928; repr., Milford House, 1971. 1364p.) was first published in 1912 as *Cyclopedia of American Medical Biography*. It covers 2,049 American physicians from colonial times to 1927. Somewhat less scholarly is *American Men of Medicine* (3rd ed. Institute for Research in Biography, 1961. 768p.) with the first edition published in 1945, covering some ten thousand physicians from the United States, Canada, and parts of Latin America. The most scholarly medical biography was prepared by the Royal College of Physicians of London and published under different titles, e.g., *The Roll of the Royal College of Physicians of London* (3v. London, The College, 1878) and subsequent editions published in 1955 and 1968, titled *Lives of the Fellows of the Royal College of Physicians of London*.

Most medical dictionaries, e.g., *Black's Medical Dictionary* (33rd ed. Barnes & Noble, 1981. 982p.), *Butterworths Medical Dictionary* (Butterworths Publishers, 1978. 1942p.), or *Dorland's Illustrated Medical Dictionary* (26th ed. Saunders, 1981. 1485p.) do not include biographical information. Brief biographies (thirty lines on the average) of famous physicians are found in *The Penguin Medical Encyclopedia*, edited by P. Wingate (Penguin, 1972. 465p.), or in more specialized dictionaries, e.g.,

B. Walker's *Encyclopedia of Metaphysical Medicine* (Routledge & Kegan Paul, 1978. 323p.) or the *American Psychiatric Association's Psychiatric Glossary* (American Psychiatric Press, 1984. 142p.). There are a number of indexing and abstracting services in the field of medicine, notably *Index Medicus* (National Library of Medicine, 1960-) and its previous cumulations that are now based on MEDLARS (Medical Literature Analysis and Retrieval System). Among several bibliographic guides in this area, still the best is Blake and Roos's *Medical Reference Works, 1679-1966: A Selected Bibliography* (Medical Library Association, 1967. 343p.) with its supplements published in 1970, 1973 and 1975, and *Handbook of Medical Library Practice* by G. L. Annan and J. W. Felter (Medical Library Association, 1970. 411p.). More recent titles are L. T. Morton's *How to Use a Medical Library* (6th ed. Heinemann Medical Books, 1979. 118p.) that is good for describing existing indexing and abstracting services, and F. Roper and J. A. Boorkman's *Introduction to Reference Sources in Health Sciences* (Medical Library Association, 1980. 252p.)

MEDICINE

319.   **Biographical Directory of the American Academy of Pediatrics, 1980.** Compiled by Jaques Cattell Press. New York, R. R. Bowker, 1980. 940p. index. $95.00. LC 80-65349. ISBN 0-8352-1282-3.

This typical Bowker medical biographical directory lists over eighteen thousand pediatric specialists. The biographies are arranged geographically, first by state then by city or town. Also represented are the Canal Zone, Puerto Rico, the Virgin Islands, and a variety of other countries. The profiles list name, membership status, year of election to the academy, pediatric specialty, birthplace and date, date of marriage, number of children, education, past professional experience, professional and academic activities, honors and awards, and mailing address and telephone. A few entries on each page contain only a mailing address.

There are several very specific medical biographical directories on the market today, e.g., *Biographical Directory of the American Podiatry Association, 1980* (R. R. Bowker, 1980. 268p. $49.95), but their prices tend to run high. This book is no exception. Except for large medical collections with unlimited budgets, this type of volume is becoming too costly for the small library. These smaller collections will be better served by a more general directory such as *Directory of Medical Specialists*, by Marquis Who's Who, Inc., or *American Medical Directory*, by the American Medical Association. [R: BL, 1 July 81, p. 1410]   Charla Leibenguth Banner

320.   **Biographical Directory of the American College of Physicians, 1979.** Compiled for the College by Jaques Cattell Press. New York, R. R. Bowker, 1979. 1905p. index. $95.00. LC 79-90566. ISBN 0-8352-1145-2.

The *Biographical Directory* provides a complete biographical summary of all members of the American College of Physicians. Each biographical entry contains information on the education, training, past and present professional and academic positions, honors and awards, and number of publications of each member, as well as current mailing address and phone number. Up to three subspecialties are listed for each member; these are printed in capital letters, which greatly facilitates the search for specific specialties. The entries are arranged geographically by state, and then by city or town; members resident in Canada and other countries are also included. A complete alphabetical index of all biographical entries completes the text.

In addition to the biographical entries, the *Directory* provides a description of the American College of Physicians' membership system, its educational programs, its fellowship and scholarship opportunities, and the awards that the College administers. Perhaps most interesting is the material on the College's educational activities, which include postgraduate courses overseas, the Medical Knowledge Self-Assessment Program V continuing education series, and multi-media self-learning units. The educational section directs interested persons to the most recent bibliographical collections dealing with internal medicine. This reference book should be a great help not only to physicians but also to consumers interested in finding local medical expertise in a certain field. [R: Choice, Dec 80, p. 507; LJ, 1 Mar 80, p. 600]

Beatrice J. Kalisch

321. Holloway, Lisabeth M. **Medical Obituaries: American Physicians' Biographical Notices in Selected Medical Journals before 1907**. New York, Garland, 1981. 513p. (Garland Reference Library of Social Science, Vol. 104). $110.00. LC 81-7084. ISBN 0-8240-9368-2.

One of the most difficult and frustrating questions posed to medical librarians is a patron's request for information about American physicians who lived prior to 1906, when the American Medical Association started publishing its directory of physicians. Fortunately, Lisabeth Holloway's valuable new reference work will help fill part of this information gap.

This useful reference tool provides data on the lives and medical careers of 17,350 American physicians who practiced medicine in the era from the colonial period up to 1906. Each citation contains the following material, when available, on individual physicians: dates of birth and death, places of medical practice, military affiliation and service in wars, medical education and degrees, and citations telling where more biographical data can be found in journals, directories, and biographical compendia. Special attention is given to physicians who served during the Civil War and those who died trying to help the victims of the 1878 yellow-fever epidemic in Tennessee and surrounding states. The majority of the physicians covered in this book were the average community doctors of seventeenth-, eighteenth-, and nineteenth-century America, rather than the more recognizable physicians and medical scientists who are found in other biographical reference texts. This fact makes Holloway's compilation particularly valuable to scholars of local history and to genealogists.

Although the author states that this book is only the first step in covering the lives and careers of the typical physicians in pre-1906 America, this reviewer highly recommends the guide for all health sciences, academic, and large public libraries.

Jonathon Erlen

322. **International Medical Who's Who: A Biographical Guide in the Biomedical Sciences**. 2nd ed. Harlow, England, Longman; distr., Detroit, Gale, 1985. 2v. index. (Longman Reference on Research). $310.00/set. ISBN 0-582-90112-X.

This second edition of a work first published in 1980 is a welcome update to a well-used reference title. This edition contains biographical profiles of about twelve thousand senior biochemists and biomedical scientists in the areas of anatomy and physiology, biochemistry, biophysics, dental sciences, immunology and transplantation, clinical medicine, molecular biology, neoplasia, pharmacology and therapeutics, psychiatry, clinical psychology, and surgery and anesthesia. Individuals chosen for inclusion include officers in medical and scientific societies, directors and section leaders in industry and official laboratories, heads of relevant academic departments, and editorial board members of relevant journals. Individuals from approximately one hundred countries are included.

This reference work is divided into two sections. Part 1 lists individual profiles in alphabetical order. Part 2, a new feature not included in the first edition, presents a listing of experts in particular subject areas in each of the major countries of the world. Each biographical entry includes, where available, the following information: full name; year of birth; higher education and degrees obtained with name of granting institution and subject studied; present job, employer, and year appointed; previous professional experience; directorships held; appointments to national committees; membership of societies, year of appointment, and highest position held with years of service; major publications, including titles of books written or edited, and journals on which the individual has served in an editorial capacity; main professional and research interests; telephone number; and full postal address.

Spot checking for individuals, particularly from the United States, who might reasonably be expected to be listed, revealed some omissions. Biographical information concerning medical professionals, however, is one of the most frequently sought types of information in health sciences libraries. For that reason, this international reference book will be a welcome addition to most health sciences collections and larger general reference collections.   Sherrilynne Fuller

323. Kaufman, Martin, Stuart Galishoff, and Todd L. Savitt, eds. **Dictionary of American Medical Biography**. Westport, Conn., Greenwood Press, 1984. 2v. index. $95.00/set. LC 82-21110. ISBN 0-313-21378-X.

Some of the most frequently requested information regarding the history of medicine is the request for biographical material about an individual and his/her role in the development of health care. These two volumes represent the first large-scale reference tool to attempt to fill this need since Kelly and Burrage's *Dictionary of American Medical Biography* (1928).

Entries in this major historical resource were written by a diverse group of historians and librarians who share an interest and expertise in American medical history. Besides covering the traditional important physicians acknowledged as the leaders in American medicine, these volumes provide valuable material about prominent figures in nursing, public health, irregular medical sects, and health-care fads and quackery. Special attention is placed on black and female healers. The scope of coverage extends from the seventeenth century to individuals who died prior to 1977. Each biographical sketch presents, when available, the birth and death dates, the place of birth, marital information, key facts on career activities, main contributions, and a list of the most influential publications, both by and about the individual. Six appendixes and an index of personal and institutional names as well as journal titles, facilitate the use of this biographical guide. The only obvious weakness in this outstanding survey of health-care leaders is the inaccuracies in the very brief biographical descriptions of the contributors to these volumes. Despite this minor problem, this reference work is a long-awaited, much-needed addition to the study of American medical history. [R: LJ, 15 Mar 84, p. 576]   Jonathon Erlen

324. **Marquis Who's Who Directory of Medical Specialists, 1985-1986.** 22nd ed. Chicago, Marquis Who's Who, 1985. 3v. $235.00/set. LC 40-9671. ISBN 0-8379-0522-2.

This work includes some 305,000 specialists certified by the twenty-three boards of the American Board of Medical Specialists. Biographical information includes the following: name, education, career history, memberships, date and place of birth, military record, teaching positions, type of practice, and office address and telephone. Physicians can be located in the *Directory* by geographic location and specialty. All professional sketches are grouped alphabetically within each specialty, city, state, and foreign country. In addition, the purpose, function, and requirements of each specialty board are outlined in the introduction to each of the twenty-three specialties.

Bohdan S. Wynar

325. **Marquis Who's Who in Cancer: Professionals and Facilities.** Chicago, Marquis Who's Who, 1985. 802p. index. $150.00. ISBN 0-8379-6501-2.

One of several new interdisciplinary directories being compiled by Marquis Who's Who, this volume offers a great deal of information about cancer of interest to researchers and the public. There are professional profiles (physicians, scientists, and associated professionals) and profiles of cancer centers, arranged geographically (by state or province and city for United States and Canadian entries, by country and city for foreign entries). A series of indexes, also arranged geographically, lists individuals by treatment modality, by primary clinical emphasis, by cancer type, and by research emphasis. Also included are alphabetical indexes of individuals and centers.

Physicians who are cancer specialists may be listed as board-certified in internal medicine (often hematology), surgery, pediatrics, radiology, etc., while scientists may be listed in standard biographical directories as biochemists, endocrinologists, immunologists, etc. The arrangement of fields of investigation in this volume cuts across many of these dividing lines and offers important new access routes. Names included in the directory were drawn from major professional societies. Information was supplied by the biographee or center, and verified by staff. Unfortunately, for whatever reason, not every physician or cancer center contacted chose to participate. The weakest of the listings is that of "associated professionals" which lists mostly individuals with social service or nursing background, e.g., in one large city with several major cancer centers, only the directors of their social service departments are listed. Many of the best-known cancer centers did not choose to provide detailed information as to services and types of cancer treatment offered. When this information is not available, however, the mere listing may be helpful.

In spite of these drawbacks, *Who's Who in Cancer* provides a wealth of data and responds to a real need to find professional biographical information broken down by cancer specialty or type of treatment. It is hoped that in future editions, the difficulties mentioned above will be overcome. Suzanne K. Gray

326. **Marquis Who's Who in Rehabilitation: Professionals and Facilities.** Chicago, Marquis Who's Who, 1985. 429p. $150.00. ISBN 0-8379-6601-9.

This first edition covers some four thousand professionals as well as research and treatment facilities in the rehabilitation field. The following information is provided for professionals listed: name, professional certification, clinical emphasis, research emphasis, published works, personal background (place and date of birth, education, internships, etc.), career history, current employment, awards and honors, professional memberships, and address and telephone. Supplementary indexes assist in locating individuals by area of clinical and research emphasis and by job category. An alphabetical index provides access to the geographical listings in the book. In addition to four thousand professionals, this volume also provides information on the 687 important rehabilitation centers throughout North America.

Somewhat related is *Who's Who in Chiropractic International* (2nd ed. Chiropractic, 1980. $55.00) that covers that particular subject field without the specific standards evidenced by Marquis publications.   Bohdan S. Wynar

327. Pekkanen, John. **The Best Doctors in the U.S.** rev. ed. New York, Seaview Books; distr., Harper & Row, 1981. 355p. $5.95pa. LC 81-50319. ISBN 0-87223-732-X.

Pekkanen's project originated from an article in *Town and Country* magazine. Since then, he has come out with the first edition of *The Best Doctors in the U.S.* and now the revised edition. The present edition includes over three thousand physicians. Pekkanen compiled his information by communicating with 1,040 physicians through survey or interview, with the most-often-asked question being "Who would you consult if you or a member of your family were ill?" The physicians were asked to cite doctors who are not only knowledgeable, but have a good rapport with people as well.

As the author sees it, the purpose of this book is to guide the individual to the best medical care. Vital information should be put into patients' hands to enable them to make better medical decisions. The publication attempts to do this by describing what physicians feel are the most important qualifications for a doctor.

The bulk of the publication lists the best specialists, hospitals, clinics, and special centers in the United States and Canada. Sections citing specialists are broken down as follows: (1) Adult, Medical, Surgical, and Diagnostic Specialists, (2) Childbirth, (3) Pediatric Specialists, (4) Cancer and Blood Diseases, and (5) Special Treatment Centers.

According to Pekkanen, many physicians were omitted from the book because they lack the exposure gained from attending meetings or from publishing. This publication attempts to include those doctors known for both research and patient care. While the work names individuals as being the best, it fails to include physician credentials. This information may be obtained from the *Directory of Medical Specialists*, published by Marquis Who's Who, Inc.

This interesting book engrosses the reader immediately. An extensive table of contents refers to specific sections; however, an alphabetical as well as a geographical index would be extremely useful.   Amy Gische Lyons

328. Talbott, John H. **A Biographical History of Medicine, Excerpts and Essays on the Men and Their Work**. New York, Grune & Stratton, 1970. 1211p. illus. index. $139.00. LC 78-109574. ISBN 0-8089-0657-7.

This unique compilation consists of over 550 biographical essays on the men (and a handful of women) who have made significant contributions to the medical sciences from 2250 B.C. (Hammurabi) through the first half of the twentieth century (James Herrick, Sir Thomas Lewis, Frederick Banting, etc.). The author claims that the biographical studies are "grouped by specialists within an era." There are no format divisions, however, and such distinctions would be located only by reading the opening section of each essay or by relying upon the subject index, which is not divided by era and which is, indeed, somewhat haphazard in its selection of terms. Each entry, which is illustrated by a photograph or "composite" illustration of the biographee, includes a description of the subject's life and contributions, and an excerpt from his writings.

There is a detailed name index which covers all individuals mentioned, in any context, in the text.

The publication is, first of all, a labor of love by its author, and his analysis is marked by his predilection for the subjects. Much of the material was published earlier in issues of the *Journal of the American Medical Association* as "historical editorial material," but it has, presumably, been expanded and revised (most essays were reviewed by specialists in the field). Regardless of its editorial bias, the volume does supply ready biographical data about individuals who are often not included in other tools, not discussed in this light, or not found in any conveniently available source. It is not a professional medical history and is, in addition, priced beyond the average library market. [R: LJ, 15 Apr 71, p. 1354]   Laurel Grotzinger

329. **Who's Who in Medicine 1981**. 5th ed. Edited by Karl Strute and Theodor Doelken. New York, Unipub, 1981. 2v. (International Red Series). $120.00/set. ISBN 3-921220-40-8 (vol. 1); 3-921220-41-6 (vol. 2).

This work contains twelve thousand brief biographies covering prominent personalities in the field of medicine and pharmaceuticals in the Federal Republic of Germany, Austria, and Switzerland. Information provided is very brief, including name, address, educational background, and career. The appendix lists professional associations and research institutes.

A related work covering these same countries is *Who's Who in Medicine: Austria, Germany, Switzerland* (2v. 5th ed. Philadelphia, International Publications Service, 1983. $120.00).   Bohdan S. Wynar

PHARMACOLOGY

330. **Pharmacology and Pharmacologists: An International Directory**. New York, Oxford University Press, 1981. 387p. index. o.p. LC 79-40202. ISBN 0-19-200101-9.

This biographical directory lists about thirty-two hundred pharmacologists from all parts of the world. Also included are a list of national, regional, and international pharmacological societies and an essay which is a general discussion of the field.

The biographical entries (arranged alphabetically) provide the following information: name, work address, phone number, current position and year of appointment, general field of work, research activities, society of which the biographee is a member, year of birth, academic and professional qualifications, past appointments, and selected publications. A useful feature of the work is the Research Activities Index, which makes it possible for the user to find names of other people engaged in similar work.

The information in the directory was obtained by "circularizing over 12,500 pharmacologists worldwide." The compilers hope that the directory's appearance will encourage others to provide information about themselves for a second edition. It does appear that there are many omissions in this edition.

Theodora Andrews

PSYCHIATRY

331.   **Biographical Directory of the Fellows and Members of the American Psychiatric Association as of October, 1977.** Compiled for the APA by the Jaques Cattell Press. New York, R. R. Bowker, 1977. 1573p. bibliog. index. o.p. LC 63-12595. ISBN 0-8352-0977-6. ISSN 0065-9827.

Replete with the usual masses of abbreviations unique to one work, this volume lists all members of the American Psychiatric Association as of 1977. It also includes complete lists of past officers, a list of present officers and committee members, and the text of the Pledge of Fellowship. The alphabetically arranged entries, as may be expected, comprise the bulk of the volume. Type is small but legible, and the ample margins do make using it easy on the eye. A geographical index of members follows the main section, and the arrangement in this second section is by state names (alphabetically), with cities then listed alphabetically.   Bohdan S. Wynar

PUBLIC HEALTH AND HEALTH CARE

332.   **Biographical Directory of the American Public Health Association**. Compiled for the Association by Jaques Cattell Press. New York, R. R. Bowker, 1979. 1207p. index. $54.50. LC 79-6967. ISBN 0-8352-1160-6.

The American Public Health Association published a membership directory in 1967, but this is their first biographical directory. It provides about thirteen thousand biographical sketches of men and women who shape American public-health policy and, in addition, includes a simple listing of all members and fellows. Also included is material of historical interest, such as the organization's objectives and purpose, constitution and bylaws, officers and board members, past presidents, information on annual meetings and awards, periodicals published, membership information, and accredited schools of public health in the United States.

The biographical section is arranged alphabetically by name of the biographee. Each entry includes: year of election to the organization, birth date, association activities, memberships in national societies, professional interests, address, and office and home phone numbers. The complete list of members which follows the biographical register includes: name, code indicating APHA section, position held, and address. A geographical index to the biographical profiles has been provided. The publication is intended to serve as an archival document as well as a reference source for members, to identify individuals with specific expertise, and to stimulate interaction among disciplines in the public health field. [R: BL, 1 Dec 80, p. 530; Choice, Sept 80, p. 61; LJ, 15 Mar 80, p. 712; RQ, Summer 80, p. 389]   Theodora Andrews

333.   **Who's Who in Health Care, 1981**. 2nd ed. Rockville, Md., Aspen Systems, 1981. 612p. index. $69.95. LC 77-79993. ISBN 0-89443-092-0.

The preface of this volume states that *Who's Who in Health Care* was designed to fill the void of a single source representing the leadership in the various fields of health care, such as medicine, nursing, dentistry, and allied health. The question that remains, however, is, Does this work fill that void?

Included in this reference tool are over seven thousand biographical sketches containing personal and professional background and achievements. These selections were made from health-care leaders in educational and research institutions, hospitals, and the private sector. The stated admission criteria for selection would appear to refer to the first edition. Were these same criteria used for the second edition? If they were, how were meritorious contributions evaluated?

To assist the user of this work, a biographical reference key, a discussion of alphabetical practices used in arranging this volume, and a table of abbreviations are included. The sketches are arranged alphabetically, thus allowing easy access. The material in these brief biographies is not always current, which could be due to a publication lag time. Some examples include the information concerning Peggy L. Chinn, Donna El-Din, and Lucie Stirm Kelly. Additionally, there are leaders in health care who have not been included, such as Florence Downs, Kathryn Barnard, Marshall Klaus, and T. Berry Brazelton. The persons included are indexed according to geographic area and profession, but specific page numbers are not given. The geographic index is divided by states in, and territories of, the United States, and also contains names of a few individuals from other parts of the world. New Brunswick, a Canadian province, is not listed with the other provinces, but is instead listed separately. Developing a *Who's Who in Health Care* is no easy task; yet, such a volume does need to be done with as much precision as possible. The publishers state that if there are errors in publication, they will be responsible for correcting them in future editions.

Health-science or large public libraries might wish to consider this volume for their reference collections. Yet, because of some of the omissions, inaccuracies, and questionable inclusion standards, quite possibly other Who's Who books might be more useful reference tools. Since health care encompasses so many areas, a Who's Who related to a specific health-care field including educators, researchers, and clinicians in that area might be more useful. Judith Ann Erlen

11 History

Introduction

This chapter includes two sections, "United States" and "Latin America," with a total of three entries. Additional titles are listed in the annotations. The coverage is limited to biographical sources such as *Twentieth-Century American Historians* (see entry 335). Biographical sources that deal with historical and cultural process are to be found in part 1, "Universal and National Biographies" that includes not only general sources but is also subdivided by countries. General historiographical works, such as G. P. Gooch's *History and Historians in the Nineteenth Century* (Longmans, 1952. 547p.), R. J. Shafer's *A Guide to Historical Method* (3rd ed. Dorsey Press, 1980. 272p.), *International Handbook of Historical Studies: Contemporary Research and Theory*, edited by G. G. Iggers and H. T. Parker (Greenwood Press, 1979. 452p.), or E. Fueter's *Geschichte der neueren Historiographie* (3rd ed. Munich, Oldenbourg, 1936; repr., Johnson, 1968. 670p.) are not included.

A number of subject dictionaries offer additional biographical information. Thus, for example, A. Palmer's *The Penguin Dictionary of Modern History 1789-1945* (2nd ed. Penguin Books, 1983. 315p.) or its companion A. Palmer's *The Penguin Dictionary of Twentieth Century History* (2nd ed. Penguin Books, 1983. 411p.) include a number of biographical entries but are primarily for historical figures and not for professional historians. The same is true of dictionaries specializing in American history, e.g., R. Morris's *Encyclopedia of American History* (6th ed. Harper & Row, 1982. 1285p.) or *Webster's Guide to American History* (G. & C. Merriam, 1971. 1428p.). Much better in this respect is an older work, J. N. Larned's *New Larned History for Ready Reference, Reading and Research; The Actual Words of the World's Best Historians, Biographers and Specialists. . .* (12v. Nichols, 1922-1924) that serves as an alphabetically arranged compendium of the world's history with numerous historiographical notes. For periodicals, the most important abstracting services should be consulted: *Historical Abstracts* (ABC-Clio Press, 1955-), *America: History and Life* (ABC-Clio Press, 1964-), and *Recently Published Articles* (American Historical Association, 1976-). Other indexing and abstracting services, bibliographies, and other types of reference sources are described in several bibliographic guides, e.g., the now somewhat obsolete *Guide to Historical Literature* prepared by the American Historical Association (Macmillan, 1961. 962p.), Helen Poulton's *The Historian's Handbook* (University of Oklahoma Press, 1972. 304p.), and many others listed by Sheehy and Walford.

UNITED STATES

334. Wilson, Clyde N., ed. **American Historians, 1607-1865**. Detroit, Gale, 1984. 382p. illus. index. (Dictionary of Literary Biography, Vol. 30). $82.00. LC 84-10262. ISBN 0-8103-1708-7.

A handsome addition to the *Dictionary of Literary Biography*, volume 30 contains biographical and critical essays on forty-six early American historians. The signed articles differ somewhat in format but all give basic biographical information, criticism, and/or commentary on the writer's works, a selected bibliography of the above, and a list of references for further research. The writing style is sometimes heavy, but easily accessible to the student for whom the book is intended; illustrations are appropriate and attractive. Volume 30 complements previous ones in the *DLB* focusing on colonial and early American and antebellum literature. Several people included here are also mentioned in those previous volumes, but the current articles are fresh and the concentration is on their historical writings rather than the popular or other work they may have done. This is an excellent reference book, valuable to all early-American history and literature collections. Deborah Hammer

335. Wilson, Clyde N., ed. **Twentieth-Century American Historians**. Detroit, Gale, 1983. 519p. illus. bibliog. index. (Dictionary of Literary Biography, Vol. 17). $80.00. LC 82-24210. ISBN 0-8103-1144-5.

Twentieth-Century American Historians (Volume 17 of Gale's Dictionary of Literary Biography) contains biographical and critical essays on fifty-nine historical writers. Most of these authors are academic and professional historians. Twenty are still living. To be eligible for inclusion, writers had to be American; their historical writings had to be concentrated chiefly upon the United States; and their most important work had to fall within the twentieth century. Fourteen major writers have been selected for extended treatment, including Charles A. Beard, Daniel J. Boorstin, Richard Hofstadter, Allan Nevins, and Frederick Jackson Turner. A photograph of each historian is given, as well as a bibliography of the historian's books and a bibliography of secondary sources. The volume includes a supplementary reading list and a cumulative index to the *Dictionary of Literary Biography*.

The criteria for inclusion rule out historians like Captain Alfred Thayer Mahan, whose history of sea power was largely concentrated on Europe, and J. Fred Rippy, whose writings were mainly on U.S. foreign policy in relation to Hispanic America. On the other hand, there are some rather surprising omissions among U.S. historians: Eugene C. Barker, Dexter Perkins, and Julius W. Pratt, to name a few. However, the editor had to draw a line somewhere, and these omissions do not in any way downgrade the historical writers who were not selected.

A total of fifty-four contributors wrote the essays (three contributors wrote two biographies each). Of these, thirty-six or two-thirds are from Southern states. While this does not reflect on the competence of the contributors, it shows a rather surprising disproportion. The essays themselves are of high quality and follow the dictum of Allan Nevins that historical writing should be readable as well as factually accurate. [R: Choice, Dec 83, p. 559; WLB, Sept 83, p. 68]   Thomas S. Harding

LATIN AMERICA

336. Thomas, Jack Ray. **Biographical Dictionary of Latin American Historians and Historiography**. Westport, Conn., Greenwood Press, 1984. 420p. bibliog. index. $49.95. LC 83-8558. ISBN 0-313-23004-8.

To some extent, the title of this work is self-explanatory, except that it does not do justice to the excellent introductory essay on Latin American historiography that lays the groundwork for the biobibliographical sketches of Latin American historical writers. The introduction, a small volume in itself (seventy pages), explores the development of Latin American historiography from the colonial times to the present, showing its evolution from an avocation of men of leisure to its coming of age as a professional discipline in the twentieth century. "The focus," says the author, "is on the 19th century, when the writing of history began to forge a discipline that ultimately emerged in the 20th century." Trends are well illustrated through the historians themselves and well documented through extensive footnotes.

The heart of this useful reference book is the biobibliographical section, consisting of approximately three hundred sketches of historians who range from the colonial chroniclers to modern historians (those who died before 1983). Acknowledging that some of those included might be challenged as historians, while others should have been included, the author says that the major considerations for inclusion were "that the writer either produced a significant amount of historical writing or that a portion of his scholarly production was so important to the discipline of history that he could not be excluded."

The book features four useful appendixes: a listing by birthplace of the historians treated in the main section, a chronological listing by year of birth (from 1478 to 1917), a listing according to the careers of the historians (twenty-two were librarians, one a cosmographer), and a listing by the subjects (including famous figures in Latin American history) researched by the major historians.

This work is a long overdue contribution to the reference literature of Latin American historiography. It should supplement, and to some extent, replace A. Curtis Wilgus's *The Historiography of Latin America: A Guide to Historical Writing, 1500-1800* (Scarecrow, 1975). [R: RQ, Fall 84, pp. 100-101]   Edwin S. Gleaves

12 Law

Introduction

In this chapter the material is subdivided into four sections: "General Works," "Civil Rights," "Criminology," and "Federal Judiciary and Supreme Court," with a total of twelve entries. Most of the works are still in print and annotations contain numerous references to related titles. The standard source in this area is *Who's Who in American Law* (see entry 338) with a number of other useful titles, e.g., *Civil Rights: A Current Guide to the People, Organizations and Events* (see entry 339) or *Biographical Dictionary of the Federal Judiciary* (see entry 346). Outstanding and internationally known attorneys are obviously included in general current and retrospective sources discussed in part 1, "Universal and National Biographies," such as *Dictionary of American Biography* (see entry 43), *Dictionary of National Biography* (see entry 137), and in many Who's Who type sources, also listed there.

Directories, e.g., *American Bar Association's Directory* (American Bar Association, 1938-), *Directory of Law Teachers in American Bar Association Approved Law Schools* (West Publishing Co., 1923-), or *Lawyer's Register by Specialties and Fields of Law: A National Directory of Lawyers Listed by Fields of Law and Including a List of Corporate Counsel* (Lawyer to Lawyer Consultation Panel, 1978- . Annual) are not included because they are primarily membership directories and offer a minimum amount of biographical information. Directories that offer more biographical information are discussed with other related titles. Most law dictionaries and encyclopedias, including the most popular, e.g., *Ballentine's Law Dictionary* (Lawyers Co-Operative Publishing Co., 1969. 1429p.) or *Black's Law Dictionary* (5th ed. West Publishing Co., 1979. 1511p.) do include biographies. For biographical material published in periodicals one can use a number of indexing services. For retrospective coverage a useful source is *Index to Legal Periodical Literature* (Boston Book Co., 1888-1919, later published by several other publishers up to 1939) and *Index to Legal Periodicals* (Wilson, 1909-) that covers over 450 legal periodicals. *Index to Legal Periodicals* can be supplemented by *Index to Periodical Articles Related to Law* (Glanville, 1958) that covers articles in journals not included in the Wilson indexing service. A very comprehensive indexing service is offered by *Current Law Index* (Information Access Corporation. 1980-) covering seven hundred periodicals selected by the Committee on Indexing of Periodical Literature of the American Association of Law Libraries. *CLI* is available in paper copy and on microfilm. There are several other indexing and abstracting services published in this country and abroad, as well as numerous bibliographies. They are discussed in a number of bibliographic guides. Intended as a concise introduction to legal bibliography is M. L. Cohen's *Legal Research in a Nutshell* (4th ed. West Publishing Co., 1985. 452p.) that is not as comprehensive as M. O. Price's *Effective Legal Research* (4th ed. Little, Brown, 1979. 643p.) or J. M. Jacobstein and R. M. Mersky's *Fundamentals of Legal Research* (3rd ed. Foundation Press, 1985. 717p.). M. L. Cohen and R. C. Berring's *How to Find the Law* (8th ed. West, 1983. 790p.) also serves as a comprehensive guide to legal bibliographies.

GENERAL WORKS

337. Naifeh, Steven, and Gregory White Smith. **The Best Lawyers in America**. New York, Putnam, 1983. 248p. $15.95; $7.95pa. LC 82-19225. ISBN 0-399-31002-9; 0-399-51068-0pa.

The Best Lawyers in America lists by state two thousand attorneys judged by colleagues to be the best in their fields. Written by two Harvard Law School graduates, the lists are broken down into five specialties: domestic relations, trusts and estates, criminal defense, creditor's and debtor's rights, and civil litigation. The authors assume that only the best lawyer (and probably the most expensive) will do, comparing those on the list to the finest surgeons in their particular fields. No criteria for identifying the best lawyers were developed; that task was left to each questioned lawyer. This book is for those who require only the best legal aid, regardless of cost.

Most consumers might get more use from a directory rating lawyers on their competence and professional skills as actually experienced by their clients than from a list of the "best" chosen by their peers. In this respect we recommend *Who's Who in American Law* (see entry 338), another useful publication. *Law and Business Directory of Corporate Counsel* (Harcourt Brace Jovanovich, 1980- . Annual) is the most comprehensive directory of more than twenty-four thousand attorneys in more than five thousand companies. Brief biographical information is included in most entries. *Martindale-Hubbell Law Directory* (Martindale-Hubbell, 1931- . Annual) provides an annual listing of the bar in both the United States and Canada. The most comprehensive directory of its kind, it is geographically organized and provides the present address and educational background of each attorney. Barry Tarlow's *National Directory of Criminal Lawyers* (University Publishers, 1979. 188p.) is organized by state and provides information on education and professional experience. *United States Lawyers Reference Directory* (Legal Directories, 1977-) is also a comprehensive listing of attorneys and law firms. [R: LJ, 1 Feb 83, p. 197]

Bill Sperry and Bohdan S. Wynar

338. **Who's Who in American Law 1985-1986**. 4th ed. Chicago, Marquis Who's Who, 1985. 686p. index. $125.00. LC 77-79896. ISBN 0-8379-3504-0.

Now in its fourth edition, *Who's Who in American Law* is a well-researched and impressively assembled biographical reference tool that contains about eighteen thousand listings of professionals in the law. This edition replaces the third edition, published in 1983.

Who's Who provides biographical sketches of leading lawyers and judges, as well as legal educators, law librarians, legal historians, social scientists, and others involved in law-related fields. Biographees are selected for inclusion in the volume on the basis of position of responsibility or noteworthy achievement. The biographees provide their own biographical information.

The sketch of each biographee includes his or her vital statistics, education, career history, awards, publications, and memberships. Each biographee was asked to list up to three areas of law that reflected personal interest or practice. Consequently, each sketch provides the biographee's areas of interest, and the cumulative index is arranged by legal subject as well as geographical area.

A useful tool that should be helpful at the reference desk of most libraries, particularly law libraries and public libraries.

This work can be supplemented by *The American Bench: Judges of the Nation* (see entry 343) that offers biographical sketches on "judges of all levels of federal and state courts with jurisdictional and geographical information on courts they serve" (preface). A related title is *Judges of the United States* (2nd ed. Washington, D.C., GPO, 1983. 681p.) prepared by Judicial Conference of the United States, Bicentennial Committee. It provides brief biographical data for each individual who sat as a judge from the eighteenth century to 1981. [R: WLB, Apr 84, p. 598]

Susan Beverly Kuklin and Bohdan S. Wynar

CIVIL RIGHTS

339. Adams, A. John, and Joan Martin Burke. **Civil Rights: A Current Guide to the People, Organizations, and Events**. 2nd ed. New York, R. R. Bowker, 1974. 266p. index. (A CBS Reference Book). $17.50. LC 74-4053. ISBN 0-8352-0722-6.

Provides rather detailed information on the key people in major civil rights groups, civic groups, organizations of minorities, etc. There is also a guide to acronyms and several appendixes: Congressional Voting Records on Civil Rights Acts in the early 1970s; List of States with Civil Rights Laws and State Agencies with Civil Rights Responsibilities; Civil Rights Chronology 1954-1973; Leading Black Elected Officials in U.S.; and Suggested Bibliography (entries not annotated). Biographical sketches (about 250) usually include career information, occasionally educational background (see, for example, the entry for Abernathy), writings, some of the most important speeches, etc. The amount of information provided for organizations varies depending on their relative importance. Usually the reader will find here information on objectives, date of founding, major activities, membership, important conventions, etc. Summing up, it is a well-balanced presentation on this important topic and is highly recommended for libraries of all types as well as for the civic-minded individual. [R: Choice, May 71, p. 361; LJ, 15 Feb 71, p. 619; RQ, Spring 71, p. 261; WLB, Feb 71, p. 598]

Bohdan S. Wynar

CRIMINOLOGY

340.   Gaute, J. H. H., and Robin Odell. **The Murderers' Who's Who: Outstanding International Cases from the Literature of Murder in the Last 150 Years**. New York, St. Martin's Press, 1979. 269p. illus. bibliog. index. $17.95. LC 83-11193. ISBN 0-312-55350-1.

This is an attempt to bring together accounts of murders, from many countries, that captured headlines and have subsequently been featured in books. The authors "hope to set out those murders distinguished by the quality of their incidents"; they include crimes which led to changes in the law, added to forensic science, or have been noted for their drama or curiosity. Crimes from 1828 to recent times are included. Gangland slayings, western gunfights, and assassinations were excluded.

The murders are arranged alphabetically by the name of the murderer. Where there was no conviction, the entry is under a popular name for the case, e.g., Mullendore Case, Moors Murders, Hammersmith Nudes Murders. The facts for each case are clearly stated in about half a page, with references to the bibliography, and illustrations on almost every page. There is an author-title bibliography of more than seven hundred items. The only index is a subject index classified by the murder instrument (e.g., acid, ax) or other important aspects such as missing bodies, matricide, or trunk crimes. While the murders are mostly British, there are many from the United States and some from another sixteen countries.

This is a useful reference book on its subject, but would have been better with a more complete index and cross-references between names of murderer, murdered, and popular names of cases. For example, Bonnie and Clyde are entered under Bonnie and Clyde, with no cross-references or indexing under either of their last names.

David W. Brunton

341.   Nash, Jay Robert. **Bloodletters and Badmen: A Narrative Encyclopedia of American Criminals from the Pilgrims to the Present**. New York, M. Evans; distr., Philadelphia, Lippincott, 1973. 640p. illus. bibliog. index. $12.95pa. LC 72-95977. ISBN 0-87131-200-X.

Nash, newspaperman and author of biographies of Dillinger and Hoover, bases this account of American murderers, gangsters, and robbers on about five thousand books collected over the past fifteen years. The well-written biographies are accompanied by over three hundred photographs of the subjects, some of them action shots. Gory tales of mass murder, prison brutality, and the romantic marriage of Belle Starr to a Cherokee Indian gone bad are detailed, and a thorough bibliography and index are appended. [R: LJ, 1 May 73, p. 1471; WLB, Sept 73, p. 86]

Frances Neel Cheney

342.   Nash, Jay Robert. **Look for the Woman: A Narrative Encyclopedia of Female Poisoners, Kidnappers, Thieves, Extortionists, Terrorists, Swindlers and Spies from Elizabethan Times to the Present**. New York, M. Evans, 1981. 408p. illus. bibliog. index. $18.95. LC 81-2868. ISBN 0-87131-336-7.

This popular, not scholarly, biographical dictionary covering over three hundred infamous women criminals, written by a prolific compiler of such compendiums, employs a writing style more likely to be found in detective magazines than in a reference book. In the preface, Nash claims to have chosen the women portrayed from a list of over ten thousand names. He feels that his work represents the most definitive work on the subject of women and crime, and considers most other works in the field to be "sociological diatribes or one-side polemics." The work is well illustrated by numerous photographs and drawings. While the source of the information in individual biographical sketches is not given, Nash does list an extensive bibliography of books and journal articles at the end of the book.

The problem with this sort of reference work is that while it does not meet the criteria one normally expects of a reference source, nothing else covers the same material. Reference librarians would prefer to have had brief biographical information on the ten thousand names rather than longer and gorier descriptions of only three hundred.   Jack E. Pontius

FEDERAL JUDICIARY AND SUPREME COURT

343. **The American Bench: Judges of the Nation**. Mary Reincke, executive ed. Minneapolis, Minn., R. B. Forster and Associates, 1977. 1906p. index. o.p. ISBN 0-931-398-02-9.

The American Bench definitively fills the gap in judicial and legal directories. This first edition provides biographical information on the nation's federal and state judges along with geographical and jurisdictional data on the respective courts. The editors have organized the directory into fifty-two sections — one section for each of the fifty states and the District of Columbia and one for the federal courts. These sections are then subdivided into three parts, which provide a description of the court, biographical information, and jurisdictional maps.

The first part summarizes the legal and geographical jurisdiction of the courts, indicates court size, explains the method by which judges are selected, and outlines the length of term served by judges. Immediately below each summary, the judges and clerks of that court are listed. All federal courts are included in the federal section, and each state section includes the U.S. District Courts, courts of last resort, intermediate appellate courts, courts of general jurisdiction, and courts of special or limited jurisdiction. Local courts are not included in the directory, but counties and county seats are listed. The geographical jurisdiction of the courts described in part one is clarified by the maps in part two.

The third and final part contains alphabetical biographies of the judges. Biographies vary because the data are submitted by the judges, but each entry has at least the individual judge's position, office, address, and telephone number. Previously this information was only available by consulting several different sources, such as *United States Lawyers Reference Directory* and the *Biographical Dictionary of the Federal Judiciary*. The *American Bench* is a valuable addition to legal and general reference collections.

A more recent title prepared by the Judicial Conference of the United States, Bicentennial Committee is *Judges of the United States* (2nd ed. Washington, D.C., GPO, 1983. 681p.) serving as a biographical directory of judges of the United States from before the adoption of the Constitution to 31 December 1981. Entries provide basic information concerning employment, publications, memberships, and family. Indexes by appointing president and the year of appointment provide access to the entries. In addition, *Almanac of the Federal Judiciary* (Chicago, Law Letters, 1984-), a semiannual publication, provides useful information on all active U.S. district judges. Entries include not only information on education and previous professional experience, but also noteworthy rulings, comments from lawyers, etc. [R: BL, 1 Sept 78, p. 66; LJ, 1 Mar 78, p. 552; RQ, Fall 78, p. 90]

Patricia M. Aldrich and Bohdan S. Wynar

344.   **Attorneys General of the United States, 1789-1979**. Washington, D.C., U.S. Department of Justice; distr., Washington, D.C., GPO, 1980. 147p. illus. index. o.p. S/N 027-000-00723-6.

The formal painted portraits of seventy U.S. attorneys general serving between 1789 and 1979 are reproduced in this attractive softcover government document. Most of the portraits were painted during the incumbent's term as attorney general; however, some of the early portraits were executed before the creation of the department and were acquired later through art dealers or from heirs. The reproductions are in black and white, and the photographs of the paintings encompass the frame containing the portrait. The scale of reduction is not given; the average size of these reproductions (not including the frame) is approximately 4x5.5 inches. Portraits are on a separate page, with the facing page containing brief biographical information for both the attorney general and the portrait artist. Arrangement is chronological. An alphabetical index includes the names of the attorneys general, but not the artists. The only portrait missing from this compilation is that of John M. Mitchell, whose portrait had not yet been commissioned at the time of publication.

Many libraries received this book as a depository item. It is not a necessary purchase for most libraries since biographical information on attorneys general and American portrait artists is easily located in standard biographical sets such as the *DAB* and *The New York Historical Society's Dictionary of Artists in America, 1564-1860* (New Haven, Yale University Press, 1957). Portraits for many of these gentlemen are included in Hayward Cirker's *Dictionary of American Portraits* (New York, Dover, 1967) and *The National Cyclopedia of American Biography* (New York, White and Co., 1892-).

It can also be supplemented by *The Attorneys General of the States and Other Jurisdictions* (Lexington, Ky., Council of State Governments, 1979. o.p.). [R: BL, 15 Feb 81, p. 800]

Milton H. Crouch

345.   Barnes, Catherine A. **Men of the Supreme Court: Profiles of the Justices**. New York, Facts on File, 1978. 221p. illus. bibliog. index. $22.00. LC 78-11633. ISBN 0-87196-459-7.

This work consists of short biographies of the twenty-six men who served on the United States Supreme Court between 1945 and 1976. It grew out of the Political Profiles series published by Facts on File but, in many cases, incorporates supplementary research. As a source of information on the individual justices, it is excellent, providing factual background, a clear exposition of the role each played on the Court, and some interpretive analysis. A twenty-two-page introduction provides a useful framework by tracing the general lines of Court activity in the post-World War II era. This is not to say that some parts of this introduction are beyond dispute, but it is lucidly laid out, standing as one of the most cogent summaries of Court activities for the nonspecialist that this reviewer has encountered. A very rich bibliography allows deeper inquiry into the careers of the justices, and a chronological chart provides perspective. Barnes also provides a collection of summaries of the important decisions of the period, which in itself is a handy guide.

In sum, the book is an excellent source for information on the Court, providing in short form for the layperson the kind of background information done on a grander scale by Leon Friedman and Fred Israels in their monumental multivolume set, *The Justices of the United States Supreme Court, 1789-1969* (Bowker, 1969). Only some unfortunate editorial errors (a repeated paragraph in the introduction, a birth date that shows Abe Fortas graduating from Yale Law School at the age of 13) mar its quality. Any reference collection that does not have Friedman and Israels would do well to invest in Barnes's book. [R: BL, 1 Feb 80, p. 790; WLB, Apr 79, p. 591]

Robert C. Berring

346. Chase, Harold, and others, comps. **Biographical Dictionary of the Federal Judiciary**. Detroit, Gale, 1976. 381p. $90.00. LC 76-18787. ISBN 0-8103-1125-9.

This volume brings together concise, alphabetically arranged biographies of federal judges with lifetime tenures from Washington to Nixon. An addendum contains the biographies of judges appointed during the Nixon administration, and the appendix lists judges arranged according to the appointing president. Even though the biographies that appear in *Who's Who in America* and *Who Was Who in America* are duplicated here, the compilers have performed a valuable service by collecting accurate biographical data not readily available elsewhere.

The essay by Keith Boyum and Jerry Clark on the representation of judges in the federal judicial system includes a list of references and tabular data on the religious, political, and professional backgrounds of the judges. The authors suggest that biographical studies of the judges may provide new insights as to why and to what extent the recruitment process depends on the judges' social, economic, and educational backgrounds. A systematic examination of a judge's major opinions, they contend, may lead to a deeper understanding of the influence that his background has in the decision-making process. Careful study of the biographies may provide a valuable approach to evaluating the federal judiciary; this is the stated rationale that motivated the compilation of the biographical dictionary. While it is interesting that the backgrounds of many federal judges have been observed to be similar and that they may affect the federal judiciary, it seems questionable to include the essay in this biographical dictionary. Undoubtedly, the essay will have more relevance for scholars interested in the judiciary than it will for the user who needs information about federal judges. [R: WLB, Dec 76, pp. 364-65]

Helen Q. Schroyer

347. Friedman, Leon and Fred L. Israel, eds. **The Justices of the United States Supreme Court, 1789-1978: Their Lives and Major Opinions**. New York, Chelsea House Publishers in association with R. R. Bowker, 1980. 5v. $75.00/set pa. LC 69-13699. ISBN 0-87754-130-2.

Originally published in hardcover between 1969-1978 and now available in paperback (hardcover edition is o.p.), the set contains analytical and biographical essays of 109 judges written by forty-nine scholars. In the fifth volume we find re-evaluation of Chief Justice Warren Burger and Justice Thurgood Marshall (briefer evaluation was made earlier when they were relatively new to the Supreme Court). The resignations of Justices Douglas, Harlan, and Black during this period made it possible for the fifth volume to summarize their work, and to bid farewell to the era of the Warren Court. The new direction of the Burger Court may be detected most strongly from the section on Chief Justice Burger. However, the pieces on the Nixon and Ford appointees to the Court, Blackmun, Powell, Rehnquist, and Stevens, are enlightening in this regard also.

The format is the same in all five volumes. Pieces on particular justices are written by different authors, most of whom are professors of law or practicing attorneys. The writing styles differ, and so does the content, to some degree. Each piece is structured around a section devoted to personal and professional biographical information, and a section of representative opinions. It is a good combination for a reader eager to know individual contributions of justices to constitutional development.

Although an attempt is made to be even-handed in evaluating each justice, the authors are more critical of the newer justices and the chief justice. The index is for the most part quite good; it links justices with topics and also lists major topics handled by each justice separately. Each case is also indexed by name of plaintiff. Additional biographical references at the end of each article allow readers the option of pursuing research beyond the scope of this work.

Any general reference collection would benefit from this handy, concise source of biographical information for justices of the Supreme Court. The original four volumes published in 1969 won the 1970 Scribes Award as outstanding works on a legal subject.

Barbara Van Deventer and Bohdan S. Wynar

348.   Sevilla, Victor J. **Justices of the Supreme Court of the Philippines: Their Lives and Outstanding Decisions**. Quezon City, Philippines, New Day Publishers; distr., Detroit, Cellar Book Shop, 1984. 2v. illus. bibliog. $16.75/vol. pa. ISBN 971-10-0133-0 (vol. 1); 971-10-0136-5 (vol. 2).

The foreword to this set asserts, "Attorney Victor J. Sevilla . . . has written a collection of biographical sketches of the 106 distinguished men who served as justices in [the Philippine] Supreme Court from its establishment under the American [United States] regime, at the opening of the century, until 1984" (p. iii). After each justice's biography, the author has appended selections from his decisions. Since the biographies and selected opinions are quite brief, from one to three pages, we may consider this book as a survey of the history of Philippine jurisprudence. The book does point out the important personalities and landmarks of this history but does not treat them in depth. However, there is no biographical sketch or photo of Associate Justice Joseph F. Cooper, who was on the supreme court from 1901-1904 during the early years of the American occupation of the Philippines.

At the end of each volume are a short bibliography, a valuable complete list of the supreme court justices, and an interesting biographical bibliography.

There are black-and-white photographs of some of the justices; many of them are of poor quality. The paper the book is printed on is also of poor quality; it is difficult to believe it will hold up very well even under light library circulation conditions. The soft binding seems adequate.

Marshall E. Nunn

13 Library Science

Introduction

This chapter covers two groups, "Librarians" and "Publishers, Booksellers, and Printers," with a total of seven entries and many related titles mentioned in the annotations. Scholarly contributions in the area of librarianship are *Dictionary of American Library Biography* (see entry 349) and the widely known current biography *Who's Who in Library and Information Services* (see entry 353) that continues previously published biographical directories such as *A Biographical Directory of Librarians in the United States and Canada*, edited by Lee Ash (5th ed. American Library Association, 1970. 1250p.) and its predecessors, also published by the ALA (1st edition in 1933). *Who's Who in Librarianship and Information Science*, edited by T. Landau (Abelard-Schuman, 1972. 311p.), is dated but still occasionally useful for Great Britain. Several other countries have similar works, e.g., *Who's Who in New Zealand Libraries* (New Zealand Library Association, 1951-), *Biographical Dictionary of Australian Librarians*, edited by G. A. Kósa (2nd ed. Burwood State College, 1979. 201p.), a retrospective biographical directory—*Dizionario bio-bibliografico dei bibliotecari e bibliofili italiani dal sec. XIV al XIX* (Olschki, 1933. 705p.) and its supplement covering a more recent period, published in three volumes in 1950-1960.

There are some additional sources for publishers and booksellers, most of them only of historical value, e.g., *Dictionaries of Printers and Booksellers in England, Scotland and Ireland* (5v. London Bibliographical Society, 1905-1932) or *Lexikon des gesamten Buchwesens* (3v. Leipzig, Hiersemann, 1935-1937) that, along with brief articles on the booktrade, contains a number of biographies of printers and booksellers.

Biographies are also included in some dictionaries and encyclopedias. The most comprehensive encyclopedia, which includes several hundred entries, is *Encyclopedia of Library and Information Science*, edited by A. Kent and others (35v. Dekker, 1968-1983, plus three supplements, 1983-1985). Some biographies are also included in *ALA World Encyclopedia of Library and Information Services*, edited by R. Wedgeworth (American Library Association, 1980. 601p.) and *ALA Yearbook* (American Library Association, 1976- . Annual). Biographies in periodical articles are covered by

Library Literature (Wilson, 1934-) and its predecessors, which cover over 220 periodicals plus monographs. *Library and Information Science Abstracts* (Library Association, 1969-), which abstracts articles from over four hundred periodicals as well as books, monographs, theses, reports and conference proceedings, also contains information on biographies in periodicals, as does *Indian Library Science Abstracts* (Indian Association of Special Libraries and Information Centers, 1967-). There is no bibliographic guide on library science but, again, *Library and Information Science Abstracts* and *Library Literature* are helpful. For added information the best guide is G. Purcell and G. A. Schlachter's *Reference Sources in Library and Information Services: A Guide to the Literature* (ABC-Clio, 1984. 359p.), which lists indexing and abstracting services from around the world.

LIBRARIANS

349.   Dictionary of American Library Biography. George S. Bobinski, Jesse Hauk Shera, and Bohdan S. Wynar, eds. Littleton, Colo., Libraries Unlimited, 1978. 596p. index. $85.00. LC 77-28791. ISBN 0-87287-180-0.

The publication of *Dictionary of American Library Biography* marks the culmination of five years of planning, research, writing, and editorial work by the editorial board of *DALB*, over two hundred contributors throughout the library community, and the staff of Libraries Unlimited, Inc. *DALB*, the first scholarly dictionary of past American library leaders, contains thoroughly researched, original biographical sketches of 301 outstanding men and women who, in large measure, founded and built this country's libraries, professional associations, and library education programs, and who developed basic bibliographic tools and information networks.

Selected for inclusion in *DALB* were those individuals who made contributions of national significance to American library development, whose writings influenced library trends and activities, who held positions of national importance, who made major achievements in special fields of librarianship, or who affected American libraries through their significant scholarly, philanthropic, legislative, or governmental support or activity. To insure proper historical perspective, only those people deceased as of 30 June 1976, were included. Probably the first biographical dictionary of its kind for any profession in the United States, *DALB* is a significant contribution to library history, making it possible to gain the historical perspective necessary to better interpret the profession's resources and their origins. [R: C&RL, Sept 78, p. 403; LJ, 1 Sept 78, p. 1575; WLB, Sept 78, p. 89]   Ann Hartman

350.   Engelbarts, Rudolf. Librarian Authors: A Bibliography. Jefferson, N.C., McFarland, 1981. 276p. index. $21.95. LC 80-28035. ISBN 0-89950-007-2.

Rudolf Engelbarts has produced an excellent compilation for librarians and library school students. Although it has the title of *Librarian Authors*, the work includes a number of benefactors and friends of libraries, including Sir Thomas Bodley, Thomas Bray, Andrew Carnegie, Richard Rogers Bowker, and Halsey W. Wilson.

Engelbarts lists names and publications of 109 men and women who were outstanding both as librarians and as authors. Most of these librarian-authors were American or English, with a scattering of Europeans. The book has been divided somewhat arbitrarily into three sections: part 1, the period from 1600 to 1800, when librarianship in its modern theory and practice had not yet evolved; part 2, the period from 1800 to

1950, which saw the proliferation of libraries and the emergence of modern librarianship; and part 3, the contemporary period from 1950 to 1980, featuring a selection of librarians who are still active or have recently terminated their activities. Among the living librarians cited are Keyes D. Metcalf, Robert B. Downs, Lawrence Clark Powell, and Jesse H. Shera.

The bulk of this volume consists of vignettes of librarians and library benefactors, with a listing of their principal works. Not all the published works were on librarianship: Randolph G. Adams, William Frederick Poole, and Justin Winsor were also historians, and John Shaw Billings was a physician. There are three bibliographics: one on publications in librarianship; the second on librarians as authors; and a third, a special bibliography of the 109 librarians and benefactors with a list of their principal works, as well as their biographies.

There are a few minor flaws. Page iii of the preface lists a total of 108 librarians or library benefactors, while on page 162 the number drops to 105. The actual count is 109. On page 57, the death date of Charles Ammi Cutter is given as 1907 instead of 1903. On page 86, Herbert Putnam is reported to have succeeded Ainsworth Rand Spofford as Librarian of Congress, ignoring the administration of John Russell Young. On page 276, the index lists no pages for Louis Round Wilson, whose contributions are described on page 161. However, these errors are not sufficient to detract from a comprehensive and thoroughly researched volume. Engelbarts's book deserves a place on the shelf of every librarian and library school teacher. Thomas S. Harding

351. **Librarians of Congress, 1802-1974**. Washington, D.C., Library of Congress; distr., Washington, D.C., GPO, 1977. 273p. illus. index. o.p. LC 77-608073. ISBN 0-8444-0238-9. S/N 030-001-00080-0.

This attractive volume, unusually so for a government publication, is composed of eleven biographical essays, each dealing with one of the Librarians of Congress, from John Beckley, the first to hold that position, to L. Quincy Mumford. Each essay is by a different author, and, wisely, their selection has not been restricted to either members of the Library staff or to librarians. In a few instances (e.g., Edward N. Waters on Herbert Putnam and Ben Powell on Mumford), the authors knew their subjects intimately. In a book such as this, the portraits tend, of course, to emphasize the positive aspects of their subjects' contributions to the Library, but they are not uncritical, and a substantial amount of research has gone into their preparation. The compilation has an informative preface by Daniel Boorstin, the present Librarian of Congress, who sets forth some of his thoughts on the role of the Library in both the federal government and the library profession at large. There is no indication of the individual who planned and edited the volume, but one may properly hypothesize that Boorstin had a major responsibility for it. Throughout the work there are many illustrations of considerable historical interest.

In reading these pages, however, one cannot but regret the necessity for the omission of the name of Verner Clapp. Probably no one since Putnam himself has been more responsible for the growth in resources and for the expansion of programs than has Clapp, who served as Deputy Librarian of Congress under Putnam, Archibald MacLeish, and Luther Evans. In the world of scholarship, as well as in the library world, both within and without the boundaries of the United States, no Librarian of Congress was as well known. This is a book that every library, and many librarians, will want to own. Jesse H. Shera

352. **Who's Who in Librarianship and Information Science**. Edited by T. Landau. 2nd ed. London, Abelard-Schuman, 1972; distr., New York, Intext, 1973. 311p. o.p. LC 70-184398. ISBN 0-200-71871-1.

This directory of British librarians covers two thousand librarians and includes the following information for each person: name, highest degree earned, association memberships, title and current place of employment, home address, year and place of birth, marital status, schools attended (including high schools), previous positions, and special interests (i.e., hobbies). There is no preface or introduction, so there is no way to know what criteria were used for selection of people listed. Bohdan S. Wynar

353. **Who's Who in Library and Information Services**. Joel M. Lee, ed. Chicago, American Library Association, 1982. 559p. $150.00. LC 81-20480. ISBN 0-8389-0351-7.

The need for an update to *A Biographical Directory of Librarians in the United States and Canada* (1970) has been evident for quite some time. According to the editor, this new work is intended to meet that need.

Each entry includes the biographee's name, birth date, employment history, education, organizational memberships, honors and awards, principal publications, professional activities, and mailing address. Included for coverage are librarians, as well as information scientists, archivists, and those in fields such as publishing whose primary activity relates to librarianship and information fields. To accomplish this task, thirty-six national association membership lists were merged and questionnaires were mailed to fifty-five thousand people with extensive follow-up conducted.

However, when important individuals in the information-science field, such as Samuel Beatty, executive director of ASIS, are excluded, it appears that the emphasis is most definitely on library science. Admittedly, however, it is difficult to determine who was excluded as an oversight and who actually requested that they not be included.

Although the editors and advisory committee sought to develop a directory which would be selective, "including the most significant members of the library and information community according to a set of eligibility guidelines" (editor's introduction), the qualifications according to these guidelines seem quite vague, i.e., "substantial experience as a practitioner or educator," and "active participation in professional, educational, and service organizations . . ." (user's guide). Does simply being a current member of ALA make one eligible for inclusion? Terms of eligibility were printed on the questionnaire: "Active members of the library profession, archivists or information scientists associated with all types of libraries in the United States and Canada." The term "active members" is somewhat hard to define, and this reviewer is under the impression that all librarians that received professional education (and the questionnaire) are included. This, of course, is fine, and the directory for all practical purposes serves as a "finding list."

In spite of the questionable selection criteria, lack of coverage of the information industry, and hefty price ($150), this biographical directory will offer some assistance to librarians in making connections with others in the profession.

Essentially, this work, in spite of the more current imprint, is not that different from the fifth edition of *A Biographical Directory of Librarians in the United States and Canada* edited by Lee Ash (Chicago, American Library Association, 1970. 1250p. o.p.) that lists some twenty thousand librarians, archivists, and information specialists in both countries. [R: RQ, Fall 82, pp. 99-100; WLB, Sept 82, pp. 77-78]

Ann L. Hartman and Bohdan S. Wynar

PUBLISHERS, BOOKSELLERS, AND PRINTERS

354. Franklin, Benjamin V., ed. **Boston Printers, Publishers, and Booksellers: 1640-1800**. Boston, G. K. Hall, 1980. 545p. illus. index. o.p. LC 80-17693. ISBN 0-8161-8472-0.

Every person known to have appeared in a Boston or Cambridge, Massachusetts imprint during the first 160 years of printing and publishing in that most important North American center receives an entry in this excellent biographical dictionary. The biographies are arranged alphabetically by name. Each entry contains the subjects' dates, when they worked as printer or publisher, names of major authors or works published, partnerships, and other important characteristics about their businesses. References to histories of printing containing information about the subjects are given in many cases.

Thirty experts contributed signed articles on the more important printers and publishers, and some of these are quite lengthy. Entries for minor figures are usually very brief and have been contributed by the editor. All of the entries are useful and accurate and seem to have been thoroughly researched. Cross-references link significant partnerships and provide guides to variant spellings of names. There are two useful indexes to the work: a name index and a title index. The book is in a serviceable binding, and it is illustrated with facsimile signatures and title pages, and portraits.

Dean H. Keller

355. Hudak, Leona M. **Early American Women Printers and Publishers, 1639-1820**. Metuchen, N.J., Scarecrow, 1978. 813p. illus. bibliog. index. $40.00. LC 78-825. ISBN 0-8108-1119-7.

As a feminist librarian, Hudak has been motivated to chronologically narrate the lives of twenty-five American women printer-publishers during the Colonial period. These sketches are accompanied by fairly extensive notes on primary source material, and an enumerative bibliography of each woman's imprints is appended along with a register of library holdings. As a source book for the potential reinterpretation of these women's roles, it is a good idea. However, the work would have been more successful had an adequate definition of its scope, periodization, and selection process been provided. For example, "American" apparently means the original thirteen colonies; however, Vermont, New Hampshire, and Delaware are not represented, while Tennessee and even Nova Scotia (Elizabeth Bushell) are. No indication of the author's choice of beginning or ending dates is given (the two dates in the title represent her first and last selections). As for the selections, nowhere does the author directly address why she selected these particular women. It seems to be because other writers have written about them (she does include an appendix of forty-five lesser-studied women), but this fact may weaken her arguments about the women's movement as discussed in the preface and conclusion.

By far the most interesting and important section is the conclusion. Unfortunately, Hudak deals only summarily with the more significant points of how women became printers (overwhelming majority by the death of their printer husbands), the type of publications produced (newspapers), the quality of press production (decidedly poor), and the financial aspects of printing (decidedly poor). With less depth and more breadth, Marjorie Barlow's *Notes on Women Printers in Colonial America and the United States, 1639-1975* (New York, Hiroswitha Club, 1976) seems to be a more successful effort and is almost one-half the price. In conclusion, many users would probably prefer a more scholarly contribution to historical bibliography rather than Hudak's work, which more nearly fits the genre of "see — women did it, too," though, no doubt, this work will be of serviceable utility until someone else sees fit to undertake the former task. [R: LJ, 1 Dec 78, p. 2407]   John V. Richardson, Jr.

14 Literature

Introduction

The material in this chapter is arranged under four sections with several subdivisions. The first section, "General Works," is divided into current and retrospective biographies. It contains twenty-two entries with numerous references to related works in the annotations. One of the best-known works is Gale's *Contemporary Authors* (see entry 356) that covers not only literature, but journalism, motion pictures, and many other areas. It serves as a basic set for a number of companion volumes, such as *New Revision Series* (see entry 357), and *Something about the Author* (see entry 389). Among retrospective sources one should mention Gale's *Dictionary of Literary Biography* (see entry 362), and the well-edited Wilson series, e.g., *European Authors* (see entry 365), *Twentieth Century Authors* (see entries 367-68), and *World Authors* (see entries 373-74).

The second section, "Specific Genres," is subdivided into "Fiction," "Literary Criticism," "Poetry," and "Science Fiction, Fantasy, and Horror," with a total of eleven entries. It contains a number of St. Martin's publications, such as *Contemporary Novelists* (see entry 378), as well as outstanding works produced by Scribner's, e.g., *Supernatural Fiction Writers* (see entry 384) and *Science Fiction Writers* (see entry 386).

The third section, "Children's and Young Adults' Literature," consists of twelve entries, among them a comprehensive annotation of five volumes of Wilson's *Junior Book of Authors* (see entries 392-96) and outstanding works such as *Twentieth-Century Children's Writers* (see entry 397).

The last section, "National Literatures," is subdivided by nationality and includes sixty-six entries with an additional several hundred titles mentioned or discussed in the annotations. The largest groups are "American Literature" (thirty-eight entries) and "British Literature" (sixteen entries). This section includes a number of outstanding biographical sources such as Scribner's *American Writers* (see entry 406), *Encyclopedia of Frontier and Western Fiction* (see entry 429), Ungar's *American Women Writers* (see entries 432-33), Scribner's *British Writers* (see entry 442), Scribner's *Ancient Writers* (see entry 460), Scribner's *European Writers* (see entries 461-63), and many others. A total of 111 entries is included in "Literature" with several hundred related titles discussed or mentioned in the annotations.

In addition to this substantial number of biographical dictionaries, the reader may also consult many subject dictionaries and encyclopedias. Thus, for example, *Cassell's Encyclopedia of World Literature* (3v. Beekman, 1973) may be useful for world coverage. The last two volumes of this set are exclusively devoted to biographies. In addition to personal data each entry provides a bibliography of biographical writings as well as critical comments about literary accomplishments. Essential biographical information is also provided in the *Encyclopedia of World Literature in the 20th Century*, edited by L. G. Klein (4v. Frederick Ungar, 1981-1984), which covers all the major world literature in articles up to fourteen thousand words as well as a number of biographical sketches, e.g., Virginia Woolf (5½ pages), Indian Nobel-Prize-winner Rabindranath Tagore (4½ pages), or William Butler Yeats (6 pages). Biographical articles are followed by critical excerpts and bibliographies, with sources in English, German, French, and Spanish. Briefer biographical information is offered by Pergamon's *A Dictionary of Literature in the English Language from Chaucer to 1940*, edited by R. Myers (2v. Pergamon Press, 1970), and its companion, *A Dictionary of Literature in the English Language from 1940 to 1970* (Pergamon Press, 1978. 519p.). In addition, *Columbia Dictionary of Modern European Literature*, edited by J. A. Bédé (2nd ed. Columbia University Press, 1980. 895p.), presents short biographies of over eighteen hundred European writers. There are also several older dictionaries that still may be useful for biographical information. Thus, for example, *The Reader's Encyclopedia*, by W. R. Benét (Crowell, 1965. 1118p.), offers a number of brief biographies on writers of all periods.

Outstanding foreign sources include the Italian *Dizionario universale delle letteratura contemporanea*, edited by A. Mondadori (5v. Milan, Mondadori, 1959-1963), which covers the period of 1870-1960 and includes many biographical entries. Substantial information is also offered by a Spanish dictionary by F. C. Sainz de Robles, *Ensayo de un diccionario de la literatura* (3rd ed. 3v. Madrid, Aguilar, 1964-1967), containing hundreds of biobibliographical sketches of authors of all periods. Most German dictionaries and encyclopedias offer reliable biographical information, and here, as examples, we can mention only two works. H. W. Eppelsheimer's *Handbuch der Weltliteratur von der Anfängen bis zur Gegenwart* (3rd ed. Frankfurt, Klostermann, 1960. 808p.) covers literature of Europe, as well as other parts of the world. The first edition of this standard work was published in 1937. *Meyers Handbuch über die Literatur—ein Lexikon der Dichter und Schriftsteller aller Literaturen* (2nd ed. Mannheim, Allgemeiner Verlag, 1970. 987p.) covers, in brief biobibliographical sketches, all major and some minor literary figures from all periods and all countries. The first edition of this standard work was published in 1964.

In addition to general works, there are a number of specialized dictionaries, for example, *McGraw-Hill Encyclopedia of World Drama*, edited by Stanley Hochman (2nd ed. 5v. McGraw-Hill, 1984). According to the introduction, its objective is to bring "into focus the accomplishments of the world's major dramatists." Each article about a major dramatist is divided into several sections: factual discussions of the author's life; short synopses of several, if not all, of the plays; and biographical information. In addition to some three hundred articles on major figures, there are almost a thousand briefer biographies on lesser-known authors. McGraw-Hill's biographical coverage far exceeds such one-volume works as, for example, *The Reader's Encyclopedia of World Drama*, edited by Gassner and Quinn (Thomas Y. Crowell, 1969. 1029p.), or

M. Matlaw's *Modern World Drama: An Encyclopedia* (E. P. Dutton, 1972. 960p.). Only the Italian work *Enciclopedia dello spettacolo* (9v. Rome, Casa Ed. Le Maschere, 1954-1962) approaches the biographical coverage of the McGraw-Hill work.

Other specialized dictionaries deal with science fiction, e.g., *The Science Fiction Encyclopedia*, edited by Peter Nicholls (Doubleday, 1979. 672p.), or *The Encyclopedia of Science Fiction and Fantasy*, compiled by D. H. Tuck (3v. Advent, 1974-1982), offering rich biographical information in their subject fields. The reader will find a good listing of other such works in Sheehy and Walford, but unfortunately some annotations are very brief and occasionally may not adequately describe the scope of a given work.

Current biographical information is found in many periodicals, and in this respect, existing indexing services are of primary importance. In addition to such well-known Wilson indexes as, for example, *Humanities Index* (Wilson, 1974-), there are specialized indexes such as *The American Humanities Index* (Whitston, 1975-), *Index to Little Magazines* (Swallow, 1949-), and many others. Several bibliographic guides to literature discuss indexes in some detail, also providing information about current and retrospective bibliographies and other types of reference sources. For example, A. P. Seidel's *Literary Criticism and Authors' Biographies: An Annotated Index* (Scarecrow, 1978. 209p.), provides references contained in collective works, literary histories, works of literary criticism, etc., supplementing R. E. Combs's *Authors: Critical and Biographical References; A Guide to 4,700 Critical and Biographical Passages in Books* (Scarecrow, 1971. 221p.). P. P. Havlice's *Index to Literary Biography* (2v. Scarecrow, 1975) covers fifty biographical reference works and is useful for locating biographical information on approximately sixty-eight thousand authors from antiquity to the present. A supplement to this work was prepared by Havlice in 1983 (2v. Scarecrow, 1983) covering an additional fifty-three thousand authors.

Several general or specialized bibliographic guides provide useful information, such as M. C. Patterson's *Literary Research Guide* (Gale, 1976. 385p.), *MLA International Bibliography of Books and Articles on the Modern Languages and Literatures* (Modern Language Association of America, 1921-), R. D. Altick and A. Wright's *Selective Bibliography for the Study of English and American Literature* (6th ed. Macmillan, 1979), L. Lewis and J. Auchard's *American Literature: A Study and Research Guide* (St. Martin's Press, 1976), A. G. Kennedy and D. B. Sands's *A Concise Bibliography for Students of English* (5th ed. Stanford University Press, 1972. 300p.), V. K. Fenster's *Guide to American Literature* (Libraries Unlimited, 1983. 243p.), and several others.

GENERAL WORKS

Current Biographies

356. Contemporary Authors: A Bio-Bibliographical Guide to Current Writers in Fiction, General Nonfiction, Poetry, Journalism, Drama, Motion Pictures, Television and Other Fields. Detroit, Gale, 1962- . In progress. Frequency and prices vary. LC 62-52046. ISSN 0010-7468. Beginning with volume 101, all new *CA* volumes are numbered singly rather than as 4-volume units. (Vol. 111. 1984. 600p. $82.00. ISBN 0-8103-1911-X.)

This well-known biographical dictionary covers a wide range of subjects, omitting scientific and technical writers. Entries are preponderantly for American writers, although some British and Canadian writers are also included, as well as samplings from other nationalities. The series started in 1962 and has been published semi-annually since 1964. Frequency of publication of individual volumes varies, and during the years a number of by-products developed. Thus, for example, there are a number of revisions, as well as "permanent" volumes. Volumes 9-12, published in 1974, represent a complete revision and consolidation into one alphabet of biographical material which originally appeared in *CA*, volumes 9 and 10, published in 1964, and volumes 11 and 12, published in 1965. In order to achieve this, the editors submitted the sketches to the biographees for revision and updating; if a biographee failed to respond, the editorial staff at Gale updated the sketch using available sources. Checking and sampling of the entries shows that this process was accomplished to a varying degree. A series of "permanent volumes" has also been established (starting in 1975) for biographical sketches of retired and deceased authors. These sketches normally will not require further change. Volume 1 of *Permanent Series* was edited by Clare D. Kinsman, and volume 2 (published in 1978) was edited by Christine Nesso.

For a volume dedicated to preserving biographical information on authors either dead or deemed to be inactive (for whatever reason) to contain notes about biographees' "works in progress" is a bit jarring. Nevertheless, the second and final volume in the *Permanent Series* does contain such entries (e.g., Victor Ernest, and others—even ones with a death date added at the end of an entry!); the attempt to explain this away is inadequate. Perhaps these and similar editorial difficulties, combined with the ongoing revisions of *Contemporary Authors* sketches, convinced Gale to discontinue this series after this volume. Henceforth, the latest revision of a regular *CA* volume will be the authority, and all people originally represented in that volume will be retained there, rather than sorted through in order to produce a spinoff of widely varying quality in the information presented. (But the latter continues to be a problem in an enterprise that depends largely upon authors supplying and/or verifying information on themselves—authorial diffidence and ego being what they are.)

CA also includes cross-references to *Contemporary Literary Criticism*, a companion series to *Contemporary Authors*. With the addition of other companion series, e.g., *Something about the Author*, *New Revision Series* (substitute for *Permanent Series*), etc., a great deal of experience is required to find out where certain names overlap.

Broadening the scope of this familiar reference work seems to be a continuing goal of the editors. In earlier volumes, the editors extended the definitions of "author" to include individuals involved in the communication field (as reflected in the subtitle), but starting with volume 104 (1982), the editors included "authors deceased since 1900 whose works are still of interest to today's reader" (preface). (Prior to this volume, *CA* covered only living writers and authors deceased since 1960.) Although authors such as Leo Tolstoy, Mark Twain, and Virginia Woolf are covered in brief entries in volume 104, future volumes will contain full-length sketches.

Provided in most of the longer entries are personal and professional facts; writings; "sidelights," which can include critical summaries of works and additional biographical information; and citations to biographical and critical sources. Obituary notices are also included for deceased authors who fall within the scope of *CA*. A feature which began in volumes 89-92, an interview with the subject, is continued occasionally. Volume 113 brings the total coverage to over eighty thousand writers and new volumes are now edited by Hal May. Cumulative indexes to the entire series appear in alternate new units, including volume 112. Indeed, *CA* is a substantial biographical source and is widely used by all types of libraries, primarily for information in the area of humanities and literature. Bohdan S. Wynar

357. **Contemporary Authors: A Bio-Bibliographical Guide to Current Writers. New Revision Series**. Linda Metzger, ed. Detroit, Gale, 1981- . In progress. $85.00/vol. LC 62-52046. ISSN 0275-7176.

Gale's *Contemporary Authors* (*CA*) has tried various methods to keep information on its biographees up to date—the *New Revision Series* (*NRS*) is the latest effort. Libraries possessing the entire *CA* set will have three distinct sets of volumes: the basic volumes (volume 114 appeared in 1984); the *First Revision Series* (volumes 41-44 appeared in 1979); and the *CA Permanent Series* (only two volumes were published). The *Permanent Series*, abandoned after two volumes, was established to remove from the regular volumes the biographies of deceased or retired authors. The *First Revision Series* (started in 1975) combined several of the original volumes, listed the biographies in one alphabetical sequence, and offered revisions in various degrees of depth and comprehensiveness. Since not all of the entries included in the *First Revision Series* actually required revision, it became obvious that this was an inefficient and costly system.

The *New Revision Series* relieves Gale of "The need to publish entries with few or no changes," since it includes only entries that require revision. Unlike the *First Revision Series*, *NRS* will not replace single volumes of *CA*; libraries must keep the existing (and ongoing) volumes as well as the *NRS* volumes. The *CA* cumulative index will provide access to both sets. So far there are twelve volumes of the *NRS* in print.

Volume 12 of the Contemporary Authors New Revision series contains updated biographical and bibliographical information on thirty-three authors who had originally been included in previous editions of *Contemporary Authors* volumes. For three of the authors, each of whom died during the last four years (Marshall McLuhan, R. Buckminster Fuller, and Julio Cortazar), the update is final. The others, we can assume, are indeed among the ranks of "today's active authors."

Each volume of the New Revision series provides a handy chart indicating which volumes of *Contemporary Authors* and of the First Revision series can, in fact, be replaced by subsequent volumes.

The entries in the New Revision series do not direct the user to previous volumes in which an author appeared. *CA*'s *Cumulative Index* must be consulted for this information.

All libraries having the original and the First Revision series will find the New Revision series valuable for its current updating of descriptions of authors who continue to be productive. Lawrence Grieco and Bohdan S. Wynar

358. **Contemporary Authors Autobiography Series. Volume 1**. Dedria Bryfonski, ed. Detroit, Gale, 1984. 431p. illus. index. $70.00. ISBN 0-8103-0004-1; ISSN 0748-0636.

This volume marks the beginning of yet another Gale literary series. Each volume in the *Contemporary Authors Autobiography Series* will contain from twenty to thirty autobiographical essays by important contemporary writers. Although volume 1 includes only creative writers, the preface indicates that subsequent volumes will also include writers of nonfiction.

Among the twenty-three authors who contributed autobiographies to this initial volume are Kay Boyle, Erskine Caldwell, Stanislaw Lem, and Irving Wallace. Essays generally range from fifteen to twenty pages in length and are liberally illustrated with informal photographs. The diversity among these contemporary writers is reflected in their sketches, some of which are deeply personal and extremely revealing, while others are matter-of-fact, even detached. Following each essay is a chronological bibliography of the author's works. An index provides entries for all proper names and titles mentioned in the essays.

Obviously, the strength of this series lies in the uniqueness of the information it contains, that is, those insights into the life, ideas, and works of an author which only he or she can provide. For many libraries, the standard biographical sources for writers will continue to be sufficient. However, libraries that support strong research programs in literature will want to consider adding this series. [R: WLB, Dec 84, p. 291]

Marie Ellis

359. Gaster, Adrian, ed. **The International Authors and Writers Who's Who, Ninth Edition**. Cambridge, England, International Biographical Centre; distr., Detroit, Gale, 1982. 1093p. $120.00. ISBN 0-900332-45-X (International Biographical Centre); 0-8103-0426-0 (Gale).

In 1976, Melrose Press Ltd., the publishing house of the International Biographical Centre at Cambridge, England, produced its first edition of *The International Authors and Writers Who's Who*. Since the firm had acquired the editorial rights to *The Authors and Writers Who's Who*, previously compiled and published in six editions by Burke's Peerage Ltd., the International Biographical Centre issued its work as the seventh edition. The title under review is, therefore, the second volume published under the auspices of the Centre, although its title page indicates the "eighth edition" imprint. The title is now distributed in America by Grand River Books, a division of Gale Research Company.

The latest edition is a continuation of the format and selection approach found in the earlier IBC publication. There is clear evidence that the coverage has been expanded significantly: the seventh edition had some ten thousand entries in 676 pages; this work has an estimated fourteen thousand entries in the biographical section. The present editor, Adrian Gaster, does not state the criteria by which individuals are identified and selected for inclusion, as was true of the earlier work. However, "every included biographee was sent a typescript of his or her entry, and though some were not returned to us, every care has been taken to ensure the accuracy of each biography" (foreword). In addition, the editor reports that "we have, as before, omitted a considerable number of authors of the one-off book, pamphleteers and highly technical writers" (foreword).

A sampling of entries in the biographical section reveals a better international balance than that of the eighth edition. Although the United Kingdom and the United States still dominate entries, any given page of ten to thirteen entries has from three to five biographees from other geographical locations. The editors can reasonably claim international scope despite their emphasis on the Western world as opposed to the Far East or the Third World. There is, however, an unexpected degree of coverage of individuals whose major claim to writing fame lies in educational publications.

Inevitably, the unusual activity of the International Biographical Centre, which has, in recent years, issued one biographical directory after another, raises questions regarding selectivity and/or vanity press connotations. Although inclusion in their publications is *not* tied to purchase of the volume, the Centre does offer considerable inducement to prospective biographees in the form of pre-publication discounts, luxury editions, special certificates, and international "conference" invitations. The number and overlapping coverage of their tools also suggest a lack of basic selection criteria or valid publication role. As a result, a publication such as this one, which does have legitimate value in terms of its expanded and updated coverage, may well be rejected along with other titles which, when viewed collectively, appear undistinguished and inappropriate for any reference collection whose librarian must allocate his or her budget carefully. [R: BL, 15 Nov 78, p. 574] Laurel Grotzinger

360. Seymour-Smith, Martin. **Who's Who in Twentieth Century Literature**. New York, Holt, Rinehart and Winston, 1976. 414p. index. o.p. LC 75-21470. ISBN 0-03-013926-0.

Approximately seven hundred poets, dramatists, novelists, biographers, essayists, and philosophers are included in this comprehensive guide to twentieth-century writers. Arranged alphabetically by author, the selections are consciously "biased towards British and American authors" but also include "major foreign authors" and "some less-well-known writers" felt by Seymour-Smith to "have been undeservedly neglected." Writers of children's literature and authors of detective stories are excluded.

The focus is primarily literary. Sigmund Freud, for example, is included because of "his influence on literature"; this is "not the place to discuss his theories." Mark Twain is listed as "a nineteenth-century figure who need be mentioned here only to draw attention to his importance to modern literature."

The inadequacy of the two-page index, the only unsatisfactory aspect of this highly praiseworthy reference guide, is partially overcome by numerous cross-references in the text itself.

Although most of the selections follow the same format (professional status, biographical details, intellectual achievements, critical analysis, major themes, important influences and selected bibliography), these entries are by no means dull compendia of facts. By isolating, defining, and analyzing each author's universe and scope, whether it be the regionalism of John Steinbeck or the "electronic media" of Marshall McLuhan, by presenting varied critical opinions, tracing the writer's development, explaining significant movements, and summarizing key ideas, Seymour-Smith successfully appeals to a general audience as well as to students of literature. [R: BL, 15 Sept 76, p. 205; Choice, Oct 76, p. 962] Colby H. Kullman

361. **World Authors 1975-1980**. Vineta Colby, ed. New York, H. W. Wilson, 1985. 829p. illus. (Wilson Authors Series). $65.00. LC 85-10045. ISBN 0-8242-0715-7.

Three hundred and seventy writers are included in this volume of the Wilson Authors series. The authors included are from many fields—literary writers, scientists, historians, and biographers to name a few. One criterion for inclusion was that the authors would have come to prominence during the 1975-1980 time period. In many instances the authors themselves contributed autobiographical sketches that provide additional insight to their body of work.

A typical entry includes a photograph, basic biographical information, a critique by an expert, and statement by the author (in one-third of the entries). Recommended for most reference collections in academic libraries.　　Jennifer Cargill

Retrospective Biographies

362. **Dictionary of Literary Biography**. Matthew J. Bruccoli, ed. director. Detroit, Gale, 1978- . In progress. $85.00/vol.

The *Dictionary of Literary Biography*, started in 1978, is a multi-volume series designed to fill a significant gap in literary biographical scholarship. Each volume in the DLB series focuses on a specific period or literary movement. It is projected that the entire series, when completed, will ultimately encompass all authors who made significant contributions to literature in the United States, Canada, England, and other countries. Individual volumes are edited by recognized scholars with contributions by subject specialists.

Each volume follows a similar format. Major biographical-critical essays are presented for the most important figures of each era. Each of these master essays includes a career chronology, list of publications, and a bibliography of works by and about the subject for easy reference. The main portion of each essay is a chronologically arranged personal and career summary with discussions of all major works. Entries for lesser figures deal with each subject's life, work, and critical reputation, all chronologically arranged in one section. All entries are arranged in a single alphabetic sequence.

Most of these volumes are reviewed separately in this work by our subject specialists. Here we are reproducing a list of available volumes in print:

Vol. 1—**The American Renaissance in New England**. Edited by Joel Myerson. 1978. 224p. LC 77-82803. ISBN 0-8103-0913-0.

Vol. 2—**American Novelists since World War II**. Edited by Jeffrey Helterman and Richard Layman. 1978. 557p. LC 77-82804. ISBN 0-8103-0914-9.

Vol. 3—**Antebellum Writers in New York and the South**. Edited by Joel Myerson. 1979. 383p. LC 79-15481. ISBN 0-8103-0915-7.

Vol. 4—**American Writers in Paris, 1920-1939**. Edited by Karen Lane Rood. 1980. 254p. LC 79-26101. ISBN 0-8103-0916-5.

Vol. 5—**American Poets since World War II**. Edited by Donald J. Greiner. 1980. 2v. $170.00/set. ISBN 0-8103-0924-6.

Vol. 6—**American Novelists since World War II**. Second Series. Edited by James E. Kibler, Jr. 1980. 404p. ISBN 0-8103-0908-4.

Vol. 7—**Twentieth-Century American Dramatists**. Edited by John MacNicholas. 1981. 2v. $170.00/set. ISBN 0-8103-0928-9.

Vol. 8—**Twentieth-Century American Science Fiction Writers**. Edited by David Cowart and Thomas Wymer. 1981. 2v. $170.00/set. ISBN 0-8103-0918-1.

Vol. 9—**American Novelists, 1910-1945**. Edited by James J. Martine. 1981. 3v. $255.00/set. ISBN 0-8103-0931-9.

Vol. 10—**Modern British Dramatists, 1900-1945**. Edited by Stanley Weintraub. 1982. 2v. $170.00/set. ISBN 0-8103-0937-8.

Vol. 11—**American Humorists, 1800-1950**. Edited by Stanley Trachtenberg. 1982. 2v. $170.00/set. ISBN 0-8103-1147-X.

Vol. 12—**American Realists and Naturalists**. Edited by Earl Harbert and Donald Pizer. 1982. 486p. ISBN 0-8103-1149-6.

Vol. 13—**British Dramatists since World War II**. Edited by Stanley Weintraub. 1983. 2v. $170.00/set. ISBN 0-8103-0936-X.

Vol. 14—**British Novelists since 1960**. Edited by Jay L. Halio. 1983. 2v. $170.00/set. ISBN 0-8103-0927-0.

Vol. 15—**British Novelists, 1930-1959**. Edited by Bernard Oldsey. 1983. 2v. $170.00/set. ISBN 0-8103-1637-4.

Vol. 16—**The Beats: Literary Bohemians in Postwar America**. Edited by Ann Charters. 1983. 2v. $170.00/set. ISBN 0-8103-1148-8.

Vol. 17—**Twentieth-Century American Historians**. Edited by Clyde N. Wilson. 1983. 519p. ISBN 0-8103-1144-5.

Vol. 18—**Victorian Novelists after 1885**. Edited by Ira B. Nadel and William E. Fredeman. 1983. 392p. ISBN 0-8103-1143-7.

Vol. 19—**British Poets, 1880-1914**. Edited by Donald E. Stanford. 1983. 486p. ISBN 0-8103-1700-1.

Vol. 20—**British Poets, 1914-1945**. Edited by Donald E. Stanford. 1983. 431p. ISBN 0-8103-1702-8.

Vol. 21—**Victorian Novelists before 1885**. Edited by Ira B. Nadel and William E. Fredeman. 1983. 417p. ISBN 0-8103-1701-X.

Vol. 22—**American Writers for Children, 1900-1960**. Edited by John Cech. 1983. 412p. ISBN 0-8103-1146-1.

Vol. 23—**American Newspaper Journalists, 1873-1900**. Edited by Perry J. Ashley. 1983. 392p. ISBN 0-8103-1145-3.

Vol. 24—**American Colonial Writers, 1606-1734**. Edited by Emory Elliott. 1984. 415p. ISBN 0-8103-1703-6.

Vol. 25—**American Newspaper Journalists, 1901-1925**. Edited by Perry J. Ashley. 1984. 385p. ISBN 0-8103-1704-4.

Vol. 26—**American Screenwriters**. Edited by Robert E. Morsberger, Stephen O. Lesser, and Randall Clark. 1984. 388p. ISBN 0-8103-0917-3.

Vol. 27—**Poets of Great Britain and Ireland, 1945-1960**. Edited by Vincent B. Sherry Jr. 1984. 393p. ISBN 0-8103-1705-2.

Vol. 28—**Twentieth-Century American Jewish Fiction Writers**. Edited by Daniel Walden. 1984. 367p. ISBN 0-8103-1706-0.

Vol. 29—**American Newspaper Journalists, 1926-1950**. Edited by Perry J. Ashley. 1984. 410p. ISBN 0-8103-1707-9.

Vol. 30—**American Historians, 1607-1865**. Edited by Clyde N. Wilson. 1984. 382p. ISBN 0-8103-1708-7.

Vol. 31—**American Colonial Writers, 1735-1781**. Edited by Emory Elliott. 1984. 421p. ISBN 0-8103-1709-5.

Vol. 32—**Victorian Poets before 1850**. Edited by Ira B. Nadel and William E. Fredeman. 1984. 417p. ISBN 0-8103-1710-9.

Vol. 33—**Afro-American Fiction Writers after 1955**. Edited by Trudier Harris and Thadious Davis. 1984. 350p. ISBN 0-8103-1711-7.

Vol. 34—**British Novelists, 1890-1929: Traditionalists**. Edited by Thomas F. Staley. 1985. 378p. ISBN 0-8103-1712-5.

Vol. 35—**Victorian Poets after 1850**. Edited by William E. Fredeman and Ira B. Nadel. 1985. 437p. ISBN 0-8103-1713-3.

Vol. 36—**British Novelists, 1890-1929: Modernists**. Edited by Thomas F. Staley. 1985. 387p. ISBN 0-8103-1714-1.

Vol. 37—**American Writers of the Early Republic**. Edited by Emory Elliott. 1985. 374p. ISBN 0-8103-1715-X.

Vol. 38—**Afro-American Writers after 1955: Dramatists and Prose Writers**. Edited by Thadious M. Davis and Trudier Harris. 1985. 390p. ISBN 0-8103-1716-8.

Vol. 39—**British Novelists, 1660-1880**. Edited by Martin C. Battestin. 1985. 350p. ISBN 0-8103-1717-6.

Bohdan S. Wynar

363.   **Dictionary of Literary Biography Documentary Series: An Illustrated Chronicle**. Margaret A. Van Antwerp, ed. Detroit, Gale, 1982- . In progress. (A Bruccoli Clark Book). $92.00/vol. LC 82-1105.

Designed to complement the biographies in other volumes of the *Dictionary of Literary Biography*, each volume in the *Documentary Series* includes selected photographs, manuscript facsimiles, letters, notebooks, interviews, and contemporary reviews of major books for a few authors of prominence. Volume 1 covers Sherwood Anderson, Willa Cather, John Dos Passos, Theodore Dreiser, F. Scott Fitzgerald, Ernest Hemingway, and Sinclair Lewis. Revealing glimpses of authors' perceptions and contemporary critical opinions abound. For this reviewer, Willa Cather's comments on her research for *Death Comes for the Archbishop* and her angry denunciation of those who would make literature subservient to propaganda were particularly rich in human interest.

Scholars and doctoral students will need to go far beyond the samples here, but undergraduates writing term papers and faculty preparing lectures for survey courses will find much of value. So, of course, will reference librarians seeking to help these clients. Each selection on a given author begins with a cross-reference to the appropriate biographical volumes of *DLB* and a short bibliography. Contributors are identified in the "acknowledgments" section.

The second volume makes readily available contemporary evidence concerning the works of seven authors: James Gould Cozzens, James T. Farrell, William Faulkner, John O'Hara, John Steinbeck, Thomas Wolfe, and Richard Wright.

With volume 3, the focus becomes more contemporary. Of the six representative and influential post-World War II writers chosen, five have had long and distinguished careers. Saul Bellow, winner of the Nobel Prize for Literature in 1976, published his first novel in 1944; Norman Mailer began in 1948 with *The Naked and the Dead*; John Updike's first short story appeared in 1954; and Kurt Vonnegut's debut as a novelist was in 1952. Vladimir Nabokov was a special case: writing novels in Russian in the 1920s, first publishing in English in 1941, and dazzling critics until his death in 1977. The remaining figure in the volume, Jack Kerouac, was essentially limited to the Beat Movement of the 1950s. There are, of course, other significant postwar writers who could have been included in this volume, e.g., Baldwin, Capote, Cheever, or Malamud; but these six form a splendidly diverse, and eclectic, group.

Unlike the previous three volumes in this series, volume 4 (published in 1984) focuses exclusively on one writer: Tennessee Williams. It is intended as a concise illustrated biography, presenting in chronological order documents that illustrate specific events in the author's literary and personal life, i.e., diverse "materials that have heretofore been accessible to a limited group of researchers." However, most of the materials reprinted here are readily available to scholars. Many reviews of the plays, novels, and poems are taken from major New York papers; most of the interviews (eighteen) are also available in other published sources. Three brief interviews are printed for the first time, but add little to our understanding of the man or his work. Of eleven reprinted letters, four are from the published Williams/Donald Windham correspondence, and all but three of the remainder are from newspapers or other published collections. Most disappointing is the lack of examples showing corrected manuscript copy.

The hundreds of illustrations (photographs, dust jackets, playbills) are of interest. However, the reduction of some of the printed illustrations makes them difficult to read.

The volume does not make an important contribution to Williams scholarship and, like the author's *Memoirs*, concentrates too much on biographical information and not enough on the plays. However, there is more emphasis here on the plays than there is in *Memoirs*. Smaller libraries with limited newspaper and periodical holdings will make good use of this collection of documents. Students of Williams will continue to start with Dreway W. Gunn's *Tennessee Williams: A Bibliography*. [R: Choice, Dec 82, p. 554; Choice, May 83, p. 1263; Choice, July-Aug 83, p. 1593; LJ, 15 Sept 82, p. 1744; LJ, 1 Mar 83, p. 489; WLB, Oct 82, pp. 171-72]

Milton H. Crouch and A. Robert Rogers

364. **Dictionary of Literary Biography Yearbook 1980-** . Karen L. Rood, Jean W. Ross, and Richard Ziegfeld, eds. Detroit, Gale, 1981- . In progress. $92.00/vol. LC 81-4188.

The purpose of these yearbooks, which began in 1980, is to update and supplement entries in the various sets of volumes that comprise the *Dictionary of Literary Biography* (1978-). The first section consists of updated entries, which give specific references to the originals and begin where they concluded. New works by living authors as well as new criticism of deceased authors may result in updates. The second section consists of new entries (authors not previously included). Each new entry typically begins with a bibliography of major works by the author, continues with a biographical and critical segment, and concludes with a brief bibliography of other relevant works. A typical entry is signed, runs to five or six pages, and includes both a photograph of the author and a reproduction from a manuscript or typescript.

So far published are: *Dictionary of Literary Biography Yearbook: 1980* (334p. ISBN 0-8103-1600-5); *1981* (312p. ISBN 0-8103-1625-0); *1982* (416p. ISBN 0-8103-1626-9); and *1983* (355p. ISBN 0-8103-1627-7).

Libraries which have purchased other volumes of the *Dictionary of Literary Biography* and found them useful will probably wish to update by means of the yearbooks. Others may wish to consider whether potential duplication with other sources may make the high prices too great a disadvantage. [R: Choice, May 82, p. 1214; LJ, 1 Apr 82, p. 719; WLB, Mar 82, p. 542] A. Robert Rogers

365. **European Authors 1000-1900. A Biographical Dictionary of European Literature**. Edited by Stanley J. Kunitz and Vineta Colby. New York, H. W. Wilson, 1967. 1016p. $40.00. LC 67-13870. ISBN 0-8242-0013-6.

Another volume in Wilson's well-known author series, this book provides 967 biographical sketches of the most influential literature figures, poets, philosophers, humanists, and others from thirty-one different literatures. Biographies concentrate on lives and accomplishments of their subjects and incorporate lists of their books translated into English with dates of original publication, and critical and biographical sources. Portraits of some three hundred individuals are appended. It should be noted that Wilson also published *Index to the Wilson Authors Series* (New York, H. W. Wilson, 1976. 72p. $7.00. LC 76-20444. ISBN 0-8242-0609-6) that assists the reader in searching through several volumes of the series to find a biography of an author whose nationality or dates may not be known. It provides access to some seventy-five hundred sketches (excluding *World Authors 1970-1975*) with cross-references to variant forms of authors' names. Bohdan S. Wynar

366. Todd, Janet, ed. **A Dictionary of British and American Women Writers 1660-1800**. Totowa, N.J., Rowman & Allanheld, 1985. 344p. index. $45.00. LC 84-2123. ISBN 0-8476-7125-9.

Here is a must-have reference for academic libraries. In it are well-written biographies of women who wrote between 1660 and 1800. Unpublished writers appear alongside those published, as women who feared social sanctions often put pen to paper but never released their work for public consumption. Playwrights, poets, essayists, translators, even letterwriters (such as Abigail Adams) join profiles of novelists in the *Dictionary*. Todd and her contributors are impressive in their careful research—they identify and provide cross-references to authors with multiple pseudonyms, and eliminate men who used feminine pen names to sell romantic novels. Bibliographical references are written into the sketches, and an alphabetical index completes the volume. Diane J. Cimbala

367. **Twentieth Century Authors: A Biographical Dictionary of Modern Literature**. Edited by Stanley J. Kunitz and Howard Haycraft. New York, H. W. Wilson, 1942. 1577p. $52.00. LC 43-51003. ISBN 0-8242-0049-7.

368. **Twentieth Century Authors: A Biographical Dictionary of Modern Literature. First Supplement**. Edited by Stanley J. Kunitz. New York, H. W. Wilson, 1955. 1223p. $43.00. LC 43-51003. ISBN 0-8242-0050-0.

The main volume of this well-known "author series" covers 1,850 authors from around the world whose work has been published in English and who flourished from 1900 to 1942. Each profile covers the author's life and artistic accomplishments, and includes lists of principal works and biographical and critical sources for each biographee. Portraits accompany seventeen hundred of the sketches.

The supplement provides updated biographical and bibliographic information on most of the authors covered in *Twentieth Century Authors*, as well as approximately seven hundred sketches of writers who became prominent between 1942 and 1955. Portraits accompany 670 of the sketches, and lists of the authors' works and of biographical and critical works written about them complement each entry.

Bohdan S. Wynar

369. Vinson, James, ed. **Dramatists**. D. L. Kirkpatrick, associate ed. New York, St. Martin's Press, 1979. 648p. (Great Writers of the English Language). $50.00. LC 78-78303. ISBN 0-312-34570-4.

370. Vinson, James, ed. **Novelists and Prose Writers**. D. L. Kirkpatrick, associate ed. New York, St. Martin's Press, 1979. 1367p. (Great Writers of the English Language). $55.00. LC 78-78302. ISBN 0-312-34624-7.

371. Vinson, James, ed. **Poets**. D. L. Kirkpatrick, associate ed. New York, St. Martin's Press, 1979. 1141p. (Great Writers of the English Language). $55.00. LC 78-78299. ISBN 0-312-34640-9.

"The selection of writers included . . . is based on the recommendations of the advisers listed on page ix." This is the only statement of criteria for this series, and it appears in each volume. It is as disconcerting here as it was in St. Martin's Contemporary Writers series. But as in the earlier series, the boards of advisers for these volumes are composed of figures with a stature conducive to such recommendations — F. W. Bateson, Roy Harvey Pearce, Walter Allen, et al.

The scope is international, and the alphabetized lists include representatives of a great many English-writing cultures. The format is much like that of Contemporary Writers. For each of the authors (about five hundred novelists, an equal number of poets, and about 130 dramatists), the series provides a capsule biography, a more or less complete bibliography, a brief list of major critical works, and an evaluative essay. Approximately two hundred contributors to *Novelists* and *Poets* (fewer than one hundred for *Dramatists*) more often than not provide perceptive, well-informed evaluations of their subjects, although occasionally this is simply prorogation of critical dispute. Still, while rarely over two pages long, the essays approach the major aspects of the author's life and works — the issues and the style.

Dispute will arise about the names included in the lists of the great, but writers like Edgar Rice Burroughs, Monk Lewis, and Earl Stanley Gardner are at least significant figures in the development of literary genres, as is Ogden Nash. Even Paddy Chayefsky must be considered a significant representative of the unavoidable attempt of popular culture to equate the audiences of drama, film, and television. Others included here may be harder to defend.

Likely, dispute over omissions will center upon contemporary figures. Perhaps excluding John Gardner is at this time as fashionable as including Thomas Pynchon, but some writers not appearing here were treated in the earlier series, and some judgments require a little distance. More troubling is the omission of figures like

William James and John Dewey; in fact, one wonders why the *Novelists and Prose Writers* volume was not simply limited to fiction writers. Still, the contributors seem to have defended well the advisers' recommendations; perhaps their omissions are also justifiable. [R: BL, 1 Sept 80, p. 68; Choice, Mar 80, p. 50; LJ, 15 Jan 80, p. 188]

F. W. Ramey

372.   Vinson, James, and Daniel Kirkpatrick, eds. **Great Foreign Language Writers**. New York, St. Martin's Press, 1984. 714p. index. $39.95; $25.00pa. LC 83-40552. ISBN 0-312-34585-2.

This book provides information about 253 foreign-language authors, ranging from Arthur Adamov to Émile Zola and from Homer to Octavio Paz. Among the 253 are fifteen anonymous works or works of unknown authorship such as the Bible and the *Romance of the Rose*.

For each author there is a brief listing of standard biographical information, a list of separately published books, a standard bibliography, a selected list of critical works, and a brief evaluative essay. There is little to be found here that is not already available in a general encyclopedia or a biographical dictionary. The list of critical studies could be helpful for the study of some of the lesser-known writers, but it is very limited, usually including only book-length studies, in English, since about 1960. The critical essays were written by individual contributors and vary considerably in quality. All of them, however, are only introductory; none is longer than two pages, and many are less than one.

As a handy gathering-together of rather obvious data on these writers, this book is useful. High school students will no doubt find it a ready starting point. It will not, however, provide them with much they could not find elsewhere in their school's library.

Philip R. Rider

373.   Wakeman, John, ed. **World Authors 1950-1970: A Companion Volume to Twentieth Century Authors**. Ed. consultant, Stanley J. Kunitz. New York, H. W. Wilson, 1975. 1594p. illus. $75.00. LC 75-172140. ISBN 0-8242-0419-0.

This new addition to the Wilson Company's well-known author series is called a "companion" rather than a supplement to *Twentieth Century Authors* because the writers treated in the latter are not carried over to the new volumes. *World Authors* is concerned with writers who have come to prominence in the twenty-year period of 1950 to 1970. To be precise, this statement must be amended to read "writers who have come to the prominent attention of the English-speaking world." The book does include creators of literature writing in languages other than English, but it considers them only to the extent that their works have been translated into English or evaluated by English-speaking critics. A writer of the importance of the Swiss dramatist Friedrich Dürrenmatt is presented only as he has been perceived by English and American critics. The great bulk of the significant criticism on Dürrenmatt is in German and appears in German, Austrian, and Swiss scholarly journals. With this considerable critical literature, *World Authors* is not concerned.

This is not intended as criticism but merely as a means of defining the scope and purpose of the book. *World Authors*, like its predecessor volumes, is a popular, not a scholarly, reference work, but as such it fulfills its purpose reasonably well. Each entry follows a standard pattern: names, dates, brief biography (usually containing a quote from the writer), and then typically two to three columns that are mixtures of biography and criticism. Also included is a list of principal works, or, for non-English writers, "principal published works in English translation." The citations are brief, consisting of titles and dates only.

Lastly, there is an "About" section consisting of a few biographical and critical references. It is this last section that is the weakest element in the book. Even confining them to English-language citations, Mr. Wakeman could and should have provided fuller bibliographies for all his writers—but especially for non-English language writers on whom English criticism is relatively more difficult to locate. What he offers is not sufficient to meet the needs of the serious, though non-scholarly, student of modern Continental literature. [R: Choice, Dec 75, p. 1294; LJ, July 75, p. 1308; RQ, Fall 75, p. 83; WLB, Oct 75, pp. 117-18]　　　　　Richard A. Gray

374.　Wakeman, John, ed. **World Authors, 1970-1975**. Stanley J. Kunitz, ed. consultant. New York, H. W. Wilson, 1980. 894p. illus. (Wilson Authors Series). $52.00. LC 79-21847. ISBN 0-8242-0641-X.

As the latest book in the Wilson Authors series, which began with Kunitz and Haycraft's *British Authors of the Nineteenth Century* (1936) and includes, among other titles, *Twentieth Century Authors* (1942) and its supplement, and *World Authors 1950-1970*, this publication does not update biographies of authors dealt with elsewhere in the series, but is called a "companion" (rather than a supplement) to the preceding volumes. Based on the general selection of subjects included in the volume, the general policies of the series were followed in that the 348 authors biographically described are considered "imaginative" writers—poets, novelists, dramatists—of literary importance and/or of exceptional popularity. A number of philosophers, historians, biographers, critics, scientists, journalists, and others whose work seemed of "sufficiently wide interest, influence, or literary merit" are also included. The majority of these 348 writers came to prominence between 1970 and 1975. Several authors omitted from previous volumes in the series "because of lack of biographical information, or because their work was not familiar to readers of English" are also included. The editor of this work no longer considers this a very significant criterion, "thanks to the vast increase in translations from all languages."

Approximately one-fifth of the authors included have provided autobiographical articles which are reproduced without alteration, except those that have been translated from foreign languages. Included with some autobiographical material, the author provides a "philosophy" of writing, e.g., Erica Jong describes herself as "self-mythologying" rather than a "confessional" writer. The text includes very brief synopses of an author's major works, with excerpts from a variety of critical reviews for most works. These are well written, scholarly, and literary. The editorial notes were written by specialists in the literature concerned, and checked and updated by independent researchers. Critical comment is fuller than in the earlier volumes in the series, a condition of *World Authors 1950-1970*, but the editor states that this is not "an independent appraisal but . . . a fair summation of representative critical response."

The lists of principal works are intended to include all of the author's published books in English, with dates of first publication. The lists of writings about authors and their work are selective. In the text, foreign titles are followed by an English version of the title and a date in parentheses. Each entry includes name ("see" references are provided for pseudonyms), dates, brief biography with a possible quote from the writer, followed by a mixture of biography and criticism, each covering two to four pages per author, and in some cases a black-and-white photographic headshot of the author is included. A key to pronunciation is provided. Authors are listed alphabetically by last name. The book is not indexed. Some works published after 1975 are included. A title index would expand the usefulness of this book to the stated intended audience, that of "students and common readers." [R: Choice, Sept 80, p. 72; LJ, 1 May 80, p. 1071; RQ, Summer 80, pp. 400-401; WLB, May 80, pp. 592-93] Donald D. Foos

375. **Who Was Who among English and European Authors 1931-1949**. Detroit, Gale, 1978. 3v. (Gale Composite Biographical Dictionary Series, No. 2; An Omnigraphics Book). $185.00/set. LC 77-280. ISBN 0-8103-0040-7.

Much like the companion set to these volumes, *Who Was Who among North American Authors 1921-1939*, these works claim great scope both geographically and temporally. The coverage provided certainly does include the obscure, but it usually fails to include the famous and does so spottily, if at all. Therefore, one has every reason to question the information provided on the obscure, and precious little reason to waste nearly $200 on this set. Entries, some twenty-three thousand of them, contain—if complete—name, education, marriage, memberships, religion, works published, mailing address (as of some time ago). Entries represent the last entry in either the *Author's and Writer's Who's Who and Reference Guide* (1934-1949) or *Who's Who among Living Authors of Older Nations* (1931). No attempt was made to collate entries; evidently, cut-and-paste was the editorial method employed.

Thomas Mann, W. H. Auden, and T. S. Eliot have biographies of four lines, six lines, and seven lines, respectively. Mann's omits his Nobel Prize, lists his obscure works, and notes his residence in California (1940s). On the other hand, Samuel Guy Inman of Trinity, Texas has found his way into this book, although his biography fails to indicate that he ever crossed the Atlantic. And Edward Keble Chatterton receives forty-five lines, limning his career for all time. But Herman Hesse didn't get in at all. [R: Choice, Dec 78, p. 1354; LJ, 1 Mar 79, p. 620] Koert C. Loomis, Jr.

376. **Who Was Who in Literature, 1906-1934**. Detroit, Gale, 1979. 2v. (Gale Composite Biographical Dictionary Series, No. 5; An Omnigraphics Book). $170.00/ set. LC 78-25583. ISBN 0-8103-0402-3.

Part of the Composite Biographical Dictionary series, *Who Was Who in Literature, 1906-1934* employs the same format and editorial approach as the other volumes although it is based on different sources. The editors (usually) extracted the last sketch appearing in the *Literary Yearbook*, *Literary Yearbook and Author's Who's Who*, and/or *Who's Who in Literature*. Although they note that the 1923 edition of *Literary Yearbook* was not used, no reason is given for not doing so. "Substantially all" of the entries in the original volumes are said to have been included herein, but who was omitted (and on what basis) is never discussed in the one-page foreword.

Claim is laid to the set's being valuable for providing "life details" on some 10,400 writers; the claim does not hold up under even the most cursory examination. The reviewer cannot call complete entries that supply only a birth year (perhaps), a career summary (if present at all, usually less than five words), a list of titles of works produced (without claim of comprehensive coverage), and a (usually incomplete) home address (e.g., Entebbe, Uganda, or Winnipeg, Canada, although London addresses are usually more precise). For "life details," one might expect to see a date of birth (not just year); parentage and place of birth; educational history; family information (marriage, children); career summary of some depth (rather than the usual "author of . . ." or "editor of . . . ," followed by a list of titles); awards; honors; etc. Such items appear so infrequently as to cause surprise when they do. As for completeness of title listings,

E. M. Forster's entry does not list either *A Passage to India* (1924) or *Aspects of the Novel* (1927), two of his three major works and both well within the time span encompassed in these volumes.

It could be said that the fault lay in the original series, but that argument does not hold for long. The editors here simply took the last entry for each person represented in the series and made no attempt to combine information from all of the volumes into a truly comprehensive sketch of the subject. Cut-and-paste (the method used to assemble the text, as attested to by the variety of typefaces on any page) precluded that approach. [R: LJ, July 79, p. 1443]   Koert C. Loomis, Jr.

377.   Wilson, Katharina M., ed. **Medieval Women Writers**. Athens, Ga., University of Georgia Press, 1984. 366p. $30.00; $12.50pa. LC 82-13380. ISBN 0-8203-0640-1; 0-8203-0641-Xpa.

Researching women writers from the Middle Ages is no simple task. However, with the publication of this critical anthology, and a few scattered articles and similar anthologies, women writers from the Middle Ages are becoming more accessible to the interested student and scholar. This volume covers fifteen women writers from seven centuries and many nationalities. The writers included are Dhuoda, Hrotsvit of Gandersheim, Marie de France, Heloise, Hildegard of Bingen, Castelloza, Mechthild of Magdeburg, Hadewijch, Marguerite Porete, Saint Bridget, Saint Catherine of Siena, Julian of Norwich, Margery Kempe, Florencia Pinar, and Christine de Pizan. The editor, Katharina Wilson, provides the historical context from which the "religious, didactic, and visionary genres" of the women writers come. Each of the fifteen chapters is written by a different noted literary or historical scholar. Biographical and critical material, selections of the women's works in translation, and bibliographies are included for each writer. The anthology is extremely valuable because it introduces some outstanding, but obscure, women writers of the Middle Ages, providing an in-depth understanding of the literary achievements of both religious and secular women writers. [R: LJ, Jan 84, p. 94]   Maureen Pastine

SPECIFIC GENRES

Fiction

378.   **Contemporary Novelists**. 3rd ed. James Vinson, ed. New York, St. Martin's Press, 1982. 750p. (Contemporary Writers of the English Language). $65.00. LC 75-189694. ISBN 0-312-16766-0.

Contemporary Novelists contains information about 564 novelists (living or deceased since the 1950s) and is international in scope. Each author entry includes a brief biography, a bibliography of works by the author, a bibliography of works about the author, comments by the author for about half of the entries, and a signed critical essay on the author's novels.

The third edition contains fifty-five fewer entries than the second (published in 1976); a check of approximately the first third of the entries showed that thirty-two names from the second edition had been dropped and seventeen new names added. Authors are selected "based upon the recommendations" of sixteen advisers. Of course, no one book can include all modern novelists, but one does wish for an indication of the criteria upon which the advisers recommend. It would be enlightening to know on what basis Agatha Christie, J. R. R. Tolkien, and Richard Wright were dropped and Frank Yerby and Margaret Walker retained.

Other changes include a new preface and the practice of listing each author's novels written for children or young adults separately. Another change is that "as a rule" (editor's note), all books written about an author (rather than just those the author suggests) are listed, while the reviews and essays listed are limited to those recommended by the entrant. Finally, the most obvious and welcome change is in the book's format; a larger two-column page is used, resulting in a volume that is easier to handle than the unwieldy, thick second edition.

The third edition of what has come to be a standard reference work, this revision is disappointing. Although some essays are new or extensively revised, other revisions consist of adding two or three sentences to cover the author's newer novels, even when as many as three new novels have been published since the last essay (see Anne Tyler). Some revisions suffer from lack of careful editing, such as the essay for Brian Aldiss, which is reprinted verbatim from the second edition with the addition of a final paragraph beginning, "More recent novels. . . ." However, left unchanged in an earlier paragraph is a sentence which reads, "In recent years . . ." and refers to a 1969 novel! Although the book has a 1982 publication date, one cannot rely on coverage through 1981; *Hotel New Hampshire* is listed, but *Rabbit Is Rich* is not, despite the fact that they both came out in the fall of 1981.

However, even with its faults, the information in this work and the addition of authors such as John Irving and E. L. Doctorow make it hard to imagine an academic or large public library without it.

An older related work is *Novels and Novelists: A Guide to the World of Fiction*, edited by Martin Seymour-Smith (New York, St. Martin's Press, 1980. 288p. o.p.) that covers fourteen hundred novelists. Coverage is international, although English-language novelists predominate.   Susan Dedmond Casbon and Bohdan S. Wynar

Literary Criticism

379. **Contemporary Literary Critics**. 2nd ed. By Elmer Borklund. Detroit, Gale, 1982. 600p. $64.00. LC 77-88429. ISBN 0-8103-0443-0.

The first edition of this work was published in 1978 and contained 115 entries of practicing British and American critics. Unlike similar works, the unique feature of this work is that all of the entries were written by one person, Elmer Borklund.

This new edition provides, for each of 124 modern critics, brief biographical information (à la *Directory of American Scholars*), a bibliography (complete only for the more important works), and an essay summarizing the critical stance of each writer. The essays (two to six pages each) contain substantial quotations from the critics' works, and are intended to be descriptive; Borklund writes: "I have tried to indicate what [each critic] wants to do, what assumptions he makes about the nature and function of literature, and what he is able to accomplish, given his analytical tools." Borklund freely admits that the essays are not without judgments; he is not afraid to point out obvious shortcomings in style or thought.

This second edition adds nine critics (including Stanley Fish, C. H. Sisson, Norman Holland, and Ian Watt) to those covered in the first edition, and updates the biographical and bibliographical information. Although there is some danger of the book being used as a "pony," it is more likely to be a valuable starting point for the student interested in exploring the jungles of modern critical theory. [R: LJ, 1 Dec 82, p. 2248]   Philip R. Rider

Poetry

380. **Contemporary Poets**, 4th ed. James Vinson, ed. New York, St. Martin's Press, 1985. 1850p. $70.00. LC 78-165556. ISBN 0-312-16837-3.

Information about some one thousand poets is provided in this edition of *Contemporary Poets*. Living poets, and a select group of poets who have died since 1950, are included, and the selection is international, although English-language poets represent the majority. Entries are alphabetical and range from one to several pages. The name under which a person usually publishes is used as the entry, with full name and pseudonyms provided. Brief biographical data are listed, followed by a bibliography of publications (by genre, then chronologically). A signed essay on the poet's work (and sometimes the poet's own comments) forms the bulk of the entry. The bibliographies appear to be up to date. Many of the essays have been rewritten or revised for the fourth edition. Much of the biographical and bibliographic information is duplicated in Gale's *Contemporary Authors* series, but *Contemporary Poets* is valuable for the critical essays. Poets who also work in other genres are criticized as poets; *Contemporary Authors* does not stress one genre, since it is a more general work.

Because a number of poets included in the third edition were dropped for the fourth edition, libraries will want to keep both editions (as well as the first and second editions). The first edition (1971) of this biographical dictionary was edited by Rosalie Murphy and was titled *Contemporary Poets of the English Language*. It is universal in its coverage of English language poets. The second edition contains fewer but longer entrics (eight hundred in the second edition; eleven hundred in the first edition). Biographical entries, arranged alphabetically, give Who's Who type data, an autobiographical note, and a signed critical article about the poet and his or her works. An index by nationality would enhance the utility of *Contemporary Poets*, but it remains a concise and critical reference tool appropriate for most libraries.

A somewhat related title is Karl Malkoff's *Crowell's Handbook of Contemporary American Poetry: A Critical Handbook of American Poetry since 1940* (New York, Thomas Y. Crowell, 1974. o.p.) that is divided into nine major portions: Contexts; From Imagism to Projectivism; Three Major Poems; Beat Poetry; The New York Poets; The Confessional Poets; The New Black Poetry; Deep Imagism; and The Formal Poets. [R: BL, 15 July/Aug 81, pp. 1458, 1461]   Janet H. Littlefield

381. Kay, Ernest, ed. **International Who's Who in Poetry**. 5th ed. Cambridge, England, International Biographical Centre; distr., Totowa, N.J., Rowman and Littlefield, 1977. 712p. $45.00. LC 59-16302. ISBN 0-900332-42-5.

This is the fifth edition of the *International Who's Who in Poetry* and is dedicated to Dr. Amado M. Yuzon, president of the United Poets Laureate International. It offers biographies and bibliographies of living poets in, as it claims, "all corners of the globe." The appendixes are full of useful information: they enumerate all the poets laureate of the United Kingdom; the official state poets of the United States; poetry societies, their addresses and programs; publishers of poetry; awards available to poets; recorded poetry. A particularly valuable section cites the Library of Congress recordings of poetry readings and discussions, many of which now have historic value: James Whitcomb Riley reading his poems, a 1950 reading by Muriel Rukeyser of her work, Anne Sexton discussing poetry in 1961. The penultimate section reports on the Third International Congress of Poets, held in June 1976 in Baltimore; the final section indexes those poets covered herein who use pseudonyms.

A random check indicates that entries are fairly extensive and accurate. Past omissions noted by reviewers of the fourth edition have been incorporated here. The coverage is still not exhaustive, however; still missing are Gordon Symes, Marcus Cumberlege and Dora Weir, and a glance through *Contemporary Authors* yields several other names not noted here. Moreover, Dr. Yuzon, the dedicatee, has had his name misspelled on the frontispiece and excluded from the roster of poets. A useful improvement for future editions might be a necrology of poets cited in past editions. Despite these problems, the editor has undertaken a mammoth and worthwhile task: everything anyone might want to know about contemporary poetry. In the main, it is somewhat better than most other International Bibliographical Centre publications, but libraries should use it with much caution.   Dorothy E. Litt

Science Fiction, Fantasy, and Horror

382.   Ash, Brian. **Who's Who in Science Fiction**. New York, Taplinger, 1976. 219p. bibliog. $10.95; $4.95pa. LC 76-11667. ISBN 0-8008-8274-1; 0-8008-8279-2pa.

Some four hundred biobibliographies of science fiction writers are included in this volume, with an emphasis on American and British authors. The coverage is not very impressive. Donald Tuck's *The Encyclopedia of Science Fiction and Fantasy and Weird Fiction through 1968* (Advent, 1974) offers much more. A useful volume on this subject is R. Reginald's *Contemporary Science Fiction Writers* (repr. Arno, 1975). In addition to its skimpy coverage, Ash's compilation is also uneven in terms of the length of the biobibliographies; although they range in length from only a few lines to two or three pages, their length does not always reflect the relative importance of the particular writer. Nevertheless, this work is inexpensive . . . will do for most smaller libraries. Larger and medium-sized libraries have several other options, including the Gale and St. Martin's Press publications mentioned in this section. [R: LJ, 15 Dec 76, p. 2557]
                                                          Bohdan S. Wynar

383.   Ashley, Mike. **Who's Who in Horror and Fantasy Fiction**. New York, Taplinger, 1978 (c1977). 240p. bibliog. $10.95; $4.95pa. LC 77-4608. ISBN 0-8008-8275-X; 0-8008-8278-4pa.

Who's Who in Horror and Fantasy Fiction presents brief biobibliographical sketches of some four hundred writers of fantasy fiction from the early 1700s to the present. Editor Ashley defines this difficult-to-define genre as including "anything [fictional] that happens contrary to accepted laws and observations," in particular, stories of the supernatural, psychological horror stories, and heroic and humorous fantasy. Within this broad area, Ashley has attempted to limit inclusion to individuals who wrote primarily within the field, or produced at least one well-known or influential work. As he readily admits, however, the distinctions are neither easily drawn nor followed. Thus, one will find within this volume such names as Ray Bradbury, Henry James, Ivan Turgenev, and Oscar Wilde, but not Jack Williamson, Harlan Ellison, Alan Gunn, C. S. Lewis, or James Thurber. The first two are covered in Brian Ash's *Who's Who in Science Fiction* and Donald Tuck's *Encyclopedia of Science Fiction*, Alan Gunn appears in *Who's Who in Children's Literature*, and the last two may be found in many reference sources.

In addition to the main section, the volume has several supplementary features that enhance its usefulness: a chronology covering the development of fantasy and horror fiction from 2000 B.C. to 1977, an alphabetical index to key stories and books, a selected, partially annotated checklist of principal anthologies and magazines in the field, a list of awards, and a selected bibliography of about twenty related reference works. Ashley's introduction provides a good, general overview of the subject, and includes brief mention of several dealers who specialize in out-of-print materials. Although carefully limited in scope, this small volume should serve librarians, collectors, researchers, and general readers as a basic guide to writers and books in the nebulous realms of horror and fantasy.

The same publisher also has *Who's Who in Spy Fiction* ($4.95pa. ISBN 0-8808-8280-6). [R: Choice, Mar 79, p. 53; WLB, Feb 79, p. 468]

Mary Jo Walker

384. Bleiler, E. F., ed. **Supernatural Fiction Writers: Fantasy and Horror**. New York, Scribner's, 1985. 2v. bibliog. index. $130.00. LC 84-27588. ISBN 0-684-17808-7.

Spanning a wide range of space and time, *Supernatural Fiction Writers* provides in-depth biobibliographical essays on some 145 selected authors who have contributed significantly to the development of horror or fantasy fiction. Among those chosen for major entries are Brackett, Ellison, Coppard, Lewis, Hoffman, Zelazny, Apuleius, Poe, Tolkien, Bradbury, Dunsany, and Henry James. A few of the choices may represent surprises, as may some of the omissions, particularly of several women writers mentioned below. Because of the scope and quality of the essays, however, readers can expect to find at least some useful material on authors who did not meet the criteria for a main entry.

The two-volume set does not include photographs, but is handsomely bound with large clear print on good paper, two columns of text per page. Individual entries, prepared by specialists as well known as Thomas Clareson and editor E. F. Bleiler himself, vary in approach yet cover the same basic territory: biographical information, analyses of notable works, comparison with other authors, evaluation of the "historical position" of the writer discussed, and a selected bibliography of books and shorter pieces by or about that writer. Bleiler has organized the set in chronological and geographical sections, subdivided alphabetically by entry name. This arrangement, though useful for a historical survey, is awkward for reference purposes. But an unusually detailed index compensates for the inconvenience.

The set complements Bleiler's *Science Fiction Writers*, a single-volume biographical cyclopedia published in 1982, also by Scribner's. The two works show some minor overlapping. Seventeen main entries appear in both, a few by the same contributors, but written from different perspectives with varying emphases. Criticism of the earlier work focused on its neglect of certain women writers such as Bradley, McCaffrey, Norton, and Wilhelm. Norton is included in the present set, but the others (plus Dinesen, Yarbro, and others) remain in limbo except for scattered material found through the indexes. Both sources, nevertheless, offer insights and information difficult to locate elsewhere. Used together or singly, they provide a valuable contribution to scholarship in their complementary genres.

Mary Jo Walker

385. Reilly, John M., ed. **Twentieth-Century Crime and Mystery Writers**. 2nd ed. New York, St. Martin's Press, 1985. 1094p. index. $69.95. LC 84-40813. ISBN 0-312-82418-1.

The first edition of this highly acclaimed biographical dictionary garnered several awards when it was published in 1980. The second edition includes 640 entries on English-language crime and mystery writers of this century. One hundred and nine of these entries are new while the remaining entries have been revised and updated wherever appropriate.

Each entry includes Who's Who-level biographical information, a bibliography, a signed critical essay, details on manuscript collections and works about the author, and whenever possible, a comment from the author on his or her work. There are an excellent 130-page title index and special appendixes on influential nineteenth-century and foreign-language writers.

A random sample of one hundred entries from this work found that eighty-four authors were also covered in *Contemporary Authors* (Gale, 1962-). The essays in *Twentieth-Century Crime and Mystery Writers*, however, were longer and more perceptive, the bibliographies generally more complete, and the biographical information and other details more up-to-date.

For those libraries which can afford it, it is difficult to imagine a more useful, better-organized, or more comprehensive single volume reference work on English-language mystery writers. For extensive bibliographical research in this genre the undisputed bible will continue to be Allen J. Hubin's *Crime Fiction 1749-1980: A Comprehensive Bibliography* (Garland, 1984). Reilly's second edition, though, is a glittering companion piece to Hubin's bibliography, and one that is unequaled in its thoroughness, ease-of-use, and insightful commentary on the writers of this genre.

Dennis Dillon

386. Science Fiction Writers: Critical Studies of the Major Authors from the Early Nineteenth Century to the Present Day. E. F. Bleiler, ed. New York, Scribner's, 1982. 623p. index. $65.00. LC 81-51032. ISBN 0-684-16740-9.

This substantial work offers essays on seventy-six notable science fiction authors. Important earlier figures, from Mary Shelley to Aldous Huxley, are included, but the greatest number of articles deal with contemporary writers. With twenty-five contributors drawn from active authors (Brian W. Aldiss, Colin Wilson) as well as academics, a variety of viewpoints is assured.

The predominant approach concentrates on thematic analysis and critical evaluation. Essential biographical information is included. Reflecting the unique nature of this form of fiction, the influences traced are as likely to derive from "hard" science, philosophy, or anthropology as from prior literary tradition. The reader new to science fiction will be fascinated by the enormous part played by magazine editors, preeminently John W. Campbell, Jr., of *Astounding Stories—Analog*, in shaping the field.

In a work of such ambitious scope, the provision of only a selected bibliography for each author must be questioned. It is true that some of the authors have been extremely prolific, and complete bibliographic treatment would require considerable detection and many more pages of text. The listed works include the most famous and presumably the best of each author's output. Still, reliable bibliographic data is especially elusive for science fiction authors. Failure to attempt this task limits the usefulness of what is otherwise an exemplary reference book.

Until recently, science fiction was very much a male preserve, and unfortunate traces of a sexist attitude linger in a few of the articles. Judith Merril in particular seems to be the victim of a double standard. She is condemned for the high emotional content of her writing (elsewhere Sturgeon is praised for a comparable quality); for the implausibility of a habitable Mars setting (in male authors from Burroughs to Bradbury it is viewed as an acceptable convention); and for the unimportance of the husbands in "Daughters of Earth" (when this is the whole point of the story). Selections on LeGuin, Russ, and Tiptree, in contrast, give a favorable and balanced treatment. (The Russ article is especially illuminating of this difficult author.) But one is puzzled at the inclusion of Margaret S. Clair, when so many accomplished and popular female authors of the past two decades are excluded: Bradley, Charnas, McCaffrey, Norton, Wilhelm.

In spite of these shortcomings, this book is a major addition to the reference shelf of science fiction. It brings together for the first time detailed and judicious literary assessments of many of the field's important authors. In most cases, the essays will be equally valuable as a "road map" prior to delving into the analyzed works, or for further reflection and study afterwards.

The physical format is both attractive and easy to use. Altogether, *Science Fiction Writers* illustrates how far science fiction has come since the days of the early pulps. [R: LJ, 15 May 82, p. 983; WLB, June 82, p. 786]   Emily J. Alward

387. **Twentieth-Century Science-Fiction Writers**. Curtis C. Smith, ed. New York, St. Martin's Press, 1981. 642p. bibliog. (Twentieth-Century Writers of the English Language). $65.00. LC 81-8944. ISBN 0-312-82420-3.

This title in St. Martin's award-winning series Twentieth-Century Writers of the English Language includes six hundred authors of science fiction novels and stories published between 1895 and 1981. While the majority of authors are American, thirty-five are foreign writers whose works have been translated into English. The essays, averaging one thousand words in length, are signed; over 140 international contributors are identified at the back of the volume along with the essays they prepared. Each entry contains detailed biographical information and an exhaustive bibliography of each writer's science fiction and non-science fiction output. Many mainstream authors are also included, even if they wrote only a few works which can be classed as science fiction, e.g., John Barth, E. M. Forster, John Hersey, Sinclair Lewis, and Mark Twain, among others.

The citations are arranged chronologically by type of work: novels, short story collections, plays, and uncollected short stories appearing in magazines. Each author's major works are critically evaluated, and their importance within the genre is discussed. A useful special feature is a reading list of over three hundred secondary sources.

While E. F. Bleiler's *Science Fiction Writers* (Scribner's, 1981) includes much longer essays, it covers just seventy authors. No other biobibliography of science fiction is as comprehensive as this one. [R: Choice, Mar 82, p. 910; LJ, 15 Feb 82, p. 446; WLB, Feb 82, p. 464]   Gary D. Barber

388. Vinson, James, ed. **Twentieth-Century Romance and Gothic Writers**. D. L. Kirkpatrick, associate ed. Detroit, Gale, 1982. 898p. index. $95.00. ISBN 0-8103-0226-8.

Twentieth-Century Romance and Gothic Writers provides biographical data on over three hundred authors. Obscure and well-known authors alike are covered. A distinguished group of advisers, who include Rachel Anderson and Barbara Cartland, helped select the authors included.

The entries are arranged alphabetically. Each entry contains biographical information, a chronological list of published works, an essay on the author's works, and comments by the author when still living. Pseudonyms are listed in the entry and cross-referenced in the alphabetical sequence. In addition, a title index lists all works mentioned in the entries.

This volume is a useful reference work for the literature student and scholar. It provides a comprehensive look at this genre and provides coverage previously not available in one volume. [R: BL, 15 Dec 83, pp. 624-25; Choice, June 83, pp. 1438-40; LJ, 15 May 83, p. 965; LJ, 15 May 83, pp. 993-94; RQ, Summer 83, pp. 429-30; WLB, Mar 83, p. 609]   Joanne Troutner

CHILDREN'S AND YOUNG ADULTS' LITERATURE

389. Commire, Anne, ed. **Something about the Author: Facts and Pictures about Authors and Illustrators of Books for Young People**. Detroit, Gale. 1971- . In progress. Price varies. LC 72-27107. ISSN 0276-816X.

Started in 1971, each volume contains illustrated biographies on about 100-150 juvenile and young-adult authors and illustrators.

As a continuing reference series that deals with the lives and works of authors and illustrators of children's books, *Something about the Author* continues to be a most valuable biographical source. *SATA* not only includes well-known authors and illustrators, but also those who are not quite so well known.

Written primarily for children and young adults (basically for the junior-high-age reader) the biographies will be read by some who are younger. Starting with 1983, some of the more controversial authors at the young adult level have not been included; therefore the usefulness will be limited at this age level.

There are full-length entries for those appearing for the first time. Brief entries may appear for some while a full biography is being prepared or they may make a biography more current with additional information. Obituaries have been a part of *SATA* since volume 20. These not only serve as death notices but also as concise views of individuals' lives. Obituaries of authors who have not appeared previously in *SATA* may also be included. Concluding each volume is a cumulative index which consists of two parts: the illustrations index, arranged alphabetically by name, gives the volume and page where the illustrator's work appears in the current volume as well as preceding volumes; the author index gives the number of the volume in which the author's biographical entry, brief entry, or obituary appears. Cross-references to *Yesterday's Authors of Books for Children* and *Children's Literature Review* (beginning with volume 36) are also included.

Each biographical entry attempts to provide a true representation of an individual's life and work. The entries include: the most complete form of the name with pseudonyms, variations, and omissions; birth dates; career information with awards and honors received; titles, dates of publication, illustration information, and genre of each title if known. If an adaptation has been made, a full report is given. Many of the illustrations are taken from these adaptations. There is a "sidelights" section commenting on the personal life and works of the person, usually gained from the biographee or his works. Cross-references to other sources for additional information complete the biographical entries.

In this easy-to-read series, there are biographical sketches of six thousand or more authors and illustrators, more than the *Fifth Book of Junior Authors and Illustrators*. But, as in the *Fifth Book of Junior Authors and Illustrators*, the entries are noncritical.

Anna Grace Patterson

390.   Doyle, Brian, comp. **The Who's Who of Children's Literature**. New York, Schoken Books, 1970 (c1968). 380p. $14.00. LC 68-28904.

Reprint of the 1968 edition with no changes. The guide is in two parts: authors and illustrators. The first part is an alphabetical list of under two hundred British and American authors "who constitute the heritage of juvenile literature." Some European authors whose works are well known in translation are included. In addition to the early writers, some important contemporary names are provided. The entries give place and date of birth, education, career, and summary of the most important juvenile works. Similar information is given for about fifty names in the second section on illustrators. Reproductions of 104 illustrations and some stills from film versions of children's books provide interesting comparisons of illustrations by different artists for the same books. The biographical guide is a welcome addition to children's-literature reference tools. It is, however, surprising that some important omissions occur in the classified, selective bibliography. Arbuthnot's *Children and Books* is listed in the old 1947 edition; no mention is made of Haviland's *Children's Literature: A Guide to Reference Sources* (Library of Congress, 1966). [R: LJ, 15 Apr 70]

Christine L. Wynar

391.   Hopkins, Lee Bennett. **More Books by More People: Interviews with Sixty-Five Authors of Books for Children**. New York, Citation Press, 1974. 410p. illus. index. $8.95; $4.95pa. LC 73-87223. ISBN 0-590-07357-5; 0-590-09401-7pa.

Unlike some biographical directories about children's book authors and illustrators, this one is written in casual and highly personalized style. The reader has the feeling of sitting in on the conversations between Mr. Hopkins and the authors. Young readers, who often are curious about these things, should find the book most enjoyable as well as informative. As a biographical reference tool it gains importance by being a continuation of Hopkins' *Books Are by People*, which presented interviews with 104 authors and illustrators.

Smaller in scope is a biographical source of fifty contemporary author-illustrators of children's books: *Authors and Illustrators of Children's Books: Writings on Their Lives and Works* (New York, R. R. Bowker, 1972. 471p. o.p.). The articles are arranged alphabetically by biographee and include awards and honors. An appendix lists each author-illustrator's works. [R: Choice, Nov 74, p. 1272]

Bohdan S. Wynar

392.   **The Junior Book of Authors**. 2nd ed. rev. Edited by Stanley J. Kunitz and Howard Haycraft. New York, H. W. Wilson, 1951. 309p. $18.00. LC 51-13057. ISBN 0-8242-0028-4.

393.   **More Junior Authors**. Edited by Muriel Fuller. New York, H. W. Wilson, 1963. 235p. $16.00. LC 63-11816. ISBN 0-8242-0036-5.

394.   **Third Book of Junior Authors**. Edited by Doris de Montreville and Donna Hill. New York, H. W. Wilson, 1972. 320p. $18.00. LC 75-149381. ISBN 0-8242-0408-5.

395.   **Fourth Book of Junior Authors and Illustrators**. Edited by Doris de Montreville and Elizabeth D. Crawford. New York, H. W. Wilson, 1978. 370p. $22.00. LC 78-115. ISBN 0-8242-0568-5.

396.   **Fifth Book of Junior Authors and Illustrators.** Edited by Sally Holmes Holtze. New York, H. W. Wilson, 1983. 357p. $30.00. LC 83-21828. ISBN 0-8242-0694-0.

Junior Authors and Illustrators series is a standard reference work with many years of distinguished tradition. The first volume was published in 1951 (6th printing, 1970) tracing the careers and works of the pioneers of juvenile literature. Biographical and autobiographical sketches of 289 authors such as Hans Christian Andersen, Randolph Caldecott, and A. A. Milne are included, along with 232 portraits of individuals profiled. *More Junior Authors* adds 268 biographies of authors and illustrators, most of whom came to prominence since the 1951 publication. Again, portraits accompany most of the sketches. The *Third Book* provides 255 autobiographical or biographical sketches plus 249 portraits for prominent authors and illustrators who achieved recognition after 1963.

The format in this third volume is appealingly readable, with names and cross-references in an alphabetical sequence. Usually a page in length, the autobiographical or biographical excerpt is preceded by birth date, a photograph, and the authorized signature. The statements, representing a variety of styles, reflect the background for the artist's or writer's creativity, often recapturing much of the remembered child. Erik Christian Haugaard's comment is perhaps representative: "I write my books because birds must sing, as dogs are meant to bark. I write for children who were born east of the sun and west of the moon. . . ."

Taken together these statements represent a kind of collective insight and appreciation into the process of creation and the sources of inspiration; they also reflect many different values behind modern writing for children. Editorial additions provide listings of awards as well as selected works written and/or illustrated. Some older authors included in this edition are Frank Baum, Lucy Boston, "Crockett Johnson," Sterling North; among contemporary writers are Betsey Byars, Tom Feelings, Nat Hentoff, Ib Spang Olsen, Inger and Lasse Sandberg, Charles Schulz, and Brinton Turkle.

The *Fourth Book* adds 250 more names and is comparable in format and scope to the earlier volumes. Entries are arranged alphabetically by surname, with a short (three hundred to five hundred words) autobiographical essay aimed at junior readers, additional biographical data by the editors, a selected bibliography of works, and references to other biographical/critical books and articles about the author or illustrator. When the series began, only the autobiographical essay was included, with a few titles; the *Third* and *Fourth* have more usefulness for general reference, with biographical material and references to other works.

Coverage is aimed at, but not entirely limited to, living authors and illustrators. An advisory committee of five librarians and/or book people made the selections of authors and illustrators; among those they omitted are Betty Greene, Ashley Bryan, Tomie de Paola, Jamake Highwater, and Katherine Paterson.

The latest volume, fifth in the series, provides 273 biographical sketches. In addition to including Caldecott and Newbery winners, the current volume includes sketches of Ashley Bryan, Tomie de Paola, Paula Danziger, Shel Silverstein, David Macaulay, and Norma Klein, among others. The editor states this volume contains entries for authors and illustrators who "have come to prominence since 1978." It can be argued that John Donovan, Leo and Diane Dillon, and Paul Zindel, for example, do not meet this criterion. Approximately two-thirds of the sketches are autobiographical, and most contain the subject's photograph and autograph. All sketches contain lists of books by and about the biographees. A cumulative index with appropriate cross-references, to all the previous volumes enhances *Fifth Book*'s value as a reference tool. The entries are completely noncritical; that is, no negative comments were found by the reviewer. People using this volume should be aware of this bias.

Summing up, the *Junior Authors* series is a well-recognized, worthwhile purchase for most libraries. [R: BL, 15 Apr 84, p. 1198] Bohdan S. Wynar

397. Kirkpatrick, D. L., ed. **Twentieth-Century Children's Writers**. 2nd ed. New York, St. Martin's Press, 1983. 1024p. index. $55.00. LC 83-40062. ISBN 0-312-82414-9.

The first edition of this work was published in 1978 (St. Martin's Press. 1507p. $50.00). This second edition of *Twentieth-Century Children's Writers* includes biographical data and critical essays on the works of more than seven hundred English-language authors of fiction, drama, and poetry for children, an increase of one hundred over the 1978 edition. All entries are newly written or revised.

An international advisory board of twenty-five well-known authorities in the field of children's literature selected the authors to be included in the work. All twentieth-century Newbery Medal authors and many Caldecott Medal recipients are found here. Nearly two hundred contributors wrote signed critical essays on the literary works of one or more authors. Essayists and advisory board members are identified in a notes section at the end of the work.

The main body of the volume, organized alphabetically, includes for each author a short biography, a bibliography of publications, and a critical essay. Location of the author's manuscripts is noted. Many authors have contributed personal comments on their own work and on writing for children. Each critical essay is approximately one-half to one page long and analyzes the author's books and their significance to the field of children's literature.

An appendix of thirty-eight nineteenth-century writers who have had considerable influence on twentieth-century authors is included. An essay on foreign-language writers whose works have been important is followed by a list of over sixty foreign-language writers with first edition of significant titles. A comprehensive title index is a welcome addition. *Twentieth-Century Children's Writers* is a major source of outstanding quality and comprehensiveness for all libraries needing information about children's writers. [R: BL, 15 Apr 84, p. 1199; LJ, 15 Mar 84, p. 577]

Patricia Tipton Sharp

398. Ward, Martha E., and Dorothy A. Marquardt. **Authors of Books for Young People**. 2nd ed. Metuchen, N.J., Scarecrow, 1971. 579p. $22.50. LC 70-157057. SBN 8108-0404-2.

399. Ward, Martha E., and Dorothy A. Marquardt. **Authors of Books for Young People: Supplement to the Second Edition**. Metuchen, N.J., Scarecrow, 1979. 308p. $16.00. LC 78-16011. ISBN 0-8108-1159-6.

The second edition provides very brief biographical entries for some twenty-one hundred writers of juvenile books and incorporates all the biographies from the first edition (1964) and the supplement (1967). The entries, arranged alphabetically by name, give dates, profession, place of birth, education and degrees, family and residence, career, interests, and a partial list of writings. The entries vary in fullness. The second edition identifies publisher and year for each title listed and provides cross-references for pseudonyms.

The 1979 supplement, covering 1,250 authors not in the 1971 second edition, follows the former publication pattern. Hence, former reviews have validity when judging this alphabetically arranged dictionary, which provides brief information on authors with sample titles of their work. An *RQ* review called the second edition "handy . . . [includes] less prominent authors." Herein is the single strength for this set, which adds critics to the list of recent award winners and other writers of fact and fiction for the young.

Praise should be tempered by realization of shortcomings in uncontrolled scope and incomplete entries. Scope is international, covering biographees living or dead. There are, first, authors of world stature (Nathaniel Hawthorne, Dostoevsky, Graham Greene, Perrault); second, well-recognized names in children's literature (Susan Cooper, Richard Adams, Marie D'Aulnoy); and then, those less prominent names yet, or maybe never, to be memorable. People in the first two categories are better documented in any one of several biographical sources. (Many entries carry reference to two such sources, *Contemporary Authors* and *Junior Book of Authors*, an H. W. Wilson series. The intent of *Authors of Books for Young People* is to augment, not supplant, such sources.) The third category of obscure authors gives this set some claim to consideration.

The entries in this work are little more than phrases from book jackets or notes from a file in the children's department of Quincy (Ill.) Public Library, where the compilers are librarians. Some minor errors give the informed reader pause, suggesting that the information was not meticulously checked or updated. This supplement makes its small "handy" contribution, but also deserves again the adjective "disappointing" used in an earlier review. [R: BL, 1 July 79, p. 1585; JAL, May 79, p. 103; LJ, 1 May 79, p. 1045; WLB, June 79, p. 721]   Claire England and Bohdan S. Wynar

400. Yesterday's Authors of Books for Children: Facts and Pictures about Authors and Illustrators of Books for Young People, from Early Times to 1960. Anne Commire, ed. Detroit, Gale, 1977-1978. 2v. illus. index. $62.00/vol. LC 76-17501. ISBN 0-8103-0090-7.

Yet another children's authors series – this one devoted exclusively to authors and illustrators of children's books who died before 1961. *YABC* complements Gale's *Something about the Author* series, which covers authors and illustrators now living or deceased since 1961. Each volume of *YABC* covers about forty figures. Unfortunately this project stopped with the publication of volume 2.

Entries range from Andy Adams to Kate Wiggin and vary in length from one to over sixteen pages (Wiggin). Each entry includes the following categories of information: personal; career; writings; adaptations; sidelights; and references to biographies, obituaries, and other sources. The "sidelights" category consists of excerpts from letters, diaries, memoirs, and autobiographies, arranged chronologically. A portrait of each biographee and numerous black-and-white illustrations from each subject's books or adaptations are included. Omitted are references to book reviews. The editors do not provide any critical assessment of an author's work or position in the world of children's writing. This is especially puzzling in view of the editor's claim that the cutoff date of 1961 makes it possible "to offer thorough overviews of their life and work."

In selecting biographees, primary attention is given to those authors who are still being read by children; no other criteria or sources used in choosing the entrants are provided. Attractively printed and designed, the set can be expected to be popular with young people and children's librarians. [R: JAL, Nov 77, p. 298; WLB, Nov 77, p. 262]

Christine L. Wynar

NATIONAL LITERATURES

American Literature

General Works

401. **American Authors 1600-1900. A Biographical Dictionary of American Literature.** Edited by Stanley J. Kunitz and Howard Haycraft. New York, H. W. Wilson, 1938. 846p. $33.00. LC 38-27938. ISBN 0-8242-0001.

This is a standard work for more popular audiences, now in its seventh printing (1977). It includes readable biographies of nearly thirteen hundred authors who contributed to the development of American literature from the first English settlement at Jamestown to the close of the nineteenth century, which makes this volume an essential reference work on the period. Lists of principal works and critical and biographical sources follow each sketch; portraits accompany four hundred of these entries. Highly recommended for all school and public libraries.

Bohdan S. Wynar

402. Burke, W. J., and Will D. Howe. **American Authors and Books, 1640 to the Present Day**. 3rd rev. ed. Revised by Irving Weiss and Anne Weiss. New York, Crown, 1973. 719p. o.p. LC 62-11815. ISBN 0-517-501392.

American Authors and Books, first published in 1943, has become a standard reference source for those interested in American *belles lettres*. This third edition has been thoroughly updated and revised, a commendable job. Entries are very brief and not really biographical in the usual sense. Entries for persons provide birth (and, where applicable, death) dates, birthplace, occupation (e.g., anthropologist, author), and titles and years of publications. In addition to entries for authors, this guide provides information on illustrators, periodicals, publishing companies, editors, etc. Title entries sometimes give a synopsis of the work but often provide only authors' names; cross-references are provided from pseudonyms to real names. It should be noted that it encompasses more than literary figures or literature *per se* — e.g., we find entries for Craig Claiborne, H. W. Wilson, William Langer, John Holt, and Louis Shores. There are similar omissions or errors (e.g., only ten novels are listed under the entry for the Lanny Budd series, but the entry for Upton Sinclair lists the eleventh novel), but these are exceptions to the overall high quality of this work.

In all, this compilation is the most thorough work of its kind; it should certainly be in all but the smallest or most highly specialized reference collections. [R: RSR, July/Sept 73, p. 21; WLB, Mar 73, p. 611]

Sally Wynkoop

403. Elliott, Emory, ed. **American Colonial Writers, 1606-1734**. Detroit, Gale, 1984. 415p. illus. bibliog. index. (Dictionary of Literary Biography, Vol. 24). $80.00. LC 83-20577. ISBN 0-8103-1703-6.

The first of three volumes in the Dictionary of Literary Biography series that are devoted to early American writers, *American Colonial Writers, 1606-1734* contains biographical and critical essays concerning ninety-five of the writers of the period. Lengthy, in-depth articles on major writers (such as William Bradford, Anne Bradstreet, William Byrd II, Jonathan Edwards, Benjamin Franklin, Cotton and Increase Mather, Samuel Sewall, Edward Taylor, and Roger Williams) are supplemented with information commentaries about many lesser-known and recently discovered writers of the colonial period.

Following the standard *DLB* format, essays include a list of the author's separate publications, basic bibliographical and career information, and notes on the locations of the author's collected papers. Often including representative comments from earlier sources, critical commentary reflects the most recent interpretations. Entries normally include illustrations from the author's life, facsimile title and text pages, manuscript pages and letters, and an author portrait.

Providing ready access to the wealth of materials relating to the literary activities of colonial New England as well as the Middle and Southern colonies, *American Colonial Writers, 1606-1734* contributes to a more complete understanding of the complex nature of the literary achievement of the colonial writers. As an information source, it is basic enough to provide general information for a high school or college student writing a term paper and specific enough to lead the specialist scholar to valuable primary and secondary source materials. [R: WLB, May 84, p. 673]   Colby H. Kullman

404.   Elliott, Emory, ed. **American Colonial Writers, 1735-1781**. Detroit, Gale, 1984. 421p. illus. bibliog. index. (Dictionary of Literary Biography, Vol. 31). $82.00. LC 84-13533. ISBN 0-8103-1709-5.

Anyone with the least interest in American literature will find this book irresistible. From the most famous to the most obscure, this thirty-first volume of *DLB* covers sixty-two American writers in the period 1735 to 1781 with wit and authority. The ideas of six eighteenth-century philosophers that influenced American thought during this period are also profiled.

Major writers are treated in lengthy essays beginning with standard biographical and bibliographic information in outline form and followed by notes on references, biographies, papers, and letters. The essays chronicle the subjects' writing careers with critical commentary from historical and contemporary perspectives. Obscure facts and tidbits of information about the writers' quirks lend interest and often humor without detracting from the text's authority.

Dealing with a period in which writing and politics were, for the most part, inextricable, the editors wisely chose an American studies approach. Reading several entries, one gains not divorced glimpses of the individual careers and talents of colonial writers but an overview of the political, philosophical, social, cultural, and artistic scheme of the times. Drawings, portrait reproductions, and facsimiles of manuscripts enhance the overview.

The book is generally readable and accurate, although the writing is sometimes unclear and a typo in the first entry sets the publication date of some John Adams letters one hundred years too late. Regardless, the volume will be of use—and, just as important, of interest—to students on a general introductory level, as well as advanced scholars interested in the commentary and bibliographic information.

Constance Hardesty

405. Levernier, James A., and Douglas R. Wilmes, eds. **American Writers before 1800: A Biographical and Critical Dictionary**. Westport, Conn., Greenwood Press, 1983. 3v. index. $195.00/set. LC 82-933. ISBN 0-313-22229-0.

Designed to provide a convenient source of information about the works and lives of 786 early American writers, *American Writers before 1800* discusses each author in individual entries that include primary bibliographical references to the author's publications in chronological order, a brief biography that includes commentary on factors in the writer's life that relate to his or her development as a representative voice of the period, a critical appraisal of the writer's writings and their significance, and a concluding list of selected readings from secondary sources. This reference source is the collective effort of some 250 established scholars of early American culture and literature who have provided many voices and points of view in their articles.

Using anthologies, literary and cultural histories, and bibliographies, James A. Levernier and Douglas R. Wilmes carefully gleaned the names of significant early American figures. Of particular importance to scholars of the period is the fact that the entries are not scaled according to the "importance" of the writer discussed since extensive material on major writers can be found in numerous other volumes. Instead, many of the entries highlight and fill in data on figures who are mentioned only in passing in other works treating this period. Consequently, it is possible to locate invaluable information on a variety of minor writers such as Anthony Benezet, Gilbert Imlay, and James Wetmore, as well as major figures such as Benjamin Franklin, Cotton Mather, and Edward Taylor.

Of wide scope, this biographical and critical dictionary proves an excellent reference guide for students of early American literature and culture. [R: Choice, June 84, pp. 1435-37; RBB, 1 Dec 84, pp. 489-90; WLB, May 84, p. 673]   Colby H. Kullman

406. Unger, Leonard, ed.-in-chief. **American Writers. A Collection of Literary Biographies**. New York, Scribner's, 1971-1981. 8v. $495.00/set. **Supplement I**. 2v. $130.00/set. **Supplement II**. 2v. $130.00/set. (May be purchased separately). LC 73-1759. ISBN 0-684-17322-0 (set).

The eight-volume set that inspired the *British Writers, Ancient Writers*, and *European Writers* series, this collection of 156 critical studies includes every notable poet, novelist, short-story writer, playwright, critic, historian, and philosopher from the seventeenth century to the present day. Each article is the work of a distinguished scholar, who provides a basic account of the writer's life but focuses on a discussion of literary style, genre, and place within established or emerging literary tradition.

The ninety-seven articles in the original four-volume parent set were selected from a series of pamphlets published by the University of Minnesota Press. They were re-edited, bibliographies were updated, and a comprehensive index was added. Among the contributors are Louis Auchincloss ("Henry Adams," "Ellen Glasgow," "Edith Wharton"), Leon Edel ("Henry James," "Henry David Thoreau"), Granville Hicks ("James Gould Cozzens"), Mark Schorer ("Sinclair Lewis"), Charles E. Shain ("F. Scott Fitzgerald"), Lawrence Thompson ("Robert Frost"), Leonard Unger ("T. S. Eliot"), and Philip Young ("Ernest Hemingway"). With the publication of *Supplement I* (2v. 1979), edited by Leonard Unger of the University of Minnesota, and *Supplement II* (2v. 1981), edited by A. Walton Litz of Princeton University, this acclaimed series was expanded with a total of fifty-nine new articles that were commissioned especially for *American Writers*. Some of the writers included in these volumes are James Baldwin,

Lillian Hellman, Bernard Malamud, E. B. White, W. H. Auden, John Cheever, Allen Ginsberg, Joyce Carol Oates, Pearl Buck, Sylvia Plath, and Thomas Pynchon.

All the essays are well documented with a selected bibliography of works by and about a given author. A brief biographical sketch is provided in each essay, but the emphasis is on the critical evaluation and analysis of the writer's literary achievements.

As is to be expected, the supplementary volumes in this series continue the basic plan of the primary volumes. Unger's intention here has been to fill gaps in the primary set and to continue the coverage of major figures down into the twentieth century. He cites the major gap being filled as that of the omission of the Schoolroom Poets (the "bearded trinomials"), with the exception of Longfellow. That has been corrected here, with essays on each of the major figures in that grouping. Coverage also includes James Baldwin, John Cheever, Adrienne Rich, and E. B. White. Some thirty persons are covered in the first supplement and twenty-nine in the second, and the essays are lengthy (twenty pages seems a minimum). They tend to delve very heavily into individual works, and students with no knowledge of the author's entire work may be a bit put off by having *everything* dissected and explained before it's ever been encountered. However, that appears to be the fashion.

Each entry has a selected bibliography attached, one listing for works and the other of criticism. Especially in the case of contemporary authors, listing works (including essays and uncollected works) can be very helpful, as they often get so easily lost or go unnoticed in the contemporary publishing swirl of activity. The layout is handsome and easy on the eye, and the books will be used for some time to come. [R: Choice, Sept 79, p. 795; WLB, June 79, p. 721-22]   Koert C. Loomis, Jr. and Bohdan S. Wynar

407. **Who Was Who among North American Authors 1921-1939**. Detroit, Gale, 1976. 2v. (An Omnigraphics Book; Gale Composite Biographical Dictionary Series, No. 1). $160.00/set. LC 76-23545. ISBN 0-8103-1041-4.

These volumes are a composite of the entries in the seven-volume series *Who's Who among North American Authors*, as compiled by Alberta Lawrence. The end product is biobibliographical notes on over 11,200 American and Canadian novelists, poets, playwrights, historians, journalists, and editors. (An astonishing number are clergymen.) The length of each entry in the original series seems to have been determined by the number and length of titles by each author; since Lawrence's original compiler's comments are not presented, however, this assumption remains unverified, and the question of how figures were chosen for inclusion remains unanswered. The anonymous compilers of this reprint have chosen for these volumes the latest entry in the series for each figure, but they fail to identify from which volume those entries came. The reprint has come out on high quality paper (as opposed to the decaying, non-book paper of the original), and it does include over eighty-nine hundred figures "not listed in the other standard reference guides" (*Who Was Who, Dictionary of American Biography*, etc.). Additionally, authors' pen names are listed in the regular sequence and are then cross-referenced (thus, "Anonymous" refers the reader to either John William Talbot or to Gail Treat, a reference that answers, after a fashion, a question that has plagued scholars for centuries).

As to the book's physical appearance, the diversity of type styles allows conjecture as to the method of composition, but this is no large matter. More serious is the question of the value of the original work. The reprint's foreword claims that these condensed volumes have great value for someone seeking information on journalists, as such biographies are "included in this work [but] are exceedingly difficult to find elsewhere." This may well be true, but the original compiler apparently never thought of William Randolph Hearst, Adela Rogers St. Johns, or Ernest Hemingway as journalists, or as anything else. As regards novelists, of the four Faulkners listed, none is William; and of the Fitzgeralds, Harrington, James, and Mary have longer entries than F. Scott. T. S. Eliot makes it; Ezra Pound does not.

As for any claims that the volumes might have had to being exhaustive on the minor figures, they fail to mention Lynn Haines, editor of the magazine *Searchlight on Congress* and author of *Your Servants in the Senate* (1926), though he was a prominent Washington correspondent during the period. This seems especially peculiar in light of the fact that Haines's uncle by marriage, Irving Bacheller, is included, and that Haines and his wife Dora wrote an authorized biography of the Lindbergh family following Charles's flight across the Atlantic, the biography being serialized in *McCall*'s as well as printed separately. If so prominent an obscure figure is left out, doubt arises as to the scope of the original volumes.

Thus, this reviewer questions the value of the original volumes on several grounds and, in spite of the editors' claims as to the value of the work for information concerning "writers whose fame did not exceed their lifetime," also questions quite strongly both the necessity and the value of the reprinted composite, especially at such a price. A student of minutiae might consult the work, but for authoritative information, would quickly pass on to the standard reference works or to such works as *Contemporary Poets* or *Contemporary Novelists*. [R: Choice, July 77, p. 662]

Koert C. Loomis, Jr.

Children's and Young Adults' Literature

408. **American Writers for Children before 1900**. Glenn E. Estes, ed. Detroit, Gale, 1985. 441p. illus. bibliog. index. (Dictionary of Literary Biography, Vol. 42). $88.00. LC 85-15990. ISBN 0-8103-1720-6.

A companion volume to John Cech's *American Writers for Children, 1900-1960* (Detroit, Gale, 1983) this volume has the same excellent coverage and format. For each of fifty-two authors from the nineteenth century there is a list of "Selected Books," a portrait, an interestingly written bibliographical account, illustrations from the author's books, and additional helps such as listings under bibliography, biography, references, and papers. Included are such well-known writers as Jacob Abbott, Louisa May Alcott, Horatio Alger, Joel Chandler Harris, Helen Hunt Jackson, Howard Pyle, and Kate Douglas Wiggin. At the end of the volume are two useful sections: "Checklist for Further Reading" and a cumulative index of the first forty-two volumes of *Dictionary of Literary Biography*, the *Dictionary of Literary Biography Yearbook*s, 1980-1984, and the Dictionary of Literary Biography Documentary series, volumes 1-4. A list of contributors is also provided.

Biographical accounts interweave life events and commentaries on literary works. Random reading indicates the contributors and editor have successfully made this a uniform characteristic. The companion volumes are reminiscent of Anne Commire's *Yesterday's Authors of Books for Children* (Detroit, Gale, 1977), and *Something about the Author* (Detroit, Gale, 1971). However, while the two volumes of *American Writers for Children* are more literary and readable in style, they are not so inclusive in coverage as the Commire titles.

A strong binding, good quality paper, excellent print, and clear reproductions of photographs and illustrations make this an inviting book for users, especially for libraries. *American Writers for Children before 1900* is strongly recommended for all who are interested in children's authors. Ruth E. Bauner

409. Cech, John, ed. **American Writers for Children, 1900-1960**. Detroit, Gale, 1983. 412p. illus. bibliog. index. (Dictionary of Literary Biography, Vol. 22; A Bruccoli Clark Book). $78.00. LC 83-14199. ISBN 0-8103-1146-1.

This title in Gale's Dictionary of Literary Biography series focuses on "Childhood's Golden Era" in the United States. From 1900 to 1960 there was an awakening interest in and development of literature for children. "The intent of this volume is to present many of the major figures . . . as well as important though perhaps less well known writers and author-illustrators . . ." of U.S. children's books published between 1900 and 1960. Forty-three authoritative and readable entries give the subject's name, dates, portrait, and a selected bibliography of the subject's work. This is followed by a narrative containing biographical information and a description and critique of the subject's major contributions to children's literature. Such well-known authors and illustrators as Lynd Ward, Robert McCloskey, Margaret Wise Brown, and E. B. White are deservedly included. Less well-known people who contributed to or significantly influenced the development of children's literature over these six decades are also included, for example, William McCay and Watty Piper. Discussions of the author's or illustrator's work include such things as the controversy over the black-and-white rabbits in Garth Williams's *Rabbits' Wedding* and the importance of the double-page spread in Virginia Lee Burton's work. In the back, a good, current bibliography lists titles for further reading.

Although not appropriate for in-depth research, this volume can serve well as a quick reference to some of the more important people involved with children's literature during these years. It is a good tool for an academic library supporting children's literature courses, or any other libraries that can afford it. [R: BL, 15 Apr 84, p. 1196]
Carol A. Doll

410. Roginski, Jim, comp. **Newbery and Caldecott Medalists and Honor Book Winners: Bibliographies and Resource Material through 1977**. Littleton, Colo., Libraries Unlimited, 1982. 339p. index. $47.50. LC 82-20362. ISBN 0-87287-296-3.

This reference work is the only one-volume comprehensive bibliography of the works and additional resource material on the Newbery and Caldecott medalists and Honor Book winners. It is an inclusive listing of award-winning books and other works by the authors and illustrators. Additional information provided on the 266 award recipients includes media formats that have been developed from their works, library and museum collections, exhibitions, and background readings. Inclusive dates for the authors and illustrators are from the beginning of their publishing careers through the 1977 award year, or the 1976 publishing year. The information on the individuals was verified by the awardees, the awardees' estates or representatives, media producers, librarians, and museum curators.

Following an introduction, which includes a brief summary of the medals, the work is arranged alphabetically by the awardee's legal name or pseudonym used at the time of the award announcement. Life dates, when known, are also provided. This book will be useful to children's and reference librarians in answering frequently asked questions about award recipients. It also allows for beginning in-depth studies of an individual's work or for identifying children's literature publishing trends as exemplified by the medalists and Honor Book winners. The collector of children's literature will find this reference book of great value. [R: BL, 1 June 83, p. 1280; Choice, Oct 83, pp. 253-54; RQ, Summer 83, pp. 426-27; WLB, May 83, pp. 787-88]

Ann Hartman

411.   Walsar, Richard, and Mary Reynolds Peacock. **Young Readers' Picturebook of Tar Heel Authors**. 5th ed. Raleigh, N.C., Division of Archives and History, North Carolina Department of Cultural Resources, 1981. 74p. illus. bibliog. $1.00pa. ISBN 0-86526-184-9.

Now in its fifth edition, this brief booklet contains biographical sketches of seventy-four authors from North Carolina. Arranged in chronological order from colonial times to the present, the work includes several nationally known literary figures—O. Henry, Randall Jarrell, Carl Sandburg, Tom Wicker, Thomas Wolfe—as well as lesser-known writers of nonfiction, novels, poems, and short stories. Full-page sketches are descriptively written, and contain a portrait or photograph as well as educational background, a publications list, and personal and professional career information. Editions are not cumulative, so some writers appearing in earlier versions have been dropped due to space limitations. The work concludes with a listing of publications, both general and individual works, consulted in the writing of the booklet. Although published since 1957, this biographical source contains information available elsewhere, and will be of most use to those southeastern libraries with children's collections.

Ilene F. Rockman

Drama

412.   MacNicholas, John, ed. **Twentieth-Century American Dramatists**. Detroit, Gale, 1981. 2v. illus. bibliog. index. (Dictionary of Literary Biography, Vol. 7; A Bruccoli Clark Book). $160.00/set. ISBN 0-8103-0928-9.

The lives and works of seventy-eight twentieth-century American dramatists are examined in this two-volume set that is part of Gale's Dictionary of Literary Biography series. *Twentieth-Century American Dramatists* focuses on nineteen major, and fifty-seven lesser-known, American playwrights whose works have been published since 1900. Included among the entries are contemporary dramatists Tennessee Williams, Arthur Miller, Neil Simon, Edward Albee, Lillian Hellman, James Baldwin, Paul Zindel, and William Saroyan, to name a few.

Entries are arranged alphabetically and vary in length from a few pages for the lesser-known figures to between twenty and thirty pages for the more renowned. Critical essays are preceded by a list of the playwrights' works (both plays and books). The essays generally focus more on the various authors' individual works than on the psychological forces at work in their lives. Primary bibliographies at the end of each essay provide a list of the dramatists' works other than their original book-length writings. Secondary bibliographies include titles that are thought to be the most relevant books and articles about the playwrights. The textual material is illustrated with photographs of the authors, playbills of their major productions, and examples of their typescripts and manuscripts. Three appendixes heighten the value of this work by discussing Trends in Theatrical Productions (Appendix I); Major Regional Theatres (Appendix II); and Books for Further Reading (Appendix III). [R: LJ, Aug 81, p. 1526; WLB, June 81, p. 778]

Patty Wood

Ethnic Minorities

413. Bailey, Leaonead Pack, comp. and ed. **Broadside Authors and Artists: An Illustrated Biographical Directory**. Detroit, Broadside Press, 1974. 125p. illus. $9.95. LC 70-108887. ISBN 0-910296-25-1.

This unique biographical reference tool provides information on authors who have been published by Broadside Press, a publishing house in Detroit that publishes the poems and prose of black writers. The format is typical of the biographical reference work, being an alphabetical arrangement by author. Information provided for the 192 authors includes birth date, current address, marital status, education, employment, and published works. Biographical information was obtained from the biographees through the use of a questionnaire, while a few biographies were compiled from other sources (e.g., family and publications carrying the biographee's work). Significantly, over 90 percent of the names listed here cannot be found in *Who's Who in America* or *Contemporary Authors*. More of the biographees, however, are listed in Ann Shockley's *Living Black American Authors*. Nevertheless, this is a useful biographical work for most public and academic libraries, and it will supplement the three biographical sources mentioned above. The primary value of this work is that it includes many young and beginning authors whose biographies are otherwise unavailable. A major weakness is the listing of some authors with incomplete biographical information, or none at all. [R: Choice, Sept 74, p. 907]   Miles M. Jackson

414. Davis, Thadious M., and Trudier Harris, eds. **Afro-American Fiction Writers after 1955**. Detroit, Gale, 1984. 350p. illus. bibliog. index. (Dictionary of Literary Biography, Vol. 33). $82.00. LC 84-18724. ISBN 0-8103-1711-7.

Volume 33 of the *Dictionary of Literary Biography* features biobibliographies of forty-nine Afro-American fiction writers who have gained prominence since 1955. Some, like James Baldwin, have produced a lengthy bibliography while others, such as George Cain, are known for one novel.

Each signed biocritical essay discusses the author's development as a writer as well as his or her growth in reputation. Most sketches include personal experiences that shaped the author's vision and work. The articles are exceptionally well written; unlike many biographical works, this is hard to put down! The illustrations, which run from portraits to reproductions of book jackets and edited pages of typescript, enhance the already handsome volume's esthetic appeal.

The DLB series is expensive, but worth its price. The entries in each volume are consistently well written and edited; the criticism alone is of enormous value to students in college and graduate literature courses. To budget-conscious libraries, however, there may be too great an overlap between the *DLB* and *Contemporary Authors*. Forty-one of the forty-nine profiles in volume 33 also appear in *CA*, although only seventeen of them have earned space in *Contemporary Literary Criticism*. Still, when finances permit, the series is a good one, and *Afro-American Fiction Writers after 1955* is no exception to its predecessors.   Diane J. Cimbala

415. Davis, Thadious M., and Trudier Harris, eds. **Afro-American Writers after 1955: Dramatists and Prose Writers**. Detroit, Gale, 1985. 390p. illus. bibliog. index. (Dictionary of Literary Biography, Vol. 38). $85.00. LC 85-1673. ISBN 0-8103-1716-8.

Focusing on those writers whose careers developed after the *Brown* vs. *the Board of Education* decision in 1954, this collective biography includes information for many lesser-known black authors. Like other books in the DLB series, this volume offers biographical information, plot summaries, and bibliographies of published works by each author. Photographs play an important part throughout this set. Reproductions of dust jackets abound and there are many face-on views of the thirty-five authors included. However, none of these photographic portraits are dated and many are of poor quality. There is neither a subject index nor an author-title index serving to identify influential works and writers mentioned by biographees or helping to identify an author included here when one knows only the title of a work. Most essays include a list of references. However, many published articles and interviews referred to in the text are not cited among the references given. This omission will frustrate some users. Some essays concentrate on an author's work, giving a critical review that is insightful and original; others, like the one on Charles Fuller, consist almost entirely of quotations taken from other published sources. An appendix contains six reprinted articles concerning black theatre, including a preliminary listing of black theatres and theatre organizations in the United States.   Milton H. Crouch

416. Littlefield, Daniel F., Jr., and James W. Parins. **A Biobibliography of Native American Writers, 1772-1924.** Metuchen, N.J., Scarecrow, 1981. 343p. index. (Native American Bibliography Series, No. 2). $21.00. LC 81-9138. ISBN 0-8108-1463-3.

Overall, this second volume of Native American Bibliography series establishes a higher level of quality than did volume 1. If the remainder of the series maintains the current level, it will be a set well worth acquiring. Littlefield and Parins have greatly expanded the scope of Arlene Hirschfelder's *American Indian Authors.* They define a native American "as a person who had tribal affiliation or maintained tribal ties and who was recognized by his contemporaries as a native American" (p. vi). Furthermore, they checked for corroborating evidence for anyone claiming to be native American; in the absence of supporting evidence, the individual was excluded (1,015 persons are listed along with 168 "Indian Pen Names" that could not be tied to a known individual).

All types of writings are included (total entries—4,371), not just literary, although the compilers admit their coverage of newspaper articles and editorials is weak. The volume consists of three main sections: an alphabetical listing by author (name, tribal affiliation, entry number, code for type of publication—address, collection, drama, editorial, fiction, letter, myth or legend, nonfiction prose, poetry, sermon translation— and title and publication data); a listing of writers known only by a pen name; and a biographical "notes" section. The notes range from extended mini-essays to one-liners— "Adam McCarthy attended Carlisle" (p. 263). There is a tribal index as well as a subject index. The cutoff date, which is arbitrary, is the year all American Indians were given U.S. citizenship, thus marking the end of an era. That cutoff decision means that many authors, for example, Charles Eastman and Will Rogers, are not completely represented. This is the work's primary weakness, although some cut-point was necessary to keep the book to a reasonable length; had the compilers followed through on those writers who started writing before 1924 up to the writer's death date, the volume would be even more useful. [R: BL, July 82, p. 1463; Choice, Mar 82, p. 892; LJ, 15 Feb 82, p. 445; WLB, Jan 82, p. 379]   G. Edward Evans

417. Page, James A., and Jae Min Roh, comps. **Selected Black American, African, and Caribbean Authors: A Bio-Bibliography.** Littleton, Colo., Libraries Unlimited, 1985. 402p. index. $55.00. LC 85-5225. ISBN 0-87287-430-3.

This handy, compact, one-volume companion to Afro-American writing provides valuable insight into 632 African-descended authors and their works. Concerned primarily with the Afro-American literature of the United States (from its beginnings to the present), this biobibliography also attempts to give some understanding of "the literary scene on the Mother Continent itself, as well as in the Caribbean diaspora."

James A. Page and Jae Min Roh's criteria for selection require that (1) authors must have had at least one book published; (2) authors must have been included in other sources such as anthologies, critical studies, handbooks, and biographical references; (3) poets must have had more than one book of poems published; (4) playwrights should have had one or more plays either published or performed; and (5) essayists must have produced significant work in the arts, biography, criticism, history, social sciences, or other areas.

Arranged alphabetically by author's last name, each entry contains birth and death dates and places, family, education, address, career information, a list of the author's works, selected comments on his or her career, and a list of information sources.

Browsing through this informative biobibliography gives insight into well-known black authors such as James Baldwin, Lorraine Hansberry, Toni Morrison, Ntozake Shangé, Wole Soyinka, Margaret Walker, and Richard Wright and calls attention to lesser-known figures such as Evelyn Burrell and Armand Lanusse. The compilers have accomplished their objective of "presenting a broad spectrum of what is being thought about, written, and spoken of in that vast, diverse world known as Black America."

Colby H. Kullman

418.   Rush, Theressa Gunnels, Carol Fairbanks Myers, and Esther Spring Arata. **Black American Writers Past and Present: A Biographical and Bibliographical Dictionary**. Metuchen, N.J., Scarecrow, 1975. 2v. illus. $39.50. LC 74-28400. ISBN 0-8108-0785-8.

Previous work by one of the authors (Myers) on a book entitled *Black Power in the Arts* (Flint, Michigan, The Mott Foundation, 1970) convinced her and later her co-authors of the need for a dictionary, ideally as comprehensive as possible, of all black writers, past and present, of poetry, drama, fiction, children's literature, and criticism.

While stressing writers in these categories, the work also includes those who have written nonfiction that is used in black studies curricula and writers from Africa and the West Indies who either live or publish in the United States.

The entries are arranged in straight alphabetical order. Their components are biographical information (supplied exclusively by the living author, and through secondary sources for deceased writers); bibliographies of writings; citations for work published in anthologies or periodicals; and finally, biographies and critical studies. Here an effort at comprehensiveness was made for minor writers only. The work concludes with a general bibliography and two appendixes, which list, respectively, black and white critics, historians, and editors.

Unquestionably, this is the most comprehensive dictionary of its kind to be issued. This in itself has value in a culture that tends to neglect or even ignore black writers, and on this ground alone, it deserves consideration by most libraries.

Nonetheless, its execution could easily have been improved. Many of its entries are so brief that they become meaningless. An example on page 175, quoted in full: "CORBO, Dominic R., Jr. *Novel: Hard Ground* New York: Vantage, 1954." Corbo was evidently uncooperative with the compilers, who nevertheless could have made some effort to supply from secondary sources information not to be extracted from him.

The underlying criterion for inclusion in the book was the fact of having had something published. No qualitative standards of any kind were used. However, the corpus of black American literature has now become so large that qualitative standards are needed if one is to make sense of it. Fascination with sheer numbers should give way to reasoned criticism and discriminating judgment.

Somewhat related is *Living Black American Authors: A Biographical Dictionary* (New York, R. R. Bowker, 1973. 220p. o.p.). Unfortunately, its coverage is uneven in terms of content of individual entries as well as overall inclusiveness. Full entries include name, occupation, place and date of birth, education, family, professional experience, memberships, awards, publications, and mailing address. Some entries include only name and titles of publications. Many well-known writers are listed (e.g., Imamu Amiri Baraka, James Baldwin, Gwendolyn Brooks) but many equally well known have been omitted (e.g., Arna Bontemps, Angela Davis, Roy Wilkins). [R: LJ, 1 Sept 75, p. 1537; RQ, Fall 75, p. 80; WLB, Oct 75, p. 118]   Richard A. Gray and Bohdan S. Wynar

Fiction

419. **American Humorists, 1800-1950.** Stanley Trachtenberg, ed. Detroit, Gale, 1982. 2v. illus. index. (Dictionary of Literary Biography, Vol. 11; A Bruccoli Clark Book). $156.00. LC 81-20238. ISBN 0-8108-1147-X.

One of the advantages of the *Dictionary of Literary Biography* (*DLB*) is that each volume (which in this case consists of two parts) can be evaluated and purchased separately; the differences in the series are notable enough that not all libraries will want all volumes. A disadvantage is the price, made especially manifest in this two-volume set, which costs nearly $0.20 per page!

Even with the price, however, this item will be hard to resist, for here we have a very useful collection of biographical and critical essays on seventy-two notable American humorists, complete with fascinating photographs, cartoons, bibliographies of the writers' works, and references for further reading. Major humorists—such as George Ade, Robert Benchley, Finley Peter Dunne, Ring Lardner, Ogden Nash, Dorothy Parker, S. J. Perelman, James Thurber, Mark Twain, and E. B. White—are accorded master essays of fifteen to thirty pages, whereas lesser figures, many of them indeed obscure, are treated more briefly. All are considered to be *literary* figures, rather than performers, newspaper columnists, or cartoonists. Writers such as Ambrose Bierce and William Faulkner are included where there is deemed to be a "significant body of humorous writing." Appendixes embrace a historical survey by regions of the country, humorous book illustrations, newspaper syndication of American humor, a selection of humorous magazines illustrated by their covers, a supplementary reading list, and a cumulative subject index of volumes 1-11 of *DLB*.

A useful compendium of information and illustration on American humor, *American Humorists, 1800-1950* belongs in all libraries that can afford it. [R: Choice, Nov 82, p. 405; LJ, 15 Oct 82, p. 1978]   Edwin S. Gleaves

420. **American Realists and Naturalists.** Donald Pizer and Earl N. Harbert, eds. Detroit, Gale, 1982. 486p. illus. index. (Dictionary of Literary Biography, Vol. 12; A Bruccoli Clark Book). $70.00. LC 82-9258. ISBN 0-8103-1149-6.

This volume, highly useful in itself, is an important addition to the DLB series. *American Realists and Naturalists* would be valuable if it merely confined itself to presenting somewhat traditional biographies; however, the editors have made sure the volume goes much further than that. Authors are not only treated within the context of their age, but also studied as participants in an American culture that would bear their impress. As a result, the intersections of European thought, American intellectual life, and the promise of the future become underlying themes of many of the biographies. In fact, the reader wishes that the essays would somehow be longer—a sign of how fulfilling each study actually is.

The entries have a common format: citations for birth, education, death, awards, etc.; a list of selected books; and lists of bibliographies, biographies, letters, seminal critical works, papers, and the like. While these critical references are, in instances, highly selective, and I think, partisan (one person's acclaimed biography is another's unimaginative reading), they often do great justice to the subject. The entries are fleshed out with photographs of the writer, a reproduction of a page from a manuscript, or the picture of a book-jacket. In short, the essays seek to make their subjects accessible and timely. Finally, the essays themselves are quite readable; they are free from literary jargon and tight in their focus. If they are not necessarily daring, they are thoughtful and always informative.   Lewis Fried

421.   Helterman, Jeffrey and Richard Layman, eds. **American Novelists since World War II**. Detroit, Gale, 1978. 557p. illus. bibliog. (Dictionary of Literary Biography, Vol. 2; A Bruccoli Clark Book). $80.00. LC 77-82804. ISBN 0-8103-0914-9.

This volume covers some eighty figures of prominence who have established themselves since the end of World War II. It continues with the series' pattern of long essays (eighteen) as well as some shorter ones. Here, long essays are given on Baldwin, Barth, Cheever, McCullers, Nabokov, Pynchon, Updike, Vonnegut, Penn Warren, and Welty, among others. There are also bibliographies.

Here, despite the apparent attempt to follow the general pattern, the essays are overly long. This book has eighty sketches and fills 557 pages; the Myerson first volume, by contrast, covers ninety-eight figures in less than half the space—224 pages. Long sections of each essay are devoted to exegesis of individual works, sometimes detailed examination, and it seems too much here. Instead of saying, "Hey, here's a good book!," the essay reduces the books to playthings, sometimes resembling hardcover Cliff Notes. [R: Choice, July/Aug 79, p. 645; LJ, 1 Apr 79, p. 938; WLB, June 79, p. 722-23]   Koert C. Loomis, Jr.

422.   Kibler, James E., Jr., ed. **American Novelists since World War II, Second Series**. Detroit, Gale, 1980. 404p. illus. index. (Dictionary of Literary Biography, Vol. 6; A Bruccoli Clark Book). $80.00. LC 80-22495. ISBN 0-8103-0908-4.

This volume, part of the *Dictionary of Literary Biography* (*DLB*), provides seventy biographical/critical sketches of recent American novelists. It is a supplement to the previous 1978 volume in the DLB series with the same title. The value of this work is in its provision of material on many lesser-known literary figures, many of whom are still developing their reputations. While it is easy to find data on Vladimir Nabokov, James Agee, and Ray Bradbury (all treated in the 1978 edition), this volume offers the user background on such writers as Mark Steadman, a "patient craftsman" who has produced two novels since 1971, and Joan Williams, who has done three since 1961.

The sketches are well done, with considerable emphasis on plot summaries of the novels and the critical reception accorded to the authors. Although some biographies run to two or three pages, a few, like that of Isaac Bashevis Singer, are substantial. Each biography is written by an authority and is followed by a selected list of works by and about the person treated. Textually, the volume is an excellent production, with photographs of the authors and frequent reproductions of manuscript materials. Significant public collections of an author's work are noted.

A foreword by the bibliophile William Targ notes that the novel form is still healthy, and he uses the volume in hand to validate that argument. *American Novelists since World War II, Second Series* is a useful supplement to the previous volume and should find an important place in any reference collection where works of contemporary novelists are examined. [R: BL, 15 Oct 80, pp. 344-46]

Donald C. Dickinson

423. Martine, James J., ed. **American Novelists, 1910-1945**. Detroit, Gale, 1981. 3v. illus. bibliog. index. (Dictionary of Literary Biography, Vol. 9; A Bruccoli Clark Book). $240.00/set. LC 81-6834. ISBN 0-8103-0931-9.

The period 1910 to 1945, encompassing World War I, the Great Depression, and World War II, a period of conflict and turmoil in American history, gave rise to eighteen major, and more than one hundred lesser-known, American novelists. These novelists and their works are critically examined in this three-volume set of Gale's Dictionary of Literary Biography series. Among the major writers discussed are Sherwood Anderson, Willa Cather, John Dos Passos, Theodore Dreiser, William Faulkner, F. Scott Fitzgerald, Ernest Hemingway, Sinclair Lewis, Henry Miller, John O'Hara, John Steinbeck, Edith Wharton, and Thomas Wolfe. In all, 125 writers are covered in *American Novelists, 1910-1945*.

Entries are arranged alphabetically and begin with a listing of the author's work, followed by critical essays about the author and his or her writings, and listings of other relevant readings and reference material. The length of the entries varies, the editors state, depending on the writer's influence and size of canon. The shorter essays run two to three pages; the longer ones go up to twenty pages.

Illustrative material includes photographs of the authors, early drafts of their novels, and edited manuscripts. Appendixes provide additional useful information, including articles giving an "Overview of U.S. Book Publishing, 1910-1945" and examining "Southern Writers between the Wars," the "Proletarian Novel," "American Fiction and the 1930s," and "Tough-Guy Literature." Patty Wood

Poetry

424. Greiner, Donald J., ed. **American Poets since World War II**. Detroit, Gale, 1980. 2v. illus. bibliog. index. (Dictionary of Literary Biography, Vol. 5). $160.00/set. LC 80-16058. ISBN 0-8103-0924-6.

This rather frighteningly expensive set is part of *Dictionary of Literary Biography*, but is, of course, complete in itself and a very useful work. The first volume covers poets from A. R. Ammons to Maxine Kumin; the second begins with Denise Levertov and ends with Louis Zukofsky (one of the relatively few persons listed who is dead). As with any collaborative or cooperative work, the quality of articles is a bit uneven, but it is generally high. Each entry is followed by a bibliography and a list of further readings, and at the end of volume 2, there is a list (unannotated) of "Books for Further

Reading." Also at the end of that volume is a cumulative list of the entries in volumes 1 through 5. There are many illustrations, including a fascinating endpaper montage of many photographs of the poets. Also included in the illustrative material are photographs of early drafts of poems, working papers, and manuscripts in general.

Some of the poets (more than 125 are covered in the two volumes) are very well known—Daniel Berrigan, Theodore Roethke, and Frank O'Hara. Others, such as Linda Pastan, are much less well known (unless, indeed, it is just my own fault for not knowing about them).

Large libraries will certainly be acquiring the entire *DLB*, while smaller ones may well want to be selective, and these two volumes would be in a selective gathering. But, as the first sentence points out, the total price is a bit frightening. [R: Choice, Mar 81, p. 919; LJ, 15 Jan 81, p. 135]   D. Bernard Theall

Regional

425. Bain, Robert, Joseph M. Flora, and Louis D. Rubin, Jr., eds. **Southern Writers: A Biographical Dictionary**. Baton Rouge, La., Louisiana State University Press, 1979. (Southern Literary Studies). $35.00; $8.95pa. LC 78-25899. ISBN 0-8071-0354-3; 0-8071-0390-Xpa.

Designed as a reference tool to be used in conjunction with *A Bibliographical Guide to the Study of Southern Literature* (1969), the updated *Southern Literary Culture* (1979), and the annual checklist published in the spring issue of *Mississippi Quarterly*, this biographical dictionary fills the need for ready information otherwise time-consuming to attain. Compiled Southern literature, biographical sketches of 379 authors, and a bibliography of the first U.S. editions of the authors' major works are presented. The concise sketches are well balanced between factual information and evaluative commentary, and are generally uniform in quality.

Apparently, considerable effort was made to arrive at a consensus of scholars and editors as to which authors were to be included, although the final list seems to slight scholars, critics, and historians and to disproportionately favor Afro-American writers. One wonders, for instance, why such significant writers as Randall Stewart, F. Van Woodward, Frank Owsley, and Douglas Southall Freeman were omitted? Perhaps the editors felt that information about such writers was readily available elsewhere. Perhaps, too, the editors felt that past neglect of Afro-American writers called for special compensation in the present volume. However much one may wish the list to be more complete and more representative of a broader range of Southern writers, the dictionary is an extremely valuable contribution to the study of Southern literature. [R: LJ, Aug 79, p. 1552]   Robert L. Welker

426. **Fifty Western Writers: A Bio-Bibliographical Sourcebook**. Fred Erisman and Richard W. Etulain, eds. Westport, Conn., Greenwood Press, 1982. 562p. index. $45.00. LC 81-13462. ISBN 0-313-22167-1.

The editors explicitly state that this volume is intended as an introductory reference and research guide. For that purpose, it is handy and generally complete. Its design is sound, based as it is on the prototype for research guides on a limited subject, Floyd Stovall's *Eight American Authors* (1971). But because there are fifty writers covered here, not eight, and because much less has been written about these fifty than about Stovall's more famous group, the design has been changed considerably. For one thing, each writer is covered in much less detail, being treated in a chapter only about ten pages long (the longest is thirteen pages, for Robinson Jeffers). For another thing, each section has only four parts: "Biography," "Major Theories," "Survey of Criticism," and "Bibliography (Primary and Secondary)." This uniformity seems natural when applied to a few major writers, but here seems strained when applied to authors as different in productivity as Jack London and Ken Kesey or in generating critical attention as John Steinbeck and Frederick Manfred. Surely, even for the beginner, much more space could have been devoted to such writers as Willa Cather, Jeffers, London, and Steinbeck.

Otherwise, the volume deserves only praise. The writers covered are from the nineteenth century as well as the present, and they wrote in such areas as fiction, nonfiction, poetry, journalism, and the popular Western novel. The essays are cogently written, and the bibliographies are well selected. For example, the recent annotated secondary bibliographies to Bret Harte, Joaquin Miller, Zane Grey, and Owen Wister are listed. And the chapters are frequently written by authoritative scholars: Earle Labor on London, Warren French on Frank Norris, and Richard Etulain, Robert Gale, and Max Westbrook. The volume is well indexed and is, all things considered, a welcome and unpretentious aid for the beginner. [R: BL, Aug 83, p. 1487; Choice, Feb 83, p. 809]   L. Terry Oggel

427.   Knight, Lucian Lamar, comp. **Biographical Dictionary of Southern Authors**. Atlanta, Ga., Martin and Hoyt, 1929 (c1910); repr., Detroit, Gale, 1978. 487p. $70.00. LC 75-26631. ISBN 0-8103-4269-3.

Originally published in 1929 as volume XV of *Library of Southern Literature*, this is a remarkable document. Knight's admittedly polemic labor of love is aimed at redressing the neglect this region had suffered at the time and to show the "true value and extent of the South's contributions to American letters." More than a literary biography, it includes nearly thirty-eight hundred sketches of authors of works on education, history, politics, science, law, medicine, and other fields. Information provided varies widely: most entries have short biographical articles and listings of publications, but many have only a name with a title or two listed after it. Those who order this volume without owning the complete *Library* may be irritated to find that it contains many cross-references to other volumes in the set. These are mostly for well-known writers, however; the chief value of this volume lies in its coverage of more obscure writers not readily found elsewhere.   Richard J. Kelly

428.   Myerson, Joel, ed. **Antebellum Writers in New York and the South**. Detroit, Gale, 1979. 383p. illus. bibliog. (Dictionary of Literary Biography, Vol. 3; A Bruccoli Clark Book). $80.00. LC 79-15481. ISBN 0-8103-0915-7.

This volume, part of the DLB series, covers some sixty-seven writers whose major work came in the period 1820-1860. Fifteen of the entries are given the long-essay treatment, with the remainder getting coverage of from one to three pages (including illustrations). Covered are such major figures of the time as Bryant, Calhoun, Cooper, Greeley, Irving, Longstreet, Melville, Poe, and Whitman. The lesser notables include writers of short stories, sermons, popular literature, editors, humorists, translators, journalists, historians, abolitionists, scientists, etc. — in other words, all manner of scribblers. Essays are both biographical and critical, but the criticism is limited to brief expositions, not detailed analysis.

The antebellum period was particularly prolific in the production of popular literature, and a thriving literary scene was established both in New York and in the

South, with ample cross-fertilization. This volume in the series updates scholarship, especially in the provision of bibliographies for the major figures as well as the notation of references for the lesser-known figures. And in so doing, it helps to provide a clearer picture of that time of national self-delusion and concurrent stringent self-examination. On the whole, Myerson's volume is praiseworthy indeed. [R: LJ, 1 Nov 79, pp. 2331-32]

Koert C. Loomis, Jr.

429. Tuska, Jon, and Vicki Piekarski, eds. **Encyclopedia of Frontier and Western Fiction**. New York, McGraw-Hill, 1983. 365p. illus. $29.95. LC 82-14831. ISBN 0-07-065587-1.

Essentially a collection of some three hundred biographies of writers of Western fiction (hardcover, paperback, and dime novel), this work exhibits careful and thorough research. The sketches, reminiscent of those in *Contemporary Authors*, include not only complete listings of all writings (including pseudonymous authorship), but also titles of movies and/or television programs derived from the printed fiction. The writers go back as far as James Fenimore Cooper, Washington Irving, Owen Wister, and O. Henry and forward to Louis L'Amour and other present-day popularizers of the Western scene.

In addition to the three hundred-odd biobibliographical sketches there are five topical essays: "Historical Personalities"; "House Names" (meaning publishing house names of series or of protagonists in series); "Native Americans"; "Pulp and Slick Western Stories"; and "Women on the Frontier." Each of these is in itself an informative, though brief, sketch of the topic it treats, and each is, of course, related primarily to Western fiction.

From a reader's point of view the work suffers somewhat from poor editorial judgment. The five essays mentioned above are buried alphabetically within the text. They would have been more useful if they had been presented as an introduction or even as an appendix. As it stands, they are likely to be overlooked. Another defect is that all listings of fiction titles, movie titles, etc., are given in paragraph rather than in columnar form. Since these often run to thirty or forty items, they are wearisome to read. [R: BL, 1 May 83, p. 1128; Choice, Oct 83, p. 250; LJ, 1 May 83, pp. 898-99; RQ, Fall 83, pp. 104-5; WLB, Sept 83, pp. 65-66]   Raymund F. Wood

430. **Twentieth-Century Western Writers**. James Vinson, ed.; D. L. Kirkpatrick, associate ed. Detroit, Gale, 1982. 941p. index. $95.00. ISBN 0-8103-0227-6.

The actual coverage of this book is less than is implied in its title, being limited to authors of novels, short stories, plays, and occasional essays. Within these limits, however, the coverage is very good, far better than that provided for similar writers in *Southwestern American Literature: A Bibliography* (Swallow, 1980). For example, for the prolific writer S. Omar Barker, the bibliography cited above devotes only one-half page, mixing nine titles of novels, verse, and short stories, without differentiation; the work under review gives five pages to Barker, with a complete listing of titles, differentiating among novels, collected short stories, short stories in magazines, verse, juveniles, and "others."

Each entry starts with a brief biographical sketch and ends with a longer, signed critical essay. Bibliographical data are categorized by type—Western writings first, then (if any) those of other regions, such as Willa Cather's *Shadows on the Rock*. Under each type the works are then differentiated, e.g., novels, short stories, etc. Under the heading "Other" are sometimes listed autobiographies or critical works. Manuscript locations are sometimes given. Pseudonyms are listed but refer the reader to the author's proper name. An index of titles (nearly one hundred pages) completes this valuable bibliography.

Chronologically the book is limited to the twentieth century. Although the writings of Bret Harte and Helen Hunt Jackson are acknowledged in the preface, neither they nor Mark Twain are included in the book itself. [R: Choice, July/Aug 83, pp. 1578-79; LJ, 15 May 83, pp. 993-94; RQ, Summer 83, pp. 429-30; WLB, May 83, pp. 789-90]

Raymund F. Wood

Science Fiction

431. Cowart, David, and Thomas L. Wymer, eds. **Twentieth-Century American Science-Fiction Writers**. Detroit, Gale, 1981. 2v. illus. index. (Dictionary of Literary Biography, Vol. 8; A Bruccoli Clark Book). $160.00/set. LC 81-4182. ISBN 0-8103-0918-1.

This work meets one of the long-standing needs of the reference librarian and science-fiction fan for a single source of biographical information and critical discussion of the *oeuvres* of the most significant twentieth-century American SF writers. The ninety-one American SF authors discussed and evaluated in this double-columned, two-volume source are those who attained prominence between 1900 and 1970. Those SF writers who emerged as major talents during the decade of the 1970s (such as Benford, McIntyre, and Varley) are not included.

Each entry consists of a list of novels or short-story collections by the author, a few paragraphs of biographical information, a long, chronologically organized critical discussion and evaluation of the major novels (and sometimes major stories) of the author, and a selected bibliography of books and articles about the author. Heinlein, LeGuin, Bradbury, and Asimov receive the longest entries, between fifteen and twenty-one double-columned pages each. Each entry has been written by a professor who is an aficionado of both the SF genre and the particular SF author. Each entry has at least one photograph of the author, and often contains a photograph of a manuscript page or the front cover of a famous novel. There are six appendixes in volume 2, containing eight essays and four lists, including a world chronology of important SF works published between 1818 and 1979. Most entries compare the novels and themes of the author being discussed to other novels about similar subjects and themes. All profiles are very well written and enjoyable to read.

The major shortcomings of this otherwise excellent reference source are the scantiness of the biographical information, the failure to list all the novels of the more prolific authors, the failure to list all the short stories of the author, and the failure to more fully discuss the major short stories of the author (many of the classics of SF are short stories, not novels). A more complete listing of interviews with the author in fanzines would also have been helpful. Large and medium libraries should buy this work. Smaller libraries can make do with the excellent *Science Fiction Encyclopedia* (Doubleday, 1979). We now await a complementary volume for twentieth-century European SF writers and one for SF writers of the 1970s. [R: WLB, Nov 81, p. 237]

Joseph H. Cataio

Women

432. American Women Writers: A Critical Reference Guide from Colonial Times to the Present. Edited by Lina Mainiero and Langdon Lynne Faust. New York, Frederick Ungar, 1978-1982. $55.00/vol. LC 78-20945. ISBN 0-8044-3151-5 (vol. 1); 0-8044-3152-3 (vol. 2); 0-8044-3153-1 (vol. 3); 0-8044-3155-8 (vol. 4).

433. American Women Writers: A Critical Reference Guide from Colonial Times to the Present. Landgon Lynne Faust, ed. Abridged ed. New York, Frederick Ungar, 1983. 2v. index. $14.95pa/vol. LC 82-40286. ISBN 0-8044-6164-3 (vol. 1); 0-8044-6165-1 (vol. 2).

This pioneering work offers articles on women who made literature their career as well as women who wrote seriously about their work in history, psychology, theology, home economics, and other fields. It also brings to public attention many unjustly neglected writers, whose stories, journals, and poetry reflected their world. Each entry provides biographical information, a summary of the writer's career, and an examination of her works, with helpful bibliographies. A comprehensive index is included in volume 4.

Though *Notable American Women* (Edward T. James, Janet Wilson James, and Paul S. Boyer, eds., 1951) provides some overlap, *AWW* is a substantially different source because it concentrates exclusively on writers: "those who are known and read, and those who have been generally neglected or undervalued because they were women." EAch critical biography meticulously assesses the writer's contribution; provides the basic biographical information, including married and maiden names, pseudonyms, and aliases that often elude even diligent searchers; and lists complete bibliographies (the first such compilations for many of the women included). Every biography is signed by a scholar or editor working in the fields of literature, women's studies, or American studies, which may account for the excellent overall quality of the entries. The range of writers represented is considerable—from little-known names to the contemporary literary luminaries. Elizabeth Bishop, Harriette Arnow, and Louisa May Alcott are, not surprisingly, here, but so are the newer names—Olga Broumas, E. M. Broner, and Rita Mae Brown. Nor is this work confined to poets and fiction writers. Diarists, journalists, anthropologists, historians, and academicians figure into the unparalleled resource, too.

One can always find cause to quarrel with the editors' selection in a work such as *AWW*. This reviewer was disappointed by the limited attention paid to minority writers. It is perplexing not to find black writers of the caliber of Audre Lorde, June Jordan, and Ntozake Shange, and Indian writers such as Joy Harjo, Wendy Rose, and Paula Gunn Allen. The abridgment of course shrinks the coverage still further, eliminating some writers included in the full set, e.g., Leslie Marmon Silko, Alice Walker, Toni Morrison, Maya Angelou, and Maxine Hong Kingston. In the introduction to the first edition, the editors admit to not doing justice to black and lesbian writers but argue that this can be justified by the fact that "these contemporary writers . . . are getting adequate attention—they are being read, anthologized, taught. . . . We concluded that such women writers could most easily be omitted in this first edition and best be covered in a supplementary volume," However, the editors may be too quick to assume that recent anthologies of minority and lesbian writers and fledgling women's studies courses assure these writers a permanent place in U.S. letters.

One hopes to see the high quality established in the first edition and the abridgment of *A WW* enhanced in a subsequent expanded edition. [R: JAL, Nov 79, p. 304; LJ, Aug 79, p. 1551; LJ, 1 Dec 83, p. 2242]

Catherine R. Loeb, Esther F. Stineman, and Bohdan S. Wynar

434. Duke, Maurice, Jackson R. Bryer, and M. Thomas Inge, eds. **American Women Writers: Bibliographical Essays**. Westport, Conn., Greenwood Press, 1983. 434p. index. $39.95. LC 82-6156. ISBN 0-313-22116-2.

Twenty-four major American women authors, often neglected in scholarly treatments of our national literature, are the focus of this collection of bibliographical essays. This authoritative guide to women novelists, dramatists, and poets is highly selective, excluding authors who have been given similar scholarly treatment elsewhere. The essays, prepared by well-known critics of the authors, include brief introductory statements about each author and sections on bibliography, editions, manuscripts and letters, biography, and criticism, in a format similar to those of Floyd Stovall's *Eight American Authors* and *Sixteen Modern American Authors*, edited by Jackson R. Bryer (Duke, 1974). Beginning with Anne Bradstreet, the coverage extends to Sarah Orne Jewett, Gertrude Stein, Kate Chopin, Margaret Mitchell, Flannery O'Connor, Carson McCullers, Anaïs Nin, Zora Neale Hurston, Anne Sexton, and others. Historical and technical innovations in literature by women writers are reflected in choice of authors. The volume is a major accomplishment, noting areas where further research is needed. Perhaps it will promote similar efforts for coverage of other significant women writers. [R: BL, 1 Dec 83, p. 547; Choice, Oct 83, p. 270; LJ, 1 Feb 83, p. 196; WLB, June 83, p. 880]

Maureen Pastine

435. **The Living Female Writers of the South**. Philadelphia, Claxton, Remsen & Haffelfinger, 1872; repr., Detroit, Gale, 1978. 568p. index. $85.00. LC 75-44070. ISBN 0-8103-4286-3.

Living . . . Writers is a reissue of an 1872 publication, thus explaining the use of *female* instead of *women* in the title. The book can be used as a reference tool, but many of the entries are lengthy biobibliographical essays, and there are generous selections from the works of most of the 183 authors treated.

Entries are arranged by state: Kentucky, Louisiana, Georgia, Alabama, Mississippi, Florida, Tennessee, Virginia, North Carolina, South Carolina, Maryland, and Texas, in that order. Names are not in alphabetical sequence; therefore, one must consult the index, which has writers and writings in one list. The index is in standard alphabetical order by first letter, but only more or less so by second letter; it is necessary to look up and down the column to spot a name. A fifteen-page introduction discusses other writers, also indexed, who had died just before the book was compiled or about whom little was known.

Stereotypical Southern romanticism suffuses much of the writing, but the book is not froth. The memory of the Civil War was still fresh; dead babies, dead soldiers, lost loves, and slaves are recurring themes, and the expression is earnest and often poignant. There are also practicality ("If we should all commence telling the truth at once, what a grand smashup of the social machine! Why should we go peering behind the scenes, where [when?] all is so fair and specious on the outside?"); dudgeon (" 'Ward's patent, reversible, perspiration-proof paper collar. . . .' What a catalogue of shams and vulgarities!"); and constants (". . . a restless desire to find how we can make all we meet subserve our interests . . ."). The book is a mix of history and contemporary sociology, yielding overall a compelling literature.

Kathleen McCullough

436.   Rainwater, Catherine, and William J. Scheick, eds. **Contemporary American Women Writers: Narrative Strategies**. Lexington, Ky., University Press of Kentucky, 1985. 240p. $22.00. ISBN 0-8131-1558-2.

Prepared by several professors, these ten biographical essays cover such personalities as Ann Beattie, Annie Dillard, Maxine Hong Kingston, Toni Morrison, Cynthia Ozick, Grace Paley, and Marge Piercy. The emphasis is on literary style of each writer and the major "message" she may suggest to the audience. Thus, for example, the editors suggest that Beattie, Dillard, Paley, and Redmon in divergent ways rely heavily upon narrative gaps, surfaces, and silences, often suggesting depths which are frequently absent from modern literary experience. Ozick and Taylor disrupt conventional reader experience of the "anti-novel" and the "family novel" respectively. Biographical data per se are of marginal interest.   Bohdan S. Wynar

Other Topics

437.   Charters, Ann, ed. **The Beats: Literary Bohemians in Postwar America**. Detroit, Gale, 1983. 2v. illus. bibliog. index. (Dictionary of Literary Biography, Vol. 16). $160.00/set. LC 82-24257. ISBN 0-8103-1148-8.

This two-volume set continues Gale's expensively mounted (and high-priced) Dictionary of Literary Biography series. Volume 16 concerns the Beat writers; it contains sixty-six well-written and well-illustrated (with black-and-white photographs) bioliterary sketches of writers associated with that literary genre, all written by literary scholars, with help from personal friends of the biographees.

Coverage includes names all will recognize (e.g., Jack Kerouac, Gregory Corso, Allen Ginsberg) and several writers little known to most of us. The amount of space given to each subject is proportionate to the literary output of the writer and, seemingly, to the "splash" he or she made on the media and the reading public. For example, the average entry runs five or six pages, including illustrative material, but the essay on Allen Ginsberg goes almost thirty double-column pages and includes nine photographs. Then there are entries for persons who are not technically Beat writers but who either influenced or were influenced by them. Among these are such names as Bob Dylan, Timothy Leary, and Norman Mailer.

Arrangement is alphabetical by name, with the two volumes combined making a complete alphabet. Each entry contains book lists, but no claim is made to exhaustiveness, and the lists are entitled "Selected Books." Quotations from the writers are salted throughout the essays, which makes easy reading and may help to explain more mystical passages.   Bruce A. Shuman

438.   Rood, Karen Lane, ed. **American Writers in Paris, 1920-1939**. Detroit, Gale, 1980. 426p. illus. bibliog. (Dictionary of Literary Biography, Vol. 4; A Bruccoli Clark Book). $80.00. LC 79-26101. ISBN 0-8103-0916-5.

Volume 4 of the *Dictionary of Literary Biography* covers the generation of literati that, to most tastes, is the richest the United States has had—that which chose to leave home. The volume is a valuable ready reference for ninety-nine figures who defined an age. Each article begins with the writer's dates and a list of his or her major publications; this is followed by an informative and often enjoyable biobibliographical and occasionally critical essay.

Twenty of the essays are "master entries," covering those figures having the most profound effect, not only on the Lost Generation but on literature itself:

E. E. Cummings, Djuna Barnes, Edith Wharton, H. D., Henry Miller, Fitzgerald, Hemingway, Pound, Stein, et al. The remaining entries are for writers who are perhaps equally well known and integral to the period, but whose sojourns in Paris were considerably briefer: William Carlos Williams, Anaïs Nin, Katherine Anne Porter, Allen Tate, and many others. The result is a readable reference work, providing an in-depth description of the Paris cafe life between the wars. As one would expect, it is more a portrait of a scene than a source of information on individuals. Still, the brief articles are accurate and clearly written, and the volume is a place to begin. [R: Choice, Oct 80, p. 219; LJ, 1 June 80, p. 1291]   F. W. Ramey

African Literature

439.   Herdeck, Donald E. **African Authors: A Companion to Black African Writing, Volume I: 1300-1973**. Washington, D.C., INSCAPE Corp.; distr., Detroit, Gale, 1974. 605p. illus. bibliog. (A Black Orpheus Press/Inscape Book). $64.00. LC 73-172338. ISBN 0-87953-008-1.

This comprehensive biographical reference source is both biographical and bibliographical in its coverage of 594 authors. The well-written vignettes provide human-interest facts about the biographees. Entries include the basic facts about the authors' lives and careers, and complete listings of their published works. The bibliographical coverage includes the major European languages and thirty-seven African vernacular languages. The vernacular language maps are an added feature. There are also photographs and drawings. The appendixes are arranged in four parts: Part 1 includes four critical essays intended to introduce the general reader to African literature. Part 2 contains appendixes that list the authors according to chronology, genre, country of origin, African languages, and European languages. Part 3 lists publishers and their addresses. Part 4 is a critical, annotated bibliography of African writing and studies of African writing. The most important feature of this biographical reference source is that it is the only work that covers African writers who are not listed anyplace else. As a reference work, *African Authors* is unique and valuable to libraries, especially large public and academic libraries. .

A related title is *Black American Writers: Bibliographical Essays* edited by Thomas M. Inge (2v. New York, St. Martin's Press, 1978. o.p.) that covers twenty-four personalities. The earliest writer represented is Jupiter Hammon, born in 1711. The second volume is dedicated to Wright, Ellison, Baldwin, and Baraka, a quartet of major figures from our own time. The format for the essays varies slightly, as required by the individual subjects, but the treatment is carefully considered. Attention is given to bibliographies, editions, manuscripts and letters, biographies, and criticism in a terse but informative style. [R: BL, 15 Jan 74, p. 499; Choice, May 74, p. 412]

Miles M. Jackson and Bohdan S. Wynar

British Literature

General Works

440.   **British Authors before 1800. A Biographical Dictionary**. Edited by Stanley Kunitz and Howard Haycraft. New York, H. W. Wilson, 1952. 584p. $24.00. LC 52-6758. ISBN 0-8242-006-3.

441. **British Authors of the Nineteenth Century**. Edited by Stanley J. Kunitz and Howard Haycraft. New York, H. W. Wilson, 1936. 677p. $27.00. LC 36-28581. ISBN 0-8242-0007-1.

The first volume contains biographical sketches of 650 major and minor literary figures tracing English literature from its beginning to the time of Cowper and Burns. Biographies are accompanied by biographical and critical sources, plus 220 portraits. *British Authors of the Nineteenth Century* adds more than one thousand biographical profiles, focusing on literary figures with some coverage of the most eminent personalities in other fields. Again, each sketch includes a list of principal works and biographical and critical sources.						Bohdan S. Wynar

442. **British Writers**. Ian Scott-Kilvert, ed. New York, Scribner's, 1979-1984. 8v. $495.00/set. LC 78-23483. ISBN 0-684-18253-X.

The British Council has undertaken the sponsorship of this important set on major figures in British literature. It was conceived as a complement to the American Writers series. This eight-volume critical work surveys the literary tradition of Britain from the fourteenth century up to the present time. First published as pamphlets by the British Council, the biographies have been re-edited and bibliographies have been updated. Some articles, for example, "Shakespeare" and "Kipling," were commissioned especially for the series. The articles range from ten thousand to fifteen thousand words in length; each one contains a discussion of the writer's life and period, and a critical assessment of the works. Contributors include Derek Pearsall, Kenneth Muir, Frank Kermode, Stanley Wells, T. S. Eliot, and other prominent personalities, scholars, literary critics, historians, and biographers. The index volume concludes the series. Over all, British Writers is perhaps the best series of general essays available on this topic. [R: Choice, June 80, p. 536; Choice, Dec 82, p. 580; Choice, Oct 84, p. 245; WLB, June 79, p. 722; WLB, May 80, p. 588]						Bohdan S. Wynar

443. Saunders, J. W. **A Biographical Dictionary of Renaissance Poets and Dramatists, 1520-1650**. Totowa, N.J., Barnes & Noble Books, 1983. 216p. index. $35.00. LC 83-6026. ISBN 0-389-20271-1.

Roughly dating the English Renaissance from 1520 to 1650, Saunders presents 507 poets and dramatists of the approximately five thousand writers in England at that time, focusing on the 10 percent concerned with what might be called belles lettres. All of the writers in this biographical dictionary were poets, dramatists, or both, and nearly all had some connection with the court.

Each writer highlighted is listed once under the occupational heading from which he made his primary earnings and for which he is now best known: actors and men of the theatre (excluding dramatists); churchmen; country gentry; courtiers, diplomats, and their agents; dramatists; historians and antiquarians; lawyers and judges; merchants, explorers, navigators, seamen, and travel writers; misfits; musicians and composers; physicians and surgeons; poets; printers, publishers, and booksellers; soldiers; teachers; tradesmen; translators; and women writers. A concluding index of alphabetically listed names makes it easy to locate any important poet or dramatist from this period.

Information given in each biography includes dates of birth and death, parents' occupations, studies at home and abroad, positions held, family life, awards received, political affiliation, and poetic and/or dramatic writings.

The volume serves as an excellent supplement to the biographical information found in the *Dictionary of National Biography* and the *Cambridge Bibliography of English Literature*. [R: Choice, Dec 83, p. 558] Colby H. Kullman

Drama

444. British Dramatists since World War II. Stanley Weintraub, ed. Detroit, Gale, 1982. 2v. bibliog. index. (Dictionary of Literary Biography, Vol. 13; A Bruccoli Clark Book). $160.00/set. LC 82-15724. ISBN 0-8103-0936-X.

Sixty-nine of the most significant, and the potentially most significant, playwrights of postwar Britain and Ireland are presented in individual biographical and critical essays that create, as editor Weintraub suggests, "a mine of data about a vital and colorful era in the theatre still being enriched by the very makers of plays evoked in these pages."

Alan Ayckbourn, Samuel Beckett, Christopher Fry, Peter Nichols, John Osborne, Harold Pinter, Peter Shaffer, Tom Stoppard, David Storey, and Arnold Wesker are among the many British playwrights highlighted in articles that include production lists, books published, biographical data, critical commentary, production photographs, program photocopies, playscript drafts, and a selected bibliography. To be found in this theatre history treasure trove are such items as a critical analysis of Dylan Thomas's *Under Milk Wood*; biographical information about the Shaffer twins, Anthony and Peter; photographs of Diana Rigg and Michael Hordern in scenes from the first production of Tom Stoppard's *Jumpers* (1972); program cover, cast list, and credits for the first production of David Storey's *The Changing Room* (1972); and the observation that on the day of Agatha Christie's death, 12 January 1976, "*The Mousetrap* gave its 9,612th performance, and London theatres dimmed their lights in tribute to her."

Appendixes furnish additional statements about Britain's postwar theatre by David Edgar, Harold Pinter, and Tom Stoppard; essays on postwar theatre companies; a discussion of stage censorship in England; and a bibliography of books for further reading. [R: Choice, June 83, p. 1429] Colby H. Kullman

Fiction

445. British Novelists, 1660-1800. Martin C. Battestin, ed. Detroit, Gale, 1985. 2v. illus. bibliog. index. (Dictionary of Literary Biography, Vol. 39). $170.00/set. LC 85-6785. ISBN 0-8103-1717-6.

This set of volumes provides a sound introduction to fifty writers who were the formative influence on the British novel. These include not only such major figures as Fielding, Defoe, and Richardson, but also comparatively minor writers such as John Shebbeare, Mary Collyer, and Thomas Amory. For each writer is provided a list of works, a list of editions and collections, major biographies and bibliographies, a rather short list of "references," and a biographical/critical essay.

Each of the fifty (signed) essays was written by one of twelve well-known scholars. The essays are the significant feature of these volumes because they are well written and, although introductory, neither overly simplistic nor mere plot summaries. Martin Battestin's essay on Fielding, for example, occupies twenty-one double-column pages, while Jerry C. Beasley contributes twenty-two pages on Smollett. The essays are certainly appropriate for college students, and even more advanced students will find them much more informative than the usual entry in a biographical dictionary.

There are a great many illustrations throughout the books, many of them of title pages, but also portraits, manuscript pages, and at least one of some marked-up page proofs (of Fanny Burney's *Camilla*). The illustrations are large (sometimes full-page) and generally legible. The volumes conclude with a one-hundred-page section reprinting excerpts from some of the primary works. These are mainly statements about the novel as a genre, many of them drawn from the authors' prefaces to their novels.

This is an attractive set of books which certainly has a place in any undergraduate or public library.   Philip R. Rider

446. **British Novelists, 1930-1959.** Edited by Bernard Oldsey. Detroit, Gale, 1983. 2v. illus. bibliog. index. (Dictionary of Literary Biography, Vol. 15). $160.00/set. LC 82-6232. ISBN 0-8103-1637-4.

Oldsey has compiled an extraordinary two-part literary biography of contemporary British novelists. Flourishing during the 1930s, 1940s, and 1950s, these fifty-nine important British novelists carry forward the tradition of the British novel begun by Defoe, Richardson, and Fielding. Included are such well-known figures as Kingsley Amis, Samuel Beckett, Lawrence Durrell, William Golding, Graham Greene, C. S. Lewis, George Orwell, C. P. Snow, and Evelyn Waugh. Writing during the period of world economic depression, World War II, and the rapid decline of the British Empire, these novelists managed to produce some of the most illustrious fiction in the history of British literature.

Each biography lists the birth, education, marriage, awards and honors, and selected books of the novelist being described. Depending upon the importance of the novelist, six to twenty pages are allotted for a description of the novelist's life. Each biography contains photographs of the novelist and of some of the dust jackets for the novels and often contains reproductions of edited manuscripts. The biographies are thorough and personable. Indeed, the structure of the two-part series is exemplary.

In addition to the biographies, the second part also contains the following appendixes: (1) "Representative Men and Women: A Historical Perspective on the British Novel, 1930-60"; (2) "Literary Effects of World War II"; (3) "Sex, Class, Politics, and Religion"; (4) "The 'Angry Young Men' "; (5) "The Comic Tradition Continued"; (6) "Literary Prizes"; (7) "Checklist of Further Readings"; and (8) "Fiction into Film, 1928-1975: A List of Movies Based on the Works of Authors in *British Novelists, 1930-1959*." These appendixes add an important dimension to the biographies.

In this most comprehensive and thorough work, Oldsey has produced an outstanding literary biography of British novelists writing between 1930 and 1960.

Joan Sargent Sherwood

447. **British Novelists since 1960.** Edited by Jay L. Halio. Detroit, Gale, 1983. 2v. illus. bibliog. index. (Dictionary of Literary Biography, Vol. 14). $160.00/set. LC 82-2977. ISBN 0-8103-0927-0.

Biographical and critical essays on 107 contemporary British novelists appear in this expensive two-volume set in Gale's Dictionary of Literary Biography series. Included are representative writers whose work began to appear around 1960. There is some overlap with other volumes of the *DLB* for writers in other modes, such as poetry and drama.

An entry begins with a short, selected book list followed by a chronological assessment of the author's life and work. The entry for John Fowles, for example, is twenty-six pages long and contains a portrait of the author, facsimile typescript, and four book-jacket illustrations. Citations headed "Screenplay," "Other," "Periodical Publications," "Interviews," and "References" conclude the Fowles article. By way of contrast, the entry for John Noone is slightly over two pages in length, including portrait and book jacket facsimiles.

Volume 1 begins with an eight-page foreword by Malcolm Bradbury that discusses aspects of the British novel since World War II. There is a list of scholarly contributors in each volume. The second volume appendixes include an essay on British fiction of the two postwar decades by John Fletcher and a list of books for further reading. A cumulative *DLB* index rounds out the set.

Although quite expensive, the work, to libraries able to afford it, can be a valuable ready reference, informative and generally well written, that should add greater range and depth in the area of late-twentieth-century fiction. [R: WLB, June 83, p. 880]

Edward A. Richter

448. **English Fiction, 1900-1950.** Vol. I. **General Bibliography and Individual Authors: Aldington to Huxley.** Vol. II. **James Joyce to Virginia Woolf.** Thomas J. Rice, ed. Detroit, Gale, 1979-1983. 2v. (American Literature and World Literatures in English Information Guide Series, Vol. 20. Gale Information Guide Library). $55.00/ vol. LC 73-16989. ISBN 0-8103-1217-4 (vol. 1); 0-8103-1505-X (vol. 2).

Answering the needs of the specialist and the nonspecialist alike, *English Fiction, 1900-1950* provides a convenient and reliable record of the important scholarship in the field. Representing British writers of fiction who flourished during the years 1900-1950, this research guide includes: (1) all generally acknowledged "major" novelists; (2) all major men and women of letters who, though they may be better known for their achievements in other fields, have made a significant contribution to modern fiction; and (3) all so-called minor writers who have, nonetheless, attracted a tremendous amount of bibliographical, biographical, or critical commentary, and who have contributed significantly to the development of modern long and short fiction in Britain.

Colby H. Kullman

449. Nadel, Ira B., and William E. Fredeman, eds. **Victorian Novelists after 1885.** Detroit, Gale, 1983. 392p. illus. index. (Dictionary of Literary Biography, Vol. 18; A Bruccoli Clark Book). $76.00. LC 82-24200. ISBN 0-8103-1143-7.

This installment in an important Gale series offers articles on thirty-three authors who flourished in the late Victorian era. Most are novelists, though some, like Henry Mayhew and Cardinal Newman, are more important as essayists or journalists. The entries range in length from three to twenty-three pages, with the longest dwelling on Thomas Hardy, Conan Doyle, Samuel Butler, George Meredith, Lewis Carroll, and Robert Louis Stevenson. Each article contains a selective bibliography of the author's works and a shorter listing of critical works and biographies. Several of the secondary sources were published as recently as 1982. The articles are richly enhanced by photographs, sketches, cartoons, and reproductions of manuscript pages and first-edition title pages.

The primary emphasis of this volume is on biographical, not critical, sources. The book contains excellent summary discussions of the authors' lives, their chief works, the popular and critical reception, and the prevailing social values that affected their writings. The contributors discuss the perils of censorship, novel serialization, and the wrath of the Victorian critics, whom they quote extensively. Although plots and literary themes are not analyzed in great detail, there is sufficient information imparted here to inspire numerous undergraduate research papers.					John P. Schmitt

450.	Nadel, Ira B., and William E. Fredeman, eds. **Victorian Novelists before 1885.** Detroit, Gale, 1983. 417p. illus. index. (Dictionary of Literary Biography, Vol. 21). $80.00. LC 83-8848. ISBN 0-8103-1701-X.

In the same format and style as earlier volumes of this series, this book offers information on thirty British writers, from William Harrison Ainsworth to Frances Trollope. Included are the Brontës, Charles Dickens, Benjamin Disraeli, William Makepeace Thackeray, and other well-known and less-well-known novelists. There are a historical and critical foreword, an appendix of seven analytical essays on novels and novelists reprinted from contemporary journals, and an index to the twenty-one volumes in the series (entries only), the yearbooks (1980-1982), and the three-volume documentary series.

Entries include, in order, vital data; a bibliography of the author's books in all literary forms, giving first publication dates of single and collected works in the United States and Great Britain; a signed biographical and critical essay written by an academic, illustrated with photographs, personal and literary, from primary sources; and, last, a bibliography of the author's works other than books, references to secondary works, and location of the author's papers.

The essays are surveys of each author's life and work and are, therefore, necessarily expository. The book's price is high for material available elsewhere, although widely dispersed, but the writing style is readable and the material interesting; the essays develop the subjects' personality and reflect the tenor of the time.

Related titles by the same editors, *Victorian Poets before 1850* (ISBN 0-8103-1710-9) and *Victorian Poets after 1850* (ISBN 0-8103-1713-3) are also volumes in the Dictionary of Literary Biography series.					Kathleen McCullough

451.	Staley, Thomas F., ed. **British Novelists, 1890-1929: Traditionalists.** Detroit, Gale, 1985. 378p. illus. bibliog. index. (Dictionary of Literary Biography, Vol. 34). $85.00. LC 84-18723. ISBN 0-8103-1712-5.

This latest volume in the lengthy Dictionary of Literary Biography series traces the development of each particular author's works and the evolution of his or her critical reputation. As do the previous volumes, this one contains reliable information in a convenient format, and places the writers discussed in the larger view of literary history with appraisals of their achievements by qualified scholars. Drawings and photographs of the novelists at various career stages, their families, and places of residence are presented. Facsimiles of title pages and dust jackets are included as well.

In the years between 1890 and 1929 the novel in Britain became the dominant literary genre, reflecting the concerns of the time. *British Novelists, 1890-1929* includes Bennett, Chesterton, Conrad, Forster, and Wells among others whose writings come largely out of the preceding nineteenth-century tradition. These people did not view innovation or change as a first principle. Themes and preoccupations have limited the staying power of a number of these writers who were enormously popular in their own day. For example, Kipling reflected imperialist notions, but displayed social conscience as well. Chesterton's work, which dealt with then current issues, is now mostly dated. Does anyone read Bennett or Galsworthy today?

In all, the book contains thirty-two biographical-critical essays with bibliographies of books by and about each author. A supplementary reading list, a list of contributors, and a cumulative index of entries in this and previous DLB volumes, round out volume 34. Add this worthwhile volume to the others on the reference shelves.

Edward A. Richter

Poetry

452.   **Poets of Great Britain and Ireland since 1960**. Vincent B. Sherry, Jr., ed. Detroit, Gale, 1985. 2v. illus. index. (Dictionary of Literary Biography, Vol. 40). $176.00/set. LC 85-12979. ISBN 0-8103-1718-4.

This newest volume in Gale's Dictionary of Literary Biography series is cut from the same cloth as its thirty-nine predecessors. Specialists have written critical biographies of the writers of a particular period, place, and genre—in this volume, modern British and Irish poets, as the title indicates—giving the most prominent extensive treatment and the not-so-prominent more concise treatment. Because these poets have not yet really been tested by time, it is difficult to sort them out and assign relative values to their contributions to the corpus of their nations' literatures. Thus a few high-profile names—for example, Ted Hughes (appointed poet laureate in 1984) and Anthony Thwaite—tower among the other eighty-some poets who toil largely outside the limelight and receive recognition mostly from a relatively select circle of peers and professors.

The set's articles follow the pattern of other volumes in the series: a bibliography of the poet's books and significant works in other genres, a critical biography focusing on the poems, and a brief bibliography of secondary works including interviews with the poet. Because it treats living authors, many still in the prime of their productivity and whose manuscripts and other memorabilia are easily collected, this, more than most other volumes in the Dictionary of Literary Biography series, resembles its kindred Dictionary of Literary Biography Documentary series. In other words, numerous dust jackets, photographs of the poets, and facsimile pages of corrected manuscripts illustrate the four- to fifteen-page articles. This volume of the series features the standard cumulative index of authors covered by the entire series to date. Finding adequate information on these contemporary poets can be time-consuming and, in a small library, frustrating. This shortcut to that information is welcome.

James Rettig

453.   Sherry, Vincent B., Jr., ed. **Poets of Great Britain and Ireland, 1945-1960**. Detroit, Gale, 1984. 393p. illus. bibliog. index. (Dictionary of Literary Biography, Vol. 27). $80.00. LC 84-5994. ISBN 0-8103-1705-2.

An addition to the Dictionary of Literary Biography series, this volume contains essays, both critical and biographical, on forty-four of Great Britain's and Ireland's poets who have written and published from 1945 through 1960. Included are such diverse personalities as Philip Larkin, I. A. Richards, Lawrence Durrell, and Kingsley Amis. There is a wide range of "schools" represented, embracing the conservatives as well as the nonconformists.

Each of the biocritical essays follows this format: the poet's name and date of birth (and if no longer living, the date of death); a bibliography of the subject's major works; and an essay that contains much biographical information as well as critical evaluations of individual poems. At the end of each essay is a list of references consulted, interviews, and locations of the poet's manuscripts. The illustrations include portraits and some interesting facsimiles of manuscripts, dust jackets, corrected proofs, and so on.

The table of contents gives the year of the poet's birth and the name of the author of the essay. The cumulative index is useful in that it indexes all volumes of the *Dictionary of Literary Biography* that have been published, volumes 1-27; the *Dictionary of Literary Biography Yearbook*, 1980-1983; and the *Dictionary of Literary Biography Documentary Series*, volumes 1-4. The endpapers have photographs of some of the poets. No names are given here for identification.

Poets of Great Britain and Ireland, 1945-1960, will be most valuable to all university and college libraries. Students of modern poetry will find much help here.

Jefferson D. Caskey

454.   Stanford, Donald E., ed. **British Poets, 1880-1914**. Detroit, Gale, 1983. 486p. illus. (Dictionary of Literary Biography, Vol. 19). $82.00. LC 83-5717. ISBN 0-8103-1700-1.

Among the forty-three poets covered here are the major figures Rudyard Kipling, W. B. Yeats, and Thomas Hardy; imagists like T. E. Hulme, F. S. Flint, and D. H. Lawrence; Georgians such as Rupert Brooke, Walter de la Mare, and A. E. Housman; decadents Oscar Wilde, Ernest Dowson, and Lionel Johnson; Catholic apologists G. K. Chesterton and Hilaire Belloc; and religious poets Francis Thompson and Alice Meynell.

Favorable remarks made about previous DLB volumes can be duly echoed about *British Poets, 1880-1914*: The format, which contains a list of selected books, letters, biographies, references, and a note about an author's papers, is especially useful; the biocritical essays, by recognized scholars, are well crafted; photographs of the authors themselves and their manuscripts, letters, and other items are excellent. On the debit side, however, several questions come to mind. Why should Yeats rate over fifty pages and Hardy only sixteen, especially as the editor in his foreword notes that both "dominated the period and are still challenging each other" and, moreover, conjectures that Hardy's work appears to be gaining "an increasingly favorable response among readers of poetry today," whereas Yeats's reputation "may have diminished"? Then, too, should so much attention be accorded Yeats if material about him and his work is so readily available elsewhere? Is T. Sturge Moore important enough to have twenty-one pages of coverage? Would it have been better to make most entries of shorter, standardized length in order to include additional poets of the period that someone using this volume might wish to inquire about? Why have such minor figures as Richard Watson Dixson, Mary Coleridge, Henry Newbolt, and Edward Thomas been included while others such as John Gray, Richard Le Gallienne, Alfred Douglas, and John Barlas been excluded? All such questions should have been anticipated by the editor, and may be even alluded to in his foreword. At best, even though most of the individual entries are worthy of commendation, *British Poets, 1880-1914* is an uneven, incomplete guide to a most interesting and important period. [R: Choice, Dec 83, p. 549]

G. A. Cevasco

455.   Stanford, Donald E., ed. **British Poets, 1914-1945**. Detroit, Gale, 1983. 431p. illus. index. (Dictionary of Literary Biography, Vol. 20). $80.00. LC 83-5718. ISBN 0-8103-1702-8.

This volume maintains the exceptionally high standards set by the Dictionary of Literary Biography series, presenting the reader with a thorough biography of forty poets. Each biography lists the major works of the poets, describes their lives, critiques their major works, and concludes with a selected list of references and other sources. Depending upon the importance of the poet, four to thirty-two pages are allotted for this description. One of the outstanding features of the series is the extensive use of photographs and other illustrations throughout the volume, giving the reader a sense of the poet in youth and in later years plus illustrations of the manuscripts.

Among the better-known poets included in this volume are W. H. Auden, C. Day Lewis, Robert Graves, Louis MacNeice, Stephen Spender, and Dylan Thomas. Less-well-known figures include John Betjeman, Basil Bunting, Roy Fuller, Edgell Rickword, and others. The volume also includes a list of contributors and a cumulative index.

The thirty-one years covered in this volume focus upon the poets of World War I (Wilfred Owen, Siegfried Sassoon, and Graves) and the socially and politically active poets of the 1930s and 1940s (Auden, Spender, and MacNeice). This latter group of poets promoted left-wing causes, especially those centering around Marxist and Communist beliefs, and were strongly influenced by the Depression of the 1930s.

As with the other volumes in this series, *British Poets, 1914-1945* is essential for many libraries across the country and for scholars of British poetry. Stanford's edition is an outstanding literary biography of British poets writing between 1914 and 1945.

Joan Sargent Sherwood

Canadian Literature

456. **Canadian Writers and Their Works**. Toronto, ECW Press; distr., Dover, N.H., Longwood Publishing Group, 1983- . In progress. $32.00/vol. ISSN 0-920802-43-5.

This twenty-volume collection (the entire collection is projected to be completed in 1987) is devoted to Canadian fiction and poetry in the nineteenth and twentieth centuries. Ten volumes will cover fiction and ten will be devoted to poetry. Each volume has an introduction by George Woodcock followed by separate essays on specific writers. The essays, written by different critics, have the same basic format: (1) a brief biography of the writer, (2) a discussion of the tradition and milieu in which the author has worked, (3) close analysis of major works, and (4) a selective bibliography of primary and secondary works.

Six volumes have been published so far, three on fiction, volumes 1, 6, and 7, and three on poetry, volumes 2, 5, and 9. Writers such as Clark Blaise, Alice Munro, Margaret Atwood, and Patrick Lane are included. The largest part of each of the essays is the critical analysis of the author's works, although readers will find value in the biographical sections as well. David Isaacson and Gloria Palmeri Powell

457. **Profiles**. Rev. ed. Irma McDonough, ed. Ottawa, Canadian Library Association, 1975. 159p. illus. $6.00pa. ISBN 0-88802-109-7.

458. **Profiles 2: Authors and Illustrators, Children's Literature in Canada**. Irma McDonough, ed. Ottawa, Canadian Library Association, 1982. 170p. illus. bibliog. $12.00pa. ISBN 0-88802-163-1.

Profiles is a collection of biographical descriptions (no criticisms) of forty-four Canadian authors and illustrators of children's books; these descriptions were previously published in *In Review*, a quarterly review journal concentrating on Canadian books for children. Each entry is about 750 words in length and signed by the reviewer; each includes a photo (and illustration, if the subject is an artist) plus a bibliography of writings. The French-language profiles have English translations. This is a valuable book, particularly to Canadians; it should expose authors/illustrators to a wider audience and thereby get the publishers moving.

Profiles 2, a supplement to *Profiles*, contains biographies of forty-five authors and illustrators of Canadian children's books. The articles are two to six pages in length. Most are written by librarians or educators, and all but two previously appeared in *In Review* magazine. Each article includes biographical information, a description of the subject's work, a photograph of the subject, and a list of her/his works for children. Examples of illustrators' works are also included.

Dean Tudor and Gari-Anne Patzwald

Caribbean Literature

459.   Herdeck, Donald E., ed. **Caribbean Writers: A Bio-Bibliographical-Critical Encyclopedia**. Maurice A. Lubin and others, associate eds. Washington, D.C., Three Continents Press, 1979. 943p. illus. bibliog. $70.00. LC 77-3841. ISBN 0-914478-74-5.

This biobibliographical work contains biographical information on some two thousand writers, and bibliographical data on more than fifteen thousand works. The majority of entries are in English, Dutch, French, and Spanish, but a few are in creole languages. Caribbean as used here also refers to Belize, Guyana, Surinam, and French Guiana. The encyclopedia contains four parts: Spanish (37 percent), French (30 percent), English (28 percent), and Dutch (5 percent) (only writers from the Dominican Republic, Puerto Rico, and Cuba are included in the Spanish section). Each section has a single A-Z listing of writers.

The entries include brief biographical data (some have a photo or drawing of the person), a list of writings, and for some authors, biographical and critical sources. Most entries are less than one column, but some extend to a page or two. Included with each section are essays on the literature of that language in each country or area, a list of writers arranged by country or island, bibliographies of critical studies and anthologies, and bibliographies of that particular literature. Containing many biographies of writers that could be difficult to locate in other sources, this work can be highly recommended for libraries desiring biographical and bibliographical information on writers from the Caribbean from colonial times to the present day. [R: Choice, Dec 79, p. 1315]

Donald J. Lehnus

European Literature

460.   **Ancient Writers: Greece and Rome**. T. James Luce, ed.-in-chief. New York, Scribner's, 1982. 2v. bibliog. index. $130.00/set. LC 82-50612. ISBN 0-684-16595-3.

Forty-six American, Canadian, British, and Israeli classicists have contributed to this extensive handbook of Greek and Roman literature. The forty-seven articles, arranged chronologically from Homer to Ammianus Marcellinus, vary in length from ten to over fifty pages; most deal with a single author, though a few cover a group of similar authors, e.g., "Greek Lyric Poets." The articles typically include a short biography (or at least the traditional account of the author's life, since little is known with certainty about most classical writers beyond their works); an extended critical analysis of the author's works; and a bibliography listing the important currently available editions of the author in the original Greek or Latin, major contemporary translations into English (and in some instances into other Western European languages), and selected critical studies (predominantly recent works in English). Greek words are given in romanized form, and most quotations from both Greek and Latin are translated into English, so the work is accessible to those who cannot read the originals.

The *Oxford Classical Dictionary* and Michael Grant's *Greek and Latin Authors, 800 B.C.-A.D. 1000* are more extensive in coverage than this work and are more useful for general libraries, but neither begins to approach the depth of coverage in *Ancient Writers*: its excellence of both scholarship and writing commends it to the attention of all academic and secondary school libraries supporting programs in classical or comparative literature. [R: WLB, Dec 82, p. 346] Paul B. Cors

461. **European Writers: The Middle Ages and the Renaissance**. William T. H. Jackson and George Stade, eds. New York, Scribner's, 1983. 2v. (vols. 1-2). $130.00/set. LC 83-16333. ISBN 0-684-16594-5.

462. **European Writers: The Age of Reason and the Enlightenment**. George Stade, ed. New York, Scribner's, 1984. 2v. (vols. 3-4). $130.00/set. LC 83-16333. ISBN 0-684-17914-8.

463. **European Writers: The Romantic Century**. Jacques Barzun and George Stade, eds. New York, Scribner's, 1985. 3v. (vols. 5-7). $195.00/set. LC 83-16333. ISBN 0-684-17915-6.

It is useful to begin a review of these volumes with a few words about the context in which they are published. Not only are they part of a projected 11-volume series on European writers, they are also part of a much larger group of similar literary reference works issued by Scribner's. Completing the series will be a four-volume work, *The Twentieth Century*. The omission of British writers is explained by the publication of an eight-volume set entitled *British Writers* (1979-1984). Beginning with the medieval period avoids duplication with the two-volume *Ancient Writers: Greece and Rome* (1982). Mention should also be made of the eight-volume *American Writers* (1974-1981).

The first two volumes are paged consecutively and contain thirty-six essays of about thirty pages each on such noted figures as Augustine, Aquinas, Boccaccio, Luther, and Montaigne or genres such as medieval satire and Renaissance pastoral poetry. All articles are signed and the academic affiliations of the authors are given in the front of volume 1. Each essay ends with a selected bibliography that usually includes major editions of original works, translations, and books of history and criticism. An additional reference feature is the "Chronology of Medieval and Renaissance Europe." Volumes 3 and 4 are shorter, with only fourteen and thirteen essays respectively. Except for a concentration on individuals, the pattern is similar to that of the first two volumes and a "Chronology of the Age of Reason and the Enlightenment" is provided in volume 3. The three volumes constituting *The Romantic Century* include seventy entries on such figures as Nietzsche, Goethe, Berlioz, Delacroix, and Balzac. A chronology highlights major events of the period, from Goethe's birth (1749) to 1890.

The essays (and this term is used advisedly) contain essential biographical information and discussion of major works. They do not cover all of the writings of a given author—still less do they provide conventional plot summaries. What is provided by this international team of scholars is much more important—critical analyses that set each writer's major works in the context of the time and make illuminating comparisons with other writers, ideas, and movements in other centuries. Though numerous exact citations to original sources are provided (in closed parentheses within the text), the essays are far from pedantic. In fact, those sampled were clearly written and enjoyable to read. This set will be especially useful to upper-division undergraduates and graduate students as starting points for further research. Educated general readers searching for more than routine biographical and bibliographical information will find that these civilized essays are sources of pleasure and illumination. [R: LJ, 1 Mar 84, p. 478; RBB, 15 Sept 84, p. 117; RQ, Summer 84, p. 475; WLB, Feb 84, pp. 451-52]

A. Robert Rogers

464.   Grant, Michael. **Greek and Latin Authors, 800 B.C.-A.D. 1000**. New York, H. W. Wilson, 1980. 490p. illus. (Wilson Author Series). $32.00. LC 79-27446. ISBN 0-8242-0640-1.

Why another handbook of classical studies, this one containing information on authors only? Pauly-Wissowa is hardly practical for ready reference. *Der kleine Pauly* and the *Lexikon der alten Welt* are accessible only to the dwindling number of scholars who read German easily. The *Oxford Classical Dictionary* provides adequate biographies (and much else). Grant updates the *OCD* (2nd ed., 1970) bibliographies and provides more detail in the biographies. (A total of 376 sketches is included.) Most libraries need both Grant and the *OCD*.

There are several special values in Grant's book besides the longish biographies (not quite as long as the still useful ones in older editions of the *Britannica*). Most important, Grant goes to the millennium. The classical tradition did not peter out, only sputtered after the fall of the Empire and the rise of Christianity. Grant has carefully selected some sixty-odd authors from the period 500-1000 A.D., the majority Western, for inclusion—in all about a fifth of the total. Other selections for inclusion have been judicious, particularly in view of Latin and Greek authors whom we know only by name or from a few fragments.

Like other Wilson author biographical dictionaries, this one is practical for readers on almost any level. It is also a practical desk tool for the non-classicist and even for librarians in research collections. [R: BL, 1 Dec 80, p. 534; Choice, Oct 80, p. 222; LJ, Aug 80, p. 1621; RQ, Fall 80, pp. 96-97; WLB, Sept 80, p. 62]

Lawrence S. Thompson

465.   Ward, Robert E. **A Bio-Bibliography of German-American Writers 1670-1970**. White Plains, N.Y., Kraus International, 1985. 377p. $72.00. LC 84-17140. ISBN 0-527-94444-0.

The author, well known for his work as a German-Americanist, has based this book on his 1978 *Dictionary of German-American Creative Writers, Volume I*. The latter was to serve as the beginning to a multivolume series which was later abandoned in favor of this biobibliography. Although an enormous amount of bibliographic compilation has occurred in the field of German-Americana, certainly since the mid-1970s, this work serves as the only relatively up-to-date work of its kind specifically geared to belles lettres and containing biographical as well as bibliographical material.

("German-American," by the way, is used by the author here as pertaining to any work composed in the German language by a person who has resided in the United States.)

Each of the entries contains a short biographical sketch of a German-American author or poet along with a list of his or her literary works, with pertinent publication data and relevant secondary sources. Also included in the book are a list of eighteenth- and nineteenth-century collections and anonymous works, a list of anthologies, and a short treatise on periodicals that featured or continue to feature German-American literature. Appended is an excellent list of recommended secondary sources. In short, the work is a comprehensive treatment: not only are there over three thousand entries, but almost seven hundred different periodicals and sources are exhumed to bring these authors and their works to light.   Ronald W. Dunbar

Japanese Literature

466. Hisamatsu, Sen'Ichi. **Biographical Dictionary of Japanese Literature**. New York, Kodansha International in collaboration with the International Society for Educational Information; distr., New York, Harper & Row, 1976. 437p. bibliog. index. $37.00. LC 75-14730. ISBN 0-87011-253-8.

Designed to acquaint English-speaking peoples with the riches of Japanese literature, this dictionary has been divided into parts corresponding with the major periods defined for that literature (Archaic, Early, Middle, Early Modern, and Modern). Entries, arranged alphabetically within each of those divisions, include birth and death dates (if known) and a brief sketch of the figure's personal life and literary achievements. Including 320 people (women are well represented in Japanese literary tradition, the star being, of course, Murasaki Shikibu), the book spans the time from the Emperor Jimmu (legendary as the founder of the imperial line) to Kawabata Yasunari and Mishima Yukio (the name form here duplicates that utilized in the book, and the Japanese practice of giving surname first). A chart following the main entries details several schools of literary practice, a short glossary explains primarily literary terms, and a bibliography provides references for each figure. (The "apology" preceding the bibliography explains that all material was found in the Japanese National Diet Library, and thus some unpublished material might be found only there.) An index in English, transliterated Japanese, and Japanese characters is also included. The book is a wealth of information, but the researcher who does not read Japanese might find much of it useless, for while terms are translated, titles of individual works are usually only transliterated, translation being reserved for the most famous (*Tale of Genji*, the *Sea of Fertility* tetralogy, etc.). For anyone seriously studying the literary tradition of Japan, however, the book should prove constantly enlightening, combining as it does the evaluation of individuals and various schools of thought. One might also consult *Who's Who among Japanese Writers* (1957), a UNESCO/Japanese P.E.N. publication, but only for contemporary figures. [R: Choice, Dec 76, p. 1272]

                                                  Koert C. Loomis, Jr.

15 Military Science

Introduction

The material in this section is arranged under two headings—"General Works" and "United States Armed Forces," with a total of nine entries plus several other titles mentioned or discussed in the annotations. Some standard works in this area are *World Military Leaders* (see entry 467) that can be supplemented by *Webster's American Military Biographies* (see entry 473) or *Dictionary of American Military Biography* (see entry 474). The reader is advised to consult our chapter on history, where a number of biographical sources and subject dictionaries include outstanding military personalities, as well as part 1, "Universal and National Biographies" that includes a number of general biographical dictionaries that cover military science.

The included biographical dictionaries were published since 1970 and there are a number of older works available on this subject. Most of them are discussed by Hardin Craig, Jr., in *A Bibliography of Encyclopedias and Dictionaries Dealing with Military, Naval and Maritime Affairs, 1577-1971* (4th rev. ed. Rice University, Dept. of History, 1971. 134p.) that provides a chronological listing on a worldwide basis. There are a number of older biographical registers, e.g., G. W. Cullum's nine-volume *Biographical Register of the Officers and Graduates of the U.S. Military Academy at West Point, N.Y., since Its Establishment in 1802. . .* (3rd ed. Boston, publisher varies, 1891-1950) that provides an extensive listing on this subject but a minimum of biographical data. A similar work is W. H. Powell's *List of Officers of the Army of the United States from 1779-1900 Embracing a Register of All Appointments. . .* (New York, Hamersly, 1900. 863p.) and, also by the same author, *Officers of the Army and Navy (Volunteer) Who Served in the Civil War* (Philadelphia, Hamersly, 1893. 419p.) and W. H. Powell and E. Shippen's *Officers of the Army and Navy (Regular) Who Served in the Civil War* (Philadelphia, Hamersly, 1892. 487p.). In comparison to Washington's work, Powell provides a little more biographical information. A truly biographical source is F. DuPre's *U.S. Air Force Biographical Dictionary* (Watts, 1965. 273p.) that includes brief biographies of deceased and living (as of 1965) members of the Air Force; unfortunately, no bibliographical references are provided with the biographical sketches. Most subject dictionaries, including such outstanding works as R. E. Dupuy and T. N. Dupuy's *The Encyclopedia of Military History; from 3500 B.C. to the Present* (rev. ed. Harper & Row, 1977. 1464p.), concentrate on military affairs, including major battles, but do not provide adequate biographical information about outstanding military leaders. The same is true of R. Parkinson's *The Encyclopedia of Modern War* (Stein and Day, 1977. 226p.) that covers the period from 1793 to 1976. The only exception is the eight-volume Russian work *Sovetskaia voennaia entsiklopediia*, edited by A. A. Grechko (Moscow, Voenizdat, 1976-1982) that emphasizes military biography, obviously from the Soviet point of view.

In addition to general indexing and abstracting services listed in the history chapter, *Air University Library Index to Military Periodicals* (Air University Library, 1949-) should be consulted for periodical literature. *A Short Research Guide on Arms and Armed Forces* (Facts on File, 1980. 112p.) adequately describes the existing literature, including most important reference sources.

GENERAL WORKS

467.   Martell, Paul, and Grace P. Hayes, eds. **World Military Leaders**. New York, R. R. Bowker, 1974. 268p. index. o.p. LC 74-78392. ISBN 0-8352-0758-4.

A somewhat uneven but useful compilation of Who's Who among world military leaders. This biographical directory contains nearly twenty-two hundred entries of senior military officers, civilian defense ministers, and astronauts for 118 countries. The eight hundred entries for the United States occupy nearly half the book, since all U.S. entries are complete with the following information: name, rank, current position and date of assignment, date and place of birth, college education and significant professional training, date of commission, experience in active theatres of war, recent assignments, most important honors, decorations and awards, date of promotion to general grades, and publications. Many of the entries for other countries give only name and current position. Russia has the second largest number of entries (nearly three hundred), but the additional information that most of these give is only marginally useful: e.g., "Duty on the Soviet-German Front in WWII. Member, Communist Party of the Soviet Union." Most of the fifty-seven entries for Communist China give complete biographical information. The major participants in the 1973 Yom Kippur War in the Middle East rate only twenty-two brief entries: Egypt, nine; Syria, one; and Israel, twelve. Peaceful and traditionally neutral Switzerland has forty-two entries.

The criterion for entry of U.S. military officers appears to be those at the rank of Major General and above, or comparable flag rank, on active duty in the Army, Navy, Air Force, Marine Corps, and Coast Guard. Retired General Westmoreland, U.S. commander in the Vietnam War, is not listed. Except for military astronauts, only two U.S. Brigadier Generals (Director, Women's Army Corps, and DCS Logistics, Military Airlift Command) and one Colonel (Air Attache to Venezuela) are listed. There are entries for forty-five military and civilian astronauts, as well as sixteen Soviet cosmonauts.

Entries are arranged alphabetically. Index is arranged by country, with breakdown by branch of service for the United States, the USSR, and the United Kingdom.
[R: WLB, Nov 74, p. 252]   LeRoy C. Schwarzkopf

UNITED STATES ARMED FORCES

468. Coletta, Paolo, ed. **American Secretaries of the Navy**. Annapolis, Md., Naval Institute Press, 1980. 2v. $59.95. illus. index. LC 78-70967. ISBN 0-87021-073-4.

Students of American naval history, government, and political science will welcome these volumes which sketch the lives, times, and influence of the secretaries of the navy from the early beginnings through the tenure of Nixon's secretary of the navy, John Hubbard Chafee. The editor, a distinguished historian with an impressive list of publications, teaches at the U.S. Naval Academy. The contributors are all able naval historians with felicitous writing styles. The front matter includes a list of the contributors and their credentials. The editor contributed seven of the sixty-two chapters in the work.

Each sketch includes a portrait of the man being considered. The format of the sketches includes: biography, problems, success in solving problems, influences affecting naval administration, and a summary of the man's achievements in operational and administrative fields. The documentation is contained in numbered notes at the end of each chapter. Various bibliographical references in the body of the text cite additional works for further study. The sketches (including notes) vary in length, with one page for Goff, who served two months; and three pages for Gilmer, who was killed after serving nine days; however, Gideon Welles gets forty-two pages, Josephus Daniels fifty-eight pages, and Knox fifty-two pages. On the average, the sketches run to more than ten pages.

Volume 1 covers the period 1775 to 1913, or from the beginnings of our nation to the eve of World War I. The first secretary of the navy was Benjamin Stoddert, who was appointed by President Adams. The volume ends with George Von Lengerke Meyer, who served from 1909 to 1913 and was appointed by Teddy Roosevelt. Volume 2 begins with Josephus Daniels, secretary of the navy under Wilson during the First World War, and ends with John Chafee, who served from 1969 to 1972. Front matter of preface, introduction, contributors, and abbreviations is included in both volumes. There is a twenty-five-page, two-column index to both volumes at the end of volume 2. The volumes are fine examples of handsome design and quality book manufacturing and are contained in a sturdy, cloth-covered slip case. The Naval Institute Press deserves a "well done" for this publication. [R: Choice, Feb 81, p. 627]   Frank J. Anderson

469. **The Congressional Medal of Honor: The Names, the Deeds**. Forest Ranch, Calif., Sharp & Dunnigan, 1984. 1105p. index. $27.50. LC 84-51095. ISBN 0-918495-01-6.

This is a reprint of a noncopyrighted U.S. government publication, *Medal of Honor Recipients, 1863-1978* published in 1979 by the Senate Committee on Veterans Affairs (SuDocs Class No. Y4.V64/4:M46/3/863-978). The publisher claims a copyright for "original material in this book," of which there is relatively little. The publisher does not mention it is a reprint, but in acknowledgments does thank the members of the Senate Committee on Veterans Affairs "for having the foresight to have commissioned" the title cited above.

The major part of the book is citations for the award of the Medal of Honor, which are grouped into twenty-two sections by war, campaign, conflict, or era. Here the publisher makes a major change by reversing the chronological sequence. The government publication begins with the section on the Civil War and ends with Vietnam; this book reverses the sequence and starts with the section on Vietnam. In this part is found most of the "original material," namely the addition of five citations: "Vietnam" (two), "World War II" (two), and "Unknowns" (one). The additions are noticeable, since typeface for the addition is different from that of the original, and some blank space has been left to adjust pages to the original text. The names of the four known additional recipients have been incorporated into the indexes and alphabetical listings. The black-and-white sketches and text that appeared at the beginning of most historical sections have been eliminated. A color photograph of the three versions of the medal has been added.

The government document version was priced at $9.50 (S/N 052-070-04866-2) when it went out of print in January 1982. This is a valuable and unique reference book which deserves to remain in print. This reprint is manufactured with good quality paper and with sturdy binding, so the price is not exorbitant in comparison with that of the government paperback.

A related title is *Hispanics in America's Defense* (Washington, D.C., Dept. of Defense, 1982. 156p.) that provides biographies on all Hispanic American recipients of the Medal of Honor.   LeRoy C. Schwarzkopf

470. Great Civil War Heroes and Their Battles. Walton Rawls, ed. New York, Abbeville Press, 1985. 303p. illus. (part col.). map. index. $39.95. LC 85-1404. ISBN 0-89659-522-6.

About the only book not yet written about the War between the States is a good unprejudiced account from the Southern viewpoint. It would probably have more reference value than this handsome work, an eligible decorative piece for coffee tables in parvenu homes. Biographies of fifty generals, both unionist and Confederate, comprise the text. They are reprints from a late nineteenth-century album, *The Heroes of the Civil War*, put together from separate pieces on each individual, originally compliments of Washington Duke and his fledgling American Tobacco Company. Full color portraits of the generals and (largely imaginary) color plates of battle scenes (unidentified by artist or publisher; many from the Kurz and Allison set) are reproduced in impeccable color separation. The biographies are undocumented and in quaint nineteenth-century journalese, hardly dependable for reference or any other purpose. There are reliable books and other studies on nearly all of the fifty generals.

Lawrence S. Thompson

471. Greene, Robert Ewell. **Black Defenders of America: 1775-1973**. Chicago, Johnson Publishing Company, 1974. 415p. illus. bibliog. index. $17.95. LC 73-15607. ISBN 0-87485-053-3.

Schools across the country should try to add this biographical dictionary to their libraries, and, of course, any collection of black materials will consider it an essential item. The preface states the purpose as follows: "This partial account of Negro military personnel in the armed forces from 1775 until 1973 is presented as a reference and guide for those who want to learn the truth about America's neglected black soldiers, sailors, marines and airmen. Using pictures and documented biographies, an attempt has been made to illustrate the black American's presence in past and present wars."

Ten separate chapters cover U.S. wars in chronological order from the American Revolution and the Indian Campaigns through Vietnam. Each chapter is introduced by a five- to six-hundred-word statement on the status of blacks in the military services during the particular war. Each biographical sketch cites the authority for the information. References are given at the end of each chapter. Photos appear on nearly every page. Appendix 1 is a photo album of black commissioned officers and non-commissioned officers. Appendix 2, Black Military Milestones, is a chronology of important contributions blacks have made to U.S. military history. A small collection of documents and statistical information is provided in appendix 3. At the end is an extensive bibliography of books, articles, and government documents. An index of names completes the work. [R: BL, 1 Sept 74, p. 52; Choice, 1 Dec 74, p. 1456]

Christine L. Wynar

472.   Love, Robert William, Jr., ed. **The Chiefs of Naval Operations**. Annapolis, Md., Naval Institute Press, 1980. 448p. illus. index. $28.95. LC 80-12253. ISBN 0-87021-115-3.

This book is a collection of short (ten to thirty pages average) biographical essays on the men who have held the post of Chief of Naval Operations, U.S. Navy. This position was established in 1915 with the intent of centralizing the process of making military decisions within the navy. As created, it was the military counterpart to the civilian post of secretary of the navy, and thus redressed the balance of power between the civilian and military aspects of the navy. As might be expected, the nature of the position changed over time as a function of the personalities of the men involved and in response to the course of international events.

The individual biographies are written by separate specialists. While each provides a sketch of the entire life of the CNO in question, the essays concentrate on the time of office. The presentation is highly factual, and often employs documents or words of the individual in question. A portrait of the individual heads each chapter, but these are the only illustrations. The book is really a study of the growth of U.S. naval policy in the twentieth century as seen from the military perspective.

This volume can be supplemented by *Secretaries of War and Secretaries of the Army: Portraits and Biographical Sketches* by William Gardner Bell (Washington, D.C., American Center for Military History, 1982. 176p. $12.00). This biographical source contains a reproduction of the official color portrait and brief biography of each Secretary of War and Secretary of the Army from 1789 to 1982. Also of interest is another volume by William Gardner Bell, *Commanding Generals and Chiefs of Staff, 1775-1983: Portraits and Biographical Sketches of the United States Army's Senior Officers* (Washington, D.C., Army Center of Military History, 1983. 285p.) that includes biographies of the U.S. Army's senior officers who were known as the Commanding Generals from 1775 to 1903, and since then, as Chiefs of Staff. [R: Choice, Feb 81, p. 848]   Bruce H. Tiffney and Bohdan S. Wynar

473.   McHenry, Robert, ed. **Webster's American Military Biographies**. Mineola, N.Y., Dover, 1984. 548p. $10.95pa. LC 77-18688. ISBN 0-486-24758-9.

This valuable reference book, originally published in 1978 by G. & C. Merriam, presents 1,033 biographies of men and women who have figured notably in the military history of the United States. Arranged in alphabetical order, the subjects served the nation (or fought against it) from the Pequot War of 1636-1637 to the evacuation of South Vietnam in 1975. The average length of entries is 450 words; the information is detailed and accurate. Happily, the publisher allowed editor Robert McHenry to define "military" in its broadest sense. Thus the book covers the expected battlefield heroes—Eisenhower, Pershing, Grant, York, Murphy—but also such welcome additions as Confederate spy Belle Boyd, astronaut Neil Armstrong, inventor Richard Gatling,

Swiss adventurer Henry Bouquet, historian Samuel Eliot Morison, and naval hero Robert Smalls.

Following the biography of Admiral Elmo Zumwalt are fifty pages of useful and interesting addenda—lists of the secretaries of war, navy, and defense; tables of major commanders in the major wars; chronological listings of wars, battles, expeditions, etc., together with the biographies associated with that particular event. There are also lists of various career categories from adventurers to veterans' officials. The book is well designed and manufactured. [R: Choice, Oct 78, p. 1032; LJ, 15 June 78, p. 1259; WLB, Sept 78, p. 88]   David Eggenberger

474. Spiller, Roger J., Joseph G. Dawson III, and T. Harry Williams, eds. **Dictionary of American Military Biography**. Westport, Conn., Greenwood Press, 1984. 3v. index. $145.00/set. LC 83-12674. ISBN 0-313-21433-6.

Nearly four hundred biographical sketches of persons prominent in American military history from the French and Indian Wars through Vietnam. They include not only soldiers, sailors, and airmen but also politicians, scientists, and others who exercised significant influence on U.S. military matters. Essays, written by some two hundred specialists, are arranged alphabetically, cross-referenced meticulously, and accompanied by brief bibliographies. Of particular note is the effort to accentuate the interaction between the biographee and his contemporaries, especially as it affected strategic (as opposed to tactical) results. Prose styles vary, but skillful editing assures a commendable degree of readability combined with dispassionate appraisals encountered too infrequently in the genre.

Appendixes comprise a chronology of American military developments, rank designations, military organizations, birthplaces of biographees, a roll of contributors, and an index. This latter is a paragon of comprehensiveness, listing persons, places, units, battles, campaigns, and government agencies. Its primary value lies in the numerous references that guide the reader to cogent information not completely covered in a specific biographee's entry. The *DAMB* is a superior work of scholarship and a remarkable reference source in the U.S. military history field.

Lawrence E. Spellman

475. **Who Was Who in American History: The Military**. Chicago, Marquis Who's Who, 1975. 652p. $57.50. LC 75-29616. ISBN 0-8379-3201-7.

Contents comprise brief biographical sketches of ten thousand deceased Americans whose service in or connections with the military from 1607 through 1972 are considered significant. Entries on listees who died before 1899 were developed by Marquis editors. Post-1898 decedents, in most cases, provided requisite data during their lifetimes. Entry lengths are imbalanced; e.g., Eisenhower rates twenty-four lines, Hugh Drum is accorded triple that amount. Additionally, no mention is made of such figures as Admiral Dewey or Colin Kelly. Historians and buffs will question the inclusion of numerous personalities whose relations with American armed forces proved tangential at best. Conclusive verification of material has been accomplished in about 90 percent of all entries. Where not done, this is so indicated. A table of abbreviations (much used throughout) is appended. Summation: a none-too-selective compilation based on Marquis's original *Who Was Who in America* and containing additional recent biographies. [R: Choice, Sept 76, p. 802]   Lawrence E. Spellman

16 Music

Introduction

In this chapter we discuss sixty-one biographical sources, with several hundred related titles mentioned in the annotations. The material is arranged under three sections: "General Works," "Composers and Musicians," and "Popular and Country and Western Music." "General Works" includes a number of standard and well-known titles, e.g., *Who's Who in American Music* (see entry 477) and, of course, *The New Grove Dictionary of Music & Musicians* (see entry 482). Under "Composers and Musicians" we find a number of current and retrospective biographical dictionaries including such outstanding works as *Baker's Biographical Dictionary of Musicians* (see entry 485), *A Dictionary of American Composers* (see entry 487), and several titles dealing with women musicians and composers, e.g., *Women of Notes* (see entry 505). "Popular and Country and Western Music" includes a number of noted specialized works, e.g., *Blues Who's Who* (see entry 529), *The Rock Who's Who* (see entry 530), and *Who's Who in Rock Music* (see entry 536).

There are a number of older biographical dictionaries that still might be useful for biographical coverage. Limited to the United States is *The ASCAP Biographical Dictionary of Composers, Authors and Publishers* (3rd ed. American Society of Composers, Authors and Publishers, 1966. 845p.), that lists 5,238 brief biographies of members. In addition there are a number of subject dictionaries and encyclopedias that contain biographical information. Brief biographies are covered in *The New Oxford Companion to Music* (2v. Oxford University Press, 1983), and biographical material is well represented in *The Concise Oxford Dictionary of Music* (3rd ed. Oxford University Press, 1980. 724p.). A. Jacob's *A New Dictionary of Music* (3rd ed. Penguin, 1974. 424p.) provides good coverage of European musicians, but much more extensive coverage is to be found in O. Thompson's *The International Cyclopedia of Music and Musicians* (11th ed. Dodd, Mead, 1985. 2609p.), covering a wide range of outstanding musicians not only in Europe but also in America. There are also a number of subject dictionaries and encyclopedias that cover specific topics, e.g., popular music and jazz are covered by R. D. Kinkle's *The Complete Encyclopedia of Popular Music and Jazz,*

1900-1950 (4v. Arlington House, 1974), with two volumes of biographical sketches (international in coverage). *Lillian Roxon's Rock Encyclopedia*, compiled by E. Naha (Grosset and Dunlap, 1978. 565p.), was first produced in 1969 and became the standard reference source for popular music and rock, although it is now somewhat unreliable. Most current biographical information on individuals (and groups) in the United States is presented in the two-volume *Rock On: The Illustrated Encyclopedia of Rock N' Roll*, by Norm Nite (Harper & Row, 1982-1984). Adequate biographical coverage is also provided in *Encyclopedia of Pop, Rock and Soul*, by I. Stambler (St. Martin's Press, 1976. 609p.), that updates *The Encyclopedia of Popular Music* by the same author (St. Martin's Press, 1966). Few reference sources that are limited to one country provide very reliable biographical data. A good example of such a work, however, is H. Kallmann's *Encyclopedia of Music in Canada* (University of Toronto Press, 1981. 1076p.).

A number of non-English works are extremely informative. Thus, for example, one should consult *Dictionnaire de la musique*, edited by M. Honegger (4v. Paris, Bordas, 1970-1976), that covers in the first two volumes not only musicians from France, but worldwide. Also strong in biography is another French work, the three-volume *Encyclopédie de la musique* (Paris, Fasquelle, 1958-1961) primarily emphasizing Europeans. There are a number of outstanding German works, e.g., H. Riemann's three-volume *Riemann musik Lexikon* (12th ed. Schott Music Corp., 1959-1967), first published in 1882, that covers biography in the first two volumes. *Kürschners deutsches Musiker-Kalender* (2nd ed. Berlin, Walter de Gruyter, 1954) covers forty-five hundred German, Swiss and Austrian musicians. International coverage is provided by *Brockhaus-Riemann-Musiklexikon* (Wiesbaden, Brockhaus, 1978- . In progress), as well as *Grosse Lexikon der Musik in acht Bänden* (Basel, Herder, 1978- . In progress). For serious research one may use Italian works such as *Enciclopedia della musica*, edited by C. Sartori (4v. Milan, Ricordi, 1963-1964), or *Enciclopedia della musica Rizzoli* (6v. Milan, Rizzoli, 1972-1978), one of the strongest for European coverage.

For journal articles there are a number of indexing services that are discussed by J. M. Meggett in *Musical Periodical Literature: An Annotated Bibliography of Indexes and Bibliographies* (Scarecrow, 1978. 116p.) and especially in a number of excellent bibliographic guides, notably V. H. Duckles's *Music Reference and Research Materials: An Annotated Bibliography* (3rd ed. Free Press, 1974. 526p.) and G. Marco's three-volume *Information on Music: A Handbook of Reference Sources in European Languages* (Libraries Unlimited, 1975-1984).

Also of interest is *Composers on Record: An Index to Biographical Information on 14,000 Composers Whose Music Has Been Recorded*, by Frank Greene (Scarecrow, 1985. 604p.).

GENERAL WORKS

Current Biographies

476. **International Who's Who in Music and Musicians' Directory**. 10th ed. Cambridge, England, International Who's Who in Music; distr., Detroit, Gale, 1984. 1178p. $85.00.

The 1985 edition of *International Who's Who in Music* contains biographical data on over ten thousand musicians. This updated volume has two thousand new entries and includes informational revisions of those entries previously cited in the former (1980) edition. The 1985 edition is an improvement over the 1980 edition in that the type is larger and the many classification abbreviations have disappeared. All in all, those changes make reading easier.

Most of the biographees included in the volume are professionals who responded through the years to a questionnaire that is periodically sent out. Response to this questionnaire keeps the series up-to-date. A shortcoming of the work is that it does not include the names of some very famous worldwide performers, such as Horowitz and Previn. The reader or researcher should be aware of this and look elsewhere for needed information on celebrities.

The *International Who's Who in Music* is a good source for tracking down music educators, as there seems to be a preponderance of teachers in the volume. I found the appendixes (six) a worthwhile addition to the volume (although not new to this edition). They list information and data on international orchestras (not all data up-to-date), music organizations, music competitions, music libraries, and conservatories. If unable to track down the sought-after subject, the researcher may investigate one of the many music directories at hand (i.e., *New Grove Dictionary* and *Baker's Biographical Dictionary*). Robert Palmieri

477. **Who's Who in American Music**. 2nd ed. Compiled and edited by Jaques Cattell Press. New York, R. R. Bowker, 1985. 1200p. $149.95.

A typical Cattell publication covering eight thousand men and women active in classical and semi-classical music in the world today. Entries are brief, containing factual personal data including education, major accomplishments, writings, and address. The coverage is very broad; this directory includes not only musicians, but also prominent musical critics, publishers, editors, etc. Entries are alphabetical and are accompanied by geographical and professional classifications indexes.

Bohdan S. Wynar

478. **Who's Who in Music: And Musicians' International Directory**. 6th ed. New York, Hafner, 1972. 498p. o.p.

If you accept that this is a British — not really international — directory, you will be better disposed toward what you find, or don't find, in it. There is a useful section which describes about fifty music schools and performing organizations in Britain; there is a directory section which identifies agents, impresarios, festivals, opera companies, old music dealers, music journals, etc. (This is mostly British, but there is an overseas directory of some twenty pages. However, this overseas part cannot be relied on if we may judge from the listing of orchestras in Ohio that fails to mention the Cleveland Orchestra.)

Most of the book is devoted to individual biographical sketches, around five thousand of them, primarily British but with courtesy inclusions from other countries. As in the directory section, it would seem that this biographical compilation is more dependable for its British than for its non-British people. Many notable Americans are left out, and information on those included is often minimal (e.g., nothing on Val Cliburn except his agent's address). Some Europeans fare much worse than that—the entire entry for Iannis Xenakis is "Romanian Composer. b:1922."

However, for checking into the basic career facts of thousands who seemingly survive the musical rat race in the U.K., this volume will serve. [R: Choice, Nov 72, p. 1116; WLB, Oct 72, p. 196]   Guy A. Marco

Retrospective Biographies

479.   Claghorn, Charles Eugene. **Biographical Dictionary of American Music**. West Nyack, N.Y., Parker, 1973. 491p. o.p. LC 73-5534. ISBN 0-13-076331-4.

It was the author's intention to be all-inclusive, and he has gathered together within the pages of this dictionary a modicum of information about more than fifty-two hundred individuals who were musically active in this country from the seventeenth century down to the present day. Claghorn, an enthusiastic amateur music lexicographer, brings together the oddest people: musicologist Manfred Bukofzer rubs elbows with psalmodist Amos Bull; conductor Karl Krueger jostles jazz drummer Gene Krupa; the Ultimate Spinach shares the same page with music critic George P. Upton. There's someone here for everybody.

But, if you're looking for detailed information about an American musical figure, you'll have to go elsewhere. Claghorn's entries are very short—most of them less than a dozen lines in length. But if you're looking for a little information about somebody you're not likely to run across in the standard biographical dictionaries, it will pay you to check Claghorn. You won't find much, it's true, but what there is appears to be more accurate than one might expect from a field that might well be termed folk musicology. [R: BL, 1 Feb 75, p. 580]   Irving Lowens

480.   Cohen, Aaron I. **International Encyclopedia of Women Composers**. New York, R. R. Bowker, 1981. 597p. illus. bibliog. $145.00. LC 81-12233. ISBN 0-8352-1288-2.

Some four thousand women composers, from ancient to modern times and from all countries, are identified in this comprehensive, well-designed volume. Biographies for thirty-seven hundred composers are presented in the main section, along with lists of their works (including literary works where appropriate), bibliographies of books and articles on the composer, and references to items appearing in the appended bibliography of general works. Photographs of 360 of the composers are presented in a separate section.

Appendixes include listings of the sources used in compiling the encyclopedia, a bibliography for further reading on women in music, and an index of composers by country, which is subdivided by century. At the back is a list of composers for whom the author was unable to locate sufficient information; readers are invited to aid in the search so that these women can be included in the supplement, which is now in preparation. [R: Choice, Mar 82, p. 889; LJ, 15 Jan 82, p. 165; WLB, Feb 82, p. 463]
Bohdan S. Wynar

481.   Pulver, Jeffrey. **A Biographical Dictionary of Old English Music**. London, Kegan Paul; New York, Dutton, 1927; repr., New York, Da Capo, 1973. 537p. index. $49.50. LC 69-16666. ISBN 0-306-71103-6.

A violinist and prolific author, Jeffrey Pulver is best known for the present work and its companion, the *Dictionary of Old English Music and Musical Instruments*—two very useful books indeed. There is no better source than the volume in hand for facts about lesser-known Britishers of the thirteenth through the seventeenth centuries. (Professor Blount notes, in the new interesting introductory essay, that only some 20 percent of the performers, composers, printers, theorists, and instrument makers included are to be found in *Baker's Biographical Dictionary*.) Pulver writes in a genial, anecdotal mode, but he does give hard information too, such as names of works—although these are not listed systematically—and manuscript locations. In the fine index we can locate references to types of music associated with various persons, names of compositions cited in the text, places mentioned, performers on different instruments, and even quotations from Pepys's diary. Pulver belongs on every serious biography shelf.   Guy A. Marco

482.   Sadie, Stanley, ed. **The New Grove Dictionary of Music & Musicians**. 6th ed. Washington, D.C., Grove's Dictionaries of Music, 1980. 20v. illus. bibliog. $2,100.00/ set. LC 79-26207. ISBN 0-333-23111-2.

The sixth edition of the standard multivolume music encyclopedia in English was published in 1980, and its new title reflects a major revision, the most thorough since the work was first published in the nineteenth century. The 9-volume fifth edition (1954) had a very strong British bias and was still aimed quite frankly at the musical amateur. By contrast, this new edition is designed for both the informed lay person and the professional musicologist. It seeks an international scope and perspective, by and large successfully. Clearly, the conception of the set has been influenced strongly both by the *New Encyclopaedia Britannica* and by *Die Musik in Geschichte und Gegenwart* (*MGG*), a 16-volume work with signed articles written by specialists from throughout the world.

Volumes of *The New Grove* average well over 750 pages each. According to the publisher's prospectus, the set contains approximately eighteen million words, 22,500 articles and seventy-five hundred cross-references, three thousand illustrations (occupying about 7 percent of the total space), and twenty-five hundred musical examples. It is claimed that 97 percent of the text is new. With a few exceptions (mainly entries for families of musicians), arrangement of the encyclopedia is alphabetical. Volume 20 contains an index of approximately nine thousand terms used in non-Western and folk music with references to the articles in which they occur.

Twice the size of the fifth edition of *Grove's Dictionary*, this new edition both extends its scope to new areas and expands the treatment of most traditional subjects. Important new areas of emphasis include popular music, jazz, non-Western music, and dance. Articles on early music (European music before the mid-eighteenth century) and contemporary music have been greatly amplified. Latin America, Spain, Portugal, and Eastern Europe are much more thoroughly covered. As might be expected, less enduring aspects of the nineteenth century in general, and of Victorian England in particular, receive less space than in previous editions. Those libraries concerned with supporting historical research will want to retain all earlier editions.

Most signed articles are written by well-known authorities and are highly reliable. More than a third of the contributors are American, and approximately a fifth are from Britain. The prospectus explains the relatively smaller representation of authors from the world's other most important musicological center, the German-speaking community, by noting that they had contributed heavily to *MGG*.

The senior editors and consultants responsible for the planning, solicitation, and review of articles are recognized scholars. Undoubtedly in part because of the team approach, *The New Grove* does not seem to have major gaps in coverage. It must be said, however, that the junior editorial staff was not always up to the job. This can be seen in minor slips and inconsistencies of various sorts, which generally result from insufficient knowledgeable checking. Reliability thus depends in no small part on the care with which individual authors read galleys and were able to follow through in the correction process. In a work of this size, naturally some articles are perfunctory or inadequate, but in general, coverage of assigned topics is thorough and the level quite high.

The encyclopedia is printed in double-column format in a legible typeface on paper with a reasonable opacity. The volumes for the first part of the alphabet were printed in Hong Kong; the others, in the United States; and the quality of printing in these latter volumes is noticeably higher. Reproductions of illustrations (all are black and white) vary in quality from acceptable to poor. Many are too gray and too small to show the required detail clearly. Illustrations in *MGG* are far superior. The binding is handsome and appears serviceable.

The New Grove represents a major advance over earlier editions. Any library that answers even casual questions about music should have it available in the reference section. *MGG* contains many biographies and by far is the most important source for information on this subject. For example, earlier-twentieth-century composers are all included in this set. In addition, many younger men and women and even minor composers are also represented with short biographies. Major biographical articles include not only actual material, but also stylistic criticism and numerous critical comments from recognized authorities. [R: BL, 1 Oct 80, p. 273; LJ, 15 Dec 80, p. 2562]   George R. Hill and Bohdan S. Wynar

483. Southern, Eileen. **Biographical Dictionary of Afro-American and African Musicians**. Westport, Conn., Greenwood Press, 1982. 478p. (Greenwood Encyclopedia of Black Music). $55.00. LC 81-2586. ISBN 0-313-21339-9.

Biographical data on more than fourteen hundred musicians of Afro-American and African descent who were born between 1640 and 1945 are brought together in this thoroughly researched and comprehensive volume. Represented are pioneers in the various fields of musical activity: folk, popular, jazz, religious, and classical. Bibliographies and discographies are usually included with each biographical entry. The author is professor of Afro-American studies and of music at Harvard University and has added much information which has been previously unpublished. Three useful appendixes group the names by period of birth, place of birth, and musical occupation. [R: LJ, 1 Jan 82, pp. 85-86]   Bohdan S. Wynar

COMPOSERS AND MUSICIANS

484. Anderson, E. Ruth. **Contemporary American Composers: A Biographical Dictionary**. 2nd ed. Boston, G. K. Hall, 1982. 578p. $65.00. LC 81-7047. ISBN 0-8161-8223-X.

In this expanded second edition of *Contemporary American Composers*, emphasis is still on composers of "serious" concert music. As before, a birth date no earlier than 1870 and American citizenship or extended residence in the United States are prerequisites. However, composers who have written only one or two compositions and those who did not respond to questionnaires have been dropped. Still, with the many new names added, well over forty-five hundred composers are listed, major and minor, born after 1870.

Format is more uniform than in the first edition. Included in each brief entry are birth/death dates (where applicable), "studied with" information, academic degrees (if any), professional and academic appointments, awards/commissions received, and mailing address. Works lists have been reorganized under capitalized headings (e.g., BAND, ORCHESTRA, CHORUS, etc.), with the result that they are much easier to read. As in the first edition, composer-provided information, elicited by questionnaire, was accepted with a minimum of verification.

This remains an excellent source of basic information on lesser-known contemporary American composers. In many instances, their entries, due to the compiler's reliance on information provided by the biographees, are as extensive as those of their better-known colleagues. Entries for some older or recently deceased composers show minimum revision. Nevertheless, this edition does improve on and expand the first edition and offers substantial information on hundreds of composers whose biographies and compositional output can be difficult to learn. [R: WLB, Oct 82, p. 172]
                                                    Avery T. Sharp

485. **Baker's Biographical Dictionary of Musicians**. 7th ed. Revised by Nicolas Slonimsky. New York, Schirmer Books/Macmillan, 1984. 2577p. $95.00. LC 84-5595. ISBN 0-02-870270-0.

Baker's has long been known as a kind of lovable maverick among music reference works, and the seventh edition finds lexicographer Nicolas Slonimsky, age ninety-one, dispensing biographical data and amusement with his usual aplomb. The dictionary's thirteen thousand entries, ranging in length from a few lines to a few pages, cover a broad range of personalities both past and present: composers, conductors, scholars, performers, educators, and librarians. Some one thousand entries have been added in response to the criticism that the sixth edition (1978) was weakest in its coverage of living performers. Many of these are for popular musicians: "crooners, songstresses . . . in fact, everyone with an operative larynx short of singing whales." Fully 80 percent of the biographies have been revised or rewritten, according to the publisher, but a number of the bibliographies and lists of composers' works have unfortunately not been updated from the previous edition.

If Slonimsky's pen can occasionally be acidic, and even crude to the point of scandal (see entries for Elton John and Wendy Carlos for examples), his observations are more often good-humored, accurate, and insightful. Perhaps no comparable work combines objectivity and opinion in quite so attractive a fashion. The infrequent errors of fact — Poulenc wrote but one work for the organ; music does survive from Debussy's

Fall of the House of Usher, and so on — do not significantly undermine the trustworthiness of the whole.

Once again, the publisher's trade binding does not seem up to the task of supporting so large a volume under heavy use. One wonders why this opportunity was not taken to divide the dictionary, hand-wrenching seven pounds, into two volumes. The typeface has been redesigned slightly for easier readability. All told, this edition of Baker's is sure to be as indispensable on the quick-reference shelf as its predecessors were.   Ross Wood

486.   Bingley, William. **Musical Biography: Or Memoirs of the Lives and Writings of the Most Eminent Musical Composers and Writers Who Have Flourished in the Different Countries of Europe during the Last Three Centuries.** 2nd ed. London, R. Bentley, 1834; repr., New York, Da Capo, 1971. 2v. index. (Da Capo Press Music Reprint Series). $75.00. LC 70-127286. SBN 306-70032-8.

The author originally compiled the work in 1822 for his "own information and amusement," in chronological and geographic order. This edition adds "such further anecdotes and memoirs as he has been able to derive from every authentic source. . . ." The preface acknowledges indebtedness to the writings of Sir John Hawkins and Dr. Burney, as well as "other English authors" and "the works of the continental writers."

With more than a little help from his friends, what we have here is a chatty, early-nineteenth-century Englishman's view of music and musicians. An introductory chapter outlines historical developments through the sixteenth century, and brief surveys continue throughout, preceding the time and area blocks of biographical entries. Some sources are identified in sparse footnotes, and an index identifies main articles on individual composers. Occasionally rather extensive lists of compositions are included (Cimarosa, Geminiani, Purcell, Thomas Attwood). Theoreticians mentioned also include non-musicians who wrote on musical matters (the astronomer, Kepler; the philosopher, Descartes). It is not surprising that the greatest number of entries are Englishmen, with space for Handel and Purcell far outdistancing all the rest. The Italians number somewhat less, followed by succeedingly smaller numbers of Germans, Frenchmen and Spainiards. That Henry Carey ("God Save the King" and "Sally in Our Alley") should receive more attention than J. S. Bach was not inappropriate in 1834. Acknowledging that the book is neither unique in content nor scholarly by today's standards, the interest in such a reprint resides more in its idiosyncrasies than in its contribution to the corpus of musical knowledge.   Clara Steuermann

487.   Butterworth, Neil. **A Dictionary of American Composers**. New York, Garland, 1984. 523p. (Garland Reference Library of the Humanities, Vol. 296). $75.00. LC 81-43331. ISBN 0-8240-9311-9.

This compilation of biographic and related information on 558 American composers from the eighteenth century to today is a solid contribution to our own music history as centered squarely on our composers — both native and foreign-born. The compiler, a Scottish lexicographer, combines factual data with critical opinion in an easy, readable text. In many instances, the composers themselves revised their own biographic entries and this most certainly firms up the accuracy of the whole project. Composers of "light music and jazz" have been left out unless they also composed in other media. This policy, alas, leaves out many notable American composers who have contributed so much to music in the twentieth century. One only needs to mention such world-class figures as Irving Berlin, Jerome Kern, Cole Porter, and Stephen Sondheim to prove the point. However, the compiler notes that many other composers have been inadvertently excluded and that subsequent editions will assuage this problem. Ample entries are found for John Cage, Aaron Copland, Charles Ives, Virgil Thomson, and Gian Carlo Menotti, while others less notable are covered by a few brief paragraphs. An appendix lists notable teachers and their American pupils. In the past, composers of serious music in America were largely unheralded; this carefully researched and substantial listing does much to correct the situation. [R: Choice, May 84, p. 1272; LJ, Jan 84, p. 74]					William J. Dane

488. Canadian Broadcasting Corporation. International Service. **Thirty-Four Biographies of Canadian Composers**. St. Clair Shores, Mich., Scholarly Press, 1972; repr. of 1964 ed. 110p. illus. $29.00. LC 75-166224. ISBN 0-403-01351-8.

This volume was originally published in 1964. Its purpose, as stated in the introduction at that time, was to help music producers in other countries to prepare appropriate continuity by providing biographical notes on some of Canada's contemporary composers. The work includes a fairly detailed biography of each composer in English and French, a listing of his works, and a small portrait.

Since the volume has long been out of print, its reappearance has to be applauded. But why simply reprint a publication in a field where new faces and new developments come thick and fast? The most recent "new work" listed was published in 1963; many of the composers have composed their most worthwhile works since that time. Several of the thirty-four have died, and many new exciting people have appeared on the scene — all of which clearly adds up to a need for an updating of what once was a worthy tool for broadcasters, music catalogers, etc.

The only comparable work is the *Catalogue of Canadian Composers*, published by the CBC in 1947, revised and enlarged in 1952 by Helmut Kallmann. Its biographies are much briefer, but its coverage is vastly greater, covering 356 composers "from the earliest-known examples to the present (1952)," and including much useful information on Canadian music. Of the thirty-four people listed in the publication being reviewed here, only five are not included in the Kallmann book. To this reviewer it seems that it would have been wiser if the publisher had attempted a more useful, updated revision; such a work would have been a welcome addition to every music library in North America as well as abroad.					Eldo Neufeld

489. Carlson, Effie B. **A Bio-Bibliographical Dictionary of Twelve-Tone and Serial Composers**. Metuchen, N.J., Scarecrow, 1970. 233p. bibliog. o.p. (Available from Books on Demand, UMI. $58.00). LC 79-8959.

While this work is not as comprehensive as its title would indicate, the author has gathered together in it a good deal of information concerning composers and their works for piano in these idioms. This choice of limitation "to a single channel which could provide a representative cross-section of serial music" (p. 10) is well made. The first published serial music of consequence was Schoenberg's *Three Pieces for Piano*, Op. 11 (1908), and since that time, works for the piano have consistently mirrored new developments. They have the added advantage of being readily accessible to the student.

The work is divided into four sections. The first is a discussion of the origins of the serial idea and its development by the Viennese school of Schoenberg, Berg, and Webern. The second section consists of eighty alphabetically arranged biobibliographical articles on other representative composers. The information given includes composers' addresses, lists of published scores of their serial piano works and select bibliographical references. The ideas of the composers and the influences they received and exerted are stressed. A brief discussion of the geographical spread of serial ideas constitutes the third section. The last section is a twenty-two-page "general bibliography listing the most important scholarly publications related to the emergence of serial composition" (p. 9), including both historical and theoretical writings. The work's fairly simple organization very nearly compensates for the lack of an index. [R: Choice, Nov 70, p. 1217; LJ, July 70, p. 2447]   Dennis North

490. Claghorn, Gene. **Women Composers and Hymnists: A Concise Biographical Dictionary**. Metuchen, N.J., Scarecrow, 1984. 272p. bibliog. $22.50. LC 83-20429. ISBN 0-8108-1680-6.

Gene Claghorn has produced a useful complement to such recent references as Cohen's *International Encyclopedia of Women Composers* and Stern's *Women Composers: A Handbook*. While Cohen and Stern concentrated on women composers of concert music, Claghorn has identified six hundred women hymnists and 155 composers of church and sacred music. Of the composers who are included, most were native to the British Isles or the United States. France, Germany, Ireland, and Italy are each represented by several names, and individuals represent Canada, The Netherlands, Poland, South Africa, Spain, and Sweden. The names and works of the hymnists were drawn from numerous Protestant and Catholic and a few Jewish hymnals published between the seventeenth and mid-twentieth centuries. Much of the biographical information on the women was drawn from newspaper obituaries, church and cemetery records, and personal letters from the musicians or their children. Only a small portion came from published sources.

The entries in the dictionary are designed to emphasize each biographee's hymnic contribution(s). Each musician's name is followed by a hymn title or titles, or a hymn tune name. At the end of most entries is a list of hymnals or song collections in which the individual's hymns have appeared. In many cases Claghorn also lists a hymnist's poetic or prose publications. Entries are brief, as little biographical information was available on many of the lesser-known hymnists.

Women Composers and Hymnists is a handy compilation of otherwise scattered, difficult-to-obtain information. [R: Choice, Nov 84, pp. 398-99]

Avery T. Sharp

491. Cross, Milton and David Ewen. **The Milton Cross New Encyclopedia of the Great Composers and Their Music**. Garden City, Doubleday, 1969. 2v. index. $29.95. LC 70-87097.

Messrs. Cross and Ewen have pooled their resources to provide a reference work of uneven and frequently negligible value. The bulk of the two volumes is devoted to an alphabetically arranged guide to the "great" composers of the world. Under each composer entry there are four subsections: (1) place and date of birth and death plus a listing of major works, (2) general biography, (3) a statement as to the musical genres in which the composer worked, and (4) analytical notes regarding specific "major" works (organized by type, e.g., orchestral, chamber, choral, etc.).

The overall approach is one designed to appeal to the relatively uninformed layman (and, unfortunately, this approach frequently succeeds in doing little more than providing either inadequate information or mere anecdotal material for cocktail parties).

What is odd to this reviewer is the inclusion of such "great" composers as Roy Harris, Meyerbeer, Respighi, and Scriabin to the exclusion of others like Janáček, Ives, Carl Philip Emanuel Bach, or John Cage.

Far better to own the full set of Grove's *Dictionary of Music & Musicians* or, if your library can't afford it, Scholes's *Oxford Companion to Music*. [R: LJ, 1 Mar 70, p. 882]   Kenyon C. Rosenberg

492. Ewen, David. **American Composers: A Biographical Dictionary**. New York, Putnam, 1982. 793p. index. $50.00. LC 81-7362. ISBN 0-399-12626-0.

The author of eighty books on music, both serious and popular, Ewen has probably surpassed the total output of many other more specialized and academically oriented musicologists. Ewen's success is as much due to his straightforward writing style as it is to his fundamental impulse to communicate the diverse facets of the field of music to the large music-loving public. Indeed, the author has answered a need with the present volume. *American Composers* contains three hundred composer entries going as far back as colonial days and including present-day artists who have achieved recognition. (Stephen Foster, John Philip Sousa, and Scott Joplin are purposely omitted due to their "popular" status.) The biographies are presented in orderly fashion: Each begins with a brief paragraph or two identifying the composer's musical style; continues with his or her individual accomplishments, influences, principal works, and newspaper and magazine quotes about the composer; and concludes with the heading "The Composer Speaks." This last feature is most unusual as well as revealing since a composer's artistic statement gives added insight into his or her musical thinking; these statements were for the most part written and prepared by the composers themselves for this book, and others were culled from articles, lectures, and some interviews. Rounding off each biography is a select bibliography. The handsome volume, like most of Ewen's other works, deserves to be on both school and public library shelves. [R: BL, 15 Dec 82, p. 610]   Frederic Schoettler

493. Ewen, David. **Composers of Tomorrow's Music: A Non-Technical Introduction to the Musical Avant-Garde Movement**. New York, Dodd, Mead, 1971; repr., Westport, Conn., Greenwood Press, 1980. 176p. illus. index. $24.75. ISBN 0-313-22107-3.

The prolific Mr. Ewen (more than twenty books on *affaires de musique*) has selected ten twentieth-century composers deemed sufficiently important to be treated. This book was first published in 1971 by Dodd and Mead and recently reprinted by Greenwood. The list is comprised of Ives, Schoenberg, Webern, Boulez, Varèse, Stockhausen, Xenakis, Babbitt, Cage, and Partch. No one will argue with such a list except, perhaps, to wonder why just these, why not another four or five and have the book more complete? Why not, indeed, except that another four or five can lead to another ten or twenty, and so on. There is, for each composer, a goodly amount of anecdotal biographical material plus a non-condescending but layman-level explanation of the musical contributions of each. A "photographic supplement" providing pictures of each composer is gratuitous but welcome; the index is thorough and affords one the ability to trace textual references to composers other than the ones treated in depth. The work is eminently readable and recommended for junior high, high school, public, and college libraries. [R: WLB, May 71, p. 888]   Kenyon C. Rosenberg

494. Ewen, David, comp. and ed. **Composers since 1900**. New York, H. W. Wilson, 1969. 639p. illus. $28.00. LC 72-102368. ISBN 0-8242-0400-X.

495. Ewen, David, comp. and ed. **Composers since 1900: A Biographical and Critical Guide, First Supplement**. New York, H. W. Wilson, 1981. 328p. illus. $22.00. LC 81-14875. ISBN 0-8242-0664-9.

Composers since 1900 is a companion volume to *Great Composers 1300-1900* published by H. W. Wilson in 1966 that contains informative biographical sketches of some two hundred of the most important composers for that period. As a matter of fact, *Great Composers* is the initial volume in the Wilson Composers and Musicians series. *Composers since 1900* contains biographical sketches of 220 composers who have written music in this century. The range of coverage includes traditionalists, innovators, eclectics, romanticists, and the avant-garde—those producing significant work with aleatoric, electronic, and directional music, organized sound, and other contemporary methods of composition. More than half of the subjects profiled were personally interviewed. Each sketch lists the composer's principal works and critical and biographical sources; most also contain a portrait. An appendix lists the biographees by major school of composition and specific techniques, idioms, and styles.

The first supplement includes forty-seven new biographies of composers who came into prominence since 1969, and updates information in the original 172 biographies. The criteria for inclusion remain the same as in *Composers* and *Great Composers:* significance of the composer's work, conferred honors, and frequency of performance in opera houses, concert halls, and on records. Recommended as standard works for all types of libraries. [R: Choice, Sept 82, p. 52; JAL, July 82, p. 186; WLB, June 82, p. 782] Bohdan S. Wynar

496. Ewen, David, comp. and ed. **Great Composers 1300-1900**. New York, H. W. Wilson, 1966. 429p. $23.00. LC 65-24585. ISBN 0-8242-0018-7.

One of the earlier works of this prolific author, *Great Composers 1300-1900* provides biographical sketches on two hundred "most important worldwide composers" (preface) for the period described in the title. Actually, this is the initial volume of Wilson's well-known Composers and Musicians series, and in addition to biographical data includes lists of principal works and bibliographies as well as published biographies of and about the biographee. Recommended for school and public libraries.

Bohdan S. Wynar

497. Ewen, David, comp. and ed. **Musicians since 1900: Performers in Concert and Opera**. New York, H. W. Wilson, 1978. 974p. $50.00. LC 78-12727. ISBN 0-8242-0565-0.

David Ewen has been one of the most prolific writers on music, generally addressing the lay audience on subjects of broad appeal: Gershwin, popular music, musical theatre, and the like. Within these areas, he is quite sober and scholarly. Such is the case with this work, which in fact is designed to supersede his 1940 *Living Musicians* and its 1957 supplementary volume. Libraries that have acquired the recent edition of *Baker's Biographical Dictionary of Musicians* might wonder if the Ewen volume would be a redundant purchase. If *Baker's* has any shortcoming, it is exactly in the area of Ewen's coverage, and even entries that are duplicated are worth it.

Ewen includes a vast amount of information, from repertoire to marriages and divorces, which will appeal even to the casual reader. He does not avoid reference to scandal, to personality conflicts, or to political and social factors, thus often providing insights which other references might ignore. This is a reference book of quality, which will be most helpful to the librarian, the music student, the radio broadcaster, and, in fact, almost anyone interested in contemporary biography. [R: Choice, June 79, pp. 507-8; LJ, 1 Mar 79, pp. 616-17; RQ, Fall 79, p. 89; WLB, May 79, p. 655]

Dominique-René de Lerma

498.   Ewen, David. **Popular American Composers from Revolutionary Times to the Present: First Supplement; A Biographical and Critical Guide.** New York, H. W. Wilson, 1972. 121p. illus. ports. index. $8.00. LC 62-9024. ISBN 0-8242-0436-0.

This volume updates the biographies of those composers represented in the earlier volume, *Popular American Composers from Revolutionary Times to the Present* (H. W. Wilson, 1962. 217p. $12.00). That original volume includes biographical sketches of 130 of the most popular composers. An appendix includes a chronological list of composers and index to more than thirty-five hundred songs. The 1972 supplement includes thirty-one new biographies of composers who have come into prominence since 1962. While the updated articles for George Gershwin and George Cohan do reveal that much use is being made of their tunes for recent Broadway productions, these composers do not fit Mr. Ewen's first requisite, since they have not, in fact, been productive since 1937 and 1942, respectively. The thirty-one new sketches, with accompanying photographs, expose some of the creative talents working for the Broadway musical theatre, motion pictures, and the popular front (including country western). This supplement is conspicuously lacking in American jazz figures; Duke Ellington was the single inclusion. Apparently Mr. Ewen believes either that American jazz composers are not popularly received or that popular American composers do not compose jazz. The articles, in the Ewen tradition, are written in a popular style. They are much lengthier than the biographical sketches in the ASCAP dictionary, and they divulge much personal information that borders on intimate detail (e.g., Bobbie Gentry's change of hair color; Paul Simon's financial solvency; Henry Mancini's working habits). There is a title index for songs, productions, and record albums of composers noted in the text. Overall, the book is a compendium of success stories; it will be moderately useful to librarians who are asked to provide a single source of popular information.   Sharon L. Paugh

499.   Gelatt, Roland. **Music Makers: Some Outstanding Musical Performers of Our Day.** New York, Knopf, 1953; repr., New York, Da Capo, 1972. 286p. illus. index. $29.50. LC 72-2334. ISBN 0-306-70519-2.

Roland Gelatt's *Music Makers* is not, strictly speaking, a reference book. Its scope is limited to twenty individual performers and a quartet chosen from among those "who have interested me [the author] over the years." Its arrangement is nonalphabetical, and it contains evaluative biographical essays rather than straight factual information. Nonetheless, *Music Makers* is a worthwhile supplement to the standard biographical dictionaries.

Baker's Biographical Dictionary cites it as bibliography for no fewer than five of the performers Gelatt discusses: Bernac, Szigeti, Kell, Segovia, and Landowska. This means that many people will turn to Gelatt's book as a prime source of biographical data for these performers. The essays on singer-teacher Pierre Bernac and clarinetist Reginald Kell are particularly useful since written literature on these artists is sparse.

This reviewer was struck by the fact that of the individual performers dealt with in this reprint of a 1953 work, all but two were born in the latter decades of the nineteenth century, and many are now dead. Thus, the book's subtitle now has less meaning. Nevertheless, interest in these artists will not wane as long as their art is preserved on recordings. While there are few surprises among Gelatt's choices of performers, every one is in some way unique; all have made distinctive contributions to the music of their times, so fusing their personalities and their art as to be memorable beyond the span of their own lives. Carole Franklin

500. Greene, David Mason. **Greene's Biographical Encyclopedia of Composers**. New York, Doubleday, 1985. 1382p. $27.95. ISBN 0-385-14278-1.

International in coverage, Greene's compendium presents some twenty-four hundred biographical sketches of "history's most important composers" from ancient times to the 1980s. Each biography contains: personal data, including personal traits and habits; an analysis of the composer's major works; and a listing of the music's availability in recorded form. All entries are arranged chronologically which supposedly should assist the user in better understanding the existing relationships between various composers and different schools of music. Biographical data in Greene's work are somewhat richer in personal detail in comparison to *The Oxford Dictionary of Music*, edited by Michael Kennedy (New York, Oxford University Press, 1985. 825p. $35.00), that contains about ten thousand entries, among them two thousand biographies of prominent composers, 450 entries on conductors, plus eighteen hundred sketches of performers. Bohdan S. Wynar

501. Handy, D. Antoinette. **Black Women in American Bands and Orchestras**. Metuchen, N.J., Scarecrow, 1981. 319p. illus. bibliog. index. $18.50. LC 80-19380. ISBN 0-8108-1346-7.

The author, a gifted flutist, administrator, and teacher, provides essays and biographical sketches on women who, in the past, struggled to gain recognition, as well as those who are achieving success in the current generation. There are four main sections in this important book. The first is a historical overview which describes the development of the bands, jazz ensembles, and orchestras in America; the second provides profiles of black female instrumentalists and orchestral leaders who, despite social problems, made enormous contributions to the history; the third section provides information on those in administrative and managerial positions, also providing statistical data on female involvement in the major and regional orchestras; the final section is devoted to the younger generation and youth orchestras of the United States, including biographical vignettes. Excellent and unusual photographs are included. The extensive bibliography and detailed index add to the reference value of this significant publication, which contains information unavailable in any other source. [R: Choice, May 81, p. 1275; RQ, Spring 81, p. 306; WLB, May 81, p. 699] Betty Malkus

502. Hodson, Phillip. **Who's Who in Wagner: An A-to-Z Look at His Life and Work**. New York, Macmillan, 1984. 182p. $14.95. LC 84-11302. ISBN 0-02-552030-X.

Phillip Hodson offers a novel approach to understanding Richard Wagner, by compiling information about the composer and presenting it in the form of a Who's Who volume. Hodson states that his purpose in writing a book of this type is to attempt to dispel some misconceptions about Wagner and, he hopes, to widen the appreciation of this great composer. *Who's Who in Wagner* gives a chronology of the composer's life; an alphabetically arranged description and account of the composer by critics, musicians, and colleagues; entries describing the operas and characters in the operas; and other pertinent data. Hodson effectively encapsulates information and comments by Wagner's contemporaries previously set forth in Robert Hartford's *Bayreuth: The*

Early Years (1980) and captures the composer's musical and philosophical involvement with decadence, symbolism, and myth dealt with in depth in Raymond Furness's *Wagner and Literature* (1982). *Who's Who in Wagner* also contains lists of Wagner's nonoperatic music and his literary works, as well as offering a view of the Wagner family tree. There is no index.

Phillip Hodson is effective in dispensing a great amount of information on Wagner and cleverly wrapping it up in such a neat and attractive package. The volume would make a fine gift, especially to one who is solely engrossed in Italian opera, for this volume will enkindle an interest or a renewal of interest in an ingenious and profound composer. [R: LJ, 1 Sept 84, p. 1662; RBB, 1 Oct 84, p. 196]   Robert Palmieri

503.   Holmes, John L. **Conductors on Record**. Westport, Conn., Greenwood Press, 1982. 734p. bibliog. $49.95. LC 80-28578. ISBN 0-313-22990-2.

This biographical dictionary presents an overview of some fifteen hundred orchestral conductors, both living and dead, who have made their mark by recording (and thus there is some aural evidence of their styles). It is, of course, necessarily restricted to the twentieth century since this is the only time period in which recordings were possible.

Arrangement is alphabetical by surname; material covered includes life dates, career progressions, some reckoning of accomplishments, a discussion of styles and influences, and so forth. The length of each profile varies according to the importance of the conductor, and as far as I can tell, this importance is measured in direct proportion to the quantity of each one's recordings. The area I know best — Canada — was checked under appropriate surnames, and I can safely report that Canadian conductors are meticulously written about.

Still, the book is a bit of a curate's egg. While there is otherwise hard-to-find material on conductors' lives and on their styles, there is very little in the way of the raison d'être: the recordings themselves. Some narrative listings are given for the major recording events of each conductor, but that's all. This book does not have a discography, for there is no real mention of recording dates, release dates, orchestras led, recording companies, and label numbers; Holmes gives only a brief note of *some* of each conductor's recordings through 1977. This is the major failure — or incompleteness — of the book. An alternative source for this data would be the triennial "Artist Issue" of the *Schwann Catalog*, under the conductor's name, but Schwann covers only current record availability in the United States. [R: Choice, Sept 82, p. 54; LJ, July 82, p. 1314; WLB, Sept 82, pp. 72-73]   Dean Tudor

504.   Kutsch, K. J. and Leo Riemens. **A Concise Biographical Dictionary of Singers**. Translated from German, expanded and annotated by Harry Earl Jones. Philadelphia, Chilton, 1969. 487p. o.p. LC 79-94106. SBN 8019-5516-5.

A translation from German of *Unvergängliche Stimmen* (1962 and rev. ed. 1965) listing fifteen hundred important singers in the twentieth century from some forty countries, and providing Who's Who type information, e.g., biographical sketch, famous roles, recordings, professional and personal data. Some omissions were indicated by *Library Journal* and *Saturday Review* of established Western concert artists. To this one can add that with the possible exception of Russia, Eastern European countries are poorly represented, even opera stars of international reputation being omitted: for example, from the Sofia Opera House, such names as Christina Morfova, Anna Todorova, Peter Raichev, Tsvetana Tabakova. It is hoped that many names will be added in a future edition to make this book fill the need for a truly international dictionary. [R: LJ, 15 Oct 69; SR, 6 Dec 69]

Bohdan S. Wynar

505.   Laurence, Anya. **Women of Notes: 1,000 Women Composers Born before 1900.** 1st ed. New York, Richards Rosen Press, 1978. 101p. illus. bibliog. $15.00. LC 78-7862. ISBN 0-8239-0263-6.

The main body of this book, following three preliminary essays, is a "biographical bibliography" (i.e., an alphabetical listing of the composers by country, with a brief sketch of their lives and mention of some works). It is a very unfortunate shortcoming that the most recent title cited in the bibliography comes from 1970, well in advance of a wave of new publications on the subject, such as Hixon's and Hennessee's *Women in Music*, Skowronski's *Women in American Music*, and Stern's *Women Composers*, to refer only to issues from Scarecrow Press, and that evidence of original research is very scanty. Furthermore, the index of names is faulty. We learn that a man, Septimus Winner, wrote "Listen to the Mocking Bird" under the alias of Alice Hawthorne, but we are not told that the actual composer was Richard Milburn, an Afro-American victim of piracy.

A new area of study such as this is destined to see the release of remedial and provisional publications. To some extent, the Scarecrow volumes might fit in this category, or should eventually. *Women of Notes* falls far short of even these preliminary standards. What we need now is original research, and a detailed bibliography and union list of the music, not any more restatements of data which have been around for a long time. Those frustrated by the many problems of *Women of Notes* may be stimulated to meet these challenges.   Dominique-René de Lerma

506.   LePage, Jane Weiner. **Women Composers, Conductors, and Musicians of the Twentieth Century: Selected Biographies.** Metuchen, N.J., Scarecrow, 1980. 388p. illus. index. $20.00. LC 80-12162. ISBN 0-8108-1298-3.

507.   LePage, Jane Weiner. **Women Composers, Conductors, and Musicians of the Twentieth Century: Selected Biographies. Volume II.** Metuchen, N.J., Scarecrow, 1983. 373p. illus. index. $21.50. LC 80-12162. ISBN 0-8108-1597-4.

LePage's first volume contains biographical sketches of seventeen "gifted women musicians of the twentieth century," including the following composers, conductors, and performers: Victoria Bond, Antonia Brico, Radie Britain, Ruth Crawford Seeger, Emma Lou Diemer, Margaret Hillis, Jean Eichelberger Ivey, Betsy Jolas, Barbara Anne Kolb, Wanda Landowska, Thea Musgrave, Pauline Oliveros, Eve Queler, Marga Richter, Louise Talma, Rosalyn Tureck, and Nancy Van de Vate. The biographies are based both on research and on the author's interviews with the musicians, or, in the case of those deceased, with persons who have an intimate knowledge of their work. A black-and-white photo of each artist is given, as are lists of works and recordings.

The idea of writing such a book was a good one, and there may be enough interest in the subjects to merit purchase, but the defects almost outweigh the merits. The writing is unbelievably poor (examples: "The audience was mesmerized by the expressiveness of the conductor; each movement sparked with creativity. . . ," or "The performance offered a contemporary composition that is unfamiliar to a critic when reflected in a review") and laden with superlatives ("creative genius," "musical giant"). The book is filled with subjective and dubious statements, such as: "The only sexists in the concert world are outside the membership of the orchestras." The book also contains many errors. Victoria Bond's "Canons" is spelled "Cannons" (an explosive work no doubt!). In a lengthy quotation from Henry Cowell's *American Composers on American Music* on Ruth Crawford Seeger, several sentences are incorrectly printed, resulting in meaningless statements such as, "All three of these songs are comparatively heterophonic by complete heterophony."

The author refers to New York Public Library as New York City Library and the Lincoln Center for the Performing Arts as Lincoln Arts Center; she wrongly locates several special collections. The archives of Hans Moldenhauer (not Moldenhouer) are now in Northwestern University Library in Evanston, Illinois, not in Spokane, Washington, and the Fleisher Collection has been in the Free Library of Philadelphia since 1929. One might well ask why Scarecrow let this volume get into print with so many errors.

Another flaw is the frequent use of quotations from poorly written newspaper reviews and the total lack of references to the work of other scholars, for example, Adrienne Fried Block and Carol Neuls-Bates, whose *Women in American Music: A Bibliography of Music and Literature* was published in 1979. For most libraries, Christine Ammer's *Unsung: A History of Women in American Music* (1980) is a better investment, even if a bit more expensive.

In the second volume in what the author hopes will be an ongoing project, the women musicians covered are Beth Anderson, Dalia Atlas, Sarah Caldwell, Pozzi Escot, Vivian Fine, Kay Gardner, Miriam Gideon, Peggy Glanville-Hicks, Doris Hays, Frederique Petrides, Marta Ptaszynska, Daria Semegen, Susan Smeltzer, Julia Smith, Elinor Remick Warren, Judith Lang Zaimont, and Ellen Taaffe Zwilich. LePage personally interviewed all of them, and she has quoted liberally from these interviews. The musicians' comments about their backgrounds and artistic philosophies provide a special insight into their work. Lengthy excerpts of published reviews of the compositions or performances are also given. In some cases whole articles by a composer are reprinted (such as Beth Anderson's "Beauty Is Revolution," first published in the avant-garde *Ear Magazine*). When applicable, a list of scores (selected by the composer), a discography, and the addresses of music publishers and recording companies that have issued the works are given for each musician.

The field of women's studies is still young; thus, reference works that cover this kind of material are needed. LePage seems genuinely interested in her subject and committed to providing greater visibility for the musicians she has selected. It is thus unfortunate that this second volume, like the first, is marred by poor writing (incorrect grammar, overuse of slang and clichés, and overuse of superlatives, such as "genius"). Stronger editorial guidance could have helped. It is also annoying to find once again a sloppy attitude toward citations; also, names of institutions and organizations are not always correctly given. There are too many cases of careless mistakes.

Carole Franklin Vidali

508. MacMillan, Keith, and John Beckwith, eds. **Contemporary Canadian Composers**. New York, Oxford University Press, 1975. 248p. illus. o.p.

Probably the most comprehensive work on the subject, this biographical source lists 144 composers who have "produced all or most of their works since 1920." Biographical information goes far beyond the typical Who's Who, including not only the usual vita but also an evaluation of the composer, an analysis of his or her most important work, and citations from critical writings. Many biographies are signed.

There is also a helpful listing of Canadian organizations, performing groups, publishers, schools of music, etc., that have been mentioned in the text. *Creative Canada: A Biographical Dictionary of Twentieth Century Creative and Performing Artists* (2v. University of Toronto Press, 1971-1972) also covers some of the composers, but its coverage in this area is much inferior to that of *Contemporary Canadian Composers*. [R: BL, 1 July 76, pp. 1550-51] Bohdan S. Wynar

509. Osborne, Charles, ed. **The Dictionary of Composers**. New York, Taplinger, 1978 (c1977). 380p. illus. (A Crescendo Book). $14.95; $9.95pa. LC 78-58291. ISBN 0-8008-2194-7; 0-8008-2195-5pa.

This is one biographical dictionary of composers that libraries can well afford not to own. Many of the contributions are turgidly or confusingly written; an example is this excerpt from the entry for Aleksandr Borodin: "Work on the opera progressed fitfully throughout the 1870s, but it remained incomplete at the time of Borodin's death from a burst artery in the heart (as did also the Third Symphony)." This kind of thing is far worse than mere infelicity; it is gross neglect displayed toward communication. Notable omissions in this volume are John Cage, Mario Castelnuovo-Tedesco, Joaquin Rodrigo, Jacques Ibert, and Krzystof Penderecki, while the likes of Arthur Sullivan, Jacques Offenbach, and Charles Gounod are given about three pages each.

Recommended instead of this volume are either Harold Schonberg's *Lives of the Great Composers* or Brockway and Weinstock's *Men of Music* (Simon and Schuster, 1950), both relatively inexpensive. The *sine qua non* in this field, however, remains Slonimsky's *Baker's Biographical Dictionary of Musicians*. [R: Choice, Apr 79, p. 202; WLB, Feb 79, p. 468] Kenyon C. Rosenberg

510. Pedigo, Alan. **International Encyclopedia of Violin-Keyboard Sonatas and Composer Biographies**. Limited edition of 500. Booneville, Ark., Arriaga Publications, 1979. 135p. illus. bibliog. $30.00. LC 79-84899. ISBN 0-686-34312-3. (Publisher's address: P.O. Box 652, Booneville, AR 72927).

This volume may or may not appeal to the violinists in the audience. The author, a violinist and duo recitalist, has assembled what may seem to be on first glance a hodgepodge of material relating to the violin/piano area. Fortunately, the title "encyclopedia" would tend to justify all that is presented.

Although much research effort has gone into this work, this reviewer feels that only two of the five sections of the book warrant praise. One encompasses composer biographies (arranged alphabetically), where, in addition to the better-known composers such as Mozart and Beethoven, there are presented over three hundred biographies of composers that do not appear in any of the standard encyclopedias and dictionaries of music such as *Grove's*, *Baker's*, and *Oxford*—the slipcover blurb asks us to "look in your favorite music dictionaries for Frances Ralston, Erno Gyulai, James Lates, Anton Puringer, Joachim Mendelsohn. . . . After you have given up, try *this* book." In this section is cited not only each composer's available violin sonata output, but also his accomplishments in other musical genres, as well as data regarding birth, death, training, position, and honors. The other chapter, entitled "Music Schools and Lists of Composers by Nations," presents what the title indicates, and each composer is referenced to the biographical section.

In the remainder of the book, the author attempts to be comprehensive, but merely skims the surface. We are grateful for the discussions on the evaluation and form of the sonata, the structure of recital programs, and the violin and keyboard sonatas of

Wolfgang Mozart. However, it seems unnecessary to include information on the medieval modes, modal interval structure, a dictionary of tempo and dynamic markings, the clef ladder, and diatonic scales—all fundamentals that are well-known to a musician. As for the thirty-two-page section of portraits (photographs) of national composers, one does not often see a picture of Bohuslav Martinu; on the other hand, Beethoven's visage is all too familiar. Also of value are the "Key to Music Publishers," "Phonograph Records," and the "Key to Recording Companies" found among the appendixes.   Frederic Schoettler

511.   Schonberg, Harold C. **The Lives of the Great Composers**. 2nd ed. New York, W. W. Norton, 1981. 653p. illus. bibliog. index. $24.95. LC 80-15058. ISBN 0-393-01302-2.

The author states that some of the material in this book originally appeared in his weekly *New York Times* column and as *Times* magazine pieces and is presented here in a revised and amplified version. This revised edition begins with Monteverdi and ends with Schoenberg. A final chapter briefly touches on composers Varese, Messiaen, Boulez, Stockhausen, Cage, Carter, and others. There are chapters on nationalistic schools and light classical composers such as Offenbach, Johann Strauss, Jr., and Sullivan. Schonberg hasn't missed many composers. They are presented chronologically, and the *life* of each composer is stressed rather than his output. Detailed descriptions of the composers' works will not be found here, although a large bibliography (over four hundred items) is included so that the person who desires to look at a composer in more depth is given guidelines for a search. *The Lives of the Great Composers* is light reading and anecdotal in concept, but it does capture the interest of the readers, so that they might read on and discover other composers.

                                                                                    Robert Palmieri

512.   Schwarz, Boris. **Great Masters of the Violin: From Corelli and Vivaldi to Stern, Zukerman and Perlman**. New York, Simon & Schuster, 1983. 671p. illus. bibliog. index. $24.00. LC 83-11996. ISBN 0-671-22598-7.

Only a violinist—with a sensitivity for the emotional, intellectual, and physical requirements for playing the instrument—could have written this book. Schwarz is a performer, was formerly a professor at Queens College, and is the author of several books and numerous articles in *The New Grove Dictionary of Music & Musicians*.

This unparalleled survey of violinists is the latest volume in an occasional series from Simon and Schuster featuring histories of musical performance. The emphasis here is on violinists' lives and performances; the works of composers, such as Vivaldi, who were also violinists are mentioned only insofar as they illuminate performance style. To give an idea of what pre-twentieth-century performances were like, Schwarz uses memoirs, letters, and autobiographies for first-person accounts. For the twentieth century (which takes up over half the book) he uses reviews, recordings, and often his own recollections of performances dating from Berlin in the 1920s to the contemporary United States.

While coverage is essentially chronological from the dawn of the modern violin in the sixteenth century to performers of 1983, Schwarz highlights schools and geographical areas that have been particularly significant. The Italy that bore Corelli and Vivaldi, Paganini's influence on the conception of the virtuoso, the world-wide effects of Leopold Auer's teaching in prerevolutionary St. Petersburg, and the contemporary prominence of Oriental musicians are some of these factors that have shaped violin performance. With its anecdotal and informed style, *Great Masters of the Violin* can be read as a detailed survey or consulted as a reference work for biographies of individual performers. [R: BL, 15 Nov 83, p. 462]   William Brockman

513.   Stevenson, Victor, ed. director. **The Music Makers**. Clive Unger-Hamilton, ed. New York, Harry N. Abrams, 1979. 255p. illus. (part col.). bibliog. index. (A Harrow House Edition). o.p. LC 78-56318. ISBN 0-8109-1327-5.

Well over nine hundred composers, performers, instrument makers, impresarios, and orchestras are surveyed in this lavishly illustrated volume. Individual entries are arranged chronologically (from Guido d'Arezzo, who flourished about the year 1000, to John Lennon, born in 1940) and interspersed with essays on the broad epochs of Western music. Also included are brief articles ("Special Features"), most of which deal with musical instruments and instrumental ensembles. Heavy emphasis is placed on art music in Europe and the United States, although American jazz musicians are fairly well represented, and popular music since 1950 is given good coverage in the final essay, "The Paradox of Popular Music." A glossary of terms and an index of names and works are included.

It is obvious that this book is not intended as a vehicle for research. Entries lack lists of works and bibliographies and are mostly of the thumbnail-sketch variety. It is thus rather curious to find biographies of a fair number of relatively obscure persons (for example, Thomas Britton, Antoine Clapisson, Gottfried Finger, Jean François Lalouette, Venanzio Rauzzini, Claudio Saracini, and Francesco Turini, none of whom are listed in the sixth edition of *Baker's Biographical Dictionary of Musicians*). It might have been preferable to eliminate a few of these shadowy figures in order to expand the entries of some of the acknowledged masters. The text as a whole is reasonably well edited and up-to-date; generous amounts of anecdotal information and occasional flashes of wit keep it on the lively side.

The illustrations—there are over six hundred of them, including photographs, pictures of art works, maps, and diagrams—are quite notable in terms of variety, quantity, and quality. Some have been widely reproduced, but others, especially portraits of lesser-known composers, could be very difficult to locate elsewhere. And, finally, the layout of the text and illustrations is exceptionally attractive.

John E. Druesedow, Jr.

514.   Thompson, Kenneth. **A Dictionary of Twentieth-Century Composers (1911-1971)**. New York, St. Martin's Press, 1973. 666p. o.p. LC 78-175526.

This is an effort to list all the compositions of thirty-two moderns: Bartók, Berg, Bloch, Busoni, Debussy, Delius, Elgar, Falla, Fauré, Hindemith, Holst, Honegger, Ives, Janáček, Kodály, Mahler, Martinů, Nielsen, Poulenc, Prokofiev, Puccini, Rachmaninov, Ravel, Roussel, Satie, Schoenberg, Sibelius, Strauss, Stravinsky, Varèse, Vaughan Williams and Webern. Titles are given in chronological order, with completion dates, durations (for some), instrumentations, first performances in various countries, first broadcast, and literature about the work (this quite selectively). General bibliographies are also given about each composer.

Spot checking at several points indicates that research was in some cases incomplete, that entries are frequently confused, and that careless proofreading was not rare. Comparing the entries for Ives with those in Dominique de Lerma's *Charles Ives, 1874-1954: A Bibliography of His Music* (Kent State University Press, 1970), we find twenty-seven works dated before 1891 in de Lerma; four in Thompson. Looking at

Fred Blum's *Jean Sibelius, An International Bibliography. . .* (Information Service, 1965) we find 1,429 numbered items; Thompson offers fewer than four hundred. With regard to proofreading—or perhaps just misunderstanding—it may be noted that the Hungarian diacritical marks (") and (˘) are both rendered by the (¨)—which has about the effect of substituting *u* for *i* in English.

Nevertheless, if we are willing to accept a rather high level of imperfection, Thompson's compilation is useful for quick reference. [R: Choice, Dec 73, p. 1534; WLB, Dec 73, p. 338]   Guy A. Marco

515. Tischler, Alice, with the assistance of Carol Tomasic. **Fifteen Black American Composers: A Bibliography of Their Works**. Detroit, Information Coordinators, 1981. 328p. illus. index. (Detroit Studies in Music Bibliography, No. 45). $19.75. LC 81-1162. ISBN 0-686-81287-5.

This biobibliography is one of several off-shoots of the work initiated by the former Black Music Center. Unlike David Baker's *The Black Composer Speaks* (1977), the biographies here are quite brief, and philosophic statements are absent; the real core of Tischler's volume is the works list, whose format is ample enough to include publication and recording data—although the details are not fully provided in all instances. A check on the listings for Adolphus Hailstork, for example, reveals six works (one composed as early as 1966) which are not cited. Therein rests one of the problems in securing such information from the composer (a problem encountered with Haydn and Mozart as well). The guide is, nonetheless, well done, and the figures, at least within the context of Afro-American musical studies, are all of importance: Edward Boatner, Margaret Bonds, Rogie Clark, Arthur Cunningham, William Dawson, Roger Dickerson, James Furman, Dr. Hailstork, Robert Harris, Wendell Logan, Carman Moore, Dorothy Moore, John Price, Noah Ryder, and Frederick Tillis. Indexes are by titles, media, and publisher addresses. The volume is handsomely produced, with portraits and ample margins. A valuable book whose significance will depend on the degree of its use. [R: Choice, Dec 81, p. 492]

Dominique-René de Lerma

516. Vodorsky-Shiraeff, Alexandria. **Russian Composers and Musicians: A Biographical Dictionary**. New York, Da Capo, 1969. 158p. $19.50. LC 71-76422. ISBN 0-306-71321-7.

Reprint of the first edition published in 1940. Contains brief biographies of the most outstanding figures of the Russian musical world with bibliographical references to all sources consulted. [R: Choice, May 70, p. 371]   Bohdan S. Wynar

517. **Who's Who in Opera: An International Biographical Directory of Singers, Conductors, Directors, Designers, and Administrators. Also Including Profiles of 101 Opera Companies**. Maria F. Rich, ed. Salem, N.H., Ayer Co., 1976. 684p. (Arno Press Who's Who Series). $71.50. LC 75-7963. ISBN 0-405-06652-X.

This carefully compiled work, whose well-defined criteria for inclusion are outlined at the front of the book, will be welcomed by all opera buffs and musicians. Prepared by Maria Rich, who has been editor of *Central Opera Service Bulletin* for the past ten years, it is "a reference source on the professional activities and personal data of currently active artists and on international operatic trends" (preface, p. ix). Not limited to singers, it also lists conductors, stage directors/producers, designers, and administrators. The minimum requirements for inclusion vary according to the occupation (e.g., singers: five major roles since the beginning of the 1971-1972 season; designers: at least two new productions; etc.). As pointed out in the preface, the criteria "exclude some important living singers who have retired or are no longer singing leading roles in major opera houses. However, their complete repertoire is mainly of historical interest and many of them are discussed in other books" (p. x). In addition, composers are omitted, to avoid duplicating the three Central Opera Service directories of contemporary operas (1967, 1969, 1975).

In all, there are over twenty-three hundred entries (1,553 singers) in the biographical section. The information provided is based on questionnaires sent to the members of 144 opera companies and festivals in thirty-three countries (the companies were chosen by an advisory board from the editor's initial list of 225). The "Guidelines to Biographical Entries" section gives detailed information on the kinds of data provided (and the reasons for omitting certain other data; for example, birth date is given only if the biographee included it on the questionnaire). For each entry, the following information is usually given: type of voice (for singers) or profession (e.g., "scenic and costume designer for opera, theater, television"); nationality; country and date of birth; spouse, spouse's occupation, and number of children; where and with whom the biographee studied; debut; awards; major companies with which the biographee performed; roles (composer in capital letters, role in medium, and name of opera in italics); world premiere; whether the biographee has done recordings, recitals, and/or teaching; residence (when supplied in the questionnaire); agent.

Following the biographical section is a sixty-five-page section of profiles of 101 opera companies. These represent the responses to a questionnaire sent to the 144 companies and festivals on which the biographical section is based. Included here, besides the expected directory-type data, is information on the two most recent seasons (opening and closing dates, number of performances, of operas, of new productions, and of non-opera performances); budget; repertory; number of persons engaged by the company in 1975; orchestra and sets; and trustees.

A list of the 144 companies and festivals follows the section of profiles, with asterisks denoting companies for which profiles are given. This is followed by a directory of international agents and their addresses, showing for each the abbreviation used in the biographical entries.

An excellent source of information on currently active performers and administrators in the field of opera. [R: Choice, Nov 76, pp. 1121-22]

Ann J. Harwell

518. Zaimont, Judith Lang, and Karen Famera, comps. and eds. **Contemporary Concert Music by Women: A Directory of the Composers and Their Works**. Westport, Conn., Greenwood Press, 1981. 355p. illus. index. $25.00. LC 80-39572. ISBN 0-313-22921-X.

Significant biographical data on seventy-two female composers are presented in this directory, which focuses predominantly on the United States. Each composer receives a paragraph to a full page in an attractive format, a black-and-white photograph, and an unidentified sample of her music. Six additional female musicians are given a page each, a photo, and a biographical sketch, although this section appeared to be a moot choice—or do all significant women musicians but six compose?

The second half of the book is devoted to a music list of the compositions organized by type—solo vocal, chamber vocal, solo instrumental, chamber instrumental, electronic, orchestral, band, choral, stage works, and music for young people, each further delineated by subdivisions (i.e., harpsichord, organ, piano, etc.). The addenda include a publisher/archive/composer address list, a discography, program listings for "Expressions: The Radio Series of the International League of Women Composers" available for airing with contact address, a record company address list, and an index, which provides access by listed women's names. No index to composition title is provided.

The directory is, as the editors point out, a pioneering work and belongs in significant music and women's collections. Furthermore, supplements are planned. We may yet get our second index, labelled samples, and more plain performers, or none (either would make more sense).   Helen Gregory

POPULAR AND COUNTRY AND WESTERN MUSIC

519.   Bane, Michael. **Who's Who in Rock**. New York, Facts on File, 1981. 259p. illus. index. $17.95. LC 80-20304. ISBN 0-87196-465-1. Also published by Dodd, Mead in 1982. $10.95pa.

Most academic music references cover the classical, the historical, and maybe the respectable pop. *The New Grove Dictionary of Music & Musicians* yields to popular artists if they have had a discernible influence on the course of musical events. Hence, Elvis Presley is included. By way of comparison, *Grove's*, in a 2½-inch entry, supplies the staid information that Presley's ". . . voice covered two and a third octaves, from *G* to *b*", with an upward extension to *d'''* in falsetto." Bane's *Who's Who*, in thirty inches with a two-column photo, tells us: "Girls fainted; parents fretted and Elvis rocked like no one had ever rocked before." Later: "He continued making movies—one bubble-headed film after another. . . ." The writing is lively, befitting the subject, and intelligent.

Bane's intent, to distinguish his work from others, was to show "how a person or group fits into the overall scheme of rock." To that end, the main section is an alphabetical listing of some twelve hundred solo and group performers with commentary that includes history, notable recordings, present work, and a candid critical evaluation. The content is current—he has Linda Ronstadt in the 1981 Broadway production of *The Pirates of Penzance*; detailed—he notes Bruce Springsteen's appearance on the covers of *Time* and *Newsweek*; historical—included are precursory styles exemplified by Tab Hunter, Big Bill Broonzy, Teresa Brewer, Bing Crosby, and the Kingston Trio, among others; and comprehensive (the informed judgment of a junior colleague is hereby acknowledged). There is an index of song titles, groups and performers not listed separately, and real names for professional.

Well done and browseable, the *Who's Who* lists the likes of The Quicksilver Messenger Service, Creedence Clearwater Revival, Thin Lizzy, Joy of Cooking, Pearls before Swine, Spooky Tooth, Meat Loaf, etc., etc. [R: BL, 1 Dec 81, p. 476]
                                                                 Kathleen McCullough

520.   Bianco, David, comp. and ed. **Who's New Wave in Music: An Illustrated Encyclopedia, 1976-1982 (The First Wave)**. Ann Arbor, Mich., Pierian Press, 1985. 430p. illus. index. (Rock & Roll Reference Series, No. 14). $29.50; $39.50 (institutions). LC 84-61228. ISBN 0-87650-173-0.

The aim of this publication is to provide comprehensive information on new-wave rock music, 1976-1982, and in terms of providing detailed information, the work is a success. It is composed of five sections: (1) "Bands and Artists" (including name, location, date band formed, style, personnel, chronology, discography), done with entry numbers, so once found in the index an entry is easy to track down in the body; (2) "Record Companies," a listing, by company, of records of new-wave music; (3) appendixes, including lists of books, major periodicals, fanzines, compilation albums, flexidisc discography, record and book dealers, and chronology and necrology; (4) the glossary; and (5) indexes (personal name, record label, song and album title, and geographic). An important minority of rock groups listed here is now very substantial indeed (e.g., Duran Duran; Pretenders; Police; Go-Go's).

Merely to look through this work will boggle the mind of anyone who has ever labored over a bibliography. The only improvements that come to mind revolve around the strong suspicion of this critic that the author very much wants to write a history of this time period; even a brief one — say, ten pages — would be of considerable assistance in correcting the few problems marring this excellent reference work. For example, the glossary is ridiculous — the phrases following the words supposedly being defined are lead sentences for nonexistent paragraphs discussing each word. The term *new wave* is not defined in the preface, as it should have been, neither is the geographical scope of the study (that finally comes as the very last section of the book). In addition, the author asserts that new wave rock is the most vital form of rock of its time period, but gives no proof.

For public libraries and for libraries supporting rock music curricula.

Mary Larsgaard

521. Chilton, John. **Who's Who of Jazz: Storyville to Swing Street**. 4th ed. New York, Da Capo, 1985. 375p. illus. $25.00; $11.95pa. LC 84-20062. ISBN 0-306-76271-4; 0-306-80243-0pa.

In the past fifteen years American jazz has increasingly become a subject of study and appreciation for music enthusiasts. Jazz not only embodies the spirit of twentieth-century America, it is seen by many critics as this nation's contribution to "classical" music. To fully appreciate the idiom, students must have access to information about the musicians who created and developed this unique style of music.

Written by John Chilton, a jazz trumpeter and arranger, the 1985 *Who's Who of Jazz* is the fourth edition of a reference classic. Over one thousand biographies are included, and these are limited to musicians born prior to 1920 who were raised in the United States. Sketches vary in length from short paragraphs to two pages, and emphasize the performer's career and musical growth over his or her personal life. At the end of some entries is a short list of recommended further readings, films, etc., about the musician. There are two inserts of black-and-white photographs, as well as a short list of jazz periodicals, arranged by country of publication. Recommended for all libraries.

Diane J. Cimbala

522. Claghorn, Charles Eugene. **Biographical Dictionary of Jazz**. Englewood Cliffs, N.J., Prentice-Hall, 1982. 377p. $25.00. LC 82-10409. ISBN 0-13-077966-0.

Jazz is a unique form of popular music because it has a classic tradition that is consciously invoked by most of today's performers. Claghorn has attempted to document this tradition and its modern interpreters with this dictionary of thirty-four hundred biographical entries, ranging widely over the history of jazz, from Jellyroll Morton to Wynton Marsalis. It is arranged alphabetically by personal name and has an appendix of small jazz groups. The entries tend to be very brief and factual: birth/death dates and places, associated players and groups, significant engagements. Occasionally there are quotes from critics and players illuminating the more important figures.

For most reference purposes this will be an inadequate guide. Claghorn's book has no discographies or photographs and rarely indicates the playing style of the performer. Although it does include many obscure musicians, the book has left out such prominent younger players as Anthony Davis, Chico Freeman, and Richie Cole. Also excluded were figures with a more broadly popular appeal, such as Pat Metheny, Joni Mitchell, and Al Jarreau. The selective information imparted frequently does not do justice to the subject, as in the forty-three-word description of "Jazz at the Philharmonic." Reference librarians are better served by Brian Case and Stan Britt's *Illustrated Encyclopedia of Jazz* or Leonard Feather and Ira Gitler's *Encyclopedia of Jazz in the Seventies* and its predecessors. [R: BL, 15 Dec 83, p. 611]   John P. Schmitt

523.   Colman, Stuart. **They Kept on Rockin': The Giants of Rock 'n' Roll**. Poole, England, Blandford Press; distr., New York, Sterling Publishing, 1982. 160p. illus. index. $9.95pa. ISBN 0-7137-1217-1.

This slim volume provides biographical sketches of approximately thirty rock-and-roll pioneers of the 1950s. Those covered in the first section, "They Really Kept on Rockin'," are performers like Chuck Berry and Jerry Lee Lewis, who made it big in the beginning and are still performing. The second section, "They Could Have Kept on Rockin'," profiles rockers whose careers were cut short, like Buddy Holly and Eddie Cockran. Next are sketches of Elvis, Little Richard, and the Everly Brothers ("They Should Have Kept on Rockin' "). Since all these are indeed "giants of rock 'n' roll," the material is pretty familiar, though the author's unpretentious style makes for engaging reading. The best section is the last, "Did Britain Keep on Rockin'?," where Colman's experience in British show business serves him well. Some of the performers covered in this section, such as Terry Dene and Other Understudies, are largely unknown in the United States and absent from standard rock biographical reference sources. But overall there is too little new information to warrant this volume's purchase, except for comprehensive subject collections.   Richard W. Grefrath

524.   Craig, Warren. **Sweet and Lowdown: America's Popular Song Writers**. Metuchen, N.J., Scarecrow, 1978. 645p. bibliog. index. $32.50. LC 77-20223. ISBN 0-8108-1089-1.

This interesting survey of 114 American composers and lyricists takes its title from a song in the 1925 Broadway production, *Tip-Toes*, by George and Ira Gershwin. Individuals such as the Gershwins are included by virtue of having written a certain number of hit songs, as determined by the author through reference to standard sources on popular music. Songs that could be classified as country and western or rock are excluded. Separate entries, each providing a biographical sketch and a chronological list of songs (linked with stage, movie, and television production titles when applicable), are grouped according to three chronological categories: (1) "Before Tin Pan Alley" (from the early nineteenth century to about 1895), (2) "Tin Pan Alley" (from 1895 to the establishment of sound motion pictures, i.e., the late 1920s), and (3) "After Tin Pan Alley" (from the late 1920s through the 1960s). To qualify for inclusion, songwriters must have written a minimum number of hits according to the chronological category in which they are placed: six for the first category, fifteen for the second, and forty for the third. With regard to the third category, for example, Richard Rodgers and Oscar Hammerstein, II, both qualify easily, but not Alan Jay Lerner and Frederick Loewe.

The author also provides a list of 129 prominent composers and lyricists (among them — in addition to Lerner and Loewe — Leonard Bernstein, Vernon Duke, Johnny Green, W. C. Handy, Henry Mancini, Stephen Sondheim, Dmitri Tiomkin, and Kurt Weill) who did not write enough songs of sufficiently wide popularity to be included.

Separate indexes are provided for the approximately seven thousand songs and twenty-seven hundred productions listed in the text. In an appendix, comparative rankings for individuals in each of the three chronological categories are also provided (winners: Stephen Collins Foster, Harry Von Tilzer, and Irving Berlin, respectively). While other reference tools are more comprehensive, this one has a more convenient format than most for scanning the hit songs and productions of a particular writer. Even so, it is regrettable that a number of well-known songwriters were omitted because of the author's guidelines. [R: LJ, 15 Dec 78, p. 2504]   John E. Druesedow, Jr.

525. Feather, Leonard. **From Satchmo to Miles**. New York, Stein and Day, 1972; repr., New York, Da Capo, 1984. 258p. $25.00. LC 70-187311. ISBN 0-306-76230-7.

Encyclopedist, newspaper columnist, critic, occasional composer, editor, record-producer, and disc jockey, Leonard Feather is now into his fifth decade of writing about jazz and jazz musicians.

In *From Satchmo to Miles*, a collection of thirteen pieces about major citizens of the jazz community, Feather draws upon his personal recollections of such diverse and colorful traditional, mainstream, and modern jazz artists as Louis Armstrong, Duke Ellington, Billie Holiday, Ray Charles, and Miles Davis.

While they are not at all "in-depth studies," Mr. Feather's profiles offer the kind of revealing insights that can come only from someone who has been permitted inside the insulated private world of the jazz musician; from someone who has "paid his dues" by learning the language and the rules of what has been an almost underground art form.

From Satchmo to Miles may not be an indispensable addition to the literature of jazz, but it certainly is an entertaining and informative collection of footnotes, anecdotes, and insights by the dean of jazz writers in the United States.

Nat Shapiro

526. Gitler, Ira. **Jazz Masters of the Forties**. New York, Da Capo, 1982. 290p. illus. index. (The Macmillan Jazz Masters Series). $25.00; $8.95pa. LC 66-17874. ISBN 0-306-76155-6; 0-306-80224-4pa.

This is actually a reprint of the 1966 edition, originally published by Collier Books. Ira Gitler's knowledgeable and affectionate study of the jazz revolution of the 1940s is a worthy addition to the growing list of books dealing with the history of America's most vital and only original art form.

One of the most valuable volumes thus far in the admirable Jazz Masters series, Mr. Gitler's book is a thorough survey of the origins, development, and leading personalities of modern jazz in the United States. Dealing, as he does, with all of the principal instrumentalists, composers, and arrangers of the decade, the author has drawn largely upon his own observations and personal interviews with a large number of the major musical figures of the period — including Charlie Parker, Dizzy Gillespie, Thelonius Monk, and Bud Powell.

Mr. Gitler, a prolific annotator of record albums, a respected reporter and critic for jazz periodicals, and a musician himself, writes with an understanding not only of the creative currents flowing through this dynamic decade, but also of the extra-musical elements, including the pernicious influence of drugs. In all, this is probably the best book thus far on modern jazz music and musicians.

A related title that is also part of the Jazz Masters series is *Jazz Masters of the Fifties*, by Joe Goldberg (New York, Da Capo, 1980. 246p. $25.00).   Nat Shapiro

527.   Hadlock, Richard. **Jazz Masters of the Twenties**. New York, Collier Books, 1974 (c1965); repr., New York, Da Capo, 1985. 225p. illus. index. (The Macmillan Jazz Masters Series). $25.00. LC 65-18469. ISBN 0-306-76283-8.

Jazz in the 1920s was both unrecognized and ignored as an art form, and its colorful practitioners functioned with remarkable lack of self-consciousness as craftsmen in the somewhat tawdry world of commerical popular entertainment.

There were no critics and just a very few devotees; and only the haphazardly and often primitively produced recordings (made mostly in the latter half of the decade) offer evidence of the enormous energy and creativity of the pioneers dealt with in Richard Hadlock's contribution to the Jazz Masters series.

The dominant stylistic currents are dealt with by Mr. Hadlock through biographies of Louis Armstrong, Bix Biederbeck, Fletcher Henderson, Jack Teagarden, Fats Waller, Bessie Smith, and, among others, the large group of white Dixieland musicians known as "The Chicagoans."

While very little new is added to existing jazz scholarship in Mr. Hadlock's retrospective, this volume is nonetheless an informative and responsible piece of work.

Nat Shapiro

528.   **The Harmony Illustrated Encyclopedia of Rock**. 4th ed. Edited by Mike Clifford. New York, Harmony/Crown Publishers, 1984. 256p. illus. (part col.). index. $19.95; $11.95pa. LC 81-20297. ISBN 0-517-54661-2; 0-517-53995-3pa.

The original edition by Logan and Woffinden published in 1977 is this reviewer's favorite rock-and-roll biographical directory. The more than eight hundred entries are copiously illustrated with spectacular color photos and reproductions of album covers and brimming with outrageously opinionated commentary. It appears to rate high with legions of fans as well, if one library's demolished first edition is any indication: binding hopelessly broken from overuse, entire articles razored out, and perceptive observations underlined.

Sad to say, this updated edition of more than eight hundred entries is an uninspired and downright sloppy job. Most of the original 250 pages of Logan and Woffinden's text has been retained, which is fine as far as it goes. The updating has been accomplished in two ways, neither satisfactory. First, amendments are tacked on to already existing articles, like the mention of Keith Moon's death in 1978. Typically, earlier in the same article the comment that Moon "has remained irrepressible" has been left as is. Carly Simon's marriage to James Taylor is mentioned, but the revision fails to note their subsequent split. The other revision mechanism is an appendix called "The 80's," which profiles about one hundred recent groups. The nuisance of two A-Z sections is the result, partially ameliorated by an index. The quality of writing is lackluster compared to that of the high-spirited Logan and Woffinden. Chrissie Hynde is acknowledged to be the "focal point" of the Pretenders, but no insights are offered about the nature of her act. A far cry from the original edition, which understood the significance of such matters as Rolling Stone Brian Jones's having "further enhanced his local notoriety by fathering two illegitimate children by the time he was 16." Kate Bush is profiled in the supplement, but the author fails to mention whether she's British or American.

Nevertheless, this revised edition will be welcome in libraries not owning the original edition, and in those whose copy looks like it's been trampled by the crowd at a Led Zeppelin concert. [R: WLB, Feb 83, p. 524]   Richard W. Grefrath

529.   Harris, Sheldon. **Blues Who's Who: A Biographical Dictionary of Blues Singers**. New Rochelle, N.Y., Arlington House, 1979; repr., New York, Da Capo, 1981. 775p. illus. bibliog. index. $18.95pa. LC 78-27073. ISBN 0-306-80155-8.

The names Chester Burnett, McKinley Morganfield, Riley King, and Peter Chatman may not ring any bells of recognition for blues enthusiasts until it is realized that these performers usually are billed under the names Howlin' Wolf, Muddy Waters, B. B. King, and Memphis Slim. The entries in this colossal work are the real names of the singers, who seem more often than not to adopt a clever alias or to acquire another name from earlier days. What is important in this regard is that there are copious cross-references from all of these variations to the correct names.

The scope of *Blues Who's Who* goes beyond the above-mentioned singers. Dinah Washington, Ethel Waters, Richie Havens, Janis Joplin, Jimi Hendrix, Woody Guthrie, Jimmie Rodgers, Ray Charles, and the more popular blues stylists Joe Williams, Joe Turner, Lou Rawls, plus Paul Butterfield and Little Richard are all here. Curiously, Billie Holiday and Mahalia Jackson are missing from such a broad cross section of blues performers. Most of the performers treated here, however, are the local city and rural singers who gained national and international recognition.

For each performer the book gives brief biographical information: his or her birth date and place, marriages, children, instruments played, songs composed, influences, reference sources, and critical quotations describing music and careers. The bulk of each entry comprises a substantially complete accounting of all professional performances in concerts, television and radio shows, films, and other media; for such prolific performers as Sonny Terry and Brownie McGhee, these lists cover many pages. Appendixes include a selected bibliography, film, radio, TV, and theatre indexes, a name and place index, and an incredibly comprehensive song index. This is the most substantial and complete source for blues performers available. [R: LJ, July 79, pp. 1441-42]   Stephen M. Fry

530.   Helander, Brock. **The Rock Who's Who: A Biographical Dictionary and Critical Discography**. New York, Schirmer Books/Macmillan, 1982. 686p. bibliog. index. $25.00; $14.95pa. LC 82-80804. ISBN 0-02-871250-1; 0-02-871920-4pa.

Helander has compiled a well-researched biographical reference work that belongs in most rock-and-roll collections. The three hundred entries each provide a biographical sketch, followed by a detailed discography. Coverage includes disk jockeys, music industry luminaries, songwriting-production teams, as well as performers. Those selected for inclusion "contributed significantly to the development of contemporary popular music." Accordingly, most of the coverage is of well-known or commercially successful bands, nearly all of which have been profiled in similar works, such as *Lillian Roxon's Rock Encyclopedia*. The most important features of Helander's compilation are the detailed discographies following each biographical sketch, which include record label, number, date of release, current availability, and indication of RIAA gold and platinum awards. Though meticulous discographies such as this have already been published for specific supergroups, such as the Beatles, the reference value of this painstaking treatment for three hundred artists is formidable.

The biographical sketches are competently written, but they follow a rather odd format. The first one-fourth or so of each is a summary of the band's career, and the rest of the sketch is a more complete version of that summary. This format can be found in newspaper articles, but it's annoying in a reference book. The unfortunate result is that much detail from the first few paragraphs is repeated later on. For instance, in the piece on the Jefferson Airplane, we are told twice that *Surrealistic Pillow* "launched" the San Francisco Sound, we're told twice that Grace Slick wrote "White Rabbit," and we're told twice that Marty Balin's "Miracles" was the group's first "smash" (or "major") hit in eight years. The book could probably be reduced in size by one-fourth if this unnecessary duplication were eliminated.

Much of the fun in a compilation like this is jousting with the author's opinions. It's easy to agree that Ringo Starr's movie *Caveman* is "inane," but harder to concur that the Doors' "Hello, I Love You" is "puerile." Overall, though, the historical perspective is excellent, as in the discussion of the Kingston Trio's "clean-cut college image that enabled them to avoid the politically suspect stigma attached to early fifties folk artists."

The index attempts to provide a cross-reference from an individual performer's name to the group that person performed with (e.g., "Stevie Nicks" see "Fleetwood Mac,") but it's carelessly done. For instance, there's no cross-reference from Linda Ronstadt to the Stone Poneys nor any from Ron Wood to the Rolling Stones, though each artist is discussed in the piece on the respective group. The bibliography, on the other hand, is excellent. One section is arranged by name of artist; following each name is a listing of relevant biographical material, including periodical articles and interviews. [R: LJ, 1 Oct 82, p. 1866; WLB, Feb 83, p. 524]   Richard W. Grefrath

531. Kingsbury's Who's Who in Country & Western Music. Kenn Kingsbury, ed. Culver City, Calif., Black Stallion Country Press, 1981. 304p. illus. (part col.). bibliog. index. $24.95.

This is a useful biographical dictionary, for it covers country music industry people as well as performers and artists. Indeed, any artist, record company, or music publisher who made the *Billboard, Cash Box, Record World,* or *Radio & Records* "charts" of bestsellers and playlists during 1979-1980 was eligible for inclusion. Material was gathered by the questionnaire method, calling for standard information. The book is printed on glossy paper, and each biographee gets a 4x3-inch section of a page (twelve people to a page), which includes about one square inch for a black-and-white photo. In separate sections, then, there is detail for 220 currently active recording artists, 224 studio musicians, 100 disc jockeys, 36 composers, 36 record producers, 29 agents, 35 "great" performers who have died, and 36 "industry-related" people—for a total of 716 persons. There is an index at the front in case the user does not know if someone is a composer, singer, musician, or other.

Also included are valuable listings and addresses for some two thousand radio stations that program twelve or more hours of country music a day (arranged by state), record companies, music publishers, talent agencies, self-help organizations, and award winners. And there is still more: short scattered essays on various aspects of country music such as television and radio shows, the John Edwards Memorial Foundation, Hollywood films (but not a complete listing), the Grand Ole Opry, the Louisiana Hayride, books and periodicals, and country music in other lands (but nothing for Canada).

Unfortunately, there is no listing of recommended long-playing records, and there are many misspellings and typographical errors. However, because of its "trade" data, this book has unique reference value for popular-music or country-music collections.

Dean Tudor

532. Shestack, Melvin. **The Country Music Encyclopedia**. New York, Thomas Y. Crowell, 1977. 560p. illus. $12.95; $7.95pa. LC 74-9644. ISBN 0-690-01220-9.

It is useful to compare *The Country Music Encyclopedia* with Irwin Stambler's *Encyclopedia of Folk, Country, and Western Music*, published in 1969. Shestack, unlike Stambler, limited his entries to stars—performers and song writers whose commercial success brought them to the top one hundred charts in *Billboard* and *Cash Box* magazines. Excluded are other important names in country music—the promoters, producers, collectors, etc.—and groups or archives such as the Country Music Association and the John Edwards Memorial Foundation.

Shestack's style is chatty and subjective and holds obvious appeal for country-music fans. Unfortunately, this rambling often fills space while leaving out much of the factual information presented in Stambler's more straightforward account. However, some new and some additional material make this reference work worth having. Definite pluses are: (1) entries for current stars, most born in the 1930s to the 1950s, some children of stars; (2) fuller coverage and lengthier articles on certain stars (Merle Haggard, for instance); (3) biographies of influential or otherwise historically significant old-time country performers; and (4) more photos (many full-page), and photos generally superior to those in Stambler.

Appendixes include a discography of titles "representative of the artist's work and . . . readily available"; a list of country-music stations in the United States (by state), Puerto Rico, and Canada; and a "Sampling of Country Songs" chosen to "reflect the changes country music has gone through." [R: LJ, July 74, p. 1822; WLB, Dec 74, p. 315]

Carole Franklin

533. Stambler, Irwin, and Grelun Landon. **The Encyclopedia of Folk, Country and Western Music**. 2nd ed. New York, St. Martin's Press, 1984. 902p. illus. bibliog. $17.95pa. ISBN 0-312-248199.

This 902-page volume updates a previous edition of the same title published in 1969. This updated edition provides biographies and musical histories of over six hundred musicians, including: Woody Guthrie; Roy Acuff; Alabama; Joan Baez; Bob Dylan; Crosby, Stills & Nash; The Kingston Trio; and Juice Newton.

The information for this work was obtained from some six hundred questionnaires to individuals or groups selected for coverage (in the case of deceased individuals, the questionnaire was sent to the estate or other representative). Direct interviews were used when obtainable; otherwise background information was procured from literature and through materials provided by the music industry.

Although the entries are often lengthy and appear on the surface to be quite detailed, much of the information provided is pre-1980s, although the copyright date is 1984. Several artists, such as Joan Baez, have been active in the eighties; but these facts are not available here. Entries are often very interesting and informative, but many are killed in the last sentences with meaningless quotes from the artists. For example, the entry on Charley Pride ends with a paragraph about racial prejudice at an all-white country club in Dallas. Pride is quoted as having said after being refused membership: ". . . I'm not concerned—there are plenty of places I can play golf." Perhaps the authors felt quotes like this helped show the artists' character; but this reviewer feels they ruined many entries.

Sixty-seven pages of this revised edition consist of music awards from various music associations, such as the Academy of Country and Western Music, the Country Music Association, the Country Music Hall of Fame, the Nashville Songwriters Association (International), the National Academy of Arts & Sciences, and the Recording Industry Association of America. This section alone makes the work invaluable.

An extensive bibliography concludes this hefty reference volume. The $17.95 price tag of this paperbound edition makes it affordable to most libraries and is recommended for all.   Janet R. Ivey

534.   Tobler, John, and Stuart Grundy. **The Guitar Greats**. New York, St. Martin's Press, 1984. 191p. illus. index. $10.95pa. LC 83-15926. ISBN 0-312-35319-7.

The book's title is misleading; its scope is better stated in the introduction: "The fourteen guitarists profiled in this book are simply amongst the greatest rock/blues players alive today." This caveat and the book's original publication in Britain largely determine the choice of guitarists profiled here. B. B. King's wide-ranging influence and popularity make him a natural choice for the first sketch. The selection of other names, while including the expected Eric Clapton, Jimmy Page, and Carlos Santana, is obviously a result of the preferences of the writers. Hank Marvin, for instance, while a phenomenon in Britain, is unknown to most Americans. It could easily be argued that Ritchie Blackmore and Brian May are not on a par with omitted rock musicians like Frank Zappa and Andy Summers. Ry Cooder is a refreshing inclusion; his playing style is understated but highly original.

While the selection may be quirky, the verve and clarity of the writing and the use of interview material bring the subjects to life and make the profiles enjoyable and informative. By focusing on professional concerns such as bands, recordings, and instruments, the book avoids the fawning praise and obsession with gossip that often characterize writing about rock musicians. Black-and-white photographs, a brief discography for each guitarist, and a reasonably detailed index contribute to making this a useful survey. [R: LJ, 1 Feb 84, p. 182]

William Brockman

535.   White, Mark. **"You Must Remember This..."**: **Popular Songwriters 1900-1980**. New York, Scribner's, 1985. 304p. bibliog. index. $14.95. LC 85-1974. ISBN 0-684-18433-8.

"You Must Remember This. . ." is a collection of biographies of over 130 popular song composers writing between 1900 and 1980. According to the author's introduction, the selection of songwriters was a personal one, although he did systematically exclude writers who have composed only a few songs, and songwriters who compose exclusively for a single performing group. The popularly written biographies are approximately one-half to one page in length and mention most of the composers' greatest song hits. White has also provided indexes to song titles, composers and lyricists, performers, and shows and films. David Ewen's *Popular American Composers* (H. W. Wilson, 1962) and its supplement offer similar information, although Ewen's biographical information is more detailed, begins with Revolutionary United States, and includes only American composers. White's volume also includes British composers, such as John Lennon and Elton John, and is more current. There is considerable duplication in these books for songwriters between 1900 and 1972, but each volume includes some composers omitted by the other.

"You Must Remember This. . ." offers a useful one-volume source of information on popular songwriters. It may not, however, be a necessary purchase for libraries owning the Ewen volume and its supplement, unless a library's needs dictate more up-to-date information.   Allie Wise Goudy

536.   York, William. **Who's Who in Rock Music**. New York, Scribner's, 1982. 413p. $29.95; $14.95pa. LC 81-21368. ISBN 0-684-17342-5; 0-684-17343-3pa.

Ladies and Gentlemen: the Rolling Stones . . . and every other rock group, group member, solo artist, and musician who sat in on a session can be found here — over twelve thousand entries, alphabetically arranged. An individual's entry includes name, instrument(s), birth and death dates (as late as Bob Marley's death in May 1981), group association(s) and years, sessions played, and discography. Group entries include musicians' names, instruments, years with group if limited, early names of group if changed, and discography through 1980 (predominantly alphabetical, though some are chronologically arranged). Further background is supplied on performers and groups who have made a major impact on the rock scene. Rock-and-roll, rhythm and blues, acid rock, folk rock, country rock, punk and new wave — it's all here. Disco, excepting the BeeGees, is omitted. Folk performers who influenced rock, such as Ledbelly, Woody Guthrie, and gospel singer Mahalia Jackson, are included. This book is so thorough and well organized that when we couldn't find The Cheers and/or Ronnie Graham (small but loud in the 1950s) we could only assume that they'd cut singles but no albums.

York's original *Who's Who. in Rock Music* was self-published in 1978, and contained six thousand entries. With twice as many entries, this highly readable book is the most complete in its field and a must for pop-music historians, discographers, disc jockeys, industry personnel, and the millions of rock fans in the United States and Great Britain, especially trivia buffs. No popular music collection should be without it. Future supplements should be looked forward to with great anticipation. [R: Choice, Sept 82, p. 62; LJ, 1 Apr 82, p. 720; WLB, Sept 82, p. 78]   Helen Gregory

17 Performing Arts

Introduction

The chapter "Performing Arts" covers "Dance," "Drama," and "Theatre" with a total of twelve entries plus related titles discussed in annotations. The first section, "Dance," includes only one work, *Biographical Dictionary of Dance* (see entry 537), that deals exclusively with this topic in recent times. Several biographical sources mentioned in the section on "Theatre" also include biographies of dancers. The second section, "Drama," includes a number of contemporary sources on playwrights, e.g., *Contemporary Dramatists* (see entry 538) or the *McGraw-Hill Encyclopedia of World Drama* (see entry 539). Our last section, "Theatre," includes the standard work *Who's Who in the Theatre* (see entry 547), complementing *Notable Names in the American Theatre* (see entry 545). A number of specialized works are also included, e.g., *A Biographical Dictionary of Actors, Actresses, Musicians, Dancers, Managers and Other Stage Personnel in London, 1660-1800* (see entry 541), to be published in ten volumes.

An older American biographical dictionary may also be useful: W. Rigdon's *The Biographical Encyclopedia and Who's Who of the American Theatre* (Heineman, 1966. 1101p.) that served as a contemporary biographical source to 3,350 individuals, including foreign actors who made significant contributions to American theatre. One of the best older British dictionaries is D. E. Baker's *Biographia Dramatica. . .* (3v. Longmans, 1812; repr., AMS Press, 1966).

A number of subject dictionaries may assist in locating biographical information. *The Concise Oxford Dictionary of Ballet*, edited by H. Koegler (2nd ed. Oxford University Press, 1982. 459p.), covers biographies of outstanding performers, and there are also a number of older works. *The Dance Encyclopedia*, compiled by A. Chujoy and P. W. Manchester (Simon and Schuster, 1967. 992p.), briefly covers most important performers and is more scholarly than *The Book of the Dance*, by A. De Mille (Golden Press, 1963. 252p.). A good international coverage is provided by *Dictionary of Modern Ballet*, edited by F. Gadan and R. Maillard (Tudor, 1959. 360p.), that was originally published in French as *Dictionnaire du ballet moderne* (1957). The modern period is covered in D. McDonagh's *The Complete Guide to Modern Dance*

(Doubleday, 1976. 534p.), emphasizing choreographers; each biographical sketch is followed by a selection of representative works. The same ground is also covered by *The Encyclopedia of Dance and Ballet*, edited by M. Clarke and D. Vaughan (Putnam, 1977. 376p.).

M. Matlaw's *Modern World Drama: An Encyclopedia* (E. P. Dutton, 1972. 960p.) includes biographical articles on playwrights who lived in the twentieth century. Less comprehensive is *Crowell's Handbook of Contemporary Drama*, by M. Anderson (Thomas Y. Crowell, 1971. 505p.), that also includes playwrights, emphasizing the written drama rather than theatre. A popular *The Oxford Companion to American Theatre*, edited by G. Bordman (Oxford University Press, 1984. 734p.) contains a large number of biographical entries and can be supplemented by *The Oxford Companion to the Theatre* (4th ed. Oxford University Press, 1983. 934p.), that provides international coverage. A useful source for biographical information is also S. Green's *Encyclopedia of Musical Theatre* (Dodd, Mead, 1976. 488p.), covering some six hundred individuals. A more specialized work is A. Woll's *Dictionary of the Black Theatre: Broadway, Off-Broadway and Selected Harlem Theatre* (Greenwood Press, 1983. 359p.), which covers personalities and organizations in the second part.

There are also a number of biographical sources published in other languages, e.g., *Kürschners biographisches Theater-Handbuch* (Berlin, Walter de Gruyter, 1956. 840p.), edited by H. A. Frenzel and H. J. Moser, that covers German, Swiss, and Austrian figures. Much more comprehensive is W. Kosch's *Deutsches Theater-Lexikon; biographisches und bibliographisches Handbuch* (Klagenfurt, Kleinmayr, 1951- . In progress), providing substantial coverage of personalities in theatre.

British theatre is covered by a serial, *Who's Who in the Theatre: A Biographical Record of the Contemporary Stage* (London, Pitman, 1912-), that unfortunately is not published on a regular basis. Separately published indexes, as well as other serial publications, are described along with other reference sources in *Performing Arts Research: A Guide to Information Sources* (Gale, 1976. 280p.) and other guides listed in Sheehy and Walford.

DANCE

537. Cohen-Stratyner, Barbara Naomi. **Biographical Dictionary of Dance**. New York, Schirmer Books/Macmillan, 1982. 970p. (A Dance Horizons Book). $75.00. LC 81-86153. ISBN 0-02-870260-3.

A comprehensive work in its field, this volume profiles more than twenty-nine hundred performers, choreographers, composers, impresarios, designers, theorists, and teachers in an attempt to include anyone who is responsible for having developed or expanded dance in Europe or the Americas. The work spans the history of dance from its European origins through the modern and contemporary periods.

For each entry, basic personal and professional biographical information is presented, including the individual's beginnings, training, and evolution through the world of dance, as well as contributions. A list of works composed, performed, or choreographed is appended to many of the entries. These include concert works, operas, theatre works, films, television shows, and other formats. A select bibliography of works about a particular individual is also appended to many entries.

For the dance enthusiast, the student, and the researcher in the performing arts, this volume should prove to be valuable in identifying and providing basic biographical information about many minor and less-well-known people from the field of dance, both past and present. Despite the lack of illustrations, this work should prove to be a valuable addition to most performing-arts collections, whether exhaustive or representative. [R: BL, Aug 83, p. 1484; LJ, 1 Jan 83, p. 41]

Edmund F. SantaVicca

DRAMA

538. **Contemporary Dramatists**. 3rd ed. James Vinson, ed. D. L. Kirkpatrick, associate ed. New York, St. Martin's Press, 1982. 1104p. index. (Contemporary Writers of the English Language). $55.00. LC 76-54628. ISBN 0-312-16664-8.

This current edition of a valuable reference work includes compact personal and critical biographies of over three hundred significant playwrights of the English language and contains forty new entries and one hundred new or revised essays regarding authors continued from the previous edition published in 1973.

In addition to standard biographical and directory information, each entry contains a full bibliography of all published works of a writer, as well as selected listings of critical studies of the author's works. Locations of manuscript collections, where applicable, are provided. Each entry also contains a signed critical essay by a scholar or critic familiar with the work of the writer, and a comment or statement (if provided) by the author. In a supplementary section, separate categories of screen writers, radio writers, television writers, librettists, and theatre groups are listed. For each section, entries consist of personal names and listings of works published or produced. When necessary, the reader is referred by cross-reference to the central corpus of the work.

An appendix includes complete entries for important playwrights who have died since the 1950s but whose reputations are considered "contemporary" by the compilers. A full index by title of all plays listed in the volume completes the work. Selective and authoritative, *Contemporary Dramatists* remains a key tool for librarians, scholars, writers, and others connected with the theatre and dramatic arts. [R: LJ, 1 Mar 83, p. 491]

Edmund F. SantaVicca

539. Hochman, Stanley, ed. **McGraw-Hill Encyclopedia of World Drama**. 2nd ed. New York, McGraw-Hill, 1984. 5v. illus. index. $295.00/set. LC 83-9919. ISBN 0-07-079169-4.

International in scope, the thoroughly revised and updated second edition of the *McGraw-Hill Encyclopedia of World Drama* presents detailed information on the achievements of playwrights throughout theatre history, from Sophocles to Tom Stoppard, Wole Soyinka to Cao Yu.

Although the primary emphasis is on playwrights and their works (950 of the thirteen hundred entries deal with playwrights), this encyclopedia also examines national, regional, and ethnic drama of countries around the world while providing comprehensive materials on such aspects as influential theatres and companies, dramatic genres, seminal directors, and non-Western dramatic traditions. Diverse entries cover such subjects as Arabic theatre, Iranian secular theatre, bunraku, kabuki, the Peking Opera, the Berliner Ensemble, musical comedy, and Shakespeare on film.

For dramatists of major importance (Aristophanes, Sophocles, Shakespeare, Congreve, Pirandello, Ibsen, and O'Neill), the entries offer a biographical section, an analysis of creative accomplishments, synopses of important works, a play list, and a bibliography. For playwrights of lesser significance (Caecilius, Thomas Shadwell, Jules Renard, Hans Christian Branner, and Ray Lawler), a conventional encyclopedic presentation is used. Over twenty-eight hundred photographs and drawings make browsing through this reference guide a memorable adventure.

The *McGraw-Hill Encyclopedia of World Drama* is an invaluable reference work for theatre historians, drama critics, teachers, and actors. So comprehensive is its information and so broad is its appeal that even the smallest of public libraries may wish to have it on hand as a guide to dramatic traditions throughout the world.

Colby H. Kullman

540. **Modern British Dramatists, 1900-1945**. Stanley Weintraub, ed. Detroit, Gale, 1982. 2v. bibliog. (Dictionary of Literary Biography, Vol. 10; A Bruccoli Clark Book). $164.00/set. LC 81-19234. ISBN 0-8103-0937-8.

This expensive set is part of the *Dictionary of Literary Biography*, inaugurated in 1978 under the distinguished editorial direction of Matthew J. Bruccoli. Seventy-three major British playwrights who came to prominence between 1900 and 1945 have been included. Articles are signed and range from two to more than twenty pages in length. A typical entry begins with a list of productions, continues with a biographical and critical section, and concludes with a short bibliography. Photographs of playwrights and scenes from a few productions are included. If there are major collections of papers or manuscripts, their locations have been noted. Appendixes at the end of part 2 include: "The Lord Chamberlain's Office and Stage Censorship in England," "Stage Censorship," "The Development of Lighting in the Staging of Drama, 1900-1945," "The Great War and the Theater, 1914-1918," "Dangerous Years: London Theater, 1939-1945," "The Royal Court Theatre and the New Drama," and "The Abbey Theatre and Irish Drama, 1900-1945." There is also a cumulative index to volumes 1-10 and the 1980 *Yearbook*.

The articles, by recognized scholars, are highly readable. The only unfortunate feature is the very high price. Libraries whose users might benefit may have to forego purchase of these volumes because of cost and potential duplication of information in less expensive sources. [R: WLB, Sept 82, pp. 75-76]   A. Robert Rogers

THEATRE

541. **A Biographical Dictionary of Actors, Actresses, Musicians, Dancers, Managers and Other Stage Personnel in London, 1660-1800**. By Philip H. Highfill, Jr., Kalman A. Burnim, and Edward A. Langhans. Carbondale, Ill., Southern Illinois University Press, 1973- . In progress. $40.00/vol. LC 71-157068.

Projected in sixteen volumes, with volumes 1-10, already published, this steadily emerging record of the lives and careers of London theatrical personnel from the Restoration to the Regency continues to be remarkable for both its comprehensiveness and its scholarship. According to the preface in the first volume, "the purpose of these volumes is to provide brief biographical notices of all persons who were members of theatrical companies or occasional performers or were patentees or servants of the patent theatres, opera houses, amphitheatres, pleasure gardens, theatrical taverns, music rooms, fair booths, and other places of public entertainment in London and its immediate environs from the Restoration of Charles II in 1660 until the end of the season 1799-1800" (p. vii). From a study of the ten volumes published between 1971 and 1984, it would seem that the editors have fulfilled that purpose.

Saying they have "combed every source that ingenuity could suggest," the authors proceed to enumerate a staggering list of sources (from *London Stage 1660-1800* to all sorts of original and secondary materials). The entries vary in length, from a few lines to several pages, and the information is given in a clear, narrative style, usually in chronological order. Birth and death dates and profession (if known) are given first; it would have been helpful if other standard biographical information had been listed at the beginning of the entry, but obviously so little was found about many of the subjects that any standard data format would have been virtually impossible.

Any collector of original materials of the period will find it extremely useful for checking names in letters, handbills, prints, etc. This is a truly significant product of years of research, *not* something thrown together in haste and passed off as a basic reference tool. Highly recommended. [R: Choice, Dec 82, p. 560]

Richard M. Buck and Bohdan S. Wynar

542.   Busby, Roy. **British Music Hall: An Illustrated Who's Who from 1850 to the Present Day**. Salem, N.H., Paul Elek, 1976. 191p. illus. o.p. ISBN 0-236-40053-3.

Biographical notes on 427 entertainers popular especially in and around London, from such early performers as nineteenth-century comedian Dan Leno to Tommy Steele, who started in rock-and-roll. Entries average about three hundred words, although much longer entries are written for such luminaries as Maurice Chevalier and Sophie Tucker, and much less is written for others not so well known. There are over 240 photographs. A short introduction gives a brief history of English music halls.

The entries are alphabetically arranged by stage names. Teams are found in the order they were billed: Olsen and Johnson are filed under Olsen. There are no cross-references from the second half of the team and there is no index. There are no entries for (or cross-references from) David Kaminski, Benjamin Kubelsky, Colin McCallum, and Erich Weiss, but within stage names entries for Danny Kaye, Jack Benny, Charles Coburn, and Houdini their original names are given. There is an entry for Bill Robinson, but only within the article is "Bojangles" mentioned. There is an entry for "Stan Laurel of Laurel and Hardy" but none for Oliver Hardy, although they played the Palladium as a team. There is no entry at all for Noel Coward or Gertrude Lawrence.

Entries are sometimes inadequate. "The Great Alexander Troupe" doesn't even tell how many acrobats were in the troupe, let alone the names. "The daring young man on the flying trapeze" can be found under Léotard, but his first name isn't given anywhere in the book. (It's Jules.)

The short glossary (twenty-one items) indicates whether information applies to Great Britain or the United States. However, "sand dance" is defined as "comedy burlesque of Arab dancing"; this may be so, somewhere, but more commonly, among dancers, it simply means dropping sand onstage for a soft-shoe number. In the entry "Burlesque U.S." the author implies that burlesque palaces ceased to be with a New York statute forbidding them in 1942, but actually, they continued nationwide into the sixties and even, in some places, into the seventies.

The book could use expansion, a sharp-eyed editor, and an index (or more cross-references), but it is an interesting and unusual reference tool that could provide needed information and amusing trivia for the general audience of the public library as well as limited reference in theatre research collections. [R: BL, 15 Sept 77, p. 229; Choice, Oct 77, p. 1070]

Helen Gregory

543. Mapp, Edward. **Directory of Blacks in the Performing Arts**. Metuchen, N.J., Scarecrow, 1978. 428p. bibliog. index. $23.00. LC 78-2436. ISBN 0-8108-1126-X.

Within one alphabet we are provided with professional data on a host of black people from the theatre, films, music, radio, television, church, dance, and support areas (such as choreographers, designers, producers, and agents), who are accordingly identified in the index. The entries cite birth dates and cities, location of education, career data, films, records, television appearances, hobbies, addresses, and similar matters—as available or relevant—as well as a cross-reference for wives, nephews, sisters, and the like who are also in the arts. Any book with so many facts and details on so many people is destined to be criticized for what it lacks. Where are San Francisco critic William Duncan Allen, or Detroit's Dean Nolan, or Chicago's Earl Calloway? (for examples). Where are opera stars Seth McCoy, Louise Parker, and Veronica Tyler, all of whom have recorded? Why is Tina Turner included, but Ike left out? John Amos, as Kunta Kinte (adult), makes it, but Kunta Kinte as a youth (L. Burton), does not. The preface does not specify selection techniques, nor are the entries keyed to the bibliography. Despite the inevitable shortcomings and a rather large number of typos, Mapp's directory is a most helpful guide to selected artists of the past two centuries. Although he is historian of the Negro Actors Guild, he has not hesitated to include information on a variety of musicians and dancers. Because there is presently no competition, this directory will prove a helpful supplement for reference work. [R: LJ, 15 Sept 78, p. 1730; WLB, Dec 78, p. 344]   Dominique-René de Lerma

544. Mullin, Donald, comp. and ed. **Victorian Actors and Actresses in Review: A Dictionary of Contemporary Views of Representative British and American Actors and Actresses, 1837-1901**. Westport, Conn., Greenwood Press, 1983. 571p . illus. index. $55.00. LC 83-1407. ISBN 0-313-23316-0.

This is a compilation of brief comments by their contemporaries on the abilities, characteristics, and status of 234 actors whose careers flourished during 1837-1901. Lengthier examinations of individual plays and of the techniques of individuals are omitted. The necessarily subjective selection of those who appear to be "the principal figures of the British and American stage of the time" goes beyond the most famous or notorious and includes enough secondary figures to provide a context for better understanding of acting and the theatre after the artistic watershed of the late 1830s.

The comments are drawn from a highly selective list of 151 contemporary works of actors' notes, recollections, autobiographies, biographies, and professional criticism published in books and periodicals. The preface cautions briefly on the critical evaluation of sources, and notes that the present work makes no attempt to duplicate other reference works, to summarize what "readers should be able to determine for themselves," or to discuss criticism of critcism.

A nineteen-page introduction describes the circumstances and traditions of nineteenth-century acting and play production. The index of actors, plays, character names, theatres, and periodicals is clear and thorough, with the various types of entries appropriately distinguished. This compilation is a convenient resource for theatre teachers and researchers; it is of limited value to those without the necessary background to judiciously interpret and use the material.   Joyce Duncan Falk

545. **Notable Names in the American Theatre**. 2nd ed. Raymond D. McGill. Clifton, N.J., J. T. White; distr., Detroit, Gale, 1976. 1250p. $125.00. LC 76-27356. ISBN 0-88371-018-8.

Originally published in 1966 as a second edition of Walter Rigdon's *Biographical Encyclopedia and Who's Who of the American Theatre*, this new edition of *Notable Names in the American Theatre* provides twenty-six hundred detailed biographical sketches, information on almost fifteen thousand Broadway and off-Broadway productions and other data.   Ellen C. Thompson

546. **Who Was Who in the Theatre: 1912-1976: A Biographical Dictionary of Actors, Actresses, Directors, Playwrights, and Producers of the English-Speaking Theatre**. Detroit, Gale, 1978. 4v. (Gale Composite Biographical Dictionary Series, No. 3; An Omnigraphics Book). $390.00/set. LC 78-9634. ISBN 0-8103-0406-6.

This set has one source — *Who's Who in the Theatre, 1912-1972* — and that source appears to have been well edited to begin with. The single-alphabet listings include everyone listed in that source unless still active at the time of publication; some forty-one hundred persons in all are included.

Entries include a person's original name, birth facts, education, marital career, credits, favorite parts, extra-theatrical activities and interests, and last address known. The disparities among typefaces are not nearly so noticeable as in the previous Gale efforts along this "composite book" line, and this set has even been edited to include death dates up to 1976 when they were not part of the original entry. The entries are *not* a mine of information, but they appear reasonably informative about the famous as well as the obscure. Not the stuff from which great dissertations are made, this set still could be useful to the student of theatre, even though no bibliographical information is included on the entrants. In sum, this could be valuable for minor theatrical figures more than for the major ones on whom book-length individual studies have appeared. [R: Choice, June 79, p. 514; WLB, June 79, p. 270]   Koert C. Loomis, Jr.

547. **Who's Who in the Theatre: A Biographical Record of the Contemporary Stage**. 17th ed. Edited by Ian Herbert, with Christine Baxter and Robert E. Finley. Detroit, Gale, 1981. 2v. index. $200.00/set. LC 81-6636. ISBN 0-8103-0234-9 (set).

To those familiar with this title, the format of the new edition will come as a pleasant shock. Now in two folio-sized volumes and published by Gale, the title becomes a companion volume to *Notable Names in the American Theatre*, published by James T. White Company in 1976, later co-distributed by Gale, and still in print. The arrangement for the biographical entries had always been the same for the Who's Whos covering the two worlds of the English-speaking stage, but now the uniformity of all phases of the publications leads one to suspect a future melding in which two massive volumes might cover the entire English-speaking stage.

There are so many purely American entries in the edition under review that a comparison with the 1976 *Notable Names* is superfluous. One can only note that there are hundreds of cross-overs among the nearly twenty-four hundred names and be thankful that the seventeenth *Who's Who* brings credits and necrology up to the end of the 1979-1980 theatre season. (In the *Playbills* volume the cutoff date is 31 December 1979.)

In Ian Herbert's comprehensive four-page preface to this edition (printed in both volumes), he discusses the history of *Who's Who*, the lack of availability of complete sets, and the methodology of the compilation. It is good to know that for some subjects considered important who did not answer the questionnaire, a record was reconstructed from secondary sources. He also points out that if a living person has been inactive for at least ten years and is likely to continue to be, he or she is usually dropped. At the end of the *Biographies* volume are a list of dropped names of the living with indication of which edition they were last listed in and a 1 January 1976-31 July 1980 obituary list, admittedly incomplete.

The *Playbills* volume has fifteen sections. Although the London and New York lists are the most useful and include off-West End and fringe, and off- and off-off-Broadway, the Shakespeare festivals lists, the several long-run lists, and the theatre buildings lists are valuable additions to a remarkable compilation.

This reviewer has done little checking for accuracy of entries in either volume, but a spot check of volume 1 indicates very little to quibble about in such a monumental research tool. It would be useful to have more home addresses and telephone numbers—no one wants to go through agents or Equity—but some professionals seem to need their privacy. Highly recommended for all theatre and general research collections.

This volume can be supplemented by *Theatre World* (Crown, 1946- . Annual. $60.00) edited by John Willis. *Theatre World* provides a record of performances, casts, and other information primarily for New York theatre, and includes many biographical sketches of actors and actresses.   Richard M. Buck and Bohdan S. Wynar

548.   Young, William C. **Famous Actors and Actresses on the American Stage: Documents of American Theater History**. New York, R. R. Bowker, 1975. 2v. illus. bibliog. index. $75.00/set. LC 75-8741. ISBN 0-8352-0821-4.

These two volumes contain information on 225 performers who appeared on (the operative word) the American stage from the beginnings until publication time. Mr. Young admits that the limitation is arbitrary and that "*omissions in no way signify that a performer is not or was not great or significant on the American stage, but merely that space has limited the scope of the work*" (p. xvi; the author's italics). Before this emphatic statement, Mr. Young mentions several criteria that he does use. These criteria and the rest of the preface *must* be read by any potential user who expects to find useful material in this book.

The criteria sound at least acceptable, but an examination of the content reveals that the selection is more than arbitrary; at times it is downright peculiar! For example, how can anyone call Julie Andrews "famous" and not Ruth Gordon? Carol Channing and not Billie Burke? Ilka Chase and not Marilyn Miller? One could go on.

In addition to questioning the decisions as to who is "famous," one must question the information provided on those who are chosen. Each entry includes an illustration, which is helpful, but the standard biographical data given are most meager: birth and death dates; debut, and sometimes New York debut (not always correctly); and famous roles (by whose standards? Several of the biographees checked appeared in roles more famous than those listed). This basic information is almost useless except for the most elementary research, especially since the "famous role" entry does not include where, when, or for how long and is usually not followed up by any kind of commentary.

The commentary that we do find on each performer *is* the body of the work. Young supplies some simple and often commonly known information: "The youngest son of Junius Brutus Booth is usually remembered only as the assassin of President Abraham Lincoln" (p. 118); "Noted as a gifted comedienne, Ilka Chase found her forte in high comedy" (p. 181). This information is followed by from one to half-a-dozen excerpts from reviews of the day, memoirs, biographies and autobiographies, periodical articles, interviews, old theatrical histories, etc.—hardly any of which classify as "documents" in the true research sense of the word. A more accurate subtitle for the book would be "secondary sources" or "clippings" of American theatre history. If the *Spirit of the Times*, *Theatre*, *The New York Times*, *Time*, *Life*, and *Newsweek* had not existed, Mr. Young would have had to invent them to produce these "documents."

The thirteen-page bibliography includes a simple list of hundreds of titles that Mr. Young at least knows about; it is much more valuable than the excerpts preceding it. There is a "decades" index in which performers are listed by "their active life on the American stage"; it is nearly useless. There is a general index, which is quite detailed; it is useful.

In sum, these volumes are not to be taken seriously as a research tool. They might be valuable for a secondary-school student doing elementary research on a popular star of past or present, or for a buff who likes to browse through material about theatre personalities—but this was clearly not the intention. [R: LJ, 15 Oct 75, p. 1909]

Richard M. Buck

18 Philosophy, Folklore, and Mythology

Introduction

This chapter on "Philosophy, Folklore, and Mythology" is divided into two sections, "Philosophy," and "Folklore and Mythology." It covers only four biographical dictionaries, with several additional titles mentioned in the annotations. The best work in the field of folklore and mythology is *Funk and Wagnall's Standard Dictionary of Folklore, Mythology and Legend* (see entry 550), which was first published in 1949-1950. Recently there has been limited interest in these areas, as indicated by the small number of published biographical works. However, a few older works exist and they may be consulted for retrospective searching. The best biographical work on philosophy is German: *Philosophen-Lexikon; Handwörterbuch der Philosophie nach Personen*, edited by W. Ziegenfuss and G. Jung (2v. Berlin, Walter de Gruyter, 1949-1950), that covers all periods and countries, and at the time of its publication, also included living philosophers. It is actually an update of the earlier work *Philosophen-Lexikon*, edited by R. Eisler (Berlin, Mittler, 1912. 889p.).

One of the oldest works on folklore and mythology is the thirteen-volume *Mythology of All Races* (Marshall Jones Co., 1916-1932), edited by L. H. Gray, J. A. Macculloch and G. F. Moore; probably the best is H. W. Haussig's *Wörterbuch der Mythologie* (Stuttgart, Ernst Klett, 1961- . In progress) to be published in ten volumes.

A number of subject encyclopedias incorporate biographical information and the reader is advised to consult them. Probably the most comprehensive work on philosophy is *Encyclopedia of Philosophy*, edited by P. Edwards (8v. Macmillan, 1967), that covers Western and Eastern philosophy. Out of fifteen hundred articles contributed by a group of internationally known scholars, nine hundred are biographical sketches of philosophers worldwide. Translated from Dutch is the *New Encyclopedia of Philosophy*, revised and edited by E. van den Bossche (Philosophical Library, 1972. 468p.), that is particularly useful for European philosophers. Most philosophical dictionaries also include biographical material. *A Dictionary of Philosophy*, edited by A. Flew (2nd ed. St. Martin's Press, 1984. 380p.), provides a concise treatment of this subject, with biographical articles up to four thousand words for major figures. Also very popular is *A Dictionary of Philosophy*, edited by A. R. Lacey (Scribner's, 1976. 239p.), useful for Oriental schools and philosophers. W. L. Reese's *Dictionary of Philosophy and Religion: Eastern and Western Thought* (Humanities Press, 1980. 644p.) covers even second-rank figures in philosophy and in this respect is more reliable than D. D. Runes's *Dictionary of Philosophy* (Philosophical Library, 1983, 360p.), that is actually only a slight revision of the work originally published in 1942. There are also a number of more specialized dictionaries, all covering prominent philosophers, e.g., S. E. Nauman's *Dictionary of Asian Philosophies* (Philosophical Library, 1978. 372p.) or the same author's *The New Dictionary of Existentialism* (Philosophical Library, 1971. 166p.). There are a number of scholarly works published in other languages, e.g., J. Ritter's *Historisches Wörterbuch der Philosophie* (Darmstadt, Wissenschaftliche Buchgesellschaft, 1971- . In progress) that will be published in twelve volumes. The two-volume *Diccionario de filosofía* (5th ed. Buenos Aires, Ed. Sudamericana, 1965) is also very strong in biographical coverage.

Good examples of subject dictionaries and encyclopedias on mythology include *Larousse Encyclopedia of Mythology* (Prometheus, 1959. 500p.) that was first published in France in 1935, and A. Cotterell's *A Dictionary of World Mythology* (Putnam, 1982. 256p.). For folklore the most outstanding work is *Enzyklopädie des Märchens* (Berlin, Walter de Gruyter, 1975- . In progress) to be published in twelve volumes.

Bibliographic guides provide additional information about existing reference sources and indexing services. For philosophy, one recent title is R. T. De George's *The Philosopher's Guide to Sources, Research Tools, Professional Life and Related Fields* (Regents Press of Kansas, 1980. 261p.), and for folklore, J. H. Brunvand's *Folklore: A Study and Research Guide* (St. Martin's Press, 1976. 144p.).

PHILOSOPHY

549. Cormier, Ramona, and Richard H. Lineback, eds. **International Directory of Philosophy and Philosophers 1982-1985**. 5th ed. Bowling Green, Ohio, Philosophy Documentation Center, Bowling Green State University, 1982. 287p. $33.75. LC 66-18830. ISBN 0-912632-46-1.

In this companion volume to the *Directory of American Philosophers*, information on philosophical activities in some ninety countries (excluding the United States and Canada) is arranged alphabetically by country. Most of the information was collected from questionnaires sent to philosophers. Under each country, data are given on colleges and universities, institutes and research centers, associations and societies, journals, and publishers. International organizations receive separate treatment in a section before the countries' listing.

Information provided for each university is: name, name and address of the philosophy department; names, ranks, and specialties of the faculty members; date of founding; source of financial support; university and philosophy department enrollment; degrees offered; and number of advanced degrees awarded in the past five years. Associations and societies receive similar treatment. The entries list name, address, date of founding, purpose and activities, names of principal officers, membership data, and publications. The same data are provided for institutes and research centers. Standard bibliographic data are offered for journals, plus an indication of the number of philosophical articles published each year, and the presence of a book review section. Name, address, date of founding, and journals and series issued are listed for each publisher. Access to this information is provided by six indexes—one for each of the major categories of information—in addition to an index to individual philosophers.

Directory of American Philosophers 1984-1985, 12th edition edited by Archie J. Bahm (Bowling Green, Philosophy Documentation Center, Bowling Green State University, 1984. 406p. $37.00. ISBN 0-912632-76-3), covers the United States and Canada providing similar information.   Bohdan S. Wynar

FOLKLORE AND MYTHOLOGY

550.   **Funk and Wagnall's Standard Dictionary of Folklore, Mythology and Legend**. Maria Leach, ed. Jerome Fried, assoc. ed. New York, Funk and Wagnalls, 1973. 1236p. $22.95. LC 72-78268. ISBN 0-308-40090-9.

This standard and very comprehensive encyclopedia, first published as a two-volume set in 1949-1950, covers gods, heroes, fairy tales, customs, songs, dances, and other related topics. All major cultures of the world are represented, with strong emphasis on national mythologies and customs. [R: BL, Nov 73, p. 253; RQ, Spring 78, p. 318]   Bohdan S. Wynar

551.   Kravitz, David. **Who's Who in Greek and Roman Mythology**. New York, Clarkson N. Potter; distr., New York, Crown, 1977. 246p. illus. $10.00; $3.95pa. LC 76-29630. ISBN 0-517-52746-4; 0-517-52747-2pa.

First published in Great Britain in 1975 under the title *The Dictionary of Greek and Roman Mythology*, this American edition shows a minimum of changes or updating (British spelling is retained), with the exception of fifty line drawings added by Lynne S. Mayo. Included are some three thousand brief entries, covering a wide range of mythological names and a helpful listing of the relatives and consorts of the mythological characters. Many other sources provide more in-depth information, such as *Crowell's Handbook of Classical Mythology* or *New Century Classical Handbook*.

Gods and Mortals in Classical Mythology, edited by Michael Grant and John Hazel (Springfield, Mass., G. & C. Merriam, 1973. 448p. o.p.), also provides brief biographical sketches of Greek and Roman mythological characters. [R: BL, 15 June 77, p. 1605; Choice, Sept 77, p. 833; WLB, June 77, p. 815]   Bohdan S. Wynar

552.   Monaghan, Patricia. **The Book of Goddesses and Heroines**. 1st ed. New York, E. P. Dutton, a division of Elsevier-Dutton Publishing, 1981. 318p. bibliog. (A Dutton Paperback). $10.25pa. LC 80-29355. ISBN 0-525-47664-4.

This is a handbook of goddesses and heroines drawn from a truly international context: Africa, Europe, the Americas, the East, and Oceania. It is an excellent collection, vast and varied in scope, which shows up the major encyclopedias (like, say, Larousse) for their insufficient research into the role of women in mythological tales. The entries are very well written without the blandness and matter-of-fact tone of much recounting of the myths of the classical or primitive canons. Ms. Monaghan points out ambiguities, summarizes variants, and in general succeeds in making most of the entries readable and interesting. This is an important reference text, and we should have one as well done on the gods and heroes, with the same cosmopolitanism.

There is one motive behind this text, however, which is more controversial. Ms. Monaghan's introduction seems to imply that this is also a book of sisters, a feminist righting of scholarly wrongs. True, many mythographers have been overly interested in the gods, or cloyingly worshipful of the goddess (like Graves), but Ms. Monaghan might remember that most myths are annoyingly sexist to begin with, and no handbook will set that right. To say that there has been an academic conspiracy against goddesses is to overstate the case. To find oneself identifying with the feminine experience in myth, and telling the stories as if the characters in those fictions are to be truly revered is to lapse into mere superstition. One should no more want to identify with Medusa than the Cyclops (or Zeus for that matter), for myths are, after all, only fictions told to answer impossible questions, and no god or goddess should be placed on the pedestal of sexist power. [R: LJ, July 81, p. 1405]   Eric Gould

19 Political Science

Introduction

The material in this chapter is arranged under five sections: "General Works," "International Organizations," "International Relations," "U.S. Politics and Government," with several subdivisions, and "Other Countries and Regions," subdivided by name of country, e.g., "Canada," "China," etc. A total of sixty-seven entries is included, with several hundred titles mentioned in the annotations. In political science a number of outstanding biographical sources have been published. Thus, for example, under "General" we have *Rulers and Governments of the World* (see entry 555). The comprehensive biographical dictionary *Who's Who in European Institutions and Organizations* (see entry 559) can be found in the section on "International Organizations," and in the section on "International Relations" we have *Biographical Dictionary of Internationalists* (see entry 562). The section on "U.S. Politics and Government," the largest in this chapter (forty-four entries), contains such popular sources as *Who's Who in American Politics* (see entry 567), *The Almanac of American Politics* (see entry 566) for contemporary coverage, and a number of more specialized sources, e.g., *The Complete Book of U.S. Presidents* (see entry 574) and *Biographical Directory of the American Congress* (see entry 590). Under "Other Countries and Regions" one finds such notable works as *Biographical Dictionary of Chinese Communism* (see entry 611) and *Who's Who of British Members of Parliament* (see entry 616).

In addition, the American Political Science Association is publishing, on an irregular basis, *Biographical Directory* (1945-) that provides biographical data for members of this association. Biographical sketches are also offered in a number of dictionaries in political science. The well-known W. Laqueur's *A Dictionary of Politics* (Free Press, 1974. 565p.) offers three thousand entries including several hundred biographies of politicians and scholars. There are also more specialized dictionaries, e.g., *Political Dictionary of the Middle East in the 20th Century*, edited by Y. Shimoni and E. Levine (Quadrangle/New York Times Book Co., 1974), that offers biographical information for this region. There are a number of foreign biographical dictionaries, e.g., *Dictionnaire diplomatique, comprenant les biographies des diplomates, du Moyen*

Âge à nos jours, constituant un traité d'histoire diplomatique sur six siècles, edited by A. F. Frangulis (Geneva, Académie Diplomatique Internationale, 1954. 1261p.), that covers prominent persons from the Middle Ages to the early 1950s. The most comprehensive is the twelve-volume *Handwörterbuch der Sozialwissenschaften*, edited by E. von Beckerath (Stuttgart, Fischer, 1952-1968), with its first edition published in 1890-1894. Several bibliographic guides describe those dictionaries in some detail, also providing information on existing indexing and abstracting services. An older, but still very useful work is C. Brock's *The Literature of Political Science: A Guide for Students, Librarians and Teachers* (R. R. Bowker, 1969. 232p.), and a much more comprehensive work is L. R. Wynar's *Guide to Reference Materials in Political Science* (2v. Libraries Unlimited, 1966-1968). A more recent work is F. L. Holler's five-volume *The Information Sources of Political Science* (ABC-Clio, 1975), probably the most comprehensive bibliographic guide on this subject.

GENERAL WORKS

553. Biographical Dictionary of Modern Peace Leaders. Harold Josephson, and others, eds. Westport, Conn., Greenwood Press, 1985. 1133p. index. $75.00. LC 84-26514. ISBN 0-313-22565-6.

This work includes 750 biographical essays on selected peace leaders, covering the years 1800-1980. Most of the subjects are from the United States and Western Europe although other regions are also represented. The editors included people who: fought publicly against the use of force in nation-state relations; were leaders in world peace organizations; worked to prevent or shorten a particular war; worked for nonviolence in social relations; were committed to transnational values; projected visions of peace in art and literature; or sought to promote international organizations as a substitute for national sovereignty. Two hundred and fifty authors from fifteen countries contributed to the biographies, signing the entries they wrote.

In the introduction the editor presents a brief history of organized peace societies, with emphasis on the United States and England. A selected chronology of the organized peace movement precedes the listings. Subjects listed vary widely, including both well-known and more obscure figures. Among the more famous are: Jane Addams, Mohandas Gandhi, Martin Luther King, Jr., Leo Tolstoy, Susan B. Anthony, Tristan Tzara, Dorothy Day, Andrew Carnegie, and Pope John XXIII. Each listing begins with a short summary of the biographee, including date and place of birth and death, education, and career details. The listings are uneven, usually a page or two long, concentrating more on the subject's contributions to nonviolence or social reform than other aspects of the person's life. For example, the entry on Pope John XXIII discusses his actions for peace but provides little on his life or attitudes toward church reform. Similarly, the entry on Tolstoy mentions his novels briefly but discusses in much more detail his later life and his writings on social reform.

Each listing ends with a short bibliography of books written by or about the biographee. These bibliographies give only the place of publication and not the name of the publisher, making it more complicated than necessary to locate the books mentioned. Appendixes include a listing of each biographee by country, an index, and a description of each contributor. As a reference source the book is uneven, but is appropriate for more casual reading; it is well-written, intriguing and full of interesting data.　　　　　　　　　　　　　　　　　　　　　　　　　　Gloria Palmeri Powell

554. Regents of Nations. A Systematic Chronology of States and Their Political Representatives in Past and Present. A Biographical Reference Book. Peter Truhart, ed. New York, K. G. Saur, 1984. 2980p. $200.00. ISBN 3-598-10491-X.

Actually this is not a biographical dictionary, but rather a chronology attempting to enumerate heads of state world-wide "without regard to the size or importance of the country," including legendary periods. Tens of thousands of individuals are listed, including chiefs of government, foreign ministers, cabinet members, etc. The material is divided into three parts: (1) Africa and America, (2) Asia, Australia, and Oceania, and, (3) Europe. Each part is subdivided by regions, and a decimal system facilitates investigation of names, individual states, historical periods, and other distinct elements. Entries include period in office, name, title, place and date of birth and death, relation to predecessor, and outstanding events (dates are adjusted to the Julian/Gregorian calendar).

Of interest to larger libraries only.   Bohdan S. Wynar

555. Rulers and Governments of the World. Edited by C. G. Allen. Vol. I. **Earliest Times to 1491**. Martha Ross, comp. Vol. II. **1492 to 1929**. Bertold Spuler, comp. Vol. III. **1930 to 1975**. Bertold Spuler, comp. New York, R. R. Bowker, 1977-1978. 3v. $135.00/set. ISBN 0-85935-051-7 (set).

For a generation, the handbook *Regenten und Regierungen der Welt* (sometimes known, after its publisher, as *Minister Ploetz*) has been a standard source for information on rulers and major officials of countries throughout the world. Thus, the appearance of an updated English edition is a major publishing event for reference librarians. What it attempts to do is to provide information on place and date of birth, tenure in office, and political party affiliation (if any) for major office holders in all countries. Each country's officials are listed chronologically according to the term of the head of the government; a name index enables one to locate a person if the position or country is not known.

The accuracy, meticulous editing, and, for major countries, the comprehensiveness of the work are remarkable. After some searching, it was possible to find a petty inaccuracy—Karl Grünheid, not Grünheld, was the First Deputy Chairman of the Planning Commission in East Germany in 1964—but that is more an indication of the detailed information it is possible to find than of poor editorial procedures. Still, it might be useful to reinforce here a few limitations, in large part pointed out in the work itself. Since it is a translation, one must be aware that Germanic name forms (e.g., Ludwig for Ludvik in Norwegian) are used; hence, the reader cannot automatically cite this as a name authority according to contemporary standards of scholarship. Coverage of minor countries is not extensive: Norway is allocated two pages and only its prime ministers and foreign ministers are identified. (In comparison, Italy has twenty pages and includes all officials through the level of the minister of tourism.) Since most questions do relate to major countries this may not be a hindrance, but since information is also more generally accessible about those countries, similar information on smaller countries would have been useful. There is some duplication of coverage with a few other works. For example, *Bidwell's Guide to Government Ministers* (London, Cass, 1973-) contains more names and uses correct orthography, but its typographical errors and poor organization hinder use; for the libraries that have them, annuals published by the various countries will, in many cases, be more complete, if not as accessible.

Where the real value of the work will lie is in those volumes covering the earlier periods of history, for in that, their coverage is unmatched; there simply are no comparable works. It should be noted that some of the information in the German edition, particularly on individual German states or countries no longer in existence, has been omitted; libraries with the original must retain it. Yet, one must view the set as a whole and declare it irreplaceable; no responsible library that receives questions on the type of information given herein will want to be without it. [R: Choice, Sept 78, p. 844; Choice, June 79, p. 512; LJ, 15 Oct 77, p. 2150; LJ, Aug 78, p. 1498; RQ, Fall 78, p. 104; WLB, Dec 77, p. 344; WLB, June 78, p. 810; WLB, June 79, pp. 726-27]

Erwin K. Welsch

556.   Tapsell, R. F. **Monarchs, Rulers, Dynasties, and Kingdoms of the World**. New York, Facts on File, 1983. 511p. bibliog. $35.00. LC 82-15726. ISBN 0-87196-121-0.

Long gone is the time when history was, for many people, a recital of kings, queens, and other assorted rulers (together, of course, with their deeds and misdeeds). Still, chronologies of monarchs and dynasties remain a significant framework for much of the world's history, and in many instances the chief frame of reference for dating and correlating historical events. That's one function Tapsell's work will serve surpassingly well. Other uses are suggested by G. C. Bolton's observation, in the foreword, that notwithstanding the rapid demise of royalty in modern times, "A fascination with monarchy persists among many." For such, this book should offer ample opportunity for, in Bolton's words, "pleasant dipping and browsing."

Chronologies of major dynasties and nations are not hard to come by, of course, but Tapsell's coverage is uniquely comprehensive. Tracing the mainstream line of British monarchs may be a snap, but where, without Tapsell, does one quickly put one's fingers on a chronology of the kings of Northumbria (c.547-878) or the princes of Wales? Or how about the dynasty of Dubai, the maharajas of Marwar, the amirs of Abuja, or the sultans of Sumatra?

The first third of this work is an encyclopedic alphabetical guide to dynasties and states; the remainder consists of dynastic lists, by geographic groupings. Articles in the former invariably refer to the latter. An impressive feature of the lists is an ingenious system of codes by which family relationships (sometimes very complex) are indicated.

Comprehensive, convenient, and impeccably authoritative, Tapsell's promises to be the standard reference source on its subject for years to come. [R: BL, 1 Dec 83, p. 557; Choice, Sept 83, p. 69; LJ, 15 June 83, p. 1252]   Hans E. Bynagle

INTERNATIONAL ORGANIZATIONS

557.   Lazitch, Branko, in collaboration with Milorad M. Drachkovitch. **Biographical Dictionary of the Comintern**. Stanford, Calif., Hoover Institution Press, 1973. 458p. (Hoover Institution Publications, No. 121). o.p. LC 72-187265. ISBN 0-8179-1211-8.

The Communist International (1919-1943) played an important role in the communist movement until its liquidation by Stalin. The present work, the only biographical dictionary of its leaders, contains 716 biographical sketches of members of the executive committee, speakers at the Comintern congresses, important delegates to congresses, and other members of the Comintern apparatus. The execution of a biographical dictionary of this scope and magnitude required the use of many sources; in general, the work seems to be remarkably well balanced. The few shortcomings noted are minor. For example, in the article on Mykola Skrypnyk (probably not Nikolai Skrypnik, since this prominent Ukrainian communist seldom used the Russian spelling of his name), one might expect to find more than the simple statement that he committed suicide in July 1933. An explanation of why he committed suicide is in order. Another example: although Shumsky's fate is rather well known, the author states that in 1927 "he completely disappeared, most probably a victim of political police" (p. 369). These minor points certainly do not detract from the excellence of this work; among other things, it helps to decode some 350 pseudonyms used by Comintern leaders in their activities. Bohdan S. Wynar

558. **Who's Who: European Communities and Other European Organizations, 1983/1984**. 3rd ed. Brussels, Belgium, Editions Delta; distr., New York, Unipub, 1984. 240p. $70.00.

The first edition of this directory was published in 1978 at a cost of $55. The second edition (1981. 240p.) contained longer entries in either French or English. The current edition is similar in format. A complete entry usually includes the individual's nationality, current position, personal data, education, career, publications, awards, memberships, recreational activities, and address(es). The criteria for selection remain basically the same: "Senior Civil Servants currently working within the European Communities . . . and within more than twenty other European Organizations, the members of the Permanent Representations and the Heads of Missions accredited to them, the Chairmen and Secretaries of the different branches of the European Movement and of the Professional Organizations set up at Community levels." A random check of names indicates that very few of the individuals included here are found in the more standard directories—e.g., *The International Who's Who* (Europa Publications) and *Who's Who in the World* (Marquis).

This directory is intended to complement the *European Communities and Other European Organizations Yearbook*, and libraries with a need for this information should have all three volumes. However, this is really too specialized for most libraries.
Thomas A. Karel

559. **Who's Who in European Institutions and Organizations**. Edited by Karl Strute and Theodor Doelken. Zurich, Who's Who AG; distr., Chicago, Marquis Who's Who, 1982. 1088p. index. (International Red Series). $75.00. ISBN 3-921220-42-4; ISSN 0722-916X.

This volume presents capsule biographies of more than four thousand persons active in various European organizations, such as the European Economic Community, as well as Europeans active in certain other international organizations, such as the United Nations and European Free Trade Association. In some areas it even extends beyond these already generous borders to include crowned heads of Europe and heads of state or other prominent ministers. The biographies are quite short, including only the most basic information, e.g., date of birth, nationality, and education, together with, naturally, position in a European organization. The information seems quite current and, as far as it could be checked since there is no other volume that covers quite the same territory, accurate. Less useful for many librarians will be the descriptions of the various organizations involved, although bringing together information published in various other sources does have its merits. More helpful will be the "Special Register," which is a classified list of other international and European institutions, organizations, and associations that includes, in most cases, only their addresses. As a one-volume introduction to European organizations and personnel this will be a useful acquisition for many libraries, although those needing biographical information will benefit most, for information about these officials can be difficult to find in other sources. [R: Choice, July-Aug 83, pp. 1579-80; WLB, June 83, pp. 886-95]   Erwin K. Welsch

560.   **Who's Who in the United Nations and Related Agencies.** Edited by Michael Hawkin. Salem, N.H., Ayer Co., 1975. 785p. $71.50. LC 75-4105. ISBN 0-405-00490-X.

This biographical directory is more comprehensive than Burckel's *Who's Who in the United Nations* (1951). It lists some thirty-seven hundred U.N. administrators, members of governing boards and commissions, senior delegates of member and observer states, U.N. correspondents, and some representatives of non-governmental organizations. The following information is provided for each entry: name and position, business address, language spoken, career positions, countries of service, education and professional interests, written books and articles, avocational interests, and home address. Supplementary material includes a U.N. organizational roster, a list of depository libraries, a list of member states, and a list of principal officials and their affiliations with more than 450 U.N. agencies. [R: Choice, Dec 75, pp. 1294-96; LJ, 15 Oct 75, pp. 1908-9]   Bohdan S. Wynar

INTERNATIONAL RELATIONS

561.   Crowley, Edward L., ed. **The Soviet Diplomatic Corps 1917-1967.** Compiled by the Institute for the Study of the USSR. Metuchen, N.J., Scarecrow, 1970. 240p. index. o.p. ISBN 0-9108-0290-2.

In reviewing certain publications prepared by the Institute for the Study of the USSR one is faced with a rather difficult task, primarily because they are so uneven in quality, occasionally even lacking minimal editorial attention. One of the best examples of this situation is this book, based on a comprehensive biographical file on some 125,000 prominent persons in the Soviet Union. It is the second volume in the Key Officials series of biographical directories. The first volume, *Party and Government Officials of the Soviet Union 1917-1967* was published in 1969; the third volume, *Soviet Science 1917-1967*, appeared in 1971. It is indicated in the introduction that "more complete biographical data on persons listed in this volume may be found in our other reference works such as the *Biographical Directory of the USSR*, 1958; *Who's Who in the USSR*, 1961-62 and 1965-66; *Prominent Personalities in the USSR*, 1968, its quarterly supplements, *Portraits of Prominent USSR Personalities*, issued regularly since January 1, 1968; and *Who Was Who in the USSR 1917-1967*, 1970" (preface, pp. 1-2). Why, then, publish this volume with so many disappointing biographical sketches, errors in spelling, omission of first names of important Soviet officials (e.g., Shumskiy or Meyers), etc.? Such an abridged edition will hardly serve any useful purpose, especially in smaller libraries that do not have access to standard tools on the subject. [R: LJ, Aug 70; RQ, Fall, 70]   Bohdan S. Wynar

562.   Kuehl, Warren F., ed. **Biographical Dictionary of Internationalists.** Westport, Conn., Greenwood Press, 1983. 934p. index. $75.00. LC 82-15416. ISBN 0-313-22129-4.

This is a valuable new addition to the shelf of biographical reference works. Its 680 sketches deal with the men and women who have stood out in history as advocates of world organization. The selections range from internationally famous activists to little-known visionaries.

The first subjects to be treated are individuals who were alive after 1800. For the first century or so, the predominance of entries from the United States and Great Britain reflects the flourishing of internationalist thought in democracies. After 1914, continental Europe, Asia, and Latin America produced an increased number of such leaders. Unfortunately many persons active since 1945 have been omitted by the decision to include only the deceased. The postwar period, however, does provide an imposing list: for example, Ralph Bunche, Jean Monnett, Hans Morgenthau, Paul-Henri Spaak, U Thant, and Arnold Toynbee.

Each entry opens with basic information on birth, death, education, and career. Many traditional details are omitted in favor of concentration on the subject's work, ideas, or activity as an internationalist. The bibliography also emphasizes this career bent.

The back matter is rich in reference material. A chronology traces trends and developments from the 1815 Congress of Vienna to the 1979 first general elections to the European Parliament. Appendixes provide the nation of birth for each subject, the primary career of each, and the type of approach (for example, African unity, health, food, interdependence). There is a good index and a helpful identification of contributors, most of whom are academics, including editor Warren Kuehl. The more than 250 authors include such figures as Fred Israel, Richard Leopold, Forrest Pogue, and David Trask. The one blemish on the volume is the lack of illustrations. [R: Choice, May 84, p. 1271]　　　　　　　　　　　　　　　　　　　　　　David Eggenberger

563. Parker, Thomas. **America's Foreign Policy 1945-1976: Its Creators and Critics.** New York, Facts on File, 1980. 246p. bibliog. index. $22.50. LC 80-21192. ISBN 0-87196-456-2.

Parker's volume provides a useful, though predictably superficial, overview of American foreign policy during its most complex decades. The bulk of the text is devoted to individual profiles of approximately seventy key figures who formulated and questioned this nation's foreign policy, e.g., Stettinius and Rusk, Fulbright and McGovern. Length of treatment corresponds roughly to significance of subject. Kissinger, for example, is awarded twelve pages; William Sloane Coffin is dismissed in less than one. Additional sections include a substantial introductory essay, a chronology, and several informative bibliographic essays.

Aesthetically, the book is a disaster. Print runs the gamut from ebony to pale gray. Type size fluctuates, as well. It simply does not appear to have been a carefully constructed work. The brief table of contents, for example, contains a monumental error.

The value of *America's Foreign Policy. . .* lies not in its originality but in its accessibility. Though containing little that cannot be quickly mined from other sources, it is a handy compilation—one which many academic libraries may wish to consider. [R: BL, 15 Oct 81, p. 326; WLB, Sept 81, p. 58]　　　　　　　　　　　Mark R. Yerburgh

564. Payne, Ronald, and Christopher Dobson. **Who's Who in Espionage.** New York, St. Martin's Press, 1984. 234p. bibliog. $15.95. LC 85-1790. ISBN 0-312-87432-4.

This attractive and highly readable book consists of biographical entries, arranged in alphabetical order, on over three hundred men and women spies active since World War II. In each entry the authors briefly discuss the background of the spy and give a detailed description of his or her activities. Entries range from one-half to two pages in length, seeming to depend on the particular individual's importance in the world of espionage. The entries are very intriguing and include information on many of the most infamous spy cases. Represented in the book are such figures as Richard Helms, Guy Burgess, Yuri Andropov, Muammar Qaddafi, Harold (Kim) Philby and many less well known individuals.

The entries are preceded by an introduction in which the authors discuss the development of espionage since World War II. The authors have also compiled descriptions of the major espionage organizations of seventeen countries throughout the world. The discussions here of recruiting methods, counter-espionage, famous operations, and spy techniques provide background on the biographical entries. A short glossary and a bibliography complete the book. Probably not for the serious researcher, this work, nevertheless, offers interesting information in a very accessible way to the less specialized reader.   Gloria Palmeri Powell

U.S. POLITICS AND GOVERNMENT

General Works

565.   Stineman, Esther. **American Political Women: Contemporary and Historical Profiles**. Littleton, Colo., Libraries Unlimited, 1980. 228p. bibliog. index. $27.50. LC 80-24478. ISBN 0-87287-238-6.

American Political Women contains sixty profiles of women serving in political positions in American government as congresswomen, ambassadors, governors, lieutenant governors, mayors, and presidential advisers as of 1980, and of selected women who have served in such important positions in the past. "Firsts" of all kinds are included: first woman ambassador; first woman mayor of a major U.S. city; first congresswoman; first woman in the cabinet; first woman elected governor. Among the women included in the sixty portraits are Bella Abzug, Sissy Farenthold, Dianne Feinstein, Elizabeth Holtzman, Nancy Kassebaum, Jeannette Rankin, Patricia Schroeder, and Sarah Weddington.

Sketches are accompanied by selected speeches and lists of works by and about the biographees. Particular attention is given to the biographee's views and activities regarding the women's movement, specific program accomplishments, and career preparation and development. Stineman's personal interviews and correspondence with political women and her work with archives and other historical sources bring to light much previously unpublished information.

The eighteen-page bibliography annotates major, recent reference materials and significant books and articles covering all aspects of women's political participation. It also lists selected dissertations, periodicals, indexing services, libraries, and organizations related to women in politics. The valuable appendix material includes: Women of the Congress 1917-1980; Women Currently Serving as Ambassadors of the U.S.; Women Chiefs of Mission 1933-1980; Women Currently Serving as Federal Judges; and Women Currently Serving in Government in Key Departmental, Agency, and White House Positions. [R: Choice, June 81, p. 1485; WLB, Apr 81, p. 623]

Ann Hartman

566.   Ujifusa, Grant, ed. **The Almanac of American Politics 1984: The Senators, the Representatives, the Governors—Their Records, States and Districts.** New York, National Journal, 1984. 1402p. illus. index. $35.00; $22.50pa. LC 72-96875. ISBN 0-89234-030-4; 0-89234-031-2pa.

Begun in 1972, the scope and organization of the *Almanac* remain unchanged. The new edition records the composition of Congress and the fifty statehouses as of 1983.

This work provides admirably succinct information on American politics using two basic units: the state itself and then the congressional districts within the states. Organized on a state basis, each chapter considers first the state's governor and lieutenant governor and its U.S. senators; then it proceeds to each congressional district. For both states and districts, factual data and statistics are provided for voting, population, and socioeconomic composition of the population.

The work is more than a compilation of objective political data. The compilers do not hesitate to editorialize when the occasion requires it. Read their delightful discussion on Spiro Agnew and the politics of Maryland. In general, I would say the compilers' orientation is liberal-center.

One of the principal virtues of the book consists in the extent to which it brings to national attention state political figures who are nationally obscure. In fact, this is one of the compilers' stated purposes—and an excellent purpose it is, too. Surely the vitality of American politics depends on having the national supply of major figures replenished from time to time.   Richard A. Gray

567.   **Who's Who in American Politics 1985-1986.** 10th ed. Jaques Cattell Press, ed. New York, R. R. Bowker, 1985. 1761p. index. $125.00. ISBN 0-8352-2075-3; ISSN 0000-0205.

First published in 1967, *Who's Who in American Politics* is the definitive biographical directory about Americans who are active in politics. Coverage of the tenth edition reflects results of the 1984 elections and chronicles the lives of 23,566 politically active men and women, listing the biographies of 2,657 entrants for the first time. To be included an individual must be currently participating in politics at a local, state, or national level, or must recently have been of national stature in politics or governmental service. Besides national and state elected officials and legislators, it includes cabinet and sub-cabinet officials, key presidential appointees, congressional administrative assistants and counsels to congressional committees, ambassadors, national and state political party chairs, key officers, national committee members, county chairs, minor party officials, mayors of cities with populations over fifty thousand, and those of influence behind the scenes. Arrangement of entries was changed to a state-by-state listing with the eighth edition from a former straight alphabetical listing. A complete entry may include party affiliation; date and place of birth; parents; family; education; current and past political, governmental, and business positions; military service; honors and awards; publications; memberships; religion; legal residence; and current mailing address. However, there are frequent instances of incomplete data and many entries provide only the individual's party affiliation, current position, and address.   LeRoy C. Schwarzkopf

568.   **Who's Who in Government.** 3rd ed. Chicago, Marquis Who's Who, 1977. 753p. index. o.p. LC 72-623344. ISBN 0-8379-1203-2.

The first edition of this work, published in 1972, included sixteen thousand listings and provided biographical data about key men and women in all branches of the U.S.

federal government and about a selected list of officials in local, state, and international government. The third edition of the Marquis directory has eighteen thousand listings, and its coverage remains essentially the same. Three indexes record names of biographees in each level of government (federal, state, and county), but there is no geographical index. This volume would complement Bowker's *Who's Who in American Politics*. The Marquis directory provides a more comprehensive coverage of governmental officials (i.e., officials employed in various agencies of government). The Bowker publication is stronger in the coverage of politicians, such as officials of both major parties, and also has good coverage of elected state and local officials. [R: WLB, Feb 76, p. 494]   Bohdan S. Wynar

569.   **Women in Public Office: A Biographical Directory and Statistical Analysis**. Compiled by Center for the American Woman and Politics, State University of New Jersey. 2nd ed. Metuchen, N.J., Scarecrow, 1978. 510p. index. $39.50. LC 78-7463. ISBN 0-8108-1142-1.

Quite simply the best single source for facts, figures, and biographical information on women holding appointed and elected offices in the United States during 1976 and 1977, *Women in Public Office* identifies over seventeen thousand women in local, state, and federal government. Arrangement is by state and within states by title and rank. Though United States congressional women may be easy to locate using other sources, the real virtue of *Women in Public Office* is the access that it gives to individuals in the many state, county, city, and town offices. Not merely producing a compendium of names and dates, the Center for the American Woman and Politics has analyzed the data on women in public office in a number of interesting ways, to provide profiles of the political and personal background of women serving in 1976-1977 as well as those who have left public office since 1975. Female and male officeholders are compared on a variety of issues and scales in a section that offers the first national data comparisons between men and women holding public office. Though the first edition of *Women in Public Office* (R. R. Bowker, 1976) was a landmark effort in the identification of political women, the second edition offers significantly more and different demographic data. It also once again calls attention to the surprisingly low percentage of women occupying positions of political power in the United States—only 8 percent of the offices covered as of 1977.   Esther F. Stineman

Executive Branch

570.   **Biographical Directory of the United States Executive Branch, 1774-1977**. Robert Sobel, ed.-in-chief. 2nd rev. ed. Westport, Conn., Greenwood Press, 1977. 503p. index. $45.00. LC 77-84. ISBN 0-8371-9527-6.

The first edition of this work, published in 1971, provided some five hundred biographical sketches of presidents and vice presidents of the United States, and presidents of the Continental Congress, covering the period 1774 up to Nixon's second administration. Included in the second edition are 516 career biographies for the period 1774 through the Carter administration's original appointments; among these are some fifty new or revised sketches. This volume is similar in format to the *Biographical Directory of the American Congress, 1774-1971* and was apparently designed to complement and supplement this work.

The biographical sketches are arranged alphabetically by biographees' surnames and include birth and death dates, religious affiliation, and information on career and service before and after election or appointment to office. Many of the sketches also supply information on the biographee's publications, memberships in organizations, and major accomplishments associated with his or her political career. References to primary and secondary works are cited in brief bibliographies at the end of each sketch. The indexes (125 pages) include a list of presidential administrations and separate sections on presidents, vice presidents, and cabinet officers. [R: BL, 1 Apr 78, pp. 1275-76]

Bohdan S. Wynar

571. Brownson, Charles B., ed. **Federal Staff Directory, 1985: Containing in Convenient Order Useful Information Concerning the Executive Branch and Its 28,000 Key Executives with Their Staff Assistants**. Mount Vernon, Va., Congressional Staff Directory, 1984. 1360p. index. $40.00. LC 59-13987. ISBN 0-87289-049-X.

This title is similar in content and format to the *Congressional Staff Directory* (Congressional Staff Directory, Ltd., 1983). Its focus is, however, on the executive rather than the legislative branch of government. Included are some twenty-eight thousand officials from the executive office of the president, the cabinet departments, and the independent agencies. Emphasis is on those individuals with the grade of GS-16 and above as well as key staff assistants. Typical information for the variously designated subdivisions of the departments and independent agencies includes responsible officer, position title, address, and phone number. Thus, the *Federal Staff Directory* is an important source in the identification of major administrators within the executive branch in Washington, D.C., and across the country. In addition, there are some twenty-two hundred biographical entries on selected federal executives.

Certainly, such sources as the *Government Manual*, the *Washington Information Directory* and the *Federal Regulatory Directory* also provide somewhat comparable information. However, the usefulness of this work is in its comprehensive coverage of major executive branch officials rather than in its attempt to combine a descriptive narrative of government offices with abbreviated personnel information. A computer-generated key-word subject index and an index of all listed individuals make this title easily accessible.

Frank Wm. Goudy

572. **Burke's Presidential Families of the United States of America**. 2nd ed. London, Burke's Peerage; distr., New York, Pergamon Press, 1981. 597p. illus. o.p. ISBN 0-85011-033-5.

The first edition of this work was issued in 1975 and included President Gerald Ford. This second edition adds Jimmy Carter and Ronald Reagan. Each of the chapters, one on each president, is divided into the following sections: a biography which consists of a short character sketch and historical assessment, a portrait of each president and his wife (except for Mrs. Jefferson, for whom no portrait is available), a chronology which lists a factual record of year-by-year events in the presidents' lives (strangely, the chronology stops in June 1980 for Jimmy Carter), and writings of the presidents. Also included are the president's direct male line ancestors, his male and female living and dead descendents, his brothers and sisters, and notes. The four appendixes consist of: A) a chapter on the president of the Confederacy, Jefferson Davis, which is arranged exactly like the chapters on the presidents; B) vice presidents of the United States with a paragraph summary of their genealogies; C) ancestral tables of the presidents; and D) the presidential elections, including the 1980 election. There is also a surname index with three thousand entries from the presidential pedigrees. There are some minor corrections from the first edition.

This will be a necessary purchase for genealogical libraries that don't own the first edition. Those who own the first can skip this one unless there is heavy local demand for the genealogies of Mr. Carter and Mr. Reagan.   Robert L. Turner, Jr.

573. Coy, Harold. **The First Book of Presidents**. rev. ed. (7th ed.). New York, Franklin Watts, 1981. 66p. illus. index. (A First Book). $8.40. LC 77-1600. ISBN 0-531-02906-9.

First published in 1952, with variable titles in other editions, *The First Book of Presidents* in this edition brings the listing up-to-date with Reagan. The bulk of the text consists of one- to two-page capsule facts and comments on each president. The format includes a block of basic factual data and a small drawing of each of the presidents (black-and-white photographs in the case of the last three). Preliminary information includes material on qualifications, elections, inauguration, duties, etc., supplemented by a few black-and-white photos and drawings. The two-page index is concise and helpful.

The style is lively and interesting, with material suitable for upper elementary grades.

An older title addressed to a similar audience is *Profiles and Portraits of American Presidents* by Margaret Bassett (New York, David McKay, 1976. 306p. o.p.) that provides four- to six-page accounts of each of the presidents, covering Ford through 1975. Unfortunately it is not as well done as Kane's *Facts about the Presidents*, a standard work for schools and smaller public libraries. Here one should also mention *Atlas of the Presidents* by Donald E. Cooke (Chicago, Hammond, 1983. 96p. $6.95. ISBN 0-8437-1045-4) that emphasizes more personal matters (personal stories, family tragedies, etc.) providing coverage from George Washington to Ronald Reagan.

Kathryn McChesney and Bohdan S. Wynar

574. DeGregorio, William A. **The Complete Book of U.S. Presidents**. New York, Dembner Books; distr., New York, W. W. Norton, 1984. 691p. illus. index. $22.50. LC 83-23201. ISBN 0-934878-36-6.

Though Joseph Kane's *Facts about the Presidents* has for many years been the reliable old standard that most individuals turned to for a wide range of presidential data, DeGregorio's *The Complete Book of U.S. Presidents* is an attractive, well-researched alternative. Each of the thirty-nine subjects is presented in a coherent, well-integrated, ten- to twenty-page chapter. The chapters are arranged under a wide range of fixed headings which are utilized whenever pertinent. Physical description, personality, childhood, marriage, recreation, administration, death, and extramarital affairs represent but a small sampling of these headings. One of the book's great strengths is the inclusion of copious footnoted quotes by and about the individuals presented. Though DeGregorio, unlike Kane, does not provide lists of comparative data, the index is extremely responsive.

The Complete Book of U.S. Presidents is suitable for all levels of libraries, from high school to graduate school. Those who wish to quickly check a fact, develop a biographical overview, or compare presidential administrations will intuitively realize that this volume has no peer. One can spend many pleasant hours, too, just dipping and browsing (as this reviewer did). It is all here: the 332-pound Taft stuck in the White House bathtub, Pierce's predilection for strong drink, Washington's false teeth (lead and ivory, not wood!), Coolidge's insistence on wearing baggy underwear, and the strange coincidence of John Adams and Thomas Jefferson both dying on July 4, 1826.

Although a total newcomer to the presidential reference pack, *The Complete Book of U.S. Presidents* is, as its title promises, about as complete as any one-volume source could be. It will quickly become a standard reference source. [R: Choice, Sept 84, p. 60; LJ, 1 Mar 84, p. 478; WLB, Sept 84, p. 65]   Mark R. Yerburgh

575. Graff, Henry F., ed. **The Presidents: A Reference History**. New York, Scribner's, 1984. 700p. index. $65.00. LC 83-20225. ISBN 0-684-17607-6.

The Presidents is a collection of thirty-five biographical essays, each covering the administration of a president from Washington through Jimmy Carter. Three essays combine the presidencies of Harrison and Tyler, Taylor and Fillmore, and Garfield and Arthur. Otherwise, the essays try to provide a brief life of the president integrated with a short, usually analytical history of his administration. Qualified historians or political scientists (e.g., Arthur S. Link and William W. Freehling) have written the essays which range from ten to thirty pages in length. Each essay can be read independently of the others. Annotated bibliographies are provided for each essay and there is an index for the entire volume.

Needless to say, this book is not a ready-reference tool but it does serve to provide brief authoritative introductions to each presidential administration. Especially useful are the essays covering presidents Nixon, Ford, and Carter since their administrations are too recent to be included in many survey texts. However, since these presidencies are so recent, nothing approaching a historical consensus of interpretation exists and some readers may not find themselves in agreement with the interpretation of the authors. The same lack of historical consensus applies to a lesser extent to the presidencies of Kennedy and Johnson. This situation is a natural and unavoidable part of the development of historical knowledge and the authors involved in the present volume have done an excellent job of charting uncertain ground. [R: Choice, Sept 84, p. 70; LJ, July 84, p. 1320; WLB, Sept 84, p. 65]   Ronald H. Fritze

576. Healy, Diana Dixon. **America's Vice-Presidents: Our First Forty-three Vice Presidents and How They Got to Be Number Two**. New York, Atheneum, 1984. 235p. illus. $15.95. LC 83-45490. ISBN 0-689-11454-0.

"*America's Vice-Presidents* offers witty and informative portraits," according to the dust jacket. The emphasis seems to be on "witty." The author manages to find at least one damning bit of trivia on each gentleman. Surely our vice presidents have not been that bad!

Each chapter is only a few pages long and is accompanied by a portrait of the vice president. There is insufficient information to provide anyone with the kind of material needed to answer a reference question. Each chapter is a summary of the vice president's life; numerous anecdotes are included. There is no bibliography or index. This book cannot be recommended as a reference work for any type of library. The attempt to portray all of the vice presidents as men of flawed nature does not even make the book enjoyable to read for pleasure.

A more balanced approach was used in an older work *Madmen and Geniuses: The Vice-Presidents of the United States* by Sol Barzman (Chicago, Follett, 1974. 335p. o.p.). Each individual is treated in a separate chapter, which provides background information and a brief overview of his vice presidency. A selective bibliography includes only secondary books, and there are no footnotes for the many quotations. Barzman has prepared a handy book that demonstrates the need to improve the office and to attract qualified candidates.

A more recent work by John D. and Emalie P. Feerick, *The First Book of Vice-Presidents of the United States* rev. ed., 7th ed. (New York, Franklin Watts, 1981. 94p.) includes one- to two-page accounts (with small photographs and engravings) of each vice president through George Bush.   Roberta R. Palen and Bohdan S. Wynar

577. Kane, Joseph Nathan. **Facts about the Presidents: A Compilation of Biographical and Historical Information**. 4th ed. New York, H. W. Wilson, 1981. 456p. illus. index. $30.00. LC 81-7537. ISBN 0-8242-0612-6.

Libraries that missed the third edition of this standard reference source will welcome this one. Added to the fourth edition are Presidents Ford, Carter, and Reagan. A number of minor editorial changes have also been made, especially in the entries for both Roosevelts, Harding, Hoover, Truman, Eisenhower, Kennedy, and Johnson.

While some information is rather frivolous, such as Truman being the only thirty-third degree Mason and the first to tape-record a press conference, more substantive data predominate. As with other editions, this one includes a portrait gallery and a separate section of such comparative data as presidents' zodiac signs, marriage statistics, nicknames, occupations, religious affiliations, etc. The entry for President Reagan is current up to the assassination attempt of 30 March 1981.

A related title is *The First Ladies* by Margaret Brown Klapthor (Washington, D.C., GPO, 1981. 89p. $8.00. $6.50pa.) representing a collection of brief biographical sketches, attractively packaged and obviously intended for a popular audience. Each essay of three hundred to four hundred words provides a characterization of the subject, vital statistics such as birth and death dates, family background, childhood, education, relationship to the presidents, and career, if any. The biographies are accompanied by portraits. The absence of sources and a bibliography for further reading makes this volume suitable only for the broadest of general reference libraries. [R: BL, 1 Dec 81, p. 281; Choice, Dec 81, pp. 488-89]

Gary D. Barber and Richard J. Cox

578. Lichtenstein, Nelson, ed. **Political Profiles: The Kennedy Years**. New York, Facts on File, 1976. 621p. bibliog. index. $55.00. LC 76-20897. ISBN 0-87196-450-3.

The Kennedy Years treats 502 personalities who were of recognized importance or who gained prominence during the early 1960s. It is one of a projected series of volumes containing biographical sketches of individuals prominent in American politics beginning with the Truman administration following World War II. Sketches are included not only for those who achieved prominence through government service, but also for those not directly in government, but whose political, social, or scientific activities placed them in the public eye. The sketches vary in length, but most appear to average five hundred to one thousand words; more noted personalities receive somewhat longer treatment.

Although the editors have attempted to touch on the important events in the life of each individual, they highlight the events that occurred within the time scope of the specific volume under consideration. However, since so many careers transcend a single presidential administration (particularly true of the brief Kennedy tenure), the editors have provided cross-references to other volumes in the series for additional discussion. They have also included brief bibliographical notes following each sketch. An appendix provides a chronology of events, lists of major government office-holders and of state governors, a bibliography, and a "career index" for those holding more than one position.

Although some libraries may find the time scope of this volume a little too limited for their reference collection, the volume should be a welcome addition to most biographical reference shelves. [R: Choice, July/Aug 77, pp. 554-56; LJ, 1 Feb 77, p. 370; RQ, Fall 77, p. 80; WLB, June 77, pp. 815-16]   Walter L. Newsome

579.   Lorant, Stefan. **The Glorious Burden: The American Presidency**. Lenox, Mass., Author's Edition, Inc., 1976. 950p. illus. ports. bibliog. index. $19.95. LC 76-48760. ISBN 0-918058-00-7.

A concise pictorial history of the United States in terms of our presidents and presidential elections, from Washington through Lyndon B. Johnson. Well illustrated with fifteen hundred portraits, cartoons, daguerreotypes, and photos. As in the author's earlier volume *The Presidency* (1952) many little-known illustrations, the result of some twenty years of research and searching for appropriate material, are included. The first chapter, on George Washington, shows his standing portrait, pictures of candidates, reproductions of several woodcuts, engravings, and paintings. In general, illustrations are well chosen, the text is readable and several appendixes (e.g., the election vote from 1789 to 1964, a list of sources for portraits of the presidents and presidential candidates) add to the value of this well-prepared book. In addition, it is printed on excellent heavy paper that certainly should justify its price. [R: BL, 1 June 69; LJ, 15 Mar 69]
                    Bohdan S. Wynar

580.   Melick, Arden Davis. **Wives of the Presidents**. Maplewood, N.J., Hammond, 1985. 96p. illus. (col.). bibliog. index. $6.95. LC 77-141. ISBN 0-8437-3813-8.

This volume of forty-one biographical sketches of the wives of U.S. presidents from Martha Washington to Nancy Reagan is handsomely illustrated with full-color reproductions of official portraits, photographs, and graphics. Mrs. Melick devotes four to five double-columned pages to the more prominent wives (including Martha Washington, Abigail Adams, Mary Lincoln, Edith Wilson, and Eleanor Roosevelt) and shorter articles to the others. In a readable, informal style, the author describes the social and intellectual background of the presidential wives and the main events in their personal lives. The articles, embellished with quotes from family letters and White House memorabilia, are placed in the context of larger historical events. A comparative data chart listing the dates, birthplaces, and the number of sons and daughters of the presidents' wives (including Caroline Fillmore and Mary Harrison, who were omitted from the biographies) is useful for quick reference. The index, mainly of names and places, is adequate. There is also a bibliography of sixty-four entries; one-fifth of these are articles from the *American Heritage* and other magazines and newspapers, and the rest are a selection of books which can only be described as random.

This book has a number of predecessors such as *The Woman in the White House* by Marianne Means and *First Ladies of the White House* by Gertrude Z. Books (to name two that are not mentioned in the bibliography). There will undoubtedly be successors as long as the occupants of the White House continue to hold the interest of the general public. This book is recommended for the high quality of its illustrations, for its convenient format, and for its readily accessible biographical data.
                    Marjorie K. Ho

581.   Quinn, Sandra L., and Sanford Kanter. **America's Royalty: All the Presidents' Children**. Westport, Conn., Greenwood Press, 1983. 237p. bibliog. index. $35.00. LC 82-12006. ISBN 0-313-23645-3.

America's Royalty is a biographical dictionary of all the children of the presidents through Ronald Reagan, including any alleged illegitimate children. The purpose of this work is to illuminate the human side of history for both the instruction and the amusement of the reader. Its authors recommend it especially as a source of anecdotes for the lectures of history instructors.

Arrangement is by chronological order of the father's term as president and then according to his children's order of birth. Individual entries begin by providing, when applicable, birth date, place of birth, death date, age at death, cause of death, education, profession, spouses, and number of children. This information is followed by a brief anecdotal biography with footnotes. A short bibliography, for further reading, is included for each presidential family after the individual entries. An appendix concerning the shared characteristics of presidents' children concludes the book with tables of schools attended, occupations, states of birth, longevity, and causes of death. The authors' conclusion, not surprisingly, is that presidential children have better opportunities in life than children in the general population. There is also a personal name index but no pictures to show what these people looked like, although that is no great impediment to the book's usefulness.

As a source of human interest stories and trivia, this book is a rich mine of information. Because of its light nature, however, not every public or academic library will want to add this monograph to its collection of U.S. social history. [R: Choice, Nov 83, p. 404; RQ, Fall 83, pp. 11-100; WLB, Sept 83, p. 64]   Ronald H. Fritze

582.   Schoenebaum, Eleanora W., ed. **Political Profiles: The Eisenhower Years**. Associate ed., Michael L. Levine. New York, Facts on File, 1977. 757p. bibliog. index. $55.00. LC 76-20897. ISBN 0-87196-452-3.

This is the third volume of a projected six-volume set covering the United States political scene from the Truman through the Carter presidencies. *The Kennedy Years* and *The Johnson Years* have already appeared. All volumes contain biographies of those men and women who played a significant role in U.S. politics, and those individuals with long careers may appear in several volumes. For each person, "there is a detailed account of the individual's career during a particular presidential administration. It also includes social and political background, early career and major accomplishments as well as an assessment of impact on the social, political or cultural life of the nation." There was little effort made to profile those Americans whose influence on policy was determined by their activities behind the scenes, e.g., the Mellon or DuPont families during Eisenhower's incumbency.

Appended to the book are a full chronology of the events of the period; the membership list of the eighty-third to eighty-sixth Congresses; a list of the Eisenhower cabinet; the membership of the Supreme Court; and the membership of the most important federal regulatory agencies. A general bibliography for the period is also appended, and many of the individual biographies contain references to other volumes in the series and to additional biographical or analytical studies. Used in conjunction with the other two volumes already available, this work presents a useful factual reference tool for those interested in the post-World War II American political scene.

This volume is continued by *The Johnson Years* (1978. 772p. $55.00) with identical execution. [R: LJ, May 78, p. 962; WLB, May 78, p. 732]

Margaret Anderson

583. Schoenebaum, Eleanora W., ed. **Political Profiles: The Nixon/Ford Years**. New York, Facts on File, 1979. 787p. bibliog. index. $55.00. LC 76-20897. ISBN 0-87196-454-6.

This volume may prove to be the most interesting of the entire series. The official and unofficial activities of the Nixon administration that are documented on these pages often strain credulity, and among those profiled are some of the most notorious characters ever associated with American politics: E. Howard Hunt, G. Gordon Liddy, Robert Vesco, Dita Beard, Donald Segretti, Tony Ulasewicz, and Spiro T. Agnew. The selection of individual entries was determined by two major considerations: "Did the man or woman have a lasting impact on politics broadly defined? Or did the individual capture the political attention of the nation?" Such criteria permit space for the likes of Carl Bernstein, Norman Mailer, Ralph Nader, Billy Graham, and Katharine Graham in addition to the obligatory politicians. The longest entries are those for Nixon and Kissinger (each over 12 pages); Agnew and Rockefeller each receive about 4½ pages; Ford 6½; Ehrlichman 7; Haldeman 5; McGovern 4; and about 3 pages each for Sam Ervin, John Dean, and Howard Hunt. The average entry is only 1-2 pages. Many of the profiles contain references to entries in other volumes of the set, and in some cases selected references are cited.

The editors have written a twenty-page introduction that provides an excellent overview of the period. The appendixes to the book include: a chronology of important events from 1969 through 1976; the members of Congress, the Supreme Court, executive departments, regulatory commissions, and independent agencies; a listing of governors; and an extensive bibliography (twenty-two pages, divided into nine broad areas). There are two indexes: a career index, which categorizes the profiled individuals "according to their most important public activity," and a traditional name-and-subject index. Despite the cost, all but the smallest libraries should acquire the Political Profiles series. This particular volume will be additionally useful when memories of the scandals and personnel of the Nixon era begin to fade.   Thomas A. Karel

584. Schoenebaum, Eleanora W., ed. **Political Profiles: The Truman Years**. New York, Facts on File, 1978. 714p. bibliog. index. $55.00. LC 76-20897. ISBN 0-87196-453-8.

The Truman Years provides biographical sketches for 435 men and women who played publicly recognized significant roles in U.S. politics during the late forties and early fifties. It is the fourth volume of a projected six-volume set, covering the years of the Truman through the Carter administrations.

Sketches are included not only for those who served in elective or appointive government offices, but also those whose social and political interactions in public affairs brought them prominence — labor leaders, civil-rights leaders, and scientists, for example. Those whose careers transcend more than one presidential administration receive treatment in all appropriate volumes, with sketches weighted toward accomplishments of the time period covered by each volume. Cross-references allow the user to follow the career of an individual throughout the set. Many entries include brief bibliographical notes.

Each volume includes an appendix with the following information for the time period covered by the volume: a chronology of important events; the names of state congressional delegations, Supreme Court justices, cabinet members and other chief executive officials, members of regulatory commissions and independent agencies, and state governors; and a bibliography. [R: Choice, June 79, p. 513]

Walter L. Newsome

585.   Southwick, Leslie H., comp. **Presidential Also-Rans and Running Mates, 1788-1980**. Jefferson, N.C., McFarland, 1984. 722p. bibliog. index. $49.95. LC 83-25577. ISBN 0-89950-109-5.

While it is easy to find biographical information on the individuals who have attained the presidency and vice presidency of the United States, it is arduous to locate information on those who were nominated but who lost the election. This book fully satisfies the need for such information.

Arranged in chronological order by election up to 1980, the biographies are informative and readable. Details are given, yet the author attempts to portray "a human side to the candidates." The author provides an analysis of each individual's qualifications, as well as background information on family, education, personal characteristics, and public offices held. Each biography is at least three thousand words long. A brief bibliography ends each section.

In addition, dates of party conventions, popular vote, and electoral vote are provided for each election.

This book is a worthy companion to Irving Stone's *They Also Ran* (Doubleday, 1966). Stone's book includes readable sketches and is an attempt to capture "the vital essence of each man." However, it ends with the 1964 election. Although Stone's book is valuable, Southwick's provides more substantive information and should quickly become the standard reference work in the field.

Although the price of this book may seem high for smaller libraries, it should not deter any librarian from purchasing it. The book is highly recommended for all libraries.

Another title, less recent, *'If Elected. . .': Unsuccessful Candidates for the Presidency, 1796-1968* put out by the U.S. National Portrait Gallery (Washington, D.C., GPO, 1972. 512p. $9.50. S/N 4706-0008) is a roster of names including those who became president as well as unsuccessful candidates. Major-party candidates who tried two or three times and third-party candidates are also included. Each entry contains an account of the life and philosophy of each candidate, accompanied by a portrait. [R: WLB, Dec 84, p. 293]   Roberta R. Palen

586.   Taylor, Tim. **The Book of Presidents**. Salem, N.H., Ayer Co., 1972. 744p. illus. index. $12.95. LC 74-164708. ISBN 0-405-00226-2.

Tim Taylor, author and journalist, has been collecting facts on the nation's presidents since 1944. After mining his collected files of information for one thousand articles and parts of two books, Mr. Taylor then set about organizing his incredible wealth of factual information. *The Book of Presidents*, containing over 500,000 facts and figures on thirty-seven chief executives in chronological order, is the result. To make the information accessible and comparisons easy, Mr. Taylor has followed the same format throughout: first there is biographical information including ancestry, birth, religion, marriage, and information on each president's parents and wife. Next the "Early Years" describes schooling and military and pre-political careers. "National Prominence" lists the pre-presidential offices, then the presidential conventions, campaigns, and voting results. The "Presidential Years" describes the inauguration, Cabinet and Supreme Court appointments, proclamations, State of the Union messages, acts passed and vetoed—in sum, a very concise yet complete factual summary of each man's tenure in office. There is finally a brief section on the "Post-Presidency Years" listing experiences, jobs, travels, correspondence, and death.

Certainly this is a handy, compact reference tool and should be in every school, college, and public library, as well as on the bookshelves of the countless amateur politicos and trivia fanatics. I wonder if sometimes Mr. Taylor, in an effort at completeness, does not go to rather ridiculous extremes. Yet, if anyone really does care, for instance, that John F. Kennedy was the seventeenth of nineteen presidents who had middle names or initials, this book is the place to find such a fact. [R: BL, 15 Mar 73, p. 699; LJ, 15 Jan 73, p. 152]   Nancy G. Boles

587. U.S. National Park Service. **Signers of the Declaration**. Washington, D.C., GPO, 1974. 310p. illus. index. (National Survey of Historic Sites and Buildings, Vol. 18). $5.65. S/N 2405-00496. (I 29.2:H62/9/v.18).

This book includes a brief biography of every signer of the Declaration of Independence. The book also includes thirty pages of historical background on the signing of the Declaration, with pictures and text describing the events that led to the final break with Britain.

There is a section of photographs and descriptions of the principal buildings associated with the signers of the Declaration, including the White House (home of John Adams and Thomas Jefferson), Jefferson's Monticello, Elbridge Gerry's birthplace in Massachusetts, and others.

The book concludes with a special appendix that contains the text of the Declaration of Independence and a history of the document.   Bohdan S. Wynar

588. Vexler, Robert I. **The Vice-Presidents and Cabinet Members: Biographies Arranged Chronologically by Administration**. Dobbs Ferry, N.Y., Oceana, 1975. 2v. index. o.p. LC 75-28085. ISBN 0-379-12089-5 (vol. 1); 0-379-12090-9 (vol. 2).

This two-volume work is a significant reference tool deserving consideration as an essential acquisition for all libraries. Biographical sketches of vice presidents and cabinet members from the administration of George Washington to that of President Ford present basic, concise, and detailed information concerning the public and private lives of each individual. The editor has established 31 December 1974 as the concluding date for information contained therein. As an aid to the researcher, bibliographic references are cited to guide one's search to more detailed sources. These volumes have been planned by the publishers to be used with their Presidential Chronology series through a system of cross-checking. The editor has diligently cited the most accurate dates and other pertinent information through consultation with diaries and original documents. The appendix includes a listing of members of the various presidential administrations by term. This work appears to be more comprehensive and scholarly (albeit less entertaining) than Sol Barzman's *Madmen and Geniuses: The Vice Presidents of the United States* (Chicago, Follet, 1974). [R: BL, 1 Sept 76, p. 58; Choice, Mar 76, p. 50; RQ, Spring 76, p. 281]   Bernard D. Reams, Jr.

589. Whitney, David C. **The American Presidents**. New York, Doubleday, 1982. 576p. illus. index. $14.95. LC 81-43923. ISBN 0-385-18525-1.

A revised and expanded edition of a work that first appeared in 1967, this volume contains biographical sketches of all U.S. presidents from Washington through Reagan. The narratives are written in a popular style, and treatment is generally balanced and noncontroversial. More space is devoted to twentieth-century administrations than those of the earlier period: the chapter on Nixon, for example, is the longest in the book. In addition to updating the coverage, Whitney has provided several new sections:

"Key Facts about the Presidents"; "What Presidents Have Said about the Presidency"; and "Presidential Historical Sites."

The major defects of the book are the lack of statistical information in summary or tabular format, and the lack of a bibliography. As a ready reference on the presidency, *The American Presidents* cannot substitute for the standard works: Joseph Kane's *Facts about the Presidents* and Tim Taylor's *The Book of Presidents*.   Jane A. Benson

Legislative Branch

590. **Biographical Directory of the American Congress, 1774-1971**. Washington, D.C., GPO, 1971; repr., 1977. 1972p. $40.00. S/N 052-071-00249-9. (92-1:S.doc.8)

More than 10,800 biographical sketches of senators and representatives elected or appointed to the Continental Congress (5 September 1774-21 October 1788) and to the Congress of the United States from the First to the Ninety-first Congress (4 March 1789, to 3 January 1971) are included in this authoritative directory. Lists of the officers of the executive branch of the government from the first administration of George Washington to the administration of Richard M. Nixon are also provided. Other lists are: delegates to the Continental Congress; all members of Congress from the First to the Ninety-first; and members of the Ninety-second Congress serving their first term. A new addition to this volume is the biographies of Presidents of the United States who never served as members of Congress.

A related work covering a shorter time period is Marjorie G. Fribourg's *The U.S. Congress: Men Who Steered Its Course, 1787-1867* (Philadelphia, Macrae Smith, 1973. $5.95. LC 72-1751. ISBN 0-8255-3410-0). [R: BL, 15 Mar 72, p. 594]

Bohdan S. Wynar

591. **Congressional Pictorial Directory: Ninety-Eighth Congress**. Compiled under the direction of the Joint Committee on Printing. Washington, D.C., GPO, 1983. 194p. illus. $6.00pa. S/N 052-070-05818-8.

The *Congressional Pictorial Directory* provides the following: (1) photographs of the Senate and House leaders, Senate and House officers and officials, Capitol officials, Senate and House members by state, and delegates from the District of Columbia and U.S. territorial possessions; (2) a list of Senate and House state delegations by districts; and (3) an alphabetical list of senators and representatives, including their home post office. However, such sources as *Politics in America* and the *Almanac of American Politics* also provide photographs of each Senate and House member as well as a vast amount of additional information about all of the legislators and their districts. Of course, the *Congressional Pictorial Directory* does have photographs of such officials as the nonvoting delegate from Guam and Samoa or the House doorkeeper, which are not easily found elsewhere. Overall, however, this title is of limited usefulness, and librarians should carefully consider their particular needs before purchasing it.

Other related titles regarding specific U.S. Congresses include George Douth's *Leaders in Profile: The United States Senate. 1972 Edition. The Ninety-Second Congress* (New York, Sperr and Douth, 1972. 472p. o.p.), a journalistic account that provides biographical sketches of each senator. *Leaders in Profile: The United States Senate. 1975 Edition. The Ninety-Fourth Congress* (New York, Sperr and Douth, 1975. 923p. o.p.) provides similar sketches of members of the Ninety-fourth Congress. Biannually updated, it also includes retired members of the Ninety-third Congress. The journalistic profiles found in these works may be of interest to some, but most of the information can be found in other, less rambling sources.

Frank Wm. Goudy

592. **Congressional Staff Directory, 1984: Containing . . . 3,200 Staff Biographies**. Charles B. Brownson, ed. Mount Vernon, Va., Congressional Staff Directory, 1984. 1210p. index. $40.00. LC 59-13987. ISBN 0-87289-058-9.

For more than twenty-five years, the *Congressional Staff Directory* has provided biographical and locational information on the staffs of the members of Congress. Each directory is particularly useful for its listing of names, room locations, phone numbers, and positions of all (not just selected!) staff members. In addition, names, positions, and phone numbers of key personnel of executive departments and independent agencies are listed.

Biographical information on key congressional staff experts is provided by the staff members themselves. Not all staff are included in this section and there are no stated criteria concerning the selection of "key experts."

The directory contains a wealth of other information, much of which is found in other sources. There is merit, however, in having all of this information in one volume.

Biographical information about state delegations in Congress includes names of cities within each district and addresses and telephone numbers of district offices. One section lists all cities with more than fifteen hundred population and their congressional district number and name of representative. Another section lists governors and their office addresses and phone numbers.

In addition to the expected index of names, there is a keyword subject index which, for example, leads the user to any executive agency or committee concerned with nuclear energy. Each section of the *Directory* is printed on a different color paper, providing easier access to information.

The directory can be useful in any library.

Roberta R. Palen

593. Engelbarts, Rudolf. **Women in the United States Congress, 1917-1972: Their Accomplishments; with Bibliographies**. Littleton, Colo., Libraries Unlimited, 1974. 184p. o.p. LC 73-93278. ISBN 0-87287-083-9.

The burgeoning interest in and study of the status of women in the United States will be assisted by this volume. Mr. Engelbarts concentrates first on the accomplishments of the eighty-one women who were members of the U.S. Congress during the period from 1917 through 1972. Beginning with Jeannette Rankin and ending with Elizabeth B. Andrews of Alabama, the author initially discusses the women who served in the House of Representatives, arranged chronologically by the year of their entry into the Congress. Subsequently, a listing of female Senators is supplied in a similar format. In addition to discussing their accomplishments, Mr. Engelbarts provides a bibliography of books and articles about or by each of the Congresswomen. To improve access to his work, the author provides, in tabular form, a chronological and alphabetical list of the women members of each house of the Congress; to assist understanding, a set of abbreviations and definitions of terms is appended. Finally, Mr. Engelbarts has included a selected, classified bibliography of books and magazine articles on topics concerned with women, as well as an alphabetical author listing for the same bibliography.

A related title of less reference value is Hope Chamberlin's *A Minority of Members: Women in the U.S. Congress* (New York, Praeger, 1973. 374p. o.p.). It contains a chronological arrangement, with an appended alphabetical list of Congress-women indicating political party, state, and pertinent dates for each. [R: Choice, Oct 74, pp. 1108-9; LJ, Aug 74, p. 1962; WLB, Oct 74, p. 181]   Ann Hartman

594. **Members of Congress since 1789**. 3rd ed. Washington, D.C., Congressional Quarterly, 1985. 180p. $9.95pa. LC 76-57729. ISBN 0-87187-335-4.

The book lists alphabetically all senators, representatives, resident commissioners, and territorial delegates who served in Congress from 1789 through the Ninety-ninth Congress that meets in 1985-1986. Dates of birth and death, time and type of service in Congress, party affiliation, and service as president, vice president, cabinet officer, speaker or other high government office are given. Separate tables list new members of Congress for the Ninety-ninth Congress, leaders in the Senate and House, statistics on the sessions of Congress and party affiliations in Congress and the presidency. One of the most interesting features of this book is the chapter which gives a good overview of the characteristics of members of Congress: occupations of members, average age, names of and statistics on women and black members, turnovers in membership, and members who became president. A short bibliography is included.

More complete biographical information is contained in *Biographical Directory of the American Congress, 1774-1971*. In fact, much of the material in this book was distilled from that well-known work. And since current biographical and statistical information is also available in the *Congressional Directory*, this work reviewed here is of marginal value to libraries having the other two works. Its main virtue is that it is inexpensive. [R: Choice, Oct 77, p. 1022]   Maggie Johnson

595. Morris, Dan, and Inez Morris. **Who Was Who in American Politics: A Biographical Dictionary of Over 4,000 Men and Women Who Contributed to the United States Political Scene from Colonial Days up to and including the Immediate Past**. New York, Hawthorn Books, 1974. 637p. o.p. LC 76-39620. ISBN 0-8015-8624-0.

A very valuable and useful biographical dictionary of political figures, most of them deceased, others still alive but no longer active in politics. The work is a handy, one-volume guide to information about prominent political figures in American politics at the national, state, and local levels.

The general structure of this reference work consists of alphabetical listings for the biographees. Information is included on birth and death dates, place of birth, occupation, elective offices held or appointed posts, or role in the political process, with appropriate dates. Information is sketchy for little-known individuals, and no references or footnotes to additional sources of biographical information are provided. The reference sources at the beginning of this work indicate that standard and highly reliable biographical materials were consulted to prepare this biographical dictionary.

Although it is expensive, it would be a very worthwhile addition to any library. *Who Was Who in American Politics* is a perfect complement to *Who's Who in American Politics*. Highly recommended for purchase by all libraries. [R: Choice, Dec 74, p. 1458]   Robert P. Haro

596. **Official Congressional Directory: 98th Congress, 1983-1984**. Washington, D.C., GPO, 1983. 1177p. index. $12.00pa. ISSN 0160-9890.

Published since 1809, the *Official Congressional Directory*, is one of the two indispensable directory reference sources for the U.S. government (the other is the *United States Government [Organization] Manual*). Although there is substantial overlapping between the two works, a point that cost-conscious government officials might well investigate further, each is essential for the unique elements it contains. Although both works have listings of executive agencies, the *Congressional Directory*, as would be expected, has much fuller coverage of matters pertaining to the Congress: personnel of Congressional committee staffs, maps of Congressional districts, representatives of the press and other media officially accredited to the Congress, etc. It also includes brief biographies of members of Congress, arranged by state. Despite the steadily escalating costs of the biennial volumes, this work is still a bargain.

Richard A. Gray

597. **Politics in America: Members of Congress in Washington and at Home**. Alan Ehrenhalt, ed.; Robert E. Healy, associate ed. Washington, D.C., Congressional Quarterly Press, a division of Congressional Quarterly, 1983. 1734p. illus. index. $29.95. LC 83-7640. ISBN 0-87187-259-5.

This new CQ publication is similar in format to the highly regarded *Almanac of American Politics*. There is a two- to three-page profile of each member of Congress arranged alphabetically by state. Within each state the two U.S. senators are profiled first, followed by the congressional districts in numerical order. Emphasized are the representative's performance on Capitol Hill and the amount of influence in his/her home district. *Politics in America* has more thorough coverage of the senators than the *Almanac*, but descriptions of the districts tend to be sketchy. This volume is current through mid-1982.

The statistical data accompanying each profile are generally less complete than similar data found in the *Almanac*. For example, the ratings from only four interest groups are given here, while eleven groups are used in the *Almanac*. Although the *Almanac* lists more key congressional votes, CQ has compiled several useful voting studies which analyze the member's entire tenure in Congress. The three categories measured are support for the president, party unity, and affinity with the conservative coalition in Congress. One area where *Politics in America* is superior concerns campaign finances. The total receipts, contributions from political action committees, and total expenditures are listed for the two most recent elections in each district.

Some of the other features in this volume are: a brief socio-political overview of each state; a comprehensive list of committee and subcommittee members; a state-by-state tally of the presidential vote; and the votes from the 1983 presidential primaries. Maps showing the congressional districts for each state are included, but these are much smaller and less useful than the maps in the *Almanac*.

Although *Politics in America* is highly objective, very readable, and often entertaining, the *Almanac of American Politics* remains the superior reference source in this field. Its writing has more verve, and generally provides greater insights into the operation of the U.S. Congress. Hence, this work should not be viewed as a replacement for the *Almanac*, but libraries with a demonstrated need for such material might consider acquiring it for supplementary or comparative use.   Thomas A. Karel

598. Warner, Ezra J., and W. Buck Yearns. **Biographical Register of the Confederate Congress**. Baton Rouge, La., Louisiana State University Press, 1975. 319p. illus. bibliog. $27.50. LC 74-77329. ISBN 0-8071-0092-7.

In their introduction, the compilers acknowledge that the Confederate Congresses were for the most part impotent, almost ceremonial gatherings. Confederate President Jefferson Davis guarded his prerogatives jealously. In addition, in a nation at war, power always gravitates to the Executive. So inconsequential did Confederate congressmen consider their legislative service that, after the War, surviving members often suppressed accounts and memoirs. Certainly no member rose to fame and prominence *because* he was a senator or representative.

Nonetheless, this scholarly volume, with its alphabetically arranged series of biographies of all men who served in the three Confederate Congresses (the Provisional Congress in five sessions from 4 February 1861 to 17 February 1862; the First Congress in four sessions from 18 February 1862 to 17 February 1864; and the Second Congress in two sessions from 2 May 1864 to 18 March 1865) fills a gap in our knowledge of Southern Civil War history.

Each biographical sketch is itself a solid piece of historical research. Moreover, because of the already alluded to fact that ex-members were not proud of their legislative service, the research effort was extraordinarily difficult. All possibly relevant primary and secondary sources were combed for clues. Often the only source that yielded hard biographical data was the 1850 census, the first census to record heads of households by name.

Sources are cited at the end of most sketches; those that lack source citations were compiled from such standard sources as the *Biographical Directory of the American Congress*. The latter work was particularly fruitful because many of the men who served as Confederate legislators had previously served in the U.S. Congress.

The work concludes with four appendixes (Sessions of the Confederate Congress, Standing Committees, Membership, and Maps of Occupied Confederate Territory, 1861-1864), and a bibliography of the manuscripts, newspapers, government documents, and other materials used as sources. [R: Choice, Feb 76, p. 1554; LJ, 15 Mar 76, p. 803]   Richard A. Gray

States, Regions, and Cities

599.   Atwood, Evangeline, and Robert N. DeArmond, comps. **Who's Who in Alaskan Politics: A Biographical Dictionary of Alaskan Political Personalities, 1884-1974**. 1st ed. Portland, Oreg., Binford and Mort for the Alaska Historical Commission, 1977. 109p. $10.00. LC 77-76025. ISBN 0-8323-0287-2.

This is the first attempt at a comprehensive, retrospective biographical directory of Alaskan politicans, civil servants, and "personalities who have made substantial imprints on Alaskan politics" (preface). The time frame is from 1884 (when Congress provided a civil government for Alaska) to 1974; listings include governors, judges, legislators, U.S. marshals, directors of departments, and other assorted governmental employees. There are a number of appendixes, arranged by office, which include chronological lists of officeholders (e.g., attorneys general, collectors of customs, Alaska Railroad general managers, etc.). The eleven hundred entries, in alphabetical order, vary in size and appear on double-column pages. Though some of the information can be located in other sources, this title is the most complete source for Alaskan political biographical data. The information is accurate and appears in a traditional Who's Who format. Unfortunately, the compilers have not clearly defined their criteria for inclusion, with the subsequent problem that many who should have been included are not and some entries perhaps could have been omitted. There are also some minor problems, such as the lack of entries for individuals listed in the appendixes, misspellings, and incorrect filing. However, *Who's Who in Alaskan Politics* is a good start toward providing both contemporary and retrospective biographical coverage for the Great Land. [R: BL, 15 Dec 77, p. 711; RQ, Winter 77, p. 183]

Alan Edward Schorr

600. **Biographical Directory of the South Carolina House of Representatives.** Edited by N. Louise Bailey and others. Columbia, S.C., University of South Carolina Press, 1973-1984. 4v. $14.95/vol. (vols. 1-3). $24.95/vol. 4. LC 73-13630. ISBN 0-87249-406-3.

Biographical sketches of members of legislative bodies are basic for ultimate dictionaries of state biographies such as the exemplary *Dictionary of North Carolina Biography.* Among other states, Indiana, Tennessee, and here, South Carolina, have provided works of this type. The entries in this set are arranged alphabetically, and each sketch is in four parts, viz., the heading with dates of birth and death (when known) and names of relatives who were also members of the House; the sketch itself with all basic information that can be documented; a list of assemblies to which the member was elected; and source notes. There is a comprehensive index of names.

This is a basic resource for South Carolina history, and genealogists will find here a major reference work to trace Southern family history. The present reviewer, in checking it against his records of South Carolina ancestors, found no error, but discovered some new sources. The bibliography of "Source Notes" is a useful guide to reference works on South Carolina history, especially for the eighteenth century. Within its defined limits, the work meets the best standards of historical scholarship.

Lawrence S. Thompson

601. Crawford, Charles W., ed. **Governors of Tennessee, I: 1790-1835.** Memphis, Tenn., Memphis State University Press, 1979. 212p. illus. index. (The Tennessee Series, Vol. 3). $12.95. ISBN 0-87870-075-7.

This volume contains biographies of the first eight governors (one territorial) of the second trans-Appalachian state (1796) after Kentucky (1792). Each biography is by a single author and represents an epitome of what is known about that statesman and his times, fully documented and with extensive selective bibliographies. This work is virtually a history of Tennessee for the half century that saw the state develop from a frontier to a prosperous plantation economy in the middle and western sections. The authors range from graduate students to established academic people, and Mr. Crawford has enforced an effective uniformity in scope and style. There is an index, for which a cumulation will be needed at the end of the series to fulfill the set's very considerable potential as a reference work.

Similar volumes have been produced for other states. The following list provides some examples.

> **Governors of Alabama.** John C. Stewart. 1975. 232p. $13.95. LC 75-8763. ISBN 0-88289-067-0.

> **Governors of Arkansas: Essays in Political Biography.** Edited by Timothy P. Donovan and Willard B. Gatewood, Jr. 1981. 320p. $20.00. LC 81-50374. ISBN 0-938626-00-0.

> **Governors of Georgia.** James F. Cook. 1979. 320p. $12.95. LC 77-71397. ISBN 0-686-83449-6.

Governors of Louisiana. 3rd ed. Miriam G. Reeves. Edited by James Calhoun. 1980. 128p. $13.95. LC 72-89969. ISBN 0-911116-71-0.

Governors of Maryland, 1777-1970. Frank F. White, Jr. 1970. $12.00. ISBN 0-942370-01-5.

Governors of Minnesota: 1849-1971. Committee for the Inauguration of Wendell R. Anderson. 1971. 22p. $2.00pa. ISBN 0-685-47097-0.

Governors of Mississippi. Cecil L. Sumners. 1980. 164p. $13.95. ISBN 0-88289-237-1.

Governors of Texas. Ross Phares. 1976. 184p. $13.95. LC 76-7013. ISBN 0-88289-078-6.

Governors of Virginia. 1860-1978. Edited by Edward Younger and James T. Moore. 1982. 428p. $17.95. LC 81-16359. ISBN 0-8139-0920-1.

Lawrence S. Thompson and Bohdan S. Wynar

602.   Glashan, Roy R., comp. **American Governors and Gubernatorial Elections, 1775-1978**. Westport, Conn., Meckler Books/Microform Review, 1979. 370p. bibliog. $45.00. LC 79-15021. ISBN 0-930466-17-9.

American Governors and Gubernatorial Elections, 1775-1978 is an updated edition of a work that first appeared in 1975. Arranged alphabetically by name of state, the book contains brief biographical data on governors of states and territories, including date of birth, birthplace, residence, occupation, party affiliation, date and age at death, and date and age on assuming office. A second set of tables for each state includes election statistics by party for all gubernatorial elections. Rather than relying heavily upon state manuals, Glashan has compiled the data from a wide variety of standard primary and secondary sources; an extensive bibliography lists both general works and references for each state.

An additional feature of the book is the inclusion of excerpts from the speeches and writings of the governors. The quotations are interspersed with the tables and identified in a separate listing of sources. Unfortunately, there is no author or subject index to the material, so that what might have proved a useful addition seems instead an afterthought.

This book is the only one-volume reference work on the subject. It updates Gately's *Register of the Governors of the States of the United States of America*, covering the period 1776-1974, and Solomon's *The Governors of the States* covering the period 1900-1974. An alternative source is Kallenbach and Kallenbach, *American State Governors 1776-1976*. The Kallenbachs' book is a three-volume set that includes election statistics and biographical sketches, although the latter are in narrative rather than tabular format. [R: RQ, Summer 80, p. 387; WLB, Apr 80, p. 523]

Jane A. Benson

603.   Holli, Melvin G., and Peter d'A. Jones, eds. **Biographical Dictionary of American Mayors, 1820-1980: Big City Mayors**. Westport, Conn., Greenwood Press, 1981. 576p. index. $69.50. LC 80-1796. ISBN 0-313-21134-5.

This directory provides brief biographies of all mayors of fifteen representative large American cities from 1820, or from the very beginnings when the office assumed a modern shape in that city, until 1980. The following cities, with starting date, which represent all regions of the country, are covered: Baltimore (1808), Boston (1822), Buffalo (1832), Chicago (1837), Cincinnati (1815), Cleveland (1836), Detroit (1824),

Los Angeles (1850), Milwaukee (1846), New Orleans (1812), New York (1833), Philadelphia (1832), Pittsburgh (1816), San Francisco (1846), and Saint Louis (1823).

The biographies of 647 American mayors were prepared by over one hundred scholars of American urban history, mostly professors from nearby universities who worked mainly with original sources in local city archives. Arranged alphabetically, each entry includes a list of major sources consulted and the name of the researcher. This comprehensive directory of all mayors includes many influential politicans not covered in other biographical directories; the researchers even uncovered some mayors not listed in official compilations. The twelve very useful appendixes include a chronological list of mayors by city; mayors by political party, ethnic background, religious affiliation, and place of birth; and statistical tables with selected data by decennial census on population, rank, and increase or decrease between censuses. [R: BL, 15 Dec 82, pp. 580-81; C&RL, July 82, p. 333; RQ, Summer 82, pp. 412-13; WLB, May 82, p. 699]   LeRoy C. Schwarzkopf

604. Kallenbach, Joseph E., and Jessamine S. Kallenbach. **American State Governors, 1776-1976**. Dobbs Ferry, N.Y., Oceana, 1977-1982. 3v. $135.00/set. LC 76-51519. ISBN 0-379-00665-0.

Reference sources that provide brief factual information on the states, from the beginning of statehood to the present, perform a useful function. They lessen the need to search state bluebooks, constitutions, histories, and a variety of other sources for a listing of governors and the practices used for selecting them. *American State Governors* describes on a state-by-state basis the constitutional provisions regarding the governorship ("mode of choice," "term and reeligibility," "time of election," "beginning of term," "qualifications" for the position, "removal" procedures, and "succession arrangements"). For each state, the governors are listed and their political party and dates of term are given. If a term was less than that legally specified, the fact has been noted and an explanation given. The sources from which the information was taken have been identified; these are official state publications, primarily state bluebooks. The reference value of this publication would have been enhanced by the inclusion of an index to governors and of a table showing similarities and dissimilarities among the states as to length of term, etc. In spite of minor weaknesses, however, this publication offers a valuable collection of data and is well researched. [R: BL, 15 Nov 78, p. 568; Choice, Sept 77, p. 833; RQ, Spring 78, p. 274]   Peter Hernon

605. Papenfuse, Edward C., and others. **A Biographical Dictionary of the Maryland Legislature, 1635-1789**. Baltimore, Md., Johns Hopkins University Press, 1979, 1985. 2v. (Studies in Marland History and Culture). $29.50 (vol. 1); $35.00 (vol. 2). LC 78-18042. ISBN 0-8018-1995-4 (vol. 1); 0-8108-3265-9 (vol. 2).

Certain information is expected from any biographical dictionary: birth and death dates, family background, marriage, children, education, military service, religion, and public and private careers. In this dictionary the information is more structured than in most. All the elements listed above are labeled in boldface or capitals for all biographees (as appropriate). For Arthur Turner (1622-1667), for example, we have Born, Immigrated, Married, Children, Private Career, Education, Religious Affiliation, Occupational Profile, Public Career, Legislative Service. Particulars about Turner follow each heading. This is not all, however. One of the purposes of this dictionary is to present the characteristics of these early legislators in such a way that they may be compared and analyzed. One such characteristic is that of family ties among legislators.

These connections, rather frequent in fact, are extensively reported for each biographee. Another characteristic is that of wealth: how much land, how many slaves, how much other property each man owned at various stages of his life. With these and the other elements mentioned earlier, the reader gets a sharp picture of the class of men who served in the Maryland legislature during its first 150 years.

The editors do not provide sources for their data in this work, but documentation is available at the Maryland Hall of Records in Annapolis. The work includes maps and lists of all legislators in each house for each session, 1635-1789. Historians, looking more and more at social and family history in their research, will find this attractive work a most fruitful source. The publication of its second volume completes this remarkable work. Eric R. Nitschke

606. **Profiles of Black Mayors in America**. Compiled and edited by the Joint Center for Political Studies, Jeanne J. Fox, associate director of research. Washington, D.C., Joint Center for Political Studies; Chicago, Johnson Publishing, 1977. 247p. illus. index. $10.00pa. LC 76-40949. ISBN 0-87485-082-7.

This volume consists of three major sections: "The Black Mayor," "Profiles of Black Mayors," and "Appendices and Statistical References." Part 1 provides a historical survey of both black political involvement and black mayors; it includes several statistical tables on communities that have had black mayors from the period of Reconstruction to the present. Part 2 contains individual profiles and is arranged by state and then by name of the mayor. Each profile supplies the name, population, and date of incorporation of the community; date of election, length of term, and method of election (popular, commission, etc.) of the mayor; and a short narrative, similar to the typical Who's Who entry, of each of the mayors cited. A total of 178 mayors are listed, 10 of whom are women. Black-and-white photographs are provided for 139. A second section in part 2 lists 28 mayors not included in the main profile section because of a lack of information; most held office either prior to 1900 or for a relatively short period. Several tables and charts (e.g., "Cities with Black Mayors Ranked by Population," "Majority White Communities with Black Mayors and Method of Election," etc.) make up part 3. The index is not very satisfactory; page numbers are incorrect for many entries, and other information is often misrepresented. Many other reference sources provide material concerning well-known mayors; however, for the mayors listed, this is the best source of information. [R: BL, 1 Sept 78, pp. 80-81]
G. Edward Evans

607. Raimo, John W. **Biographical Directory of American Colonial and Revolutionary Governors, 1607-1789**. Westport, Conn., Meckler Books/Microform Review, 1980. 521p. maps. index. $75.00. LC 80-13279. ISBN 0-930466-07-1.

The format of *Biographical Directory of American Colonial and Revolutionary Governors, 1607-1789* makes the volume accessible to both students and the lay reader. The colonies are presented in alphabetical order, while the biographies within a colony appear chronologically. A chronological listing of each colony's governors is given, but page numbers are not included. The index, therefore, is the only key to the location of the material. A general bibliography of pertinent works appears at the beginning of each colony, while a concise bibliography follows each entry. The entries provide dates of birth and death, place of birth, names of parents, family, religion, political and private careers, and some accomplishments in office. However, if a governor served in more than one colony (e.g., Sir Edmund Andros – nine colonies), the identifical information is published for each colony. It would have been more beneficial to the user if pertinent achievements in each colony had been given rather than redundant material.

The term "governor" is interpreted to include "anyone who held effective executive power in those British colonies which in 1776 became the first thirteen states." Thus, the volume contains the lives and careers of approximately four hundred individuals who met this criterion. Of these men, roughly 50 percent are not represented in either the *Dictionary of American Biography* (*DAB*) or the *Dictionary of National Biography* (*DNB*). For those who are listed in the *DAB* and *DNB*, considerable new information has been added by the discovery of additional genealogical and historical data. This could account for the differences in length of the biographies; some contain more information than others. Nevertheless, any college or university library whose faculty or students do research in American history should obtain this volume. In addition, large public libraries would do well to add this to their collections of reference works. [R: BL, 15 Apr 81, p. 1168; Choice, Dec 80, p. 510; LJ, 15 Sept 80,. p. 1849]

Irene Wood Bell

608.   Sobel, Robert, and John Raimo, eds. **Biographical Directory of the Governors of the United States 1789-1978**. Westport, Conn., Meckler Books/Microform Review, 1978. 4v. index. $225.00. LC 77-10435. ISBN 0-930466-00-4.

Although the format in each biography here begins in typical Who's Who fashion, the political summaries are presented in narrative form rather than as abbreviated information. This might seem to increase its utility, except that the narratives provide not only facts but interpretation; thus, separating the two would be essential for the scholar. Some two thousand governors are listed, first under state name, then chronologically by term within each state. Incumbents at time of publication are included, even though a full summary is obviously not possible. Sketches include information as to parentage, place of birth, religion, marriage and family, education, general career (jobs before politics as well as in that area), electoral results, a summary of political achievements or efforts, date of death, and bibliographical data (including the location of pertinent collections of primary source material). The sketches usually were written by a state or local historian, by a librarian, or by a professor of history. Sources include state archives, biographies, accounts in newspapers and magazines, theses and dissertations, items held by state historical societies, and standard state directories and histories. The source cited most often is Roy Glashan's *American Governors and Gubernatorial Elections, 1775-1975* (1975), but even it doesn't appear to have been used consistently by contributors. Entries are unsigned, and the list of contributors fails to identify who wrote precisely which sketches. Colonial governors are covered in a separate volume, *Biographical Directory of American Colonial and Revolutionary Governors, 1607-1789*, (1980).

Given the fact that the narratives do become interpretive rather than simply reportorial, it would be wise to supplement this work with other material. First would be *Dictionary of American Biography* and *Who Was Who in America*, at least for the most outstanding figures. James Gately's *Register of the Governors of the States of the United States of America, 1776-1974* provides a chronological listing.

Students will *not* be able to obtain a thorough understanding of the political climate and trends within any given state by reading these biographies. Certainly, the tendency of governors of Colorado (and of other states) to be elected and serve, then to spend time out of office, then to be re-elected, makes for confusion when reading the articles in strict entry order. (And following the cross-references in such cases — only the name is listed for any term after the first — confuses as well because of the dense nature of the articles.) The only index is of governors' names, and it fails to identify even party affiliation, giving only state, volume number in the set, and page number for the sketch of which that person is the subject. Thus, for all of this set's bulk, and for $225.00, a purchaser would get the most use from this set in its coverage of obscure personages — or at least a place to start. But in and of itself, this is not the standard work that the publisher would have us believe it to be. [R: Choice, Dec 78, p. 1344; LJ, 1 Oct 78, p. 1968; WLB, Oct 78, p. 189]   Koert C. Loomis, Jr.

OTHER COUNTRIES AND REGIONS

Canada

609.   Ondaatje, Christopher, and Donald Swainson, eds. **The Prime Ministers of Canada 1867-1968**. Toronto, Pagurian Press; distr., Brattleboro, Vt., Stephen Greene Press, 1970 (c1968). 191p. illus. bibliog. index. $7.95.

Brief, interestingly written personal biographies of the fifteen men who have been prime minister of Canada. The biographies average about eight pages in length. The level of writing would make the book most useful at the upper elementary or secondary school level. An index, a brief selected bibliography, and pencil-sketched portraits of the prime ministers are included.

A related title is Gwynneth Evans's compilation, *Women in Federal Politics: A Bio-bibliography/Les Femmes au Fédéral: Une Bio-bibliographie* (edited by Marion C. Wilson. Ottawa, National Library of Canada, 1975). Now out-of-print, this bilingual book contains biobibliographical sketches of forty-one women who served in the Canadian Parliament from 1920-1974. [R: LJ, 1 Feb 71, p. 466]

Ralph M. Edwards

China

610.   Bartke, Wolfgang, and Peter Schier. **China's New Party Leadership: Biographies and Analysis of the Twelfth Central Committee of the Chinese Communist Party**. Armonk, N.Y., M. E. Sharpe, 1985. 289p. illus. (A Publication of the Institute of Asian Affairs in Hamburg). $50.00. LC 84-14130. ISBN 0-87332-291-9.

The Twelfth National Congress of the Chinese Communist Party in China, which took place in Beijing 1-11 September 1982, demonstrated the decisive victory of the Deng Xiaoping faction over its Maoist opponents within the party. Nearly 1,600 delegates from among the 39-million party members elected 210 members and 138 alternates to the Twelfth Central Committee. With few exceptions, the Central Committee members represented the political, military, and economic top leadership of the People's Republic of China. A clear majority belong to the anti-Maoist coalition led by Deng. Immediately following the Congress, the Twelfth Central Committee elected the actual leadership of the party, the Politboro, which included only four members of the Maoist faction among its twenty-eight members (including alternates).

Divided into three parts, this valuable reference work provides detailed and up-to-date biographical information about each of the 210 full- and 138-alternate members of the Central Committee as well as the authors' analyses of and insights into the political background and power structure prior to and during the Twelfth National Congress.

The ten chapters in part 1 serve as an introduction to the Twelfth National Congress of the Chinese Communist Party and the new party leadership. The biographies given in part 2, some with personal photographs, are current to September 1983. The third part provides various diagrams and tables of the party, state, and military leadership of China as of 1 January 1984.

With its focus on the party, this one-volume work complements Wolfgang Bartke's *Who's Who in the People's Republic of China*. It is a very important reference source for information on the current top political leaders of China.

Hwa-Wei Lee

611. **Biographical Dictionary of Chinese Communism, 1921-1965**. Donald W. Klein and Anne B. Clark, eds. Cambridge, Mass., Harvard University Press, 1971. 2v. $65.00. LC 69-12725. ISBN 0-674-07410-6.

Taking into consideration the political realities of these times, this biographical directory with a selected listing of 433 biographical sketches of prominent leaders of the People's Republic of China will probably be one of the most popular reference books. Biographical sketches vary in length, depending on the relative importance of a given individual and, as one can expect, the availability of information. Appended to the biographical sketches is a list of sources used, occasionally even interviews, but primarily secondary sources—books and articles in many languages including Russian. There is also a selected bibliography and a glossary-name index, which lists 1,750 persons found in the text. The many appendixes show that all information gathered in this work is current to 1965. Thus, the events of the Cultural Revolution are not included. Perhaps there will be a supplement to update some of the information.

This is truly a work of significant proportion—the first such undertaking in the West. In comparison to the monumental *Biographical Dictionary of Republican China*, this work is obviously not as detailed and its biographical sketches often lack the wealth of documentation provided by its counterpart on Republican China. But again, at this point in our study of Chinese Communism, it might be impossible to prepare such a work, with so much information simply not available. In the meantime this is by far the best biographical source on this important subject.

Not as elaborate, Robert Elegant's *China's Red Masters: Political Biographies of the Chinese Communist Leaders* (New York, Twayne, 1951; repr., Westport, Conn., Greenwood Press, 1971) contains informal biographical information on twelve Chinese Communist leaders and includes a four-page bibliography. [R: Choice, Nov 71, p. 1162; LJ, 15 June 71, p. 2071]

Bohdan S. Wynar

Europe

612. Central Services European Consortium for Political Research, University of Essex, comp. and ed. **Directory of European Political Scientists**. 4th fully rev. ed. Munich, New York, Hans Zell/K. G. Saur, 1985. 627p. index. $75.00. ISBN 3-598-10317-0.

Greatly expanded from the previous edition, the *Directory* contains twenty-five hundred biographical entries for political scientists of European origin (or those non-Europeans who are primarily employed in Europe). The entries are arranged alphabetically and are numbered consecutively to facilitate indexing. The publisher's claim that this is a "fully revised edition" is not entirely correct, however. Some entries (especially for well-known individuals like Karl Deutsch and Jean Lacouture) have simply been repeated from the third edition if the latest questionnaire was not returned. These entries are indicated by an asterisk after the name.

The entries are fairly brief and contain standardized data: birth date, nationality, address, degrees, doctoral thesis, appointments, publication (limited to eight), research areas, and fields of interest. For a general American audience, few names of those included here will be familiar. Among those that do stand out, most are British: Richard Rose, Bernard Crick, David Butler, Peter Reddaway. Others include Michel Crozier, Jean Blondel, Maximilien Rubel, Giovanni Sartori, and Herbert J. Spiro (an American who is currently teaching in Berlin). There are, of course, omissions; two names that this reviewer looked for in vain were Wolfgang Leonhard and Mihaly Vajda. Also, some historians who dabble in political matters (such as E. P. Thompson) are not included.

The index to this directory is extremely useful. It contains thirty-three broad subject fields, each with long listings of entry numbers. Many of the broad fields (e.g., "International Relations," "Policy Analysis," "Area Politics") are divided into several more specific sections. For instance, field number 27, "Political Theory," is divided into ten sub-fields—among them are "Marxism and Socialism," "Eurocommunism," "Ideology," and "Classical Political Thought." Unfortunately, there is no geographic index to the individuals, so one cannot readily identify, say, all of the Greek political scientists who are included.

The *Directory* is most suitable for large research libraries where the writings of European scholars are likely to be collected. One bright note: although this new edition contains nearly two hundred additional pages, the price has not increased since 1979!

Thomas A. Karel

613. Who's Who in European Institutions and Organizations. Edited by Karl Strute and Theodor Doelken. Zurich, Who's Who AG; distr., Chicago, Marquis Who's Who, 1982. 1088p. index. (International Red Series). $75.00. ISBN 3-921220-42-4; ISSN 0722-916X.

This volume presents capsule biographies of more than four thousand persons active in various European organizations, such as the European Economic Community, as well as Europeans active in certain other international organizations, such as the United Nations and European Free Trade Association. In some areas it even extends beyond these already generous borders to include crowned heads of Europe, heads of state, and other prominent ministers. The biographies are quite short, including only the most basic information, e.g., date of birth, nationality, and education, together with, naturally, position in a European organization. The information seems quite current and, as far as it could be checked since there is no other volume that covers quite the same territory, accurate. Less useful for many librarians will be the descriptions of the various organizations involved, although bringing together information published in various other sources does have its merits. Most helpful will be the "Special Register," which is a classified list of other international and European institutions, organizations, and associations that includes, in most cases, only their addresses. As a one-volume introduction to European organizations and personnel this will be a useful acquisition for many libraries, although those needing biographical information will benefit most, for information about these officials can be difficult to find in other sources. [R: Choice, July/Aug 83, pp. 1579-80; WLB, June 83, pp. 886-95]

Erwin K. Welsch

Germany

614. **Who's Who in German Politics: A Biographical Guide to 4,500 Politicans in the Federal Republic of Germany**. Compiled by Karl-Otto Saur. Munich, Verlag Dokumentation; distr., New York, R. R. Bowker, 1971. 342p. o.p. ISBN 3-7940-3219-5.

This German-language biographical directory of West German political leaders will assist in piecing together the political mosaic of this pivotal European nation. Biographical information about politicans at various levels is presented, including ministers and state secretaries of the federal and state governments, members of the Bundestag and the Landtage, or state parliaments, members of various representative bodies of West Berlin, mayors and city directors of cities over fifty thousand population, state council members, and all county directors. The information, which includes political affiliation, education, past and present political posts, and publications, was obtained from questionnaires sent to the individual political leaders. A list of members of the Bundestag and the various Landtage is provided. In future editions, it would be useful to designate the party affiliation of each member appearing in these lists and to indicate the numerical strengths of the parties represented. The bilingual list of abbreviations used and the English table of contents and preface increase the work's effectiveness. The biographical descriptions, such as that for Walter Hallstein, are not as extensive as those found in *International Who's Who*. Nevertheless, this volume does provide worthwhile current information similar to that found in *Wer Ist Wer*, concerning political leaders of various governmental levels in West Germany. [R: Choice, Sept 72, p. 795; LJ, 1 May 72, p. 1697; RQ, Summer 72, p. 390]

Don D. Insko

Great Britain and Commonwealth

615. Hellicar, Eileen. **Prime Ministers of Britain**. North Pomfret, Vt., David and Charles, 1978. 159p. illus. index. $7.50. LC 77-85014. ISBN 0-7153-7486-9.

The author has succeeded in her intention to compile a readable survey of the lives of the prime ministers that might serve as a "shortcut" for students. Libraries above the high-school level need not add this work to their reference collections, however, because the biographies are so brief that they will answer few of the questions likely to be asked about any prime minister. Where Hellicar provides three pages on William Pitt the Younger, for example, the *Dictionary of National Biography* (*DNB*) has twenty-eight; Herbert Van Thall's *Prime Ministers from Sir Robert Walpole to Edward Heath*, twenty pages; and *Who's Who in History*, eleven pages. The *DNB*, which lacks biographies of eight of forty-eight prime ministers, may be supplemented with John Mackintosh, *British Prime Ministers in the Twentieth Century*, which is complete through Callaghan. Although Hellicar claims that her work was intended to lead students on to further reading, she provides no bibliography, in contrast to the other works cited. [R: BL, 1 July 78, p. 1672; LJ, July 78, p. 1396]   Elliot Palais

616. **Who's Who of British Members of Parliament**. Michael Stenton, ed. Sussex, England, Harvester Press; distr., Atlantic Heights, N.J., Humanities Press, 1971-1981. 4v. $52.00/vol. 1. $60.00/vol. 2. $86.50/vol. 3. $84.00/vol. 4.

The purpose of this set is to provide biographical information on all members of the House of Commons from 1832 to 1975. The biographical information is based on *Dod's Parliamentary Companion*, which began publication in 1932 and provides contemporary information on members of Parliament (MPs). Since many individuals appeared in *Dod's* for a number of years, the editor for this set has taken the fullest entry from *Dod's*, adding to it material such as the reason for leaving the House of Commons, important events of the individual's subsequent career, and death date. Entries are arranged alphabetically by last name. The first volume covers MPs who ended their parliamentary careers before 1885 (with a few notable exceptions, such as Gladstone, who is listed in volume II as well as in this volume). The second volume covers the years 1886 to 1918, the third up to 1945 and the fourth from 1946 to 1979.

Since *Dod's* is not readily available, this source is particularly useful. The biographies are fascinating, including as they do such interesting features as stances taken on political issues of the day. There is not much overlap between this source and other existing major British biographical sources. [R: BL, 15 Sept 77, p. 238; Choice, June 77, p. 516; LJ, 1 May 77, p. 1005]   Mary Reichel

Latin America

617.   Corke, Bettina, ed. **Who Is Who in Government and Politics in Latin America. Quien es Quien en la Political y los Gobiernos de America Latina**. New York, Decade Media Books, 1984. 509p. index. $65.00. LC 84-070526. ISBN 0-91365-02-4.

This is the first "Who's Who in Latin America" since 1945 and the first to deal specifically with government and politics. The editors' objective was to provide biographical information on individuals in government and politics who had gained prominence on a national or regional level. They include more than one thousand entries drawn from twenty-three countries with Argentina having the most entries (eighty-five), followed by Mexico (seventy-two) and Brazil (seventy-one). Bilingual English/Spanish entries are arranged alphabetically, first by country and then within each country. The majority of entries were compiled from questionnaires filled out by the biographees themselves, with supplemental information added from secondary sources.

Although this is certainly a laudable undertaking, random checks of some of the largest countries suggest that the desire to include a representative sample has not been entirely met. Of eighty-five entries for Argentina, more than thirty-eight individuals listed were either economists or bankers. There was no entry for the vice president and not a single entry for any of the nine members of the president's cabinet. For Brazil, only eight of twenty-two cabinet members are included and none of the twenty-one governors warranted an entry. Similar patterns were found in checking entries for other countries.

Another criticism concerns the length of the various entries; it seems to bear no relationship to the importance (political) of the individual. While some entries for academics consume more than half a page, entries for presidents are sometimes as short as four lines thus providing little if any useful information. For future editions the editors might set as a minimum goal the inclusion of the president and vice president of each country along with important members of the cabinet, the president of the chamber or senate, important governors, mayors of major cities, prominent leaders of the opposition, editors of the major presses, and prominent church leaders. In conclusion, although this is an ambitious undertaking, the objectives set by the editors themselves were not entirely met in this first edition. Librarians might prefer to await future revised editions.

A related title is Glen Taplin's *Middle American Governors* (Metuchen, N.J., Scarecrow, 1972) which, in outline form, lists those who have governed in Panama, Mexico, Guatemala, El Salvador, British Honduras, Honduras, Nicaragua, and Costa Rica. Also listed are Spanish monarchs from 1492 to 1814. It is written in chronological order, under each country, providing a historical guide to the countries. Unfortunately this work is now out-of-print. Brian E. Coutts and Bohdan S. Wynar

Soviet Union

618. **Biographical Dictionary of Dissidents in the Soviet Union, 1956-1975**. S. P. de Boer, E. J. Driessen, and H. L. Verhaar, comps. and eds. Boston, Martinus Nijhoff, 1982. 679p. bibliog. $165.00. LC 81-22433. ISBN 90-247-2538-0.

Unlike other biographical dictionaries, this unique biographical source includes biographies only of unofficial, oppositionist Soviet citizens of various social backgrounds and nationalities. The dictionary is the result of a project started in 1975 at the Institute of Eastern European Studies of the University of Amsterdam, and it is dedicated to Sergej Dedjulin, Leningrad biographer of the dissident movement in the Soviet Union, whose files were confiscated by the KGB in 1979. Many sources were used in this compilation, including such well-known documents as the thirty-volume *Sobranie dokumentov samizdata*, published in Munich by Radio Liberty, and thirty-eight issues of *Khronika tekuščikh sobytij*. This well-edited work will complement such standard sources as *Who's Who in the Socialist Countries: A Biographical Encyclopedia of 10,000 Leading Personalities in 16 Communist Countries* (Verlag Dokumentation, 1978) and should be recommended as a priority purchase to all larger libraries.

Bohdan S. Wynar

619. **Party and Government Officials of the Soviet Union 1917-1967**. Compiled by the Institute for the Study of the USSR. Metuchen, N.J., Scarecrow, 1969. 214p. o.p. LC 71-5797. SBN 8108-0285-6.

Essentially a register of names that will supplement *Prominent Personalities in the USSR. A Biographic Directory* (Scarecrow, 1968) with annual *Supplements* (1968 and 1969). Chapter 1, Party Officials, begins its coverage in 1898 with the founding of the Russian Social Democratic Workers Party. Names of attending officials, meeting dates and highlights of each of the chronologically arranged Congresses and Conferences are presented. Chapter 2, Government Officials, lists heads of state, heads of the government, and officials of the various departments and offices, with dates of tenure in office. Bohdan S. Wynar

20 Religion

Introduction

This chapter contains sections on "General Works" (current and retrospective biographical dictionaries), "Bible Studies," and "Saints," with a total of eighteen entries and many more titles mentioned in the annotations. Among the titles discussed we should mention the well-known *Who's Who in Religion* (see entry 623) and *American Catholic Who's Who* (see entry 620) for current coverage, as well as *Dictionary of American Religious Biography* (see entry 625) and the more specialized *Dictionary of American Catholic Biography* (see entry 626) for retrospective coverage. There are a few older biographical dictionaries, e.g., W. B. Sprague's nine-volume *Annals of the American Pulpit; or Commemorative Notices of Distinguished American Clergymen of Various Denominations, from the Early Settlement of the Country to the Close of the Year 1855* (New York, R. Carter, 1857-1869), which covers most denominations in biographical sketches of two or three pages per biographee.

In addition, many religious dictionaries and encyclopedias contain biographical information. Of the more recent works one should mention *Abingdon Dictionary of Living Religions*, edited by K. Crim (Abingdon, 1981. 830p.), which has a large number of biographical articles complementing an older work of S. G. F. Brandon's, *Dictionary of Comparative Religion* (Scribner's, 1970. 704p.). Both dictionaries are more scholarly than the recent *The Facts on File Dictionary of Religions*, edited by J. R. Hinnells (Facts on File, 1984. 550p.), which tries to cover all of the world's religions in 550 pages, including some biographies. *World Christian Encyclopedia: A Comparative Study of Churches and Religions in the Modern World, A.D. 1900-2000*, edited by D. B. Barrett (Oxford University Press, 1982. 1010p.), is an uneven work but contains a small Who's Who section covering 480 prominent figures. A much better work is *The Oxford Dictionary of the Christian Church*, edited by F. L. Cross and E. A. Livingstone (2nd ed. Oxford University Press, 1974. 1518p.), first published in 1957 with six thousand entries ranging from just a few lines to about twenty-five hundred words. Many biographical entries are included.

A number of religious dictionaries and encyclopedias concentrate primarily on one denomination, are written from a somewhat parochial point of view, or specialize in one particular area. A few examples of such works should be mentioned here. *The Westminster Dictionary of Church History*, edited by J. C. Brauer (Westminster Press, 1971. 887p.), is generally an excellent work emphasizing the modern period, with a relatively small number of Roman Catholic contributors. Another is *The Brethren Encyclopedia*, edited by D. F. Durnbaugh (3v. Brethren Encyclopedia, 1983-1984), which presents information on churches that trace their origins to the German Baptist Brethren (1708-). The first two volumes consist of alphabetically arranged articles about significant Brethren, deceased or past usual retirement age. *The Catholic Encyclopedia*, edited by R. C. Broderick (Thomas Nelson, 1976. 612p.), is written from the Catholic point of view and includes some four thousand entries, including notable theologians. The *New Catholic Encyclopedia: An International Work of Reference on the Teachings, History, Organization, and Activities of the Catholic Church and on All Institutions, Religions, Philosophies, and Scientific and Cultural Developments Affecting the Catholic Church from Its Beginning to the Present*, prepared by the editorial staff at the Catholic University of America (15v. McGraw-Hill, 1967. *Supplement XVI*, 1974. 520p. and *Supplement XVII*, 1979. 812p.), is the most comprehensive Catholic work, containing some seventeen thousand articles with many biographies. The *Evangelical Dictionary of Theology*, edited by W. A. Elwell (Baker Book House, 1984. 1204p.), has a total of twelve hundred entries, many of them biographical. A more concise work is *The Westminster Dictionary of Christian Spirituality* (Westminster Press, 1983. 400p.), containing 354 articles on this subject with numerous biographies. There are a number of dictionaries that cover non-Christian religions and most of them provide biographical entries. Examples of such works are *Dictionary of Non-Christian Religions*, edited by G. Parrinder (Westminster Press, 1973. 320p.), *Harper's Dictionary of Hinduism: Its Mythology, Folklore, Philosophy, Literature and History* (Harper & Row, 1977. 372p.), etc.

There are, of course, a number of older dictionaries and encyclopedias that can be consulted for retrospective information. One of the best known is *Schaff-Herzog Encyclopedia*, edited by S. M. Jackson (12v. and index. Funk and Wagnalls, 1908-1912), based on the third edition of the twenty-four-volume *Realencyklopädie für protestantische Theologie und Kirche* (3 Auf. Leipzig, Hinrichs, 1896-1913), founded by J. J. Herzog, a classical German work written from the Protestant point of view. A new comprehensive work intended as a continuation of the *Realencyklopädie* is the *Theologische Realenzyklopädie* (Berlin, Walter de Gruyter, 1976- . In progress), with eight volumes published and twenty-five volumes projected. It offers a well-balanced interpretation of theology, not necessarily only from the viewpoint of Protestant churches. Another German work is *Die Religion in Geschichte und Gegenwart: Handwörterbuch für Theologie und Religionswissenschaft* (3rd ed. Tübingen, Mohr, 1957-1965), written from the Protestant viewpoint. The Roman Catholic point of view is represented by *Lexikon für Theologie und Kirche*, edited by J. Höfer and K. Rahner (10v. 2nd ed. Freiburg, Herder, 1957-1965. *Ergänzungsband*, 3v. Teil 1-3. Herder, 1966-1968). One of the most comprehensive French works is A. Baudrillart's *Dictionnaire d'histoire et de géographie ecclésiastiques. . .* (Paris, Letouzey, 1912- . In progress) with some twenty volumes published. It covers all subjects from the point of view of the Catholic church, from the beginning of Christianity to the present time. Biographical articles are also included, covering all of the major and some minor figures in the Catholic church.

Unfortunately there is no bibliographic guide that covers all aspects of religion. One should consult Sheehy and Walford for specialized guides, e.g., J. P. McCabe's *Critical Guide to Catholic Reference Books* (2nd ed. Libraries Unlimited, 1980. 282p.). J. R. Kennedy's *Library Research Guide to Religion and Theology: Illustrated Search Strategy and Sources* (Pierian Press, 1974. 53p.) is intended for undergraduate students but offers some information on existing indexing and abstracting services.

GENERAL WORKS

Current Biographies

620.   **American Catholic Who's Who.** Washington, D.C., U.S. Catholic Conference, 1982. 1v. $24.95. ISBN 0-686-11131-1.

This annual was first published in 1911 as a monograph and since 1935 was issued on an annual basis and later on a biennial basis. Starting with 1980 it substantially increased its coverage and at the present time provides more than six thousand brief biographical sketches of archbishops, bishops, priests and many lay persons involved in church affairs in leadership positions. It includes a list by diocese of members of the National Council of Catholic Bishops, geographical index, necrology, and occasional essays on recent canonizations. Beginning with the 1981 volume the coverage includes Canada.

Similar, but not as comprehensive, works are available for other denominations. A few examples: *Who's Who among Free Will Baptists* (Randall House, 1978. $24.95. ISBN 0-89265-052-4) provides good coverage of this denomination and S. Bacote's *Who's Who among the Colored Baptists of the United States* (Philadelphia, Ayer Co., 1980. 307p. $28.50. LC 79-52588. ISBN 0-405-12455-4) is a reprint of the 1913 edition providing historical coverage of blacks. A better work on this subject is *Biographical Directory of Negro Ministers*, 3rd edition by Ethel L. Williams (G. K. Hall, 1975. 854p.). Although now out-of-print it provides information on over two thousand black clergymen alive in the United States in 1975 that was unavailable from any other source at that time.   Bohdan S. Wynar

621.   Beebe, Tom. **Who's Who in New Thought: Biographical Dictionary of New Thought—Personnel, Centers, and Authors' Publications**. Lakemont, Ga., CSA Press, 1977. 318p. bibliog. o.p. LC 76-4718. ISBN 0-87707-189-6.

"New Thought," with roots in New England transcendentalism, dates from the time of Phineas P. Quimby, who flourished in Maine in the middle of the last century. The thrust of New Thought appears to be mental "healing" and a positive, hopeful approach to life's problems. Unlike Christian Science, whose origins it shares, it does not deny the existence of evil and sickness and many New Thought believers are also members of traditional Protestant denominations.

In the title under review, coverage is limited to ministers, practitioners, and other officials in New Thought's four modern major divisions: United Church of Religious Science, Religious Science International, Unity Churches, and Divine Science Churches. Also considered are people in independent organizations with obvious New Thought sympathies, and a few historical characters who espoused New Thought teachings—such as Mary Baker Eddy and Emanuel Swendenborg, even though these are the springs of separate ecclesiastical movements.

In addition to biographical sketches, the work contains an international directory of New Thought churches and centers, a bibliography of some New Thought authors, and a list of New Thought schools and colleges. Though well intentioned and filling a gap in religious biographical and directory material, this *Who's Who* is seriously flawed by poor editing, uneven use of source material, and the avoidance of consistent formats for the bibliographical and biographical material. Nevertheless, collections requiring thorough coverage of personalities and organizations in religion will need to have this title. The coverage of New Thought in available, standard directories is poor to non-existent.   Joseph McDonald

622. **A Biographical Directory of Clergymen of the American Lutheran Church.** Edited by Arnold R. Mickelson and Robert C. Wiederaenders. Minneapolis, Augsburg, 1972. 1054p. illus. o.p. LC 72-80314. ISBN 0-8066-9293-6.

This pictorial directory is the second biographical directory published by the American Lutheran Church. The first was issued in 1962, and another is projected. The directory includes for each clergyman a small photograph, full name, date and source (church body) of ordination, date and place of birth, names of parents, immigration/naturalization year (where applicable), name of wife and year of marriage, education, honorary degrees, selected published works, offices held, church/denominational service, and (again where applicable) date of retirement. Six entries are given per page, the typography is pleasing, and the photographic reproductions are of exceptionally high and uniform quality. A separate section (one page at the beginning) provides similar information regarding the general officers of the ALC, and a ten-year listing of "Removals from the ALC Clergy Roster" appears at the back of the volume.

Glenn R. Wittig

623. **Who's Who in Religion.** 3rd ed. Chicago, Marquis Who's Who, 1985. 439p. $99.50. LC 76-25357. ISBN 0-8379-1603-8.

The lack of a current biographical dictionary of religious leaders in America has frequently been a source of regret for reference librarians. Not since the early 1940s has there been a general Who's Who approach to the clergy of all denominations as well as to lay persons and teachers. *Who's Who in Religion*, Marquis's third edition, ought to find a ready response from American librarians.

Despite its title, the present work is limited to religious leaders now active in the United States. The some seven thousand biographies are distributed over the following categories: church officials, both national and regional, clerical and lay; clergy—leading priests, rabbis, and ministers; professors of religion, theology, or divinity in seminaries and universities; and lay leaders.

In a field where for so many years there has been literally nothing, the Marquis volume is most welcome.   Bohdan S. Wynar

Retrospective Biographies

624. Barker, William P. **Who's Who in Church History.** Grand Rapids, Mich., Baker Book House, 1977. 319p. o.p. LC 74-85306. ISBN 0-8010-0705-4.

This popular reference work offers the biographies of more than fifteen hundred men and women—educators and theologians, priests and nuns, kings and popes, missionaries and preachers, martyrs and mystics, writers and musicians, doctors and scientists, even a clockmaker—all of whom left an imprint on the history of the church.

Each entry provides a biographical sketch along with a summary of how and why the person achieved prominence in the church. Inclusion in this book was based on three requirements: persons who thought of themselves as part of the Christian community, persons who had some effect on the ministry of the church, and persons no longer living. This type of inclusion, however, excluded those of other faiths and millions of valiant Christians who lived obscure lives. Some persons included are not conventional or orthodox churchmen nor persons who furthered Christ's ministry. With all the exclusions, however, the book serves as a good tool for historical purposes and provides a concise reference tool recommended in libraries for the churchman and layman.

Ina J. Weis

625.   Bowden, Henry Warner. **Dictionary of American Religious Biography**. Westport, Conn., Greenwood Press, 1977. 572p. index. $45.00. LC 76-5258. ISBN 0-8371-8906-3.

With a text of no more than 540 pages, this dictionary contains no fewer than 425 biographies. Representing all denominations significant in some four hundred years of American religious history, biographies cover Indians, blacks, Asians, laymen, women, theists, free-thinkers, and cultists. Henry Bowden is associate professor of religion at Douglass College, Rutgers University. He stresses the pluralism of America's past and suggests that "in the latter part of the twentieth century, we are slowly realizing that Protestant Christianity, controlled by ordained white clergymen, never enjoyed exclusive rights over American citizens with religious interests."

Each biography has about four hundred words (one to one-and-a-half pages). Each has a select bibliography that gives citations to nine standard reference works and contains no more than six works by, and five biographies about, each subject. About 80 percent of the entries are also in the *Dictionary of American Biography*. A few non-Americans are included. The clergy predominate (of fifty-seven Roman Catholics, only six or seven are laymen). Treatment is objective and factual, since the editor seems deliberately to avoid polemics. For example, the controversies about the late Cardinal Spellman are not mentioned, and Cardinal Cushing is characterized as a prelate whose pronouncements on public affairs were unpredictable. Perhaps the most interesting and valuable sections are given to the various cults and minority groups. [R: Choice, Sept 77, p. 826; LJ, 15 May 77, p. 1167; RQ, Fall 77, pp. 70-71; WLB, Sept 77, p. 89]

Theodore M. Avery, Jr.

626.   Delaney, John J. **Dictionary of American Catholic Biography**. Garden City, N.Y., Doubleday, 1984. 621p. $24.95. LC 83-25524. ISBN 0-385-17878-6.

The most noteworthy men and women from all walks of life who helped expand and evolve American Catholicism are profiled in this *Dictionary of American Catholic Biography*. Consisting of biographies spanning time from the colonial period to the present, this volume cites the contributions made by some fifteen hundred eminent individuals. In addition to distinguished ecclesiastics, leading Catholics from the arts, literature, politics, education, science, sports, and entertainment are listed. Prominent among the most famous are Jacques Marquette, Giovanni da Verrazano, and the Marquis de Lafayette; Rose Hawthorne, Mother Cabrini, and Dorothy Day; Thomas Merton, Flannery O'Connor, and Tennessee Williams; James Farley, John Fitzgerald Kennedy, and Robert Kennedy; John La Farge and Ivan Mestrovic; Arturo Toscanini and Meredith Wilson; Babe Ruth and Knute Rockne; Bing Crosby, Spencer Tracy, Pat O'Brien, Gracie Allen, and Jimmy Durante.

Having been drawn from secondary sources, the biographies contain nothing new, but the idea of collecting them into a single reference tool seems unique and worthwhile since the mass of information this dictionary contains could be located formerly only by searching through hundreds of sources. Each entry supplies date and place of birth, educational background, activities, achievements, and place and date of death. (Only the deceased are listed, allowing for a possible sequel—*Dictionary of* Living *American Catholics*.) If the subject accomplished something especially notable in the arts, titles of works are given.

An attempt has been made to include those Catholics who played a truly important role in the development of the church in America as well as those who made a contribution through their profession or activity. Listing is not meant to signify full approbation, however, for even a few Catholics whose lives may have been somewhat less than exemplary have been included. Among the more controversial or less "loyal" can be found Senator Joseph McCarthy, Dorothy Kilgallen, and the excommunicated Father Leonard Feeney, S.J., who preached the pernicious doctrine "outside the Church there is no salvation."

G. A. Cevasco

627. Hammack, Mary L. **A Dictionary of Women in Church History**. Chicago, Moody Press, 1984. 167p. bibliog. $11.95. LC 84-14710. ISBN 0-8024-0332-8.

Though the preface describes the sources searched for names to be included in this dictionary, the compilation appears somewhat random. Those sources yielded names, but the method for selecting sources tends toward inclination rather than strictly defined research. Biographees must have had some influence on church history, and information about them must be substantiated. Only deceased persons are included. While the criteria are clearly stated, the overall focus seems far too general.

A chronological index preceding the body of the work arranges entries into five major periods of the Christian era. One thousand biographies range from identifications to more detailed entries. Treatments vary from factual to vague; some entries straightforward, others imitating a style reminiscent of nineteenth-century devotional literature. What results is uneven coverage, perhaps reflecting differences among the sources listed in the two-page bibliography.

This is a work intended not for scholars, but for popular use.

Bernice Bergup

628. Hatfield, Edwin F. **The Poets of the Church: A Series of Biographical Sketches of Hymn-Writers with Notes on Their Hymns**. New York, Anson D. F. Randolph; repr., Detroit, Gale, 1978. 719p. index. (A Firenze Book). $110.00. LC 78-19045. ISBN 0-8103-4291-X.

A reprint of Hatfield's work, first published in 1884, this source contains information on slightly less than three hundred writers whose poetry contributed to the development of hymnody within the Christian tradition. The work has no preface, so no criteria are outlined as a basis for inclusion. Poets range from the early Church Fathers, such as Ambrose, through Bernard of Clairvaux in the twelfth century, to Bishop Christopher Wordsworth, a contemporary of Hatfield's. In addition to a basic biographical sketch, each entry focuses on the individual's contribution to hymnology. An index of the principal hymns of the biographees follows the main section. Because of its particular coverage, the work will have a rather specialized use within collections.

Bernice Bergup

629. Moyer, Elgin. **Wycliffe Biographical Dictionary of the Church**. Revised and enlarged by Earle E. Cairns. Chicago, Moody Press, 1982. 449p. $19.95. LC 81-22578. ISBN 0-8024-9693-8.

This biographical dictionary compiles information (some two thousand entries) from other reference sources likely to appear in many collections. According to the preface, the scope includes persons from the Roman Catholic, Eastern, and Protestant churches, from the evangelical tradition, and black leaders of Africa and the United States. However, the criteria for inclusion and exclusion are never clearly stated, an omission which raises some questions about coverage, and about the distinctive character of this reference work.

Preceding the biographical entries is a "Chronological Index and Outline of Church History." Here biographees' names are alphabetically arranged in broad chronological periods such as "Apostolic to Old Catholic Church 5 B.C. – A.D. 313" and "Roman Catholicism, Revivals, Reform, Missions and Liberalism 1789-1914." In this listing, biographees are assigned a key letter purportedly identifying the person's major contribution to church history. However, such designations are so general and the time periods so broad that neither are significantly helpful. Several persons are identified as "He" (for "Heretic"); but it is unclear just what standard of orthodoxy was used to determine that status.

The writing style leaves much to be desired, the choppy prose and incomplete sentences more nearly resembling notes taken in a lecture class. Nor is one impressed by this capsule summary describing the period from 1914 to the present: "Ecumenical fusion by nondenominational and interdenominational agencies, organic reunion, and national and international confederations replaced the fission of the reformation" (p. xxvii).

Although the volume may be helpful for basic information on some otherwise obscure church figures, a work such as the *Oxford Dictionary of the Christian Church* (which is given as a source for the Wycliffe dictionary) gives fuller entries in clear prose along with bibliographical references. [R: Choice, Oct 82, p. 245; LJ, 1 Sept 82, p. 1649]   Bernice Bergup

630. Young, Henry J. **Major Black Religious Leaders since 1940**. Nashville, Tenn., Abingdon, 1979. 160p. $5.95pa. LC 79-11646. ISBN 0-687-22914-6.

The most important institution in black-American society has traditionally been the church, with the minister being *ex officio* a major figure within the community. In this compact paperback, fourteen of these individuals receive biographical, theological, and philosophical notice. Among the more celebrated ministers, almost all of whom were active in some aspect of civil rights, are W. E. B. DuBois, Benjamin Mays, Howard Thurman, Adam Clayton Powell, Jr., Elijah Muhammad, Malcolm X, C. Eric Lincoln, Jesse Jackson, and, of course, Martin Luther King, Jr. It then becomes redundant to observe that such persons had an effect on the totality of American society and were sometimes influential in foreign policy. In not one instance do we have a minister whose orientation can be fully equated with non-black theological traditions. They all speak of social justice, with their ideas stimulated by religion, and by racial experiences and observations. Apparently, the question of ultimate salvation is assumed to result from social salvation and good works of the human confraternity. The book's reference value rests in its terse, almost outlined, format. The bibliography appears only in the footnotes, and there is no index. [R: BL, 1 Mar 80, p. 932; Choice, Mar 80, p. 98; LJ, 1 Dec 79, p. 2578]   Dominique-René de Lerma

BIBLE STUDIES

631. Brownrigg, Ronald. **Who's Who in the New Testament**. New York, Holt, Rinehart and Winston, 1971. 448p. illus. maps. o.p. LC 75-153654. SBN 03-086262-0.

A companion volume to Comay's *Who's Who in the Old Testament* (Holt, 1971), this work deals with fewer names and is able to give more space to each person. The articles on Jesus, Mary, Peter, Paul, and other major figures are quite long and profusely illustrated with photographs of paintings, statues, landscapes, etc. The biographies usually explain differing doctrines about each person when appropriate and maintain a moderate and objective tone. The value of this work, as of its companion, will depend on a library's need for theological materials and the extent of its holdings in Biblical dictionaries and encyclopedias containing similar information.

James P. McCabe

632. Buechner, Frederick. **Peculiar Treasures: A Biblical Who's Who**. New York, Harper & Row, 1979. 181p. illus. $11.49. LC 78-20586. ISBN 0-06-061157-X.

An alphabetical arrangement of short, witty analyses of over one hundred Biblical characters ranging from Aaron to Zaccheus. Buechner has accomplished his purpose of making Biblical characters seem human, and has done so with humor and insight. But for reference work, there is too little hard fact and too much clever interpretation in each short sketch. The author is really giving his own opinion of each character and drawing contemporary lessons of a moral and religious nature. Buechner is at his best with minor figures like Goliath or Rahab the harlot, where there is little solid fact to report and an informed imagination can have full play to spark the readers' interest. With more important figures like Abraham or Moses, however, the coverage is much too brief and the interpretation too one-sided. A tendency to use anachronisms to bring stories up-to-date is dramatically effective but can be factually confusing and sometimes overly cute. In the end, despite its title, the author seems to have intended this work as a series of very original and entertaining meditations, and as such it is delightful, but of little value as a reference source for even the smallest library.

Cleon Robert Nixon, III

633. Coggins, Richard. **Who's Who in the Bible**. Totowa, N.J., Barnes & Noble Books, 1981. 232p. $23.50. ISBN 0-389-20183-9.

This work is another in a long tradition of popular and scholarly Bible biography aids. In it, Coggins, a British lecturer and author of Old Testament studies, reports how scholars are currently evaluating the historical evidence regarding more than five hundred men and women named in the Bible. The author relies heavily on modern critical scholarship but incorporates neither footnotes nor bibliographies. Because of this critical historical approach, the work is considerably different from others in this genre which adhere strictly to what is known from the Biblical account (e.g., George M. Alexander, *Handbook of Biblical Personalities*, 1962; and William P. Barker, *Everyone in the Bible*, 1966) or contain historical inaccuracies (Joan Comay, *Who's Who in the Old Testament Together with the Apocrypha*, 1971; and Ronald Brownrigg, *Who's Who in the New Testament*, 1971. A succinct survey of what is known historically of the events described in the Bible is also offered in the introduction. For these reasons this work can be a useful addition, if desired, for large general collections. But for reference, a good Bible dictionary, e.g., *Interpreter's Dictionary of the Bible* is the better choice for biography and a whole lot more.

The work is divided into two sections: Old Testament and Apocrypha, and New Testament, each arranged alphabetically. Also included are a list of abbreviations and a chronological table. Black-and-white line maps of the Old Testament and New Testament worlds appear as end pages.

Related works are *Who's Who in the Bible*, edited by Albert E. Sims and George Dent (Philosophical Library, 1982. $4.95), and *Who's Who among Bible Women*, edited by Peggy Musgrove (Gospel Pub., 1981. $3.95), which are not as well executed.

Glenn R. Wittig and Bohdan S. Wynar

634.   Wright, J. Stafford. **Revell's Dictionary of Bible People**. Old Tappan, N.J., Fleming H. Revell, 1978. 239p. illus. maps. o.p. LC 78-20810. ISBN 0-8007-1038-X.

Revell's Dictionary provides entries for over four hundred individuals in the Bible, both Old and New Testaments, excluding only those persons appearing in genealogical and other lists. Arranged alphabetically, the entry for each individual contains a brief summary of the individual's life and important relationships, with appropriate scriptural references, cross-references, and in most cases the meaning of the name. The Revised Standard Version is the primary version cited; when necessary, different translations are supplied as well.

The author states in "A Word to the Reader" that he was asked to do something "with a light touch." What has resulted is an informal, oftentimes overly simplistic, approach. Some of the definitions are extremely sketchy. For example, under the entry "Abed-nego," there is no mention of Shadrach and Meshach, and no cross-references appear, although the definition begins "One of Daniel's three friends." Entries for Shadrach and Meshach do appear, with cross-references to Abednego. Under the entry for "John" (John the Baptist) the definition merely states that he is "the son of old parents"; no mention or cross-reference appears for either Elisabeth or Zechariah. The foreword indicates that the volume includes a short subject index, but no such index exists. Needless to say, the volume offers very little to serious students of the Bible.

Susan C. Holte

SAINTS

635.   Attwater, Donald. **The Penguin Dictionary of Saints**. Baltimore, Md., Penguin Books, 1970. 362p. (Penguin Reference Books). $1.95pa.

This book was first published in hardcover in 1965. It provides in a concise form, brief biographical sketches of some 750 saints, from Christ's apostles to the men and women who have been canonized in recent times. The author, a well-known authority in hagiology, edited *Catholic Dictionary* (3rd ed. Macmillan, 1961) and revised Butler's standard work, *Lives of the Saints*. The coverage in this dictionary is universal; however, special attention has been paid to the saints of Great Britain and Ireland.

A related work is the *Dictionary of Saints*, edited by John J . Delaney (Doubleday, 1980. 647p. $22.50), which is much more comprehensive in comparison to Attwater, covering five thousand saints. It is intended for a general audience and can safely be recommended for all public libraries. The only drawback to this otherwise satisfactory compilation is alphabetization under surnames that may frustrate some users. In 1983, Doubleday published an abridged edition (fifteen hundred entries) of this work for $6.95.

Bohdan S. Wynar

636. Farmer, David Hugh. **The Oxford Dictionary of Saints**. New York, Oxford University Press, 1978. 435p. index. $17.50; $8.95pa. ISBN 0-19-869120-3; 0-19-283036-8pa.

A former Benedictine monk, presently a reader in history at Reading University, has compiled about one thousand interesting and concise biographies of saints, alphabetically arranged, usually with appended bibliographies. Saints who lived, died, or were venerated in Great Britain or Ireland are included, as well as those who appear in the calendars of the *Book of Common Prayer*, the Sarum Rite, the modern Roman Missal, and those to whom a church is dedicated. The *Oxford Dictionary* contains an introductory evaluation of earlier sources of saints' lives, an appendix giving brief biographies of Englishmen for whom there is some evidence of a popular cult but whose canonization was not achieved, and an index of places in Great Britain and Ireland associated with particular saints. Well edited, with cross-references to variant spellings of proper names and to names of saints mentioned in the biographical sketches of other saints, this work is very useful for brief identification.

The author acknowledges his debt to many sources, among them Butler's *Lives of the Saints* (Christian Classics, 1976), a more comprehensive work that covers most saints of the Roman Martyrology. Entries in Butler's work are arranged by date of feast according to the Roman calendar but there is no index. One could also consult *A Biographical Dictionary of the Saints, with a General Introduction on Hagiology*, by Frederick George Holweck (St. Louis, Mo., Herder, 1924; repr., Detroit, Gale, 1969. 1053p. $75.00), which presents the known data of a saint's life, the particular line of Christian activity in which he or she was prominent, and brief bibliographical notices. [R: C&RL, July 79, p. 347; WLB, June 79, p. 725]

Frances Neel Cheney and Bohdan S. Wynar

637. Habig, M. A. **Saints of the Americas**. Huntington, Ind., Our Sunday Visitor, 1974. 384p. illus. (part col.). bibliog. index. o.p. LC 74-15269. ISBN 0-87973-880-4.

The biographies of forty-five saints and *beati*, most of whom are rather obscure, are given in this work along with a treatment of the place of the Virgin Mary in the Western Hemisphere. Although the biographies are clearly written and readable, they are done in the style of hagiography reminiscent of the nineteenth century and pre-Vatican II spirituality; i.e., they are filled with details, sometimes absurd, gleaned from uncritical sources which frequently serve only to alienate the modern reader rather than generate admiration or the desire to imitate the virtues of the saint. Nevertheless, all of the information is documented, and the book is supplied with an index and numerous appendixes.

James P. McCabe

21 Science and Technology

Introduction

The "Science and Technology" chapter includes "General Works," "Aviation and Aerospace," "Biochemistry," "Chemistry," "Computer Science," "Electronics," "Energy and Nuclear Sciences," "Engineering and Technology," and "Physics," with a total of forty-one entries plus several hundred additional titles mentioned in the annotations. "General Works" includes a number of well-known works such as *American Men and Women of Science: Physical and Biological Sciences* (see entry 638), and the monumental *Dictionary of Scientific Biography* (see entry 648). A number of well-known works are included in the subject-oriented sections, e.g., *American Chemists and Chemical Engineers* (see entry 659), *Marquis Who's Who Directory of Computer Graphics* (see entry 661), *Marquis Who's Who Directory of Online Professionals* (see entry 662), *McGraw-Hill's Leaders in Electronics* (see entry 663), *Who's Who in Technology Today* (see entry 676), *Who's Who in Frontier Science and Technology* (see entry 675), and *Pioneers of Science: Nobel Prize Winners in Physics* (see entry 678).

In addition to those more recently published directories there are a number of older biographical and reference sources, some of them published in foreign languages. From the early 1950s a biennial was published, the eight-volume *Leaders in American Science*, edited by Robert C. Cook (Who's Who in American Education, 1953-1968). Each volume contained about fifteen thousand biographical sketches plus photographs covering prominent personalities in science research, as well as governmental officials in the United States and Canada. The two-volume *McGraw-Hill Modern Men of Science* (McGraw-Hill, 1966-1968), later published in a revised three-volume edition as *McGraw-Hill Modern Scientists and Engineers* (see entry 652), is intended to serve as a biographical supplement to the *McGraw-Hill Encyclopedia of Science and Technology* (various editions). The first edition covered 1,426 leading contemporary scientists in the first volume and 420 in the second. The second edition, intended as a supplement to the fourth edition of the *McGraw-Hill Encyclopedia* (1977), revised a number of sketches and added three hundred new biographies. According to the preface, "The individuals were selected by the editors from recipients of major awards and prizes given by the leading societies, organizations, and institutions of the world. The scope is international and extends in time from the leaders of the 1920s to the 1978 Nobel Prize winners." Both editions are cross-referenced with the *Encyclopedia. A Biographical Dictionary of Scientists*, edited by T. I. Williams (A. & C. Black and Wiley-Interscience, 1969. 592p.), which is international in scope providing brief biographical sketches in science and technology, medicine, and mathematics. Only deceased persons are included. The Royal Society of London, for several years published *Obituary Notices of Fellows of the Royal Society* (Royal Society, 1932-1954) consisting of long biographical articles of the deceased members, including many foreign members.

Probably the most famous biographical work is J. C. Poggendorff's *Biographisch-literarisches Handwörterbuch zur Geschichte der exakten Wissenschaften* (Leipzig, Barth, 1863-1904; Verlag Chemie, 1925-1940, repr., 11v. Edwards, 1945), which contains scholarly biographies of mathematicians, astronomers, physicists, chemists, geologists, and other scientists of all countries. The biographical sketches are well-documented with detailed bibliographies. This work is supplemented by *Biographisch-literarisches Handwörterbuch der exakten Naturwissenschaften, unter Mitwirkung der Akademien der Wissenschaften zu Berlin, Göttingen, Heidelberg, München und Wien. . .* , edited by R. Zaunick and H. Salié (Berlin, Akademie-Verlag, 1955- . In progress, with seven volumes published). An important work from the Soviet point of view is *Biograficheskii slovar' deiatelei estestvoznaniia i tekhniki*, edited by A. A. Zvorykin (2v. Moscow, Bol'shaia sovetskaia entsiklopediia, 1958-1959), which contains forty-five hundred biographies providing international coverage. Living scientists are included in this work, which also has an English abridged version, namely *Who's Who in Soviet Science and Technology*, edited by I. Telberg (2nd ed. Telberg Book Co., 1964. 301p.). A handy compendium of biographical sketches arranged by country is J. Turkevich and L. B. Turkevich's *Prominent Scientists of Continental Europe* (American Elsevier, 1968. 204p.) covering.primarily members of national academies and faculty at leading universities.

Some biographical information can also be found in subject encyclopedia and dictionaries that are simply too numerous to mention here. Biographical sources, subject dictionaries and encyclopedias, as well as indexing and abstracting services, are all adequately discussed in several bibliographic guides, e.g., S. Herner's *A Brief Guide to Sources of Scientific and Technical Information* (2nd ed. Information Resources Press, 1980. 160p.), H. R. Malinowsky and J. M. Richardson's *Science and Engineering Literature: A Guide to Reference Sources* (3rd ed. Libraries Unlimited, 1980. 342p.), and many others, most of which are listed in Sheehy and Walford.

GENERAL WORKS

Current Biographies

638.   American Men and Women of Science: Physical and Biological Sciences. 15th ed. Edited by Jaques Cattell Press. New York, R. R. Bowker, 1982. 7v. index. $495.00/ set. LC 6-7326. ISBN 0-8352-1413-3 (set).

The fourteenth edition of this standard source was published in eight volumes in 1979, providing brief biographical data on 130,500 scientists. The present edition has an almost identical number of entries (130,000). Seventy-five hundred entries are new in this set and many obsolete entries have been removed. Selection criteria remain the same as in earlier editions — "achievement by reason of experience and training, of a stature in scientific work equivalent to that associated with the doctoral degree, coupled with presently continued activity in such work" or "research activity of high quality in science as evidenced by publication in reputable scientific journals, or, for those whose work cannot be published because of governmental or industrial security, research activity of high quality in science as evidenced by the judgment of the individual's peers" or "attainment of a position of substantial responsibility. . . ." The information is based on data forms submitted by the biographees. Included are living U.S. and Canadian scientists in all physical and biological fields as well as engineers, mathematicians, and computer scientists. This information is now also available on Bowker's *AMWS* database that has been developed with the cooperation of the National Academy of Sciences. *AMWS* is currently available from DIALOG and BRS. In 1983 Bowker published *American Men and Women of Science Editions 1-14 Cumulative Index* (1264p. $125.00) that provides alphabetical access to 297,000 scientists. Each entry provides the full name of the scientist and the editions in which it appears. *American Men and Women of Science* is a well-established and reliable reference source, useful to libraries of all types as an important fact-finding tool for biographical data for most scientists in this country and Canada. Most research libraries should have a standing order for this publication. [R: LJ, 1 Mar 80, p. 602]   Bohdan S. Wynar

639.   Who's Who in Science in Europe: A Biographical Guide in Science, Technology, Agriculture, and Medicine. 4th ed. Harlow, England, Longman; distr., Detroit, Gale, 1984. 3v. index. (Longman Reference on Research Series). $500.00/set. ISBN 0-582-90109-X.

Previous editions of this standard biographical directory were published in 1967, 1972, and 1978. As the introduction notes, "each edition has been an entirely new compilation going to original sources for society officers, industrial scientists and engineers, and senior academic postings." Europe is defined as Western and Eastern Europe, excluding the USSR; thirty countries are included, with Turkey classed as a part of Europe.

The latest three-volume set is expanded significantly from the original 1967 edition, but has been reduced by one volume and a number of entries from the 1978 edition (an estimated fifty thousand down to thirty thousand). The format of the fourth edition is highly readable with each entry subdivided by the following labels: Born, Higher Education, Job, Experience, Appointments, Societies, Publications, Interests, Telephone, and Address. Since the data, in general, are obtained directly from the biographees, not all entries are complete in terms of dates or data. For example,

H. G. Van Eyk does not identify his "higher education," but is a professor on the faculty of medicine, Erasmus Universiteit Rotterdam.

A number of entries are marked with an asterisk and contain only data on job and address. These biographees did not respond to questionnaires, but are included with the information taken from "recently published sources" (introduction).

Part 1, an A to Z listing by name of the biographee, makes up the first two volumes and part of the third volume. Part 2, "Country and Subject Index," concludes volume 3 (pages 2469-2556), and is a simple listing by country (Austria to Yugoslavia), and then by subject (e.g., "Agriculture and Food Science," "Earth and Astronomical Sciences," "Engineering, Mechanical and Civil," "Physics and Nuclear Sciences") of individuals who have "allocated themselves into one or more of eight subject areas" (introduction).

The volume's subtitle indicates the parameters of inclusion: well-known individuals in the natural and physical sciences including agriculture, engineering, and medicine. Those fields omitted are: "The social sciences, economics, political science, social medicine, law, and education. . ." (introduction). Despite its relatively high cost, it is a basic reference source for any library that needs access to data on leaders in numerous scientific occupations.

As part of the Longman Reference on Research series this volume complements *European Research Centres: A Directory of Organizations in Science, Technology, Agriculture, and Medicine*, published in November 1982.   Laurel Grotzinger

640. Who's Who of British Scientists, 1980/81. 3rd ed. Dorking, Surrey, England, Simon Books; distr., New York, St. Martin's Press, 1980. 589p. $75.00. ISBN 0-312-87433-2.

Although the first and second editions of *Who's Who of British Scientists* were published in 1969 and 1971, it took nine years for the third edition to appear. This meant that the new edition had to practically start from scratch and suffer a few compromises in the process. Since the editors had to rely upon voluntary submission of entries, biographies of recent winners of Nobel prizes in science, as promised, are scarce. Also, they had to abandon plans for a cross-reference list of scientists by scientific specialization. The book, however, is a wealth of information on over six thousand scientists in universities, polytechnics, research establishments, and industry, mostly under the age of fifty. Documented are the birth dates, current position, past appointments, selected publications, professional interests, and current address for each entry. The selected publications, although limited, give shortened citations, but they are sufficient for most librarians to track down. Abbreviations and lists of research establishments, scientific societies, and professional institutions in Great Britain are also given. Larger reference libraries will find this volume useful.

Robert J. Havlik

Retrospective Biographies

641. Abbott, David, ed. **The Biographical Dictionary of Scientists: Astronomers**. New York, Peter Bedrick; distr., New York, Harper & Row, 1984. 204p. illus. index. $18.95. LC 84-9236. ISBN 0-911745-80-7.

642. Abbott, David, ed. **The Biographical Dictionary of Scientists: Biologists**. New York, Peter Bedrick; distr., New York, Harper & Row, 1984. 182p. illus. index. $18.95. LC 84-10972. ISBN 0-911745-82-3.

643. Abbott, David, ed. **The Biographical Dictionary of Scientists: Chemists.** New York, Peter Bedrick; distr., New York, Harper & Row, 1984 (c1983). 203p. illus. index. $18.95. LC 84-9284. ISBN 0-911745-81-5.

644. Abbott, David, ed. **The Biographical Dictionary of Scientists: Physicists.** New York, Peter Bedrick; distr., New York, Harper & Row, 1984. 212p. illus. index. $18.95. LC 84-9211. ISBN 0-911745-79-3.

This four-volume reference work provides brief biographical sketches of scientists world-wide from antiquity to the present. Each volume contains more than two hundred entries, one-half to a full page in length, and is arranged alphabetically by the last name of the subject. Each book begins with a succinct, well-written historical overview of the topic to provide perspective for the reader. The entries themselves are clearly presented and very informative, making interesting browsing or providing useful information to students. Because of the short length of the entries, this set is more appropriate for lay people, high school students, and beginning college students. Advanced students and scholars will wish to consult other sources such as the fourteen-volume *Dictionary of Scientific Biography* (Scribner's, 1970-1976) to obtain more detailed information.

Other features in each volume include a glossary, an author-subject index, and a small number of black-and-white photographs and line drawings. A few scientists appear in more than one volume (e.g., Galileo who made contributions in both astronomy and physics); but this only serves to enhance the set's value. *The Biographical Dictionary of Scientists* is appropriate for the reference collection in public, high school, and college libraries.   Robert A. Seal

645. Asimov, Isaac. **Asimov's Biographical Encyclopedia of Science and Technology: The Lives and Achievements of 1510 Great Scientists from Ancient Times to the Present, Chronologically Arranged.** 2nd rev. ed. New York, Doubleday, 1982. 941p. illus. index. $29.95. LC 81-47861. ISBN 0-385-17771-2.

This volume was first published in 1964 and revised in 1972; the revised edition was published in paperback by Avon in 1976 ($5.95), indicating its popularity. Over 300 new biographies have been added for a total of 1,510 entries, chronologically arranged. The biographees are listed alphabetically in the table of contents for easy accessibility. The articles are primarily concerned with the achievements of the individuals. Through the index one can find subjects and persons only mentioned in the text.

Although there is some duplication in subject matter, *The Concise Dictionary of Scientific Biography* covers many more scientists (more than five thousand), but not in as much depth as Asimov's book. [R: LJ, 1 Mar 83, p. 449; SLJ, May 83, p. 25]
                                                                         Bohdan S. Wynar

646. **Concise Dictionary of Scientific Biography.** By the American Council of Learned Societies. James F. Maurer, managing ed. New York, Scribner's, 1981. 773p. $100.00; $66.67 (libraries). LC 81-5629. ISBN 0-684-16650-X.

As noted in the preface, Scribner's has used the sixteen-volume *Dictionary of Scientific Biography* as a basis for a one-volume abridgment which includes "essential facts from all the entries, set forth briefly and clearly and in significant proportion to the scope of the original articles." The original set is a superb reference work comparable in authority and coverage to the *Dictionary of American Biography* except that it deals only with deceased scientists selectly chosen from all periods. In the parent set, each article is authored by a distinguished scientist and/or historian, and includes an interpretative analysis of the biographee's contributions with appropriate documentation. In this single volume, each entry provides "the subject's places and dates of birth and death, areas of research, major phases and aspects of his or her career, and a brief statement of outstanding achievements. When pertinent, educational and social-cultural connections are mentioned, as well as family relationships to other scientists treated in the volume" (preface, p. vii). The editors state that the entries are approximately one-tenth as long as the original, " but the scale of reduction has been varied liberally, both to ensure clarity and to reflect the comparative judgments embodied in the larger set." The work is arranged alphabetically by name with appropriate cross-references, covers slightly more than five thousand individuals, and is well designed and printed.

It is difficult to conclude that Scribner's has prepared a work which may be of limited worth, especially given the fact that it is reasonably priced and is based on a superb master set. However, the question must be asked as to the audience to which it is addressed, i.e., those who will want this information in this format. Any reasonably sized library serving patrons interested in scientific contributions has already acquired the sixteen-volume set. There would be minimal need for an abridgment if the user had access to the full, original article. If it is intended for smaller libraries that cannot afford the master set, then it must be questioned in terms of what it could add that a good encyclopedia does not provide, since the work has selectively identified obviously renowned scientists.

As a result, the final question relates to the content of the entries, and here the one-volume work raises other concerns. The original articles have been abridged according to an editorial formula which emphasizes, as described earlier, a synthesis of key data. They have been rewritten by an editorial staff which does not pretend to duplicate the original author's style or "flavor." The result is a mixture of semi-awkward prose, heavy use of a straight subject/verb sentence structure often followed by multiple clauses, and a dubious attempt to reduce authoritative, interpretive material to a brief evaluation. Since many of the biographical facts on the subjects are available in standard directories or, as mentioned above, in encyclopedias, the need for or value of the synthesis is a crucial issue. As the editors point out, "for the history of science in fullest detail, and to appreciate the interconnections among the workers in one or more fields, the large DSB must be referred to beginning with its extensive and minute indexing of the fifteen volumes." Given this comment, few librarians may wish to acquire this ready-reference volume even though it provides basic facts "about the life, the scientific thought, and the contribution to knowledge of more than 5,000 scientists." [R: BL, 1 June 82, p. 1328; Choice, Jan 82, p. 603]   Laurel Grotzinger

647.   Daintith, John, Sarah Mitchell, and Elizabeth Tootill. **A Biographical Encyclopedia of Scientists**. New York, Facts on File, 1981. 2v. bibliog. index. $80.00. LC 80-23529. ISBN 0-87196-396-5.

The editors of this publication have produced an excellent ready-reference dictionary of scientists from ancient times to the space age. They have concentrated on the traditional pure sciences—physics, chemistry, biology, astronomy, and the earth sciences. The editors have also added mathematics and medicine, as well as scientists who have made important contributions to anthropology, psychology, and engineering and technology. A small number of philosophers like Plato and Aristotle are also included. The encyclopedia is international in scope.

The main part of this two-volume set contains an alphabetic list of 1,966 scientists with descriptions of their lives and contributions. Of these scientists, 452, or 23 percent, are still living, or have died within the past two years (1980-1981). While the entries contain basic biographical data, the emphasis has been placed on the principal achievements of these scientists, and the significance of their achievements. The editors have attempted to include people who have produced major advances in theory, or have made influential discoveries, being guided by lists of prizes and awards made by scientific societies. There are a number of cross-references, especially in cases where two or more people have collaborated on a research project.

Supplementing the biographical section are a chronology of scientific discoveries and publications arranged under year and subject, from the time of the earliest Greek philosopher, Thales (590 B.C.), to the first reusable spacecraft in 1981; a short list of scientific books particularly influential in the development of science; an index to the biography section listing the names of scientists who are mentioned in the text, but do not have entries of their own; and an index to the biography section listing important scientific topics and the scientists associated with them.

This publication has benefitted from meticulous editing. One of the few noticeable errors was the designation of Joseph Priestley as a Presbyterian minister (actually he was a Unitarian minister). One surprising omission in the biography section is Vannevar Bush, who was director of the Office of Scientific Research and Development during World War II.

A Biographical Encyclopedia of Scientists will be a valuable addition to the shelves of small and medium-sized libraries. In larger libraries it should be useful as a ready-reference supplement to the *Dictionary of Scientific Biography* (Scribner's) and the *McGraw-Hill Encyclopedia of Science and Technology*. [R: Choice, Apr 82, p. 1044, WLB, Dec 81, p. 300]   Thomas S. Harding

648. **Dictionary of Scientific Biography**. Charles Coulston Gillispie, ed.-in-chief. New York, Scribner's, 1970-1981. 16v. $695.00/set. ISBN 0-684-151448.

The set, over seventeen years in preparation, comprises fourteen basic volumes, a supplement, and the index. The *DSB*, edited under the auspices of the American Council of Learned Societies, is a comprehensive reference work in the history of science. Some five thousand biographies of mathematicians and natural scientists cover all regions and historical periods, including such topics as Japanese, Egyptian, Mesopotamian, Indian, and pre-Columbian sciences. The biographies, ranging in length from five hundred to twenty thousand words, were written by fifteen hundred authors from ninety countries. *DSB* had the full cooperation of the Academy of Sciences of the USSR. All articles were specially commissioned for *DSB*, and cover scientists from antiquity to the mid-twentieth century.

In terms of selection, this dictionary is patterned on the *Dictionary of National Biography*; it lists well-documented biographical sketches of scientists no longer living, and the selection criteria are influenced by "contributions to science . . . sufficiently distinctive to make an identifiable difference to the profession or community of knowledge." The scope is international, but, as indicated in the preface, some countries (India, China, Japan) will not be as well represented as Western scientists.

This highly praised work is completed by the index, which contains over seventy-five thousand entries. Eight indexers worked for ten years preparing it. References to biographees comprise only a small portion of this comprehensive work. All but the most trivial and isolated references to other individuals are indexed. Periodicals, societies, universities, museums, medals, lectureships, and prizes are accessed. When a topic is pertinent to a particular country, the country is indexed. Scientific topics and concepts are fully indexed, including chronological and topical subheadings. The index is both logical and legible, and is in itself a contribution to scientific scholarship. Since its appearance in 1970, the *Dictionary of Scientific Biography* has been an invaluable tool; its completion makes it indispensable. [R: Choice, July 73, p. 754; Choice, Dec 73, p. 1526; LJ, 19 Sept 76, p. 1845; LJ, 1 June 80, p. 1292; WLB, June 80, pp. 669-70]

Bohdan S. Wynar

649. Downs, Robert B. **Landmarks in Science: Hippocrates to Carson.** Littleton, Colo., Libraries Unlimited, 1982. 305p. bibliog. index. $23.50. LC 82-154. ISBN 0-87287-295-5.

Robert Downs presents a survey of the great masterworks in science from ancient to modern times. The seventy-four sketches, covering more than two millennia, reveal the major trends in science as well as the development of scientific ideas and their interaction over the centuries. Isaac Newton, for example, built upon the works begun by Copernicus and carried forward by Brahe, Kepler, and Galileo.

Arranged according to the birth dates of the authors, the sketches comment on the lives and most important individual works of the scientists. The book begins with notable scientific advances during the fourth and third centuries B.C. by Hippocrates, Aristotle, and Theophrastus and ends with those in modern times by Pavlov, Freud, and Rachel Carson. All branches of science, including medicine, are represented. Bibliographical notes at the end provide information on the various editions and series of English translations of the works included, a record of the earlier works' first appearances in printed form, and a list of recommended general histories of science. [R: C&RL, Sept 83, p. 429; JAL, Nov 83, p. 309; SBF, Mar/Apr 85, p. 188]

Ann Hartman

650. Elliott, Clark A. **Biographical Dictionary of American Science: The Seventeenth through the Nineteenth Centuries.** Westport, Conn., Greenwood Press, 1979. 360p. index. $55.00. LC 78-4292. ISBN 0-313-20419-5.

As so often noted before, biographical directories or dictionaries are an indispensable element in most reference collections. No matter how large the collection, the unique range of human endeavor invariably produces a request that cannot be answered by the resources at hand. However, this particular volume has a special value for most libraries since it is "deliberately designed as a retrospective companion to *American Men of Science*, which has been recognized as the chief directory of living scientists since its first edition appeared in 1906" (preface). The coverage of some six hundred scientists who predate *AMS*, whose birth dates range from 1606-1867, with entries that average between three hundred and four hundred words, provides a useful synthesis of persons who "were noted for their contributions to scientific knowledge. . . . The term *science* has been somewhat narrowly defined to mean chiefly work in such areas as mathematics, astronomy, physics, chemistry, botany, zoology, geology, and their allied specialties, and including some aspects of applied science. In general, engineers, inventors, physicians, social scientists, cultural anthropologists, ethnologists, explorers, and the like have not been included" (preface).

Each major sketch includes standard biographical data: full name, birth and death dates, specialization, genealogy, education, honors, career data, society memberships, scientific contributions, works, and manuscripts and citations to resources used in the compilation of the biographical material. Needless to say, certain limitations are evident, such as restricting the number of publications cited, the actual assessment of the individual's scientific contribution, and, of course, omissions. The author, Clark A. Elliott, who is associate curator at the Harvard University Archives, with access to an impressive number of resources, both published and human, would readily admit his own key role in the selection and elimination of candidates for inclusion. There are a number of briefer entries that do not give an evaluation of the contribution or other significant biographical details; these entries provide an additional three hundred names beyond the six hundred longer articles noted above. As described in the preface, "these are persons who had reached a significant stage in their careers before 1900 and who therefore were closely identified with science in the late nineteenth century"; they *were* included in the first editions of *American Men of Science*, but are cross-referenced or briefly noted here, e.g., Charles Loring Jackson and Washington Irving Stringham, respectively a chemist and a mathematician, who are covered in *AMS* and *DAB*.

Five useful appendixes, arranged by year of birth, place of birth, education, occupation, and fields of science, give extra content access to the tool, while its well-designed layout and clear typography make visual use easy. There is an index that provides subject, publication, and other kinds of references as well as a list of abbreviations, an introductory analysis of the coverage, and a preface that precisely defines the scope of the volume. All in all, the tool is difficult to fault and should serve well as a basic reference source that effectively complements *American Men of Science*. [R: Choice, Oct 79, p. 992; WLB, Sept 79, p. 65]   Laurel Grotzinger

651.   Feldman, Anthony, and Peter Ford. **Scientists and Inventors**. New York, Facts on File, 1979. 336p. illus. (part col.). index. $24.95. ISBN 0-87196-410-4.

Human scientific and technical progress is made by the contributions of thousands of individuals and their ideas and labors. Only a few, however, are recognized in their lifetime or after their death. Some contribute a single idea that may change the paradigm of a science, while others may contribute multiple inventions for the sole purpose of man's benefit. The authors have selected over 150 scientists and inventors through history for inclusion in this book; the selected scientists range from Democritus (c. 460-370 B.C.) to Christiaan Barnard (1922-) and James Watson (1928-).

To show the account of human progress, the selected individuals are presented in chronological order, and each receives a two-page spread that includes a portrait (when available), a picture or diagram of the scientific principle or the equipment or product discovered or invented, and in some cases a photograph of a contemporary application. Many of the pictures, diagrams, and photos are in color. Several paragraphs sketch out the person's life, influences, and major contributions. Captions on the illustrations contribute to the text and do not repeat data in the sketches. There is an alphabetic list of individuals included as well as a subject index to the articles, illustrations, and captions. Although the illustrations and captions are clear and attractive, the print of the articles is occasionally thin. The British origin of the book is recognizable from the source of contemporary photographs, but spelling, with a few exceptions, follows American usage. Most pleasing, however, is the price of the book, which is well within the range of all types of libraries. [R: LJ, 1 Nov 79, p. 2362]   Robert J. Havlik

652.   **McGraw-Hill Modern Scientists and Engineers**. New York, McGraw-Hill, 1980. 3v. index. o.p. LC 79-24383. ISBN 0-07-045266-0.

McGraw-Hill Modern Scientists and Engineers is an expanded and revised edition of *McGraw-Hill Modern Men of Science* (published in two volumes, 1966 and 1968). Some three hundred new articles have been added and 45 percent of the original articles are revised, resulting in a three-volume work comprising 1,140 biographies. The scope is international and covers leading scientists from the 1920s to the 1978 Nobel Prize winners. Biographees are selected from recipients of major awards and prizes given by leading societies, organizations, and institutions of the world. Biographees, whenever possible, were asked to write their own articles (the autobiographical articles are coded with a solid star). The remaining articles were prepared by subject specialists and submitted to the biographees for approval, if possible (many of these articles are, of course, about deceased persons). Articles carried over from *Modern Men of Science* have been reviewed, and biographical details were supplied (recent prizes, date of death, etc.). Each biography is illustrated with a portrait of the subject. Articles contain cross-references to other biographies in the set, and users needing background information are referred to the parent work, the *McGraw-Hill Encyclopedia of Science and Technology*. The set concludes with a field index, listing biographees under the appropriate scientific disciplines; and an analytical index, covering topics, concepts, and references to biographees.

Modern Scientists and Engineers is not as inclusive as Bowker's *American Men and Women of Science*, but the articles contain far more than the Who's Who information found in the Bowker set. Its most obvious competition is Scribner's *Dictionary of Scientific Biography*. *DSB* extends its coverage only into the mid-twentieth century, so *Modern Scientists and Engineers* will serve as an extension of *DSB*. However, there is overlap, and in most cases, *DSB* will be the preferred source. The autobiographical nature of *Modern Scientists and Engineers* insures accurate articles, but also leads to unevenness in audience perception. Some biographies can be understood by the average high school student, while others assume more than a basic scientific background. *DSB* is presented in a more even style, and has the added benefit of containing extensive bibliographies for each biography. Nonetheless, *McGraw-Hill Modern Scientists and Engineers* is a comprehensive examination of leading contemporary scientists. [R: BL, 1 Dec 80, pp. 534-35; LJ, July 80, p. 1502; RQ, Fall 80, pp. 99-100; WLB, Sept 80, p. 64]

Janet H. Littlefield

653. Siegel, Patricia Joan, and Kay Thomas Finley. **Women in the Scientific Search: An American Bio-Bibliography, 1724-1979**. Metuchen, N.J., Scarecrow, 1985. 399p. index. $32.50. LC 84-20290. ISBN 0-8108-1755-1.

This biobibliography was designed to assist the scholar in choosing and locating resource material about women scientists and also to provide the reader with biographies of women who were pioneers in seeking equality for women in science. Some of the women are quite well-known, others less so or almost unknown. The compilers hope they have provided a starting point for future work. They have consulted innumerable sources, some very obscure, and have sought the help of librarians, archivists, and alumnae directors to complete their work.

The first section presents annotated general biographical works arranged by date. Then information on individual women is given in sections divided as follows: archaeologists, anthropologists, ethnologists, and folklorists; astronomers; bacteriologists; biologists; botanists; chemists and biochemists; educators; embryologists; engineers; entomologists; geographers; geologists; home economists; marine scientists; mathematicians; medical scientists, general; anatomists; geneticists; histologists;

microbiologists; pathologists; physiologists; ornithologists; philosophers and historians of science; physicists; psychologists; science writers and artists; and zoologists. The entries include brief biographical information and references to places where further material can be found.

The authors are professors of French and chemistry respectively at the State University of New York College at Brockport.   Theodora Andrews

654.   **Who Was Who in American History—Science and Technology**. Chicago, Marquis Who's Who, 1976. 688p. $57.50. LC 76-5763. ISBN 0-8379-3601-2.

A selective biographical reference work comprising abbreviated sketches of those American men and women now deceased whose contributions to the advance of science and/or technology during the past 350 years are considered notable. Ten thousand engineers, inventors, and scientists are included, their résumés extracted from Marquis's six-volume *Who Was Who in America*. Entries for pre-1898 decedents were compiled by Marquis staffers; most others are autobiographical, with some posthumous updating by executors or surviving relatives. Unverified entries, of which there are relatively few, are so indicated. Data consist of facts on birth and death, parentage, education, marriage and offspring, academic/business positions and accomplishments, major publications, honors, and awards. Frequently mispronounced surnames are spelled phonetically, and an abbreviations table is appended. As in other Who's Who works, the small print may prove irksome to some readers. Summation: brief biographies of American (i.e., United States) sci-tech personalities of the past, gathered in single-volume format for the first time. [R: WLB, Dec 76, p. 364]

Lawrence E. Spellman

655.   Williams, Trevor I., ed. **A Biographical Dictionary of Scientists**. 3rd ed. New York, John Wiley, 1982. 674p. (A Halsted Press Book). $29.95. LC 74-12374. ISBN 0-470-27326-7.

Any single-volume biographical dictionary that presumes to select and describe some one thousand eminent scientists and technologists from early times to the present must occasionally omit a key figure. Moreover, the volume is admittedly the result of the "Editor's subjective choice of entries" and "reflect[s] the Editor's own interests and assessments." However, this is the third edition (first, 1969 and second in 1974) edited by Williams. And despite its obvious inability to be all things to all users, it does present well-written, reasonably complete sketches that include such essential elements as birth and death data, classification as to field of specialization and major accomplishments, and a narrative entry that notes family background, experiences, and contributions. The *Dictionary* is alphabetically arranged by the scientist's last name; each entry is signed with initials, which refer to a distinguished list of over fifty contributors who actually prepared the majority of the biographical sketches. The sketches average approximately three hundred to four hundred words, arranged in two-column pages. Of special value are brief bibliographies appended to each entry, which cite sources of the biographical data and key works. Many have only a single citation but others list up to six resources and note items that include a portrait.

The fields from which the scientists were selected include agriculture, astronomy, biochemistry, botany, chemistry, geology, mathematics, medicine, physics, technology, and all branches of engineering. All entries are cross-referenced by "see" and "q.v." references. A special appendix entitled "Anniversaries" is actually a chronological table that lists the birth and death dates of each scientist mentioned. A special section, labelled "Appendix," adds the names of scientists who are mentioned in the book but for whom no full biographies are included, with references to the entry or entries in which each appears—e.g., Fowler, R. H. (1889-1944). *See* Milne, E. A.

The volume, as Williams notes, "is strictly historical and no names of living subjects are included." The major purpose of this edition is to add scientists who died since 1981; entries prepared for 1980 have not been rewritten. The value of the new biographies must be weighed against the cost of the new edition. [R: Choice, June 75, p. 516; WLB, Oct 75, p. 126] Laurel Grotzinger

AVIATION AND AEROSPACE

656. **Astronauts and Cosmonauts Biographical and Statistical Data**. Revised by Marcia S. Smith. Washington, D.C., GPO, 1983. 335p. $6.00. S/N 052-070-05856-1.

This directory was first published in 1976 and contained portraits and brief biographical data on all designated U.S. astronauts as follows: seventy-three astronauts in the National Aeronautics and Space Administration space program from 1959 to the present; twelve astronauts in the X-15 program from 1958 to 1969; six astronauts in the joint Air Force-NASA X-20 Dyna-Soar program from 1961 to 1963; and seventeen astronauts in the Department of Defense Manned Orbiting Laboratory program from 1963 to 1969. It also included portraits and brief biographical data on thirty-nine Russians who were identified as cosmonauts. The portrait and biographical sketch of each individual occupied a single page.

Comparative data on American and Soviet spaceflights were provided in a series of tables: a list of U.S. and USSR manned spaceflights with information on name of spacecraft, launch date, crew, payload, and flight time; a list of crew members by program for U.S. and USSR spaceflights; a list of comparative time spent on space missions for individuals; a summary of manned spaceflights by program, both U.S. and USSR; and a summary table of individuals participating in the U.S. astronaut programs.

This work was revised in 1983 by Marcia S. Smith. Most of the information is substantially updated, including all present and former astronauts from NASA, X-15, X-20, Dyna-Soar and Manned Orbiting Laboratory programs in the U.S. It contains similar information on known cosmonauts from the USSR and spacenauts from other countries. [R: BL, 15 Sept 76, p. 307] LeRoy C. Schwarzkopf

657. **Who's Who in Aviation and Aerospace**. By the editors of the National Aeronautical Institute. New York, Grey House, 1983. 1415p. $95.00. ISBN 0-939300-10-9.

This directory contains some fifteen thousand brief biographical sketches of aviation and aerospace executives, leading aeronautical engineers, designers and technical specialists, government and military officials, and members of the aviation press. Selections were made by the National Aeronautical Institute and Jane's Publishing Company. Professionals in each sector of the industry are represented, including: aerospace engineering and manufacturing, air traffic control, airline and airport management, aviation/aerospace education, aviation publishing, commercial and general aviation manufacturing, commercial and corporate aviation, federal regulation, flight instruction, military aviation, private aviation, professional association administration, research, experimentation and testing, sales and distribution, and state regulation. A previous work, entitled *Who's Who in Aviation* was published by Harwood and Charles Publishing Company in 1973. Bohdan S. Wynar

BIOCHEMISTRY

658.　Fruton, Joseph S. **A Bio-Bibliography for the History of the Biochemical Sciences since 1800**. Philadelphia, Pa., American Philosophical Society, 1982. 885p. $20.00. LC 82-72158. ISBN 0-87169-983-4.

The debt historians of science owe to Professor Fruton for sharing his prodigious efforts in preparing a new and enlarged biobibliography is comparable to the debt statisticians have owed R. A. Fisher for his statistical tables. The alphabetical listing of names with dates of birth and death followed by a complete listing of biographical and bibliographical reference works is straightforward, and the listing is far more inclusive than the subtitle would suggest. Inclusion of names of living persons born before 1911 presents problems; Nobel Laureate G. D. Snell (1903-), for example, is missing. In areas in which Fruton had to rely on archivists and librarians, there is less critical selection than in his own areas of interest. If C. C. Little is to be omitted because he was best known as an administrator, there seems little reason to include Thomas Barbour. Also, we find C. D. Davenport but not E. C. MacDowell; Raymond Pearl but not R. A. Fisher; Karl Sax but not P. Manglesdorf; W. M. Wheeler but not R. H. Wetmore; H. H. Plough but not J. W. Gowen; etc.; but these represent prejudices of this reviewer and are not to be taken too seriously as criticism. It is hoped that this valuable work will give rise to further editions.　　　　　　　　　　　　　　　　　Brower R. Burchill

CHEMISTRY

659.　Miles, Wyndham D., ed. **American Chemists and Chemical Engineers**. Washington, D.C., American Chemical Society, 1976. 544p. index. $29.95. LC 76-192. ISBN 0-8412-0278-8.

This biographical dictionary provides information about 517 prominent men and women who have made significant contributions to chemistry and related fields in America. Covering a span of three hundred years, from alchemists of early colonial times to chemists who have died recently, entries include educators, editors of professional journals, influential writers, consultants, and persons who have applied chemistry to other professions. Biographies range from two hundred to one thousand words in length and were prepared by authoritative persons with knowledge of the subject field. Selected references appended to the biographies document the writer's data and provide sources for additional information. Indexes include a list of contributors and a list of persons mentioned in the biographies.

Considering the broad range of activities and occupations represented, a subject index would have lent greater value to the work. The volume attempts to cover too broad an area and presents information that could be found more readily in standard biographical reference sources or major indexes such as *Chemical Abstracts*. Selection of entries is quite subjective and serious omissions occur due to failure of contributors in meeting publication deadlines. Biographical information about the contributors would also have been desirable, since many of them have already gained prominence in their respective fields.

On the positive side, the volume offers insight into the personal lives of chemists and provides good coverage of American Nobel Prize winners in chemistry and related fields. [R: Choice, Oct 76, p. 955; RQ, Summer 77, p. 353]

Andrew G. Torok

COMPUTER SCIENCE

660. Directory of Consultants in Computer Systems. 3rd ed. Woodbridge, Conn., Research Publications, 1985. 1v. $75.00. ISBN 0-943692-08-3.

The boom in the computer industry has been instrumental in the mushrooming of several reference publications including this annual biographical directory. It provides brief biographical information on some twenty-five hundred consultants and consulting firms in the United States that should assist micro, mini, and mainframe users to find the proper individual (or firm) for their computer needs. Entries are arranged alphabetically by name under the state in which the consultants are located and provide brief data on credentials, area of specialization, etc. The *Directory* includes a key-word index providing multiple cross-references to each consultant. Users may select a consultant or firm by software application, hardware brands and models, exact specialties, and programming languages.

Research Publications also publishes other biographical directories, including: *Directory of Consultants in Biotechnology* (2,100 profiles, $85.00), *Robotics and Mechanics* (1,960 profiles, $75.00), *Lasers and Physics* (2,240 profiles, $85.00), *Electronics* (2,700 profiles, $85.00), *Environmental Science* (1,375 profiles, $75.00), *Plastics and Chemicals* (2,765 profiles, $85.00) and *Energy Technologies* (1,100 profiles, $75.00). All of them are primarily directories with a minimum of biographical data, but useful in pinpointing specific information about the individuals listed.

Bohdan S. Wynar

661. Marquis Who's Who Directory of Computer Graphics. Chicago, Marquis Who's Who, 1984. 549p. index. $125.00. ISBN 0-8379-5901-2.

The editorial work on this first edition started in Fall 1982 by Marquis with the assistance of the National Computer Graphics Association. The mailing of the questionnaires was accomplished in Spring 1983 and a respondent had to be an active participant in the computer-graphics field employed by government, private sector, or research and academic institutions. Brief biographical sketches of some forty-five hundred individuals provide the following: name and birth date, education, professional certification, career history and career-related activities, creative works, professional memberships and mailing address. There are supplementary indexes at the end of the volume, including: computer graphics area of interest and expertise, computer graphics application area, computer graphics product expertise, and geographic listing. A related title, *Who's Who in Microcomputing*, edited by Datapro Research Corporation (New York, McGraw-Hill, 1982. $39.95), offers additional information in this particular area.

Bohdan S. Wynar

662. Marquis Who's Who Directory of Online Professionals. Chicago, Marquis Who's Who, 1984. 829p. index. $85.00. ISBN 0-8379-6001-0.

This directory covers some six thousand individuals with brief biographical sketches, usually indicating current online position, previous experience, systems currently used, hours of searching per month, equipment used, databases frequently used, consulting experience, if any, as well as the usual information about education, career-related activities, and address and telephone number. There are several indexes that should facilitate the use of this work, including: online function index, subject expertise index and geographic index.

The sketches are typical of Marquis publications; biographee-supplied, much abbreviated, in small print. Questionnaires were mailed to members of professional societies, journal subscribers, attendees at conferences, and users of online services. The only criteria for inclusion were "employment in the industry or use of the industry's products and systems." This includes librarians, computer scientists, publishers, professors, consultants, market researchers, executives, and the like. This, then, is a directory, not a Who's Who. Some thirty-five fields are covered in this directory, including library and information science. A computerized version of the *Directory*, known as the Marquis PRO-FILES Database is available on DIALOG.

A. Neil Yerkey and Bohdan S. Wynar

ELECTRONICS

663. **McGraw-Hill's Leaders in Electronics**. New York, McGraw-Hill, 1979. 651p. index. $47.50. ISBN 0-07-019149-2.

Compiled jointly by McGraw-Hill and *Electronics* magazine, this specialized biographical work includes some fifty-two hundred current notables from private industry, government agencies, academia, and the consulting and military worlds. The editors boldly claim it to be "the only volume documenting the worldwide electronics industries through the people who influence them most. . . ." The contents are arranged in the common alphabetical sequence of capsule collections of facts about the biographees. The component bits of information usually encountered in such a source are presented in an easy-to-read format and are nicely illustrated by the "key" found in the preliminary pages. Not too surprisingly, the entries vary greatly in length, from one or two lines to three-fourths of a column.

There are no photographs, but the volume has an index that lists all the names of persons affiliated with a given organization. This part is useful because it permits one to determine the balance in the distribution of affiliations. Bell Telephone Labs, for example, has 202 entries, while IBM shows 87 and RCA 86, but Sony only 6 names. The "Table of Abbreviations" is another feature, indispensable for a work of this type. Although the exact basis for inclusion is not readily apparent, the preface indicates that the questionnaire method was used, with each participant "given the chance to update or correct . . . the listing." A close examination reveals that in some 40 percent of the cases, where no other data are given, entries were presumably made by virtue only of position held. Hewlett and Packard (calculator company) are included, but Brattain (transistor pioneer) is not.

A more recent title is *Who's Who in Electronics*, edited by Kathie Graeser and Carolyn Hamilton (New York, Harris Pub., 1982. 912p. $75.00). Other relevant titles are *Electrical Who's Who*, a British publication; *Who's Who in Computers and Data Processing* (3v. Quadrangle Books, 1971. o.p.) and *Who's Who in Computer Education and Research*. For the larger science or engineering collections that may already have one or more of these and that also hold tools such as *American Men and Women of Science* and *Dictionary of Scientific Biography*, the volume at hand should be quite suitable as a supplementary source, with little overlap. It would also be a valuable addition for electronics special libraries.

Philip H. Kitchens

ENERGY AND NUCLEAR SCIENCES

664. **International Who's Who in Energy and Nuclear Sciences**. Compiled by the Longman Editorial Team. Harlow, England, Longman; distr., Detroit, Gale, 1983. 531p. (Longman Reference on Research Series). $195.00. ISBN 0-582-90110-3.

This directory provides biographical profiles of over thirty-eight hundred individuals involved in the generation, storage, and efficient use of energy in some seventy countries. In addition to research chemists, physicists, and engineers, the directory includes economists, lawyers, and architects. This work is an obvious spinoff for the Longman Group, which also publishes the *World Energy Directory* and the *World Nuclear Directory*.

The directory consists of two parts. The first and major portion is an alphabetical listing of biographees, from whom information was obtained by questionnaire. However, many entries are incomplete because individuals failed to respond. Such entries, marked with an asterisk, provide only brief information: name, job title, and address. Complete entries include name, year of birth, degrees, present job title, professional experience, appointments, society memberships, publications, research interest, and address. Part 2, entitled "Country and Topic Listing," serves as an index. Arrangement is by country, with subdivisions by specialization such as coal and coal products, geothermal energy, and nuclear fuels. Under each specialization, individuals are listed alphabetically. Instead of listing surnames first, as in part 1, the editors have for some unexplained reason presented names in this index section in "normal" order: initial(s) of given name(s), followed by surnames. This is a minor inconvenience for short listings but could be quite annoying to someone consulting a heavily populated specialty such as solar energy, energy conversion, or nuclear reaction technology.

The book is international in scope, but coverage is very uneven from country to country. For example, there is only one entry for the USSR and less than a page for Japan, but the U.S. listing takes four-and-one-half pages. Future editions may correct the uneven coverage, lack of complete biographical information, and awkward format. Unless libraries need international coverage, association directories like *Guide to Energy Specialists* (World Environment Center, 1981) or the *AEE Directory of Energy Professionals*, 1982-1983 (Association of Energy Engineers) will be sufficient. [R: RQ, Fall 83, p. 106]   Victoria L. Young

665. Pernet, Ann, ed. **Who's Who in Atoms**. 6th ed. Guernsey, England, F. Hodgson; distr., Philadelphia, International Publications, 1977. 620p. $250.00. ISBN 0-85280-201-3.

This work was first published in 1959 as *World Nuclear Directory*. This latest edition contains biographical sketches of approximately seven thousand international nuclear scientists, including information on the present position held by each scientist.

Another related British publication is *Who's Who in Atoms: An International Reference Book* (6th ed., London, Harrap, 1974). This two-volume work contains over twenty thousand entries on nuclear scientists working in seventy-six countries.

Ellen C. Thompson

ENGINEERING AND TECHNOLOGY

666.   Carvill, James. **Famous Names in Engineering**. Woburn, Mass., Butterworths, 1981. 93p. illus. bibliog. index. $23.95; $14.95pa. ISBN 0-408-00539-4; 0-408-00540-8pa.

This book contains one-page biographies of eighty-three famous people connected with the theories, laws, formulae, and inventions that form the foundation of engineering practice. The writing is designed to stimulate interest in the person behind the name, and thus is directed toward students, lay persons, professional engineers, or instructors who want a brief but informative account of someone whose name has been immortalized in courses. The basic background information on birth, death, contemporaries, historical setting, achievements, and the impact of the person's work on events is nicely interwoven into a readable, interesting piece without sacrificing accuracy or professionalism. Anecdotes provide a glimpse of the biographee's personal life and interests. Each article includes a portrait and the appropriate equation, diagram, or illustration. The book has a table of contents, a list of famous people by subject, and a chronological table. A bibliography of further reading at the end of the book lists approximately six sources for each person, including primary source material and references to other biographical reference works.

Although few individuals will purchase this paperback book for themselves, it definitely belongs in the collection of any school with an engineering or pre-engineering program. Reference librarians will continue to consult the *Dictionary of Scientific Biography*, which is more comprehensive, and the *Biographical Dictionary of Scientists*, as well as such sources as the *Dictionary of Named Effects and Laws in Chemistry, Physics, and Mathematics*. However, for the price, this book would be especially suited to the junior or community college collection, a public library sci/tech section, or an undergraduate-level reference or regular collection. [R: Choice, Jan 82, p. 646; SBF, Sept/Oct 82, p. 25]   Karen L. Andrews

667.   **Directory of Expert Witnesses in Technology**. Woodbridge, Conn., Research Publications, 1985. 936p. $95.00. ISBN 0-89235-085-7.

This directory provides brief biographical sketches of some nine thousand individuals prominent in science, engineering and technology. Biographical information includes: name, current address, area of specialization, past affiliations, major achievements, education, publications, patents, memberships, and honors and awards, if any. The volume is accompanied by a key-word index that allows information on the individuals to be located by name, field of expertise and discipline (fifteen thousand specialized areas), or even by city or state.   Bohdan S. Wynar

668.   **Great Engineers and Pioneers in Technology, Volume 1: From Antiquity through the Industrial Revolution**. Roland Turner and Steven L. Goulden, eds. New York, St. Martin's Press, 1981. 488p. illus. index. $69.50. LC 80-28986. ISBN 0-312-34574-7 (vol. 1).

The first volume of *Great Engineers*, a biographical dictionary that is projected to be issued in three volumes, lists 373 engineers who were born before the year 1800. The biographical profiles are chronologically listed in five sections: (1) engineering in the ancient world, (2) medieval engineering: Islam and Europe, (3) engineering in the Far East in historical times, (4) engineering in the Renaissance, and (5) the Industrial Revolution. Each of the five sections is preceded by an essay that sets the historical background. For instance, the essay on the Industrial Revolution discusses its origins in terms of the sociopolitical and economic conditions that favored it; the interrelationship between coal, iron, and steam that ushered it in; and its impact on textile industry as well as the globalization of the Industrial Revolution. This 12½-page essay is followed by biographical sketches of engineers from Thomas Newcomen to Benoit Paul Emile Clapeyron. Each biographee is described under the headings "Life and Times," "Outstanding Engineering Achievement," and "Further Reading." Numerous illustrations of engineers and inventions are included in this volume. At the end, there are a glossary of technical terms, a chronology of important engineering events from ancient times to 1850, a bibliography of works on engineering, a list of illustrations, and a name-subject index.

Overall, *Great Engineers* provides a wealth of information about the achievements of numerous engineers and does so in a pleasant and informative manner. It should be in public libraries and in academic libraries with strong engineering collections.

Rao Aluri

669. **International Who's Who in Optical Science and Engineering**. 1st ed. Chicago, Marquis Who's Who, 1985. 745p. $150.00. ISBN 0-8379-7001-6.

This directory includes biographies of some sixty-five hundred persons in the international optics and engineering communities. Brief biographies include name, birth date, career, career-related activities, published works, awards and honors, current professional memberships, educational background, professional certifications, areas of interest and expertise, industrial application areas, product and consulting experience, telephone number, and address. Four indexes are provided: area of expertise, application area, product expertise, and city, state or country. Optical scientists and engineers are at the forefront of medicine, communications, electronics, and data processing. This volume, with typical Marquis biographical profiles, will be of interest to many special libraries.

Bohdan S. Wynar

670. Kay, Ernest, ed. **International Who's Who in Engineering**. Cambridge, England, International Biographical Centre; distr., Totowa, N.J., International Biographical Centre, 1984. 589p. $115.00. ISBN 0-900332-71-9.

Promoted as "the only global biographical reference work in its field," this volume is the first of a new series by the publisher, who has a number of similar titles in its list. About thirty-five hundred names are listed, with the usual biographical data—birth date and place, present position, education, previous positions, honors, publications, hobbies, and current address.

Inclusion was by invitation, and biographees were not charged. Unfortunately, criteria for inclusion are not specified—one can infer from the editorial introduction, however, that universities, "learned societies," and professional institutions were polled.

Spot checking for well-known American engineers revealed that coverage is quite poor. Most of the major engineering societies such as ASME and IEEE are missing from the list of cooperating institutions in the back of the book. Scanning some of the entries leads one to wonder how some qualified for a Who's Who type of publication!

In summary, the work is seriously flawed, and it is difficult to ascertain what type of library would benefit from its presence on the shelf.

Edwin D. Posey

671. **Leading Consultants in Technology**. 2nd ed. Woodbridge, Conn., Research Publications, 1985. 2v. index. $195.00/set. ISBN 0-89235-089-X; ISSN 0749-9000.

This two-volume reference work lists more than seventeen thousand self-designated consultants from the United States and Canada. The individuals were selected from another Research Publications volume, *Who's Who in Technology Today*. Volume 1 consists of the biographical sketches of the consultants, and volume 2, the "Expertise Index" and the index of names. The biographical sketches are organized first by area, then alphabetically by state, and finally alphabetically by consultant. Each listing includes name, telephone number, present position, address, areas of expertise along with past affiliations, education, publications, patents, achievements, and memberships and honors. Many of the entries note which article or book was considered the most significant by the biographee. This is a nice touch.

The entries emphasize consultants associated with universities or officers of major companies rather than people employed by consulting firms. This point is clearly demonstrated in the area entitled "Environmental Science/Engineering." Under the subheading "Texas" there are twenty-four consultants listed of whom sixteen are university faculty. There are no listings for consultants from the firm of Espey-Huston which is a major Texas environmental consulting firm.

The areas used to organize volume 1 are quite broadly stated; for example, the area of electronics is subdivided into "Electrical Engineering," "Electronic," "Computer Science," "Control Systems," and "Magnetics and Related Electronic Technologies." The other areas of technology are handled in a similar fashion.

The "Expertise Index" in volume 2 is an alphabetical listing of phrases used by the biographee to describe his areas of specialization and an alphabetical listing of all names which appear in volume 1. This listing of names is very important, since each biographee is listed only once. Because of the broad subject organization of volume 1, a user might have trouble finding a particular biography. The book has two major weaknesses; first, there is no listing of consultants by employer or firm and there is no listing of consultants by city. As a result, it is impossible to find a consultant whose name you have forgotten but who works in Dayton, Ohio. It is also impossible to find consultants who work for a particular university or company. These types of things are just what a user of this book might want.

The set is bound in an eye-catching way. The covers are bright glossy blue and buff with orange accents. They should stand out on most reference shelves. While there are a few people listed twice and a few people have died since the original data were collected for *Who's Who in Technology*, this set serves the purpose for which it was designed. It is a listing of primarily scientific faculty, researchers, and company managers who see themselves as consultants.   Susan B. Ardis

672. Marshall, John. **A Biographical Dictionary of Railway Engineers**. North Pomfret, Vt., David and Charles, 1978. 247p. index. $15.95. LC 77-85011. ISBN 0-7153-7489-3.

Designed for the use of railroad historians and "rail fans," this volume contains biographical sketches of railway engineers from all over the world. Averaging two hundred to four hundred words in length, each sketch provides vital data for, and catalogs the achievements of, each of the individuals listed. Abbreviated bibliographical notes indicate the source(s) of information for the sketches.

Potential American users of this tool should be aware of two important points. First, although the volume is world-wide in scope, British engineers overwhelmingly predominate, reflecting the work's British origins. The second point involves the use of the word "engineer." For many, a railway engineer is one who sits in the locomotive and runs the train, á la the legendary Casey Jones (who, by the way, is not included). However, the dictionary includes civil and mechanical engineers as well—those who designed and supervised the building of railroads, railroad bridges, locomotives, and the like. As a matter of fact, probably the names in the volume most familiar to American rail fans are those associated with the design and/or building of locomotives—Matthais Baldwin and Ephraim Shay, for example.

Walter L. Newsome

673. Strute, Karl, ed. **Who's Who in Technology 1984**. 2nd ed. Zurich, Who's Who AG; distr., New York, Unipub, 1984. 3v. (International Red Series). $160.00/set. ISSN 0170-7116.

The first two volumes of this hardbound three-volume set provide brief biographical sketches of individuals from eighteen European countries. This represents a 50 percent increase over the 1979 edition which covered only Germany, Austria, and Switzerland. The engineering professions account for many of the entries, but the business, government, and academic communities are well represented. Entries are arranged alphabetically by last name and include full name, title, pseudonym, birthday, place of birth, parents' names, marital status, spouse's name, number of children, address, present position, career information, membership in professional associations, and recreational activities. The entries are in many cases incomplete, particularly with respect to personal information.

The third volume is an appendix which presents both a directory of names listed alphabetically under major fields and subfields, and a corporate directory consisting of government agencies, businesses, and academic and professional institutions. Numerous advertisements throughout the third volume comprise the bulk of its 1,260 pages. An index of advertisements completes the volume.

American libraries will find this compilation of limited value. Considering the price, even large research libraries and corporate information centers may have second thoughts. This volume is also available from International Publications Service at $240.00 (ISBN 0-8002-3837-0).

Another related title available from International Publications Service is *Who's Who in Technology: Austria, Germany, Switzerland*, edited by Otto J. Groeg (2v. 1979. $195.00).

Andrew G. Torok

674. **Who's Who in Engineering**. 5th ed. New York, American Association of Engineering Societies, 1982. 1900p. $200.00 ($120.00 to members). ISBN 0-87615-013-X.

The first edition of this directory was published in 1970 as *Engineers of Distinction: Including Scientists in Related Fields*. The current edition lists over fifteen thousand brief biographies of members of the engineering societies that belong to the association. A list of the member societies is found in the front of the work. The volume contains supplementary listings such as a society index and an awards index. There is also an index of individuals by state and by specialization. An essential reference book for all parties seeking information on distinguished engineers employed in private industry, government, and their own consulting firms.

Bohdan S. Wynar

675.　**Who's Who in Frontier Science and Technology, 1984-1985**. Chicago, Marquis Who's Who, 1984. 846p. index. $84.50. LC 82-82015. ISBN 0-8379-5701-X.

Contains 16,500 biographical sketches of scientists and technologists working in North America in the frontier areas of their specialties. Includes an index of fields and subspecialties.

The sketches are typical of Marquis Who's Who publications: biographee-supplied, much abbreviated, small print. Selection was made on the basis of incumbency as heads of research facilities, members of honorary organizations, or recipients of awards. Selection was also based on significant achievement, although that criterion is not explained.

The method of defining "frontier science and technology" is not satisfactorily explained, either. Apparently, the Marquis staff asked scientists and journal editors for "current descriptions of fields at the cutting edge." The resultant list of 24 fields and 350 subfields includes both new directions in traditional fields and work using the most advanced technology.

A sample of entries revealed about a 60 percent overlap with *American Men and Women of Science* (Bowker, 1982, 15th ed.). The reference value of this work will depend on the need to locate information about people working in newer areas of research. [R: Choice, Oct 84, p. 255; LJ, 1 Oct 84, p. 1841; RBB, 15 Nov 84, p. 426; WLB, Oct 84, p. 149]　　　　　　　　　　　　　　　　　A. Neil Yerkey

676.　**Who's Who in Technology Today**. 4th ed. Barbara A. Tinucci and Louann Chaudier, eds. Lake Bluff, Ill., J. Dick Publishing/Woodbridge, Conn., Research Publications, 1984. 5v. index. $425.00/set. LC 80-644137. ISBN 0-943692-15-6; ISSN 0190-4841.

This fourth edition continues the original purpose of identifying the people who have made significant contributions to technological progress. Most of the biographees apply and furnish data to the editors; additional nominees are suggested by professional and technical societies. Entries are then screened by the editors; inclusion is based on patents, publications, honors and/or achievement, and expertise in an important area of technology.

The entries include the person's name and employer, educational background, membership in organizations, honors and awards, principal area of expertise, and personal information. Entries are arranged under broad categories, with narrower fields listed therein. Some thirty-two thousand North American scientists and technologists are listed.

Volumes 1-4 are arranged by discipline and each contains an alphabetical index. The broad subject fields covered include: electronics and computer science; physics and optics; chemistry and biotechnology; mechanical engineering; civil engineering; and earth sciences. These areas are also further subdivided. The fifth volume comprises the "Expertise Index," with a list of key-word headings, an index of principal expertise (including fifteen hundred fields of specialization), and an index of names.

Despite the formidable price, this set is an essential acquisition for most research libraries, large public libraries, and special libraries supporting high technology clienteles.　　　　　　　　　　　　　　　　　　　　　　　　Edwin D. Posey

677.　**Who's Who of British Engineers, 1980**. Athens, Ohio, Ohio University Press, 1981. 352p. $55.00. LC 68-55655. ISBN 0-312-87413-8.

This directory provides the usual biographical data about some six thousand British engineers in government, research, teaching, and industry. Included are details of their academic qualifications, civil honors, past and present appointments, memberships, and specific areas of professional interest. Of special interest to the users is information on published works, including some important articles and research papers. This work can be supplemented by *Who's Who in Technology*, edited by Karl Strute (2nd ed. 3v. distr., New York, Unipub, 1984. $160.00) that lists some twenty thousand individuals from Western Europe.   Bohdan S. Wynar

PHYSICS

678.   Weber, Robert Lemmerman. **Pioneers of Science: Nobel Prize Winners in Physics**. J. M. A. Lenihan, ed. London, Institute of Physics; distr., Philadelphia, Heyden, 1980. 272p. illus. bibliog. index. $23.00. ISBN 0-9960020-1-4.

Bisographies of 114 Nobel Prize winners in physics are included in this excellent book. Presented chronologically by date of the award, the sketches average two pages in length and are accompanied by portraits of the laureates. The biographies are current through the 1979 Nobel Prizes. Scientific achievement is stressed, but there is also much information about the personalities of the laureates, making the book interesting for the general reader as well as the student of physics. A bibliography and an index conclude the work. *Pioneers of Science* is appropriate for most general science collections. [R: Choice, Apr 81, p. 1121]   Bohdan S. Wynar

22 Social Sciences

Introduction

The material in this chapter covers recently published biographical dictionaries arranged as follows: "Social Sciences in General," "Anthropology," "Community Service, Social Welfare, and Social Work" and "Psychology," with a total of thirteen entries plus several related titles mentioned in the annotations. It should be pointed out, however, that most biographical sources pertaining to social scientists will be found in other chapters, primarily part 1, "Universal and National Biographies," as well as such chapters as "History," "Geography," and "Political Science." In addition, many dictionaries in the social sciences incorporate biographies, e.g., *A New Dictionary of the Social Sciences*, edited by G. D. Mitchell (Aldine, 1979. 244p.), which unfortunately is not so comprehensive as *A Dictionary of Social Sciences*, edited by J. Gould and W. Kolb and compiled under the auspices of UNESCO (Free Press, 1964. 761p.). As a matter of fact, older sources offer substantial biographical data—notably two outstanding encyclopedias: the fifteen-volume *Encyclopaedia of the Social Sciences*, edited by E. R. A. Seligman (Macmillan, 1930-1935) is a classic, prepared under the auspices of ten learned societies with international scholarly contributions. The biographical sketches are very sound and this encyclopedia, in addition to social sciences in general, also covers political science, economics, law, anthropology, sociology, penology, and social work, as well as the social aspects of ethics, education, psychology, philosophy, biology, geography, medicine, art, and other subjects. This encyclopedia is complemented, but not superseded by, the seventeen-volume *International Encyclopedia of Social Sciences*, edited by D. L. Sills (Free Press/Macmillan, 1968). Biographical sketches in this newer work are limited to six hundred entries (compared to four thousand in the earlier set), including living persons born before 1890.

There are several bibliographic guides in this area that provide adequate descriptions of existing reference sources, including indexing and abstracting services. One of the most comprehensive is J. B. Mason's *Research Resources: Annotated Guide to the Social Sciences* (2v. ABC-Clio, 1968-1971). An older guide, *Sources of Information in the Social Sciences: A Guide to the Literature*, edited by C. M. White (American

Library Association, 1973. 702p.), was first published in 1964, and a new edition is in preparation. White's work is much superior to Mason's with the exception of coverage of indexing and abstracting services.

SOCIAL SCIENCES IN GENERAL

679.   **American Reformers: An H. W. Wilson Biographical Dictionary.** Alden Whitman, ed. New York, H. W. Wilson, 1985. 930p. illus. (H. W. Wilson Biographical Dictionary). $75.00. LC 85-636. ISBN 0-8242-0705-X.

This biographical dictionary includes 508 American men and women who have sought to raise public consciousness about a variety of social issues and causes, e.g., industrial reform, racial and gender equality, temperance, abolition, education, and religious freedom. The editor, Alden Whitman, has selectively chosen individuals concerned with issues of national—as opposed to local or regional—importance from the seventeenth century to contemporary times in America. They include well-known reformers such as Susan B. Anthony, Martin Luther King, Jr., Earl Warren, Harriet Tubman, and Samuel Langhorne Clemens, as well as less prominent, sometimes obscure, pioneers of various reform movements.

Historians and subject specialists, who are the contributors of *American Reformers*, have provided extensive bibliographies which follow each biographical essay. Entries are initialed and a list of the contributors appears in the front of the book. Typically, an entry consists of statistical information, vocational background, writings, travels, religious affiliation, and the significant contributions and activities relative to the specific cause(s) toward which the indivudal worked.

The essays, which vary in length from one to four pages, are listed in alphabetical order by the last name of the biographee. There is no index per se, though biographees are listed under broad subject categories (e.g., black rights, ecology, education, populism, women's rights) following the text of the book. A picture accompanies virtually every entry, and there is a photographic-credits section at the end of the volume.

This well-written, documented work is recommended for college, public, and high school libraries—large and small.   Dianne B. Catlett

680.   **International Encyclopedia of the Social Sciences Biographical Supplement.** New York, Free Press/Macmillan, 1979. **Supplement to the 17 Volume IESS.** 1979. $90.00. LC 68-10023. ISBN 0-02-895510-2. **Supplement to the 8 Volume IESS.** 1979. $85.00. LC 77-72778. ISBN 0-02-895690-7.

Biographies of the 215 most important figures in current social sciences are included in this volume. The *Biographical Supplement* updates the original *International Encyclopedia of the Social Sciences* (*IESS*), published in 1968 and edited by David L. Sills (17v. New York, Free Press, 1968-1979. $275.00). *IESS* includes only eminent social scientists who are deceased or had reached the age of seventy-five at time of publication, and therefore does not include many modern social scientists; the *Supplement* follows the same criteria. Social science fields represented are: anthropology, criminology, demography, economics, history, linguistics, philosophy, political science and legal theory, psychology and psychiatry, religion, sociology, and statistics. Each biography is a signed work of original scholarship, written by a leading social scientist. Entries contain basic biographical information, as well as an in-depth discussion of the subject's work, contributions, and influence on other scholars. Most entries contain two bibliographies: one of the subject's own work, and another of works related to the subject. The *Biographical Supplement* is available in two formats: to accompany the seventeen-volume *IESS* or the eight-volume *IESS*.

                                                                    Bohdan S. Wynar

681.   Nijhawan, N. K., ed. **National Register of Social Scientists in India**. [By] Indian Council of Social Science Research. New Delhi, India, Concept Publishing; distr., Atlantic Highlands, N.J., Humanities Press, 1983. 976p. index. $80.50. ISBN 0-391-02493-0.

The Indian Council of Social Science Research worked hard to prepare the *National Register of Social Scientists in India* and has succeeded in providing a useful source for getting information on Indian social scientists. This reference volume has been divided into four parts. Part 1 includes biographical information on 7,527 Indian social scientists working in India; part 2 has a list of 250 areas of specialization under which the biographies fall; part 3 is an alphabetical index under various subject headings with a list of social scientists who specialize in those subjects and their branches; and part 4 is an appendix that includes the questionnaire sent to the social scientists. Part 1 has been further divided into seventeen sections under various subjects, such as anthropology, demography, education, history, international relations, management, public administration, social work, and communication. Entries in each section have been arranged alphabetically by last name. The information in each entry includes the social scientist's date of birth, education beyond bachelor's degree, publications, current position, and complete office address. There are many cross-references in the volume.

The register will help in identifying the Indian social scientists. It must be added, however, that the register does not give complete information about each person included. For example, place of birth has not been included, and only the current position is listed. Previous positions, other interests, honors or grants, other contributions to the field, etc., are not mentioned. The index does not give any page numbers. Only 35 percent of working Indian social scientists have been included in the register. Therefore, it is not a very comprehensive reference work. Nevertheless, a good beginning has been made.   Ravindra N. Sharma

ANTHROPOLOGY

682.   **Fifth International Directory of Anthropologists**. Preface by Sol Tax. Chicago, University of Chicago Press, 1975. 496p. index. (Current Anthropology Resource Series). $29.95. LC 74-11615. ISBN 0-266-79077-0.

The fourth edition of this now standard biographical directory was published in 1967. The data for the current edition were obtained through questionnaires sent to all fellows of the American Anthropological Association, to associates of "Current Anthropology," to registrants of the IXth International Congress of Anthropology, and to institutions, universities, museums, etc., in the United States and abroad.

In his preface, Professor Sol Tax, of the University of Chicago, devotes substantial space to a consideration of the completeness of his results. Far from claiming completeness, he acknowledges that while the *Directory* lists 4,765 anthropologists, an informed estimate of the world total qualified for inclusion is 5,525. Judged by the standards of performance achieved by other compilers of directories, his results are excellent and no apologies are called for.

The *Directory* is arranged in straight alphabetical order. For indexing purposes, all biographical entries are serially numbered. The entries themselves are gratifyingly full, with bountiful details on the subjects' education, research interests, publications, job experiences, and language competencies.

The indexing is excellent. Specific approaches are geographical (i.e., geographic orientation of the subjects' research interests, not their residences) and chronological (i.e., time period of research interests, ranging from Paleolithic to ethnographic present and contemporary). A minutely detailed Subject/Methodological Index is itself subdivided into cultural anthropology and archaeology. All index references are to serial entry numbers.

A necessary purchase for libraries having substantial research collections in anthropology. Richard A. Gray

COMMUNITY SERVICE, SOCIAL WELFARE, AND SOCIAL WORK

683. **International Who's Who in Community Service: Incorporating Directory of Public Affairs, Repertoire d'Affaires Publiques, Who's Who in Public Affairs, Dictionnaire Biographique de Service Publique, and Who's Who in Sussex (Established 1935).** 3rd ed. Totowa, N.J., International Biographical Centre, c/o Biblio Distribution Center, 1979. 409p. $50.00. ISBN 0-85649-023-7.

This third edition of the *International Who's Who in Community Service* is devoid of any prefatory matter. Therefore, users in libraries lacking previous editions will have no clue as to its scope, criteria for inclusion, or even what is meant by "community service." As this edition now incorporates five other directories, the omission of such vital information is an additional handicap. The first edition (published in 1974) did indicate that community service was broadly defined, encompassing individuals in national and local government, social welfare, medicine, education, the arts and sciences, church life, leisure activities, etc. The entries in the new edition seem to reflect this same scope.

Since about twelve individuals are sketched per double-columned page, the volume contains between five thousand and six thousand entries. Information provided includes: birth date, nationality, profession, position, community service activities, address, and telephone number. As with earlier editions, no selection criteria are indicated. Also, many important community figures are omitted, while minor figures are listed. An example of the latter is a person whose only community service is membership in the American Temperance Society and in a regional church conference. This is another poorly conceived and overpriced biographical tool from the publishers of the *Dictionary of International Biography*. [R: WLB, Oct 74, p. 180]

Gary D. Barber

684. Lender, Mark Edward. **Dictionary of American Temperance Biography: From Temperance Reform to Alcohol Research, the 1600s to the 1980s.** Westport, Conn., Greenwood Press, 1984. 572p. index. $45.00. LC 83-12589. ISBN 0-313-22335-1.

This is a biographical encyclopedia of men and women active since the colonial period in the United States in movements related to regulating or studying drinking of alcohol. The 373 entries represent all ethnic and religious groups, both sexes, and all philosophical stances regarding drinking regulation/reform.

The arrangement is nearly identical to that of Henry Bowden's *Dictionary of American Religious Biography*. Each entry includes three parts: a Who's Who-type summary; a one- to one-and-a-half-page narrative, emphasizing the subject's role related to alcohol; and a bibliography. The latter may list up to six works by, and six works about, the subject (including standard general biographies). The narratives include cross-references to other entries. Access is by a subject/name/organization index. There are also lists of the biographees by birthplace and by religious affiliation.

While no detailed criteria for inclusion are given, nearly all listees died before 1980, and all are significant as leaders or intellectual contributors, or as typical of aspects of the movements.

Much of the information here parallels the biographical entries in the six-volume *Standard Encyclopedia of the Alcohol Problem* (1925-1930), although the information is fresher and the writing better. The index could have been better (e.g., nicknames rarely have entries), but it is more complete than what one usually finds in such reference works.

This would be a useful purchase for libraries with major collections or user interest in temperance, or social reform in general. [R: Choice, Oct 84, p. 250; WLB, Nov 84, p. 225]   James H. Sweetland

685. Lord, Benjamin, ed. **America's Wealthiest People: Their Philanthropic and Nonprofit Affiliations**. Washington, D.C., Taft Corporation, 1984. 78p. index. $57.50pa. ISBN 0-914756-57-5.

From Josephine Abercrombie to Mortimer Zuckerman, this book claims to list the five hundred or so wealthiest people in the United States, together with any philanthropic associations to which they may have laid claim. For each person, the compiler lists birth date, education, present employment, corporate and philanthropic affiliations, addresses, club, estimates of wealth and a section called "Notes," which recounts how each person amassed his or her fortune. The amount of information varies considerably from one individual to another, reflecting, presumably, how much information about each can be found in the open press, or to put it another way, how successful each has been in keeping his or her activities hidden. The names and data are drawn from files maintained by the Taft Corporation, a Washington, D.C., firm that specializes in corporate and foundation philanthropy. Indexes are provided for state of residence, philanthropic affiliations, and broad categories (e.g., "Arts and Humanities") at which the rich may be presumed to be disposed to throw money.

This book is aimed at fund-raisers and development officers, dangling before them the hope that knowing who the rich are will make it simpler to squeeze funds from foundations with which they are associated. To be sure, there are disclaimers: "We do not encourage you to believe that there is a scientific rationale on which you can base strategies for reaching and cultivating the people listed in this book. . ." (p. i). But the message is clear – here are the fat cats, go get them. Why else bother to publish?

The Taft Corporation has based its reputation on the notion that successful fund-raising depends on knowing as much as one can about the foundation officers who make funding decisions, so that presentations can be tailored to their known inclinations. Perhaps; but the grant seeker will do well to concentrate instead on building a solid proposal as the best way to influence foundation officers. The intelligent fund-raiser will also avoid this book, whose price of $57.50 for seventy-eight meanly printed pages is plainly aimed at helping to hoist the officers of the Taft Corporation into place among the nation's wealthiest people.

Robert Balay

686. **NASW Professional Social Workers' Directory, 1978**. Washington, D.C., National Association of Social Workers, 1978. 1733p. o.p. LC 78-58684. ISBN 0-87101-078-X.

This is the fourth edition of the directory of the National Association of Social Workers. The brief biographical information on about seventy-five thousand members was gathered from a questionnaire or from membership records if the form was not returned. The *Directory* gives the person's name, religious or military title, membership in Academy of Certified Social Workers, address, telephone number, degrees (date and place), present position, employer's name or whether the person is in private practice, social-work state license, certificates, or regulations. A code is used to indicate student or associate members, those members who are also listed in the *NASW Register of Clinical Social Workers*, or members who did not return the original questionnaire (approximately one-third of the entries are based on membership records). About one entry in forty contains "optional biographical information," which allows members to list additional information about themselves (social-work honors, prior work experience, additional degrees, etc.).

New editions of this directory are published every six years. Since social workers must move, change jobs, etc., as often as the rest of the population, a considerable portion of the information is already out of date. Also, the *Directory* would be more useful if it had geographical or speciality indexes. It would be important to know which social workers work in Altoona or who specializes in alcoholism treatment. It is puzzling as to why so few entries contain the "optional biographical information." Additional background information, particularly job experience, would make the *Directory* more important. As it is, it can be recommended only for large applied social science reference collections.

Jack E. Pontius

687. **NASW Register of Clinical Social Workers, 1985**. 4th ed. Washington, D.C., National Association of Social Workers, 1985. 626p. index. $60.00. LC 75-42777. ISBN 0-87101-126-3.

This is a revision of the third edition that was published in 1982. Entries were checked and revised as needed and new registrants added. Listings are compiled through a system of voluntary application of prospective entrants, who submit certified credentials to the Register Board. The board reviews the credentials according to stipulated procedures to ascertain whether the applicants indeed qualify for entry. The "introduction" clearly disclaims any attempt to or ability to judge the competencies of the listees.

The *NASW Register* is divided into two parts. Part 1 is an alphabetical name index containing such information as name, address, and phone numbers, an indication of whether the individual is engaged in private practice or is affiliated with an institution, the affiliation, education, specialization, and a listing of experience. Part 2 is an alphabetically arranged geographical index arranged by state and subarranged by cities, towns, etc. Under each is found a listing of clinical social workers in that area. After using the geographical index, the user must refer to part 1. Use of the directory is facilitated by introductory matter consisting of definitions, descriptions, and directions for use. Tables of abbreviations and social-work state licenses, certifications, and registrations are also helpful. Entries are allotted generous space and are easy to read. A check of local entries when compared with the Buffalo phone book seemed to indicate accurate information. One caveat should be mentioned—since entrants are chosen through voluntary submission of data, the register is in no way complete.

Harry S. Otterson, Jr.

688. **People in Philanthropy: A Guide to Philanthropic Leaders, Major Donors, and Funding Connections**. Yvette Henry and others, eds. Washington, D.C., Taft Corporation, 1984. 361p. index. $187.00. LC 84-50482. ISBN 0-914756-60-5.

Successful fund-raising is not always done by those who have the best ideas or presentation. As in many other fields, knowing the right people has a greater influence on the outcome. To help identify the powerful and influential people in philanthropy, the Taft Corporation has compiled this list which is divided into four sections: "Wealthy People," "Foundation Donors," "Foundation Officers," and "Corporate Officers." Each section has alphabetically arranged, brief biographical sketches that include information about the individual's dates and state of birth, education, current employment, corporate and nonprofit affiliations. The profiles have many abbreviations that are explained in the "Key to Abbreviations Used in Biographies." In addition, three special indexes provide lists of all individuals in the previous sections by philanthropic affiliations, state of birth, and by their alma mater. These lists identify names of those on foundation or corporate boards that are important to your request strategy, as well as those with geographical or school ties. These connections are useful when applying for funds since one needs all the assistance possible to insure acceptance of a fund-raising proposal.

Jean Herold

689. Watkins, Nina, ed. **International Who's Who in Community Service. 1973-74**. London, Eddison Press, 1973; distr., Totowa, N.J., Rowman & Littlefield, 1974. 851p. $37.50. LC 78-189467. ISBN 0-85649-012-1.

The information for this book was obtained through the distribution of a questionnaire; there was evidently no follow-up on those individuals who failed to respond. Perhaps that explains why, among a random check of U.S. legislators, we find entries for Hiram Fong, Daniel Inouye, and Shirley Chisholm but none for Senators Eastland and Mansfield or Congressman Garry Brown. All of the above, happily, can be found in *Who's Who in American Politics*.

The definition of "community service" used here is broad, including individuals in national and local government, social welfare, medicine, education, the arts and sciences, church life, leisure activities, community life, etc. Indeed, one would be hard put to exclude any field of human endeavor as long as it is within the boundaries of law and propriety. The information provided includes date of birth, nationality, current and past positions, education, professional and social affiliations, and business and home addresses.

According to the preface, more than two thousand of the sixty-four hundred biographees listed in this volume went on to express an interest in the gold and silver medals, wall plaques, and diplomas promoted by the publishers. [R: WLB, Oct 74, pp. 180-81]

Marjorie K. Ho and Bohdan S. Wynar

PSYCHOLOGY

690. **Directory of the American Psychological Association**. 1981 ed. Washington, D.C. American Psychological Association, 1981. 1659p. $57.50pa. LC 49-3998. ISBN 0-912704-46-2.

The *Directory* lists biographical information for more than forty thousand psychologists who are members of the American Psychological Association (APA). Entries include typical information: name, address, office and home phone numbers, birth date, highest degree, major field, psychological specialty areas, licensure or certification as a psychologist, employment information, APA membership information, and a symbol indicating when the entry was most recently updated. If the psychologist is in private or group practice, that fact is shown under employment. In addition to the biographies, documents of interest to psychologists, such as the APA bylaws and "Ethical Standards of Psychologists," a geographical index, and a divisional membership roster, are included. A new edition of the *Directory* is issued every three years, and it is updated by an annual membership register.

This source will be useful for locating short biographical information, especially addresses and phone numbers, and for identifying psychologists who are in private or group practice. The geographical index will facilitate location of private-practice psychologists in an area, even though the usefulness of a symbol that was designed for this purpose was destroyed due to a typesetting error. The *Directory* is a standard source that should be in the reference collection of every major library. Mary Reichel

691. Zusne, Leonard. **Biographical Dictionary of Psychology**. Westport, Conn., Greenwood Press, 1984. 563p. index. $49.95. LC 83-18326. ISBN 0-313-24027-2.

The *Biographical Dictionary* is a revised edition of Zusne's *Names in the History of Psychology: A Biographical Sourcebook*. For the first edition, a total of 526 eminent psychologists, all deceased, was selected. The selection was made by nine panelists, all of whom are prominent psychologists themselves. Included in the selection were also scholars from other professions who have significantly contributed to the development of psychology.

The present edition includes most of the entries from the first edition, with 101 new names added. While about one-half of the newly included names relate to those personalities in psychology who died after the publication of the first edition, the other half come from the more distant past. The relative eminence of all historical figures included in the present work was established according to the space given to them by sixteen authors of the histories of psychology. The rationale for this method of evaluation, differing from that in the first edition, is explained. Each biography, after stating the nationality and profession of the biographee and his/her standard biographical data (birth, death, highest degree, positions held), lists "the main points of theoretical contributions; philosophies held; inventions and discoveries made; methodologies initiated; books and seminal articles written; research conducted; laboratories, journals and institutions founded; and influence exercised" (p. vii).

In contrast to the first edition, individual entries in the *Biographical Dictionary* are arranged alphabetically, not chronologically according to birth dates. In addition to Appendix A, giving a chronological listing of birth dates (starting with Thales, born ca. 624 B.C.), new information is provided in other appendixes. Specifically, new ranking information on the relative eminence of names in the history of psychology is provided in Appendix B, while Appendix C relates to nineteenth- and twentieth-century contributors in academic and research institutions, arranged geographically and chronologically.

Zusne's *Biographical Dictionary of Psychology* is an exceptional work which can be considered a good reference companion to the study of the history and systems of psychology. It brings together information that in most instances would require time-consuming searching in scattered sources. The first edition of this work has been considered unique in the field and received positive recommendations and acceptance as a Who's Who in the history of psychology. The current edition which provides more extensive information undoubtedly is an invaluable reference tool whose usefulness will be appreciated by psychology students and professionals on different levels and in diverse settings. [R: LJ, Aug 84, p. 1438]   Miluse Soudek

23 Sports

Introduction

The chapter on "Sports" is arranged in several sections: "General Works," "Aeronautics," "Baseball," "Basketball," "Boxing," "Football," "Golf," "Hockey," "Showjumping and Equestrianism," "Tennis," and "Track and Field," with a total of twenty-seven biographical works, plus many more mentioned in the annotations. The "General Works" include such titles as *Quest for Gold: The Encyclopedia of American Olympians* (see entry 694) and *The Lincoln Library of Sports Champions* (see entry 693) for juvenile audiences. Most biographical works dealing with individual sports are for a general audience, with only a few showing a more scholarly execution. However, some sports dictionaries that also contain biographical information are of a high quality. An example is *The Oxford Companion to World Sports and Games*, edited by John Arlott (Oxford University Press, 1975. 143p.), that, in keeping with the tradition of Oxford Companions in other areas, provides brief but well-researched biographical information on prominent sports figures. Similar works are Z. Hollander's *The Modern Encyclopedia of Basketball* (2nd ed. Doubleday, 1979. 624p.), *Fischler's Hockey Encyclopedia* (Thomas Y. Crowell, 1975. 628p.), and R. Henshaw's *The Encyclopedia of World Soccer* (New Republic Books, 1979. 828p.).

There are only a few bibliographic guides in this area that discuss reference sources and indexing services. Dated, but still the best, is M. Nunn's *Sports* (Libraries Unlimited, 1976. 217p.). The reader is advised to consult Sheehy and Walford for information on indexing services.

GENERAL WORKS

692. Hickok, Ralph. **Who Was Who in American Sports**. New York, Hawthorn Books, 1971. 338p. o.p. LC 72-158009.

This is a reliable, fairly detailed volume containing biographical sketches of approximately fifteen hundred of America's most important and colorful sports figures. As one might expect, athletes from the popular spectator sports dominate the entries. Baseball and football personalities comprise 58 percent of the entries; the former is represented by 635 persons and the latter by 248. Among the forty-two sports covered, several have only one or two persons represented. With few exceptions, all deceased members of the major sports' halls of fame are listed. Some devotees of archery, field hockey, softball, polo, and several other minor sports may question the absence of figures from their specialities. In addition to athletes and coaches, some well-known broadcasters, managers, sportswriters, officials, and rule-makers are included. The entries give birth and death dates, place of birth, career highlights, records established, life-time averages when appropriate, and the name of the hall of fame to which the athlete was elected. The year in which this honor was bestowed is not listed. References to sources containing additional biographical information on the individuals would have been useful. Index of personalities by sports is included. [R: LJ, July 71, p. 2294]

Robert Van Benthuysen

693. **The Lincoln Library of Sports Champions**. 4th ed. Columbus, Ohio, Frontier Press, 1985. 20v. illus. (part col.). index. $327.50/set. LC 84-81800. ISBN 0-912168-11-0.

Nearly five hundred sports personalities in more than fifty sports are profiled in this multivolume work. Set in 11-point type and containing over three thousand photographs and illustrations, the set is designed for elementary and junior high school students. The champions selected represent a wide range of sports and are mainly contemporary figures.

Although the set will undoubtedly be popular, it does suffer from inconsistent selection of biographees, as well as slightly advanced vocabulary. The Rutgers readability graph indicates a seventh-grade reading level; the print size suggests that the editors had hoped for a lower reading level, perhaps fifth or sixth grade. The last volume of the set is a glossary of sports terminology. It is a helpful feature, but the text consists largely of long, complex sentences that a younger reader may have difficulty understanding, even with the help of the glossary.

The basic shortcoming of the set is its selection of sports figures. The emphasis on modern sportsmen is acceptable in a popular juvenile work, and the editors have chosen mainly recognizable names. However, the editors have also chosen to include figures for "educational" reasons: "There are also lessons to learn from studying the lives of these sports stars. Struggling against great odds; living through impoverished early lives; learning to live in a world of widespread prejudice; learning to live with defeat and victory; knowing love and understanding; wrestling with one's self; and the importance of confidence, courage, desire, and determination are lessons for all." And, "sheer ability was not the only reason for the choice of a particular person, nor is it intended that the men and women are the absolute best in sports. The individual's significance and contributions to his sport were equally important." With this standard in mind, one wonders how Evel Knievel ended up in this set. Moral character is a rather subjective basis to determine inclusion in the ranks of sports champions. The editors do not seem to have defined the distinction between champions and heroes. The concept that students can learn lessons from the lives of sports heroes is disturbing. Certainly many sports figures have overcome great obstacles to achieve stardom, but is this a proper criterion for selection as a champion? Perhaps the editors would have produced a more balanced group of champions if they had used performance instead of popularity as the basis of selection. Or the publishers could rename the set "The Lincoln Library of Sports Heroes."

The set is useful for its illustrations and biographies, which provide more than statistical data. There is nothing comparable available for juvenile audiences. It should provide interesting reading for younger sports fans if the vocabulary does not prove too advanced.

This work can be supplemented by *The Big Book of Halls of Fame in the United States and Canada: Sports*, edited by Jaques Cattell Press (R. R. Bowker, 1977. 1042p. o.p.) that covers forty sports, providing biographical information on some ten thousand persons and animals.

James P. Heitzer, Janet H. Littlefield, and Bohdan S. Wynar

694. Mallon, Bill, and Ian Buchanan. **Quest for Gold: The Encyclopedia of American Olympians**. With Jeffrey Tishman. New York, Leisure Press; distr., New York, Scribner's, 1984. 495p. illus. $19.95pa. LC 84-966. ISBN 0-88011-217-4.

American participation in the Olympic games is a cause for intense pride among most citizens, not just those who follow the various events which are such an integral part of the meeting of the world's finest athletes. *Quest for Gold* records the Olympic feats of those medal winners representing the United States from 1896, when the modern games were reinstituted, to the fateful 1980 team which boycotted the Moscow games.

Only medal winners are included, and the brief biographical sketches range from very short one-line entries (mostly from 1904 participants) to a lengthy sympathetic view of Jim Thorpe, the 1912 Olympian who was stripped of his medals because of "professional" status only to have them restored posthumously in 1983. Six appendixes include Olympic records, the rosters of the 1940 team (when the games were cancelled but a team was named) and the 1980 team, as well as a thorough sport-by-sport index.

The sketches of the Olympians are a little uneven. For example, the entry for basketball player Kenny Carr does not indicate that he has become a mainstay with the Portland franchise in the National Basketball Association. In contrast, the entry for Larry Brown, also a participant in basketball, mentions that Brown coaches at the University of Kansas, a position he assumed only a few years ago. Despite this minor criticism, *Quest for Gold* is a useful addition to Olympic literature, surpassing the *Guinness Book of Olympic Records* and the *Olympic Sports Offical Album*. It can also be supplemented by *Who's Who in the Nineteen Eighty-Four Olympics*, edited by David Emery (Tapsfield, Mass., Merrimack, 1984. 192p. $9.95pa.) that covers 694 athletes.

Boyd Childress and Bohdan S. Wynar

AERONAUTICS

695. Jones, Mel R. **Above and Beyond: Eight Great American Aerobatic Champions**. Blue Ridge Summit, Pa., TAB Books, 1984. 150p. illus. index. $11.95pa. LC 84-8531. ISBN 0-8306-2353-1.

This collective biography includes coverage of eight current U.S. stunt pilots: Bob Herendeen, Charlie Hillard, Gene Soucy, Tom Poberezny, Henry Haigh, Kermit Weeks, Betty Stewart, and Leo Loudenslager. Both their personal and professional lives are discussed. Many of the illustrations are candid photographs of people and equipment; there are also a few sketches of stunt sequences.

Appendixes list the U.S. National Aerobatic Champions, 1964-1983; the biennial World Aerobatic Championships, 1960-1982; and the names of the U.S. participants in the World Aerobatic Championships, 1960-1984. The book is unique in its focus on currently active stunt pilots and offers a glimpse of a very unusual, high-risk lifestyle.

Betty Gay

696. **Who's Who of Ballooning: 1783-1983**. South Gate, Calif., Rechs Publications, 1983. 362p. $20.00. ISBN 0-937568-26-0.

Prepared jointly by the National Balloon Museum and the Balloon Federation of America, this directory contains biographical information on some fifty-three hundred world aeronauts. Unfortunately this work is not professionally edited and serves as a good example of rather numerous biographical publications sponsored by organizations interested in sports activities. Two other examples are *Who's Who in the Martial Arts and Directory of Black Belts* (New York, R. A. Wall, 1975. 275p. $7.95) and *Who's Who in Karate*, edited by Harold Long and Allen Wheeler (New York, National Paperback, 1981. 110p. $3.95).   Bohdan S. Wynar

BASEBALL

697. Allen, Maury. **Baseball's 100: A Personal Ranking of the Best Players in Baseball History**. New York, A&W Visual Library, 1981. 316p. illus. $14.95; $7.95pa. LC 80-70369. ISBN 0-89104-200-8; 0-89104-208-3pa.

Allen, a well-known and competent sports writer, has taken an interesting idea and turned it into a fascinating book. But it is not a reference book; instead it is a very good general interest sports book. His idea is to select one hundred of the best baseball players of the twentieth century and rank them in order of their skills and performance. There have been over ten thousand major-league baseball players since 1900, so how did Allen select and rank them? He draws upon his forty years as an inveterate baseball fan (fanatic?) and his extensive reading for a lot of his conclusions; and he has interviewed several old-timers of the game, such as Casey Stengel, to help him fill in the information on superstars of the early twentieth century.

Allen has assembled all of this information, and the result is a book of his personal evaluations of the greatest of the greatest. He doesn't expect everyone to agree with his rankings (why should Hank Aaron be number 1 instead of Babe Ruth?), but his book will generate a lot of interest and controversy.

His capsule biographies of each player are one-and-one-half pages long and include full-page black-and-white photos for all one hundred entries. A brief appendix section has Allen's choices for the ten best managers, ball parks, and other miscellaneous listings.

Allen's book is well written and edited and makes lively reading from cover to cover. Put it in the circulating sports collection where it will surely reach a large and appreciative audience. Marshall E. Nunn

698. Appel, Martin, and Burt Goldblatt. **Baseball's Best: The Hall of Fame Gallery.** 2nd ed. New York, McGraw-Hill, 1980. 448p. illus. $29.95. LC 80-12628. ISBN 0-07-002148-1.

This compilation concerns members of major league baseball's Hall of Fame: players, managers, owners, umpires, league presidents, and even one sportswriter. Coverage includes 1979 inductees, although in an addendum. Entries run from two to five pages each, but length is based on no readily apparent criteria. All inductees are treated equally, according to the preface, regardless of manner of induction. Arranged alphabetically, entries include: a portrait and one or more other photos of the member; a brief biography, including a narrative of the highlights of each player's career; and major league pitching and/or batting totals. This last item represents the major problem in using the book as a reference tool: major league totals, even if complete, are often insufficient for reference use, and these are not complete. For pitchers, the totals lack shutouts, games started, complete games, etc. For batters, the totals lack bases on balls, stolen bases, total bases, slugging averages, etc. Far more satisfactory would have been a complete major league record, year by year, including the categories noted above, plus others. The ample white space in the book would have accommodated these statistics without an excessive number of additional pages.

As it is, the user seeking more than minimal information must look elsewhere, probably to McGraw-Hill's own *Baseball Encyclopedia*. No records of inductees from the old Negro leagues are included, the indication being "no records available." It seems probable that there are some records available somewhere, possibly in the box scores found in newspapers of the era of those leagues. This could be a project for some baseball historian. Binding, paper, typography, and quality of photos are all excellent. Typographical errors are at a minimum. [R: BL, 1 Sept 78, p. 70] Jerry Cao

699. Campbell, Dave, and others. **The Scouting Report: 1985: An In-depth Analysis of the Strengths and Weaknesses of Every Active Major League Baseball Player**. Edited by Marybeth Sullivan. New York, Harper & Row, 1985. 666p. illus. index. $14.95pa. ISBN 0-06-091245-6; ISSN 0743-1309.

The Scouting Report: 1985 is a remarkable book. Every one of 674 active major leaguers are represented here, most getting a whole page to themselves. The report for each player is almost entirely narrative, containing the following sections: for pitchers—pitching, fielding, and overall; for non-pitchers—hitting, fielding, baserunning, and overall. There are also pictures of each player, position, number, whether he bats right- or left-handed, height, weight, number of years in the majors, birth date and place, and 1984 and lifetime stats. For the hitters there is also a diagram showing batting strengths and weaknesses, and the area of the field toward which they are likely to hit.

The comments in the narratives are at times painfully honest, which lends a lot of credibility to the book. Much effort to achieve objectivity and fairness seems evident on every page, yet a certain amount of subjectivity is inevitable. The beauty of the book is that it contains the same kind of information baseball fans have always talked about among themselves (i.e., the past, present, and future performances of players from the rawest rookies to the most seasoned veterans). The book would enrich any fan's knowledge of the game. Its presentation is refreshingly straightforward and logical. As a librarian and a fan, I hope the editors continue this unique player report for many years to come.   Lawrence Grieco

700.   Karst, Gene, and Martin J. Jones. **Who's Who in Professional Baseball.** New Rochelle, N.Y., Arlington House, 1973. 919p. o.p. LC 73-11870. ISBN 0-87000-220-1.

Provides biographical sketches for some fifteen hundred players, managers, coaches, and other officials. The coverage is, of course, selective, in view of the fact that over ten thousand men have played major league baseball—not to mention the thousands of league officials and club owners. Nevertheless, the selection seems to be sound; included are not only such superstars as Cy Young and Willie Mays, but also men like Doc Hyland or Charles Ebbets, whose names might be less familiar to younger fans.

There are other reference books on this subject. *The Baseball Encyclopedia* is probably the most authoritative, and *Baseball Record Book*, published annually, contains complete official major league records, including year-by-year leaders and all-time great individual career records. On a more comprehensive scale, this is also done by *Official Encyclopedia of Baseball*, which provides a register of all players from the beginning of professional playing down through the 1970 season. Nevertheless, this biographical directory, with its informal approach, presents "some unusual, colorful personality facets of the great and not so great" (preface).

Bohdan S. Wynar

701.   **Official Baseball Register, 1985.** Barry Siegel, ed. St. Louis, Mo., Sporting News, 1985. 560p. $9.95pa. ISBN 0-89204-177-3.

The *Official Baseball Register* is a listing of statistics for major league players, managers, and coaches. Published annually in March, before the baseball season begins, the *Register* includes the lifetime statistics of all players on the spring training rosters as well as those who played in the major leagues the previous season.

Each entry contains five sections. The first section includes the vital statistics: date of birth, height and weight, left or right handed, hobbies, and colleges attended. Next is a list of the times the player led his league in a batting, pitching, or fielding category, and awards (such as most valuable player). The main section is the lifetime statistics of the player, including both minor and major leagues. Following the statistics all transactions involving the player are listed; this includes the player drafts and free-agent signings. The last section is the All-Star Game and post-season records and statistics, including the years that a player was selected for the All-Star Game but did not participate.

The main attribute of the *Official Baseball Register* is its accuracy. The entries are reset every year, instead of tacking new information on at the end. This makes the book very readable. The only annoying feature is that two important statistics, saves for pitchers and stolen bases for hitters, are in the achievement section instead of the statistics section; this arrangement highlights the exceptional players, but precludes comparison with the average player.

James P. Heitzer

BASKETBALL

702. **Complete Handbook of Pro Basketball 1984**. Zander Hollander, ed. New York, New American Library, 1983. 272p. illus. (A Signet Book). $3.95pa. ISBN 0-451-12528-2.

This one is for the statistics buffs. Introduced by three articles on players, refereeing, and the NBA, and concluded by NBA TV/Radio roundup, team statistics for both the NBA and the ABA, the ABA dispersal draft, and the NBA schedule, the individual player histories and statistics are the main meat of this compilation. Team by team, the players are listed with age, height, weight, and playing position. In addition to a photograph, there is a brief history of each one's career plus comments on abilities, or lack thereof, and in some cases a prediction is made about a player's probable future in the game for the coming year. Wording of the profiles sounds somewhat like the comments made by a sportscaster needing filler during a game. Below the history, career figures are given in tabular form. These include years played, teams played for, total games played, field goals and free throws attempted and made, percentages, rebounds, total points, and average points per game. The top rookie is named, history of the career of the coach is summarized, the "Great Moment" for the team is described, and all-time team leaders are listed. This book will be a good argument stopper — or starter — and is small and easy to carry along to work or to games.

Cecil F. Clotfelter

703. Mendell, Ronald L. **Who's Who in Basketball**. New Rochelle, N.Y., Arlington House, 1973. 248p. o.p. LC 73-11871. ISBN 0-87000-22-8.

There is a lot of biographical information about basketball players and coaches scattered through a multitude of the game's histories and reference sources, but this is the first publication to bring all the information together between two covers. There are over nine hundred biographical sketches, including pro and college players, coaches and officials, from 1891 to 1973. Entries are alphabetically arranged; besides including the essential outlines of lives and careers, they frequently bring us up-to-date on the biographees after they left basketball. One small criticism: there is no cross-indexing, so how are we to find Lew Alcindor or Walt Hazzard if we don't recall their new names (Kareem Abdul-Jabbar and Mahdi Abdul-Rahman)? Binding and typography are acceptable. No illustrations.

Marshall E. Nunn

704. **NBA Register**. 1984-1985 ed. Mike Douchant and Alex Sachare, eds. St. Louis, Mo., Sporting News, 1984. 352p. illus. $9.95pa. ISBN 0-89204-162-5; ISSN 0739-3067.

Attached to every sport are statisticians who make it their business to compile absurdly complete records on the performance of teams or individuals, in the apparent belief that a player's reputation and value to his team may be shown by the numbers he has compiled. This book is one of the end products of that cottage industry. It lists, for every player active in the National Basketball Association during the 1983-1984 season, a bewildering array of statistics: games played, minutes played, field goals attempted and made, free throws attempted and made, offensive and defensive rebounds, etc., etc. The dense columns of figures are headed by abbreviations (FGM = field goals made) but no list of abbreviations is provided; only the initiated will understand. A small photograph of each player is provided, and full-page shots of players in action are interspersed for filler. There are special sections for the records compiled by NBA coaches, by all-time great players, and—to reassure everyone that the sport and its statistics will endure—by promising newcomers to professional basketball.

If there were assurance that the numbers were a genuine indication of a player's value, all this effort would not have been in vain; but alas, every fan knows that a collection of talented players does not necessarily a great team make, and that a player's numbers do not define his value. How else to explain that great scorers often labor for losing teams, or that teams without overwhelming talent contrive to win championships?

This book will be seized upon eagerly by devoted students of the game, but no others need apply. Robert Balay

705. Padwe, Sandy. **Basketball's Hall of Fame**. Englewood Cliffs, N.J., Prentice-Hall, 1970. 193p. illus. $6.95. LC 76-99451. ISBN 0-13-072322-3.

The Basketball Hall of Fame has been in the planning stages for many years. In 1968, the building was opened to the public for the first time. This volume is the official account of the Hall of Fame published with their cooperation. Fifteen chapters are devoted to some of the all-time great innovators and personalities of the basketball world, with a final chapter giving biographical data and photographs of the members of the Hall of Fame. Players and coaches from the ranks of professional, collegiate, amateur, military, and high school teams are included. The introduction is most informative on the organization, history, and method of selection to the Basketball Hall of Fame. [R: LJ, July 70, p. 2509] Judith Armstrong

706. Winick, Matt, ed. **Official National Basketball Association Register, 1984**. Howard M. Balzer and John Duxbury, contributing eds. St. Louis, Mo., Sporting News, 1983. 456p. illus. $9.95pa. ISSN 0271-8170.

The *National Basketball Association Official Guide* is the primary and most essential reference tool for libraries needing material on professional basketball. The *Register*, on the other hand, is a supplementary tool of more marginal value to libraries and can be recommended only for those libraries with a large and active body of patrons interested in the sport. The *Guide* contains all of the detailed records and statistics, and is team- and record-oriented. The *Register* is player-oriented. It is primarily an alphabetical listing by player of the individual career records for all players who appeared in at least one game in the 1979/1980 season or who were on the injured list for the entire year. It also contains a summary of the collegiate records of the players selected in the first three rounds of the 1983 draft and some other notable newcomers. Finally, it contains a year-by-year summary of the East-West All-Star Game since its inception in 1951 and other statistics and records relating to the All-Star Game. For almost all libraries, the *Guide* is perfectly adequate, and the *Register* is of marginal value. Don't confuse the two or feel that you need both. Norman D. Stevens

BOXING

707. Burrill, Bob. **Who's Who in Boxing**. New Rochelle, N.Y., Arlington House, 1974. 208p. o.p. LC 73-13020. ISBN 0-87000-232-5.

Biographical sketches, in a Who's Who format, of over four hundred boxers, managers, promoters, and others associated with the fight game. International in coverage; time period is from the late nineteenth century to the present; entries are arranged alphabetically. Comparison of the entries for three fighters with the

Encyclopedia Americana's entries for the same three reveals these results: (1) Jack Dempsey—*Americana* states his birth date as 25 June 1895, whereas Burrill gives it as June 24; *Americana* says that after losing a decision to King Levinsky in 1932, Dempsey retired from the ring, whereas Burrill lists his last fight in 1940 against Ellis Bashara. (2) Gene Tunney—birth dates differ again, with *Americana* giving 27 May 1897, and Burrill giving May 25; the encyclopedia states that he won the light-heavyweight world crown by defeating Georges Charpentier, retired in 1929 as undefeated champion, and wrote two books, *A Man Must Fight* (Boston, 1932) and *Arms for Living* (New York, 1941); Burrill makes no mention of the Charpentier fight, of the retirement date, or of the two books. (3) James Corbett—*Americana* lists his first major contest as a twenty-eight-round bout on a barge in San Francisco Bay on 5 June 1889, in which he defeated Joe Choynski. On 21 May 1891, he fought Peter Jackson to a sixty-one-round draw. Burrill does not give the month, date, and location of the Choynski fight and does not record the Jackson fight at all. These discrepancies and omissions are serious; the book should be used with caution. [R: WLB, May 74, p. 762]   Marshall E. Nunn

FOOTBALL

708.   Allen, George, with Ben Olan. **Pro Football's 100 Greatest Players: Rating the Stars of Past and Present**. Indianapolis, Ind., Bobbs-Merrill, 1982. 238p. illus. $14.95. LC 82-4254. ISBN 0-672-52723-5.

Deciding who are the one hundred greatest professional football players is an awesome task, but no one is more qualified for this task than George Allen. This is a very readable and controversial reference work in the field of sports. Allen has picked players from 1933, the year the NFL really came into existence, to the present. Factors considered were versatility, longevity, career statistics, performance, consistency, and leadership. The work is divided into categories for each playing position. A brief biography is given, as well as Allen's comments on the player. A list of George Allen's picks for an all-time team is presented at the end, as are player statistics for each person in the book. There is no index, nor are the individual players listed in the table of contents.

Well-documented and readable, this work will be of interest to professional football fans, but does not merit a place on the reference shelf. The statistical information contained here can be found in other standard reference works. [R: BL, 1 Sept 82, p. 20; LJ, 1 Sept 82, p. 1672]   Joanne Troutner

709.   Balzer, Howard and Barry Siegel, eds. **Football Register 1984**. St. Louis, Mo., Sporting News, 1984. 496p. illus. $9.95pa. ISBN 0-89204-156-0.

Revised annually, this handy compendium is a roster of currently active players in the National Football League (there is no information within its covers on players or coaches in the rival, fledgling United States Football League).

The book's main section contains this information on each active player: personal data, educational background, and playing career (including statistics). The data are complete and authoritative and are current through the 1983-1984 season. Illustrations are not a prominent feature of this publication; there are a few good black-and-white action photos to relieve the almost five hundred pages of personal data and statistics.

This title, along with other Sporting News rosters on professional sports (such as the one on hockey) is a basic reference book acquisition for all libraries.
                Marshall E. Nunn

710.   Lamb, Kevin. **Football Stars, 1985**. Chicago, Ill., Contemporary Books, 1985. 120p. illus. $5.95pa. LC 85-14912. ISBN 0-8092-5141-8.

Football Stars, 1985 takes a close-up look at forty of football's hottest players. Kevin Lamb chose at least one player for each of the twenty-eight NFL teams. The majority selected are quarterbacks, running backs, and receivers, simply because they receive the most attention. No one injured at the time of writing was included. Twenty-four of the forty were first-round draft choices, with seven others second-round draft choices.

Each entry includes the player's vital statistics (date and place of birth, weight, and height), each year and team performed in, and statistics for each of those years. Those players having played in the CFL have those statistics included also. Statistics include the number of games played, rushing, pass receiving, passing, sacks, place kicking, and punt returns.

Among the players included are Mark Clayton, Dan Marino, and Dwight Stephenson of the Miami Dolphins; Art Monk and Joe Theismann of the Washington Redskins. Everyone from 1984 rookie Lewis Lipps of the Pittsburgh Steelers to ten-year veteran Walter Payton of the Chicago Bears to eighteen-year veteran Jan Stenrud (the only place kicker represented), currently of Minnesota. Surprisingly, only one of "America's team" — Dallas Cowboys' Randy White, is represented.

This $5.95 paperback will be an excellent addition to any library's sports collection; but this reviewer believes it would be best used in the circulating collection.

Janet R. Ivey

711.   Mendell, Ronald L., and Timothy B. Phares. **Who's Who in Football**. New Rochelle, N.Y., Arlington House, 1974. 395p. o.p. LC 74-17336. ISBN 0-87000-237-6.

Who's Who in Football lists approximately fourteen hundred football players, coaches, officials, administrators, and owners. It covers both collegiate and professional football. Selection of persons seems well balanced, although problems are apparent (e.g., there are two identical entries for Robert C. Hubbard).

Information for each person is limited to career data. The only personal data are birth dates and birthplaces. Will be a useful addition to public library sports collections.

Bohdan S. Wynar

GOLF

712.   Alliss, Peter. **The Who's Who of Golf**. Englewood Cliffs, N.J., Prentice-Hall, 1983. 381p. illus. index. $24.95; $14.95pa. LC 83-11047. ISBN 0-13-958497-8; 0-13-958489-7pa.

This biographical directory includes the outstanding male and female golfers from the middle of the last century through the end of 1982. Entries are listed alphabetically by world regions (e.g., "North America," "Great Britain and Ireland," "South and Central America"). Each entry gives the golfer's full name, year and place of birth, and year of death if appropriate. The biographical essays covering each individual's golfing career are delightful and informative. Mention is made of number of wins and money that was won. There is no other biographic directory of golf personalities that is as comprehensive and enjoyable to read. Even though some photographs are included, it would have made the work more impressive if a photograph had been included for every entry.

It can be supplemented by *Who's Who in Golf* (New Rochelle, N.Y., Arlington House, 1976. 208p. o.p.) that lists over six hundred golfing greats, including both amateurs and professionals who had won a national championship. Less coverage is provided in *Who's Who in International Golf* by David Emery (Facts on File, 1983. 128p. $12.95) which lists only 182 individuals with excellent photographs.

H. Robert Malinowsky and Bohdan S. Wynar

HOCKEY

713. **Complete Handbook of Pro Hockey 1984.** Edited by Zander Hollander. New York, New American Library, 1983. 320p. illus. (A Signet Book). $3.95pa. ISBN 0-451-12527-4.

Overall format for this volume is almost identical to that of the 1982 *Complete Handbook of Pro Basketball*. There are five articles on the game or on players of hockey, records, and statistics of the AHL, CHL, WHA, and NHL. The balance of the book tells about the players, their names, ages, heights, weights, positions, and histories with career statistics in tabular form. Coaches are profiled, "Great Moments" are described, and all-time team leaders are listed. There are lots of photographs. This book, like the one on basketball, can be easily carried in the pocket when going to games for a quick check on a favorite or to settle arguments with friends about who has done what.

Cecil F. Clotfelter

714. **Hockey Register.** 1984-1985 ed. Larry Wigge, ed. Frank Polnaszek, comp. St. Louis, Mo., Sporting News, 1984. 384p. $9.95pa. ISBN 0-89204-128-5; ISSN 0090-2292.

The *Hockey Register* is a companion volume to another Sporting News annual volume, the *Football Register*. Its intent is similar: to present up-to-date personal data and statistics on active players in the National Hockey League. It includes information on players who participated in at least one NHL game in the 1983-1984 season as "selected invitees to training camps" (p. 2).

The main section of the book is a roster of forwards and defensemen, alphabetically arranged by name. Each entry lists personal data, positions played, and a year-by-year statistical summary of the player's hockey career. The same format is repeated for the smaller section on goalkeepers. This volume is a must purchase for most libraries.

Marshall E. Nunn

SHOWJUMPING AND EQUESTRIANISM

715. Emery, David, ed. **Who's Who in International Showjumping & Equestrianism.** New York, Facts on File, 1983. 128p. illus. (part col.). (Who's Who in Sport Series). $12.95. ISBN 0-87196-791-X.

This attractive small book is a volume in the Who's Who in Sport series. It covers both showjumping, which can be lucrative with prize money, and equestrianism or eventing, which is a sport for those with independent means (such as Britain's Princess Anne). The 138 entries are arranged alphabetically by name of rider, giving place and date of birth, place of residence, height, weight, and career highlights. This section is followed by a narrative that discusses the riding accomplishments of the rider and names some of the more important horses that each has ridden or owned. There are excellent action photographs of about one-third of the riders. The book is not an exhaustive Who's Who but "is intended to be a balanced mixture of the established names, some in semi-retirement, and the up-and-coming stars."

H. Robert Malinowsky

TENNIS

716.   Emery, David, ed. **Who's Who in International Tennis**. New York, Facts on File, 1983. 128p. illus. (part col.). (Who's Who in Sport Series). $12.95. ISBN 0-87196-789-8.

This well-illustrated and compact guide should be very useful to anyone who follows the increasingly popular sport of tennis. There are 220 alphabetically arranged entries that give place and date of birth, residence, height, weight, and career highlights. The brief narrative on each player describes the accomplishments of the player. Good action photographs are included for about one-third of the entries. The editor indicates that the book "contains all the famous figures, plus an introduction to the would-be champions" of both sexes.

H. Robert Malinowsky

717.   Wade, Virginia, with Jean Rafferty. **Ladies of the Court: A Century of Women at Wimbledon**. New York, Atheneum, 1984. 192p. illus. (part col.). index. $16.95. ISBN 0-689-11468-0.

This is a reference book only in the sense that any well-indexed, informative publication can be used for reference. In this very specialized work the "ladies of the court" referred to in the title are those women who have won the singles or doubles championships in the open division at the Wimbledon tournament, one of the most notable annual competitions in the sport of tennis.

Wade, herself a Wimbledon winner, and Rafferty, a sports writer, have gathered information and photographs reflecting personalities and styles of each competitor, as well as the public's attitude toward the players, the tournament, and the game itself. Arranged chronologically, the book traces the history of women's entry into Wimbledon and the development of the players and their impact on the tournament.

The book concludes with a two-page chronological list of winners and a six-page biographical section, arranged alphabetically, with entries for both maiden and married names. Herein lies its only true reference value.

Marjorie N. Nelson

TRACK AND FIELD

718.   Hanley, Reid M. **Who's Who in Track and Field**. New Rochelle, N.Y., Arlington House, 1973. 160p. o.p. LC 73-11872. ISBN 0-87000-219-8.

An important biographical reference source for some 420 international track-and-field athletes, from the 1870s to 1973. It's the only book of its kind, and it will be an important addition to any sports reference section. Alphabetically arranged entries give biographical data, records established, and details of personal lives. Packed with information otherwise unobtainable.

Marshall E. Nunn

Author/Title Index

Unless otherwise indicated, reference is to entry number. References to authors or titles mentioned only in an annotation are identified by an *n* following the entry number (e.g., 102n). References to authors or titles mentioned in introductory material are to page number and are identified by a *p* (e.g., p. 4).

Initial articles have been deleted from foreign-language as well as from English titles.

Subject Index

Unless otherwise indicated, reference is to entry number. References to subjects mentioned only in an annotation are identified by an *n* following the entry number (e.g., 102n). References to subjects mentioned in introductory material are to page number and are identified by a *p* (e.g., p. 4).